Ford Galaxy
Owners Workshop Manual

M R Storey

Models covered

(5556 - 320)

Galaxy MPV
Petrol: 2.3 litre (2295cc) 4-cylinder
Turbo-Diesel: 1.9 litre (1896cc)

Does NOT cover models with 2.0 litre 4-cyl or 2.8 litre V6 petrol engines
Does NOT cover revised model range introduced March 2006

© Haynes Publishing 2012

A book in the **Haynes Owners Workshop Manual Series**

ABCDE
FGHIJ
KLMNO
PQRST

ISBN **978 0 85733 556 2**

British Library Cataloguing in Publication Data
A catalogue record for this book is available from the British Library.

Printed in the USA

Haynes Publishing
Sparkford, Yeovil, Somerset BA22 7JJ, England

Haynes North America, Inc
861 Lawrence Drive, Newbury Park, California 91320, USA

Haynes Publishing Nordiska AB
Box 1504, 751 45 UPPSALA, Sverige

Contents

LIVING WITH YOUR FORD GALAXY

Roadside repairs

Weekly checks

Lubricants and fluids

Tyre pressures

MAINTENANCE

Routine maintenance and servicing

Contents

REPAIRS & OVERHAUL

First introduced in August 2000, the second generation Ford Galaxy departs significantly from its Volkswagen and Seat stablemates. Whilst still retaining the basic floor pan and mechanicals of the Volkswagen-Audi Group (VAG) variants, the Mark 2 Galaxy adopted some features of the corporate exterior 'kinetic design' of the Ford motor company. The interior is all new and shares little in common with earlier Galaxy models.

This multi-purpose vehicle (MPV) is available in one body shape, and equipped with a variety of engine sizes. This manual covers the 4-cylinder 2.3 litre petrol engines and all diesel engine models. The petrol engine is double overhead camshaft (DOHC) 16-valve unit, equipped with balance shafts. The diesel engines (of VW origin) are unit injector PD (Pumpe-Duse) engines. All diesel engines are turbocharged and are available in a variety of power outputs.

A five-speed manual gearbox is fitted as standard to all petrol models, with an optional four-speed automatic unit also available. Diesel models feature a 5- or 6-speed manual gearbox depending on the engine output, with an automatic gearbox also available for the 114 bhp (AUY) engine.

Fully-independent front suspension is fitted, with the components attached to a subframe assembly; the rear suspension is semi-independent, with separate coil springs, dampers and trailing arms. All models feature power steering, ABS brakes and front airbags. Side airbags, traction control and electronic stability programming feature on higher specification models. Three trim levels are available: LX, Zetec and Ghia, with various special editions trim levels also available.

For the home mechanic, the Galaxy is quite straightforward to maintain, and most of the items requiring frequent attention are easily accessible.

Your Ford Galaxy Manual

The aim of this manual is to help you get the best value from your vehicle. It can do so in several ways. It can help you decide what work must be done (even should you choose to get it done by a garage). It will also provide information on routine maintenance and servicing, and give a logical course of action and diagnosis when random faults occur. However, it is hoped that you will use the manual by tackling the work yourself. On simpler jobs it may even be quicker than booking the car into a garage and going there twice, to leave and collect it. Perhaps most important, a lot of money can be saved by avoiding the costs a garage must charge to cover its labour and overheads.

The manual has drawings and descriptions to show the function of the various components so that their layout can be understood. Tasks are described and photographed in a clear step-by-step sequence. The illustrations are numbered by the Section number and paragraph number to which they relate – if there is more than one illustration per paragraph, the sequence is denoted alphabetically.

References to the 'left' or 'right' of the vehicle are in the sense of a person in the driver's seat, facing forwards.

Acknowledgements

Certain illustrations are the copyright of the Ford Motor Company, and are used with their permission. Thanks are due to Draper Tools Limited, who provided some of the workshop tools, and to all those people at Sparkford who helped in the production of this manual.

We take great pride in the accuracy of information given in this manual, but vehicle manufacturers make alterations and design changes during the production run of a particular vehicle of which they do not inform us. No liability can be accepted by the authors or publishers for loss, damage or injury caused by any errors in, or omissions from, the information given.

Working on your car can be dangerous. This page shows just some of the potential risks and hazards, with the aim of creating a safety-conscious attitude.

General hazards

Scalding

• Don't remove the radiator or expansion tank cap while the engine is hot.
• Engine oil, transmission fluid or power steering fluid may also be dangerously hot if the engine has recently been running.

Burning

• Beware of burns from the exhaust system and from any part of the engine. Brake discs and drums can also be extremely hot immediately after use.

Crushing

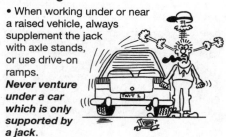

• When working under or near a raised vehicle, always supplement the jack with axle stands, or use drive-on ramps. *Never venture under a car which is only supported by a jack*.
• Take care if loosening or tightening high-torque nuts when the vehicle is on stands. Initial loosening and final tightening should be done with the wheels on the ground.

Fire

• Fuel is highly flammable; fuel vapour is explosive.
• Don't let fuel spill onto a hot engine.
• Do not smoke or allow naked lights (including pilot lights) anywhere near a vehicle being worked on. Also beware of creating sparks (electrically or by use of tools).
• Fuel vapour is heavier than air, so don't work on the fuel system with the vehicle over an inspection pit.
• Another cause of fire is an electrical overload or short-circuit. Take care when repairing or modifying the vehicle wiring.
• Keep a fire extinguisher handy, of a type suitable for use on fuel and electrical fires.

Electric shock

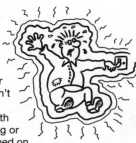

• Ignition HT and Xenon headlight voltages can be dangerous, especially to people with heart problems or a pacemaker. Don't work on or near these systems with the engine running or the ignition switched on.

• Mains voltage is also dangerous. Make sure that any mains-operated equipment is correctly earthed. Mains power points should be protected by a residual current device (RCD) circuit breaker.

Fume or gas intoxication

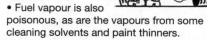

• Exhaust fumes are poisonous; they can contain carbon monoxide, which is rapidly fatal if inhaled. Never run the engine in a confined space such as a garage with the doors shut.
• Fuel vapour is also poisonous, as are the vapours from some cleaning solvents and paint thinners.

Poisonous or irritant substances

• Avoid skin contact with battery acid and with any fuel, fluid or lubricant, especially antifreeze, brake hydraulic fluid and Diesel fuel. Don't syphon them by mouth. If such a substance is swallowed or gets into the eyes, seek medical advice.
• Prolonged contact with used engine oil can cause skin cancer. Wear gloves or use a barrier cream if necessary. Change out of oil-soaked clothes and do not keep oily rags in your pocket.
• Air conditioning refrigerant forms a poisonous gas if exposed to a naked flame (including a cigarette). It can also cause skin burns on contact.

Asbestos

• Asbestos dust can cause cancer if inhaled or swallowed. Asbestos may be found in gaskets and in brake and clutch linings. When dealing with such components it is safest to assume that they contain asbestos.

Special hazards

Hydrofluoric acid

• This extremely corrosive acid is formed when certain types of synthetic rubber, found in some O-rings, oil seals, fuel hoses etc, are exposed to temperatures above 4000C. The rubber changes into a charred or sticky substance containing the acid. *Once formed, the acid remains dangerous for years. If it gets onto the skin, it may be necessary to amputate the limb concerned*.
• When dealing with a vehicle which has suffered a fire, or with components salvaged from such a vehicle, wear protective gloves and discard them after use.

The battery

• Batteries contain sulphuric acid, which attacks clothing, eyes and skin. Take care when topping-up or carrying the battery.
• The hydrogen gas given off by the battery is highly explosive. Never cause a spark or allow a naked light nearby. Be careful when connecting and disconnecting battery chargers or jump leads.

Air bags

• Air bags can cause injury if they go off accidentally. Take care when removing the steering wheel and trim panels. Special storage instructions may apply.

Diesel injection equipment

• Diesel injection pumps supply fuel at very high pressure. Take care when working on the fuel injectors and fuel pipes.

 Warning: Never expose the hands, face or any other part of the body to injector spray; the fuel can penetrate the skin with potentially fatal results.

Remember...

DO

• Do use eye protection when using power tools, and when working under the vehicle.

• Do wear gloves or use barrier cream to protect your hands when necessary.

• Do get someone to check periodically that all is well when working alone on the vehicle.

• Do keep loose clothing and long hair well out of the way of moving mechanical parts.

• Do remove rings, wristwatch etc, before working on the vehicle – especially the electrical system.

• Do ensure that any lifting or jacking equipment has a safe working load rating adequate for the job.

DON'T

• Don't attempt to lift a heavy component which may be beyond your capability – get assistance.

• Don't rush to finish a job, or take unverified short cuts.

• Don't use ill-fitting tools which may slip and cause injury.

• Don't leave tools or parts lying around where someone can trip over them. Mop up oil and fuel spills at once.

• Don't allow children or pets to play in or near a vehicle being worked on.

The following pages are intended to help in dealing with common roadside emergencies and breakdowns. You will find more detailed fault finding information at the back of the manual, and repair information in the main chapters.

If your car won't start and the starter motor doesn't turn

☐ Open the bonnet and make sure that the battery terminals are clean and tight.

☐ Switch on the headlights and try to start the engine. If the headlights go very dim when you're trying to start, the battery is probably flat. Get out of trouble by jump starting (see next page) using a friend's car.

If your car won't start even though the starter motor turns as normal

☐ Is there fuel in the tank?

☐ Has the engine immobiliser been deactivated? This should happen automatically, on inserting the ignition key. However, if a replacement key has been obtained, it may not contain the transponder chip necessary to deactivate the system.

☐ Check that none of the engine-related fuses have blown.

☐ Is there moisture on electrical components under the bonnet? Switch off the ignition, then wipe off any obvious dampness with a dry cloth. Spray a water-repellent aerosol product (WD-40 or equivalent) on ignition and fuel system electrical connectors like those shown in the photos. Pay special attention to the ignition coil wiring connector and HT leads.

A Check the security and condition of the battery connections.

B Check the fuses and fusible links in the underbonnet fusebox.

C Check the HT lead connections at the ignition coil on the left of the engine.

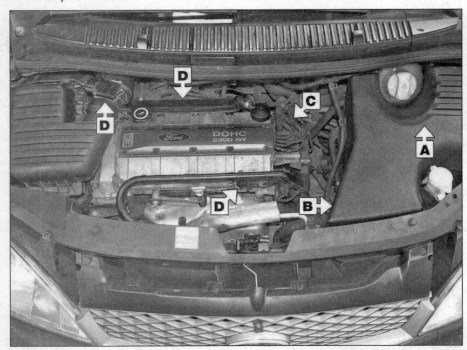

D Check the security of any accessible electrical connectors.

Check that electrical connections are secure (with the ignition switched off) and spray them with a water-dispersant spray like WD-40 if you suspect a problem due to damp.

Jump starting

HAYNES HiNT *Jump starting will get you out of trouble, but you must correct whatever made the battery go flat in the first place. There are three possibilities:*

1 *The battery has been drained by repeated attempts to start, or by leaving the lights on.*

2 *The charging system is not working properly (alternator drivebelt slack or broken, alternator wiring fault or alternator itself faulty).*

3 *The battery itself is at fault (electrolyte low, or battery worn out).*

When jump-starting a car, observe the following precautions:

✓ Before connecting the booster battery, make sure that the ignition is switched off.

Caution: Remove the key in case the central locking engages when the jump leads are connected

✓ Ensure that all electrical equipment (lights, heater, wipers, etc) is switched off.
✓ Take note of any special precautions printed on the battery case.
✓ Make sure that the booster battery is the same voltage as the discharged one in the vehicle.

✓ If the battery is being jump-started from the battery in another vehicle, the two vehicles MUST NOT TOUCH each other.
✓ Make sure that the transmission is in neutral (or PARK, in the case of automatic transmission).

HAYNES HiNT *Budget jump leads can be a false economy, as they often do not pass enough current to start large capacity or diesel engines. They can also get hot.*

1 Connect one end of the red jump lead to the positive (+) terminal of the flat battery

2 Connect the other end of the red lead to the positive (+) terminal of the booster battery.

3 Connect one end of the black jump lead to the negative (-) terminal of the booster battery

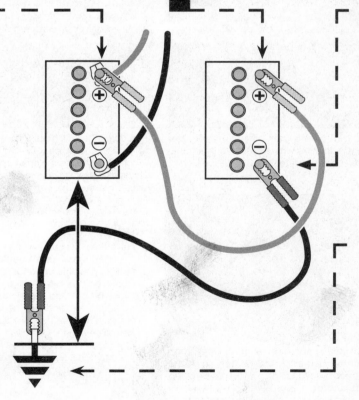

4 Connect the other end of the black jump lead to a bolt or bracket on the engine block, well away from the battery, on the vehicle to be started.

5 Make sure that the jump leads will not come into contact with the fan, drive-belts or other moving parts of the engine.

6 Start the engine using the booster battery and run it at idle speed. Switch on the lights, rear window demister and heater blower motor, then disconnect the jump leads in the reverse order of connection. Turn off the lights etc.

Wheel changing

⚠️ *Warning: Do not change a wheel in a situation where you risk being hit by other traffic. On busy roads, try to stop in a lay-by or a gateway. Be wary of passing traffic while changing the wheel – it is easy to become distracted by the job in hand.*

Preparation

- ☐ When a puncture occurs, stop as soon as it is safe to do so.
- ☐ Park on firm level ground, if possible, and well out of the way of other traffic.
- ☐ Use hazard warning lights if necessary.

- ☐ If you have one, use a warning triangle to alert other drivers of your presence.
- ☐ Apply the handbrake and engage first or reverse gear.
- ☐ Chock the wheel diagonally opposite the

one being removed – a couple of large stones will do for this.
- ☐ If the ground is soft, use a flat piece of wood to spread the load under the jack.

Changing the wheel

1 The jack and wheel brace are stored behind the right-hand side trim panel of the luggage compartment. Open the cover, unscrew the retaining bolt and remove the jack and wheel brace. Detach the wheel brace from the jack.

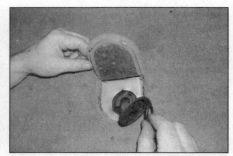

2 The spare wheel is in a cradle under the rear of the vehicle. Pull up the cover in the luggage compartment for access to the spare wheel cradle securing screw. Using the wheel brace, lower the spare wheel to the ground.

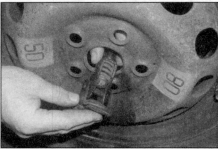

3 Lift up the spare wheel, rotate the toggle and unhook the cable.

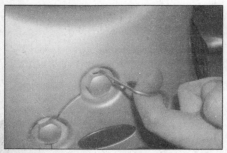

4 Where fitted, use the hook in the tool kit to remove the wheel trim. Some models have plastic caps covering the wheel bolts.

5 Loosen each wheel bolt by half a turn. Where locking wheel bolts are fitted, use the special adapter.

6 Locate the jack head below the reinforced jacking point nearest the wheel to be changed. Place the spare wheel under the vehicle as a precaution against the jack failing. Ensure that the lug on the jack head engages with the cut-out in the jacking point. Turn the handle to raise the wheel clear of the ground.

Finally . . .

- ☐ Have the wheel bolts tightened to the specified torque (see Chapter 10) at the earliest possible opportunity.
- ☐ Remove the wheel chocks.
- ☐ Stow the jack and tools in the luggage compartment, and refit the removed wheel in the cradle. Raise the cradle before driving the vehicle.
- ☐ Check the tyre pressure on the wheel just fitted. If it is low drive slowly to the nearest garage and inflate the tyre to the right pressure.
- ☐ Have the punctured wheel repaired at the earliest opportunity.

7 Fully remove the wheel bolts and remove the wheel. Place the wheel under the sill and remove the spare from under the vehicle.

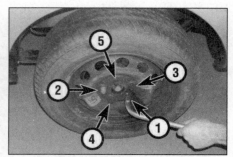

8 Locate the spare wheel on the studs and tighten the bolts moderately with the wheel brace. Lower the vehicle to the ground, and then securely tighten the wheel bolts progressively in diagonal sequence.

Identifying leaks

Puddles on the garage floor or drive, or obvious wetness under the bonnet or underneath the car, suggest a leak that needs investigating. It can sometimes be difficult to decide where the leak is coming from, especially if an engine undershield is fitted. Leaking oil or fluid can also be blown rearwards by the passage of air under the car, giving a false impression of where the problem lies.

 Warning: Most automotive oils and fluids are poisonous. Wash them off skin, and change out of contaminated clothing, without delay.

 The smell of a fluid leaking from the car may provide a clue to what's leaking. Some fluids are distinctively coloured. It may help to remove the engine undershield, clean the car carefully and to park it over some clean paper overnight as an aid to locating the source of the leak.
Remember that some leaks may only occur while the engine is running.

Sump oil

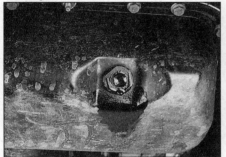

Engine oil may leak from the drain plug...

Oil from filter

...or from the base of the oil filter.

Gearbox oil

Gearbox oil can leak from the seals at the inboard ends of the driveshafts.

Antifreeze

Leaking antifreeze often leaves a crystalline deposit like this.

Brake fluid

A leak occurring at a wheel is almost certainly brake fluid.

Power steering fluid

Power steering fluid may leak from the pipe connectors on the steering rack.

Towing

When all else fails, you may find yourself having to get a tow home – or of course you may be helping somebody else. Long-distance recovery should only be done by a garage or breakdown service. For shorter distances, DIY towing using another car is easy enough, but observe the following points:
☐ Use a proper tow-rope – they are not expensive. The vehicle being towed must display an ON TOW sign in its rear window.
☐ Always turn the ignition key to the 'on' position when the vehicle is being towed, so that the steering lock is released, and the direction indicator and brake lights work.

☐ The front towing eye is located behind the lower air intake on the front bumper.
☐ Before being towed, release the handbrake and make sure the transmission is in neutral. On models with automatic transmission, special precautions apply: The vehicle speed must not exceed 30 mph and towed distance must not exceed 30 miles.
☐ Note that greater-than-usual pedal pressure will be required to operate the brakes, since the vacuum servo unit is only operational with the engine running.
☐ The driver of the car being towed must keep the tow-rope taut at all times to avoid snatching.

☐ Make sure that both drivers know the route before setting off.
☐ Only drive at moderate speeds and keep the distance towed to a minimum. Drive smoothly and allow plenty of time for slowing down at junctions.

Introduction

There are some very simple checks which need only take a few minutes to carry out, but which could save you a lot of inconvenience and expense.

These *Weekly checks* require no great skill or special tools, and the small amount of time they take to perform could prove to be very well spent, for example:

☐ Keeping an eye on tyre condition and pressures, will not only help to stop them wearing out prematurely, but could also save your life.

☐ Many breakdowns are caused by electrical problems. Battery-related faults are particularly common, and a quick check on a regular basis will often prevent the majority of these.

☐ If your car develops a brake fluid leak, the first time you might know about it is when your brakes don't work properly. Checking the level regularly will give advance warning of this kind of problem.

☐ If the oil or coolant levels run low, the cost of repairing any engine damage will be far greater than fixing the leak, for example.

Underbonnet check points

◄ 2.3 litre petrol engine

A *Engine oil level dipstick*

B *Engine oil filler cap*

C *Coolant expansion tank*

D *Brake (and clutch) fluid reservoir – hidden*

E *Power steering fluid reservoir – under cover*

F *Screen washer fluid reservoir*

G *Battery – under cover*

◄ 1.9 litre diesel engine

A *Engine oil level dipstick*

B *Engine oil filler cap*

C *Coolant expansion tank*

D *Brake (and clutch) fluid reservoir – hidden*

E *Power steering fluid reservoir – under cover*

F *Screen washer fluid reservoir*

G *Battery – under cover*

Engine oil level

Before you start
✔ Make sure that the car is on level ground.
✔ Check the oil level before the car is driven, or at least 5 minutes after the engine has been switched off.

 HAYNES HiNT *If the oil is checked immediately after driving the vehicle, some of the oil will remain in the upper engine components, resulting in an inaccurate reading on the dipstick.*

The correct oil
Modern engines place great demands on their oil. It is very important that the correct oil for your car is used (see *Lubricants and fluids*).

Car care
● If you have to add oil frequently, you should check whether you have any oil leaks. Place some clean paper under the car overnight, and check for stains in the morning. If there are no leaks, then the engine may be burning oil.
● Always maintain the level between the upper and lower dipstick marks (see photo 3). If the level is too low, severe engine damage may occur. Oil seal failure may result if the engine is overfilled by adding too much oil.

1 The dipstick top is brightly-coloured for easy identification (see *Underbonnet check points* for the exact location). Withdraw the dipstick.

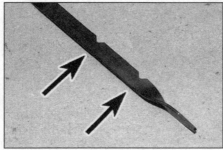

3 Note the oil level on the end of the dipstick, which should be between the upper MAX mark and lower MIN mark. If the oil level is only just above, or below, the MIN mark, topping-up is required.

2 Using a clean rag or paper towel wipe all oil from the dipstick. Insert the clean dipstick into the tube as far as it will go, then withdraw it again.

4 Oil is added through the filler cap aperture. Lift off the cap using a twisting motion. Top-up the level taking care not to spill the oil. Add the oil slowly, checking the level on the dipstick often, and allowing time for the oil to flow to the sump. Add oil until the level is just up to the MAX mark on the dipstick – don't overfill (see *Car care*).

Coolant level

 Warning: Do not attempt to remove the expansion tank pressure cap when the engine is hot, as there is a very great risk of scalding. Do not leave open containers of coolant about, as it is poisonous.

Car care
● With a sealed-type cooling system, adding coolant should not be necessary on a regular basis. If frequent topping-up is required, it is likely there is a leak. Check the radiator, all hoses and joint faces for signs of staining or wetness, and rectify as necessary.

● It is important that antifreeze is used in the cooling system all year round, not just during the winter months. Don't top up with water alone, as the antifreeze will become diluted.

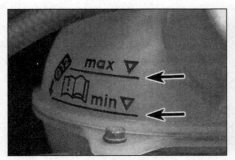

1 The coolant level varies with the temperature of the engine. MIN and MAX marks are shown on the side of the tank. When the engine is cold, the coolant level should be between the two marks, but ideally on the MAX mark. When the engine is hot, the level will rise above the MAX mark slightly.

2 If topping-up is necessary, **wait until the engine is cold**. Slowly unscrew the expansion tank cap, to release any pressure present in the cooling system, and remove it.

3 Add a mixture of water and antifreeze to the expansion tank until the coolant level is on the MAX mark. Refit the cap and tighten it securely.

Brake (and clutch) fluid level

⚠️ **Warning:**
- **Brake fluid can harm your eyes and damage painted surfaces, so use extreme caution when handling and pouring it.**
- **Do not use fluid that has been standing open for some time, as** it absorbs moisture from the air, which can cause a dangerous loss of braking effectiveness.

Safety first!

● If the reservoir requires repeated topping-up this is an indication of a fluid leak somewhere in the system, which should be investigated immediately.

● If a leak is suspected, the car should not be driven until the braking system has been checked. Never take any risks where brakes are concerned

1 The MAX and MIN marks are indicated on the side of the reservoir, which is located at the rear right-hand side of the engine compartment. The fluid level must be kept between these two marks. Note that access is poor. We removed the air filter cover and outlet pipe to check the level.

2 If topping-up is necessary, first wipe the area around the filler cap with a clean rag, then hold the fluid level sensor wiring plug as the cap is unscrewed. When adding fluid, it's a good idea to inspect the reservoir. The fluid should be changed if dirt is visible or if it is more than two years old.

3 Carefully add fluid, avoiding spilling it on surrounding paintwork. If the air filter and outlet pipe are left in place a length of hose and a funnel can be used to top-up the level. Use only the specified hydraulic fluid; mixing different types of fluid can cause damage to the system and/or a loss of braking effectiveness. Bear in mind that the level in the reservoir will rise slightly when the cap/float assembly is refitted. After filling to the correct level, refit the cap securely. Wipe off any spilt fluid.

Power steering fluid level

✔ Park the vehicle on level ground.
✔ Set the steering wheel straight-ahead.
✔ The engine should be turned off.

Safety first!

● The need for frequent topping-up indicates a leak, which should be investigated immediately.

1 The reservoir is located next below the battery cover at the left-hand corner of the engine compartment. Remove the filler cap, which incorporates the dipstick

2 With the engine at operating temperature the level should be within the 'hot' range of the dipstick. If the engine is cold, then check the level on the cold side of the dipstick. If necessary, wipe the dipstick clean and recheck the level.

3 If topping-up is required, wipe clean the area around the reservoir filler neck and unscrew the filler cap from the reservoir. When topping-up, use the specified type of fluid and do not overfill the reservoir. When the level is correct, securely refit the cap.

Washer fluid level*

The underbonnet reservoir also serves the tailgate washer.

● Screen wash additives not only keep the windscreen clean during bad weather, they also prevent the washer system freezing in cold weather – which is when you are likely to need it most. Don't top-up using plain water, as the screen wash will become diluted, and will freeze in cold weather.

Warning: On no account use engine coolant antifreeze in the screen washer system – this may damage the paintwork.

1 The screen/tailgate washer fluid reservoir filler neck is located at the front of the battery cover. The screen washer level cannot easily be seen. Remove the filler cap, and look down the filler neck – if fluid is not visible, topping-up is required.

2 When topping-up the reservoir, add a screen wash additive in the quantities recommended on the bottle.

Wiper blades

1 Check the condition of the wiper blades; if they are cracked or show any signs of deterioration, or if the glass swept area is smeared, renew them. For maximum clarity of vision, wiper blades should be renewed annually.

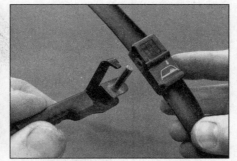

2 To remove a windscreen wiper blade, pull the arm fully away from the screen until it locks. Swivel the blade through 90°, then lift it off the wiper arm. Fit the new blade using a reversal of the removal procedure.

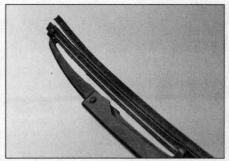

3 Don't forget to check the tailgate wiper blade as well. To remove the tailgate wiper blade, pull the arm away from the window until it locks. Carefully prise the blade from the arm using the fingers only until it is released. Fit the new blade using a reversal of the removal procedure.

Tyre condition and pressure

It is very important that tyres are in good condition, and at the correct pressure - having a tyre failure at any speed is highly dangerous. Tyre wear is influenced by driving style - harsh braking and acceleration, or fast cornering, will all produce more rapid tyre wear. As a general rule, the front tyres wear out faster than the rears. Interchanging the tyres from front to rear ("rotating" the tyres) may result in more even wear. However, if this is completely effective, you may have the expense of replacing all four tyres at once! Remove any nails or stones embedded in the tread before they penetrate the tyre to cause deflation. If removal of a nail does reveal that the tyre has been punctured, refit the nail so that its point of penetration is marked. Then immediately change the wheel, and have the tyre repaired by a tyre dealer.

Regularly check the tyres for damage in the form of cuts or bulges, especially in the sidewalls. Periodically remove the wheels, and clean any dirt or mud from the inside and outside surfaces. Examine the wheel rims for signs of rusting, corrosion or other damage. Light alloy wheels are easily damaged by "kerbing" whilst parking; steel wheels may also become dented or buckled. A new wheel is very often the only way to overcome severe damage.

New tyres should be balanced when they are fitted, but it may become necessary to re-balance them as they wear, or if the balance weights fitted to the wheel rim should fall off. Unbalanced tyres will wear more quickly, as will the steering and suspension components. Wheel imbalance is normally signified by vibration, particularly at a certain speed (typically around 50 mph). If this vibration is felt only through the steering, then it is likely that just the front wheels need balancing. If, however, the vibration is felt through the whole car, the rear wheels could be out of balance. Wheel balancing should be carried out by a tyre dealer or garage.

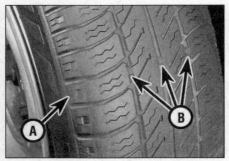

1 *Tread Depth - visual check*
The original tyres have tread wear safety bands (B), which will appear when the tread depth reaches approximately 1.6 mm. The band positions are indicated by a triangular mark on the tyre sidewall (A).

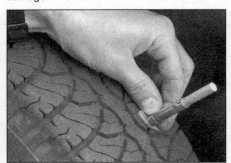

2 *Tread Depth - manual check*
Alternatively, tread wear can be monitored with a simple, inexpensive device known as a tread depth indicator gauge.

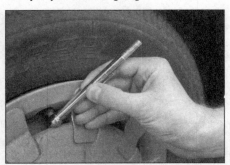

3 *Tyre Pressure Check*
Check the tyre pressures regularly with the tyres cold. Do not adjust the tyre pressures immediately after the vehicle has been used, or an inaccurate setting will result.

Tyre tread wear patterns

Shoulder Wear

Underinflation (wear on both sides)
Under-inflation will cause overheating of the tyre, because the tyre will flex too much, and the tread will not sit correctly on the road surface. This will cause a loss of grip and excessive wear, not to mention the danger of sudden tyre failure due to heat build-up.
Check and adjust pressures
Incorrect wheel camber (wear on one side)
Repair or renew suspension parts
Hard cornering
Reduce speed!

Centre Wear

Overinflation
Over-inflation will cause rapid wear of the centre part of the tyre tread, coupled with reduced grip, harsher ride, and the danger of shock damage occurring in the tyre casing.
Check and adjust pressures

If you sometimes have to inflate your car's tyres to the higher pressures specified for maximum load or sustained high speed, don't forget to reduce the pressures to normal afterwards.

Uneven Wear

Front tyres may wear unevenly as a result of wheel misalignment. Most tyre dealers and garages can check and adjust the wheel alignment (or "tracking") for a modest charge.
Incorrect camber or castor
Repair or renew suspension parts
Malfunctioning suspension
Repair or renew suspension parts
Unbalanced wheel
Balance tyres
Incorrect toe setting
Adjust front wheel alignment
Note: *The feathered edge of the tread which typifies toe wear is best checked by feel.*

Battery

Caution: Before carrying out any work on the vehicle battery, read the precautions given in 'Safety first!' at the start of this manual.

✔ Make sure that the battery tray is in good condition, and that the clamp is tight. Corrosion on the tray, retaining clamp and the battery itself can be removed with a solution of water and baking soda. Thoroughly rinse all cleaned areas with water. Any metal parts damaged by corrosion should be covered with a zinc-based primer and then painted.

✔ Periodically (approximately every three months), check the charge condition of the battery as described in Chapter 5A.

✔ On batteries which are not of the maintenance-free type, periodically check the electrolyte level in the battery – see Chapter 1.

✔ If the battery is flat, and you need to jump start your vehicle, see *Roadside Repairs.*

1 The battery is located in the left-hand front corner of the engine compartment. Remove the cover to access the battery. The exterior of the battery should be checked for damage such as cracks.

2 Lift the cover from the positive terminal and check the tightness of the clamps to ensure good electrical connections. You should not be able to move them. Check cables for cracks and frayed conductors.

HAYNES HINT

Battery corrosion can be kept to a minimum by applying a layer of petroleum jelly to the clamps and terminals after they are reconnected.

3 If corrosion (white, fluffy deposits) is evident, remove the cables from the battery terminals, clean them with a small wire brush, and then refit them. Automotive stores sell a tool for cleaning the battery post . . .

4 . . . as well as the battery cable clamps.

Electrical systems

✔ Check all external lights and the horn. Refer to the appropriate Sections of Chapter 12 for details if any of the circuits are found to be inoperative.

✔ Visually check all accessible wiring connectors, harnesses and retaining clips for security, and for signs of chafing or damage.

HAYNES HINT

If you need to check your brake lights and indicators unaided, back up to a wall or garage door and operate the lights. The reflected light should show if they are working properly.

1 If a single indicator light, brake light or headlight has failed, it is likely that a bulb has blown and will need to be renewed. Refer to Chapter 12 for details. If both brake lights have failed, it is possible that the switch has failed (see Chapter 9).

2 If more than one indicator light or tail light has failed, it is likely that either a fuse has blown or that there is a fault in the circuit (see Chapter 12). The fuses are located in the fusebox, below the driver's side of the facia. For access to the fuses, pull down the fusebox cover.

3 To renew a blown fuse, use the plastic tool provided to pull the fuse from its location then fit the new one. If the fuse blows again, it is important that you find out why – a complete checking procedure is given in Chapter 12.

Lubricants and fluids

Engine

Petrol. . . . .
Ford Formula E SAE 5W/30
Alternative 5W/30 oils may be used provided that they meet
Ford specification WSS-M2C913-B (or A)

Diesel . . . .
Ford Formula SD SAE 5W/40
Alternative 5W/40 oils may be used provided they meet
Ford specification WSS-M2C917-A

Cooling system. . . . .
Motorcraft Super Plus antifreeze (orange) to
Ford specification WSS-M97 B44-D*

Manual transmission

Five-speed transmission. . . . .
SAE 75W/90 synthetic oil to
Ford specification WSD-M2C200-C

Six-speed transmission . . . .
Ford NO52171 VX00

Automatic transmission

AG4 transmission . . . .
Ford NO52162 VX00

AG4 transmission final drive. . . . .
Ford NO52145 VX00 or SAE 75W/90

AG5 transmission . . . .
Ford NO52990 VX00

Brake (and clutch) hydraulic system . . . .
DOT 4 hydraulic fluid to Ford specification SAM-6C9103-A

Power steering . . . .
Hydraulic fluid to Ford specification WSS-M2C204-A

* Do not mix coolant types, nor top-up with any other type of coolant.

Tyre pressures

Tyre pressures (cold):	Front	Rear
Normally-laden (up to 3 people):		
195/60 R16 H tyres	3.2 bars (46 psi)	2.9 bars (42 psi)
205/55 R16 H tyres	3.3 bars (48 psi)	3.0 bars (44 psi)
215/55 R16 H tyres	2.8 bars (41 psi)	2.6 bars (38 psi)
225/45 R17 V tyres	2.8 bars (41 psi)	2.6 bars (38psi)
Fully-laden (with more than 3 people):		
195/60 R16 H tyres	3.3 bars (49 psi)	3.6 bars (52 psi)
205/55 R16 H tyres	3.5 bars (51 psi)	3.8 bars (55 psi)
215/55 R16 H tyres	3.0 bars (44 psi)	3.2 bars (46 psi)
225/45 R17 V tyres	3.0 bars (44 psi)	3.4 bars (49 psi)

Note: *Pressures apply to original-equipment tyres, and may vary if any other make of tyre is fitted; check with the tyre manufacturer or supplier for the correct pressures if necessary.*

Chapter 1 Part A:
Routine maintenance and servicing – petrol models

Contents

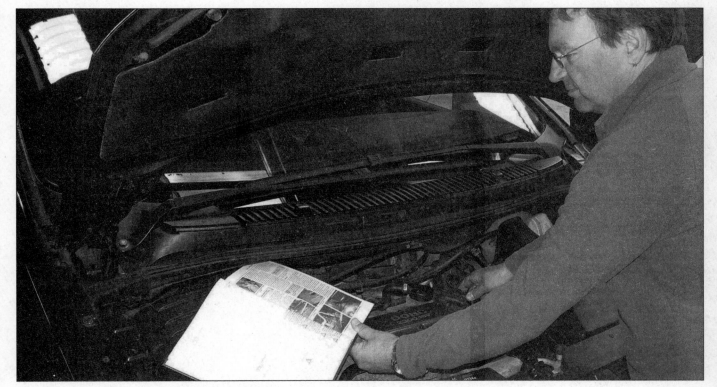

Degrees of difficulty

| Easy, suitable for novice with little experience | 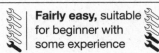 | Fairly easy, suitable for beginner with some experience | 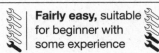 | Fairly difficult, suitable for competent DIY mechanic | 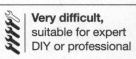 | Difficult, suitable for experienced DIY mechanic | 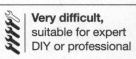 | Very difficult, suitable for expert DIY or professional | |

Lubricants and fluids. . . . .   Refer to end of *Weekly checks* on page 0•16

Capacities

Engine oil (including filter). . . . .   4.0 litres

Cooling system
With one heater . . . .   8.7 litres approx
With two heaters . . . .   10.5 litres approx
With two heaters and auxiliary heater . . . .   11.2 litres approx

Transmission
Manual transmission . . . .   2.25 litres
Automatic transmission:
   Initial filling . . . .   5.5 litres
   Fluid change. . . . .   3.5 litres
Automatic transmission final drive (filled for life) . . . .   0.8 litres

Fuel tank . . . .   70 litres approx

Cooling system

Antifreeze mixture:
   50% antifreeze . . . .   Protection down to –35°C

Ignition system

Spark plugs . . . .   Motorcraft AGPS 22P1
Spark plug electrode gap. . . . .   1.0 mm

Brakes

Brake pad minimum thickness (including backing) . . . .   7.0 mm

Auxiliary drivebelt

Tension adjustment . . . .   Automatically adjusted

Torque wrench settings

	Nm	lbf ft
Automatic transmission drain plug.	15	11
Final drive filler plug (automatic transmission).	20	15
Ignition coils.	10	7
Ignition coils/HT lead cover	5	4
Manual transmission drain plug.	35	26
Manual transmission filler/level plug	35	26
Roadwheel bolts.	170	125
Spark plugs	18	13
Sump drain plug.	25	18

The maintenance intervals in this manual are provided with the assumption that you, not the dealer, will be carrying out the work. These are the minimum intervals recommended by us for vehicles driven daily. If you wish to keep your vehicle in peak condition at all times, you may wish to perform some of these procedures more often. We encourage frequent maintenance, since it enhances the efficiency, performance and resale value of your vehicle.

When the vehicle is new, it should be serviced by a dealer service department (or other workshop recognised by the vehicle manufacturer as providing the same standard of service) in order to preserve the warranty. The vehicle manufacturer may reject warranty claims if you are unable to prove that servicing has been carried out as and when specified, using only original equipment parts or parts certified to be of equivalent quality.

Service interval display

All Ford Galaxy models are equipped with a service interval display indicator in the instrument panel. As a service approaches, the tripmeter will display SERVICE IN 2000 M when the ignition is turned on. This will be displayed for approximately 1 minute. The mileage will decrease until the display reads: SERVICE NOW. After servicing the service interval display should be reset – see Section 5.

Every 250 miles or weekly
- [ ] Refer to Weekly checks

Every 5000 miles or 6 months (whichever occurs first)
- [ ] Renew the engine oil and filter (Section 3)

Note: *Frequent oil and filter changes are good for the engine. We recommend changing the oil at least twice a year.*

Every 10 000 miles or 12 months (whichever occurs first)
- [ ] Check condition of the auxiliary drivebelt (Section 4)
- [ ] Reset the service interval display (Section 5)
- [ ] Check the operation of the windscreen/tailgate washer system(s) (Section 6)
- [ ] Lubricate all hinges and locks (Section 7)
- [ ] Check the battery electrolyte level (Section 8)
- [ ] Check the cooling system for antifreeze content (Section 9)
- [ ] Engine management ECM memory fault code check (Section 10)
- [ ] Check the tyre wear (Section 11)
- [ ] Check all underbonnet components and hoses for fluid leaks (Section 12)
- [ ] Check all brake flexible hoses and rigid pipes for condition (Section 13)
- [ ] Check the front brake pad thickness and disc condition (Section 14)
- [ ] Check the rear brake pad thickness and disc condition (Section 15)
- [ ] Check the condition of the exhaust system and its mountings (Section 16)
- [ ] Check and if necessary adjust the handbrake (Section 17)
- [ ] Check the steering and suspension components for condition and security (Section 18)
- [ ] Carry out a road test (Section 19)
- [ ] Check the tightness of the roadwheel bolts (Section 20)
- [ ] Renew the pollen filter (Section 21)
- [ ] Check the underbody sealant (Section 22)

Every 2 years (regardless of mileage)
- [ ] Renew the remote handset battery (Section 23)
- [ ] Renew the brake/clutch fluid (Section 24)
- [ ] Renew the coolant (Section 25)

Every 30 000 miles or 3 years (whichever occurs first)
Note: *Carry out the following work in addition to that described for the 10 000 miles/12 months interval.*
- [ ] Check manual transmission oil level (Section 26)
- [ ] Check the headlight beam adjustment (Section 27)
- [ ] Renew the spark plugs (Section 28)
- [ ] Check the automatic transmission final drive level (Section 29)
- [ ] Check the automatic transmission fluid level (Section 30)
- [ ] Renew the secondary air injection filter (Section 31)
- [ ] Carry out an exhaust emissions check (Section 32)

Every 40 000 miles or 4 years (whichever occurs first)
- [ ] Renew the air filter element (Section 33)

Every 80 000 miles
- [ ] Renew the auxiliary drivebelt (Section 34)

Underbonnet view

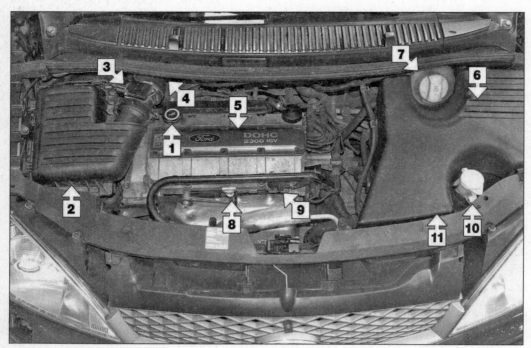

1 Engine oil filler cap
2 Air cleaner
3 Mass airflow meter
4 Brake/clutch fluid
   reservoir – hidden
5 Ignition coils/spark plugs
   cover
6 Battery
7 Coolant expansion tank
8 Engine oil level dipstick
9 Camshaft position sensor
10 Washer fluid reservoir
11 Power steering fluid
   reservoir – below cover

Front underbody view

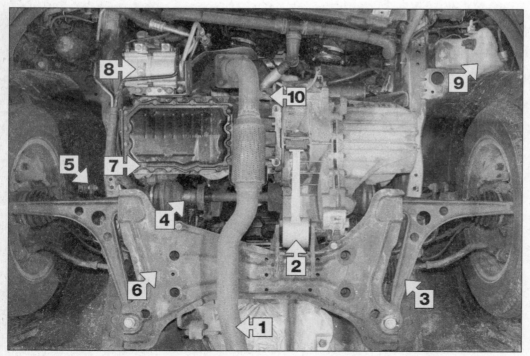

1 Exhaust front pipe
2 Engine roll restrictor
3 Lower suspension arm
4 Driveshaft
5 Anti-roll bar
6 Front crossmember
7 Engine sump oil drain
   plug
8 Air conditioning
   compressor
9 Washer fluid reservoir
10 Oxygen sensor

Rear underbody view

1 Exhaust tail pipe and
  silencer
2 Suspension trailing arm
3 Coil spring
4 Shock absorber
5 Anti-roll bar
6 Fuel tank

Maintenance procedures

1 Introduction

This Chapter is designed to help the home mechanic maintain his/her vehicle for safety, economy, long life and peak performance.

The Chapter contains a master maintenance schedule, followed by Sections dealing specifically with each task in the schedule. Visual checks, adjustments, component renewal and other helpful items are included. Refer to the accompanying illustrations of the engine compartment and the underside of the vehicle for the locations of the various components.

Servicing your vehicle in accordance with the mileage/time maintenance schedule and the following Sections will provide a planned maintenance programme, which should result in a long and reliable service life. This is a comprehensive plan, so maintaining some items but not others at the specified service intervals will not produce the same results.

As you service your vehicle, you will discover that many of the procedures can – and should – be grouped together, because of the particular procedure being performed, or because of the proximity of two otherwise unrelated components to one another. For example, if the vehicle is raised for any reason, the exhaust can be inspected at the same time as the suspension and steering components.

The first step in this maintenance pro-gramme is to prepare yourself before the actual work begins. Read through all the Sections relevant to the work to be carried out, then make a list and gather all the parts and tools required. If a problem is encountered, seek advice from a parts specialist, or a dealer service department.

2 Regular maintenance

1 If, from the time the vehicle is new, the routine maintenance schedule is followed closely, and frequent checks are made of fluid levels and high-wear items, as suggested throughout this manual, the engine will be kept in relatively good running condition, and the need for additional work will be minimised.
2 It is possible that there will be times when the engine is running poorly due to the lack of regular maintenance. This is even more likely if a used vehicle, which has not received regular and frequent maintenance checks, is purchased. In such cases, additional work may need to be carried out, outside of the regular maintenance intervals.
3 If engine wear is suspected, a compression test (refer to Chapter 2A) will provide valuable information regarding the overall performance of the main internal components. Such a test can be used as a basis to decide on the extent of the work to be carried out. If, for example, a compression test indicates serious internal engine wear, conventional maintenance as described in this Chapter will not greatly improve the performance of the engine, and may prove a waste of time and money, unless extensive overhaul work is carried out first.
4 The following series of operations are those most often required to improve the performance of a generally poor-running engine:

Primary operations

a) Clean, inspect and test the battery (See 'Weekly checks').
b) Check all the engine-related fluids (See 'Weekly checks').
c) Check the condition of the auxiliary drivebelt (Section 4).
d) Renew the spark plugs (Section 28).
e) Inspect the ignition system components (Chapter 5B).
f) Check the condition of the air filter, and renew if necessary (Section 33).
g) Check the condition of all hoses, and check for fluid leaks (Sections 12 and 13).

5 If the above operations do not prove fully effective, carry out the following secondary operations:

Secondary operations

All items listed under Primary operations, plus the following:

a) Check the charging system (Chapter 5A).
b) Check the ignition system (Chapter 5B).
c) Check the fuel system (Chapter 4A).

3.2 Remove the engine undershield

As the drain plug releases from the threads, move it away quickly so that the stream of oil running out of the sump goes into the drain pan and not up your sleeve.

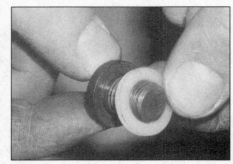

3.3 Recover the sealing ring from the drain plug

Every 5000 miles or 6 months

3 Engine oil and filter renewal

1 Frequent oil and filter changes are the most important maintenance procedures which can be undertaken by the DIY owner. As engine oil ages, it becomes diluted and contaminated, which leads to premature engine wear.

2 Before starting this procedure, gather all the necessary tools and materials. Also make sure that you have plenty of clean rags and newspapers handy, to mop-up any spills. Ideally, the engine oil should be warm, as it will drain better, and more built-up sludge will be removed with it. Take care, however, not to touch the exhaust or any other hot parts of the engine when working under the vehicle. To avoid any possibility of scalding, and to protect yourself from possible skin irritants and other harmful contaminants in used engine oils, it is advisable to wear gloves when carrying out this work. Access to the underside of the vehicle is possible if it can be raised on a lift, driven onto ramps, or jacked up and supported on axle stands (see *Jacking and vehicle support*). Whichever method is chosen, make sure that the vehicle remains level, or if it is at an angle, that the drain plug is at the lowest point. With the vehicle raised,

remove the engine compartment undershield **(see illustration)**.

3 Using a socket and wrench or a ring spanner, slacken the drain plug about half a turn. Position the draining container under the drain plug, then remove the plug completely **(see Haynes Hint)**. Recover the sealing ring from the drain plug **(see illustration)**.

4 Allow some time for the old oil to drain, noting that it may be necessary to reposition the container as the oil flow slows to a trickle.

5 After all the oil has drained, wipe off the drain plug with a clean rag, and fit a new sealing washer. Clean the area around the drain plug opening, and refit the plug. Tighten the plug to the specified torque.

6 Move the container into position under the oil filter, which is located on the left-hand rear side of the cylinder block.

7 Using an oil filter removal tool if necessary, slacken the filter initially, then unscrew it by hand the rest of the way **(see illustration)**. Empty the oil in the filter into the container.

8 Use a clean rag to remove all oil, dirt and sludge from the filter sealing area on the engine. Check the old filter to make sure that the rubber sealing ring has not stuck to the engine. If it has, carefully remove it.

9 Apply a light coating of clean engine oil to the sealing ring on the new filter, then screw it into position on the engine. Tighten the filter firmly by hand only – **do not** use any tools.

10 Remove the old oil and all tools from under the car then refit the undershield and lower the car to the ground.

11 Remove the dipstick, then unscrew the oil filler cap from the cylinder head cover **(see illustration)**. Fill the engine, using the correct grade and type of oil (see *Lubricants and fluids*). An oil can spout or funnel may help to reduce spillage. Pour in half the specified quantity of oil first, then wait a few minutes for the oil to settle in the sump. Continue adding oil a small quantity at a time until the level is up to the lower mark on the dipstick. Adding around 1.0 litre will bring the level up to the upper mark on the dipstick. Refit the filler cap.

12 Start the engine and run it at idle speed for a few minutes; check for leaks around the oil filter seal and the sump drain plug. Note that there may be a few seconds delay before the oil pressure warning light goes out when the engine is started, as the oil circulates through the engine oil galleries and the new oil filter before the pressure builds-up.

13 Switch off the engine, and wait a few minutes for the oil to settle in the sump once more. With the new oil circulated and the filter completely full, recheck the level on the dipstick, and add more oil as necessary.

14 Dispose of the used engine oil safely, with reference to *General repair procedures* in the *Reference* section of this manual.

3.7 Using a filter removal tool if necessary, slacken the filter

3.11 Unscrew the oil filler cap from the cylinder head cover

Every 10 000 miles or 12 months

4 Auxiliary drivebelt condition and tension check

1 The auxiliary drivebelt drives the alternator, coolant pump, power steering pump, and where fitted, the air conditioning compressor.

2 For access to the drivebelt, apply the handbrake, then jack up the front of the vehicle and support it on axle stands (see *Jacking and vehicle support*). Undo the bolts and remove the engine undershield **(see illustration 3.2)**.

3 Examine the auxiliary drivebelt along its entire length for damage and wear in the form of cuts and abrasions, fraying and cracking. The use of a mirror and possibly an electric torch will help, and the engine may be turned with a spanner on the crankshaft pulley in order to observe all areas of the belt.

4 If a drivebelt requires renewal, refer to Chapter 2A for the removal, refitting and adjustment procedure.

5 Service interval display resetting

1 In order to reset the service interval display, Ford technicians use specialist diagnostic equipment. In the absence of this equipment, the display can be reset as follows.

2 Turn the ignition on and hold down the trip button for 2 seconds. The display will reset. Turn the ignition off.

6 Washer system(s) operation check

1 Check that each of the washer jet nozzles are clear and that each nozzle provides a strong jet of washer fluid. The jets should be aimed to spray at a point slightly above the centre of the screen. The washer jets aim can be cleaned with a fine pin.

2 Carry out a check of all wiper blades. Look for splits or cracks on the wiping surface and renew as necessary. Check that the wipers clean efficiently across their entire sweep; any gaps in the swept area may be caused by defective wiper blade hinges, preventing the blade from following the contours of the screen/lens surface. Check that the wiper blades do not overshoot the edge of the screen/lens at the end of their sweep and that the blades park in the correct position when switched off. If this is not the case, or if the blades overlap each other at the midpoint of their stroke, the wiper arms may be incorrectly fitted (see Chapter 12).

7 Hinges and locks lubrication

1 Lubricate the hinges of the bonnet, doors and tailgate with a light general-purpose oil. Similarly, lubricate all latches, locks and lock strikers. At the same time, check the security and operation of all the locks, adjusting them if necessary (see Chapter 11).

2 Lightly lubricate the bonnet release mechanism and cable with a suitable grease.

8 Battery electrolyte level check

1 Where a non-maintenance free battery is fitted, the level of the electrolyte may be checked and if necessary topped-up. On some batteries, MIN and MAX marks are printed on the side of the battery and the level may be checked without removing the cell covers. Where there are no exterior marks, remove the cover(s) from the top of the cells and check that the level of the electrolyte is approximately 2 or 3 mm above the internal plates. Some batteries may have a plastic internal level indicator.

2 If necessary, top-up the cells using distilled or de-ionised water.

3 Refit the cell cover(s).

9 Cooling system antifreeze concentration check

⚠️ **Warning: Wait until the engine is cold before starting this procedure. Do not allow antifreeze to come in contact with your skin, or with the painted surfaces of the vehicle. Rinse off spills immediately with plenty of water.**

1 Note that a tester will be required to check the coolant strength; these can be obtained relatively cheaply from most motor accessory shops.

10.1 Checking the ECM for stored fault codes

2 With the engine completely cold, unscrew and remove the filler cap from the coolant expansion tank. Follow the instructions supplied with the tester and check the coolant mixture is sufficient to give protection down to temperatures well below freezing. If the coolant has been renewed regularly this shouldn't be a problem. However, if the coolant mixture is not strong enough to provide sufficient protection it will be necessary to drain the cooling system and renew the coolant (see Section 25).

3 Once the test is complete, check the coolant level is correct (see *Weekly checks*) then securely refit the expansion tank cap.

10 Engine management ECM memory fault code check

Rudimentary fault code readers are now available for a modest cost. These tend to only display the mandatory emissions-related fault codes. More expensive models may be able to access the engine management (and other systems) in greater depth **(see illustration)**. For a fully comprehensive check a professional tool will be required. Ford's own IDS diagnostic tool is the obvious choice here, as it is also capable of updating the vehicles software as well as listing any fault codes stored within the various control modules. Many independent garages will own this or similar professional tools.

11 Tyre wear check

1 Raise and securely support the relevant side of the car in turn to allow a thorough check of each tyre to be performed; refer to *Jacking and vehicle support* for reference.

2 Turn the tyre slowly by hand and carry out an inspection as described in *Weekly checks*.

3 Lower the vehicle to the ground.

12 Underbonnet/underbody components and hoses fluid leak check

1 For access to the bottom of the engine, jack up the front of the vehicle and support it on axle stands (see *Jacking and vehicle support*). Undo the two retaining nuts and four bolts (two each side), and remove the undershield. Visually inspect the engine joint faces, gaskets and seals for any signs of water or oil leaks. Pay particular attention to the areas around the camshaft cover, cylinder head, oil filter and sump joint faces. Bear in mind that, over a period of time, some very slight seepage from these areas is to be expected – what you are really looking for is any indication of

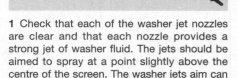
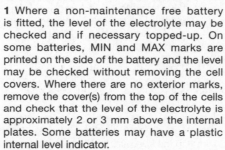

A leak in the cooling system will usually show up as white- or antifreeze-coloured crusty deposits on the area surrounding the leak.

a serious leak. Should a leak be found, renew the offending gasket or oil seal by referring to the appropriate Chapters in this manual.

2 Also check the security and condition of all the engine-related pipes and hoses. Ensure that all cable-ties or securing clips are in place and in good condition. Clips which are broken or missing can lead to chafing of the hoses, pipes or wiring, which could cause more serious problems in the future.

3 Carefully check the radiator hoses and heater hoses along their entire length. Renew any hose which is cracked, swollen or deteriorated. Cracks will show up better if the hose is squeezed. Pay close attention to the hose clips that secure the hoses to the cooling system components. Hose clips can pinch and puncture hoses, resulting in cooling system leaks.

4 Inspect all the cooling system components (hoses, joint faces, etc) for leaks **(see Haynes Hint)**. Where any problems of this nature are found on system components, renew the component or gasket with reference to Chapter 3.

5 Where applicable, inspect the automatic transmission fluid cooler hoses for leaks or deterioration.

6 With the vehicle raised at the rear, inspect the petrol tank and filler neck for punctures, cracks and other damage. The connection between the filler neck and tank is especially critical. Sometimes a rubber filler neck

14.2 The thickness of the brake pad, including the backing plate, must not be less than 7 mm

or connecting hose will leak due to loose retaining clamps or deteriorated rubber.

7 Carefully check all rubber hoses and metal fuel lines leading away from the petrol tank. Check for loose connections, deteriorated hoses, crimped lines, and other damage. Pay particular attention to the vent pipes and hoses, which often loop up around the filler neck and can become blocked or crimped. Follow the lines to the front of the vehicle, carefully inspecting them all the way. Renew damaged sections as necessary.

8 From within the engine compartment, check the security of all fuel hose attachments and pipe unions, and inspect the fuel hoses and vacuum hoses for kinks, chafing and deterioration.

9 Check the condition of the power steering fluid hoses and pipes.

10 On completion, refit the undershield, and lower the vehicle to the ground.

13 Brake flexible hoses and rigid pipes condition check

1 Inspect all the braking system flexible hoses and metal pipes for signs of damage or deterioration. Any faulty pipe/hoses must be renewed (see Chapter 9).

14 Front brake pad thickness and disc condition check

1 Firmly apply the handbrake, loosen the front roadwheel bolts, then jack up the front of the car and support it securely on axle stands (see *Jacking and vehicle support*). Remove the front roadwheels.

2 For a comprehensive check, the brake pads should be removed and cleaned. The operation of the caliper can then also be checked, and the condition of the brake disc itself can be fully examined on both sides. Refer to Chapter 9 **(see illustration)**.

3 If any pad's friction material is worn to the specified thickness or less, *all four pads must be renewed as a set.* **Note:** *If any pad is approaching the minimum thickness, consider renewal as a precautionary measure in case the pads wear out before the next service.*

16.2 Check the condition of the exhaust mountings

4 On completion, refit the roadwheels and lower the vehicle to the ground.

15 Rear brake pad thickness and disc condition check

1 Firmly chock the front wheels and select first gear or Park, then jack up the rear of the vehicle and support it securely on axle stands (see *Jacking and vehicle support*). Remove the rear roadwheels.

2 For a quick check, the pad thickness can be carried out via the inspection hole on the rear of the caliper. Using a steel rule, measure the thickness of the pad lining including the backing plate. This must not be less than that indicated in the Specifications.

3 The view through the caliper inspection hole gives a rough indication of the state of the brake pads. For a comprehensive check, the brake pads should be removed and cleaned. The operation of the caliper can then also be checked, and the condition of the brake disc itself can be fully examined on both sides. Chapter 9 contains a detailed description of how the brake disc should be checked for wear and/or damage.

4 If any pad's friction material is worn to the specified thickness or less, *all four pads must be renewed as a set.* **Note:** *If any pad is approaching the minimum thickness, consider renewal as a precautionary measure in case the pads wear out before the next service.* Refer to Chapter 9 for details.

5 On completion, refit the roadwheels and lower the vehicle to the ground.

16 Exhaust system and mountings condition check

1 With the engine cold, check the complete exhaust system from the engine to the end of the tailpipe. The exhaust system is most easily checked with the vehicle raised on a hoist, or suitably-supported on axle stands, so that the exhaust components are readily visible and accessible.

2 Check the exhaust pipes and connections for evidence of leaks, severe corrosion and damage. Make sure that all brackets and mountings are in good condition, and that all relevant nuts and bolts are tight **(see illustration)**. Leakage at any of the joints or in other parts of the system will usually show up as a black sooty stain in the vicinity of the leak.

3 Rattles and other noises can often be traced to the exhaust system, especially the brackets and mountings. If the components are able to come into contact with the body or suspension parts, secure the system with new mountings. Otherwise separate the joints (if possible) and twist the pipes as necessary to provide additional clearance.

17 Handbrake check and adjustment

1 With the vehicle on level ground, chock the front wheels and release the handbrake lever. Gradually apply the handbrake, counting the number of clicks from the ratchet mechanism until the handbrake is fully applied. If the adjustment is correct, there should be 3 to 6 clicks before the handbrake is fully applied. If this is not the case, adjust as follows.

2 Ensure the front wheel chocks are still in place, jack up the rear of the vehicle and support it on axle stands (see *Jacking and vehicle support*). Fully release the handbrake lever.

3 Working underneath the vehicle, rotate the adjuster locknut in the required direction to achieve the correct lever adjustment **(see illustration)**.

4 With the handbrake fully released, check that the rear wheels rotate freely, with no signs of binding or resistance.

5 Once the adjustment is correct, lower the vehicle to the ground.

18 Steering and suspension components condition/ security check

Suspension and steering

1 Raise the front of the vehicle, and securely support it on axle stands.

2 Visually inspect the balljoint dust covers and the steering rack gaiters for splits, chafing or deterioration. Any wear of these components will cause loss of lubricant, together with dirt and water entry, resulting in rapid deterioration of the balljoints or steering gear.

3 On vehicles with power steering, check the fluid hoses for chafing or deterioration, and the pipe and hose unions for fluid leaks. Also check for signs of fluid leakage under pressure from the steering gear rubber gaiters, which would indicate failed fluid seals within the steering gear.

4 Grasp the roadwheel at the 12 o'clock and 6 o'clock positions, and try to rock it **(see illustration)**. Very slight free play may be felt, but if the movement is appreciable, further investigation is necessary to determine the source. Continue rocking the wheel while an assistant depresses the footbrake. If the movement is now eliminated or significantly reduced, it is likely that the hub bearings are at fault. If the free play is still evident with the footbrake depressed, then there is wear in the suspension joints or mountings.

5 Now grasp the wheel at the 9 o'clock and 3 o'clock positions, and try to rock it as before. Any movement felt now may again be caused by wear in the hub bearings or the steering track rod balljoints. If the inner or outer balljoint is worn, the visual movement will be obvious.

6 Using a large screwdriver or flat bar, check for wear in the suspension mounting bushes by levering between the relevant suspension component and its attachment point. Some movement is to be expected as the mountings are made of rubber, but excessive wear should be obvious. Also check the condition of any visible rubber bushes, looking for splits, cracks or contamination of the rubber.

7 With the car standing on its wheels, have an assistant turn the steering wheel back-and-forth about an eighth of a turn each way. There should be very little, if any, lost movement between the steering wheel and roadwheels. If this is not the case, closely observe the joints and mountings previously described, but in addition, check the steering column universal joints for wear, and the rack-and-pinion steering gear itself.

Strut/shock absorbers

8 Check for any signs of fluid leakage around the suspension strut/shock absorber body, or from the rubber gaiter around the piston rod. Should any fluid be noticed, the suspension strut/shock absorber is defective internally, and should be renewed. **Note:** *Suspension struts/shock absorbers should always be renewed in pairs on the same axle.*

9 The efficiency of the suspension strut/shock absorber may be checked by bouncing the vehicle at each corner. Generally speaking, the body will return to its normal position and stop after being depressed. If it rises and returns on a rebound, the suspension strut/shock absorber is probably suspect. Examine also the suspension strut/shock absorber upper and lower mountings for any signs of wear.

Driveshafts

10 With the vehicle raised and securely supported on stands, turn the steering onto full lock then slowly rotate the roadwheel. Inspect the condition of the outer constant velocity (CV) joint rubber gaiters while squeezing the gaiters to open out the folds. Check for signs of cracking, splits or deterioration of the rubber which may allow the grease to escape and lead to water and grit entry into the joint. Also check the security and condition of the retaining clips. Repeat these checks on the inner CV joints. If any damage or deterioration is found, the gaiters should be renewed as described in Chapter 8, Section 3.

11 At the same time check the general condition of the CV joints themselves by first holding the driveshaft and attempting to rotate the wheel. Repeat this check by holding the inner joint and attempting to rotate the driveshaft. Any appreciable movement indicates wear in the joints, wear in the driveshaft splines or loose driveshaft retaining bolt.

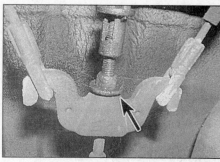

17.3 Turn the adjuster locknut (arrowed) to adjust the handbrake lever

19 Road test

Instruments and electrical equipment

1 Check the operation of all instruments and electrical equipment.

2 Make sure that all instruments read correctly, and switch on all electrical equipment in turn, to check that it functions properly.

Steering and suspension

3 Check for any abnormalities in the steering, suspension, handling or road feel.

4 Drive the vehicle, and check that there are no unusual vibrations or noises.

5 Check that the steering feels positive, with no excessive sloppiness, or roughness, and check for any suspension noises when cornering and driving over bumps.

Drivetrain

6 Check the performance of the engine, clutch (where applicable), gearbox/transmission and driveshafts.

7 Listen for any unusual noises from the engine, clutch and gearbox/transmission.

8 Make sure that the engine runs smoothly when idling, and that there is no hesitation when accelerating.

9 Check that, where applicable, the clutch action is smooth and progressive, that the drive is taken up smoothly, and that the

18.4 Check for signs of wear in the hub bearings by grasping the roadwheel at the 12 o'clock and 6 o'clock positions

pedal travel is not excessive. Also listen for any noises when the clutch pedal is depressed.

10 On manual gearbox models, check that all gears can be engaged smoothly without noise, and that the gear lever action is smooth and not abnormally vague or notchy.

11 On automatic transmission models, make sure that all gearchanges occur smoothly, without snatching, and without an increase in engine speed between changes. Check that all the gear positions can be selected with the vehicle at rest. If any problems are found, they should be referred to a Ford dealer or specialist.

Braking system

12 Make sure that the vehicle does not pull to one side when braking, and that the wheels do not lock when braking hard.

13 Check that there is no vibration through the steering when braking.

14 Check that the handbrake operates correctly without excessive movement of the lever, and that it holds the vehicle stationary on a slope.

15 Test the operation of the brake servo unit as follows. With the engine off, depress the footbrake four or five times to exhaust the vacuum. Hold the brake pedal depressed, then start the engine. As the engine starts, there should be a noticeable give in the brake pedal as vacuum builds-up. Allow the engine to run for at least two minutes, and then switch it off. If the brake pedal is depressed now, it should be possible to detect a hiss from the servo as the pedal is depressed. After about four or five applications, no further hissing should be heard, and the pedal should feel considerably harder.

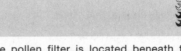

20 Roadwheel bolts tightness check

1 With the vehicle wheels on the ground and the handbrake applied, prise off the wheel trims (where applicable), and check the tightness of the wheel bolts using a torque wrench. The correct torque setting is given at the start of this Chapter.

2 When all the bolts have been checked, refit the wheel trims (where applicable).

21 Pollen filter renewal

1 The pollen filter is located beneath the windscreen cowl panels; it is located on the right-hand side on left-hand drive models, and on the left-hand side on right-hand drive models.

2 Remove the battery compartment cover and then remove the side panel. With reference to Chapter 11 remove the windscreen cowl panel and then remove the bulkhead panel **(see illustration)**.

3 Unbolt the coolant expansion tank and move it to one side. Access is considerably easier if the windscreen wiper motor and linkage is removed as described in Chapter 12.

4 Ensure that the area around the filter is cleared of all leaves, debris, etc, as when the filter is removed, this will be able to enter the vehicle interior.

5 Release the retaining clip, and slide the element with the frame out of the guide towards the centre of the vehicle. Manoeuvre the frame and element under the wiper linkage (if left in place) and out from the engine compartment **(see illustrations)**.

6 Remove the filter element from the frame.

7 Fit the new element onto the frame, with the airflow arrows pointing towards the vehicle interior, ensuring that the left and right ends of the frame fit into the first laminations at each end of the element. Ensure also that the square pegs of the frame locate in the filter laminations **(see illustrations)**.

8 Guide the frame and element under the wiper linkage and slide it into position, ensuring that the guide lugs on the frame engage correctly with the guide slots in the housing, and the retaining clip locks the assembly in place **(see illustration)**.

9 The remainder of the refitting procedure is a reversal of removal.

22 Underbody sealant check

Raise and support the vehicle on axle stands (see *Jacking and vehicle support*).

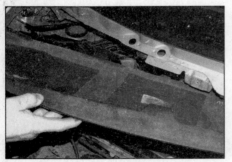

21.2 Remove the bulkhead panel

21.5a Release the pollen filter retaining clip (arrowed) . . .

21.5b . . . and remove the filter

21.7a Fit the new element into the frame with the airflow arrows pointing to the vehicle interior . . .

21.7b . . . and the ends of the frame located into the first and last laminations of the filter

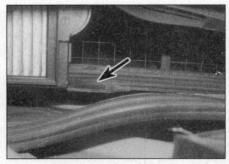

21.8 The lugs on the frame must engage with the guide slots in the housing (arrowed)

Using an electric torch or lead light, inspect the entire underside of the vehicle, paying particular attention to the wheel arches. Look for any damage to the flexible underbody coating, which may crack or flake off with age, leading to corrosion. Also check that the wheel arch liners (where fitted) are securely attached with any clips provided – if they come loose, dirt may get in behind the liners and defeat their purpose. If there is any damage to the underseal, or any corrosion, it should be repaired before the damage gets too serious.

Every 2 years

23 Handset battery renewal

1 Carefully prise the handset body from the key blade **(see illustration)**.
2 Using a small screwdriver release the retaining clips and separate the halves of the handset body **(see illustration)**.
3 Gently push back the clips and lift the first battery, dividing plate, and second battery from the handset.
4 Insert the first new battery, positive side up, into the handset **(see illustration)**.
5 Place the dividing plate on top of the first battery **(see illustration)**.
6 Insert the second battery, again positive side up, making sure it is held in place by the retaining clips.
7 Fit the halves of the handset together, and slide it back into the key blade.
8 It may be the case that the handset will not function correctly after battery renewal. If this is the case the handset must be resynchronised as follows:
a) *With the key in the driver's lock, turn it three times anti-clockwise within twenty seconds. Hold the key in the unlock position for half a second between turns.*
b) *Remove the key from the lock – the LED in the driver's door will now be flashing.*
c) *Point the key at the rear view mirror and press the lock button. This must be performed within five seconds of removing the key.*
d) *Whilst still holding the locking button down, press the unlock button three times and then release the locking button.*
e) *The LED in the driver's door will flash to confirm that coding is complete.*
f) *The above procedure must be completed within 20 seconds.*
g) *If another key with remote locking is available then follow points 'c' and 'd' within fifteen seconds of programming the previous key.*

24 Brake/clutch fluid renewal

⚠ *Warning: Brake hydraulic fluid can harm your eyes and damage painted surfaces, so use extreme caution when handling and pouring it. Do not use fluid that has been standing open for some time, as it absorbs moisture from the air. Excess moisture can cause a dangerous loss of braking effectiveness.*

Brakes

1 The procedure is similar to that for the bleeding of the hydraulic system as described in Chapter 9.
2 On right-hand drive models, remove the air ducting assembly as described in Chapter 4A, to gain access to the master cylinder reservoir.
3 Working as described in Chapter 9, open the first bleed screw in the sequence, and pump the brake pedal gently until nearly all the old fluid has been emptied from the master cylinder reservoir. Top-up to the MAX level with new fluid, and continue pumping until only the new fluid remains in the reservoir, and new fluid can be seen emerging from the bleed screw. Tighten the screw, and top the reservoir level up to the MAX level line.
4 Work through all the remaining bleed screws in the sequence until new fluid can be seen at all of them. Be careful to keep the master cylinder reservoir topped-up to above the MIN level at all times, or air may enter the system and greatly increase the length of the task. The bleed screw sequence is:
a) *Left-hand front brake.*
b) *Right-hand front brake.*
c) *Right-hand rear brake.*
d) *Left-hand rear brake.*
5 When the operation is complete, check that all bleed screws are securely tightened, and that their dust caps are refitted. Wash off all traces of spilt fluid, and recheck the master cylinder reservoir fluid level. Check the operation of the brakes before taking the car on the road.

Clutch

6 Because the clutch hydraulic system shares the same fluid reservoir as the brake system, we recommend that the clutch hydraulic fluid is renewed at the same time. Working as described in Chapter 6, remove the dust cap from the slave cylinder bleed screw. Fit a spanner and tube to the screw, place the other end of the tube in a jar, and pour in sufficient fluid to cover the end of the tube.
7 Ensure that the fluid level is maintained at least above the lower level line in the reservoir throughout the procedure.
8 Have an assistant fully depress the clutch pedal several times to build-up pressure, then maintain it on the final downstroke.
9 While pedal pressure is maintained, unscrew the bleed screw (approximately one half of a turn) and allow the compressed fluid to flow into the jar. The assistant should maintain pedal pressure and should not release it until instructed to do so. When the flow stops, tighten the bleed screw again,

23.1 Prise the handset body from the key blade

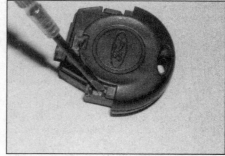
23.2 Release the retaining clips and separate the halves of the body

23.4 Insert the first battery, positive (+) side up

23.5 Place the dividing plate on the first battery

have the assistant release the pedal slowly, and recheck the reservoir fluid level.

10 Repeat the steps given in paragraphs 8 and 9 until the new fluid emerges from the bleed screw. If the master cylinder has been drained and refilled, allow approximately five seconds between cycles for the master cylinder passages to refill.

11 Tighten the bleed screw securely, remove the tube and spanner, and refit the dust cap. Do not overtighten the bleed screw.

12 Wash off all traces of spilt fluid, and recheck the fluid level.

25 Coolant renewal

⚠️ *Warning: Wait until the engine is cold before starting this procedure. Do not allow antifreeze to come in contact with your skin, or with the painted surfaces of the vehicle. Rinse off spills immediately with plenty of water. Never leave antifreeze lying around in an open container, or in a puddle in the driveway or on the garage floor. Children and pets are attracted by its sweet smell, but antifreeze can be fatal if ingested.*

Cooling system draining

1 With the engine completely cold, cover the expansion tank cap with a wad of rag, and slowly turn the cap anti-clockwise to relieve the pressure in the cooling system (a hissing sound may be heard). Wait until any pressure remaining in the system is released, then continue to turn the cap until it can be removed.

2 Release the fasteners (four bolts, two nuts) and remove the engine/transmission undershield. Position a suitable container beneath the radiator bottom hose connection, then release the retaining clip and ease the hose from the radiator stub. If the hose joint has not been disturbed for some time, it will be necessary to gently manipulate the hose to break the joint. Do not use excessive force, or the radiator stub could be damaged. Allow the coolant to drain into the container (see illustration).

3 If the coolant has been drained for a

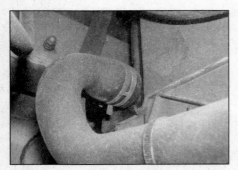

25.2 Release the retaining clip, and ease the bottom hose from the radiator stub

reason other than renewal, then provided it is clean and less than two years old, it can be re-used if there is no alternative, but this is not recommended. **Note:** *If an aluminium engine component which comes into contact with the coolant has been renewed, then the coolant must also be renewed. Used coolant will not protect new aluminium from corrosion.*

4 Once all the coolant has drained, reconnect the hose to the radiator and refit the retaining clip.

Cooling system flushing

5 If coolant renewal has been neglected, or if the antifreeze mixture has become diluted, then in time, the cooling system may gradually lose efficiency, as the coolant passages become restricted due to rust, scale deposits, and other sediment. Flushing the system clean can restore the cooling system efficiency.

6 The radiator should be flushed independently of the engine, to avoid unnecessary contamination.

Radiator flushing

7 To flush the radiator, disconnect the top and bottom hoses and any other relevant hoses from the radiator, with reference to Chapter 3.

8 Insert a garden hose into the radiator top inlet. Direct a flow of clean water through the radiator, and continue flushing until clean water emerges from the radiator bottom outlet.

9 If after a reasonable period, the water still does not run clear, the radiator can be flushed with a good proprietary cooling system cleaning agent. It is important that their manufacturer's instructions are followed carefully. If the contamination is particularly bad, insert the hose in the radiator bottom outlet, and reverse-flush the radiator.

Engine flushing

10 To flush the engine, remove the thermostat as described in Chapter 3, then temporarily refit the thermostat cover.

11 With the top and bottom hoses disconnected from the radiator, insert a garden hose into the radiator top hose. Direct a clean flow of water through the engine, and continue flushing until clean water emerges from the radiator bottom hose.

12 On completion of flushing, refit the thermostat and reconnect the hoses with reference to Chapter 3.

Cooling system filling

13 Before attempting to fill the cooling system, make sure that all hoses and clips are in good condition, and that the clips/connections are secure. Note that an antifreeze mixture must be used all year round, to prevent corrosion of the engine components (see following sub-Section).

14 Remove the expansion tank filler cap, and fill the system by slowly pouring the coolant into the expansion tank to prevent airlocks from forming.

15 If the coolant is being renewed, begin by

pouring in a couple of litres of water, followed by the correct quantity of antifreeze, then fill with more water.

16 Once the level in the expansion tank starts to rise, squeeze the radiator top and bottom hoses to help expel any trapped air in the system. Once all the air is expelled, top-up the coolant level to the MAX mark, refit the expansion tank cap.

17 Start the engine and run it at a fast idle for about three minutes. After this, allow the engine to idle normally until the bottom hose becomes hot.

18 Check for leaks, particularly around disturbed components. Check the coolant level in the expansion tank, and top-up if necessary. Note that the system must be cold before an accurate level is indicated in the expansion tank. If the expansion tank cap is removed while the engine is still warm, cover the cap with a thick cloth, and unscrew the cap slowly to gradually relieve the system pressure (a hissing sound will normally be heard). Wait until any pressure remaining in the system is released, then continue to turn the cap until it can be removed. Never remove the cap when the engine is still hot.

Antifreeze mixture

Caution: All vehicles were originally filled with Ford's own Motorcraft Super Plus 2000 (orange in colour). If the coolant visible in the expansion tank is any colour other than orange, then the cooling system may have been topped-up with coolant containing the wrong type of antifreeze. If you are unsure of the type of antifreeze used, or if you suspect that mixing may have occurred, the best course of action is to drain, flush and refill the cooling system. Note that Ford specify the coolant should be changed after a period ten years. However, we consider it prudent to consider changing the coolant after two years and definitely changing it after five years.

19 The antifreeze should always be renewed at the specified intervals. This is necessary not only to maintain the antifreeze properties, but also to prevent corrosion, which would otherwise occur as the corrosion inhibitors become progressively less effective.

20 The quantity of antifreeze and levels of protection are indicated in the Specifications.

21 Before adding antifreeze, the cooling system should be completely drained, preferably flushed, and all hoses checked for condition and security.

22 After filling with antifreeze, a label should be attached to the expansion tank, stating the type and concentration of antifreeze used, and the date installed. Any subsequent topping-up should be made with the same type and concentration of antifreeze.

Caution: Do not use engine antifreeze in the washer system, as it will cause damage to the vehicle paintwork.

Every 30 000 miles or 3 years

26 Manual transmission oil level check

1 The oil filler/level plug is located on the front side of the manual transmission.
2 Apply the handbrake, then jack up the front and rear of the vehicle and support it on axle stands (see *Jacking and vehicle support*). To ensure an accurate check, make sure that the vehicle is level. Undo the two retaining nuts and four bolts (two each side), and remove the engine/transmission undershield.
3 Unscrew and remove the filler/level plug (see illustration).
4 Check that the oil level is to the bottom lip of the filler hole.
5 If necessary, add the specified oil through the filler/level hole. If the level requires frequent topping-up, check for leaks.
6 Refit the plug and tighten to the specified torque. Refit the engine/transmission undershield, then lower the vehicle to the ground.

27 Headlight beam adjustment

1 Accurate adjustment of the headlight beam is only possible using optical beam setting equipment, and this work should therefore be carried out by a Ford dealer or suitably-equipped workshop. All MOT test centres have this equipment.
2 For reference, the headlights can be adjusted using the adjuster screws, accessible via the top of each light unit (see the illustrations given in Chapter 12, Section 9).
3 All models are equipped with an electrically-operated headlight beam adjustment system which is controlled through the switch in the facia. On these models, ensure that the switch is set to the basic 0 position before adjusting the headlight aim.

28 Spark plug renewal

1 The correct functioning of the spark plugs is vital for the correct running and efficiency of the engine. It is essential that the plugs fitted are appropriate for the engine (a suitable type is specified at the beginning of this Chapter). If this type is used and the engine is in good condition, the spark plugs should not need attention between scheduled renewal intervals. Spark plug cleaning is rarely necessary, and should not be attempted unless specialised equipment is available, as damage can easily be caused to the firing ends.
2 Undo the retaining bolts and remove the ignition coils/HT lead cover from the top of the engine (see illustration).
3 Release the wiring harness from the retaining clips on the coils, and disconnect the wiring plugs (see illustration). Some models have a single ignition coil pack fitted to the end of the cylinder head, on these models remove the HT leads to access the spark plugs.
4 Release the HT leads from the retaining clips on the coils, and disconnect the HT lead connectors from the spark plugs. Pull the leads from the plugs by gripping the end fitting, not the lead, otherwise the lead connection may be fractured (see illustrations).
5 Slacken and remove the retaining screws, and remove the ignition coils (see illustration). Note that the HT connections on the underside of the coils locate directly onto the spark plugs beneath them.
6 It is advisable to remove the dirt from the spark plug recesses using a clean brush, vacuum cleaner or compressed air before removing the plugs, to prevent dirt dropping into the cylinders.
7 Unscrew the plugs using a spark plug spanner, suitable box spanner or a deep socket and extension bar (see illustration). Keep the socket aligned with the spark plug – if it is forcibly moved to one side, the ceramic insulator may be broken off. As each plug is removed, examine it as follows.
8 Examination of the spark plugs will give a good indication of the condition of the

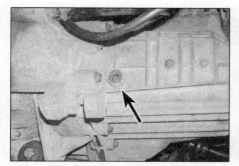

26.3 Unscrew and remove the filler/level plug (arrowed)

28.2 Remove the cover (arrowed) from the ignition coils/HT leads

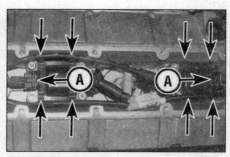

28.3 Release the wiring from the retaining clips (arrowed), then disconnect the wiring plugs (A) from the coils

28.4a Squeeze the retaining tabs and disconnect the HT leads from the coils . . .

28.4b . . . then pull the HT leads from the spark plugs

28.5 Undo the coil retaining screws (arrowed)

28.7 Unscrew the spark plugs using a deep socket or similar

28.12a Check the electrode gap using a feeler gauge . . .

28.12b . . . or wire gauge

engine. If the insulator nose of the spark plug is clean and white, with no deposits, this is indicative of a weak mixture or too hot a plug (a hot plug transfers heat away from the electrode slowly, a cold plug transfers heat away quickly).

9 If the tip and insulator nose are covered with hard black-looking deposits, then this is indicative that the mixture is too rich. Should the plug be black and oily, then it is likely that the engine is fairly worn, as well as the mixture being too rich.

10 If the insulator nose is covered with light tan to greyish-brown deposits, then the mixture is correct and it is likely that the engine is in good condition.

11 The spark plug electrode gap is of considerable importance as, if it is too large or too small, the size of the spark and its efficiency will be seriously impaired. On engines fitted with multi-electrode spark plugs, it is recommended that the plugs are renewed rather attempting to adjust the gaps. With other spark plugs, the gap should be set to the value given by the manufacturer.

12 To set the gap, measure it with a feeler

blade and then bend open, or closed, the outer plug electrode until the correct gap is achieved. The centre electrode should never be bent, as this may crack the insulator and cause plug failure, if nothing worse. If using feeler blades, the gap is correct when the appropriate-size blade is a firm sliding fit **(see illustrations)**.

13 Special spark plug electrode gap adjusting tools are available from most motor accessory shops, or from some spark plug manufacturers.

14 Before fitting the spark plugs, check that the threaded connector sleeves are tight, and that the plug exterior surfaces and threads are clean. It's often difficult to screw in new spark plugs without cross-threading them – this can be avoided using a piece of rubber hose **(see Haynes Hint)**.

15 Remove the rubber hose (if used), and tighten the plug to the specified torque using the spark plug socket and a torque wrench. Refit the remaining spark plugs in the same manner.

16 The remainder of refitting is a reversal of refitting.

29 Final drive oil level check (automatic transmission)

1 The final drive oil filler/level plug is located on the right-hand side of the automatic transmission, behind the right-hand driveshaft inner joint **(see illustration)**. Apply the handbrake, then jack up the front of the vehicle and support it on axle stands (see *Jacking and vehicle support*). Undo the two retaining nuts and four bolts (two each side), and remove the engine undershield. To ensure an accurate check, make sure that the vehicle is level.

2 Unscrew and remove the filler/level plug and check that the oil level is on the bottom lip of the filler hole. If necessary, add the specified oil through the filler/level hole. If the level requires constant topping-up, check for leaks and repair.

3 Refit the plug and tighten to the specified torque, then lower the vehicle to the ground.

30 Automatic transmission fluid level check

Note: *For an accurate fluid level check, Ford technicians use an electronic tester which is plugged into the vehicle's diagnostic socket, and establishes that the temperature of the fluid is between 35° and 45°C via a sensor within the transmission casing. In view of this, it is recommended that the vehicle is taken to a Ford dealer or automatic transmission specialist to have the level checked.*

1 Jack up the front and rear of the vehicle and support it on axle stands (see *Jacking and vehicle support*). Undo the two retaining nuts and four bolts (two each side), and remove the engine undershield.

2 Note that the transmission must be refilled from below the vehicle, so make sure that the vehicle is supported in a level position.

3 Start the engine and move the selector lever through all gear positions. Switch off the engine.

4 At this point the Ford technician connects the IDS tester to the vehicle's diagnostic socket, and establishes that the temperature

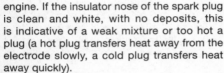

It is very often difficult to insert spark plugs into their holes without cross-threading them. To avoid this possibility, fit a short length of hose over the end of the spark plug. The flexible hose acts as a universal joint to help align the plug with the plug thread, the hose will slip on the spark plug, preventing thread damage to the aluminium cylinder head.

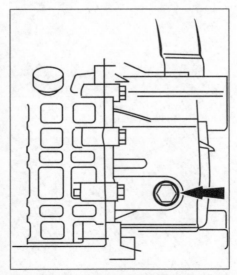

29.1 On automatic transmissions, the final drive oil filler/level plug is located on the right-hand side, behind the driveshaft inner joint (arrowed)

of the transmission fluid is between 35° and 45°C. **Note:** *If the level is checked when the temperature is too low, overfilling will occur. If the level is checked when the temperature is too high, underfilling will occur.*

5 With the vehicle still on level ground, start the engine and unscrew the level plug from under the transmission **(see illustration)**. If the level is too high, fluid will escape down the overflow pipe. Refit and tighten the level plug when the fluid ceases to drip. If the level is too low, no fluid will escape.

6 If the fluid level is too low, pull out the retaining clip and pull off the filler pipe blanking plug from the front of the transmission casing **(see illustration)**. On some models, the filler plug is secured by a cap. Prise the cap off with a screwdriver. Using a funnel, add fluid until it begins to drip from the overflow pipe, then tighten the level plug. Always renew the sealing washer.

7 With the fluid level correct, refit the filler plug and secure it in place with the retaining clip or cap.

8 Refit the engine/transmission undershield, and lower the vehicle to the ground.

31 Secondary air injection pump filter renewal

1 Remove the battery compartment upper panel.

2 Reach down and slacken the secondary air injection pump filter retaining clip.

3 Pull the filter from the hose.

4 Refitting is a reversal of removal.

32 Exhaust emissions check

This check is part of the manufacturer's maintenance schedule, and involves testing the exhaust emissions using an exhaust gas analyser. Unless a fault is suspected, this test is not essential, although it should be noted that it is recommended by the manufacturers. Exhaust emissions testing is included as part of the MOT test.

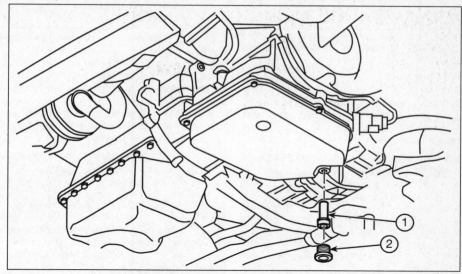

30.5 **Transmission level plug (1) and drain plug (2)**

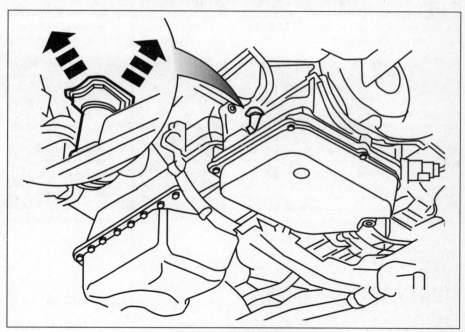

30.6 **Pull out the filler cap**

Every 40 000 miles or 4 years

33 Air filter element renewal

1 Disconnect the mass airflow sensor wiring plug, then release the retaining clips, and separate the sensor from the air filter cover **(see illustrations)**.

2 Lift up and remove the right-hand headlight shield.
3 Release the air filter cover retaining clips, remove the cover, and lift out the element **(see illustrations)**. Note which way around the element is fitted.
4 With the filter removed, check the condition of the PCV filter **(see illustration)**. This filter is normally supplied with a new air filter.

5 Wipe clean the main body, then fit the new air filter, making sure it is the correct way round.
6 Refit the upper cover and secure with the retaining clips. Where applicable refit the headlight shield.
7 Reconnect the mass airflow sensor, secure the retaining clips, then refit the wiring plug.

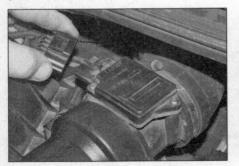

33.1a Disconnect the mass airflow sensor wiring plug . . .

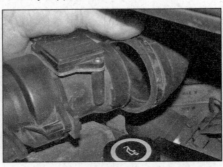

33.1b . . . then remove the outlet hose

33.3a Remove the air filter cover screws (arrowed) . . .

33.3b . . . then remove the filter cover . . .

33.3c . . . and remove the air filter

33.4 Check the PCV filter

Every 80 000 miles

34 Auxiliary drivebelt renewal

Refer to Chapter 2A, Section 6.

Chapter 1 Part B:
Routine maintenance and servicing – diesel models

Contents

Degrees of difficulty

| Easy, suitable for novice with little experience | Fairly easy, suitable for beginner with some experience | Fairly difficult, suitable for competent DIY mechanic | Difficult, suitable for experienced DIY mechanic | Very difficult, suitable for expert DIY or professional |

Lubricants and fluids . . . . Refer to end of *Weekly checks* on page 0•16

Capacities

Engine oil (including filter) . . . . 4.3 litres

Cooling system . . . . 9.5 litres (approx)

Transmission
Manual transmission . . . . 2.5 litres
Automatic transmission . . . . 7.5 litres

Fuel tank . . . . 70 litres

Cooling system

Antifreeze mixture:
  50% antifreeze . . . . Protection down to –35ºC

Brakes

Brake pad minimum thickness (including backing) . . . . 7.0 mm

Torque wrench settings

	Nm	lbf ft
Automatic transmission drain plug	15	11
Manual transmission drain plug	35	26
Manual transmission filler/level plug	35	26
Roadwheel bolts	170	125
Sump drain plug	30	22

Maintenance schedule

The maintenance intervals in this manual are provided with the assumption that you, not the dealer, will be carrying out the work. These are the minimum intervals recommended by us for vehicles driven daily. If you wish to keep your vehicle in peak condition at all times, you may wish to perform some of these procedures more often. We encourage frequent maintenance, since it enhances the efficiency, performance and resale value of your vehicle.

When the vehicle is new, it should be serviced by a dealer service department (or other workshop recognised by the vehicle manufacturer as providing the same standard of service) in order to preserve the warranty. The vehicle manufacturer may reject warranty claims if you are unable to prove that servicing has been carried out as and when specified, using only original equipment parts or parts certified to be of equivalent quality.

Service interval display

All Ford Galaxy models are equipped with a service interval display indicator in the instrument panel. As a service approaches, the tripmeter will display SERVICE IN 2000 M when the ignition is turned on. This will be displayed for approximately 1 minute. The mileage will decrease until the display reads: SERVICE NOW. After servicing the service interval display should be reset – see section 6.

Every 250 miles or weekly
☐ Refer to *Weekly checks*

Every 10 000 miles or 12 months (whichever occurs first)
☐ Renew the engine oil and filter (Section 3)
Note: *Frequent oil and filter changes are good for the engine. We recommend changing the oil at least twice a year.*

Every 10 000 miles or 12 months (whichever occurs first)
☐ Check condition of the auxiliary drivebelts (Section 4)
☐ Check the timing belt condition and wear (Section 5)
☐ Reset the service interval display (Section 6)
☐ Check the operation of the windscreen/tailgate washer system(s) (Section 7)
☐ Check the tyre wear (Section 8)
☐ Lubricate all hinges and locks (Section 9)
☐ Check the battery electrolyte level (Section 10)
☐ Check the cooling system for antifreeze content (Section 11)
☐ Drain water from the fuel filter (Section 12)
☐ Renew the pollen filter (Section 13)
☐ Check and if necessary adjust the handbrake (Section 14)
☐ Check the tightness of the roadwheel bolts (Section 15)
☐ Engine management ECM memory fault code check (Section 16)
☐ Check all underbonnet components and hoses for fluid leaks (Section 17)
☐ Check all brake flexible hoses and rigid pipes for condition (Section 18)
☐ Check the front brake pad thickness and disc condition (Section 19)
☐ Check the rear brake pad thickness and disc condition (Section 20)
☐ Check the condition of the exhaust system and its mountings (Section 21)
☐ Check the steering and suspension components for condition and security (Section 22)
☐ Carry out a road test (Section 23)
☐ Check the underbody sealant (Section 24)

Every 20 000 miles or 2 years (whichever occurs first)
Note: *Carry out the following work in addition to that described for the 10 000 miles/12 months interval.*
☐ Renew fuel filter (Section 25)
☐ Renew the air filter element (Section 26)

Every 2 years (regardless of mileage)
☐ Renew the remote control handset battery (Section 27)
☐ Renew the coolant (Section 28)
☐ Renew the brake/clutch fluid (Section 29)

Every 30 000 miles or 3 years (whichever occurs first)
Note: *Carry out the following work in addition to that described for the 10 000 miles/12 months interval.*
☐ Check manual transmission oil level (Section 30)
☐ Check the headlight beam adjustment (Section 31)
☐ Check the automatic transmission fluid level (Section 32)
☐ Carry out an exhaust emissions check (Section 33)

Every 40 000 miles or 4 years (whichever occurs first)
☐ Renew the timing belt – vehicles built up to 06/2003 (Section 34)
Note: *It is strongly recommended that the timing belt renewal interval is reduced to 30 000 miles on vehicles which are subjected to intensive use, ie, mainly short journeys or a lot of stop-start driving. The actual belt renewal interval is therefore very much up to the individual owner, but bear in mind that severe engine damage will result if the belt breaks.*
Note: *Timing belt change intervals are subject to constant updating by the vehicle manufacturer. Always check for the latest manufacturer recommended renewal intervals, or follow the advice given above.*

Every 60 000 miles
☐ Renew the timing belt – vehicles built from 06/2003 (Section 35)
Note: *It is strongly recommended that the timing belt renewal interval is reduced to 30 000 miles on vehicles which are subjected to intensive use, ie, mainly short journeys or a lot of stop-start driving. The actual belt renewal interval is therefore very much up to the individual owner, but bear in mind that severe engine damage will result if the belt breaks.*
Note: *Timing belt change intervals are subject to constant updating by the vehicle manufacturer. Always check for the latest manufacturer recommended renewal intervals, or follow the advice given above.*

Every 80 000 miles
☐ Renew the auxiliary drivebelts (Section 36)

Underbonnet view

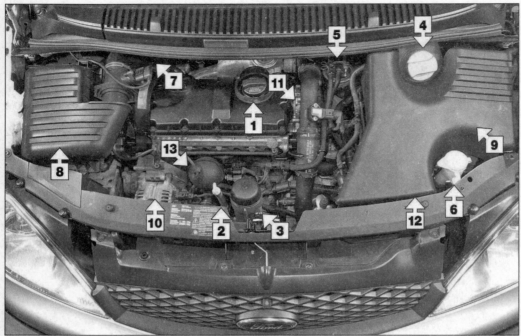

1 Engine oil filler cap
2 Engine oil dipstick
3 Oil filter
4 Coolant expansion tank
5 Fuel filter
6 Windscreen/headlight washer fluid reservoir
7 Master cylinder brake fluid reservoir – hidden
8 Air cleaner housing
9 Battery – under cover
10 Alternator
11 Brake vacuum pump
12 Power steering fluid reservoir – under cover
13 Vacuum reservoir for inlet manifold flap valve

Front underbody view

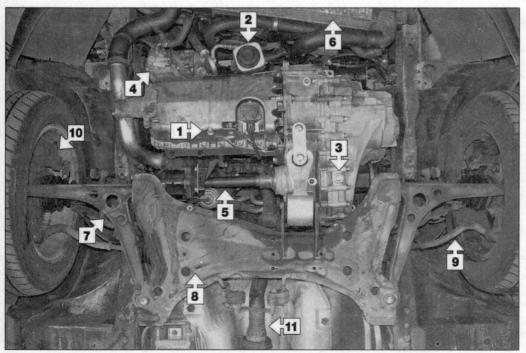

1 Sump drain plug
2 Oil cooler/filter base cap
3 Manual transmission drain plug
4 Air conditioning compressor
5 Driveshaft
6 Intercooler
7 Front suspension lower arm
8 Crossmember
9 Steering track rod
10 Front brake caliper
11 Exhaust pipe

Rear underbody view

1 Fuel tank
2 Rear axle assembly
3 Rear suspension coil spring
4 Rear shock absorber
5 Exhaust rear silencer
6 Rear anti-roll bar
7 Handbrake cables
8 Hydraulic brake line
9 Spare wheel

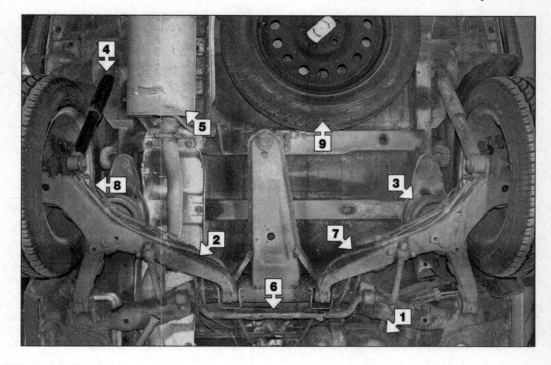

Maintenance procedures

1 Introduction

This Chapter is designed to help the home mechanic maintain his/her vehicle for safety, economy, long life and peak performance.

The Chapter contains a master maintenance schedule, followed by Sections dealing specifically with each task in the schedule. Visual checks, adjustments, component renewal and other helpful items are included. Refer to the accompanying illustrations of the engine compartment and the underside of the vehicle for the locations of the various components.

Servicing your vehicle in accordance with the mileage/time maintenance schedule and the following Sections will provide a planned maintenance programme, which should result in a long and reliable service life. This is a comprehensive plan, so maintaining some items but not others at the specified service intervals will not produce the same results.

As you service your vehicle, you will discover that many of the procedures can – and should – be grouped together, because of the particular procedure being performed, or because of the proximity of two otherwise unrelated components to one another. For example, if the vehicle is raised for any reason, the exhaust can be inspected at the same time as the suspension and steering components.

The first step in this maintenance programme is to prepare yourself before the actual work begins. Read through all the Sections relevant to the work to be carried out, then make a list and gather all the parts and tools required. If a problem is encountered, seek advice from a parts specialist, or a dealer service department.

2 Regular maintenance

1 If, from the time the vehicle is new, the routine maintenance schedule is followed closely, and frequent checks are made of fluid levels and high-wear items, as suggested throughout this manual, the engine will be kept in relatively good running condition, and the need for additional work will be minimised.
2 It is possible that there will be times when the engine is running poorly due to the lack of regular maintenance. This is even more likely if a used vehicle, which has not received regular and frequent maintenance checks, is purchased. In such cases, additional work may need to be carried out, outside of the regular maintenance intervals.
3 If engine wear is suspected, a compression test (refer to Chapter 2B) will provide valuable information regarding the overall performance of the main internal components. Such a test can be used as a basis to decide on the extent

of the work to be carried out. If, for example, a compression test indicates serious internal engine wear, conventional maintenance as described in this Chapter will not greatly improve the performance of the engine, and may prove a waste of time and money, unless extensive overhaul work is carried out first.
4 The following series of operations are those most often required to improve the performance of a generally poor-running engine:

Primary operations

a) Clean, inspect and test the battery (See 'Weekly checks').
b) Check all the engine-related fluids (See 'Weekly checks').
c) Check the condition of the auxiliary drivebelts (Section 4).
d) Check the condition of the air filter, and renew if necessary (Section 26).
e) Renew the fuel filter (Section 25).
f) Check the condition of all hoses, and check for fluid leaks (Sections 17 and 18).
5 If the above operations do not prove fully effective, carry out the following secondary operations:

Secondary operations

All items listed under Primary operations, plus the following:
a) Check the charging system (Chapter 5A).
b) Check the preheating system (Chapter 5C).
c) Check the fuel system (Chapter 4B).

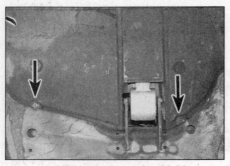

3.2 Remove the undershield (rear bolts arrowed)

3.3 Sump drain plug

As the plug releases, move it away sharply so the stream of oil issuing from the sump runs into the container, not up your sleeve.

Every 5000 miles or 6 months

3 Engine oil and filter renewal

1 Frequent oil and filter changes are the most important preventive maintenance procedures which can be undertaken by the DIY owner. As engine oil ages, it becomes diluted and contaminated, which leads to premature engine wear.

2 Before starting this procedure, gather all the necessary tools and materials. Also make sure that you have plenty of clean rags and newspapers handy, to mop-up any spills. Ideally, the engine oil should be warm, as it will drain better, and more built-up sludge will be removed with it. Take care, however,

not to touch the exhaust or any other hot parts of the engine when working under the vehicle. To avoid any possibility of scalding, and to protect yourself from possible skin irritants and other harmful contaminants in used engine oils, it is advisable to wear gloves when carrying out this work. Access to the underside of the vehicle will be greatly improved if it can be raised on a lift, driven onto ramps, or jacked up and supported on axle stands (see *Jacking and vehicle support*). Whichever method is chosen, make sure that the vehicle remains level, or if it is at an angle, that the drain plug is at the lowest point. Undo the retaining screws and remove the engine undershield **(see illustration)**.

3 Slacken the sump drain plug about half a

turn. Position the draining container under the drain plug, then remove the plug completely **(see Haynes Hint)**. The sealing ring is captive on the drain plug and a new drain plug should be fitted **(see illustration)** however it may be possible to remove the old seal and fit a suitable replacement.

4 Allow some time for the old oil to drain, noting that it may be necessary to reposition the container as the oil flow slows to a trickle.

5 After all the oil has drained, wipe off the drain plug with a clean rag, and fit a new sealing washer. Clean the area around the drain plug opening, and refit the plug. Tighten the plug securely.

6 Remove the engine top cover to gain access to the oil filter housing. Place absorbent cloths around the filter housing to catch any spilt oil.

7 Unscrew and remove the cap from the top of the oil filter housing using an oil filter strap wrench or the correct tool. Recover the large sealing ring from the cap, and the small sealing ring from the centre rod. Lift out the filter element **(see illustrations)**. Dispose of the element.

8 Using a clean rag, wipe all oil and sludge from the inside of the filter housing and cap.

9 Insert the new element. Fit new sealing rings to the cap, then refit it and tighten securely. Also, as applicable, refit the lower cap and drain plug and tighten securely. Wipe up any spilt oil before refitting the engine top cover.

10 Remove the old oil and all tools from under the car then refit the undershield(s) and lower the car to the ground. Also refit the engine top cover.

11 Remove the dipstick, then unscrew the oil filler cap from the cylinder head cover. Fill the engine, using the correct grade and type of oil (see *Lubricants and fluids*). An oil can spout or funnel may help to reduce spillage. Pour in half the specified quantity of oil first **(see illustration)**, then wait a few minutes for the oil to run to the sump (see *Weekly checks*). Continue adding oil a small quantity at a time until the level is up to the maximum mark on the dipstick. Refit the filler cap.

12 Start the engine and run it for a few minutes; check for leaks around the oil filter

3.7a Unscrew the cap . . .

3.7b . . . and remove the filter element

3.7c Remove the sealing ring from the cap

3.11 Pour in half the specified quantity of oil first, wait, then add the rest

cap and the sump drain plug. Note that there may be a few seconds delay before the oil pressure warning light goes out when the engine is started, as the oil circulates through the engine oil galleries and the new oil filter (where fitted) before the pressure builds-up.

⚠️ **Warning: Do not increase the engine speed above idling while the oil pressure light is illuminated, as considerable damage can be caused to the turbocharger.**

13 Switch off the engine, and wait a few minutes for the oil to settle in the sump once

more. With the new oil circulated and the filter completely full, recheck the level on the dipstick, and add more oil as necessary.

14 Dispose of the used engine oil safely, with reference to *General repair procedures* in the *Reference* section of this manual.

Every 10 000 miles or 12 months

4 Auxiliary drivebelts condition and tension check

1 Apply the handbrake, then jack up the front of the vehicle and support it on axle stands (see *Jacking and vehicle support*).
2 Using a socket on the crankshaft pulley bolt, turn the engine slowly clockwise so that the full length of the auxiliary drivebelt can be examined. Look for cracks, splitting and fraying on the surface of the belt; check also for signs of glazing (shiny patches) and separation of the belt plies. If damage or wear is visible, or if there are traces of oil or grease on it, the belt should be renewed (see Section 36).

5 Timing belt condition and wear check

1 Release the spring clips and remove the upper timing belt cover from the engine (refer to Chapter 2B, Section 7).
2 Inspect the timing belt for signs of excessive wear, fraying, cracking and damage. Also check for traces of oil which may have come from a faulty oil seal. The full length of the timing belt should be checked by turning the engine with a spanner on the crankshaft pulley bolt.
3 Using a steel rule or vernier calipers, measure the width of the timing belt in several places **(see illustration)**. If it varies by more than 2.0 mm at any point, the timing belt must be renewed with reference to Chapter 2B.
4 On completion of the check, refit the upper timing cover.

6 Service interval display resetting

1 In order to reset the service interval display, Ford technicians use specialist diagnostic equipment. In the absence of this equipment, the display can be reset as follows.
2 Turn the ignition on and hold down the trip button for 2 seconds. The display will reset. Turn the ignition off.

7 Washer system(s) operation check

1 Check that each of the washer jet nozzles are clear and that each nozzle provides a strong jet of washer fluid. The jets should be aimed to spray at a point slightly above the centre of the screen. The washer jets aim can not be adjusted, but they can be cleaned with a fine pin.
2 Carry out a check of all wiper blades. Look for splits or cracks on the wiping surface and renew as necessary. Check that the wipers clean efficiently across their entire sweep; any gaps in the swept area may be caused by defective wiper blade hinges, preventing the blade from following the contours of the screen/lens surface. Check that the wiper blades do not overshoot the edge of the screen/lens at the end of their sweep and that the blades park in the correct position when switched off. If this is not the case, or if the blades overlap each other at the midpoint of their stroke, the wiper arms may be incorrectly fitted (see Chapter 12).

8 Tyre wear check

1 Raise and securely support the relevant side of the car in turn to allow a thorough check of each tyre to be performed; refer to *Jacking and vehicle support* for reference.

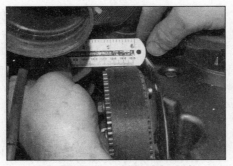

5.3 Check the width of the belt

2 Turn the tyre slowly by hand and carry out an inspection as described in *Weekly checks*.

9 Hinges and locks lubrication

1 Lubricate the hinges of the bonnet, doors and tailgate with a light general-purpose oil. Similarly, lubricate all latches, locks and lock strikers. At the same time, check the security and operation of all the locks, adjusting them if necessary (see Chapter 11).
2 Lightly lubricate the bonnet release mechanism and cable with a suitable grease.

10 Battery electrolyte level check

1 Where a non-maintenance free battery is fitted, the level of the electrolyte may be checked and if necessary topped-up. On some batteries, MIN and MAX marks are printed on the side of the battery and the level may be checked without removing the cell covers. Where there are no exterior marks, remove the cover(s) from the top of the cells and check that the level of the electrolyte is approximately 2 or 3 mm above the internal plates. Some batteries may have a plastic internal level indicator.
2 If necessary, top-up the cells using distilled or de-ionised water.
3 Refit the cell cover(s).

11 Cooling system antifreeze concentration check

⚠️ **Warning: Wait until the engine is cold before starting this procedure. Do not allow antifreeze to come in contact with your skin, or with the painted surfaces of the vehicle. Rinse off spills immediately with plenty of water.**

1 Note that a tester will be required to check the coolant strength; these can be obtained relatively cheaply from most motor accessory shops.
2 With the engine completely cold, unscrew

12.2 Remove one of the hoses

12.3 Attach a short length of hose

and remove the filler cap from the coolant expansion tank. Follow the instructions supplied with the tester and check the coolant mixture is sufficient to give protection down to temperatures well below freezing. If the coolant has been renewed regularly this shouldn't be a problem. However, if the coolant mixture is not strong enough to provide sufficient protection it will be necessary to drain the cooling system and renew the coolant (see Section 28).

3 Once the test is complete, check the coolant level is correct (see *Weekly checks*) then securely refit the expansion tank cap.

12 Fuel filter draining

1 Remove the battery cover and the upper section of the battery compartment panel.

2 Remove one of the fuel filter hoses **(see illustration)**.

3 Position a suitable container beneath the filter and then attach a short length of hose to the filter drain plug **(see illustration)**.

4 Loosen the drain cap under the filter, and drain off approximately 0.1 litre of liquid. Tighten the drain cap.

5 Refit the hose and move the spring clip back into position.

6 Start the engine and check for fuel leaks.

7 Refit the upper section of the battery compartment panel and the battery cover.

13 Pollen filter renewal

1 The pollen filter is located beneath the windscreen cowl panels; it is located on the right-hand side on left-hand drive models,

and on the left-hand side on right-hand drive models.

2 Remove the battery compartment cover and then remove the side panel. With reference to Chapter 11 remove the windscreen cowl panel and then remove the bulkhead panel **(see illustration)**.

3 Unbolt the coolant expansion tank and move it to one side. Access is considerably easier if the windscreen wiper motor and linkage is removed as described in Chapter 12.

4 Ensure that the area around the filter is cleared of all leaves, debris, etc, as when the filter is removed, this will be able to enter the vehicle interior.

5 Release the retaining clip, and slide the element with the frame out of the guide towards the centre of the vehicle. Manoeuvre the frame and element under the wiper linkage (if left in place) and out from the engine compartment **(see illustrations)**.

6 Remove the filter element from the frame.

7 Fit the new element onto the frame, with the airflow arrows pointing towards the vehicle interior, ensuring that the left and right ends of the frame fit into the first laminations at each end of the element. Ensure also that the square pegs of the frame locate in the filter laminations **(see illustrations)**.

8 Guide the frame and element under the wiper linkage and slide it into position, ensuring that the guide lugs on the frame engage correctly with the guide slots in the housing, and the retaining clip locks the assembly in place **(see illustration)**.

9 The remainder of the refitting procedure is a reversal of removal.

13.2 Remove the bulkhead panel

13.5a Release the pollen filter retaining clip (arrowed) . . .

13.5b . . . and remove the filter

13.7a Fit the new element into the frame with the airflow arrows pointing to the vehicle interior . . .

13.7b . . . and the ends of the frame located into the first and last laminations of the filter

13.8 The lugs on the frame must engage with the guide slots in the housing (arrowed)

14 Handbrake check and adjustment

1 With the vehicle on level ground, chock the front wheels and release the handbrake lever. Gradually apply the handbrake, counting the number of clicks from the ratchet mechanism until the handbrake is fully applied. If the adjustment is correct, there should be 3 to 6 clicks before the handbrake is fully applied. If this is not the case, adjust as follows.

2 Ensure the front wheel chocks are still in place, jack up the rear of the vehicle and support it on axle stands (see *Jacking and vehicle support*). Fully release the handbrake lever.

3 Working underneath the vehicle, rotate the adjuster locknut in the required direction to achieve the correct lever adjustment **(see illustration)**.

4 With the handbrake fully released, check that the rear wheels rotate freely, with no signs of binding or resistance.

5 Once the adjustment is correct, lower the vehicle to the ground.

15 Roadwheel bolts tightness check

1 With the vehicle wheels on the ground and the handbrake applied, prise off the wheel trims (where applicable), and check the tightness of the wheel bolts using a torque wrench. The correct torque setting is given at the start of this Chapter.

2 When all the bolts have been checked, refit the wheel trims (where applicable).

16 Engine management ECM memory fault code check

Rudimentary fault code readers are now available for a modest cost. These tend to only display the mandatory emissions-related fault codes. More expensive models may be able to access the engine management (and other systems) in greater depth. For a fully comprehensive check a professional tool will be required. Ford's own IDS diagnostic tool is the obvious choice here, as it is also capable of updating the vehicle's software as well as listing any fault codes stored within the various control modules. Many independent garages will own this or similar professional tools.

17 Underbonnet/underbody components and hoses fluid leak check

1 For access to the top and bottom of the engine, remove the engine top cover, then jack up the front of the vehicle and support it on axle stands (see *Jacking and vehicle support*).

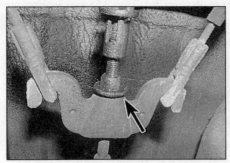

14.3 Turn the adjuster locknut (arrowed) to adjust the handbrake lever

Undo the two retaining nuts and four bolts (two each side), and remove the undershield. Visually inspect the engine joint faces, gaskets and seals for any signs of water or oil leaks. Pay particular attention to the areas around the camshaft cover, cylinder head, oil filter and sump joint faces. Bear in mind that, over a period of time, some very slight seepage from these areas is to be expected – what you are really looking for is any indication of a serious leak. Should a leak be found, renew the offending gasket or oil seal by referring to the appropriate Chapters in this manual.

2 Also check the security and condition of all the engine-related pipes and hoses. Ensure that all cable-ties or securing clips are in place and in good condition. Clips which are broken or missing can lead to chafing of the hoses, pipes or wiring, which could cause more serious problems in the future.

3 Carefully check the radiator hoses and heater hoses along their entire length. Renew any hose which is cracked, swollen or deteriorated. Cracks will show up better if the hose is squeezed. Pay close attention to the hose clips that secure the hoses to the cooling system components. Hose clips can pinch and puncture hoses, resulting in cooling system leaks.

4 Inspect all the cooling system components (hoses, joint faces etc) for leaks **(see Haynes Hint)**. Where any problems of this nature are found on system components, renew the component or gasket with reference to Chapter 3.

5 Where applicable, inspect the automatic transmission fluid cooler hoses for leaks or deterioration.

6 With the vehicle raised at the rear, inspect the fuel tank and filler neck for punctures, cracks and other damage. The connection between the filler neck and tank is especially critical. Sometimes a rubber filler neck or connecting hose will leak due to loose retaining clamps or deteriorated rubber.

7 Carefully check all rubber hoses and metal fuel lines leading away from the fuel tank. Check for loose connections, deteriorated hoses, crimped lines, and other damage. Pay particular attention to the vent pipes and hoses, which often loop up around the filler neck and can become blocked or crimped. Follow the lines to the front of the vehicle, carefully inspecting them all the way. Renew damaged sections as necessary.

A leak in the cooling system will usually show up as white- or antifreeze-coloured crusty deposits on the area surrounding the leak.

8 From within the engine compartment, check the security of all fuel hose attachments and pipe unions, and inspect the fuel hoses and vacuum hoses for kinks, chafing and deterioration.

9 Where applicable, check the condition of the power steering fluid hoses and pipes.

10 On completion, refit the undershield and engine top cover, and lower the vehicle to the ground.

18 Brake flexible hoses and rigid pipes condition check

1 Inspect all the braking system flexible hoses and metal pipes for signs of damage or deterioration. Any faulty pipe/hoses must be renewed (see Chapter 9).

19 Front brake pad thickness and disc condition check

1 Firmly apply the handbrake, loosen the front roadwheel bolts, then jack up the front of the car and support it securely on axle stands (see *Jacking and vehicle support*). Remove the front roadwheels.

2 For a comprehensive check, the brake pads should be removed and cleaned. The operation of the caliper can then also be checked, and the condition of the brake disc itself can be fully examined on both sides. Refer to Chapter 9 **(see illustration)**.

3 If any pad is worn to the specified thickness

19.2 The thickness of the brake pad, including the backing plate, must not be less than 7 mm

or less, *all four pads must be renewed as a set*. **Note:** *If any pad is approaching the minimum thickness, consider renewal as a precautionary measure in case the pads wear out before the next service.*

4 On completion, refit the roadwheels and lower the vehicle to the ground.

20 Rear brake pad lining thickness and disc condition check

1 Firmly chock the front wheels and select first gear or Park, then jack up the rear of the vehicle and support it securely on axle stands (see *Jacking and vehicle support*). Remove the rear roadwheels.

2 For a quick check, the pad thickness can be carried out via the inspection hole on the rear of the caliper. Using a steel rule, measure the thickness of the pad lining including the backing plate. This must not be less than that indicated in the Specifications.

3 The view through the caliper inspection hole gives a rough indication of the state of the brake pads. For a comprehensive check, the brake pads should be removed and cleaned. The operation of the caliper can then also be checked, and the condition of the brake disc itself can be fully examined on both sides. Chapter 9 contains a detailed description of how the brake disc should be checked for wear and/or damage.

4 If any pad is worn to the specified thickness or less, all four pads must be renewed as a set. **Note:** *If any pad is approaching the minimum thickness, consider renewal as a precautionary measure in case the pads wear out before the next service.* Refer to Chapter 9 for details.

5 On completion, refit the roadwheels and lower the vehicle to the ground.

21 Exhaust system and mountings condition check

1 With the engine cold, check the complete exhaust system from the engine to the end of the tailpipe. The exhaust system is most easily checked with the vehicle raised on a hoist, or suitably-supported on axle stands, so that the

22.4 Check for signs of wear by grasping the roadwheel at the 12 o'clock and 6 o'clock positions, and trying to rock it

exhaust components are readily visible and accessible.

2 Check the exhaust pipes and connections for evidence of leaks, severe corrosion and damage. Make sure that all brackets and mountings are in good condition, and that all relevant nuts and bolts are tight. Leakage at any of the joints or in other parts of the system will usually show up as a black sooty stain in the vicinity of the leak.

3 Rattles and other noises can often be traced to the exhaust system, especially the brackets and mountings. If the components are able to come into contact with the body or suspension parts, secure the system with new mountings. Otherwise separate the joints (if possible) and twist the pipes as necessary to provide additional clearance.

22 Steering and suspension components condition/ security check

Suspension and steering

1 Raise the front of the vehicle, and securely support it on axle stands.

2 Visually inspect the balljoint dust covers and the steering rack gaiters for splits, chafing or deterioration. Any wear of these components will cause loss of lubricant, together with dirt and water entry, resulting in rapid deterioration of the balljoints or steering gear.

3 On vehicles with power steering, check the fluid hoses for chafing or deterioration, and the pipe and hose unions for fluid leaks. Also check for signs of fluid leakage under pressure from the steering gear rubber gaiters, which would indicate failed fluid seals within the steering gear.

4 Grasp the roadwheel at the 12 o'clock and 6 o'clock positions, and try to rock it **(see illustration)**. Very slight free play may be felt, but if the movement is appreciable, further investigation is necessary to determine the source. Continue rocking the wheel while an assistant depresses the footbrake. If the movement is now eliminated or significantly reduced, it is likely that the hub bearings are at fault. If the free play is still evident with the footbrake depressed, then there is wear in the suspension joints or mountings.

5 Now grasp the wheel at the 9 o'clock and 3 o'clock positions, and try to rock it as before. Any movement felt now may again be caused by wear in the hub bearings or the steering track rod balljoints. If the inner or outer balljoint is worn, the visual movement will be obvious.

6 Using a large screwdriver or flat bar, check for wear in the suspension mounting bushes by levering between the relevant suspension component and its attachment point. Some movement is to be expected as the mountings are made of rubber, but excessive wear should be obvious. Also check the condition of any visible rubber bushes, looking for splits, cracks or contamination of the rubber.

7 With the car standing on its wheels, have an assistant turn the steering wheel back-and-forth about an eighth of a turn each way. There should be very little, if any, lost movement between the steering wheel and roadwheels. If this is not the case, closely observe the joints and mountings previously described, but in addition, check the steering column universal joints for wear, and the rack-and-pinion steering gear itself.

Strut/shock absorber

8 Check for any signs of fluid leakage around the suspension strut/shock absorber body, or from the rubber gaiter around the piston rod. Should any fluid be noticed, the suspension strut/shock absorber is defective internally, and should be renewed. **Note:** *Suspension struts/shock absorbers should always be renewed in pairs on the same axle.*

9 The efficiency of the suspension strut/shock absorber may be checked by bouncing the vehicle at each corner. Generally speaking, the body will return to its normal position and stop after being depressed. If it rises and returns on a rebound, the suspension strut/shock absorber is probably suspect. Examine also the suspension strut/shock absorber upper and lower mountings for any signs of wear.

Driveshafts

10 With the vehicle raised and securely supported on stands, turn the steering onto full lock then slowly rotate the roadwheel. Inspect the condition of the outer constant velocity (CV) joint rubber gaiters while squeezing the gaiters to open out the folds. Check for signs of cracking, splits or deterioration of the rubber which may allow the grease to escape and lead to water and grit entry into the joint. Also check the security and condition of the retaining clips. Repeat these checks on the inner CV joints. If any damage or deterioration is found, the gaiters should be renewed as described in Chapter 8, Section 3.

11 At the same time check the general condition of the CV joints themselves by first holding the driveshaft and attempting to rotate the wheel. Repeat this check by holding the inner joint and attempting to rotate the driveshaft. Any appreciable movement indicates wear in the joints, wear in the driveshaft splines or loose driveshaft retaining bolt.

23 Road test

Instruments and electrical equipment

1 Check the operation of all instruments and electrical equipment.

2 Make sure that all instruments read correctly, and switch on all electrical equipment in turn, to check that it functions properly.

Steering and suspension

3 Check for any abnormalities in the steering, suspension, handling or road feel.
4 Drive the vehicle, and check that there are no unusual vibrations or noises.
5 Check that the steering feels positive, with no excessive sloppiness, or roughness, and check for any suspension noises when cornering and driving over bumps.

Drivetrain

6 Check the performance of the engine, clutch (where applicable), gearbox/transmission and driveshafts.
7 Listen for any unusual noises from the engine, clutch and gearbox/transmission.
8 Make sure that the engine runs smoothly when idling, and that there is no hesitation when accelerating.
9 Check that, where applicable, the clutch action is smooth and progressive, that the drive is taken up smoothly, and that the pedal travel is not excessive. Also listen for any noises when the clutch pedal is depressed.
10 On manual gearbox models, check that all gears can be engaged smoothly without noise, and that the gear lever action is smooth and not abnormally vague or notchy.
11 On automatic transmission models, make sure that all gearchanges occur smoothly, without snatching, and without an increase in engine speed between changes. Check that all the gear positions can be selected with the vehicle at rest. If any problems are found, they should be referred to a Ford dealer.

Braking system

12 Make sure that the vehicle does not pull to one side when braking, and that the wheels do not lock when braking hard.
13 Check that there is no vibration through the steering when braking.
14 Check that the handbrake operates correctly without excessive movement of the lever, and that it holds the vehicle stationary on a slope.
15 Test the operation of the brake servo unit as follows. With the engine off, depress the footbrake four or five times to exhaust the vacuum. Hold the brake pedal depressed, then start the engine. As the engine starts, there should be a noticeable give in the brake pedal as vacuum builds-up. Allow the engine to run for at least two minutes, and then switch it off. If the brake pedal is depressed now, it should be possible to detect a hiss from the servo as the pedal is depressed. After about four or five applications, no further hissing should be heard, and the pedal should feel considerably harder.

24 Underbody sealant check

Raise and support the vehicle on axle stands (see *Jacking and vehicle support*). Using an electric torch or lead light, inspect the entire underside of the vehicle, paying particular attention to the wheel arches. Look for any damage to the flexible underbody coating, which may crack or flake off with age, leading to corrosion. Also check that the wheel arch liners (where fitted) are securely attached with any clips provided – if they come loose, dirt may get in behind the liners and defeat their purpose. If there is any damage to the underseal, or any corrosion, it should be repaired before the damage gets too serious.

Every 20 000 miles or 2 years

25 Fuel filter renewal

1 Remove the battery cover and the upper section of the battery compartment panel.
2 Remove the control valve retaining clip, and lift off the valve with the hoses still attached (see illustrations).
3 Release the retaining clips and disconnect the fuel supply and outlet hoses from the top of the filter. Note the fitted positions of the hoses.
4 Depress the locking tab and lift the filter up and out of the mounting bracket (see illustrations).
Caution: Do not allow diesel fuel to contact any of the coolant hoses. Mop-up any spilt fuel immediately.
5 Note the position of the filter in relation to the housing and then remove the bolt. Remove the filter from the housing.
6 Refit the filter into the housing and tighten the clamp screw. Slide the new filter into the mounting bracket. Reconnect the supply and outlet hoses, and tighten the retaining clips.
7 Refit the control valve, and secure it in place with the retaining clip.
8 Start the engine and rev it a few times to bleed the filter through. Check for leaks.

25.2a Remove the clip . . .

25.2b . . . and lift out the valve

25.4a Depress the locking tab (arrowed) . . .

25.4b . . . and remove the filter

9 Refit the upper section of the battery compartment panel and refit the battery cover.

26 Air filter element renewal

1 Remove the fixing screws from the air filter cover **(see illustration)**.
2 Where fitted disconnect the vacuum pipe from the upper air filter cover.
3 Work the cover free from the housing.
4 Remove the air filter element, noting which way round it is fitted **(see illustration)**.
5 Check the main housing for any debris – use a vacuum cleaner to remove the debris

26.1 Remove the screws (arrowed)

if necessary – and then fit the new air filter, making sure it is the correct way round.
6 Refit the upper cover.

26.4 Remove the air filter

7 Tighten the fixing screws with care as they only bite into the plastic section of the lower housing.

Every 2 years

27 Handset battery renewal

1 Carefully prise the handset body from the key blade **(see illustration)**.
2 Using a small screwdriver release the retaining clips and separate the halves of the handset body **(see illustration)**.
3 Gently push back the clips and lift the first battery, dividing plate, and second battery from the handset.

27.1 Prise the handset body from the key blade

27.4 Insert the first battery, positive (+) side up

4 Insert the first new battery, positive side up, into the handset **(see illustration)**.
5 Place the dividing plate on top of the first battery **(see illustration)**.
6 Insert the second battery, again positive side up, making sure it is held in place by the retaining clips.
7 Fit the halves of the handset together, and slide it back into the key blade.
8 It may be the case that the handset will not function correctly after battery renewal. If this is the case the handset must be resynchronised as follows:

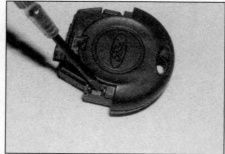

27.2 Release the retaining clips and separate the halves of the body

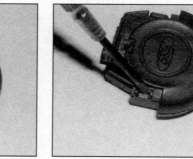

27.5 Place the dividing plate on the first battery

a) With the key in the driver's lock, turn it three times anti-clockwise within twenty seconds. Hold the key in the unlock position for half a second between turns.
b) Remove the key from the lock – the LED in the driver's door will now be flashing.
c) Point the key at the rear view mirror and press the lock button. This must be performed within five seconds of removing the key.
d) Whilst still holding the locking button down, press the unlock button three times and then release the locking button.
e) The LED in the driver's door will flash to confirm that coding is complete.
f) The above procedure must be completed within 20 seconds.
g) If another key with remote locking is available then follow points 'c' and 'd' within fifteen seconds of programming the previous key.

28 Coolant renewal

⚠ *Warning: Wait until the engine is cold before starting this procedure. Do not allow antifreeze to come in contact with your skin, or with the painted surfaces of the vehicle. Rinse off spills immediately with plenty of water. Never leave antifreeze lying around in an open container, or in a puddle in the driveway or on the garage floor. Children and pets are attracted by its sweet smell, but antifreeze can be fatal if ingested.*

Cooling system draining

1 With the engine completely cold, cover the expansion tank cap with a wad of rag, and slowly turn the cap anti-clockwise to relieve the pressure in the cooling system (a hissing sound will normally be heard). Wait until any pressure remaining in the system is released, then continue to turn the cap until it can be removed.

2 Release the fasteners (two nuts and four bolts) and remove the engine/transmission undershield. Undo the retaining clips and disconnect the intercooler right-hand hose.

3 Position a suitable container beneath the radiator bottom hose connection, then release the retaining clip and ease the hose from the radiator stub. If the hose joint has not been disturbed for some time, it will be necessary to gently manipulate the hose to break the joint. Do not use excessive force, or the radiator stub could be damaged. Allow the coolant to drain into the container.

4 If the coolant has been drained for a reason other than renewal, then provided it is clean and less than two years old, it can be re-used if there is no alternative, but this is not recommended. *Note: If an aluminium engine component which comes into contact with the coolant has been renewed, then the coolant must also be renewed. Used coolant will not protect new aluminium from corrosion.*

5 Once all the coolant has drained, reconnect the hose to the radiator and ensure the retaining clip is properly seated.

Cooling system flushing

6 If coolant renewal has been neglected, or if the antifreeze mixture has become diluted, then in time, the cooling system may gradually lose efficiency, as the coolant passages become restricted due to rust, scale deposits, and other sediment. Flushing the system clean can restore the cooling system efficiency.

7 The radiator should be flushed independently of the engine, to avoid unnecessary contamination.

Radiator flushing

8 To flush the radiator, disconnect the top and bottom hoses and any other relevant hoses from the radiator, with reference to Chapter 3.

9 Insert a garden hose into the radiator top inlet. Direct a flow of clean water through the radiator, and continue flushing until clean water emerges from the radiator bottom outlet.

10 If after a reasonable period, the water still does not run clear, the radiator can be flushed with a good proprietary cooling system cleaning agent. It is important that their manufacturer's instructions are followed carefully. If the contamination is particularly bad, insert the hose in the radiator bottom outlet, and reverse-flush the radiator.

Engine flushing

11 To flush the engine, remove the thermostat as described in Chapter 3, then temporarily refit the thermostat cover.

12 With the top and bottom hoses disconnected from the radiator, insert a garden hose into the radiator top hose. Direct a clean flow of water through the engine, and continue flushing until clean water emerges from the radiator bottom hose.

13 On completion of flushing, refit the thermostat and reconnect the hoses with reference to Chapter 3.

Cooling system filling

14 Before attempting to fill the cooling system, make sure that all hoses and clips are in good condition, and that the clips/connections are secure. Note that an antifreeze mixture must be used all year round, to prevent corrosion of the engine components (see following sub-Section).

15 Remove the expansion tank filler cap, and fill the system by slowly pouring the coolant into the expansion tank to prevent airlocks from forming.

16 If the coolant is being renewed, begin by pouring in a litre of water, followed by the correct quantity of antifreeze, then fill with more water.

17 Once the level in the expansion tank starts to rise, squeeze the radiator top and bottom hoses to help expel any trapped air in the system. Once all the air is expelled, top-up the coolant level to the MAX mark, refit the expansion tank cap, then refit the expansion tank to the bodywork.

18 Start the engine and run it at a fast idle for about three minutes. After this, allow the engine to idle normally until the bottom hose becomes hot.

19 Check for leaks, particularly around disturbed components. Check the coolant level in the expansion tank, and top-up if necessary. Note that the system must be cold before an accurate level is indicated in the expansion tank. If the expansion tank cap is removed while the engine is still warm, cover the cap with a thick cloth, and unscrew the cap slowly to gradually relieve the system pressure (a hissing sound will normally be heard). Wait until any pressure remaining in the system is released, then continue to turn the cap until it can be removed. Never remove the cap when the engine is still hot.

Antifreeze mixture

Caution: All vehicles were originally filled with Ford's own Motorcraft Super Plus 2000 (orange in colour). If the coolant visible in the expansion tank is any colour other than orange, then the cooling system may have been topped-up with coolant containing the wrong type of antifreeze. If you are unsure of the type of antifreeze used, or if you suspect that mixing may have occurred, the best course of action is to drain, flush and refill the cooling system. Note that Ford specify the coolant should be changed after a period ten years. However, we consider it prudent to consider changing the coolant after two years and definitely changing it after five years.

20 The antifreeze should always be renewed at the specified intervals. This is necessary not only to maintain the antifreeze properties, but also to prevent corrosion which would

otherwise occur as the corrosion inhibitors become progressively less effective.

21 The quantity of antifreeze and levels of protection are indicated in the Specifications.

22 Before adding antifreeze, the cooling system should be completely drained, preferably flushed, and all hoses checked for condition and security.

23 After filling with antifreeze, a label should be attached to the expansion tank, stating the type and concentration of antifreeze used, and the date installed. Any subsequent topping-up should be made with the same type and concentration of antifreeze.

Caution: Do not use engine antifreeze in the washer system, as it will cause damage to the vehicle paintwork.

29 Brake/clutch fluid renewal

⚠ *Warning: Brake hydraulic fluid can harm your eyes and damage painted surfaces, so use extreme caution when handling and pouring it. Do not use fluid that has been standing open for some time, as it absorbs moisture from the air. Excess moisture can cause a dangerous loss of braking effectiveness.*

Brakes

1 The procedure is similar to that for the bleeding of the hydraulic system as described in Chapter 9.

2 On right-hand drive models, remove the air ducting assembly as described in Chapter 4B, to gain access to the master cylinder reservoir.

3 Working as described in Chapter 9, open the first bleed screw in the sequence, and pump the brake pedal gently until nearly all the old fluid has been emptied from the master cylinder reservoir. Top-up to the MAX level with new fluid, and continue pumping until only the new fluid remains in the reservoir, and new fluid can be seen emerging from the bleed screw. Tighten the screw, and top the reservoir level up to the MAX level line.

4 Work through all the remaining bleed screws in the sequence until new fluid can be seen at all of them. Be careful to keep the master cylinder reservoir topped-up to above the MIN level at all times, or air may enter the system and greatly increase the length of the task. The bleed screw sequence is:

a) Left-hand front brake.
b) Right-hand front brake.
c) Right-hand rear brake.
d) Left-hand rear brake.

5 When the operation is complete, check that all bleed screws are securely tightened, and that their dust caps are refitted. Wash off all traces of spilt fluid, and recheck the master cylinder reservoir fluid level. Check the operation of the brakes before taking the car on the road.

Clutch

6 Because the clutch hydraulic system shares the same fluid reservoir as the brake system, we recommend that the clutch hydraulic fluid is renewed at the same time. Working as described in Chapter 6, remove the dust cap from the slave cylinder bleed screw. Fit a spanner and tube to the screw, place the other end of the tube in a jar, and pour in sufficient fluid to cover the end of the tube.

7 Ensure that the fluid level is maintained at least above the lower level line in the reservoir throughout the procedure.

8 Have an assistant fully depress the clutch pedal several times to build-up pressure, then maintain it on the final downstroke.

9 While pedal pressure is maintained, unscrew the bleed screw (approximately one half of a turn) and allow the compressed fluid to flow into the jar. The assistant should maintain pedal pressure and should not release it until instructed to do so. When the flow stops, tighten the bleed screw again, have the assistant release the pedal slowly, and recheck the reservoir fluid level.

10 Repeat the steps given in paragraphs 8 and 9 until the new fluid emerges from the bleed screw. If the master cylinder has been drained and refilled, allow approximately five seconds between cycles for the master cylinder passages to refill.

11 Tighten the bleed screw securely, remove the tube and spanner, and refit the dust cap. Do not overtighten the bleed screw.

12 Wash off all traces of spilt fluid, and recheck the fluid level.

Every 30 000 miles or 3 years

30 Manual transmission oil level check

1 The oil filler/level plug is located on the front side of the manual transmission.

2 Apply the handbrake, then jack up the front and rear of the vehicle and support it on axle stands (see *Jacking and vehicle support*). To ensure an accurate check, make sure that the vehicle is level. Undo the two retaining nuts and four bolts (two each side), and remove the engine/transmission undershield.

3 Unscrew and remove the filler/level plug.

4 Check that the oil level is to the bottom lip of the filler hole.

5 If necessary, add the specified oil through the filler/level hole **(see illustration)**. If the level requires frequent topping-up, check for leaks and repair.

6 Refit the plug and tighten to the specified torque. Refit the engine/transmission undershield, then lower the vehicle to the ground.

31 Headlight beam adjustment

1 Accurate adjustment of the headlight beam is only possible using optical beam setting equipment, and this work should therefore be carried out by a Ford dealer or suitably-equipped workshop.

2 For reference, the headlights can be adjusted using the adjuster screws, accessible via the top of each light unit (see the illustrations given in Chapter 12, Section 9).

3 Some models are equipped with an electrically-operated headlight beam adjustment system which is controlled through the switch in the facia. On these models, ensure that the switch is set to the basic 0 position before adjusting the headlight aim.

32 Automatic transmission fluid level check

Note: *For an accurate fluid level check, Ford technicians use an electronic tester which is plugged into the vehicle's diagnostic socket, and establishes that the temperature of the fluid is between 35° and 45°C via a sensor within the transmission casing. In view of this, it is recommended that the vehicle is taken to a Ford dealer or automatic transmission specialist to have the level checked.*

1 Jack up the front and rear of the vehicle and support it on axle stands (see *Jacking and vehicle support*). Undo the two retaining nuts and four bolts (two each side), and remove the engine undershield.

2 Note that the transmission must be refilled from below the vehicle, so make sure that the vehicle is supported in a level position.

3 Start the engine and move the selector lever through all gear positions. Switch off the engine.

4 At this point the Ford technician connects the IDS tester to the vehicle's diagnostic socket, and establishes that the temperature of the transmission fluid is between 35° and 45°C. **Note:** *If the level is checked when the temperature is too low, overfilling will occur. If the level is checked when the temperature is too high, underfilling will occur.*

5 With the vehicle still on level ground unscrew the level plug from under the transmission **(see illustration)**. If the level is too high, fluid will escape down the overflow pipe. Refit and tighten the level plug when the fluid ceases to drip. If the level is too low, no fluid will escape.

6 If the fluid level is too low, pull out the retaining clip and pull off the filler pipe blanking plug from the front of the transmission casing. On some models, the filler plug is secured by a cap. Prise the cap off with a screwdriver. Using a funnel, add fluid until it begins to drip from the overflow pipe, then tighten the level plug. Always renew the sealing washer.

7 With the fluid level correct, refit the filler plug and secure it in place with the retaining clip or cap.

8 Refit the engine/transmission undershield, and lower the vehicle to the ground.

33 Exhaust emissions check

This check is part of the manufacturer's maintenance schedule, and involves testing the exhaust emissions using an exhaust gas analyser. Unless a fault is suspected, this test is not essential, although it should be noted that it is recommended by the manufacturers. Exhaust emissions testing is included as part of the MOT test.

30.5 Add oil through the filler/level hole

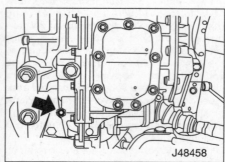

J48458

32.5 Remove the level check plug (arrowed)

Every 40 000 miles or 4 years

34 Timing belt renewal –
up to 06/2003

Refer to Chapter 2B, Section 4.

Every 60 000 miles

35 Timing belt renewal –
from 06/2003

Refer to Chapter 2B, Section 4.

Every 80 000 miles

36 Auxiliary drivebelt renewal

Refer to Chapter 2B, Section 3.

Chapter 2 Part A:
Petrol engine in-car repair procedures

Contents

Degrees of difficulty

Easy, suitable for novice with little experience 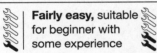	Fairly easy, suitable for beginner with some experience	Fairly difficult, suitable for competent DIY mechanic	Difficult, suitable for experienced DIY mechanic	Very difficult, suitable for expert DIY or professional

Specifications

General

Capacity	2295 cc, DOHC 16V
Bore	89.6 mm to 89.61 mm
Stroke.	91.0 mm
Engine code:*	
Stage 3 Emissions	E5SA
Stage 4 Emissions	E5SB
Power output:	
E5SA engine	107 kW @ 5500 rpm
E5SB engine	103 kW @ 5500 rpm
Torque output:	
E5SA engine.	203 Nm @ 2500 rpm
E5SB engine.	200 Nm @ 2500 rpm
Compression ratio	10.0 : 1
Firing order	1 – 3 – 4 – 2
No 1 cylinder location.	Timing chain end

* Note: *See 'Vehicle identification' at the end of this manual for the location of code markings on the engine*

Lubrication system

Oil pump type.	Bi-rotor, chain driven from the crankshaft
Oil pressure (oil temperature 80°C):	
At idle speed.	1.6 bar
At 2000 rpm	3.1 bar
Oil pressure relief valve opens at	3.7 to 4.6 bar
Oil pump clearances:	
Between rotor and housing	0.154 to 0.304 mm
Between inner and outer rotor	0.05 to 0.2 mm
Endfloat between mating face and rotor	0.039 to 0.104 mm

Camshaft

Camshaft lift:	
Inlet camshaft	9.4 mm
Exhaust camshaft	8.75 mm
Endfloat	0.02 to 0.26 mm

Torque wrench settings

	Nm	lbf ft
Accessory bracket to cylinder block	47	35
Air conditioning compressor	25	18
Alternator mounting to cylinder head	25	18
Auxiliary belt tensioner	25	18
Balancer shaft gears to shaft	19	14
Balancer shaft housing to cylinder block:		
Stage 1	5	4
Stage 2	17	13
Big-end bearing caps:*		
Stage 1	7	5
Stage 2	16	12
Stage 3	Angle-tighten a further 90°	
Camshaft bearing cap	24	18
Camshaft cover:		
Stage 1	3	2
Stage 2	9	7
Camshaft position sensor	5	4
Camshaft sprockets	59	44
Coolant outlet housing	20	15
Coolant pipe bracket to cylinder block	23	17
Coolant pump	19	14
Coolant pump blanking plug	16	12
Coolant pump pulley	25	18
Coolant temperature gauge sender unit	6	4
Coolant temperature sensor	23	17
Crankshaft oil seal housing	15	11
Crankshaft position sensor	4	3
Crankshaft pulley hub to crankshaft:		
Stage 1	52	38
Stage 2	Angle-tighten a further 85°	
Crankshaft pulley to hub (two-part pulley)	34	25
Cylinder head bolts:		
Stage 1	10	7
Stage 2	35	26
Stage 3	Angle-tighten a further 90°	
Stage 4	Angle-tighten a further 90°	
Stage 5: Three bolts at right-hand end (see text)	38	28
Driveplate mounting bolts*	87	64
Driveshaft centre bearing to cylinder block bracket	27	20
EGR/air injection pipe to exhaust manifold	35	26
Engine mountings:		
Engine support plate bracket to cylinder head	44	32
Engine support plate to engine	58	43
Left-hand mounting-to-body bolts:		
Large bolts:		
Stage 1	50	37
Stage 2	Angle-tighten a further 90°	
Small bolt	25	18
Left-hand mounting-to-transmission bolts:		
Stage 1	90	66
Stage 2	Angle-tighten a further 90°	
Right-hand mounting:		
Stud	10	7
Bolt	61	45
Nut	54	40
Engine-to-transmission bolts	44	32
Engine/transmission roll restrictor:		
To crossmember	100	74
To transmission:		
Stage 1	60	44
Stage 2	Angle-tighten a further 90°	
Exhaust downpipe to manifold	35	26
Exhaust manifold:		
Nuts	23	17
Studs	14	10
Flywheel mounting bolts*	87	64
Front crossmember to body:		
Stage 1	150	111
Stage 2	Angle-tighten a further 90°	

Torque wrench settings

	Nm	lbf ft
Fuel rail	24	18
Inlet manifold:		
Studs	14	10
Nuts/bolts	22	16
Main bearing cap	97	72
Oil baffle plate to cylinder block	19	14
Oil drain plug	25	18
Oil filter mounting	21	15
Oil pick-up pipe to balance shaft housing/cylinder block	12	9
Oil pressure switch	27	20
Oil pump cover	10	7
Oil pump drive chain lower guide	12	9
Oil pump drive chain tensioner	12	9
Oil pump drive chain upper guide	26	19
Oil pump sprocket	33	24
Oil pump to cylinder block	12	9
Power steering pump	23	17
Power steering pump pulley	23	17
Spark plugs	18	13
Sump to balancer shaft housing/cylinder block	12	9
Sump to cylinder block	12	9
Thermostat housing	20	15
Throttle body to inlet manifold	10	7
Timing chain lower cover	11	8
Timing chain lower guide bolt	26	19
Timing chain upper cover	8	6
Timing chain upper guide bolt	12	9
Wheel bolts	170	125

* New bolts/nuts must be used

1 General information

Using this Chapter

Chapter 2 is divided into three Parts: A, B and C. Repair operations that can be carried out with the engine in the vehicle are described in Part A (petrol engines) and Part B (diesel engines). Part C covers the removal of the engine/transmission as a unit, and describes the engine dismantling and overhaul procedures.

In Parts A and B, the assumption is made that the engine is installed in the vehicle, with all ancillaries connected. If the engine has been removed for overhaul, the preliminary dismantling information which precedes each operation may be ignored.

Access to the engine compartment can be improved by removing the bonnet as described in Chapter 11.

Engine description

The engine is a 2.3 litre water-cooled, double-overhead camshaft, in-line four-cylinder unit, with a cast-iron cylinder block and an aluminium-alloy cylinder head. The engine is mounted transversely at the front of the vehicle, with the transmission bolted to the left-hand of the engine.

The crankshaft is of five-bearing type, and thrustwashers are fitted to the centre main bearing to control crankshaft endfloat.

The camshafts are driven by a simplex (single row) timing chain from the crankshaft sprocket. A hydraulic tensioner is fitted to the chain. The cylinder block-mounted oil pump is also driven by a simplex chain from the crankshaft sprocket. In order to smooth the running of the engine, a housing with two balancer shafts is fitted under the cylinder block. The shafts rotate in opposite directions at twice the speed of the crankshaft, and thus produce vibrations which counter those produced by the engine itself. The shafts are driven from the crankshaft sprocket, by the same chain that drives the oil pump.

The valves are operated from the camshaft through hydraulic bucket-type tappets, and the valve clearances are adjusted automatically.

The cylinder head carries the double camshafts. It also houses the inlet and exhaust valves, which are closed by single or double coil springs, and which run in sintered guides pressed into the cylinder head. The camshaft actuates the valves directly via hydraulic tappets, mounted in the cylinder head. The cylinder head contains integral oilways which supply and lubricate the tappets. The exhaust valves are sodium-filled to provide better cooling.

Engine coolant is circulated by a pump, driven by an auxiliary drivebelt from the crankshaft pulley. For details of the cooling system, refer to Chapter 3.

Lubricant is circulated under pressure by means of a bi-rotor pump, driven by a chain from the crankshaft. Oil is drawn from the sump through a strainer, and then forced through an externally-mounted, renewable screw-on filter. From there, it is distributed to the cylinder head, where it lubricates the camshaft journals and hydraulic tappets, and also to the crankcase, where it lubricates the main bearings, connecting rod big-ends, gudgeon pins and cylinder bores.

Repairs with engine in vehicle

The following operations can be performed without removing the engine:

a) Auxiliary drivebelt – removal and refitting.
b) Camshafts – removal and refitting.
c) Camshaft sprockets – removal and refitting.
d) Coolant pump – removal and refitting (refer to Chapter 3).
e) Crankshaft oil seals – renewal.
f) Crankshaft sprocket – removal and refitting.
g) Cylinder head – removal and refitting.
h) Engine mountings – inspection and renewal.
i) Sump – removal and refitting.
j) Balancer shaft housing – removal, inspection and refitting.
k) Timing chain, sprockets and covers – removal, inspection and refitting.

2 Engine valve timing marks – general information and usage

General information

1 The crankshaft and camshafts are interconnected by the timing chain, and rotate in phase with each other. If the timing chain is removed, it is possible for the shafts to rotate independently of each other, and the correct phasing is then lost.

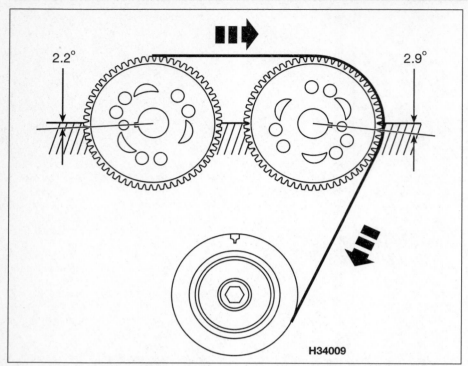

2.4 Rotate the crankshaft pulley until the notch on its circumference is in the 12 o'clock position, and the camshaft sprockets are positioned as shown

2 The design of the engine covered in this Chapter is such that piston-to-valve contact will occur if the crankshaft is turned with the timing chain removed. For this reason, it is important that the correct phasing between the camshafts and crankshaft is preserved whilst the timing chain is off the engine. This is achieved by setting the engine in a reference condition (known as Top Dead Centre or TDC) before the timing chain is removed, and then preventing the shafts from rotating until the chain is refitted. Similarly, if the engine has been dismantled for overhaul, the engine can

be set to TDC during reassembly to ensure that the correct shaft phasing is restored.

3 TDC is the highest position a piston reaches within its respective cylinder – in a four-stroke engine, each piston reaches TDC twice per cycle; once on the compression stroke, and once on the exhaust stroke. In general, TDC normally refers to No 1 cylinder on the compression stroke. Note that the cylinders are numbered one to four, starting from the timing chain end of the engine.

4 The crankshaft pulley has a marking which, when in the 12 o'clock position (vertical) in

relation to the cylinder block, indicates that No 1 cylinder (and hence also No 4 cylinder) is at TDC **(see illustration)**.

5 The camshaft sprockets are also equipped with timing marks **(see illustration)** – when these are aligned as shown, No 1 cylinder is at TDC compression.

Setting No 1 cylinder at TDC

6 Before starting work, make sure that the ignition is switched off.

7 Remove the timing chain upper cover (see Section 8).

8 Remove all of the spark plugs as described in Chapter 1A.

9 Using a socket or spanner on the crankshaft, rotate the engine clockwise until the mark on the crankshaft pulley is in the 12 o'clock position (vertical) in relation to the cylinder block **(see illustration 2.4)**.

10 Examine the camshaft sprockets, and check that the marks are aligned **(see illustration 2.5)**. If the camshaft sprocket marks are adjacent to each other, and aligned with the cylinder head surface, the engine is set to TDC on cylinder No 4 **(see illustration)**. Rotate the crankshaft pulley one complete turn to set the engine to TDC on No 1 cylinder.

3 Cylinder compression test

1 When engine performance is down, or if misfiring occurs which cannot be attributed to the ignition or fuel systems, a compression test can provide diagnostic clues as to the engine's condition. If the test is performed regularly, it can give warning of trouble before any other symptoms become apparent.

2 The engine must be fully warmed-up to normal operating temperature, the battery must be fully-charged. Remove the fuel pump fuse from below the central junction box

2.5 With the engine in position, the camshaft sprocket marks (arrowed) should be just below the upper edge of the cylinder head

2.10 If the camshaft sprocket marks (arrowed) are facing each other, the engine is at TDC on No 4 cylinder – rotate the crankshaft one complete turn

behind the fusebox cover in the driver's side of the lower facia. The 20 amp (yellow) fuel pump fuse is No 14 **(see illustration)**. Start the engine and allow it to stop.

3 Remove all the spark plugs (see Chapter 1A). **Note:** *In order to remove the spark plugs the ignition coils must be removed on some models. Prior to removing the coils disconnect the wiring plugs.*

4 Fit a compression tester to the No 1 cylinder spark plug hole – the type of tester which screws into the plug thread is preferable.

5 Have an assistant hold the throttle wide open. Crank the engine on the starter motor several seconds. After one or two revolutions, the compression pressure should build-up to a maximum figure, and then stabilise. Record the highest reading obtained.

6 Repeat the test on the remaining cylinders, recording the pressure in each. Keep the throttle wide open.

7 All cylinders should produce very similar pressures; a difference of more than 3 bars between any two cylinders indicates a fault. Note that the compression should build-up quickly in a healthy engine. Low compression on the first stroke, followed by gradually-increasing pressure on successive strokes, indicates worn piston rings. A low compression reading on the first stroke, which does not build-up during successive strokes, indicates leaking valves or a blown head gasket (a cracked head could also be the cause).

8 If the pressure in any cylinder is low, carry out the following test to isolate the cause. Introduce a teaspoonful of clean oil into that cylinder through its spark plug hole, and repeat the test.

9 If the addition of oil temporarily improves the compression pressure, this indicates that bore or piston wear is responsible for the pressure loss. No improvement suggests that leaking or burnt valves, or a blown head gasket, may be to blame.

10 A low reading from two adjacent cylinders is almost certainly due to the head gasket having blown between them.

11 If one cylinder is about 20 percent lower than the others and the engine has a slightly rough idle, a worn camshaft lobe could be the cause.

12 On completion of the test, refit the spark plugs, and fuel pump fuse.

4 Timing chain, sprockets and tensioner – removal, examination and refitting

General information

1 The primary function of the timing chain is to drive the camshafts. Should the chain break in service, the valve timing will be disturbed and piston-to-valve contact will occur, resulting in serious engine damage.

Removal

2 Before starting work, disconnect the battery negative (earth) lead. **Note:** *Before disconnecting the battery, refer to 'Disconnecting the battery' at the rear of this manual.*

3 Set the engine at TDC on No 1 cylinder as described in Section 2.

4 Remove the oil pump/balancer shaft drive chain as described in Section 5.

5 Squeeze the upper timing chain guide securing lugs together, using pliers if necessary, and withdraw the guide from the plate at the front of the cylinder head **(see illustration)**. Discard the chain guide, a new one must be fitted.

6 Hold the inlet camshaft sprocket stationary using a peg spanner (or similar) which engages with the spokes of the camshaft sprocket. Unscrew the camshaft sprocket Torx bolt, taking care not to drop the washer from the bolt **(see illustration)**. Repeat the procedure on the exhaust camshaft sprocket. Slide the sprockets from the camshafts and the timing

3.2 **The fuel pump fuse is No 14 (arrowed)**

chain, and lay the chain over the exhaust side of the timing case, having eliminated the slack in the chain. Secure the chain in place using a cable-tie or similar.

7 Using a suitable pair of pliers, extract the circlip from the chain tensioner arm pivot pin, taking care not to drop it into the timing case, then withdraw the pivot pin from the tensioner arm. If the pin is difficult to extract, an M6 bolt can be screwed into the end to facilitate removal **(see illustrations)**.

8 Lift the tensioner arm from the timing case.

9 Lift the tensioner plunger from the cylinder head, and discard it. A new one must be fitted.

10 Unscrew the bolts securing the timing chain guide, and withdraw the guide through the top of the timing case **(see illustrations)**.

11 Remove the Woodruff key from the end of the crankshaft, prising it free with a screwdriver if necessary, then slide the double chain sprocket from the crankshaft, and lift the

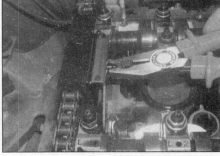

4.5 **Squeeze together the retaining lugs, and remove the timing chain guide**

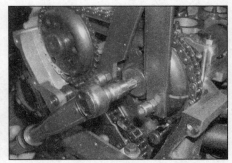

4.6 **Use a tool to hold the sprocket, and undo the Torx bolt – don't drop the washer**

4.7a **Pull out the circlip (arrowed) . . .**

4.7b **. . . and extract the pivot pin**

4.7c **If the pin is reluctant to move, screw in a 6 mm bolt, and pull it out**

4.10a Undo the upper timing chain guide bolt (arrowed) . . .

4.10b . . . and the lower bolt (note the washers)

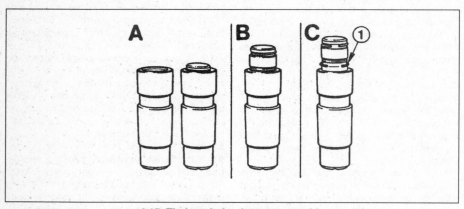

4.15 Timing chain plunger assembly

A *Piston retracted – plunger assembly usable*
B *Piston partially unlatched – discard plunger assembly*
C *Latching ring (1) visible – discard plunger assembly*

4.17 The copper-coloured link must be at the bottom (arrowed)

4.18a The notch on the sprocket (A) must align with the groove in the crankshaft (B)

4.18b The copper-coloured link (A) must align with the mark on the sprocket (B)

4.20 Insert the pivot pin, and secure it with the circlip

chain from the sprocket. Remove the chain from the top of the timing case.

Examination

12 Examine all the teeth on the camshafts and crankshaft sprockets. If the teeth are 'hooked' in appearance, renew the sprockets.
13 Check the tensioner sprocket for wear. If excessive wear is evident, the complete tensioner assembly must be renewed. Note that the tensioner plunger must be renewed whenever the chain is disturbed.
14 Examine the chain for wear. If the chain has been in operation for some time, if the chain can be pulled outwards from the sprocket teeth, or if when held horizontally (rollers vertical) it takes on a deeply bowed appearance, renew it.

Refitting

15 Install the new tensioner plunger into the cylinder head. Before fitting the plunger, take note of the position of the piston **(see illustration)**. The assembly is normally supplied with the piston protruding slightly from the cylinder, or slightly below the top surface of the cylinder (A). If the new assembly is supplied with the piston partially unlatched (B), or fully unlatched (C), it must not be used.

⚠ **Warning: Take care when installing the plunger assembly, as there is a risk of injury if the piston flies out.**

16 Ensure that the slot for the Woodruff key in the end of the crankshaft is pointing vertically downwards. If necessary, temporarily refit the crankshaft pulley bolt in order to turn the crankshaft to the required position.
17 Insert the timing chain and chain guide down through the timing case. Ensure that the single copper-coloured link is at the lower end **(see illustration)**. If desired, use a cable-tie to prevent the timing chain from dropping into the timing case, as during removal.
18 Fit the chain to the inner row of teeth, aligning the coppered link in the chain with the timing mark on the sprocket **(see illustration)**. Slide the sprocket onto the crankshaft, ensuring the notch in the sprocket aligns with the groove in the crankshaft **(see illustration)**. Refit the Woodruff key.
19 Apply a little locking compound to the threads, and fit the bolts securing the chain guide in position. Tighten the bolts to the specified torque. Note that the upper bolt is fitted with a plain and a wave washer **(see illustration 4.10b)**.
20 Refit the chain tensioner arm into position, then insert the pivot pin, and secure it with the circlip **(see illustration)**. Take care not to drop the circlip into the timing case.
21 Release the cable-tie securing the timing chain, take the slack out of the exhaust side of the chain, and fit the exhaust camshaft sprocket to the chain. The copper-coloured links must be centred around the mark on the sprocket **(see illustration)**.
22 Fit the sprocket to the exhaust camshaft, with the camshaft in the TDC position (ie, with

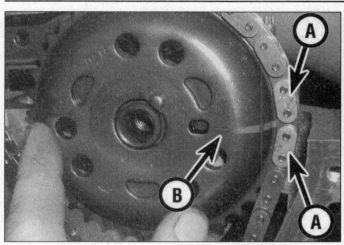

4.21 The copper-coloured links (A) must be centred around the mark on the sprocket (B)

4.22 If necessary, use a pair of pliers on the unmachined surface to rotate the camshaft

the exhaust camshaft sprocket timing mark in line with the top edge of the cylinder head, pointing to the exhaust side of the engine, refer to Section 2). If necessary, use a pair of pliers on one of the unmachined sections of the camshaft to turn the camshaft slightly. Take care not to damage the machined surfaces of the camshaft (see illustration). Note that the sprocket will only fit properly in one position – when the notch in the rear of the sprocket aligns with the groove in the end of the camshaft. Tighten the camshaft sprocket retaining bolt finger-tight only at this stage.

23 Fit the inlet camshaft sprocket to the chain. Again, the copper-coloured links must be centred around the mark on the sprocket (see illustration).

24 Refit the sprocket to the inlet camshaft, with the camshaft in the TDC position (ie, with the inlet camshaft sprocket timing mark in line with the top edge of the cylinder head, pointing to the inlet side of the engine – see Section 2). Again, if necessary, turn the camshaft to enable the sprocket to be fitted. Tighten the camshaft sprocket retaining bolt finger-tight only at this stage.

25 Turn the crankshaft clockwise slowly until the inlet camshaft begins to turn.

26 If the chain tensioner plunger piston protrudes from the cylinder, unlatch the piston by gently tapping the piston with a brass drift.

27 If the plunger is below the top surface of the cylinder, a tool must be fabricated to unlatch the piston (see illustration). It is suggested that 2.5 mm diameter welding rod is used to manufacture the tool. Use the tool to release the piston as follows.

28 Carefully lift the chain tensioner arm with a screwdriver, and insert the tool between the tensioner arm and the piston. Remove the screwdriver, and release the piston by pressing down the tensioner arm by hand. Carefully withdraw the tool once the piston has been released.

29 Hold the camshaft sprockets using the same method as used during dismantling, and tighten the sprocket bolts to the specified torque.

30 Temporarily refit the crankshaft pulley bolt, and rotate the crankshaft two full turns in a clockwise direction, and check that the sprocket marks align as described in Section 2.

31 Turn the crankshaft clockwise through another complete revolution, and check that the timing marks on the camshaft sprockets are facing each other, directly in line with the top face of the cylinder head (see illustration 2.10).

32 If the timing marks do not align as described, the chain has been incorrectly fitted, and should be removed and refitted. Note that a new tensioner plunger will be required if this is the case.

33 Once the timing marks correctly align, rotate the crankshaft clockwise one complete revolution until the crankshaft is the TDC position on No 1 cylinder (if necessary, refer to Section 2).

34 Push a new upper timing chain guide on to the bracket between the two camshaft sprockets.

35 Refit the oil pump/balancer shaft drive chain as described in Section 5.

36 Refit the timing chain upper cover and camshaft cover, as described in Sections 8 and 7 respectively.

37 Lower the vehicle to the ground, and reconnect the battery earth lead.

4.23 Centre the copper-coloured links (A) around the sprocket mark (B), and align the mark with the top edge of the cylinder head

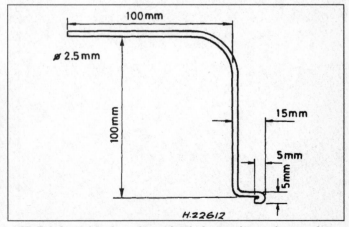

4.27 Fabricated tool used to unlatch the tensioner plunger piston

5.4 Compress the oil pump/balancer shaft chain tensioner, and lock it in place by inserting a drill bit (arrowed)

5.6a Undo the Torx bolts and remove the lower chain guide . . .

5.6b . . . and the upper guide

5 Oil pump/balancer shafts drive chain – removal and refitting

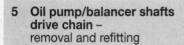

Removal

1 Apply the handbrake, then jack up the front of the vehicle and support it on axle stands (see *Jacking and vehicle support*). Undo the two retaining nuts and four bolts (two each side), and remove the undershield from under the engine compartment.

2 Set the engine to TDC as described in Section 2, then rotate the crankshaft a further half-a-turn to position it at TDC on cylinder No 2.

3 Remove the lower timing chain cover as described in Section 8.

4 Compress the oil pump drive chain tensioner, and insert a 2.5 mm drill bit into the hole in the tensioner body, to secure the tensioner arm in place **(see illustration)**.

5 Undo the retaining Torx bolt and remove the tensioner from the engine.

6 Unscrew the Torx bolts and remove both oil pump chain guides. Remove the oil pump chain leaving the oil pump sprocket in place **(see illustrations)**. Note that the upper guide is slotted at its lower end to fit over the lower Torx bolt.

Refitting

7 Fit the chain around the oil pump sprocket, balancer shaft sprocket, and outer row of teeth on the crankshaft sprocket. The copper-coloured links on the chain must be centred around the marks on the crankshaft and balance shaft sprocket **(see illustrations)**.

8 Refit the upper and lower oil pump chain guides, and tighten the bolts to the specified torque.

9 Check that the oil pump chain tensioner is still in its compressed state. If it is not, squeeze the arm into the tensioner body, and insert a 2.5 mm drill bit into the hole on the front face to hold the arm in place **(see illustration 5.4)**. Position the tensioner against the chain, insert and tighten the retaining bolts to the specified torque. Withdraw the drill bit, and allow the tensioner to extend.

10 Refit the lower timing cover as described in Section 8.

11 On all engines, refit the auxiliary drivebelt as described in Section 6.

12 Refit the timing chain upper cover and camshaft cover, as described in Sections 8 and 7 respectively.

13 Working underneath the vehicle, refit the engine undershield.

14 Lower the vehicle to the ground.

6 Auxiliary drivebelt – removal and refitting

1 The auxiliary drivebelt drives the alternator, coolant pump, power steering pump and the air conditioning compressor.

2 The drivebelt is of the Poly-Vee ribbed design.

3 The drivebelt tension is adjusted automatically by a spring-tensioned idler.

4 To remove the drivebelts first apply the handbrake, then jack up the front of the vehicle and support it on axle stands (see *Jacking and vehicle support*). Undo the four bolts and two nuts, then remove the undershield from under the engine compartment.

Removal

5 If the drivebelt is to be re-used, mark it for clockwise direction to ensure it is refitted the same way round.

6 Using a spanner on the hexagon in the centre of the tensioner pulley, rotate the tensioner clockwise to relieve the tension on the belt **(see illustration)**. Holding the tensioner in this position, disengage the belt from the pulleys.

5.7a Fit the oil pump chain with the copper-coloured link (A) over the mark on the crankshaft sprocket (B)

5.7b Take up the slack to check the timing

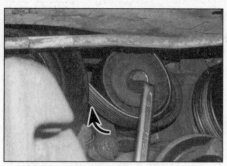

6.6 Rotate the tensioner clockwise to relieve the tension

Refitting

7 Route the drivebelt around the pulleys, holding the tensioner with a spanner. When the belt is correctly routed, release the tensioner **(see illustration)**. If a used belt is being refitted, ensure the previously-made direction of the rotation marks are observed.
8 Refit the engine undershield, and lower the vehicle to the ground.

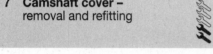

7 Camshaft cover – removal and refitting

Removal

1 Pull out the upper part of the battery compartment panel **(see illustration)**.
2 Remove the air cleaner housing with reference to Chapter 4A.

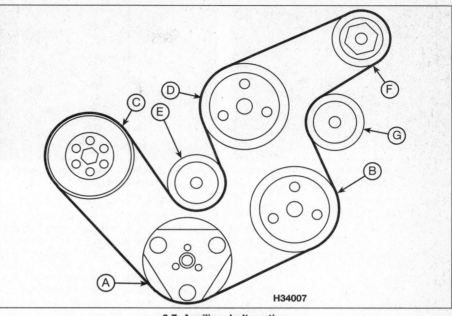

6.7 Auxiliary belt routing

A Air conditioning compressor
B Power steering pump
C Crankshaft pulley
D Coolant pump
E Tensioner
F Alternator
G Idler pulley

3 Undo the three retaining bolts, and remove the bulkhead cover **(see illustration)**. Note that the centre bolt also secures the accelerator cable support bracket. Slide the trim to the right-hand side and manoeuvre it from behind the coolant expansion tank.
4 Pull the crankcase ventilation valve/ breather tube from the camshaft cover **(see illustration)**.
5 Unscrew the ten bolts and remove the cover **(see illustration)**.
6 Where fitted, undo the coil retaining bolts, and disconnect the HT leads from the spark plugs **(see illustrations)**. Some models have a separate coil

7.1 Pull out the upper battery compartment panel

7.3 Undo the three bolts (two arrowed) and remove the bulkhead cover

7.4 Pull out the ventilation valve (arrowed)

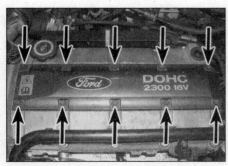

7.5 Undo the bolts and remove the cover

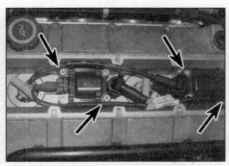

7.6a Undo the coil bolts (arrowed) . . .

7.6b . . . and pull the HT connectors from the spark plugs

7.10 Disconnect the camshaft position sensor wiring plug

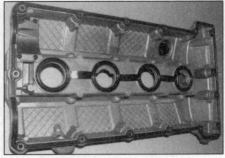

7.13a Fit the rubber gaskets to the camshaft cover . . .

7.13b . . . then fit the metal sleeves with the rubber washers to hold them in place

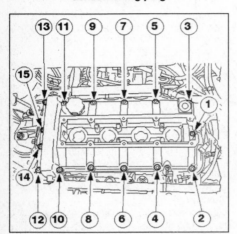

7.13c Progressively tighten the cover bolts in the sequence shown

8.3 Note the earth strap (arrowed) secured to the engine mounting bracket

8.4 Remove the small bracket from the corner of the cylinder head

8.5 Undo the three Torx screws and remove the engine mounting

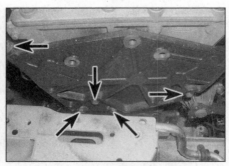

8.6 Engine support plate bolts (arrowed)

pack fitted to the end of the cylinder head – on these models remove the HT leads. **Note:** *Do not pull on the cable when disconnecting the plugs, only pull on the connectors. If the connectors are difficult to remove, twist the connector slightly prior to pulling.*

7 Remove the coils and lay them to one side.

8 If desired, using a spark plug socket and long extension, remove the spark plugs, if necessary refer to Chapter 1A.

9 Undo the two bolts securing the alternator wiring rail to the cylinder head.

10 Disconnect the camshaft position sensor wiring plug and unscrew the 15 camshaft cover retaining bolts/nuts **(see illustration)**.

11 Remove the camshaft cover, and recover the gasket(s).

Refitting

12 Clean the surfaces of the camshaft cover and cylinder head.

13 Carefully fit the gasket(s) to the camshaft cover, then fit the rubber washers over the metal sleeves to hold them in place. Position the cover on the cylinder head, then tighten the bolts/nuts progressively to the specified torque in the sequence shown **(see illustrations)**.

14 The remainder of refitting is a reversal of removal. Note that prior to reconnecting the HT leads connectors to the spark plugs, smear a little silicone grease around the inside of the connectors.

8 Timing chain covers – removal and refitting

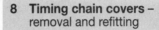

Upper cover

Removal

1 Remove the camshaft cover as described in Section 7. Undo the two retaining nuts and four bolts (two each side), and remove the engine undershield.

2 Position a jack under the engine sump, and take the weight of the engine. Use a block of wood on the jack head to prevent any damage to the sump casing.

3 Undo the three bolts and two nuts, then remove the engine mounting bracket. Where fitted, undo the nut securing the earth strap to the engine mounting bracket stud **(see illustration)**.

4 Undo the retaining bolt and stud, and remove the small engine support bracket from the front left-hand corner of the cylinder head **(see illustration)**.

5 Unscrew the three Torx screws, and remove the engine mounting from the right-hand side inner wing **(see illustration)**.

6 Using the jack, raise the engine, pushing back at the same time, until the engine support plate lower bolts are visible. Undo the retaining bolts and remove the engine support plate **(see illustration)**.

7 Remove the 7 bolts and withdraw the timing chain upper cover from the engine **(see illustration)**.

Refitting

8 Ensure the mating surfaces of the cover

and cylinder head are clean and dry. Refit the upper timing cover using a new gasket. Before finally tightening the retaining bolts, align the top edge of the cover with the upper surface of the cylinder head. The step down from the cylinder head surface to the cover must be no more than 0.13 mm **(see illustration)**. Tighten the bolts to the specified torque.

9 The remainder of refitting is a reversal of removal.

Lower cover

Removal

10 Apply the handbrake, then jack up the front of the vehicle and support it on axle stands (see *Jacking and vehicle support*). Undo the two retaining nuts and four bolts (two each side), and remove the engine undershield. With reference to Section 6, remove the auxiliary drivebelt.

11 On engines with a two-part crankshaft pulley, remove the outer ring of six bolts from the pulley, and use two M6 x 20 mm bolts in the holes provided to the force the pulley from the hub **(see illustration)**.

12 On all engines, slacken the crankshaft pulley bolt. Prevent the crankshaft from turning by engaging top gear (manual gearbox only) and having an assistant press the brake pedal hard, or by remove the starter motor and jamming the ring gear teeth with a lever or large flat-bladed screwdriver.

13 Unscrew the pulley bolt part-way, and use a suitable two-legged puller to draw the pulley hub from the crankshaft. We used two 6 mm bolts to attach the puller to the crankshaft pulley **(see illustration)**.

14 Working underneath the vehicle, remove the bolt securing the power steering pipe to the support bracket.

15 Remove the bolts securing the lower timing chain cover.

Refitting

16 Using a punch (or similar) drive the seal out from the outside of the cover. Press the new oil seal into place from the inside of the cover, ensuring that the spring side of the seal faces the inside of the cover (see Section 10). Lubricate the inside lip of the seal with clean engine oil. On original covers the oil seal was bonded into place, and although it is possible

8.7 Undo the bolts and remove the upper timing chain cover

to drive the seal out, there is a risk of distorting the cover. If this is the case, renewal of the cover is necessary.

17 Position a new timing cover gasket on the engine block. The cover has an integral vulcanised gasket, consequently, if the gasket is damaged, the cover must be renewed. Manoeuvre the cover over the crankshaft, and push it into place, taking care not to damage the inner edge of the oil seal on the shoulder of the crankshaft. Temporarily refit the crankshaft pulley/hub to 'centre' the cover and oil seal. Tighten the cover retaining bolts to the specified torque.

18 Where applicable, refit the power steering pipe to the support bracket and tighten the bolt securely.

19 On engines with a two-part crankshaft pulley, position the pulley hub over the end of the crankshaft, ensuring that the Woodruff key aligns with the slot in the hub, and press the

8.11 Use two M6 bolts to force the pulley from the hub

8.8 Check the step from the timing cover to the cylinder head with feeler gauges

pulley into place. It may be possible to gently tap the hub into place using a soft-faced hammer, although Ford specify the use of special tool No 21-214 to press the hub into place. If necessary however, it is possible to fabricate a home-made equivalent using an M12 bolt, washer and nut. Screw the bolt, washer and nut into the end of the crankshaft, and up against the hub, then tighten the nut until the hub is against the shoulder of the crankshaft **(see illustrations)**. Remove the tool. Screw in the hub retaining bolt and tighten it to the Stage 1 torque setting, and the Stage 2 angle tightening setting. Use the method employed during dismantling to prevent the crankshaft from rotating. Position the pulley on the hub, fit and tighten the retaining bolts to the specified torque. Note that one of the holes in the pulley and hub is slightly offset, so the pulley will only fit correctly in one position **(see illustration)**.

8.13 Attach the puller to the hub using two M6 bolts and washers

8.19a Fit the hub to the crankshaft, aligning the Woodruff key with the slot in the hub

8.19b Use an M12 bolt, washer and nut to press the hub into place

8.19c The crankshaft pulley holes are offset so that it will only fit on one way

9.2 Squeeze the lugs (arrowed) together and remove the upper timing chain guide

20 On engines with a one-part crankshaft pulley, position the pulley over the end of the crankshaft, ensuring that the Woodruff key aligns with the slot in the pulley, and press the pulley into place. It may be possible to tap the pulley into place with a soft-faced hammer, although Ford specify the use of special tool No 16-057 to press the pulley into place. If necessary however, it is possible to fabricate a home-made equivalent using an M12 bolt, washer and nut. Screw the bolt, washer and nut into the end of the crankshaft, and up against the pulley, then tighten the nut until the pulley is against the shoulder of the crankshaft **(see illustrations 8.19a and 8.19b)**. Remove the tool. Screw in the pulley retaining bolt and tighten it to the Stage 1 torque setting, and the Stage 2 angle tightening setting. Use the method employed during dismantling to prevent the crankshaft from rotating.
21 Refit the auxiliary drivebelt as described in Section 6.
22 Working underneath the vehicle, refit the engine undershield.
23 Lower the vehicle to the ground.

9 Camshafts and hydraulic tappets – removal, inspection and refitting

Removal

1 Set the engine to TDC on No 1 cylinder, as described in Section 2.
2 Squeeze the upper timing chain guide

9.14 Refit the hydraulic tappets to their original location

9.7 The upper timing chain guide bracket is retained by No 1 inlet and exhaust bearing cap nuts (arrowed)

securing lugs together, using pliers if necessary, and withdraw the guide from the plate at the front of the cylinder head **(see illustration)**. Discard the chain guide, a new one must be fitted.
3 Hold the inlet camshaft sprocket stationary using a peg spanner (or similar) which engages with the spokes of the camshaft sprocket. Unscrew the camshaft sprocket Torx bolt, taking care not to drop the washer from the bolt. Repeat the procedure on the exhaust camshaft sprocket. Slide the sprockets from the camshafts and the timing chain, and lay the chain over the exhaust side of the timing case, having eliminated the slack in the chain. Secure the chain in place using a cable-tie or similar.
4 Using a suitable pair of pliers, extract the circlip from the chain tensioner arm pivot pin, taking care not to drop it into the timing case, then withdraw the pivot pin from the tensioner arm. If the pin is difficult to extract, an M6 bolt can be screwed into the end to facilitate removal **(see illustrations 4.7a, 4.7b and 4.7c)**.
5 Lift the tensioner arm from the timing case.
6 Withdraw the tensioner plunger assembly from the cylinder head, and discard it. A new one must be fitted.
7 Take note of the markings on the camshaft bearing caps. It is essential that they are refitted to their original positions. Evenly and progressively slacken the bearing cap nuts, until the caps can be removed. Note that the upper timing chain guide is retained by No 1 inlet and exhaust camshaft bearing caps **(see illustration)**. Lift the camshafts from the cylinder head.

9.16a Position the camshaft, so that none of the lobes are at full lift

8 If the hydraulic tappets are to be removed, proceed as follows. Obtain sixteen small containers, or a large container divided into sixteen compartments to store the tappets. Partially fill the container(s) so that the tappets will be immersed in oil.
9 Withdraw the tappets from the cylinder head bores – a tool fitted with a rubber suction cup (such as a valve grinding tool) will aid in this operation. Store the tappets in the order that they are removed from the cylinder head, to ensure they are refitted to the their original locations. Failure to do so could result in accelerated camshaft and tappet wear after reassembly.
10 After removing all the tappets, ensure that any excess oil accidentally spilled into the camshaft bearing caps securing bolt holes is removed, using compressed air or absorbent rag. This will prevent damage to the cylinder head by hydraulic action during reassembly.

Inspection

11 Examine the camshaft bearing surfaces and cam lobes for signs of wear ridges and scoring. Renew the camshaft if any of these conditions are apparent. Examine the condition of the bearing surfaces of the bearing caps and cylinder head.
12 If available, use a micrometer to measure the lift of the camshaft lobes. Measure the diameter of the camshaft at 90° to the camshaft lobe, and in line with the camshaft lobe. Subtract the first measurement from the second, and compare the dimension to that given in the Specifications at the start of this Chapter.
13 Inspect the tappet upper surfaces for signs of wear. If evident, examine the corresponding camshaft lobe as it is likely to be worn in the same manner. Check the sides of each tappet for signs of scoring.

Refitting

14 Lubricate the hydraulic tappets with clean engine oil, and refit them into their original locations **(see illustration)**.
15 Using a spanner on the crankshaft pulley, rotate the engine clockwise approximately 45°, to eliminate the possibility of accidental piston-to-valve contact.
16 Lubricate the bearing surfaces in the cylinder head, and the bearing surfaces and lobes of the camshaft with clean engine oil. Refit the camshafts into the cylinder head, in such a position that none of the lobes are at full lift. The camshafts are marked with two identification rings between the second and third cylinder lobes **(see illustrations)**.
17 Refit the camshaft bearing caps to their original locations, noting that the inlet camshaft caps are numbered R1 to R5, and the exhaust camshaft caps are numbered L1 to L5, from the timing chain end of the cylinder head **(see illustrations)**. Note that the upper timing chain guide is fitted onto the studs of No 1 bearing cap **(see illustration 9.7)**.
18 Tighten the bearing cap nuts by hand evenly and progressively to lower the camshafts into position. Continue to tighten the bearing

caps until they contact the cylinder head, then tighten them to the specified torque setting.

19 After the camshafts bearings have been tightened down, the crankshaft must not be moved for 15 minutes.

20 Install the new tensioner plunger into the cylinder head. Before fitting the plunger, take note of the position of the piston **(see illustration 4.15)**. The assembly is normally supplied with the piston protruding slightly from the cylinder, or slightly below the top surface of the cylinder (A). If the new assembly is supplied with the piston partially unlatched (B), or fully unlatched (C), it must not be used.

 Warning: Take care when installing the plunger assembly, as there is a risk of personal injury if the piston flies out.

21 Using a spanner or socket on the crankshaft pulley, rotate the crankshaft 45° anti-clockwise, to the TDC position.

22 Refit the chain tensioner arm into position, then insert the pivot pin, and secure it with the circlip **(see illustration 4.20)**. Take care not to drop the circlip into the timing case.

23 Release the cable-tie securing the timing chain, take the slack out of the exhaust side of the chain, and fit the exhaust camshaft sprocket to the chain. The copper-coloured links must be centred around the mark on the sprocket **(see illustration 4.21)**.

24 Fit the sprocket to the exhaust camshaft, with the camshaft in the TDC position (ie, with the exhaust camshaft sprocket timing mark in line with the top edge of the cylinder head, pointing to the exhaust side of the engine, refer to Section 2). If necessary, use a pair of pliers on one of the unmachined sections of the camshaft to turn the camshaft slightly. Take care not to damage the machined surfaces of the camshaft. Note that the sprocket will only fit properly in one position – when the notch in the rear of the sprocket aligns with the groove in the end of the camshaft. Tighten the camshaft sprocket retaining bolt finger-tight only at this stage.

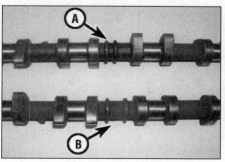

9.16b **Rings identify the inlet camshaft (A) and exhaust camshaft (B)**

25 Fit the inlet camshaft sprocket to the chain. Again, the copper-coloured links must be centred around the mark on the sprocket **(see illustration 4.23)**.

26 Refit the sprocket to the inlet camshaft, with the camshaft in the TDC position (ie, with the inlet camshaft sprocket timing mark in line with the top edge of the cylinder head, pointing to the inlet side of the engine – see Section 2). Again, if necessary, turn the camshaft to enable the sprocket to be fitted. Tighten the camshaft sprocket retaining bolt finger-tight only at this stage.

27 Turn the crankshaft clockwise slowly until the inlet camshaft begins to turn.

28 If the chain tensioner plunger piston protrudes from the cylinder, unlatch the piston by gently tapping the piston with a brass drift.

29 If the plunger is below the top surface of the cylinder, a tool must be fabricated to unlatch the piston **(see illustration 4.27)**. It is suggested that 2.5 mm diameter welding rod is used to manufacture the tool. Use the tool to release the piston as follows.

30 Carefully lift the chain tensioner arm with a screwdriver, and insert the tool between the tensioner arm and the piston. Remove the screwdriver, and release the piston by pressing down the tensioner arm by hand. Carefully withdraw the tool once the piston has been released.

9.17a **The inlet camshaft caps are labelled R1 to R5 (arrowed) . . .**

31 Hold the camshaft sprockets using the same method as used during dismantling, and tighten the sprocket bolts to the specified torque.

32 Temporarily refit the crankshaft pulley bolt, and rotate the crankshaft two full turns in a clockwise direction, and check that the sprocket marks align as described in Section 2.

33 Turn the crankshaft clockwise through another complete revolution, and check that the timing marks on the camshaft sprockets are facing each other, directly in line with the top face of the cylinder head **(see illustration)**.

34 If the timing marks do not align as described, the chain has been incorrectly fitted, and should be removed and refitted. Note that a new tensioner plunger will be required if this is the case.

35 Once the timing marks correctly align, rotate the crankshaft clockwise one complete revolution until the crankshaft is the TDC position on No 1 cylinder (if necessary, refer to Section 2).

36 Push a new upper timing chain guide on to the bracket between the two camshaft sprockets.

37 Refit the upper timing chain cover and camshaft cover as described in Sections 8 and 7 respectively.

9.17b **. . . and the exhaust caps are labelled L1 to L5 (arrowed) starting from the timing chain end**

9.33 **Check that the sprocket marks are facing each other**

10.4a From the inside of the cover, drive the seal into place . . .

10.4b . . . until it's flush with the cover outer edge

10.7 Pull on the self-tapping screws to extract the seal

10 Crankshaft oil seals – renewal

Timing chain end

1 Renewal of the seal is only possible once the lower timing cover has been removed (see Section 8).

2 With the cover on the bench, use a punch (or similar) to drive the seal from the cover from the outside. **Note:** *On original covers, the seal is bonded into place, and although the seal can be driven out, there is a high risk of distorting the cover. In which case the cover must be renewed.*

3 Clean the seal housing, and polish off any burrs or raised edges which may have caused the seal to fail in the first place.

4 Apply a smear of silicone sealant around the outside of the seal, and press the seal into place from the inside of the cover. Use a tubular drift (eg, a socket) that bears only hard outer edge of the seal **(see illustrations)**.

5 Refit the lower timing cover as described in Section 8.

Flywheel/driveplate end

6 Remove the flywheel/driveplate, with reference to Section 12.

7 The oil seal must be renewed without removing the housing. Make a note of the fitted depth of the seal in its housing. Punch or drill two small holes opposite each other in the seal. Screw a self-tapping screw into each, and pull on the screws to extract the seal **(see illustration)**.

8 Clean the seal housing, and polish off any burrs or raised edges, which may have caused the seal to fail in the first place.

9 Lubricate the lip of the new seal with clean engine oil, and carefully locate the seal on the end of the crankshaft.

10 Using a suitable tubular drift, which bears only on the hard outer edge of the seal, drive the seal into position, to the same depth in the housing as the original was prior to removal.

11 Wash off any traces of oil, and refit the flywheel/driveplate (with new bolts) as described in Section 12.

11 Cylinder head – removal and refitting

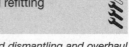

Note: *Cylinder head dismantling and overhaul is covered in Chapter 2C.*

> ⚠ **Warning: The cylinder head must have cooled to below 30ºC before unscrewing the cylinder head bolts.**

Removal

1 Before starting work, disconnect the battery negative (earth) lead. **Note:** *Before disconnecting the battery, refer to 'Disconnecting the battery' at the rear of this manual.* Depressurise the fuel system as described in Chapter 4A.

2 Remove the camshafts and hydraulic tappets as described in Section 9.

3 Undo the four nuts and disconnect the front exhaust pipe from the exhaust manifold.

4 Drain the cooling system as described in Chapter 1A.

5 On the rear side of the engine, disconnect the wiring plugs from the crankshaft position sensor and the oil pressure switch. Unclip the harness from the retaining clip.

6 Depress the retaining clips and pull off the connectors from the idle air control valve, No 4 injector and the throttle position sensor. Using a small screwdriver, prise out the retaining clips and lift off the injectors' power supply rail **(see illustration)**. Position the wiring harness to one side.

7 Where fitted, disconnect the hose from the secondary air injection filter.

8 Disconnect the coolant hose from the thermostat/coolant outlet housing at the left-hand end of the cylinder head **(see illustration)**.

9 Release the retaining clip and disconnect the heater hose from the thermostat/coolant outlet housing **(see illustration 11.8)**.

10 Disconnect the wiring plugs from the engine coolant temperature sensor, and temperature gauge sender, both located in the thermostat/coolant outlet housing. Where fitted, disconnect the wiring plug from the radio interference suppressor fitted above the thermostat housing.

11 Disconnect the inner end of the throttle cable from the quadrant, undo the three Torx screws and remove the cable from the engine, complete with the support bracket **(see illustrations)**.

12 Release any retaining clips and disconnect the vacuum lines from the inlet manifold, idle air control valve and (where

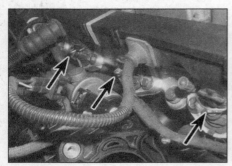

11.6 Prise out the retaining clips (arrowed) and remove injector wiring rail

11.8 Disconnect the hoses from the thermostat/coolant outlet housing

11.11a Disconnect the inner end of the accelerator cable from the quadrant

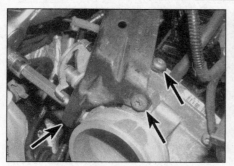

11.11b Undo the three accelerator cable bracket Torx screws (arrowed)

11.12a Disconnect the vacuum hoses from the inlet manifold . . .

11.12b . . . and the idle air control valve

11.12c The brake servo hose is released by depressing the collar

11.14 Squeeze together the tabs and disconnect the fuel supply and return couplings

11.19 Undo the three bolts at the right-hand end of the cylinder head

fitted) the EGR valve (see illustrations). Note that the brake servo hose is disconnected by depressing the collar around the connection, and pulling the hose from the manifold (see illustrations).

13 Unscrew the nut securing the alternator bracket to the cylinder head. Slacken the alternator top mounting nut and swivel the bracket away from the cylinder head.

14 Squeeze together the tabs of the quick-release connectors, and disconnect the fuel supply and return hoses (see illustration). Note that the connectors are colour-coded to aid refitment.

15 Where fitted, undo the retaining bolts and remove the EGR valve and pipe.

16 Undo the nut securing the oil dipstick guide tube to the cylinder head. Carefully pull the dipstick guide tube from the engine block.

17 Unscrew the retaining bolts and remove the exhaust manifold heat shield.

18 Slacken and remove the upper bolt securing the timing chain guide to the cylinder head (see illustration 4.10a).

19 Undo and remove the three bolts at the right-hand end of the cylinder head (see illustration).

20 Using a splined tool, unscrew the cylinder head bolts a turn at a time, in **reverse order** to the tightening sequence (see illustration 11.28) and remove them together with their washers. **Note:** *Only the cylinder head bolts with integral washers can be re-used, providing the length of the bolt below the head does not exceed 174.3 mm (see illustrations).*

21 With all the bolts removed, lift the cylinder head from the block. If it is stuck, tap it free with a wooden mallet. Do not insert a lever into the gasket joint.

22 Remove the cylinder head gasket from the block.

23 If required, remove the inlet and exhaust

manifolds from the cylinder head with reference to the relevant Part of Chapter 4.

Refitting

24 Thoroughly clean the contact faces of the cylinder head and block. Also clean any oil or coolant from the bolt holes in the block – if this precaution is not taken, not only will the tightening torque be incorrect but there is the possibility of damaging the block. Ensure the locating dowels are in place (see illustrations). Where applicable (refer to paragraph 20), clean the threads of the used cylinder head bolts.

25 Where removed, refit the exhaust and inlet manifolds to the cylinder head with reference to the relevant Part of Chapter 4.

26 Locate a new gasket on the block. The gasket will only fit one way around.

27 Carefully lower the head onto the block, making sure that it engages the location dowels

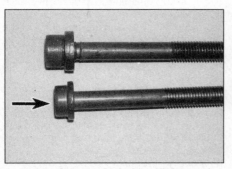

11.20a Only re-use bolts with integral washers (arrowed) . . .

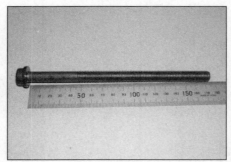

11.20b . . . providing the bolt length below the head does not exceed 174.3 mm

11.24a Ensure the locating dowels are in place at the timing chain end . . .

11.24b . . . and the flywheel end

correctly. Do not use any jointing compound on the cylinder head joint. Insert the cylinder head bolts, together with their integral washers, and initially hand-tighten them.

28 Using the sequence shown **(see illustration)** tighten all the bolts to the Stage 1 torque given in the Specifications.

29 Working in the same sequence, tighten the bolts to the Stage 2 torque, and the Stage 3 and 4 angles as given in the Specifications.

30 Insert the three bolts at the right-hand end of the cylinder head, and tighten them to the specified torque **(see illustration 11.19)**.

31 The remainder of refitting is a reversal of removal, bearing in mind the following points:
a) *After refitting the camshafts, allow 15 minutes before turning the crankshaft.*
b) *Tighten all nuts and bolts to their correct torque where specified.*

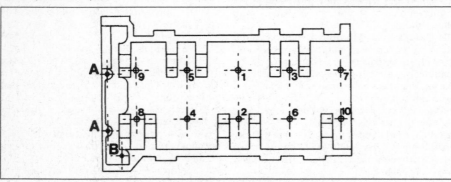

11.28 Cylinder head bolt tightening sequence

A Long M8 bolts   *B Short M8 bolt*

12.3 Flywheel locking tool

c) *Refill the cooling system as described in Chapter 1A.*
d) *Check the throttle cable adjustment as described in Chapter 4A.*
e) *Renew the oil dipstick guide tube O-ring.*

12 Flywheel/driveplate – removal, inspection and refitting

Removal

1 On manual gearbox models, remove the gearbox (see Chapter 7A) and clutch (see Chapter 6).

2 On automatic transmission models, remove the automatic transmission as described in Chapter 7B.

3 The flywheel/driveplate bolts are offset to ensure correct fitment. Unscrew the bolts while holding the flywheel/driveplate stationary. Temporarily insert a bolt in the cylinder block, and use a screwdriver to hold the flywheel/driveplate, or make up a holding tool as shown **(see illustration)**.

4 Lift the flywheel/driveplate from the crankshaft. If removing a driveplate, note the location of the shim (next to the crankshaft) and the spacer.

Inspection

5 Check the flywheel/driveplate for wear and damage. Examine the starter ring gear for excessive wear to the teeth. If the driveplate

12.6 The flywheel bolts holes are slightly offset, so it will only fit one way around

or its ring gear are damaged, the complete driveplate must be renewed. The flywheel ring gear, however, may be renewed separately from the flywheel, but the work should be entrusted to a Ford dealer or local garage. If the clutch friction face is discoloured or scored excessively, it may be possible to regrind it, but this work should also be entrusted to a Ford dealer or specialist.

Refitting

6 Refitting is a reversal of removal **(see illustration)**. Use new bolts when refitting the flywheel or driveplate, and coat the threads of the bolts with locking fluid before inserting them. Tighten them to the specified torque.

13 Engine mountings – inspection and renewal

Inspection

1 Jack up and support the front of the car securely on axle stands. Remove the engine undershield.

2 Check the mounting rubbers to see if they are cracked, hardened or separated from the metal at any point; renew the mounting if any such damage or deterioration is evident.

3 Check that all the mounting's fasteners are securely tightened; use a torque wrench to check if possible.

4 Using a large screwdriver or a crowbar, check for wear in the mounting by carefully levering against it to check for free play. Where this is not possible, enlist the aid of an assistant to move the engine/transmission back-and-forth, or from side-to-side, while you watch the mounting. While some free play is to be expected even from new components, excessive wear should be obvious. If excessive free play is found, check first that the fasteners are correctly secured, then renew any worn components as described below.

Renewal

Right-hand engine mounting

5 Apply the handbrake then jack up the front of the vehicle and support it on axle stands (see *Jacking and vehicle support*). Undo the two retaining nuts and four bolts (two each side), and remove the undershield. Support the weight of the engine/transmission using a trolley jack with a block of wood placed on its head.

6 Remove the air cleaner housing as described in Chapter 4A.

7 Undo the three horizontal bolts securing the mounting bracket to the engine support plate, and the two nuts securing the mounting bracket to the engine mounting **(see illustration)**. Note the earth strap mounted on the foremost horizontal bolt.

8 Unscrew the three bolts and remove the mounting from the inner wing **(see illustration)**.

13.7 Undo the bolts/nuts and remove the mounting bracket

13.8 Lift out the rubber insert, and undo the Torx bolts

13.12 Slacken the mounting bolts

9 Fit the new engine mounting and bracket using a reversal of the removal procedure, tightening the nuts/bolts to the specified torque.

Left-hand engine mounting

10 Apply the handbrake then jack up the front of the vehicle and support it on axle stands (see *Jacking and vehicle support*). Undo the two retaining nuts and four bolts (two each side), and remove the undershield. Support the weight of the engine/transmission using a trolley jack with a block of wood placed on its head.
11 Remove the battery, the surround and the support tray as described in Chapter 5A.
12 Slacken the five bolts and single nut securing the engine/transmission mounting to the body **(see illustration)**.
13 Using the jack, lower the engine/transmission slightly. Fully remove the retaining bolts and remove the mounting **(see illustration)**. If required, unbolt and remove the lower section of the mounting from the transmission.
14 Fit the new mounting using a reversal of the removal procedure, tightening the nuts/bolts to the specified torque.

Engine roll restrictor

15 Apply the handbrake, then jack up the front of the vehicle and support it on axle stands (see *Jacking and vehicle support*). Undo the two retaining nuts and four bolts (two each side), and remove the engine undershield.
16 Support the weight of the engine with a trolley jack and piece of wood beneath the sump.

13.13 Remove the mounting

17 Unscrew the bolt securing the roll restrictor to the transmission **(see illustration)**.
18 Slacken and remove the bolt securing the roll restrictor to the front crossmember.
19 Fit the new roll restrictor using a reversal of the removal procedure, noting the different specified torque applicable if the restrictor is made from steel or aluminium.

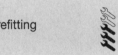

14 Sump – removal and refitting

Removal

1 Apply the handbrake, then jack up the front of the vehicle and support it on axle stands (see *Jacking and vehicle support*).
2 Undo the two retaining nuts and four bolts (two each side), and remove the undershield from under the engine.

13.17 Undo the roll restrictor transmission bolt and crossmember bolt (arrowed)

3 Position a container beneath the sump, then unscrew the drain plug and drain the engine oil. Clean the plug and if necessary renew the washer, then refit and tighten the plug after all the oil has drained. Remove the dipstick from the engine.
4 The sump plate is bolted to the underside of the balancer shaft housing. Undo the eighteen bolts and remove the sump plate **(see illustration)**.
5 If required, the baffle plate and oil pump pick-up tube can be removed by unscrewing the retaining nuts/bolts **(see illustration)**.

Refitting

6 Where removed, refit the oil pick-up tube (with a new gasket/O-ring where applicable) and oil baffle plate. Apply a little locking compound to the bolts, and tighten them to the specified torque **(see illustration)**.
7 Ensure the mating surfaces of the sump

14.4 Undo the bolts and remove the sump plate

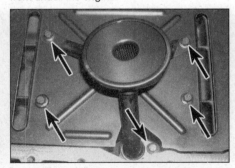

14.5 The oil pick-up tube and baffle plate is secured by five bolts (arrowed)

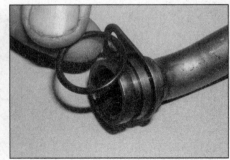

14.6 Renew the oil pick up tube O-ring

and cylinder block/balancer shaft housing are clean and dry.

8 Discard the gasket and fit a new one and then refit the sump plate, tightening the bolts to the specified torque.

9 The remainder of refitting is a reversal of removal. Refill the engine with new oil as described in Chapter 1A.

15 Balancer housing and shafts – removal, inspection and refitting

Removal

1 Located within the shaft housing are two contra-rotating balancer shafts spinning at twice crankshaft speed. The shafts produce vibrations which counter those produced by the engine. The rearmost shaft is driven by the crankshaft via a chain which also drives the oil pump. The front shaft is geared to the rear shaft **(see illustration)**.

2 The balancer shaft housing removal and refitting is much easier if the engine is removed from the vehicle. However, if the engine is in the vehicle, proceed as follows.

3 Remove the front section of the exhaust system as described in Chapter 4C.

4 Remove the flywheel/driveplate as described in Section 12. Remove the engine-to-transmission adapter plate.

5 Remove the sump plate, baffle plate and oil pump pick-up tube as described in Section 14.

6 With reference to Section 5, remove the oil pump/balancer shaft drive chain.

7 Unscrew the balancer shaft housing retaining bolts and nuts, and withdraw the housing from the engine. Do not prise between the mating faces of the sump and cylinder block. Discard the old gasket. Note that the housing is aligned with the cylinder block by two guide sleeves. The sleeves must not be interchanged, because one has an oil supply hole.

Inspection

8 Although the balancer shafts can be removed for inspection, no parts are available separately. If any component shows sign of excessive wear or damage, the complete housing and shaft assembly must be renewed. At the time of writing, no specifications regarding shaft clearances, endfloat or dimensions were available.

Refitting

9 Ensure the mating surfaces of the cylinder block and balancer shaft housing are clean and dry. Apply a bead of silicone sealant to the crankshaft oil seal housing **(see illustration)**.

10 Fit the new gasket onto the housing, using the integral retaining tags to keep the gasket in place. Push the half-round section of the gasket into place. Apply a smear of sealant to both transition zones between the metal and rubber sections of the gasket **(see illustration)**.

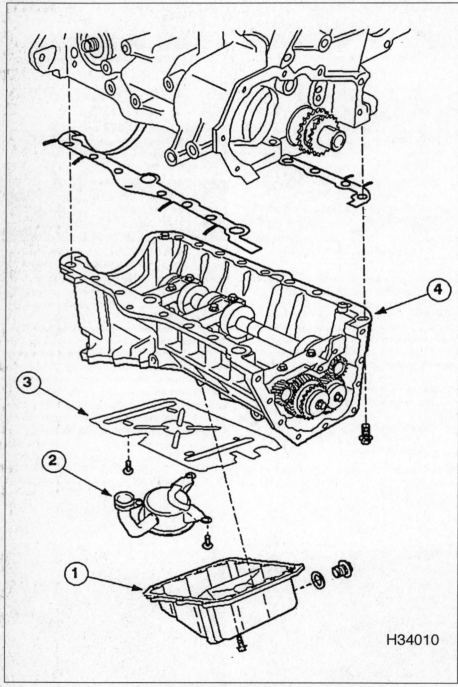

15.1 Balancer shaft housing

1 Sump plate   3 Baffle plate
2 Oil pick-up tube   4 Balancer shaft housing

H34010

15.9 Apply sealant to the areas shown (arrowed)

15.10 Apply sealant to the transition areas between the metal and rubber sections of the gasket (arrowed)

15.12 Using a straight-edge and feeler gauges, measure the difference in height between the cylinder block and the edge of the housing

11 Position the housing on the cylinder block, but do not fully-tighten the retaining nuts and bolts at this stage.
12 Align the balancer shaft housing so that its end face is between 0.25 mm below and 0.1 mm proud of the cylinder block end face. If the housing cannot be fitted so that the position is correct, measure the difference in height using a feeler gauge (see illustration).
13 Tighten the housing securing nuts and bolts to the specified torque and repeat the measurement made in the previous paragraph. If the position is still not correct, suitable shims must be fitted (available from a Ford dealer) between the housing and the transmission to eliminate the clearance when mating the engine to the transmission (see illustration). Note that the shims should be fitted at both sides of the housing. Select suitable shims from those listed below:

Adjustment value	Available shims	Colour coding
0.0 to 0.25 mm	No adjustment	
0.26 to 0.29 mm	0.15 mm	Silver
0.30 to 0.44 mm	0.30 mm	Pale blue
0.45 to 0.59 mm	0.45 mm	Red
0.60 to 0.75 mm	0.60 mm	Black
0.76 to 0.90 mm	0.75 mm	Green

14 The remainder of refitting is a reversal of removal. Refill the engine with the correct specification and quantity of oil as described in Chapter 1A.

16 Oil pump – removal, inspection and refitting

Removal
1 Remove the oil pump/balancer shaft drive chain as described in Section 5.
2 Undo the Torx bolt and remove the pump sprocket to access the retaining bolts. Undo the retaining bolts and withdraw the pump from the cylinder block. Recover the gasket (see illustration).
3 Slacken and remove the retaining bolts, and remove the outer cover from the pump assembly. Withdraw the pump rotors from the body (see illustration).

Inspection
4 Clean the components and check them for wear and damage. Using a feeler blade, check the backlash between the gears, and the clearance between the outer rotor and pump body, and compare with that given in the

15.13 If necessary, fit suitable shims to the edge of the balancer shaft housing (see text)

Specifications. Similarly check the endfloat of the gears, using a straight-edge across the end face of the pump. Note that the rotors should be fitted with the dot mark facing outwards. If outside the specified limits, the pump should be renewed, otherwise refit the cover and tighten the bolts to the specified torque (see illustrations). To remove the oil pressure relief valve, slacken and remove the Torx retaining cap and washer, then pull out the spring and plunger (see illustration). At the time of writing, no information was available concerning the free length or strength of the

16.2 Undo the bolts (arrowed) and remove the oil pump

16.3 The oil pump cover is retained by two bolts

16.4a Check for wear between the gears . . .

16.4b . . . between the outer rotor and body . . .

16.4c . . . and the rotor endfloat

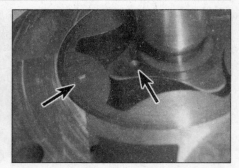

16.4d The marks on the rotors (arrowed) must face outwards

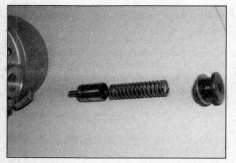

16.4e Oil pressure relief valve components

16.5 Prime the oil pump before refitting

16.7 Fit the sprocket with FRONT facing outwards

valve spring. When refitting the retaining cap, apply a few drops of locking compound to its threads, and tighten it securely.

Refitting

5 Prime the pump by pouring oil into the inlet aperture while turning the driveshaft (see illustration).
6 Clean the contact faces, then refit the pump with a new gasket, into the cylinder block recess. Ensure that the gasket is fitted correctly, and does not obstruct any of the oil pump passages. Tighten the retaining bolts to the specified torque.
7 Refit the oil pump/balancer shaft drive chain as described in Section 5. Refit the oil pump sprocket prior to refitting the drive chain. Note that to aid refitment, one side of the sprocket is marked FRONT (see illustration).

8 The remainder of refitting is a reversal of removal.

17 Oil pressure switch – removal and refitting

Removal

1 The oil pressure switch is located on the rear of the cylinder block, adjacent to the oil filter (see illustration).
2 Disconnect the wiring plug from the switch, and unscrew the switch from the cylinder block.

Refitting

3 If the original switch is to be refitted, apply a

17.1 Oil pressure switch is on the rear of the cylinder block (arrowed)

smear of sealant to the threads of the switch. Screw the switch into the cylinder block, and tighten it to the specified torque. Reconnect the wiring plug.

Chapter 2 Part B:
Diesel engine in-car repair procedures

Contents

Degrees of difficulty

| **Easy,** suitable for novice with little experience | 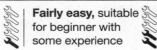 | **Fairly easy,** suitable for beginner with some experience | | **Fairly difficult,** suitable for competent DIY mechanic | | **Difficult,** suitable for experienced DIY mechanic | | **Very difficult,** suitable for expert DIY or professional | |

Specifications

General

Capacity.	1896 cc
Bore	79.5 mm
Stroke.	95.5 mm
Engine codes*	ANU, ASZ, ASZ1 and AUY
Maximum power output (at 4000 rpm):*	
Engine code ANU.	66 kW (90 PS)
Engine code AUY	85 kW (115 PS)
Engine code ASZ	96 kW (130 PS)
Engine code ASZ1	110 kW (150 PS)
Maximum torque output (at 1900 rpm):	
Engine code ANU.	240 Nm
All other engines.	310 Nm
Idle speed.	900 rpm
Maximum speed (intermittent)	5100 rpm
Compression ratio	18.0 : 1
Compression pressures:	
Standard (new engine)	25 to 31 bar
Minimum compression pressure	Approximately 19.0 bar
Maximum difference between cylinders.	Approximately 5.0 bar
Firing order	1 – 3 – 4 – 2
No 1 cylinder location.	Timing belt end

* Note: *See 'Vehicle identification' at the end of this manual for the location of engine code markings.*

Camshaft

Camshaft endfloat (maximum)	0.15 mm
Camshaft bearing running clearance (maximum).	0.11 mm
Camshaft run-out (maximum).	0.01 mm

Lubrication system

Oil pump type.	Gear type, chain-driven from crankshaft
Oil pressure (oil temperature 80°C, at 2000 rpm).	2.0 bar

Torque wrench settings

	Nm	lbf ft
Alternator mounting bolts	25	18
Auxiliary drivebelt tensioner securing bolts	25	18
Big-end bearing caps bolts:*		
Stage 1	30	22
Stage 2	Angle-tighten a further 90°	
Camshaft bearing cap nuts:*		
Stage 1	8	6
Stage 2	Angle-tighten a further 90°	
Camshaft cover nuts/bolts	10	7
Camshaft sprocket centre bolt	100	74
Camshaft sprocket outer bolts	25	18
Flywheel/driveplate mounting bolts:*	29	21
Coolant pump bolts	15	11
Crankshaft oil seal housing bolts	15	11
Crankshaft pulley bolts:		
Stage 1	10	7
Stage 2	Angle-tighten a further 90°	
Crankshaft speed/position sensor wheel-to-crankshaft bolts:*		
Stage 1	10	7
Stage 2	Angle-tighten a further 90°	
Crankshaft sprocket bolt:*		
Stage 1	120	89
Stage 2	Angle-tighten a further 90°	
Cylinder head bolts:*		
Stage 1	40	30
Stage 2	60	44
Stage 3	Angle-tighten a further 90°	
Stage 4	Angle-tighten a further 90°	
Driveplate mounting bolts:*	29	21
Engine mountings:		
Left-hand mounting-to-body bolts:		
Large bolts:		
Stage 1	50	37
Stage 2	Angle-tighten a further 90°	
Small bolt	25	18
Left-hand mounting-to-transmission bolts:		
Stage 1	90	66
Stage 2	Angle-tighten a further 90°	
Right-hand mounting:		
Stud	10	7
Bolt	61	45
Nut	54	40
Engine roll restrictor to crossmember:		
Stage 1	60	44
Stage 2	Angle tighten a further 90°	
Engine roll restrictor to transmission	100	74
EGR pipe nuts	25	18
Exhaust manifold nuts	25	18
Exhaust pipe-to-manifold/turbocharger nuts	25	18
Flywheel mounting bolts:*	29	21
Glow plugs	15	11
Injector adjusting locknut	30	22
Injector clamp bolt:*		
Stage 1	12	9
Stage 2	Angle-tighten a further 270°	
Injector rocker arm shafts:*		
Stage 1	20	15
Stage 2	Angle-tighten a further 90°	
Inlet manifold nuts	25	18
Main bearing cap bolts:*		
Stage 1	65	48
Stage 2	Angle-tighten a further 90°	
Oil baffle-to-camshaft cover bolt	5	4
Oil cooler securing plate	25	18
Oil drain plug	30	22
Oil filter cover	25	18
Oil filter housing-to-cylinder block bolts	15	11

Torque wrench settings (continued)

	Nm	lbf ft
Oil level/temperature sensor-to-sump bolts....................	10	7
Oil pick-up pipe securing bolts	15	11
Oil pressure relief valve plug	40	30
Oil pressure warning light switch	20	15
Oil pump chain tensioner bolt	15	11
Oil pump securing bolts................................	15	11
Oil pump sprocket securing bolt........................	25	18
Piston oil spray jet bolt...............................	10	7
Sump bolts..	15	11
Timing belt idler pulley bolt	20	15
Timing belt outer cover bolts:		
Lower cover	10	7
Upper cover	25	18
Timing belt rear cover bolts:		
Cover-to-cylinder head bolt	10	7
Cover-to-injection pump bolts	30	22
Timing belt tensioner roller securing nut:		
Stage 1	20	15
Stage 2	Angle-tighten a further 45°	
Turbocharger oil return pipe-to-cylinder block..................	25	18

* **Note:** *Use new bolts*

---

1 General information

Using this Chapter

Chapter 2 is divided into three Parts: A, B and C. Repair operations that can be carried out with the engine in the vehicle are described in Part A (petrol engines) and Part B (diesel engines). Part C covers the removal of the engine/transmission as a unit, and describes the engine dismantling and overhaul procedures.

In Parts A and B, the assumption is made that the engine is installed in the vehicle, with all ancillaries connected. If the engine has been removed for overhaul, the preliminary dismantling information which precedes each operation may be ignored.

Engine description

Throughout this Chapter, engines are identified and referred to by the manufacturer's code letters. A listing of all engines covered, together with their code letters, is given in the Specifications at the start of this Chapter.

The engines are water-cooled, single overhead camshaft, in-line four-cylinder units, with cast-iron cylinder blocks and aluminium-alloy cylinder heads. All are mounted transversely at the front of the vehicle, with the transmission bolted to the left-hand end of the engine.

The crankshaft is of five-bearing type, and thrustwashers are fitted to the centre main bearing to control crankshaft endfloat.

The camshaft is driven via a toothed timing belt from the crankshaft. The camshaft is mounted at the top of the cylinder head, and is secured by bearing caps. Because high pumping forces (up to 2050 bar) are required to drive the unit injectors a broad heavy duty timing belt is fitted with the tension controlled by a hydraulic tensioner.

The valves are closed by coil springs, and run in guides pressed into the cylinder head. The camshaft actuates the valves directly, via hydraulic tappets. The camshaft also features four additional cams to drive the unit injectors via roller cam followers.

The gear-type oil pump is driven via a chain from a sprocket on the crankshaft. Oil is drawn from the sump through a strainer, and then forced through an externally-mounted, renewable filter. From there, it is distributed to the cylinder head, where it lubricates the camshaft journals and hydraulic tappets, and also to the crankcase, where it lubricates the main bearings, connecting rod big-ends, gudgeon pins and cylinder bores. A coolant-fed oil cooler is fitted to the oil filter housing on all engines. Oil jets are fitted to the base of each cylinder – these spray oil onto the underside of the pistons, to improve cooling.

All engines have a tandem pump fitted, incorporating a vacuum pump (for the brake servo and various vacuum-controlled ancillaries) and a fuel pump, driven by the camshaft.

On all engines, engine coolant is circulated by a pump, driven by the timing belt. For details of the cooling system, refer to Chapter 3.

Operations with engine in vehicle

The following operations can be performed without removing the engine:

a) Compression pressure – testing.
b) Camshaft cover – removal and refitting.
c) Crankshaft pulley – removal and refitting.
d) Timing belt covers – removal and refitting.
e) Timing belt – removal, refitting and adjustment.
f) Timing belt tensioner and sprockets – removal and refitting.
g) Fuel injectors – removal, refitting and adjustment.

h) Camshaft oil seals – renewal.
i) Camshaft and hydraulic tappets – removal, inspection and refitting.
j) Cylinder head – removal and refitting.
k) Cylinder head and pistons – decarbonising.
l) Sump – removal and refitting.
m) Oil pump – removal, overhaul and refitting.
n) Crankshaft oil seals – renewal.
o) Engine/transmission mountings – inspection and renewal.
p) Flywheel/driveplate – removal, inspection and refitting.

Note: *It is possible to remove the pistons and connecting rods (after removing the cylinder head and sump) without removing the engine. However, this is not recommended. Work of this nature is more easily and thoroughly completed with the engine on the bench, as described in Chapter 2C.*

2 Compression and leakdown tests – description and interpretation

Compression test

Note: *A compression tester suitable for use with diesel engines will be required for this test.*

1 When engine performance is down, or if misfiring occurs which cannot be attributed to the ignition or fuel systems, a compression test can provide diagnostic clues as to the engine's condition. If the test is performed regularly, it can give warning of trouble before any other symptoms become apparent.

2 The engine must be fully warmed-up to normal operating temperature, the battery must be fully-charged and you will require the aid of an assistant.

3 Disconnect the injector solenoids by disconnecting the connector at the end of the

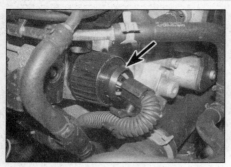

2.3 Disconnect the injector solenoids wiring plug connector (arrowed)

3.2 Release the tensioner

6 Locate the new drivebelt on the pulleys, then slowly release the tensioner. Check that the belt is located correctly in the multi-grooves in the pulleys.

7 Refit the engine cover.

---

4 Engine assembly and valve timing marks – general information and usage

cylinder head **(see illustration)**. **Note:** *As a result of the wiring being disconnected, faults will be stored in the ECM memory. These must be erased after the compression test.*

4 Remove the glow plugs as described in Chapter 5C, then fit a compression tester to the No 1 cylinder glow plug hole.

5 Have your assistant crank the engine for several seconds on the starter motor. After one or two revolutions, the compression pressure should build-up to a maximum figure and then stabilise. Record the highest reading obtained.

6 Repeat the test on the remaining cylinders, recording the pressure in each.

7 The cause of poor compression is less easy to establish on a diesel engine than on a petrol engine. The effect of introducing oil into the cylinders (wet testing) is not conclusive, because there is a risk that the oil will sit in the recess on the piston crown, instead of passing to the rings. However, the following can be used as a rough guide to diagnosis.

8 All cylinders should produce very similar pressures. Any difference greater than that specified indicates the existence of a fault. Note that the compression should build-up quickly in a healthy engine. Low

compression on the first stroke, followed by gradually increasing pressure on successive strokes, indicates worn piston rings. A low compression reading on the first stroke, which does not build-up during successive strokes, indicates leaking valves or a blown head gasket (a cracked head could also be the cause).

9 A low reading from two adjacent cylinders is almost certainly due to the head gasket having blown between them and the presence of coolant in the engine oil will confirm this.

10 On completion, remove the compression tester, and refit the glow plugs, with reference to Chapter 5C. Reconnect the electrical supply to the injectors.

Leakdown test

11 A leakdown test measures the rate at which compressed air fed into the cylinder is lost. It is an alternative to a compression test, and in many ways it is better, since the escaping air provides easy identification of where pressure loss is occurring (piston rings, valves or head gasket).

12 The equipment required for leakdown testing is widely available and considerably cheaper than a diesel engine compression tester, assuming a supply of compressed air is available.

---

3 Auxiliary drivebelt – removal and refitting

Removal

1 Remove the engine cover and disconnect the battery.

2 Using a suitable spanner, rotate the automatic tensioner clockwise. Insert a hex key or drill bit into the hole provided and lock the tensioner in place **(see illustration)**.

3 If the belt is to be refitted, mark the direction of rotation before removing it.

4 Note how the drivebelt is routed, then remove it from the crankshaft pulley, alternator pulley, power steering pump pulley, and air conditioning compressor pulley **(see illustration)**.

5 Inspect the belt for cracks and missing sections.

General information

1 TDC is the highest point in the cylinder that each piston reaches as it travels up-and-down when the crankshaft turns. Each piston reaches TDC at the end of the compression stroke and again at the end of the exhaust stroke, but TDC generally refers to piston position on the compression stroke. No 1 piston is at the timing belt end of the engine.

2 Positioning No 1 piston at TDC is an essential part of many procedures, such as timing belt removal and camshaft removal.

3 The design of the engines covered in this Chapter is such that piston-to-valve contact may occur if the camshaft or crankshaft is turned with the timing belt removed. For this reason, it is important to ensure that the camshaft and crankshaft do not move in relation to each other once the timing belt has been removed from the engine.

Setting TDC on No 1 cylinder

Note: *The timing marks on the crankshaft pulley may not be present on all engines. If the marks are absent follow the timing belt renewal procedure as described in Section 8 to locate TDC.*

4 Remove the auxiliary drivebelt as described in Section 3.

5 Remove the timing belt upper cover as described in Section 7.

6 Remove the glow plugs, as described in Chapter 5C, to allow the engine to turn more easily.

7 Using a spanner or socket on the crankshaft sprocket bolt, turn the crankshaft in the normal direction of rotation (clockwise) until the alignment mark on the face of the sprocket aligns with the mark on the lower timing belt cover **(see illustration)**.

8 The arrow (marked 4Z) on the rear section

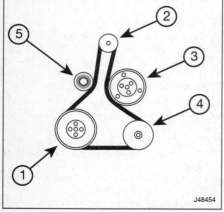

3.4 The belt routing

1 Crankshaft
2 Alternator
3 AC compressor
4 Power steering pump
5 Automatic tensioner

J48454

4.7 Align the marks (arrowed)

4.8 Align the arrow on the rear of the timing belt cover (arrowed) between the lugs on the rear of the camshaft hub sender wheel

of the upper timing belt upper cover will be in line with the two lugs on the rear of the camshaft hub sender wheel (see illustration). If the marks do not align, rotate the crankshaft one complete revolution.

9 The engine is now set to TDC on No 1 cylinder.

5 Camshaft cover – removal and refitting

Removal

1 Remove the dipstick, and prise off and remove the engine top cover, then disconnect the breather hose from the camshaft cover.
2 Unclip and then remove the upper timing belt cover.
3 Unscrew the camshaft cover retaining bolts and lift the cover away. If it sticks, do not attempt to lever it off – instead free it by working around the cover and tapping it lightly with a soft-faced mallet.
4 Recover the camshaft cover gasket (see illustration). Inspect the gasket carefully, and renew it if damage or deterioration is evident.
5 Clean the mating surfaces of the cylinder head and camshaft cover thoroughly, removing all traces of oil and old gasket – take care to avoid damaging the surfaces as you do this.

Refitting

6 Refit the camshaft cover by following the removal procedure in reverse, noting the following points:

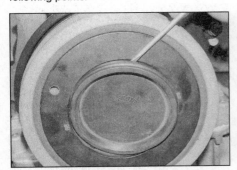

6.4 Prising out the crankshaft pulley centre cap

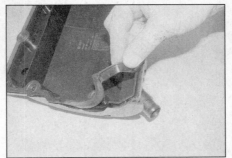

5.4 The camshaft cover gasket locates in a groove in the cover

a) Apply a 5 mm spot of suitable sealant to the points where the camshaft bearing caps contacts the cylinder head (see illustration). The sealant should be applied to both end caps.
b) Tighten the retaining nuts/bolts in sequence (see illustration).

6 Crankshaft pulley – removal and refitting

Removal

1 Disconnect the battery negative lead (see Disconnecting the battery in the Reference Chapter).
2 Jack up and support the front of the vehicle (see Jacking and vehicle support). Remove the right-hand roadwheel.
3 Remove the securing screws and withdraw the engine undershield
4 Where applicable, prise the cover from the centre of the pulley to expose the securing bolts (see illustration).
5 Slacken the bolts securing the crank-shaft pulley to the sprocket (see illustrations). If necessary, the pulley can be prevented from turning by counterholding with a spanner or socket on the crankshaft sprocket bolt.
6 Remove the auxiliary drivebelt, as described in Section 3.
7 Unscrew the bolts securing the pulley to the sprocket, and remove the pulley.

6.5a The power steering pipe can be moved to ...

5.6a Apply sealant to the points (arrowed) on the cylinder head

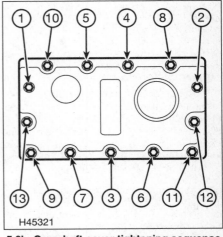

5.6b Camshaft cover tightening sequence

Refitting

8 Refit the pulley over the locating peg on the crankshaft sprocket, then refit the pulley securing bolts.
9 Refit auxiliary drivebelt as described in Section 3 of this Chapter.
10 Prevent the crankshaft from turning as during removal, then fit the pulley securing bolts, and tighten to the specified torque.
11 Refit the engine undershield.
12 Refit the roadwheel, lower the vehicle to the ground, and reconnect the battery negative lead.

6.5b ... access the crankshaft pulley bolts (arrowed)

7.2 Release the retaining clips (one arrowed)

7.6 Remove the centre cover

7.10 Remove the lower cover

7 Timing belt covers –
removal and refitting

Upper outer cover

1 Where applicable, release the retaining clips and remove the air intake hose from across the top of the timing belt cover.

2 Release the uppermost part of the timing belt outer cover by prising open the metal spring clips, then withdraw the cover away from the engine **(see illustrations)**.

3 Refitting is a reversal of removal, noting that the lower edge of the upper cover engages with the centre cover.

Centre outer cover

4 Remove the auxiliary drivebelt as described in Section 3 and then remove the automatic tensioner.

5 Remove the crankshaft pulley as described in Section 6. It is assumed that, if the centre cover is being removed, the lower cover will be also – if not, simply remove the components described in Section 6 for access to the crankshaft pulley, and leave the pulley in position.

6 With the upper cover removed (paragraphs 1 to 3), unscrew and remove the retaining bolts from the centre cover. Withdraw the centre cover from the engine, noting how it fits over the lower cover **(see illustration)**.

7 Refitting is a reversal of removal.

Lower outer cover

8 Remove the upper and centre covers as described previously.

9 If not already done, remove the crankshaft pulley as described in Section 6.

10 Unscrew the remaining bolt(s) securing the lower cover, and lift it out **(see illustration)**.

11 Refitting is a reversal of removal; locate the centre cover in place before fitting the top two bolts.

Rear cover

12 Remove the upper, centre and lower covers as described previously.

13 Remove the timing belt, tensioner and sprockets as described in Sections 8 and 9.

14 Slacken and withdraw the retaining bolts and lift the timing belt inner cover from the studs on the end of the engine, and remove it from the engine compartment.

15 Refitting is a reversal of removal.

8 Timing belt –
removal, inspection and refitting

Note: *A variety of special tools are required to fit the timing belt. Most can be easily fabricated, except Ford tool 310-085. This is essential to lock the crankshaft. These tools are widely available from specialist tool suppliers.*

Removal

1 The primary function of the toothed timing belt is to drive the camshaft, but it also drives the coolant pump. Should the belt slip or break in service, the valve timing will be disturbed and piston-to-valve contact may occur, resulting in serious engine damage. For this reason, it is important that the timing belt is tensioned correctly, and inspected regularly for signs of wear or deterioration.

2 Disconnect the battery negative lead. **Note:** *Before disconnecting the battery, refer to 'Disconnecting the battery' at the rear of this manual.*

3 Remove the air filter, ducting and the air filter housing.

4 Apply the handbrake, then jack up the front of the vehicle and support it securely on axle stands (see *Jacking and vehicle support*).

5 Remove the securing screws and withdraw the engine undershield.

6 Using a suitable jack and a block of wood to spread the load, support the right-hand end of the engine.

7 Remove the auxiliary drivebelt as described in Section 3 and then remove the automatic tensioner.

8 With the engine supported, remove the complete right-hand engine mounting assembly, with reference to Section 19. Also, unbolt the mounting bracket from the cylinder block.

9 Working from below, disconnect and remove the intercooler pipe from the sump. Remove the power steering pipe support from the rear of the engine. **Do not** disconnect the power steering pipe.

10 Set the engine to TDC on No 1 cylinder as described in Section 4.

11 Remove the crankshaft pulley as described in Section 6.

12 Remove the timing belt covers, as described in Section 7.

13 Install the special tool onto the crankshaft **(see illustrations)**. **Note:** *There are two versions of this locking tool. Ensure that the version with the index mark at the 12 o'clock position is used.*

14 Fit a 6 mm drill bit into the locking hole on the camshaft sprocket. We used a 6 mm peg, but if you are using a drill bit, tape up the flutes of the drill bit to prevent injury **(see illustration)**.

15 Two types of tensioner are fitted to the

8.13a Align the marks (arrowed) and install the locking tool . . .

8.13b . . . and fit the pin

8.14 Lock the camshaft in position

8.16a Slacken the locknut . . .

8.16b . . . and fit the damper retaining tool

diesel engines – hydraulic and mechanical. Ford suggest that the hydraulic version must be renewed if it is removed. Note that it is common practice to renew the tensioner and idler if the timing belt is renewed. Indeed, most belt manufacturers will only guarantee the timing belt if the tensioner and idler are renewed at the same time.

Hydraulic tensioner removal

16 Slacken the tensioner locking nut and rotate the tensioner anti-clockwise until the special tool (310-084) can be inserted **(see illustrations)**.

17 With the special tool in position rotate the tensioner clockwise until the belt can be removed. Discard the belt – it must be renewed.

18 Fully remove the locking nut and remove the tensioner **(see illustration)**. If required, the hydraulic part of the tensioner system can be removed.

19 Undo the bolt and remove the idler pulley **(see illustration)**.

Mechanical tensioner removal

20 Using a suitable tool to counterhold the camshaft sprocket, slacken the three camshaft sprocket bolts. **Do not** rely on the drill bit to hold the camshaft sprocket in position.

21 Slacken the tensioner locking nut and then insert special tool 303-1053 into the tensioner. This tool is a peg spanner; a pair of heavy duty 90° circlip pliers are a perfect substitute for this tool.

22 Rotate the tensioner anti-clockwise until the special tool 303-1054 can be inserted. This is a simple pin, easily fabricated from a length of welding rod or similar. Note that new tensioners are normally supplied with this tool in place.

23 Tighten the locking nut and remove the timing belt. Discard the belt – a new one must be fitted.

24 Fully remove the locking nut and remove the tensioner.

25 Remove the idler pulley.

Inspection

26 Examine the belt for evidence of contamination by coolant or lubricant. If this is the case, find the source of the contamination before progressing any further. Check the

8.18 Remove the tensioner

belt for signs of wear or damage, particularly around the leading edges of the belt teeth.

27 Replace the timing belt, noting the best practice advised in paragraph 15.

28 With the belt removed, inspect the condition of the coolant pump. Rotate it by hand whilst feeling for any play in the bearings or any undue noise from the bearings or impeller. Because the tension on the coolant pump will change with a new timing belt, it is not uncommon for the coolant pump to leak soon after the belt has been renewed. It is strongly recommended to renew the coolant pump when the timing belt is renewed. The renewal of the coolant pump is covered in Chapter 3.

29 If the timing belt is not going to be refitted for some time, it is a wise precaution to hang a warning label on the steering wheel, to remind yourself (and others) not to attempt to start the engine.

8.30 Rotate the sprocket

8.19 Remove the idler pulley

Refitting

Hydraulic tensioner refitting

30 Slacken the camshaft sprocket bolts and rotate the sprocket until it stops against the drill bit **(see illustration)**.

31 Install the idler pulley and new tensioner.

32 Install the new timing belt, starting at the camshaft sprocket followed by the tensioner, crankshaft sprocket and finally the coolant pump.

33 Fit the new hydraulic section of the tensioner.

34 Rotate the tensioner anti-clockwise and remove the special tool from the hydraulic section of the tensioner.

35 Rotate the tensioner clockwise so that the 4 mm drill bit can be inserted between the cam and the hydraulic damper **(see illustration)**. Tighten the tensioner locknut to the specified torque.

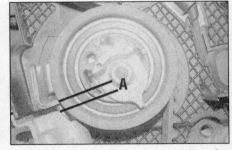

8.35 The gap between the top edge of the tensioner housing and the tensioner backplate arm (A) must be 4 mm

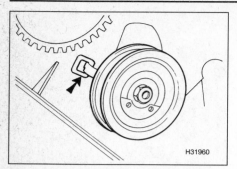

8.38 Ensure that the lug on the tensioner backplate engages with the cut-out in the rear timing belt cover

36 Use the special tool and tighten the camshaft sprocket bolts to the specified torque.

Mechanical tensioner refitting

37 Rotate the camshaft sprocket anti-clockwise until it stops.
38 Fit the tensioner with the pin installed and then fit the idler pulley **(see illustration)**.
39 Install the new timing belt, starting at the camshaft sprocket followed by the tensioner, crankshaft sprocket and finally the coolant pump.
40 Rotate the tensioner and remove the locking pin.
41 Rotate the tensioner clockwise until the marks align **(see illustration)**.
42 Use the special tool and tighten the camshaft sprocket bolts to the specified torque.

All engines

43 Remove the drill bit and the crankshaft locking tool.
44 Rotate the engine two complete revolutions clockwise and refit the drill bit and crankshaft locking tool.
45 The drill bit must fit easily into the camshaft, if not, slacken the camshaft bolts and turn the hub until the drill bit can be fitted. Tighten the bolts to the specified torque.
45 Check that the 4 mm drill bit can be fitted (hydraulic tensioner) or that the marks are aligned (mechanical tensioner).
46 If necessary repeat the tensioning procedure.
47 The remainder of the refitting procedure is a reversal of removal.

9.7 Fitting a new crankshaft sprocket securing bolt

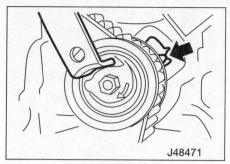

8.41 Align the marks

---

9 Timing belt sprockets – removal and refitting

Crankshaft sprocket

Note: *A new crankshaft sprocket securing bolt must be used on refitting.*

1 Remove the timing belt as described in Section 8 and then remove the crankshaft pulley – see Section 6.
2 The sprocket securing bolt must now be slackened, and the crankshaft must be prevented from turning as the sprocket bolt is unscrewed. To hold the sprocket, make up a suitable tool, and screw it to the sprocket using two bolts screwed into two of the crankshaft pulley bolt holes.
3 An alternative approach is to remove the starter motor (as described in Chapter 5A) and use a broad-bladed screwdriver or pry bar to jam the flywheel ring gear.
4 Hold the sprocket using the tool, then slacken the sprocket securing bolt. Take care, as the bolt is very tight. Do not allow the crankshaft to turn as the bolt is slackened.
5 Unscrew the bolt, and slide the sprocket from the end of the crankshaft, noting which way round the sprocket's raised boss is fitted.
6 Commence refitting by positioning the sprocket on the end of the crankshaft, with the raised boss fitted as noted on removal.
7 Fit a new sprocket securing bolt, then

9.16 Using a fabricated tool to counterhold the camshaft hub

counterhold the sprocket using the method employed on removal, and tighten the bolt to the specified torque in the two stages given in the Specifications **(see illustration)**.
8 Refit the timing belt as described in Section 8.

Camshaft sprocket

9 Remove the timing belt as described in Section 8.
10 The camshaft sprocket bolt(s) must now be slackened. Do not use the timing locking bar to hold the camshaft stationary; it must be removed before loosening the sprocket bolt. In order to eliminate any possibility of accidental piston-to-valve contact, turn the crankshaft 90º anti-clockwise so that all the pistons are halfway up the cylinder bore.
11 Unscrew and remove the three retaining bolts and remove the camshaft sprocket from the camshaft hub.
12 Refit the sprocket ensuring that it is fitted the correct way round, as noted before removal.
13 Refit the sprocket bolt(s), and tighten by hand only at this stage.
14 If the crankshaft has been turned, turn the crankshaft clockwise 90º back to TDC. Refit and tension the timing belt as described in Section 8.

Camshaft hub

Note: Ford *technicians use special tool 205-072 to counterhold the hub, however it is possible to fabricate a suitable alternative – see below.*
15 Remove the camshaft sprocket as described in this Section.
16 Engage special tool 205-072 with the three locating holes in the face of the hub to prevent the hub from turning. If this tool is not available, fabricate a suitable alternative. Whilst holding the tool, undo the central hub retaining bolt about two turns **(see illustration)**.
17 Leaving the central hub retaining bolt in place, attach Ford tool 303-338 (or a similar three-legged puller) to the hub and evenly tighten the puller until the hub is free of the camshaft taper **(see illustration)**.
18 Ensure that the camshaft taper and the hub centre is clean and dry, locate the hub on the taper, noting that the built-in key in the

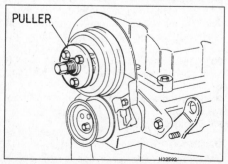

9.17 Attach a three-legged puller to the hub, and evenly tighten the puller until the hub is free of the camshaft taper

hub taper must align with the keyway in the camshaft taper (see illustration).

19 Hold the hub in this position with tool 205-072 (or similar home-made tool), and tighten the central bolt to the specified torque.

20 The remainder of refitting is a reversal of removal.

Coolant pump sprocket

21 The coolant pump sprocket is integral with the coolant pump. Refer to Chapter 3 for details of coolant pump removal.

10 Pump injector rocker shaft assembly – removal and refitting

Removal

1 Remove the camshaft cover as described in Section 5. In order to ensure that the rocker arms are refitted to their original locations, use a marker pen or paint and number the arms 1 to 4, with No 1 nearest the timing belt end of the engine. If the arms are not fitted to their original locations, the injector basic clearance setting procedure must be carried out as described in Chapter 4B, Section 5.

2 Starting with the outer bolts first, carefully and evenly slacken the rocker shaft retaining bolts. Discard the rocker shaft bolts, new ones must be fitted (see illustration).

Refitting

3 Carefully check the rocker shaft, rocker arms and camshaft bearing cap seating surface for any signs of excessive wear or damage.

4 Ensure that the shaft seating surface is clean and position the rocker shaft assembly in the camshaft bearing caps, making sure that, if re-using the original rocker arms, they are in their original locations.

5 Insert the new injector rocker shaft retaining bolts, and starting from the inner bolts, gradually and evenly tighten the bolts to the Stage 1 torque setting.

6 Again, starting with the inner retaining bolts, tighten the bolts to the Stage 2 angle as listed in this Chapter's Specifications.

7 Refit the camshaft cover as described in Section 5.

11 Camshaft and hydraulic tappets – removal, inspection and refitting

Note: A new camshaft oil seal will be required on refitting.

Removal

1 Turn the crankshaft to position No 1 piston at TDC on the firing stroke, and lock the camshaft and the fuel injection sprocket in position, as described in Section 4.

2 Remove the timing belt as described in Section 8.

9.18 The built-in key in the hub taper must align with the keyway in the camshaft taper (arrowed)

3 Remove the camshaft sprocket as described in Section 9.

4 Remove the brake tandem pump as described in Chapter 4B.

5 Remove the injector rocker arms as described in Section 10.

6 Check the camshaft bearing caps for identification markings. The bearing caps are normally stamped with their respective cylinder numbers. If no marks are present, make suitable marks using a scriber or punch. The caps should be numbered from 1 to 5, with No 1 at the timing belt end of the engine. Note on which side of the bearing caps the marks are made to ensure that they are refitted the correct way round.

7 On some engines the camshaft rotates in shell bearings. As the camshaft bearing caps are removed, recover the shell bearing halves from the camshaft. Number the back of the bearings with a felt pen to ensure that, if re-used, the bearings are fitted to their original locations. **Note:** *Fitted into the cylinder head, under each camshaft bearing cap, is a washer for each cylinder head bolt.*

8 Unscrew the securing nuts, and remove Nos 1, 3 and 5 bearing caps.

9 Working progressively, in a diagonal sequence, slacken the nuts securing Nos 2 and 4 bearing caps. Note that as the nuts are slackened, the valve springs will push the camshaft up.

10 Once the nuts securing Nos 2 and 4 bearing caps have been fully slackened, lift off the bearing caps.

11 Carefully lift the camshaft from the cylinder head, keeping it level and supported at both

11.11 Remove the camshaft oil seal

10.2 Starting with the outer bolts first, carefully and evenly slacken the rocker shaft retaining bolts (arrowed)

ends as it is removed so that the journals and lobes are not damaged. Remove the oil seal from the end of the camshaft and discard it – a new one will be required for refitting (see illustration).

12 Lift the hydraulic tappets from their bores in the cylinder head, and store them with the valve contact surfaces facing downwards, to prevent the oil from draining out. It is recommended that the tappets are kept immersed in oil for the period they are removed from the cylinder head. Make a note of the position of each tappet, as they must be refitted in their original locations on reassembly – accelerated wear leading to early failure will result if the tappets are interchanged.

13 Where fitted recover the lower shell bearing halves from the cylinder head; number the back of the shells with a felt pen to ensure that, if re-used, the bearings are fitted to their original locations.

Inspection

14 With the camshaft removed, examine the bearing caps and the bearing locations in the cylinder head for signs of obvious wear or pitting. If evident, a new cylinder head will probably be required. Also check that the oil supply holes in the cylinder head are free from obstructions.

15 Visually inspect the camshaft for evidence of wear on the surfaces of the lobes and journals. Normally their surfaces should be smooth and have a dull shine; look for scoring, erosion or pitting and areas that appear highly polished, indicating excessive wear. Accelerated wear will occur once the hardened exterior of the camshaft has been damaged, so always renew worn items. **Note:** *If these symptoms are visible on the tips of the camshaft lobes, check the corresponding tappet, as it will probably be worn as well.*

16 If the machined surfaces of the camshaft appear discoloured or blued, it is likely that it has been overheated at some point, probably due to inadequate lubrication. This may have distorted the shaft, so check the run-out as follows: place the camshaft between two V-blocks and using a DTI gauge, measure the run-out at the centre journal. If it exceeds the figure quoted in the Specifications at the start of this Chapter, renew the camshaft.

11.17 Checking camshaft endfloat using a DTI gauge

17 To measure the camshaft endfloat, temporarily refit the camshaft to the cylinder head, then fit Nos 1 and 5 bearing caps and tighten the retaining nuts to the specified torque setting. Anchor a DTI gauge to the timing belt end of the cylinder head **(see illustration)**. Push the camshaft to one end of the cylinder head as far as it will travel, then rest the DTI gauge probe on the end face of the camshaft, and zero the gauge. Push the camshaft as far as it will go to the other end of the cylinder head, and record the gauge reading. Verify the reading by pushing the camshaft back to its original position and checking that the gauge indicates zero again. **Note:** *The hydraulic tappets must **not** be fitted whilst this measurement is being taken.*

18 Check that the camshaft endfloat measurement is within the limit listed in the Specifications. If the measurement is outside the specified limit, wear is unlikely to be confined to any one component, so renewal of the camshaft, cylinder head and bearing caps must be considered.

19 The camshaft bearing running clearance should now be measured. This will be difficult to achieve without a range of micrometers or internal/external expanding calipers, measure the outside diameters of the camshaft bearing surfaces and the internal diameters formed by the bearing caps (and shell bearings where applicable) and the bearing locations in the cylinder head. The difference between these two measurements is the running clearance.

20 Compare the camshaft running clearance measurements with the figure given in the Specifications; if any are outside the specified

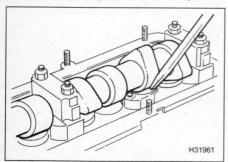

12.8 Press down on the tappet using a wooden or plastic instrument

tolerance, the camshaft, cylinder head and bearing caps (and shell bearings where applicable) should be renewed.

21 Inspect the hydraulic tappets for obvious signs of wear or damage, and renew if necessary. Check that the oil holes in the tappets are free from obstructions.

Refitting

22 Remove the crankshaft locking tool and rotate the crankshaft 90° anti-clockwise. This will lower the pistons and guard against any possibility of the valves contacting the piston crowns.

23 Smear some clean engine oil onto the sides of the hydraulic tappets, and offer them into position in their original bores in the cylinder head. Push them down until they contact the valves, then lubricate the camshaft lobe contact surfaces.

24 Lubricate the camshaft and cylinder head bearing journals (and shell bearings where applicable) with clean engine oil.

25 Carefully lower the camshaft into position in the cylinder head making sure that the cam lobes for No 1 cylinder are pointing upwards. **Note**: *The camshaft and crankshaft must not be rotated for at least 30 minutes after tightening the bearing caps.*

26 Refit a new camshaft oil seal on the front of the camshaft. Make sure that the closed end of the seal faces the camshaft sprocket end of the camshaft, and take care not to damage the seal lip. Locate the seal against the seat in the cylinder head.

27 Oil the upper surfaces of the camshaft bearing journals (and shell bearings where applicable), then fit Nos 2 and 4 bearing caps. Ensure that they are fitted the right way round and in the correct locations (see paragraph 6), then progressively tighten the retaining nuts in a diagonal sequence to the specified torque. Note that as the nuts are tightened, the camshaft will be forced down against the pressure of the valve springs.

28 Fit bearing caps 1, 3 and 5 over the camshaft and progressively tighten the nuts to the specified torque. Note that it may be necessary to locate No 5 bearing cap by tapping lightly on the end of the camshaft.

29 Refit the camshaft sprocket as described in Section 9.

30 Carry out the unit injector basic setting procedure as described in Chapter 4B.

31 Refit and tension the timing belt as described in Section 8.

32 Refit the brake tandem pump as described in Chapter 4B.

12 Hydraulic tappets – testing

⚠ *Warning: After fitting hydraulic tappets, wait a minimum of 30 minutes (or preferably, leave overnight) before starting the engine, to allow*

the tappets time to settle, otherwise the valve heads will strike the pistons.

1 The hydraulic tappets are self-adjusting, and require no attention whilst in service.

2 If the hydraulic tappets become excessively noisy, their operation can be checked as described below.

3 Start the engine, and run it until it reaches normal operating temperature, increase the engine speed to approximately 2500 rpm for 2 minutes.

4 If any hydraulic tappets are heard to be noisy, carry out the following checks.

5 Remove the camshaft cover as described in Section 5.

6 Using a socket or spanner on the crankshaft sprocket bolt, turn the crankshaft until the tip of the camshaft lobe above the tappet to be checked is pointing vertically upwards.

7 Using feeler blades, check the clearance between the top of the tappet and the cam lobe. If the play is in excess of 0.1 mm, renew the relevant tappet. If the play is less than 0.1 mm, or there is no play, proceed as follows.

8 Press down on the tappet using a wooden or plastic instrument **(see illustration)**. If free play in excess of 1.0 mm is present before the tappet contacts the valve stem, renew the relevant tappet.

9 On completion, refit the camshaft cover as described in Section 5.

13 Camshaft oil seals – renewal

Right-hand oil seal

1 Remove the timing belt as described in Section 8.

2 Remove the camshaft sprocket and hub, as described in Section 9.

3 Drill two small holes into the existing oil seal, diagonally opposite each other. Take great care to avoid drilling through into the seal housing or camshaft sealing surface. Thread two self-tapping screws into the holes, and using a pair of pliers, pull on the heads of the screws to extract the oil seal.

4 Clean out the seal housing and the sealing surface of the camshaft by wiping it with a lint-free cloth. Remove any swarf or burrs that may cause the seal to leak.

5 Do not lubricate the lip and outer edge of the new oil seal, push it over the camshaft until it is positioned in place above its housing. To prevent damage to the sealing lips, wrap some adhesive tape around the end of the camshaft.

6 Using a hammer and a socket of suitable diameter, drive the seal squarely into its housing. **Note:** *Select a socket that bears only on the hard outer surface of the seal, not the inner lip which can easily be damaged.*

7 Refit the camshaft sprocket and its hub, as described in Section 9.

8 Refit and tension the timing belt as described in Section 8.

14.6 Disconnect the central connector for the injectors

14.8 Undo the four tandem pump retaining bolts (arrowed)

14.16 Unscrew the bolt and remove the camshaft position sensor

Left-hand oil seal

9 The left-hand camshaft oil seal is formed by the brake tandem pump seal. Refer to Chapter 9 for details of brake vacuum pump removal and refitting.

14	Cylinder head – removal, inspection and refitting	

Note: *The cylinder head must be removed with the engine cold. New cylinder head bolts and a new cylinder head gasket will be required on refitting, and suitable studs will be required to guide the cylinder head into position – see text.*

Removal

1 Disconnect the battery negative lead and remove the engine top cover. Remove the soundproofing material from the valve cover. **Note:** *Before disconnecting the battery, refer to 'Disconnecting the battery' at the rear of this manual.*

2 Drain the cooling system and engine oil as described in Chapter 1B.

3 Disconnect the MAF sensor and remove the air filter, air filter housing and intake pipe from the inlet manifold.

4 With reference to Chapters 11 and 12, remove the windscreen cowl panel and the bulkhead panel. Access can be improved further by removing the wiper motor and linkage assembly.

5 Unbolt the coolant expansion tank and fuel filter support bracket. Remove the side panels from the battery tray. Access can be further improved by removing the battery.

6 At the left-hand end of the cylinder head, disconnect the wiring plug form the coolant temperature sensor, remove the spring clips and remove the coolant hoses. Disconnect the wiring plug from the end of the cylinder head **(see illustration)**.

7 Unplug the wiring connector from the manifold absolute pressure sensor (MAP) and remove the pipe. Remove the intercooler pipe.

8 Disconnect the wiring plug from the fuel temperature sensor, and then remove the fuel and vacuum lines from the tandem pump. Plug and seal the fuel lines. Alternatively leave

the pipes connected and remove the tandem pump complete with the pipework **(see illustration)**.

9 At the rear of the engine, remove the vacuum lines from the EGR valve and the anti-shudder valve.

10 At the front of the engine, remove the glow plug wiring loom, the camshaft position sensor wiring plug and the vacuum hose(s) from the vacuum reservoir.

11 Remove the camshaft cover as described in Section 5 and then remove the intake pipe and crankcase ventilation pipe from the turbocharger.

12 Jack up and support the front of the vehicle. Remove the engine undershield.

13 Disconnect the turbocharger oil return line and remove the support bracket.

14 Support the flexible section of the exhaust pipe and then remove it from the manifold. On vehicles fitted with and EGR cooler, remove

14.18a Where applicable, undo the bolt (arrowed) from the inner cover . . .

14.19 Using two nuts locked together to unscrew the tensioner mounting stud

the hose and disconnect the EGR pipe from the exhaust manifold.

15 On engines fitted with and EGR cooler (engine codes ASZ and AUY) loosen the inlet manifold bolts and remove the inlet manifold.

16 Remove the timing belt as described in Section 8 and then unbolt and remove the camshaft sensor **(see illustration)**.

17 Remove the camshaft sprocket and timing belt tensioner as described in Section 9.

18 Where applicable, unscrew the bolt(s) securing the rear timing belt cover to the cylinder head **(see illustrations)**.

19 Using two suitable nuts locked together, unscrew the timing belt tensioner mounting stud from the cylinder head **(see illustration)**.

20 Unbolt and remove the turbocharger oil supply pipe.

21 Progressively slacken the cylinder head bolts, by one turn at a time, in order **(see illustration)**. Check that nothing remains

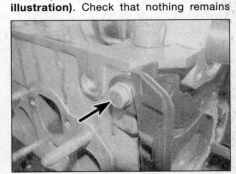

14.18b . . . and the one (arrowed) on the side of the cover

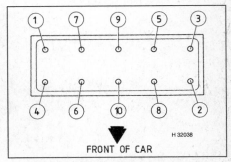

14.21 Cylinder head bolt slackening sequence

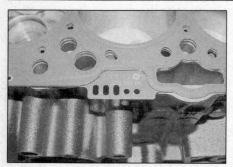

14.26 The thickness of the cylinder head gasket can be identified by notches or holes

connected and then remove the cylinder head bolts.

22 With all the bolts removed, lift the cylinder head from the block, together with the manifolds and turbocharger. If the cylinder head is stuck, tap it with a soft-faced mallet to break the joint. **Do not** insert a lever into the gasket joint.

23 Lift the cylinder head gasket from the block. Do not discard the gasket at this stage, as it will be required when determining the thickness of the new gasket required.

24 If desired, the manifolds can be removed from the cylinder head with reference to Chapter 4B (inlet manifold) or 4C (exhaust manifold).

Inspection

25 Dismantling and inspection of the cylinder head is covered in Chapter 2C.

Cylinder head gasket selection

Note: *A dial test indicator (DTI) will be required for this operation.*

26 Examine the old cylinder head gasket for manufacturer's identification markings **(see illustration)**. These will be in the form of holes or notches, and a part number on the edge of the gasket. Unless new pistons have been fitted, the new cylinder head gasket must be of the same type as the old one. In this case, purchase a new gasket, and proceed to paragraph 33.

27 If new piston assemblies have been fitted as part of an engine overhaul, or if a new short engine is to be fitted, the projection of

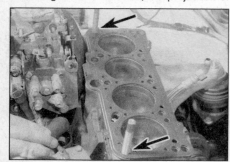

14.41 Two of the old head bolts (arrowed) can be used as cylinder head alignment guides

14.29 Measuring the piston projection at TDC using a dial gauge

the piston crowns above the cylinder head mating face of the cylinder block at TDC must be measured. This measurement is used to determine the thickness of the new cylinder head gasket required.

28 Anchor a dial test indicator (DTI) to the top face (cylinder head gasket mating face) of the cylinder block, and zero the gauge on the gasket mating face.

29 Rest the gauge probe on No 1 piston crown, and turn the crankshaft slowly by hand until the piston reaches TDC. Measure and record the maximum piston projection at TDC **(see illustration)**.

30 Repeat the measurement for the remaining pistons, and record the results.

31 If the measurements differ from piston-to-piston, take the highest figure, and use this to determine the thickness of the head gasket required as follows:

Gasket identification

Piston projection	Number of holes/ notches
0.91 to 1.00 mm	1
1.01 to 1.10 mm	2
1.11 to 1.20 mm	3

32 Purchase a new gasket according to the results of the measurements.

Refitting

Note: *If an exchange cylinder head, complete with camshaft, is to be fitted, the manufacturers recommend the following:*
a) *Lubricate the contact surfaces between the tappets and the cam lobes before fitting the camshaft cover.*
b) *Do not remove the plastic protectors from the open valves until immediately before fitting the cylinder head.*
c) *Renew the engine coolant.*

33 The mating faces of the cylinder head and block must be perfectly clean before refitting the head. Use a scraper to remove all traces of gasket and carbon, also clean the tops of the pistons. Take particular care with the aluminium surfaces, as the soft metal is easily damaged.

34 Make sure that debris is not allowed to enter the oil and water passages – this

is particularly important for the oil circuit, as carbon could block the oil supply to the camshaft and crankshaft bearings. Using adhesive tape and paper, seal the water, oil and bolt holes in the cylinder block.

35 To prevent carbon entering the gap between the pistons and bores, smear a little grease in the gap. After cleaning a piston, rotate the crankshaft to that the piston moves down the bore, then wipe out the grease and carbon with a cloth rag. Clean the other piston crowns in the same way.

36 Check the head and block for nicks, deep scratches and other damage. If slight, they may be removed carefully with a file. More serious damage may be repaired by machining, but this is a specialist job.

37 If warpage of the cylinder head is suspected, use a straight-edge to check it for distortion, as described in Chapter 2C.

38 Ensure that the cylinder head bolt holes in the crankcase are clean and free of oil. Syringe or soak up any oil left in the bolt holes. This is most important in order that the correct bolt tightening torque can be applied, and to prevent the possibility of the block being cracked by hydraulic pressure when the bolts are tightened.

39 Turn the crankshaft anti-clockwise all the pistons at an equal height, approximately halfway down their bores from the TDC position (see Section 4). This will eliminate any risk of piston-to-valve contact as the cylinder head is refitted.

40 Where applicable, refit the manifolds with reference to Chapters 4B and/or 4C.

41 To guide the cylinder head into position, screw two long studs (or old cylinder head bolts with the heads cut off, and slots cut in the ends to enable the bolts to be unscrewed) into the cylinder block **(see illustration)**.

42 Ensure that the cylinder head locating dowels are in place in the cylinder block, then fit the new cylinder head gasket over the dowels, ensuring that the part number is uppermost. Where applicable, the OBEN/TOP marking should also be uppermost. **Note:** *Only remove the gasket from its packaging immediately prior to fitting.*

43 Lower the cylinder head into position on the gasket, ensuring that it engages correctly over the guide studs and dowels.

44 Fit the new cylinder head bolts to the eight remaining bolt locations, and screw them in as far as possible by hand.

45 Unscrew the two guide studs from the exhaust side of the cylinder block, then screw in the two remaining new cylinder head bolts as far as possible by hand.

46 Working progressively, in sequence, tighten all the cylinder head bolts to the specified Stage 1 torque **(see illustrations)**.

47 Again working progressively, in sequence, tighten all the cylinder head bolts to the specified Stage 2 torque.

48 Tighten all the cylinder head bolts, in sequence, through the specified Stage 3 angle **(see illustration)**.

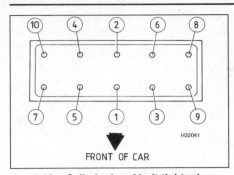

14.46a Cylinder head bolt tightening sequence

FRONT OF CAR

14.46b Using a torque wrench to tighten the cylinder head bolts

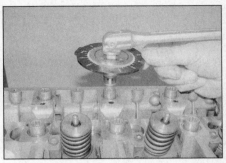

14.48 Angle-tighten the cylinder head bolts

49 Finally, tighten all the cylinder head bolts, in sequence, through the specified Stage 4 angle.

50 After finally tightening the cylinder head bolts, turn the camshaft so that the cam lobes for No 1 cylinder are pointing upwards.

51 The remainder of the refitting procedure is a reversal of the removal procedure, bearing in mind the following points.

a) *Refit the camshaft cover with reference to Section 5.*

b) *Use new sealing rings when reconnecting the turbocharger oil return pipe to the cylinder block.*

c) *Reconnect the exhaust front section to the exhaust manifold, with reference to Chapter 4C.*

d) *Refit the timing belt tensioner with reference to Section 8.*

e) *Refit the camshaft sprocket as described in Section 9, and refit the timing belt as described in Section 8.*

f) *Refill the cooling system and engine oil as described in Chapter 1B.*

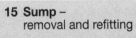
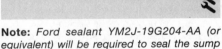

15 Sump –
removal and refitting

Note: *Ford sealant YM2J-19G204-AA (or equivalent) will be required to seal the sump on refitting.*

Removal

1 Apply the handbrake, then jack up the front of the vehicle and support securely on axle stands (see *Jacking and vehicle support*).

2 Remove the securing screws and withdraw the engine undershield.

3 Drain the engine oil as described in Chapter 1B.

4 Disconnect the wiring connector from the oil level/temperature sender in the sump **(see illustration)**.

5 Slacken and remove the bolts securing the sump to the cylinder block, and the bolts securing the sump to the transmission casing, then withdraw the sump. If necessary, release the sump by tapping with a soft-faced hammer.

6 If desired, unbolt the oil baffle plate from the cylinder block.

Refitting

7 Begin refitting by thoroughly cleaning the mating faces of the sump and cylinder block. Ensure that all traces of old sealant are removed.

8 Where applicable, refit the oil baffle plate, and tighten the securing bolts.

9 Ensure that the cylinder block mating face of the sump is free from all traces of old sealant, oil and grease, and then apply a 2.0 to 3.0 mm diameter thick bead of silicone sealant to the sump **(see illustration)**. Note that the sealant should be run around the inside of the bolt holes in the sump. The sump must be fitted within 5 minutes of applying the sealant.

10 Offer the sump up to the cylinder block, then refit the sump-to-cylinder block bolts, and lightly tighten them by hand, working progressively in a diagonal sequence. **Note:** *If the sump is being refitted with the engine and transmission separated, make sure that the sump is flush with the flywheel/driveplate end of the cylinder block.*

11 Refit the sump-to-transmission casing bolts, and tighten them lightly, using a socket.

12 Again working in a diagonal sequence, *lightly* tighten the sump-to-cylinder block bolts, using a socket.

13 Tighten the sump-to-transmission casing bolts to the specified torque.

14 Working in a diagonal sequence, progressively tighten the sump-to-cylinder block bolts to the specified torque.

15 Refit the wiring connector to the oil level/temperature sender (where fitted), then refit the engine undershield(s), and lower the vehicle to the ground.

15.4 Disconnect the wiring plug (arrowed) from the sender

16 Allow at least 30 minutes from the time of refitting the sump for the sealant to dry, then refill the engine with oil, with reference to Chapter 1A.

16 Oil pump and drive chain –
removal, inspection and refitting

Oil pump

Removal

1 Remove the sump as described in Section 15.

2 Where applicable, unscrew the securing bolts, and remove the oil baffle from the cylinder block.

3 Unscrew and remove the three mounting bolts, and release the oil pump from the dowels in the crankcase **(see illustration)**. Unhook the oil pump drive sprocket from the chain and withdraw the oil pump and oil pick-up pipe from the engine. Note that the tensioner will attempt to tighten the chain, and it may be necessary to use a screwdriver to hold it in its released position before releasing the oil pump sprocket from the chain.

4 If desired, unscrew the flange bolts and remove the suction pipe from the oil pump. Recover the O-ring seal. Unscrew the bolts and remove the cover from the oil pump. **Note:** *If the oil pick-up pipe is removed from the oil pump, a new O-ring will be required on refitting.*

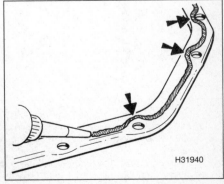

15.9 Apply the sealant around the inside of the bolt holes

Inspection

5 Clean the pump thoroughly, and inspect the gear teeth/rotors for signs of damage or wear. If evident, renew the oil pump.

6 Unscrew the retaining bolt and slide off the sprocket (note that the sprocket can only be fitted in one position).

Refitting

7 Prime the pump with oil by pouring oil into the pick-up pipe aperture while turning the driveshaft.

8 Refit the cover to the oil pump and tighten the bolts securely. Where applicable, refit the pick-up pipe to the oil pump, using a new O-ring seal, and tighten the securing bolts.

9 If the drive chain, crankshaft sprocket and tensioner have been removed, delay refitting them until after the oil pump has been mounted on the cylinder block. If they have not been removed, use a screwdriver to press the tensioner against its spring to provide sufficient slack in the chain to refit the oil pump.

10 Engage the oil pump sprocket with the drive chain, then locate the oil pump on the dowels. Refit and tighten the three mounting bolts to the specified torque.

11 Where applicable, refit the drive chain, tensioner and crankshaft sprocket using a reversal of the removal procedure.

12 Refit the oil baffle, and tighten the securing bolts.

13 Refit the sump as described in Section 15.

Drive chain and sprockets

Note: *Ford sealant YM2J-19G204-AA (or equivalent) will be required to seal the crankshaft oil seal housing on refitting, and it is advisable to fit a new crankshaft oil seal.*

Removal

14 Proceed as described in paragraphs 1 and 2.

15 To remove the oil pump sprocket, unscrew the securing bolt, then pull the sprocket from the pump shaft, and unhook it from the drive chain.

16 To remove the chain, remove the timing belt as described in Section 8, then unbolt the crankshaft oil seal housing from the cylinder block. Unbolt the chain tensioner from the cylinder block, then unhook the chain from the sprocket on the end of the crankshaft.

17 The oil pump drive sprocket is a press-fit on the crankshaft, and cannot easily be removed. Consult a Ford dealer or engine repair specialist for advice if the sprocket is worn or damaged.

Inspection

18 Examine the chain for wear and damage. Wear is usually indicated by excessive lateral play between the links, and excessive noise in operation. It is wise to renew the chain in any case if the engine is to be overhauled. Note that the rollers on a very badly worn chain may be slightly grooved. If there is any doubt as to the condition of the chain, renew it.

19 Examine the teeth on the sprockets for wear. Each tooth forms an inverted V. If worn, the side of each tooth under tension will be slightly concave in shape when compared with the other side of the tooth (ie, the teeth will have a hooked appearance). If the teeth appear worn, the sprocket should be renewed.

Refitting

20 If the oil pump has been removed, refit the oil pump as described previously in this Section before refitting the chain and sprocket.

21 Refit the chain tensioner to the cylinder block, and tighten the securing bolt to the specified torque. Make sure that the tensioner spring is correctly positioned to pretension the tensioner arm.

22 Engage the oil pump sprocket with the chain, then engage the chain with the crankshaft sprocket. Use a screwdriver to press the tensioner against its spring to provide sufficient slack in the chain to engage the sprocket with the oil pump. Note that the sprocket will only fit in one position.

23 Refit the oil pump sprocket bolt, and tighten to the specified torque.

24 Fit a new crankshaft oil seal to the housing, and refit the housing as described in Section 18.

25 Where applicable, refit the oil baffle, and tighten the securing bolts.

26 Refit the sump as described in Section 15.

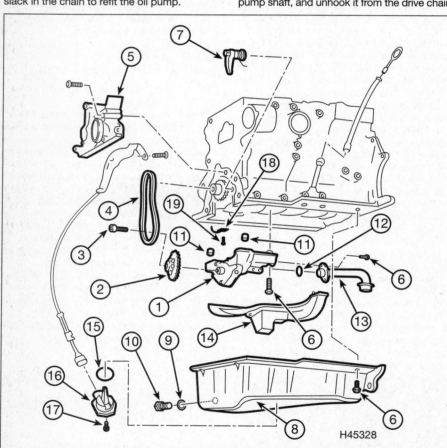

16.3 Sump and oil pump components

1 Oil pump	*7 Drive chain tensioner*	*14 Oil baffle*
2 Oil pump sprocket	*8 Sump*	*15 Seal*
3 Bolt	*9 Seal*	*16 Oil level/temperature*
4 Oil pump drive chain	*10 Sump drain plug*	*sender*
5 Crankshaft oil seal	*11 Dowels*	*17 Bolt*
housing	*12 O-ring*	*18 Oil spray jet*
6 Bolt	*13 Oil pick-up pipe*	*19 Bolt*

17 Flywheel/driveplate – removal, inspection and refitting

Note: *New flywheel/driveplate securing bolts will be required on refitting.*

Removal

1 On manual transmission models, remove the gearbox (see Chapter 7A) and clutch (see Chapter 6).

2 On automatic transmission models, remove

17.3a A fabricated tool can be used (arrowed) to hold the flywheel stationary

17.3b Align the bolts on models fitted with a dual mass flywheel . . .

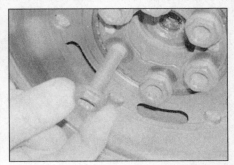

17.3c . . . and remove them (solid flywheel shown)

the automatic transmission as described in Chapter 7B.

3 The flywheel/driveplate bolts are offset to ensure correct fitment. Unscrew the bolts while holding the flywheel/driveplate stationary. Temporarily insert a bolt in the cylinder block, and use a screwdriver to hold the flywheel/driveplate, or make up a holding tool **(see illustrations)**.

4 Lift the flywheel/driveplate from the crankshaft **(see illustration)**. If removing a driveplate, note the location of the shim (where applicable – between the driveplate and the crankshaft), and the spacer under the securing bolts. Recover the engine-to-transmission plate if it is loose.

Inspection

5 Check the flywheel/driveplate for wear and damage. Examine the starter ring gear for excessive wear to the teeth. If the driveplate or its ring gear are damaged, the complete driveplate must be renewed. The flywheel ring gear, however, may be renewed separately from the flywheel, but the work should be entrusted to a Ford dealer or suitably-equipped local garage. If the clutch friction face is discoloured or scored excessively, it may be possible to regrind it, but this work should be entrusted to an automotive machine shop.

6 On vehicles fitted with an automatic transmission install the driveplate, minus the shim and using the old bolts. Working through the torque converter mounting holes measure the distance from the front of the plate to the engine block. Measure the distance at three positions and calculate the average distance. This must figure must be between 19.5 mm and 21.1 mm. Renew the driveplate if these specifications are not met.

7 Where a dual mass flywheel is fitted it must be renewed if there is any evidence of fluid or grease on the flywheel or clutch components. The following procedures are given for guidance only. If in doubt as to the condition of the flywheel a professional inspection is recommended. If the assembly passes all the checks listed and there was no juddering from the clutch when taking up the drive, the flywheel can be refitted. However if the vehicle has covered a high mileage and especially if the vehicle is on its second new clutch, then

it would be prudent to renew the dual mass flywheel.

Warpage

Check the drive surface for any signs of warpage or damage **(see illustration)**. The flywheel will normally warp like a bowl – ie, higher at the circumference. If the warpage is more than 4.0 mm consider renewing the flywheel.

Free rotational movement

This is the distance the drive surface of the flywheel can be turned independently of the flywheel primary element, using finger pressure only. Move the drive surface in one direction and make a mark where the locating pin aligns with the flywheel edge. Move the drive surface in the other direction (finger pressure only) and make another mark **(see illustration)**. The total of free movement should not exceed 10 mm. If it is more, consider renewing the flywheel.

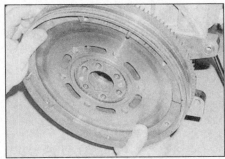

17.4 Remove the flywheel

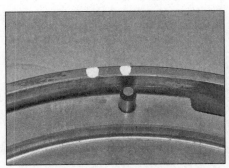

17.7b Flywheel free rotational movement check alignment marks – see text

Total rotational movement

This is the total distance the drive surface can be turned independently of the flywheel primary elements. Insert two bolts into the clutch pressure plate damper unit mounting holes and, with the crankshaft flywheel held stationary, user a pry bar between the bolts and use some effort to move the drive surface fully in one direction. Make a mark where the locating pin aligns with the flywheel edge. Now force the drive surface fully in the opposite direction, and make another mark. The total rotational movement should not exceed 44.0 mm. If it does have the flywheel professionally inspected.

Lateral movement

The lateral movement (up and down) of the drive surface in relation to the primary element of the flywheel should not exceed 2.0 mm, if it does the flywheel may need renewing. This can be checked by pressing the drive surface

17.7a Flywheel warpage check – see text

17.7c Flywheel lateral movement check marks – see text

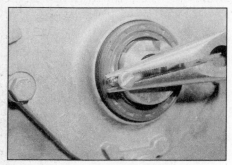

18.2 Removing the crankshaft oil seal using self-tapping screws

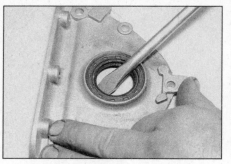

18.3 Prising the oil seal from the crankshaft oil seal housing

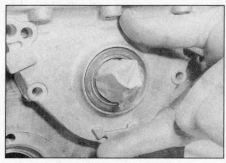

18.9 Slide the oil seal housing over the end of the crankshaft

down on one side into the flywheel (flywheel horizontal) and making an alignment mark between the drive surface and the inner edge of the primary elements. Now press down on the opposite side of the drive surface and make another mark above the original one. The difference between the two marks is the lateral movement (see illustration).

Refitting

8 Refitting is a reversal of removal, bearing in mind the following points.
  a) *Ensure that the engine-to-transmission plate is in place before fitting the flywheel/ driveplate.*
  b) *On automatic transmission models fit the shim before installing the driveplate.*
  c) *On automatic transmission models, the raised pip on the spacer under the securing bolts must face the torque converter.*
  d) *Use new bolts when refitting the flywheel or driveplate, and coat the threads of the bolts with locking fluid before inserting them. Tighten the securing bolts to the specified torque.*

---

18 Crankshaft oil seals – renewal

Note 1: The oil seals are a PTFE (Teflon) type and are fitted dry, without using any grease or oil. These have a wider sealing lip and have been introduced instead of the coil spring type oil seal.

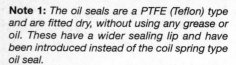

18.17 Locate the crankshaft oil seal fitting tool over the end of the crankshaft

Note 2: If the oil seal housing is removed, suitable sealant (Ford YM2J-19G204-AA or equivalent) will be required to seal the housing on refitting.

Right-hand oil seal

1 Remove the timing belt as described in Section 8, and the crankshaft sprocket with reference to Section 9.
2 To remove the seal without removing the housing, drill two small holes diagonally opposite each other, insert self-tapping screws, and pull on the heads of the screws with pliers (see illustration).
3 Alternatively, to remove the oil seal complete with its housing, proceed as follows.
  a) *Remove the sump as described in Section 15. This is necessary to ensure a satisfactory seal between the sump and oil seal housing on refitting.*
  b) *Unbolt and remove the oil seal housing.*
  c) *Working on the bench, lever the oil seal from the housing using a suitable screwdriver. Take care not to damage the seal seating in the housing (see illustration).*
4 Thoroughly clean the oil seal seating in the housing.
5 Wind a length of tape around the end of the crankshaft to protect the oil seal lips as the seal (and housing, where applicable) is fitted.
6 Fit a new oil seal to the housing, pressing or driving it into position using a socket or tube of suitable diameter. Ensure that the socket or tube bears only on the hard outer ring of the seal, and take care not to damage the seal

18.19a Fit the oil seal/housing assembly over the end of the crankshaft . . .

lips. Press or drive the seal into position until it is seated on the shoulder in the housing. Make sure that the closed end of the seal is facing outwards.
7 If the oil seal housing has been removed, proceed as follows, otherwise proceed to paragraph 11.
8 Clean all traces of old sealant from the crankshaft oil seal housing and the cylinder block, then coat the cylinder block mating faces of the oil seal housing with a 2.0 to 3.0 mm thick bead of sealant (Ford YM2J-19G204-AA or equivalent). Note that the seal housing must be refitted within 5 minutes of applying the sealant.
Caution: DO NOT put excessive amounts of sealant onto the housing as it may get into the sump and block the oil pick-up pipe.
9 Refit the oil seal housing, and tighten the bolts progressively to the specified torque (see illustration).
10 Refit the sump as described in Section 15.
11 Refit the crankshaft sprocket with reference to Section 9, and the timing belt as described in Section 8.

Left-hand oil seal

12 Remove the flywheel/driveplate as described in Section 17.
13 Remove the sump as described in Section 15. This is necessary to ensure a satisfactory seal between the sump and oil seal housing on refitting.
14 Unbolt and remove the oil seal housing, complete with the oil seal.
15 The new oil seal will be supplied ready-fitted to a new oil seal housing.
16 Thoroughly clean the oil seal housing mating face on the cylinder block.
17 New oil seal/housing assemblies are supplied with a fitting tool to prevent damage to the oil seal as it is being fitted. Locate the tool over the end of the crankshaft (see illustration).
18 If the original oil seal housing was fitted using sealant, apply a thin bead of suitable sealant (Ford YM2J-19G204-AA or equivalent) to the cylinder block mating face of the oil seal housing. Note that the seal housing must be refitted within 5 minutes of applying the sealant.
Caution: DO NOT put excessive amounts of

18.19b . . . then tighten the securing bolts to the specified torque

sealant onto the housing as it may get into the sump and block the oil pick-up pipe.
19 Carefully fit the oil seal/housing assembly over the end of the crankshaft, then refit the securing bolts and tighten the bolts progressively, in a diagonal sequence, to the specified torque **(see illustrations)**.
20 Remove the oil seal protector tool from the end of the crankshaft.
21 Refit the sump as described in Section 15.
22 Refit the flywheel/driveplate as described in Section 17.

19 Engine/transmission mountings – inspection and renewal

Refer to Section 13 in Chapter 2A for the basic procedure, however, note that the rear engine mounting is different.

20 Engine oil cooler – removal and refitting

Note: *New sealing rings will be required on refitting.*

Removal

1 The oil cooler is mounted under the oil filter housing on the front of the cylinder block **(see illustration)**.
2 Position a container beneath the oil filter to catch escaping oil and coolant.

20.1 Oil filter and oil cooler mounting details

1 Oil cooler securing plate	10 Oil pressure warning light switch
2 O-ring	
3 Oil cooler	11 Sealing washer
4 O-ring	12 Oil filter housing
5 O-ring	13 Gasket
6 Sealing washer	14 Bolt
7 Sealing plug	15 Oil filter
8 Sealing washer	16 O-ring
9 Drain tap	17 Oil filter cover

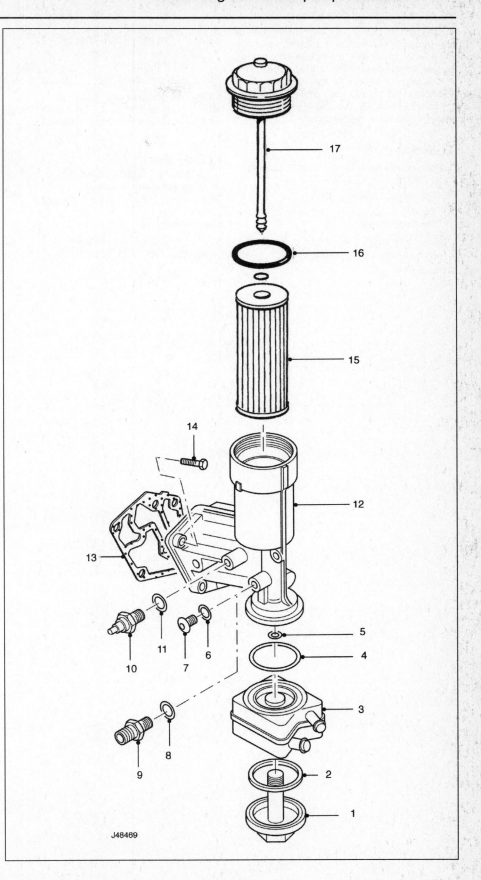

J48469

3 Clamp the oil cooler coolant hoses to minimise coolant spillage, then remove the clips, and disconnect the hoses from the oil cooler. Be prepared for coolant spillage.

4 Unscrew the oil cooler securing plate from the bottom of the oil filter housing, then slide off the oil cooler. Recover the O-rings from the top and bottom of the oil cooler.

Refitting

5 Refitting is a reversal of removal, bearing in mind the following points:

a) *Use new oil cooler O-rings.*

b) *Tighten the oil cooler securing plate to the specified torque.*

c) *On completion, check and if necessary top-up the oil and coolant levels.*

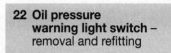

21 Oil pressure relief valve – removal, inspection and refitting

1 The oil pressure relief valve is part of the oil filter hosing assembly. If a fault develops the complete assembly must be renewed.

22 Oil pressure warning light switch – removal and refitting

Removal

1 The oil pressure warning light switch is fitted to the right-hand side of the oil filter housing (see illustration 20.1). Remove the engine top cover(s) to gain access to the switch.

2 Disconnect the wiring connector and wipe clean the area around the switch.

3 Unscrew the switch from the filter housing and remove it, along with its sealing washer. If the switch is to be left removed from the engine for any length of time, plug the oil filter housing aperture.

Refitting

4 Examine the sealing washer for signs of damage or deterioration and if necessary renew.

5 Refit the switch, complete with washer, and tighten it to the specified torque.

6 Securely reconnect the wiring connector then check and, if necessary, top-up the engine oil as described in *Weekly checks*. On completion, refit the engine top cover(s).

Chapter 2 Part C:
Engine removal and overhaul procedures

Contents

Degrees of difficulty

Easy, suitable for novice with little experience		Fairly easy, suitable for beginner with some experience		Fairly difficult, suitable for competent DIY mechanic		Difficult, suitable for experienced DIY mechanic		Very difficult, suitable for expert DIY or professional	

Specifications

Engine codes*

Petrol engines:
Stage 3 Emissions E5SA
Stage 4 Emissions E5SB
Diesel engines:
66 kW (90 PS) . . . . ANU
85 kW (115 PS) . . . . AUY
96 kW (130 PS) . . . . ASZ
110 kW (150 PS) ASZ1
* Note: *See 'Vehicle Identification' for the location of the code marking on the engine.*

Cylinder head

Cylinder head gasket surface maximum distortion . . . . 0.1 mm
Minimum cylinder head height:
Petrol engines . . . . 147.25 mm
Diesel engines . . . . Head resurfacing not possible
Cylinder head gasket selection (diesel engines):
Piston projection 0.91 to 1.00 mm . . . . 1 hole/notch*
Piston projection 1.01 to 1.10 mm . . . . 2 holes/notches*
Piston projection 1.11 to 1.20 mm . . . . 3 holes/notches*
Maximum crack width between valve seats (diesel engines) . . . . 0.5 mm
*** *Disregard single and double oval holes*

Camshaft

Maximum endfloat:
Petrol engines . . . . 0.02 to 0.26 mm
Diesel engines . . . . 0.15 mm maximum

Pistons and piston rings

Piston diameter:
  Petrol engines. . . . . 89.58 to 89.62 mm
  Diesel engines. . . . . 79.47 to 79.97 mm
Piston ring end gap clearance (ring 15 mm from bottom of bore):
  Petrol engines:
    Top compression ring. . . . . 0.30 to 0.46 mm
    Middle compression ring . . . . 0.50 to 0.76 mm
    Oil control ring . . . . 0.15 to 0.71 mm
  Diesel engines:
    New:
      Compression rings . . . . 0.20 to 0.40 mm
      Oil scraper ring . . . . 0.25 to 0.50 mm
    Wear limit . . . . 1.0 mm

Valves

Valve spring free length:
  Petrol engines. . . . . 43.6 mm
  Diesel engines . . . . Not available
Maximum valve head deflection (end of stem flush with top of guide):
  Petrol engines. . . . . Not available
  Diesel engines . . . . 1.3 mm

Cylinder block

Bore diameter:
  Petrol engines. . . . . 89.60 mm (nominal)
  Diesel engines . . . . 79.51 mm (nominal)

Connecting rods

Big-end shell-to-journal clearance:
  Petrol engines. . . . . 0.006 to 0.060 mm
  Diesel engines . . . . 0.080 mm maximum
Big-end bearing endfloat:
  Petrol engines. . . . . 0.09 to 0.31 mm
  Diesel engines . . . . 0.37 mm

Crankshaft

Endfloat:
  Petrol engines. . . . . 0.093 to 0.303 mm
    Wear limit . . . . Not specified
  Diesel engines . . . . 0.070 to 0.170 mm
    Wear limit . . . . 0.37 mm
Main bearing running clearance:
  Petrol engines. . . . . 0.020 to 0.039 mm
    Wear limit . . . . 0.15 mm
  Diesel engines . . . . 0.030 to 0.080 mm
    Wear limit . . . . 0.17 mm

Torque wrench settings

Refer to Chapter 2A or 2B.

---

1 General information

1 Included in this Part of Chapter 2 are details of removing the engine from the car and general overhaul procedures for the cylinder head, cylinder block and all other engine internal components.

2 The information given ranges from advice concerning preparation for an overhaul and the purchase of parts, to detailed step-by-step procedures covering removal, inspection, renovation and refitting of engine internal components.

3 After Section 5, all instructions are based on the assumption that the engine has been removed from the car. For information concerning in-car engine repair, as well as the removal and refitting of those external components necessary for full overhaul, refer to the relevant in-car repair procedure section (Chapters 2A or 2B) and to Section 5 of this Chapter. Ignore any preliminary dismantling operations described in the relevant in-car repair sections that are no longer relevant once the engine has been removed from the car.

4 Apart from torque wrench settings, which are given at the beginning of the relevant in-car repair procedure in Chapters 2A or 2B, all specifications relating to engine overhaul are at the beginning of this Part of Chapter 2.

2 Engine overhaul –
general information

1 It is not always easy to determine when, or if, an engine should be completely overhauled, as a number of factors must be considered.

2 High mileage is not necessarily an indication that an overhaul is needed, while low mileage does not preclude the need for an overhaul. Frequency of servicing is probably the most important consideration. An engine which has had regular and frequent oil and filter changes, as well as other required maintenance, should give many thousands of miles of reliable

service. Conversely, a neglected engine may require an overhaul very early in its life.

3 Excessive oil consumption is an indication that piston rings, valve seals and/or valve guides are in need of attention. Make sure that oil leaks are not responsible before deciding that the rings and/or guides are worn. Perform a compression test, as described in the relevant Part A or B of this Chapter, to determine the likely cause of the problem.

4 Check the oil pressure with a gauge fitted in place of the oil pressure switch, and compare it with that specified (see Chapter 2A or 2B). If it is extremely low, the main and big-end bearings, and/or the oil pump, are probably worn out.

5 Loss of power, rough running, knocking or metallic engine noises, excessive valve gear noise, and high fuel consumption may also point to the need for an overhaul, especially if they are all present at the same time. If a complete service does not remedy the situation, major mechanical work is the only solution.

6 An engine overhaul involves restoring all internal parts to the specification of a new engine. During an overhaul, the pistons and the piston rings are renewed. New main and big-end bearings are generally fitted; if necessary, the crankshaft may be renewed, to restore the journals. The valves are also serviced as well, since they are usually in less-than-perfect condition at this point. While the engine is being overhauled, other components, such as the starter and alternator, can be overhauled as well. The end result should be an as-new engine that will give many trouble-free miles. **Note:** *Critical cooling system components such as the hoses, thermostat and coolant pump should be renewed when an engine is overhauled. The radiator should be checked carefully, to ensure that it is not clogged or leaking. Also, it is a good idea to renew the oil pump whenever the engine is overhauled.*

7 Before beginning the engine overhaul, read through the entire procedure, to familiarise yourself with the scope and requirements of the job. Overhauling an engine is not difficult if you follow carefully all of the instructions, have the necessary tools and equipment, and pay close attention to all specifications. It can, however, be time-consuming. Plan on the car being off the road for a minimum of two weeks, especially if parts must be taken to an engineering works for repair or reconditioning. Check on the availability of parts and make sure that any necessary special tools and equipment are obtained in advance. Most work can be done with typical hand tools, although a number of precision measuring tools are required for inspecting parts to determine if they must be renewed. Often the engineering works will handle the inspection of parts and offer advice concerning reconditioning and renewal. **Note:** *Always wait until the engine has been completely dismantled, and until all components (especially the cylinder block and*

the crankshaft) have been inspected, before deciding what service and repair operations must be performed by an engineering works. The condition of these components will be the major factor to consider when determining whether to overhaul the original engine, or to buy a reconditioned unit. Do not, therefore, purchase parts or have overhaul work done on other components until they have been thoroughly inspected. As a general rule, time is the primary cost of an overhaul, so it does not pay to fit worn or sub-standard parts.

8 As a final note, to ensure maximum life and minimum trouble from a reconditioned engine, everything must be assembled with care, in a spotlessly-clean environment.

3 Engine removal – preparation and precautions

If you have decided that the engine must be removed for overhaul or major repair work, several preliminary steps should be taken.

Locating a suitable place to work is extremely important. Adequate work space, along with storage space for the vehicle, will be needed. If a workshop or garage is not available, at the very least a solid, level, clean work surface is required.

If possible, clear some shelving close to the work area and use it to store the engine components and ancillaries as they are removed and dismantled. In this manner, the components stand a better chance of staying clean and undamaged during the overhaul. Laying out components in groups together with their fixings, bolts, screws, etc, will save time and avoid confusion when the engine is refitted.

Clean the engine compartment and engine before beginning the removal procedure; this will help visibility and help to keep tools clean.

The help of an assistant is essential; there are certain instances when one person cannot safely perform all of the operations required to remove the engine from the vehicle. Safety is of primary importance, considering the potential hazards involved in this kind of operation. A second person should always be in attendance to offer help in an emergency. If this is the first time you have removed an engine, advice and aid from someone more experienced would also be beneficial.

Plan the operation ahead of time. Before starting work, obtain (or arrange for the hire of) all of the tools and equipment you will need. Access to the following items will allow the task of removing and refitting the engine to be completed safely and with relative ease: a heavy-duty trolley jack – rated in excess of the weight of the engine, complete sets of spanners and sockets as described in the rear of this Manual, wooden blocks, and plenty of rags and cleaning solvent for mopping-up spilled oil, coolant and fuel. A selection

of different-sized plastic storage bins will also prove useful for keeping dismantled components grouped together. If any of the equipment must be hired, make sure that you arrange for it in advance, and perform all of the operations possible without it beforehand; this may save you time and money.

Plan on the vehicle being out of use for quite a while, especially if you intend to carry out an engine overhaul. Read through the whole of this Section and work out a strategy based on your own experience and the tools, time and workspace available to you. Some of the overhaul processes may have to be carried out by a Ford dealer or an engineering works – these establishments often have busy schedules, so it would be prudent to consult them before removing or dismantling the engine, to get an idea of the amount of time required to carry out the work.

When removing the engine from the vehicle, be methodical about the disconnection of external components. Labelling cables and hoses as they are removed will greatly assist the refitting process.

Always be extremely careful when lifting the engine from the engine bay. Serious injury can result from careless actions. If help is required, it is better to wait until it is available rather than risk personal injury and/or damage to components by continuing alone. By planning ahead and taking your time, a job of this nature, although major, can be accomplished successfully and without incident.

4 Engine – removal and refitting

Note: *The engine can be removed from the car only as a complete unit with the transmission; the two are then separated for overhaul. The engine/transmission unit is lowered out of position, and withdrawn from under the vehicle. Bearing this in mind, ensure the vehicle is raised sufficiently so that there is enough clearance between the front of the vehicle and the floor to allow the engine/transmission assembly to be slid out once it has been lowered out of position. If clearance is an issue it is possible to remove the entire front panel of the vehicle, including the radiator and AC condenser. This procedure involves considerably more work and the AC system must evacuated.*

Removal

1 Select a solid, level surface to park the vehicle on. Give yourself enough space to move around it easily.

2 Disconnect the negative (earth) lead, and remove the battery, battery compartment upper and lower panels. **Note:** *Before disconnecting the battery, refer to 'Disconnecting the battery' at the rear of this manual.*

3 Apply the handbrake, slacken both front wheel bolts, then jack up the front of the

4.12 Label the wiring and hoses as they are disconnected (TPS = Throttle Position Sensor)

vehicle and support it on axle stands (see *Jacking and vehicle support*). Remove both front wheels.

4 Remove the engine/transmission under-shield, and where applicable, the top cover.

5 Remove the bonnet (see Chapter 11).

6 Carry out the following with reference to the relevant Part of Chapter 1:
  a) Drain the cooling system.
  b) Drain the engine oil.

7 Unbolt the power steering pump and tie it to one side (see Chapter 10). **Note:** *There is no need to disconnect the fluid pipes.*

8 Unbolt the AC compressor and tie it to one side (see Chapter 3). **Note:** *Although not strictly necessary, we found it preferable to remove the alternator (Chapter 5A) and the alternator/power steering pump/compressor mounting bracket (seven bolts) from the front of the engine block. This gave much greater clearance when lowering the engine/transmission.*

 Warning: Do not disconnect the air conditioning refrigerant circuit.

9 Remove the windscreen cowl panel and the bulkhead panel.

10 Remove the air cleaner housing and intake ducting with reference to the relevant Part of Chapter 4.

11 Depressurise the fuel system, and disconnect the fuel supply and return pipes from the fuel rail/injection pump. Plug or cap the open pipes/fittings to prevent fuel loss/dirt ingress.

4.20 Attach chains/straps to the lifting eyes on the cylinder head

12 Label all vacuum hoses, wiring connections, and coolant hoses to ensure correct refitment, then disconnect them. Pieces of masking tape with numbers or letters written on them work well **(see illustration)**. If there is a possibility of confusion regarding connects or routing, make a sketch or notes.

13 Where fitted, disconnect the accelerator cable from the engine (see the relevant Part of Chapter 4).

14 On manual transmission models, prise out the spring clip and disconnect the clutch hydraulic pipe (see Chapter 6). Release the pipe from the selector cable bracket, and plug the pipe openings to prevent dirt ingress and fluid loss.

15 Prise the selector cable end(s) from the balljoint(s) on the transmission, and undo the bolts securing the cable support bracket to the transmission housing (see the relevant Part of Chapter 7). Note the fitted positions of the cable(s).

16 Remove the front section of the exhaust system with reference to Chapter 4C.

17 Remove the main wiring cable and solenoid cable from the starter motor (see Chapter 5A).

18 Remove both front driveshafts as described in Chapter 8.

19 With reference to Chapter 5A remove the battery, side panel and the battery support panel.

20 Attach lifting chains/straps to the lifting eyes on the cylinder head. Attach the chains to a lifting crane or engine support beam, and take the weight of the engine and transmission **(see illustration)**.

21 Disconnect and remove the engine/transmission mountings (see the relevant Part of Chapter 2).

22 If available, a low trolley should be placed under the engine/transmission assembly, to facilitate its easy removal from under the vehicle. Make a final check to ensure that nothing else remains connected to the engine/transmission. Lower the engine/transmission assembly, making sure that nothing is trapped, taking great care not to damage the radiator/cooling fan assembly. Enlist the help of an assistant during this procedure, as it may be necessary to tilt the assembly slightly to clear the body panels. Great care must be taken to ensure that no components are trapped and damaged during the removal procedure.

23 Detach the hoist and withdraw the engine/transmission unit from under the vehicle.

Separation

24 With the engine/transmission assembly removed, support the assembly on suitable blocks of wood, on a workbench (or failing that, on a clean area of the workshop floor).

25 Remove the starter motor as described in Chapter 5A.

26 On automatic transmission models, prise out the engine adapter plate plug from the front of the engine, and unscrew the three

torque converter nuts. Turn the crankshaft to align each nut in turn with the adapter plate hole – see Chapter 7B.

27 Ensure that both engine and transmission are adequately supported, then slacken and remove the remaining bolts securing the transmission housing to the engine. Note the correct fitted positions of each bolt (and the relevant brackets) as they are removed, to use as a reference on refitting.

28 Carefully withdraw the transmission from the engine, ensuring that the weight of the transmission is not allowed to hang on the input shaft while it is engaged with the clutch friction disc.

29 If they are loose, remove the locating dowels from the engine or transmission, and keep them in a safe place.

Refitting

30 Refitting is a reversal of removal, but note the following points:
  a) On manual transmission models first smear the splines of the input shaft with a little 'white grease', manufactured specifically for this application, and normally supplied with a clutch kit. Do not use copper grease.
  b) On automatic transmission models, check that the torque converter is fully entered on the input shaft by checking that the distance between the bellhousing mounting flange and the torque converter is approximately 16.1 mm. If it is less, the torque converter is not fully entered.
  c) Ensure that all engine and transmission mountings are fitted free of strain.
  d) Tighten all nuts and bolts to the specified torque where given.
  e) Refit, and where applicable adjust, all engine related components and systems with reference to the Chapters concerned.
  f) Ensure that the engine is filled with oil and that the cooling system is refilled as described in the relevant Part of Chapter 1 before starting the engine.

5 Engine overhaul – preliminary information

It is much easier to dismantle and work on the engine if it is mounted on a portable engine stand. These stands can often be hired from a tool hire shop. Before the engine is mounted on a stand, the flywheel should be removed, so that the stand bolts can be tightened into the end of the cylinder block/crankcase. **Note:** *Do not measure cylinder bore dimensions with the engine mounted on this type of stand.*

If a stand is not available, it is possible to dismantle the engine with it blocked up on a sturdy workbench, or on the floor. Be very careful not to tip or drop the engine when working without a stand.

If you intend to obtain a reconditioned engine, all ancillaries must be removed first to be transferred to the new engine (just as they will if you are doing a complete engine overhaul yourself). These components include the following:

Petrol engines

a) *Alternator (including mounting brackets) and starter motor (Chapter 5A).*
b) *The ignition system and HT components including all sensors, distributor, HT leads and spark plugs (Chapters 1A and 5B).*
c) *The fuel injection system components (Chapter 4A).*
d) *All electrical switches, actuators and sensors, and the engine wiring harness (Chapters 4A and 5B).*
e) *Inlet and exhaust manifolds (Chapters 4A and 4C).*
f) *Engine oil dipstick and tube.*
g) *Engine mountings (Chapter 2A).*
h) *Flywheel/driveplate (Chapter 2A).*
i) *Clutch components (Chapter 6).*

Diesel engines

a) *Alternator (including mounting brackets) and starter motor (Chapter 5A).*
b) *The glow plug/preheating system components (Chapter 5C).*
c) *All fuel system components, including the fuel injectors, all sensors and actuators (Chapter 4B).*
d) *The vacuum pump (Chapter 9).*
e) *All electrical switches, actuators and sensors, and the engine wiring harness (Chapter 4B and Chapter 5C).*
f) *Inlet and exhaust manifolds, and turbocharger (Chapter 4B and 4C).*
g) *The engine oil level dipstick and its tube.*
h) *Engine mountings (Chapter 2B).*
i) *Flywheel/driveplate (Chapter 2B).*
j) *Clutch components (Chapter 6).*

All engines

Note: *When removing the external components from the engine, pay close attention to details that may be helpful or important during refitting. Note the fitted position of gaskets, seals, spacers, pins, washers, bolts, and other small components.*

If you are obtaining a short engine (the engine cylinder block/crankcase, crankshaft, pistons and connecting rods, all fully assembled), then the cylinder head, sump, oil pump, timing chain/belt (together with its tensioner and covers), auxiliary belt (together with its tensioner), coolant pump, thermostat housing, coolant outlet elbows, oil filter housing and, where applicable, oil cooler will also have to be removed.

If you are planning a full overhaul, the engine can be dismantled in the order given below:

a) *Inlet and exhaust manifolds (see the relevant part of Chapter 4).*
b) *Timing belt, sprockets and tensioner (see Chapter 2B).*
c) *Cylinder head (see Chapter 2A or 2B).*

6.4 Keep groups of components together in labelled bags or boxes

d) *Timing chains and sprockets (see Chapter 2A).*
e) *Flywheel/driveplate (see Chapter 2A or 2B).*
f) *Sump (see Chapter 2A or 2B).*
g) *Oil pump (see Chapter 2A or 2B).*
h) *Piston/connecting rod assemblies (see Section 7).*
i) *Crankshaft (see Section 8).*

6 Cylinder head – dismantling, cleaning, inspection and reassembly

Note: *New and reconditioned cylinder heads are available from Ford, and from engine specialists. Specialist tools are required for the dismantling and inspection procedures, and new components may not be readily available. It may, therefore, be more practical for the home mechanic to buy a reconditioned head, rather than to dismantle, inspect and recondition the original head.*

Dismantling

1 Remove the cylinder head from the engine block as described in Part A or B of this Chapter. Also remove the camshaft(s) and hydraulic tappets as described in Part A or B of this Chapter.
2 On diesel models, remove the injectors and glow plugs (see Chapters 4B and 5C).
3 Where applicable, remove the rear coolant outlet housing together with its gasket/O-ring.

6.6a Remove the upper spring seat . . .

6.5 Compress the valve springs with a compressor tool

4 It is important that groups of components are kept together when they are removed and, if still serviceable, refitted in the same groups. If they are refitted randomly, accelerated wear leading to early failure will occur. Stowing groups of components in plastic bags or storage bins will help to keep everything in the right order – label them according to their fitted location, eg, No 1 exhaust, No 2 inlet, etc **(see illustration)**. Note that No 1 cylinder is nearest the timing chain/belt end of the engine.
5 With the cylinder head resting on one side, using a valve spring compressor, compress each valve spring in turn, extracting the split collets when the upper valve spring seat has been pushed far enough down the valve stem to free them. If the spring seat sticks, tap the upper jaw of the compressor with a hammer to free it **(see illustration)**.
6 Release the valve spring compressor and remove the upper spring seat, and single valve springs (petrol engines) or double valve springs (diesel engines) **(see illustrations)**.
7 Use a pair of pliers or a special removal tool to extract the valve stem oil seal, then remove the lower spring seat from the valve guide. Withdraw the valve itself from the head gasket side of the cylinder head. Repeat this process for the remaining valves **(see illustrations)**.

Cleaning

8 Using a suitable degreasing agent, remove all traces of oil deposits from the cylinder

6.6b . . . and the valve spring

6.7a Use a removal tool to extract the stem oil seal . . .

6.7b . . . then remove the lower spring seat

6.13 Measure the distortion of the cylinder head

head, paying particular attention to the journal bearings, hydraulic tappet bores, valve guides and oilways. Scrape off any traces of old gasket from the mating surfaces, taking care not to score or gouge them. If using emery paper, do not use a grade of less than 100. Turn the head over and using a blunt blade, scrape any carbon deposits from the combustion chambers and ports. Finally, wash the entire head casting with a suitable solvent to remove the remaining debris.

9 Clean the valve heads and stems using a fine wire brush. If the valve is heavily coked, scrape off the majority of the deposits with a blunt blade first, then use the wire brush. On 2.3 litre petrol models, the exhaust valve stems are filled with sodium to aid cooling. If the exhaust valves are to be renewed, the old valves must be treated as special waste, and disposed of accordingly.

10 Thoroughly clean the remainder of the components using solvent and allow them to dry completely. Discard the oil seals, as new ones must be fitted when the cylinder head is reassembled.

Inspection

Cylinder head

Note: On diesel engines the cylinder heads and valves cannot be reworked (although valves may be lapped-in); new or exchange units must be obtained.

11 Examine the head casting closely to identify any damage or cracks that may have developed. Pay particular attention to the areas around the valve seats and spark plug

holes. If cracking is discovered in this area, Ford state that the diesel cylinder head may be re-used, provided the cracks between the valves are no larger than 0.5 mm wide. More serious damage will mean the renewal of the cylinder head casting.

12 Moderately pitted and scorched valve seats can be repaired by lapping the valves in during reassembly, as described later in this Section.

13 Measure any distortion of the gasket surfaces using a straight-edge and a set of feeler blades. Take one measurement longitudinally on both the inlet and exhaust manifold mating surfaces. Take several measurements across the head gasket surface, to assess the level of distortion in all planes (see illustration). Compare the measurements with the figures in the Specifications. On petrol engines, if the head is distorted out of specification, it may be possible to have it machined by an engineering works.

14 Minimum cylinder head heights (measured between the cylinder head gasket surface and the cylinder head cover gasket surface) are listed in Specifications.

Camshaft

15 Visually inspect the camshaft for evidence of wear on the surfaces of the lobes and journals. Normally their surfaces should be smooth and have a dull shine; look for scoring, erosion or pitting and areas that appear highly polished, indicating excessive wear. Accelerated wear will occur once the hardened exterior of the camshaft has been damaged, so always renew worn items. **Note:**

If these symptoms are visible on the tips of the camshaft lobes, check the corresponding tappet, as it will probably be worn as well.

16 If the machined surfaces of the camshaft appear discoloured or blued, it is likely that it has been overheated at some point, probably due to inadequate lubrication. This may have distorted the shaft, so have the camshaft inspected at an automotive engineering workshop.

17 To measure the camshaft endfloat, temporarily refit the camshaft to the cylinder head, then fit the first and last bearing caps (and shell bearings where applicable) and tighten the retaining nuts to the specified torque setting. Anchor a DTI gauge to the timing belt end of the cylinder head and align the gauge probe with the camshaft axis. Push the camshaft to one end of the cylinder head as far as it will travel, then rest the DTI gauge probe on the end of the camshaft, and zero the gauge display. Push the camshaft as far as it will go to the other end of the cylinder head, and record the gauge reading. Verify the reading by pushing the camshaft back to its original position and checking that the gauge indicates zero again (see illustration). **Note:** The hydraulic tappets must not be fitted whilst this measurement is being taken.

18 Check that the camshaft endfloat measurement is within the limit listed in the Specifications. Wear outside of this limit is unlikely to be confined to any one component, so renewal of the camshaft, cylinder head and bearing caps must be considered.

19 If it is considered necessary to establish the camshaft bearing running clearance, take the camshaft and cylinder head to an automotive engineering workshop. If the camshaft journals or cylinder head bearing surfaces are worn, they may be able to offer a solution. Otherwise renewal of the camshaft and/or cylinder head is the only course of action.

Valves and associated components

Note: On all engines, the valve heads cannot be recut, although they may be lapped-in.

20 Examine each valve closely for signs of wear. Inspect the valve stems for wear ridges, scoring or variations in diameter; measure their diameters at several points along their lengths with a micrometer (see illustration).

6.17 Check the camshaft endfloat using a DTI gauge

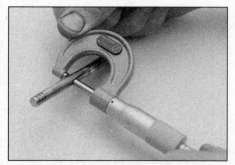

6.20 Measure the diameter of the valve stems with a micrometer

6.23 Measure the maximum deflection of the valve in its guide, using a DTI gauge

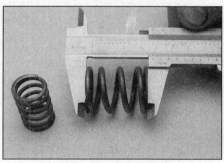

6.25 Measure the free length of each of the valve springs

6.26 Check the squareness of the valve springs

21 The valve heads should not be cracked, badly pitted or charred. Note that light pitting of the valve head can be rectified by lapping-in the valves during reassembly, as described later in this Section.

22 Check that the valve stem end face is free from excessive pitting or indentation; this would be caused by defective hydraulic tappets.

23 Insert each valve into its respective guide in the cylinder head and set up a DTI gauge against the edge of the valve head. With the end of the valve stem flush with the top of the valve guide, measure the maximum side-to-side deflection of the valve in its guide **(see illustration)**.

24 If the measurement exceeds that given in the Specifications, the valve and valve guide should be renewed as a pair. **Note:** *Valve guides are an interference fit in the cylinder head and their removal requires access to a hydraulic press. For this reason, it would be wise to entrust the job to an engineering workshop.*

25 Using vernier calipers, measure the free length of each of the valve springs. Compare the measurement obtained with that given in the Specifications. Note that valve springs are usually renewed during a major engine overhaul **(see illustration)**.

26 Stand each spring on its end on a flat surface, against an engineer's square **(see illustration)**. Check the squareness of the spring visually, and renew it if it appears distorted.

Reassembly

27 To achieve a gas-tight seal between the valves and their seats, it will be necessary to lap-in (or grind-in) the valves. To complete this process you will need a quantity of fine/coarse grinding paste and a grinding tool – this can either be of the rubber sucker type, or the automatic type which is driven by a rotary power tool.

28 Smear a small quantity of *fine* grinding paste on the sealing face of the valve head. Turn the cylinder head over so that the combustion chambers are facing upwards and insert the valve into the correct guide. Attach the grinding tool to the valve head and, using a backward/forward rotary action, grind the valve head into its seat. Periodically lift the valve and rotate it to redistribute the grinding paste **(see illustration)**.

29 Continue this process until the contact between valve and seat produces an unbroken, matt grey ring of uniform width, on both faces. Repeat the operation on the remaining valves.

30 If the valves and seats are so badly pitted that coarse grinding paste must be used, bear in mind that there is a maximum protrusion of the end of the valve stem from the valve guide. If this dimension is outside the limit due to excessive grinding-in, the hydraulic tappets may not operate correctly. Have the cylinder head inspected by an automotive engineering workshop.

31 Assuming the repair is feasible, work as described previously but use coarse grinding paste initially, to achieve a dull finish on the valve face and seat. Wash off the coarse paste with solvent and repeat the process using fine grinding paste to obtain the correct finish.

32 When all the valves have been lapped-in,

6.28 Grind-in the valves with a reciprocating rotary motion

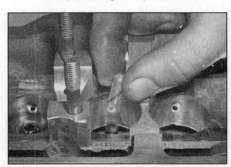

6.34 Fit a protective sleeve over the valve stem before fitting the stem seal

remove all traces of grinding paste from the cylinder head and valves with solvent, and allow them to dry completely.

33 Turn the head on its side. Fit the first lower spring seat into place, with the convex side facing the cylinder head **(see illustration)**.

34 Working on one valve at a time, lubricate the valve stem with clean engine oil, and insert it into the guide. Fit one of the protective plastic sleeves supplied with the new valve stem oil seals over the valve end face – this will protect the oil seal whilst it is being fitted **(see illustration)**.

35 Dip a new valve stem seal in clean engine oil, and carefully push it over the valve and onto the top of the valve guide – take care not to damage the stem seal as it passes over the valve end face. Use a suitable long reach socket or special installer to press it firmly into position **(see illustrations)**. Remove the protective sleeve.

6.33 Fit the lower spring seat with the convex face facing the cylinder head

6.35a Push the stem seal over the valve and onto the top of the valve guide . . .

6.35b . . . then use a long reach socket to seat the seal

6.36 Fit the valve spring(s)

6.37a Fit the upper seat over the top of the valve spring

6.37b Use grease to hold the two halves of the split collet in the groove

6.41 On petrol engines, the coolant outlet seal is integral with the housing

36 Locate the valve spring(s) over the valve stem **(see illustration)**. Ensure that the springs locate correctly on the lower seat.
37 Fit the upper seat over the top of the springs, then using a valve spring compressor, compress the springs until the upper seat is pushed beyond the collet grooves in the valve stem. Refit the split collet, using a dab of grease to hold the two halves in the grooves **(see illustrations)**. Gradually release the spring compressor, checking that the collet remains correctly seated as the spring extends. When correctly seated, the upper seat should force the two halves of the collet together, and hold them securely in the grooves in the end of the valve.
38 Repeat this process for the remaining sets of valve components. To settle the components after installation, strike the end of each valve stem with a mallet, using a block of wood to protect the stem from damage. Check before progressing any further that the split collets remain firmly held in the end of the valve stem by the upper spring seat.
39 Refit the hydraulic tappets and camshaft as described in Part A or B of this Chapter.
40 Where applicable, refit the coolant sensor and oil pressure switch to the cylinder head.
41 Where applicable, refit the thermostat/coolant outlet housing together with a new gasket/O-ring **(see illustration)**.

42 On diesel models, refit the injectors, and glow plugs (see Chapters 4B and 5C).
43 Refit the cylinder head with reference to Parts A or B of this Chapter. Also refit the camshaft sprocket as described in Part A or B of this Chapter.

7 Piston/connecting rod assemblies – removal and inspection

Removal

1 Refer to Part A or B of this Chapter (as

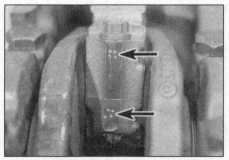

7.4 Mark the big-end caps and connecting rods with their numbers (arrowed)

applicable) and remove the cylinder head, flywheel, sump/balancer shaft housing and baffle plate, oil pump and pick-up.
2 Inspect the tops of the cylinder bores for ridges at the point where the pistons reach top dead centre. These must be removed otherwise the pistons may be damaged when they are pushed out of their bores. Use a scraper or ridge reamer to remove the ridges.
3 Using a set of feeler blades, measure the big-end-to-crankpin web thrust clearance at each connecting rod, and record the measurements for later reference.
4 Rotate the crankshaft until piston No 1 is at bottom dead centre; piston No 4 will also be at bottom dead centre. Unless they are already identified, mark the big-end bearing caps and connecting rods with their respective piston numbers, using a centre-punch or a scribe **(see illustration)**. Note the orientation of the bearing caps in relation to the connecting rod; it may be difficult to see the manufacturer's markings at this stage, so scribe alignment arrows on them both to ensure correct reassembly.
5 Unscrew the bearing cap bolts half a turn at a time, until they can be removed and the cap withdrawn. Recover the bottom shell bearing, and tape it to the cap for safe-keeping. Note that if the shell bearings are to be re-used, they must be refitted to the same connecting rod.

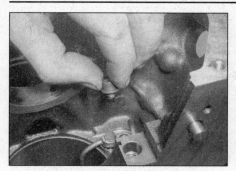

7.8a Remove the piston cooling jets retaining screws . . .

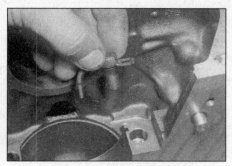

7.8b . . . and withdraw the jets from their mounting holes

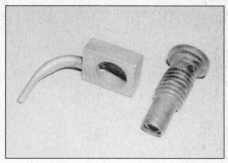

7.8c Piston cooling jet and retainer

6 Drive the piston out of the top of the bore using a piece of wooden dowel or a hammer handle. As the piston and connecting rod emerge, recover the top shell bearing and tape it to the connecting rod for safe-keeping. On engines fitted with piston cooling jets at the bottom of the cylinders, take care not to allow the connecting rod to damage the jet as the piston is being removed.

7 Remove No 4 piston and connecting rod in the same manner, then turn the crankshaft through half a turn and remove No 2 and 3 pistons and connecting rods. Remember to maintain the components in their cylinder groups whilst they are in a dismantled state.

8 If applicable, remove the retaining screws and withdraw the piston cooling jets from the bottom of the cylinder **(see illustrations)**.

Inspection

9 On petrol engines, the gudgeon pin is an interference fit in the connecting rod. If new pistons are to be fitted to existing connecting rods, the work should be carried out be a Ford dealer or specialist. Note that the F cast into the side of the connecting rod must face in the same direction as the arrow on the piston crown (the arrow on the piston crown faces towards the timing chain end).

10 On diesel engines, remove the circlips, push out the gudgeon pin, and separate the piston and connecting rod **(see illustrations)**. Discard the circlips as new items must be fitted on reassembly. If the pin proves difficult to remove, heat the piston to 60ºC with hot water – the resulting expansion will then allow the two components to be separated.

11 Before an inspection of the pistons can be carried out, the existing piston rings must be removed, using a removal/installation tool, or an old feeler blade if such a tool is not available. Always remove the upper piston rings first, expanding them to clear the piston crown. The rings are very brittle and will snap if they are stretched too much – sharp edges are produced when this happens, so protect your eyes and hands. Discard the rings on removal, as new items must be fitted when the engine is reassembled **(see illustration)**.

12 Use a section of old piston ring to scrape the carbon deposits out of the ring grooves, taking care not to score or gouge the edges of the groove.

13 Carefully scrape away all traces of carbon from the tops of the pistons. A hand-held wire brush (or a piece of fine emery cloth) can be used, once the majority of the deposits have been scraped away. Be careful not to remove any metal from the piston, as it is relatively soft. **Note:** *Make sure each piston is kept identified for position during cleaning.*

14 Once the deposits have been removed, clean the pistons and connecting rods with paraffin or a suitable solvent, and dry thoroughly. Make sure that the oil return holes in the ring grooves are clear.

15 Examine the pistons for signs of excessive wear or damage. Some normal wear will be apparent, in the form of a vertical 'grain' on the piston thrust surfaces and a slight looseness of the top compression ring in its groove. Abnormal wear should be carefully examined, to assess whether the component is still serviceable and what the cause of the wear might be.

16 Scuffing or scoring of the piston skirt may indicate that the engine has been overheating, through inadequate cooling or lubrication. Scorch marks on the skirt indicate that blow-by has occurred, perhaps caused by worn bores or piston rings. Burnt areas on the piston crown are usually an indication of pre-ignition, pinking or detonation. In extreme cases, the piston crown may be melted by operating under these conditions. Corrosion pit marks in the piston crown indicate that coolant has seeped into the combustion chamber. The faults causing these symptoms must be corrected before the engine is brought back into service, or the same damage will recur.

17 Check the pistons, connecting rods, gudgeon pins and bearing caps for cracks. Lay the connecting rods on a flat surface, and look along the length to see if it appears bent or twisted. If you have doubts about their condition, get them measured at an engineering workshop. Inspect the small-end bush bearing in the connecting rod for signs of wear or cracking.

18 Have the cylinder bores, pistons, rings and connecting rods examined and measured by an automotive engineering workshop. If renewal is necessary, they will be able to supply piston kits to match the cylinder bores.

19 The orientation of the piston with respect to the connecting rod must be correct when the two are reassembled. The piston crown is marked with an arrow (which may be obscured by carbon deposits); this must point towards the timing chain/belt end of the engine when the piston is installed. On diesel engines, the

7.10a Insert a small screwdriver into the slot and prise off the gudgeon pin circlips

7.10b Push out the gudgeon pin to separate the piston and connecting rod

7.11 Piston rings can be removed using an old feeler gauge

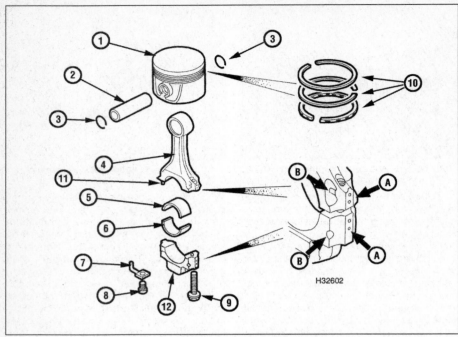

7.19 Typical piston assembly

1 Piston	5 Big-end bearing shell	9 Big-end bearing cap bolts
2 Gudgeon pin	6 Big-end bearing shell	10 Piston rings
3 Circlip	7 Oil jet for piston cooling	11 Locating dowel
4 Connecting rod	(where applicable)	12 Big-end bearing cap
	8 Oil jet retaining screw	

A Connecting rod/bearing cap identification marks
B Connecting rod/bearing cap orientation marks

8.1a Oil baffle plate – petrol engines

8.1b Oil baffle plate – diesel engines

8.4 Measure the crankshaft endfloat using a DTI gauge

8.5 If a DTI gauge is not available, measure the endfloat using feeler gauges

connecting rod and its bearing cap both have recesses/lugs machined into them, close to their mating surfaces – these recesses/lugs must both face the same way as the arrow on the piston crown (ie, towards the timing belt end of the engine) when correctly installed **(see illustration)**. On petrol engines, the connecting rod has an F cast into the side which faces the timing chain end of the engine.

20 On diesel engines, lubricate the gudgeon pin and small-end bush with clean engine oil. Slide the pin into the piston, engaging the connecting rod small-end. Fit two new circlips to the piston at either end of the gudgeon pin. Repeat this operation for the remaining pistons.

8 Crankshaft –
   removal and inspection

Note: If no work is to be done on the pistons and connecting rods, then removal of the pistons will not be necessary. Instead, the pistons need only be pushed far enough up the bores so that the connecting rods are positioned clear of the crankpins. The use of an engine stand is strongly recommended.

Removal

1 With reference to Chapter 2A or 2B as applicable, carry out the following:
   a) Remove the timing chain/belt and crankshaft sprocket.
   b) Remove the clutch components and flywheel or driveplate (as applicable).
   c) Remove the sump/balancer shaft housing, baffle plate **(see illustrations)**, oil pump and pick-up tube.
   d) Remove the crankshaft oil seals and housings.

2 Lay the engine block on its side, supporting it with wooden blocks as required.

3 Remove the pistons and connecting rods or disconnect them from the crankshaft as described in Section 7 (see Note above).

4 With the cylinder block upside down on the bench, carry out a check of the crankshaft endfloat as follows. **Note:** This can only be accomplished when the crankshaft is still installed in the cylinder block/crankcase, but is free to move. Set up a DTI gauge so that the probe is in line with the crankshaft axis and is in contact with a fixed point on the end of the crankshaft. Push the crankshaft along its axis to the end of its travel, and then zero the gauge. Push the crankshaft fully the other way, and record the endfloat indicated on the dial **(see illustration)**. Compare the result with the figure given in the Specifications and establish whether new thrustwashers are required.

5 If a dial gauge is not available, feeler blades can be used. First push the crankshaft fully towards the flywheel end of the engine, then use a feeler blade to measure the gap between cylinder No 3 crankpin web and the main bearing thrustwasher **(see illustration)**. Compare the results with the Specifications.

6 Observe the manufacturer's identification marks on the main bearing caps. The number indicates the cap position in the crankcase, as counted from the timing chain/belt end of the engine **(see illustrations)**.

7 Loosen the main bearing cap bolts half a turn at a time, until they can be removed. Using a soft-faced mallet, strike the caps lightly to free them from the crankcase. Recover the lower main bearing shells, using tape to attach them to the cap for safe-keeping. Mark them to aid identification, but do not score or scratch them in any way. Note that on diesel engines, thrustwashers are fitted either side of the upper and lower centre main bearing cap/saddle.

8 Carefully lift the crankshaft out, taking care not to dislodge the upper main bearing shells.

9 Extract the upper main bearing shells from the crankcase, and tape them to their respective bearing caps. Remove the two thrustwasher bearings from either side of No 3 bearing saddle.

10 With the shell bearings removed, observe the recesses machined into the bearing caps and crankcase – these provide location for the lugs which protrude from the shell bearings and so prevent them from being fitted incorrectly.

Inspection

11 Wash the crankshaft in a suitable solvent and allow it to dry. Flush the oil holes thoroughly, to ensure they are not blocked.

12 Inspect the main bearing and crankpin journals carefully. If uneven wear, cracking, scoring or pitting are evident then the crankshaft should be reground by an engineering workshop, and refitted to the engine with undersize bearings.

13 Rather than attempt to determine the crankshaft journal sizes, and the bearing clearances, take the crankshaft to an automotive engineering workshop. Have them perform the necessary measurements, grind the journals if necessary, and supply the appropriate new shell bearings.

14 Check the oil seal journals at either end of the crankshaft. If they appear excessively scored or damaged, they may cause the new seals to leak when the engine is reassembled. It may be possible to repair the journal; seek the advice of an engineering workshop or your Ford dealer.

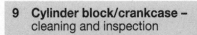

9 Cylinder block/crankcase – cleaning and inspection

Cleaning

1 Remove all external components as applicable including lifting eyes, mounting brackets, the coolant pump, oil cooler and filter mounting housing, fuel injection pump mounting bracket (where applicable) and electrical switches/sensors from the block.

8.6a Manufacturer's identification markings on the main bearing caps (arrowed) – diesel engines

For complete cleaning, the core plugs should ideally be removed. Drill a small hole in the plugs, then insert a self-tapping screw into the hole. Extract the plugs by pulling on the screw with a pair of grips, or by using a slide hammer.

2 Scrape all traces of gasket and sealant from the cylinder block/crankcase, taking care not to damage the sealing surfaces.

3 Remove all oil gallery plugs (where fitted). The plugs are usually very tight – they may have to be drilled out, and the holes retapped. Use new plugs when the engine is reassembled.

4 If the casting is extremely dirty, it should be steam-cleaned. After this, clean all oil holes and galleries one more time. Flush all internal passages with warm water until the water runs clear. Dry thoroughly, and apply a light film of oil to all mating surfaces and cylinder bores, to prevent rusting. If you have access to compressed air, use it to speed up the drying process, and to blow out all the oil holes and galleries.

 Warning: Wear eye protection when using compressed air.

5 If the castings are not very dirty, you can do an adequate cleaning job with hot, soapy water and a stiff brush. Take plenty of time, and do a thorough job. Regardless of the cleaning method used, be sure to clean all oil holes and galleries very thoroughly, and to dry all components well. Protect the cylinder bores as described above, to prevent rusting.

6 All threaded holes must be clean, to ensure accurate torque readings during reassembly. To clean the threads, run the correct-size tap into each of the holes to remove rust, corrosion, thread sealant or sludge, and to restore damaged threads. If possible, use compressed air to clear the holes of debris produced by this operation. **Note:** *Take extra care to exclude all cleaning liquid from blind tapped holes, as the casting may be cracked by hydraulic action if a bolt is threaded into a hole containing liquid.*

7 Apply suitable sealant to the new oil gallery plugs, and insert them into the holes in the block. Tighten them securely. Similarly fit new core plugs – driving them into place with a suitable close-fitting tube or socket.

8.6b On petrol engines, the caps also have an arrow to indicate which side faces the timing chain end (arrowed)

8 If the engine is not going to be reassembled immediately, cover it with a large plastic bag to keep it clean; protect all mating surfaces and the cylinder bores as described above, to prevent rusting.

Inspection

9 Visually check the casting for cracks and corrosion. Look for stripped threads in the threaded holes. If there has been any history of internal water leakage, it may be worthwhile having an engine overhaul specialist check the cylinder block/crankcase with professional equipment. If defects are found, have them renewed or if possible, repaired.

10 Check the cylinder bores for scuffing or scoring. Any evidence of this kind of damage should be cross-checked with an inspection of the pistons (see Section 7 of this Chapter). If the damage is in its early stages, it may be possible to repair the block by reboring it. Seek the advice of an engineering workshop.

11 Place the cylinder block on a level work surface, crankcase downwards. Use a straight-edge and a set of feeler blades to measure the distortion of the cylinder head mating surface in both planes. A maximum figure is not quoted by the manufacturer, but use the figure of 0.05 mm as a rough guide. If the measurement exceeds this figure, repair may be possible by machining – consult an engineering workshop for advice.

12 To allow an accurate assessment of the wear in the cylinder bores to be made, take the cylinder block (and pistons) to an automotive engineering workshop, and have them carry out the measurement procedures. If necessary, they will be able to rebore the cylinders, and supply appropriate piston kits.

13 Even if the cylinder bores are not excessively worn, the cylinder bores must be honed. This process involves using an abrasive tool to produce a fine, cross-hatch pattern on the inner surface of the bore. This has the effect of seating the piston rings, resulting in a good seal between the piston and cylinder. Again, an engineering workshop will be able to carry out the job for you at a reasonable cost.

14 Refit all the components removed in paragraph 1.

10 Main and big-end bearings – inspection and selection

Inspection

1 Even though the main and big-end bearings should be renewed during the engine overhaul, the old bearings should be retained for close examination, as they may reveal valuable information about the condition of the engine **(see illustration)**.

2 Bearing failure can occur due to lack of lubrication, the presence of dirt or other foreign particles, overloading the engine, or corrosion. Regardless of the cause of bearing failure, the cause must be corrected before the engine is reassembled, to prevent it from happening again.

3 When examining the bearing shells, remove them from the cylinder block/crankcase, the main bearing caps, the connecting rods and the connecting rod big-end bearing caps. Lay them out on a clean surface in the same general position as their location in the engine. This will enable you to match any bearing problems with the corresponding crankshaft journal. *Do not* touch any shell's internal bearing surface with your fingers while checking it, or the delicate surface may be scratched.

4 Dirt and other foreign matter gets into the engine in a variety of ways. It may be left in the engine during assembly, or it may pass through filters or the crankcase ventilation system. It may get into the oil, and from there into the bearings. Metal chips from machining operations and normal engine wear are often present. Abrasives are sometimes left

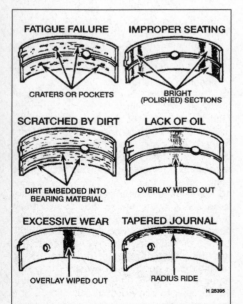

10.1 Typical bearing failures

FATIGUE FAILURE — CRATERS OR POCKETS

IMPROPER SEATING — BRIGHT (POLISHED) SECTIONS

SCRATCHED BY DIRT — DIRT EMBEDDED INTO BEARING MATERIAL

LACK OF OIL — OVERLAY WIPED OUT

EXCESSIVE WEAR — OVERLAY WIPED OUT

TAPERED JOURNAL — RADIUS RIDE

H 28395

in engine components after reconditioning, especially when parts are not thoroughly cleaned using the proper cleaning methods. Whatever the source, these foreign objects often end up embedded in the soft bearing material, and are easily recognised. Large particles will not embed in the bearing, but will score or gouge the bearing and journal. The best prevention for this cause of bearing failure is to clean all parts thoroughly, and keep everything spotlessly-clean during engine assembly. Frequent and regular engine oil and filter changes are also recommended.

5 Lack of lubrication (or lubrication breakdown) has a number of interrelated causes. Excessive heat (which thins the oil), overloading (which squeezes the oil from the bearing face) and oil leakage (from excessive bearing clearances, worn oil pump or high engine speeds) all contribute to lubrication breakdown. Blocked oil passages, which usually are the result of misaligned oil holes in a bearing shell, will also oil-starve a bearing, and destroy it. When lack of lubrication is the cause of bearing failure, the bearing material is wiped or extruded from the steel backing of the bearing. Temperatures may increase to the point where the steel backing turns blue from overheating.

6 Driving habits can have a definite effect on bearing life. Full-throttle, low-speed operation (labouring the engine) puts very high loads on bearings, tending to squeeze out the oil film. These loads cause the bearings to flex, which produces fine cracks in the bearing face (fatigue failure). Eventually, the bearing material will loosen in pieces, and tear away from the steel backing.

7 Short-distance driving leads to corrosion of bearings, because insufficient engine heat is produced to drive off the condensed water and corrosive gases. These products collect in the engine oil, forming acid and sludge. As the oil is carried to the engine bearings, the acid attacks and corrodes the bearing material.

8 Incorrect bearing installation during engine assembly will lead to bearing failure as well. Tight-fitting bearings leave insufficient bearing running clearance, and will result in oil starvation. Dirt or foreign particles trapped behind a bearing shell result in high spots on the bearing, which lead to failure.

9 *Do not* touch any shell's internal bearing surface with your fingers during reassembly as there is a risk of scratching the delicate surface, or of depositing particles of dirt on it.

10 As mentioned at the beginning of this Section, the bearing shells should be renewed as a matter of course during engine overhaul. To do otherwise is false economy.

Bearings selection

11 Main and big-end bearings for the engines described in this Chapter are available in standard sizes and a range of undersizes to suit reground crankshafts. Refer to your Ford dealer or automotive engineering workshop for details.

11 Engine overhaul – reassembly sequence

1 Before reassembly begins, ensure that all new parts have been obtained, and that all necessary tools are available. Read through the entire procedure to familiarise yourself with the work involved, and to ensure that all items necessary for reassembly of the engine are at hand. In addition to all normal tools and materials, thread-locking compound will be needed. A suitable tube of liquid sealant will also be required for the joint faces that are without gaskets. It is recommended that the manufacturer's own products are used, which are specially formulated for this purpose; the relevant product names are quoted in the text of each Section where they are required.

2 In order to save time and avoid problems, engine reassembly should ideally be carried out in the following order:

a) *Crankshaft (see Section 12).*
b) *Piston/connecting rod assemblies (see Section 13 and 14).*
c) *Oil pump (see Chapter 2A or 2B).*
d) *Sump/balancer shaft housing (see Chapter 2A or 2B).*
e) *Flywheel/driveplate (see Chapter 2A or 2B).*
f) *Cylinder head (see Chapter 2A or 2B).*
g) *Timing chain/belt tensioner, sprockets and timing chain/belt (see Chapter 2A or 2B).*
h) *Inlet and exhaust manifolds (see the relevant part of Chapter 4).*
i) *Engine external components and ancillaries (see list in Section 5 of this Chapter).*

3 At this stage, all engine components should be absolutely clean and dry, with all faults repaired. The components should be laid out (or in individual containers) on a completely clean work surface.

12 Crankshaft – refitting

1 Crankshaft refitting is the first stage of engine reassembly following overhaul. At this point, it is assumed that the crankshaft, cylinder block/crankcase and bearings have been cleaned, inspected and reconditioned or renewed. Where removed, the oil jets must be refitted at this stage and their mounting bolts tightened to the specified torque.

2 Place the cylinder block on a clean, level work surface, with the crankcase facing upwards. Wipe out the inner surfaces of the main bearing caps and crankcase with a clean cloth – they must be kept spotlessly clean.

3 Clean the rear surface of the new bearing shells with a cloth and lay them on the bearing saddles in the crankcase. Ensure that the orientation lugs on the shells engage with the recesses in the saddles, and that the oil holes are correctly aligned **(see illustration)**.

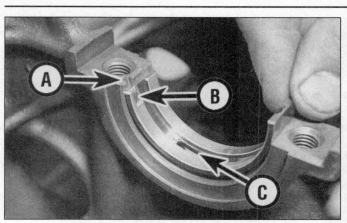

12.3 Bearing shells correctly fitted

A Recesses in bearing saddle   B Lug on bearing shell   C Oil hole

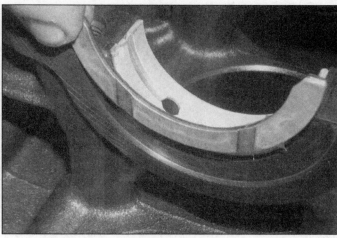

12.4a Fit the thrustwashers to the bearing saddle . . .

Do not hammer or otherwise force the bearing shells into place. It is critically important that the surfaces of the bearings are kept free from damage and contamination.

4 Fit the thrustwashers either side of the No 3 bearing saddle and/or bearing cap. On petrol engines the thrustwashers are fitted to either side of the central bearing saddle, and on diesel engines they are fitted to either side of both the central bearing saddle and the central main bearing cap. Use a small quantity of grease to hold them in place. Ensure that they are seated correctly in the machined recesses, with the oil grooves facing outwards **(see illustrations)**.

5 Give the newly-fitted main bearing shells and the crankshaft journals a final clean with a cloth. Check that the oil holes in the crankshaft are free from dirt, as any left here will become embedded in the new bearings when the engine is first started.

6 Liberally coat the bearing shells in the crankcase with clean engine oil of the appropriate grade.

7 Lower the crankshaft into position so that No 1 cylinder crankpin is at BDC, ready for fitting No 1 piston.

8 Lubricate the lower bearing shells in the main bearing caps with clean engine oil. Make sure that the locating lugs on the shells are still engaged with the corresponding recesses in the caps **(see illustration)**.

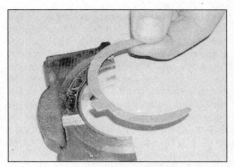

12.4b . . . and on diesel engines, fit the thrustwashers to the bearing cap

9 Fit the main bearing caps in the correct order and orientation – No 1 bearing cap must be at the timing chain/belt end of the engine and the bearing shell locating recesses in the bearing saddles and caps must be adjacent to each other **(see illustrations)**. Insert the bearing cap bolts and hand-tighten them only. The main bearing caps are labelled 1 to 5, and on petrol engines, the arrow mark points towards the timing chain end.

10 Working from the centre bearing cap outwards, tighten the new retaining bolts to their specified torques and angles in the stages given.

11 Check that the crankshaft rotates freely by turning it manually. If resistance is felt,

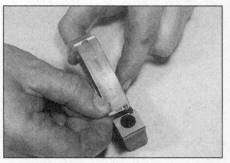

12.8 Ensure the bearing shell locating lugs engage with the recesses in the caps

having the running clearances and crankshaft measurements rechecked.

12 Carry out a check of the crankshaft endfloat as described at the beginning of Section 8. If the thrust surfaces of the crankshaft have been checked and new thrustwashers have been fitted, then the endfloat should be within specification.

13 Refit the pistons and connecting rods or reconnect them to the crankshaft as described in Section 14.

14 On petrol engines, refit the flywheel end oil seal housing to the cylinder block. Note that the housing must not be installed flush with the lower edge of the block, but with a step of up to 0.46 mm on each side **(see illustration)**.

12.9a No 3 main bearing cap – diesel engines

12.9b No 1 main bearing cap – diesel engines

12.14 The housing must be installed with a step of up to 0.46 mm on each side – petrol engines

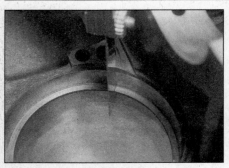

13.5 Check the piston ring end gap using feeler gauges

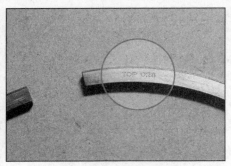

13.7 Piston ring top markings

15 With reference to Chapter 2A or 2B as applicable, carry out the following:
a) Refit the crankshaft oil seals/housing.
b) Refit the oil pump and pick-up tube, baffle plate and sump/balancer shaft housing.
c) Refit the flywheel and clutch or driveplate (as applicable).
d) Refit the crankshaft sprocket and timing chain/belt.

13 Pistons and piston rings – assembly

1 At this point it is assumed that the pistons have been correctly assembled to their respective connecting rods.
2 Before the rings can be fitted to the pistons, the end gaps must be checked with the rings fitted into the cylinder bores.
3 Lay out the piston assemblies and the new ring sets on a clean work surface so that the components are kept together in their groups during and after end gap checking. Place the crankcase on the work surface on its side, allowing access to the top and bottom of the bores.
4 Take the No 1 piston top ring and insert it into the top of the bore. Using the No 1 piston, push the ring close to the bottom of the bore, at the lowest point of the piston travel. Ensure that it is perfectly square in the bore.
5 Use a set of feeler blades to measure the gap between the ends of the piston ring. The correct blade will just pass through the gap with a minimal amount of resistance **(see illustration)**. Compare this measurement with that listed in Specifications. Check that you have the correct ring before deciding that a gap is incorrect. Repeat the operation for the remaining rings.
6 If new rings are being fitted, it is unlikely that the end gaps will be too small. If a measurement is found to be undersize, it must be corrected or there is the risk that the ends of the ring may contact each other during operation, possibly resulting in engine damage. This is achieved by gradually filing down the ends of the ring, using a file clamped in a vice. Fit the ring over the file such that both its ends contact opposite faces of the file. Move the ring along the file, removing small

amounts of material at a time. Take great care as the rings are brittle and form sharp edges if they fracture. Remember to keep the rings and piston assemblies in the correct order.
7 When all the piston ring end gaps have been verified, they can be fitted to the pistons. Work from the lowest ring groove (oil control ring) upwards. Note that the oil control ring may comprise of two side rails separated by a expander ring, or a one-piece oil control ring with an internal expander spring. Note also that the two compression rings are different in cross-section, and so must be fitted in the correct groove and the right way up, using a piston ring fitting tool. Both of the compression rings may have marks stamped on one side to indicate the top facing surface. Ensure that these marks face up when the rings are fitted **(see illustration)**.
8 Distribute the end gaps around the piston, spaced at 120° intervals to the each other.
Note: If the piston ring manufacturer supplies specific fitting instructions with the rings, follow these exclusively.

14 Piston/connecting rod assemblies – refitting

Note: At this point, it is assumed that the crankshaft has been measured, renewed/reground as necessary, and has been fitted to the engine, as described in Section 12.
1 Place the cylinder block on a clean, level work surface. Position the crankshaft such that crankpin No 1 is at BDC.

14.8 Use a hammer handle to tap the piston into its bore

2 Fit the upper big-end bearing shell to the connecting rod, ensuring that the locating lug and recess engage correctly. If new shells are being fitted, ensure that all traces of the protective grease are cleaned off using paraffin. Wipe dry the shells and connecting rods with a lint-free cloth.
3 Lubricate the cylinder bores, the pistons, piston rings and upper bearing shells with clean engine oil. Lay out each piston/connecting rod assembly in order on a work surface.
4 Where the bearing caps are secured with nuts, pad the threaded ends of the bolts with insulating tape to prevent them scratching the crankpins and bores when the pistons are refitted.
5 Start with piston/connecting rod assembly No 1. Make sure that the piston rings are still spaced as described in Section 14, then clamp them in position with a piston ring compressor.
6 Insert the piston/connecting rod assembly into the top of cylinder No 1. Lower the big-end in first, guiding it to protect the cylinder bores. Where oil jets are located at the bottoms of the bores, take particular care not to break them off when guiding the connecting rods onto the crankpins.
7 Ensure that the orientation of the piston in its cylinder is correct – the piston crown, connecting rods and big-end bearing caps have markings which must point towards the timing chain/belt end of the engine when the piston is installed in the bore – refer to Section 7 for details.
8 Using a block of wood or hammer handle against the piston crown, tap the assembly into the cylinder until the piston crown is flush with the top of the cylinder **(see illustration)**.
9 Ensure that the bearing shell is still correctly installed. Liberally lubricate the crankpin and both bearing shells with clean engine oil. Taking care not to mark the cylinder bores, tap the piston/connecting rod assembly down the bore and onto the crankpin. Oil the threads and undersides of the bolt heads. Fit the big-end bearing cap, tightening its new retaining nuts/bolts finger-tight at first. Note that the orientation of the bearing cap with respect to the connecting rod must be correct when the two components are reassembled. On diesel engines, the connecting rod and its corresponding bearing cap both have recesses/lugs machined into them – these recesses/lugs must both face in the same direction as the arrow on the piston crown (ie, towards the timing belt end of the engine) when correctly installed – refer to the illustrations in Section 7 for details.
10 On diesel engines, the piston crowns are specially shaped to improve the engine's combustion characteristics. Because of this, pistons 1 and 2 are different to pistons 3 and 4. When correctly fitted, the larger inlet valve chambers on pistons 1 and 2 must face the flywheel/driveplate end of the engine, and the larger inlet valve chambers on the

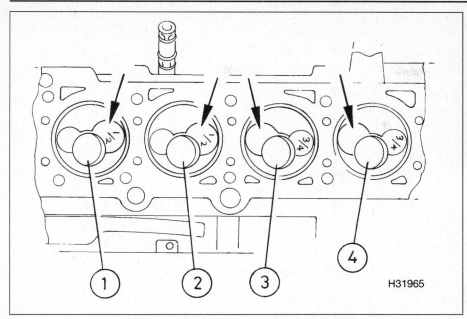

14.10 Piston orientation and coding on diesel engines

14.16 Measure the piston projection with a DTI gauge

remaining pistons must face the timing belt end of the engine. New pistons have number markings on their crowns to indicate their type – 1/2 denotes piston 1 or 2, 3/4 indicates piston 3 or 4 **(see illustration)**.

11 Tighten the retaining bolts/nuts to the specified Stage 1 torque.

12 Tighten the retaining bolts/nuts to the specified Stage 2 setting. On petrol engines, tighten the bolts to the Stage 3 setting.

13 Refit the remaining three piston/connecting rod assemblies in the same way.

14 Rotate the crankshaft by hand. Check that it turns freely; some stiffness is to be expected if new parts have been fitted, but there should be no binding or tight spots.

Diesel engines

15 If new pistons are fitted or if a new short engine is installed, the projection of the piston crowns above the cylinder head at TDC must be measured, to determine the type of head gasket that should be fitted.

16 Turn the cylinder block over (so that the crankcase is facing downwards) and rest it on a stand or wooden blocks. Anchor a DTI gauge to the cylinder block, and zero it on the head gasket mating surface. Rest the gauge probe on No 1 piston crown and turn the crankshaft slowly by hand so that the piston reaches TDC. Measure and record the maximum projection at TDC **(see illustration)**.

17 Repeat the measurement for the remaining pistons and record.

18 If the measurements differ from piston-to-piston, take the highest figure and use this to determine the head gasket type that must be used – refer to the Specifications for details.

19 Note that if the original pistons have been refitted, then a new head gasket of the same type as the original item must be fitted.

All engines

20 Refer to Part A or B of this Chapter (as applicable) and refit the oil pump and pick-up, sump/balancer shaft housing and baffle plate, flywheel and cylinder head.

15 Engine – initial start-up after overhaul and reassembly

1 Refit the remainder of the engine components in the order listed in Section 11 of this Chapter. Refit the engine to the vehicle as described in Section 4 of this Chapter. Double-check the engine oil and coolant levels and make a final check that everything has been reconnected. Make sure that there are no tools or rags left in the engine compartment.

Petrol models

2 Remove the spark plugs, referring to Chapter 1A for details.

3 The engine must be disabled such that it can be turned over using the starter motor but without starting – disable the fuel pump by removing the fuel pump fuse from the fusebox with reference to Chapter 2A and disconnect the wiring plugs from the ignition coils with reference to Chapter 5B.

Caution: To prevent damage to the catalytic converter, it is important to disable the fuel system.

4 Turn the engine using the starter motor until the oil pressure warning lamp goes out. If the lamp fails to extinguish after several seconds of cranking, check the engine oil level and oil filter security. Assuming these are correct, check the security of the oil

pressure switch cabling – do not progress any further until you are satisfied that oil is being pumped around the engine at sufficient pressure.

5 Refit the spark plugs, coil wiring plugs, and the fuel pump fuse.

Diesel models

6 Disconnect the electrical wiring plug from the left-hand side of the cylinder head and remove the fuel supply line from the tandem pump – refer to Chapter 4B.

7 Turn the engine using the starter motor until the oil pressure warning lamp goes out.

8 If the lamp fails to extinguish after several seconds of cranking, check the engine oil level and oil filter security. Assuming these are correct, check the security of the oil pressure switch cabling – do not progress any further until you are satisfied that oil is being pumped around the engine at sufficient pressure.

9 Reconnect the electrical supply to the fuel injectors and refit the fuel line to the tandem pump.

All models

10 Start the engine, but be aware that as fuel system components have been disturbed, the cranking time may be a little longer than usual.

11 While the engine is idling, check for fuel, water and oil leaks. Don't be alarmed if there are some odd smells and the occasional plume of smoke as components heat-up and burn-off oil deposits.

12 Assuming all is well, keep the engine idling until hot water is felt circulating through the top hose.

13 After a few minutes, recheck the oil and coolant levels, and top-up as necessary.

14 There is no need to retighten the cylinder head bolts once the engine has been run following reassembly.

15 If new pistons, rings or crankshaft bearings have been fitted, the engine must be treated as new, and run-in for the first 600 miles. *Do not* operate the engine at full-throttle, or allow it to labour at low engine speeds in any gear. It is recommended that the engine oil and filter are changed at the end of this period.

Notes

Chapter 3
Cooling, heating and ventilation systems

Contents

Degrees of difficulty

Easy, suitable for novice with little experience	**Fairly easy,** suitable for beginner with some experience	**Fairly difficult,** suitable for competent DIY mechanic	**Difficult,** suitable for experienced DIY mechanic	**Very difficult,** suitable for expert DIY or professional

Specifications

Thermostat

Opening temperature	85°C (approx)

Air conditioning system

Compressor clutch air gap:	
FS10 compressor	0.35 to 0.75 mm
Sanden compressor	0.4 to 0.8 mm
Refrigerant R134a	Ford specification WSH-M17B19-A
Refrigerant oil	Ford specification WSH-M1C231-B
Refrigerant capacity:	
Front air conditioning only	700 ± 50 g
Front and rear air conditioning	1050 ± 50 g
Refrigerant oil capacity:	
Front air conditioning only:	
FS10 compressor	200 ml
Sanden compressor	135 ml
Front and rear air conditioning	240 ml

Torque wrench settings	Nm	lbf ft
Petrol engines		
Bumper support bar bolts:		
Outer bolts	40	30
Inner bolt..	20	15
Compressor bolts.......................................	25	18
Compressor driveplate bolt (FS10 compressor)	13	10
Compressor driveplate nut (Sanden compressor)	20	15
Coolant outlet distribution pipe	10	7
Coolant pump pulley bolts................................	25	18
Coolant pump retaining bolts.............................	19	14
Coolant temperature sensor..............................	23	17
Coolant temperature gauge sensor	6	4
Crash bar bolts.......................................	20	15
Engine mountings......................................	Refer to Chapter 2A	
High-pressure switch	8	6
Radiator	10	7
Refrigerant pipe to compressor	20	15
Refrigerant pipe to expansion valve.......................	7	5

Torque wrench settings (continued)

	Nm	lbf ft
Diesel engines		
Bumper support bar bolts:		
Outer bolts	40	30
Inner bolt.	20	15
Compressor bolts.	45	33
Compressor driveplate bolt (FS10 compressor)	13	10
Compressor driveplate nut (Sanden compressor)	20	15
Coolant pump bolts	15	11
Crash bar bolts.	20	15
High-pressure switch	8	6
Radiator	10	7
Refrigerant pipe to compressor	22	16
Refrigerant pipe to expansion valve.	7	5
Thermostat housing retaining bolts	15	11

1 General information and precautions

The cooling system is of the pressurised type, comprising a coolant pump, an aluminium radiator, cooling fan(s), a thermostat, heater matrix, and all associated hoses and switches. The coolant pump is driven by the auxiliary drivebelt. All models are fitted with one or two electric cooling fans, located behind the radiator. The system functions as follows.

When the engine is cold, the coolant in the engine is pumped around the cylinder block and head passages, and through an engine oil cooler (where fitted). After cooling the cylinder bores, combustion surfaces and valve seats, the coolant passes through the heater, and is returned via the cylinder block to the coolant pump. The thermostat is initially closed, preventing the cold coolant from the radiator entering the engine.

When the coolant in the engine reaches a predetermined temperature, the thermostat opens. The cold coolant from the radiator is then allowed to enter the engine through the bottom hose and the hot coolant from the engine flows through the top hose to the radiator. As the coolant circulates through the radiator, it is cooled by the inrush of air when the car is in forward motion. The airflow is supplemented by the action of the cooling fan(s) when necessary. As the coolant reduces in temperature, it passes to the bottom of the radiator and the cycle is repeated.

On some models, the operation of the electrically-operated auxiliary cooling fan(s) is controlled by a thermostatic switch. Whilst on others, the fans are controlled by the engine management ECM, receiving its signal from the engine coolant temperature sensor. At a predetermined coolant temperature, the switch/sensor actuates the fan. The switch then cuts the power supply to the fan when the coolant temperature has reduced sufficiently.

⚠️ *Warning: Do not attempt to remove the expansion tank filler cap, or to disturb any part of the cooling system, while the engine is hot, as there is a high risk of scalding. If the expansion* tank filler cap must be removed before the engine and radiator have fully cooled (even though this is not recommended), the pressure in the cooling system must first be relieved. Cover the cap with a thick layer of cloth to avoid scalding, and slowly unscrew the filler cap until a hissing sound is heard. When the hissing has stopped, indicating that the pressure has reduced, slowly unscrew the filler cap until it can be removed; if more hissing sounds are heard, wait until they have stopped before unscrewing the cap completely. At all times, keep well away from the filler cap opening, and protect your hands.

⚠️ *Warning: Do not allow antifreeze to come into contact with your skin, or with the painted surfaces of the vehicle. Rinse off spills immediately, with plenty of water. Never leave antifreeze lying around in an open container, or in a puddle in the driveway or on the garage floor. Children and pets are attracted by its sweet smell, but antifreeze can be fatal if ingested.*

⚠️ *Warning: If the engine is hot, the electric cooling fan may start rotating even if the engine is not running. Be careful to keep your hands, hair, and any loose clothing well clear when working in the engine compartment.*

⚠️ *Warning: Refer to Section 10 for precautions to be observed when working on models equipped with air conditioning.*

2.3 To release the clip, squeeze together the ends

2 Cooling system hoses – disconnection and renewal

Note: *Refer to the warnings given in Section 1 of this Chapter before proceeding. Hoses should only be disconnected once the engine has cooled sufficiently to avoid scalding.*

1 If the checks described in the relevant Part of Chapter 1 reveal a faulty hose, it must be renewed as follows.

2 First drain the cooling system (see the relevant Part of Chapter 1). If the coolant is not due for renewal, it may be re-used, providing it is collected in a clean container.

3 To disconnect a hose, release the retaining clips, then move them along the hose, clear of the relevant inlet/outlet **(see illustration)**. Carefully work the hose free. The hoses can be removed with relative ease when new – on an older car, they may have stuck.

4 If a hose proves to be difficult to remove, try to release it by rotating its ends before attempting to free it. Gently prise the end of the hose with a blunt instrument (such as a flat-bladed screwdriver), but do not apply too much force, and take care not to damage the pipe stubs or hoses. Note in particular that the radiator inlet stub is fragile; do not use excessive force when attempting to remove the hose. If all else fails, cut the hose with a sharp knife, then slit it so that it can be peeled off in two pieces. Although this may prove expensive if the hose is otherwise undamaged, it is preferable to buying a new radiator. Check first, however, that a new hose is readily available.

5 When fitting a hose, first slide the clips onto the hose, then work the hose into position. On some hose connections alignment marks are provided on the hose and union; if marks are present, ensure they are correctly aligned.

6 Ensure the hose is correctly routed, then slide each clip back along the hose until it passes over the flared end of the relevant inlet/outlet, before tightening the clip securely.

7 Refill the cooling system with reference to the relevant Part of Chapter 1.

8 Check thoroughly for leaks as soon as possible after disturbing any part of the cooling system.

3.6 Disconnect the wiring plug

3.8 Remove the intercooler hoses

3.9 Remove the support bracket (arrowed)

3 Radiator –
removal, inspection and refitting

Note: *Due to the size of the radiator and the restricted access space, the help of an assistant is recommended.*

Note: *Removal of the radiator on the 90 and 115 PS diesel models requires the draining of the AC system. Consult an AC specialist or garage who will have the necessary equipment to carry out this task. It is a criminal offence to knowingly discharge the refrigerant to atmosphere.*

Removal

1 Disconnect the battery as described in Chapter 5A.

2 Jack up and support the front of the vehicle – see *Jacking and vehicle support* in the reference section of this book.

3 With reference to Chapter 11, remove the front bumper cover and the engine under tray.

4 Drain the cooling system as described in the relevant Part of Chapter 1 and then remove the upper radiator hose.

5 Where necessary, remove the cooling fan(s) and shroud as described in Section 5 of this Chapter; the fans and shroud can remain in place on the 130 and 150 PS diesel models.

6 Where fitted disconnect the wiring plug from the radiator mounted thermoswitch **(see illustration)**.

90 and 115 PS diesel engines

7 Remove the engine cover.

8 At the front of the radiator, unbolt and remove the power steering pipe from the radiator and the AC condenser. Remove the supply and return hoses from the intercooler **(see illustration)**.

9 Unbolt the AC refrigerant pipes from the bonnet slam panel **(see illustration)** and then separate the AC refrigerant pipes from the condenser. Immediately cap the refrigerant pipes and the condenser outlet and inlet.

10 Remove the AC condenser mounting bolts and support the AC condenser **(see illustrations)**.

11 Remove the radiator mounting bolts **(see illustrations)** and lower the radiator from the vehicle. Anticipate further coolant spillage as the radiator is lowered.

12 With the radiator removed from the vehicle, unbolt the intercooler, remove the thermoswitch and the rubber mounting blocks **(see illustrations)**.

3.10a Remove the bolts (arrowed) . . .

3.10b . . . and support the condenser

3.11a Remove the left hand (arrowed) . . .

3.11b . . . and the right-hand mounting bolt (arrowed)

3.12a Remove the intercooler . . .

3.12b . . . the thermoswitch . . .

3.12c . . . the upper . . .

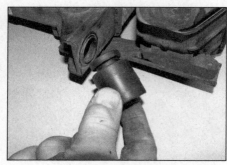

3.12d . . . and the lower rubber mountings

3.14 Unbolt and move the fusebox to one side

130 and 150 PS diesel engines

13 Remove the engine cover.

14 Unbolt and move the fusebox to one side **(see illustration)**. Tie the fusebox securely to one side using stout cord or a cable-tie.

15 Unhook the bonnet release cable from the bonnet latch.

16 Unbolt and then remove the battery side cover **(see illustration)** and then disconnect the wiring plug from the cooling fans.

17 Release the spring clamp from the intercooler hose and then remove the hose. Detach the refrigerant pipe from the cooling fan shroud **(see illustration)**.

18 If not already done so remove the radiator upper hose and then remove both the left-hand and right-hand radiator upper mounting bolts.

19 Remove the air deflector from the bottom of the radiator.

20 Unbolt and then remove the intercooler lower hose.

3.17 Remove the screw (arrowed)

3.16 Remove the battery side cover

21 If necessary support the radiator fan assembly by tying stout cord around the radiator and over the bonnet slammed panel. With the radiator secured in position, remove both the left and right-hand lower mounting bolts.

22 With the aid of an assistant release the securing cord and lower the radiator to the ground.

Petrol engines

23 At the front of the radiator, unbolt and remove the power steering pipe from the radiator and the AC condenser.

24 If not already done so remove the radiator lower coolant hose, anticipating some fluid spillage as the hose is removed.

25 Unbolt and remove the right-hand radiator mounting bolt and recover the mounting rubber. Repeat the procedure on the left-hand radiator mounting bolt.

26 With care, move the radiator and AC

3.32 Ensure the lugs engage in the upper mounting holes

condenser slightly to one side access the condenser retaining bolts. Remove the bolts and then remove the radiator.

Inspection

27 If the radiator has been removed due to suspected blockage, reverse-flush it as described in Section 25 of Chapter 1A (petrol engines) or Section 28 of Chapter 1B (diesel engines). Clean dirt and debris from the radiator fins using an airline (in which case, wear eye protection) or a soft brush. Be careful, as the fins are sharp, and easily damaged.

28 If necessary, a radiator specialist can perform a flow test on the radiator, to establish whether an internal blockage exists.

29 A leaking radiator must be referred to a specialist for permanent repair. Do not attempt to weld or solder a leaking radiator, as damage to the plastic components may result.

30 If the radiator is to be sent for repair or renewed, remove all hoses and switches.

31 Inspect the condition of the radiator mounting rubbers, and renew them if necessary.

Refitting

32 Refitting is a reversal of removal, bearing in mind the following points.

a) *Ensure that the lugs on the top edge of the radiator engage correctly with their corresponding locating holes in the front panel (see illustration).*

b) *Make sure all coolant hoses are correctly reconnected and securely retained by their clips.*

c) *Refill the cooling system as described in the relevant Part of Chapter 1.*

d) *On models with automatic transmission, on completion check the transmission fluid level and, if necessary, top-up as described in the relevant Part of Chapter 1.*

---

4   Thermostat – removal, testing and refitting

1 On petrol models, the thermostat is located on the left-hand end of the cylinder head. Note that Ford only supply the thermostat as a complete assembly including the housing. Aftermarket suppliers offer the thermostat as a separate item. On diesel models, the thermostat is located on the front right-hand corner of the cylinder block.

Removal

Petrol engines

2 Disconnect the battery negative lead, and remove the battery compartment upper and lower panels (see Chapter 5A). **Note:** *Before disconnecting the battery, refer to 'Disconnecting the battery' at the rear of this manual.*

3 Drain the cooling system as described in Chapter 1A.

4 Disconnect the wiring plug for the engine coolant temperature sensor, located on the thermostat housing **(see illustration)**.

5 Release the retaining clips and disconnect the coolant hoses from the thermostat housing **(see illustration)**.

6 Slacken and withdraw the three securing bolts and remove the thermostat housing cover. Using a screwdriver, prise out the retaining circlip, lift the thermostat from its housing and recover the sealing ring. A new sealing ring must be used on refitting **(see illustrations)**.

Diesel engines

7 Remove the engine cover.

8 Drain the cooling system as described in Chapter 1B.

9 Release the spring clip and remove the coolant hose from the thermostat housing.

10 Remove the two securing bolts and remove the housing, complete with the thermostat. Recover the O-ring if it has come loose and then remove the thermostat from the housing by rotating it 90° anti-clockwise **(see illustrations)**.

11 Discard the sealing ring; a new one must be used on refitting.

Testing

12 A rough test of the thermostat may be made by suspending it with a piece of string in a container full of water. Heat the water to bring it to the boil – the thermostat must be fully open by the time the water boils. If not, renew it.

13 If a thermometer is available, the precise opening temperature of the thermostat may be determined; compare with the figure given in the Specifications. The opening temperature should also be marked on the thermostat.

14 A thermostat which fails to close as the water cools must also be renewed.

Refitting

15 Refitting is a reversal of removal, noting the following points:
a) *Use a new thermostat housing cover sealing ring.*
b) *Tighten the housing retaining bolts to the specified torque setting, where given.*
c) *Refill the cooling system as described in the relevant Part of Chapter 1.*
d) *On completion reconnect the battery.*

---

5   Cooling fan(s) –
testing, removal and refitting

Testing

1 Vehicles may be fitted with one or two cooling fans, depending on model. The speed and operation of the fan(s) is controlled in several ways. Some models rely on a radiator-mounted thermoswitch and a control unit to operate the fan(s). Diesel models may have a thermostatic switch fitted, but most

4.4 Disconnect the coolant temperature sensors wiring plugs (arrowed)

4.6a Undo the thermostat housing Torx bolts (arrowed)

4.5 Disconnect the thermostat housing hoses

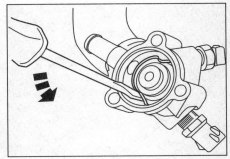
4.6b Prise out the circlips and remove the thermostat

use information gathered from the engine management sensors to control the operation of the cooling fans. All models feature a two-speed cooling fan.

2 If a fan does not appear to work, first check the fuses/fusible links. On most models check the under bonnet fusebox, fuses number 2 and 3. Also check fuse number 18 of the facia-mounted fusebox. If they are good, run the engine until normal operating temperature is reached, then allow it to idle. If the fan does not cut in within a few minutes, switch off the ignition and disconnect the wiring plug from the cooling fan switch. Note that on diesel engines if the ambient temperature is low it may not be possible to raise the engine temperature sufficiently to allow the cooling fans to operate. Bridge the relevant two contacts in the wiring plug using a length of spare wire, and switch on the ignition. If the

fan now operates, the switch is probably faulty and should be renewed.

3 If the switch appears to work, the motor can be checked by disconnecting the motor wiring connector and connecting a 12 volt supply directly to the motor terminals. Proceed with caution and ensure your hands are well clear of the fan blades. If the motor is faulty, it must be renewed, as no spares are available.

4 If the fan still fails to operate, check the cooling fan circuit wiring (Chapter 12). Check each wire for continuity and ensure that all connections are clean and free of corrosion.

5 On models with a cooling fan control unit, if no fault can be found with the fuses/fusible links, wiring, fan switch, or fan motor, then it is likely that the cooling fan control unit is faulty. Testing of the unit should be entrusted to a Ford dealer or specialist; if the unit is faulty it must be renewed.

4.10a Remove the bolts (arrowed) . . .

4.10b . . . remove the housing and rotate the thermostat to remove it

5.11a Remove the screws (upper two shown) . . .

5.11b . . . and remove the fan(s)

5.11c On the 130 and 150 PS engines unbolt the fan from the shroud

5.12 Rotate and lower the fan shroud to remove it

Removal

6 Disconnect the battery negative cable. **Note:** *Before disconnecting the battery, refer to 'Disconnecting the battery' at the rear of this manual.* On diesel engines remove the engine cover.

7 Remove the battery compartment side panels (see Chapter 5A).

8 Unbolt the fusebox from the slam panel and move it to one side. Use cable-ties or stout cord to secure it out of harms way.

9 Disconnect the cooling fan(s) wiring plug and detach the wiring loom from the fan shroud.

10 Remove the bolt from the refrigerant pipe mounted on the fan shroud. Carefully move the pipe to one side.

11 Undo the mounting screws and remove the fan(s). On the 130 and 150 PS diesel engines, remove the fans complete with the fan shroud (see illustrations).

12 If required the fan shroud can now be removed (see illustration).

Refitting

13 Fit the motor assembly to the shroud and securely tighten its retaining nuts. Ensure the motor wiring is correctly routed and clipped securely in position.

14 Refit the shroud assembly to the radiator and securely tighten its retaining bolts.

15 The remainder of refitting is a reversal of removal.

---

6 Cooling system electrical switches and sensors – testing, removal and refitting

Cooling fan(s) thermal switch
Testing

1 Testing of the switch is described in Sec-

tion 5, as part of the electric cooling fan test procedure.

Removal

Note: *The engine and radiator should be allowed to cool completely before the switch is removed.*

2 On some models, the switch is clipped into the radiator upper hose, whilst on others the switch is located in the left-hand side of the radiator, just above the bottom hose stub (see illustrations). On some models, the function of the switch is incorporated into the engine management ECM.

3 Disconnect the battery negative lead. **Note:** *Before disconnecting the battery, refer to 'Disconnecting the battery' at the rear of this manual.* Drain the cooling system to just below the level of the switch (as described in the relevant Part of Chapter 1). Alternatively, have ready a suitable bung to plug the switch aperture in the radiator/hose when the switch is removed. If this method is used, take great care not to damage the radiator/hose, and do not use anything which will allow foreign matter to enter the radiator/hose.

5 Disconnect the wiring plug from the switch.

6 Carefully unscrew the switch from the radiator, or pull out the retaining clip and remove the switch (as applicable), and recover the seal. If the system has not been drained, plug the switch aperture to prevent further coolant loss.

Refitting

7 If the switch was originally fitted using a sealing ring, use a new sealing ring on refitting. Where no sealing ring was fitted, clean the switch threads (where applicable) thoroughly and coat them with fresh sealing compound.

8 Refitting is a reversal of removal. Where applicable, tighten the switch securely and refill (or top-up) the cooling system as described in the relevant Part of Chapter 1.

9 On completion, start the engine and run it until it reaches normal operating temperature. Continue to run the engine, and check that the cooling fan cuts in and out correctly.

Coolant temperature sensor
Testing

10 On all models, the engine coolant

6.2a The thermal switch may be fitted to the upper radiator hose . . .

6.2b . . . or the radiator itself (arrowed)

6.10 The coolant temperature gauge sender is on the underside of the thermostat/coolant outlet housing – petrol models temperature sensor is located on the side or underside of the thermostat housing on the left-hand end of the cylinder head (see illustration). The correct operation of this sensor is essential for the engine management system to determine the correct fuelling and running of the engine.

11 The sensor contains a thermistor – an electronic component whose electrical resistance (or voltage) decreases at a predetermined rate as its temperature rises. If the sensor is faulty, it must be renewed.

Typical sensor values

Volts	°C
1.33	60
1.02	70
0.78	80
0.60	90
0.46	100
0.35	110
0.27	120

12 If a fault develops, backprobe the sensor and monitor the voltage returned to the ECU as the engine temperature increases. Alternatively have the vehicle's self-diagnosis memory interrogated by a Ford dealer or specialist. A faulty sensor will normally log a fault code in the ECM.

Removal

13 Either partially drain the cooling system to just below the level of the sensor (as described in the relevant Part of Chapter 1), or have ready a suitable plug which can be used to plug the sensor aperture whilst it is removed. If a plug is used, take great care not to damage the sensor unit aperture, and do not use anything which will allow foreign matter to enter the cooling system.

14 Disconnect the wiring connector from the sensor.

15 On petrol models, unscrew the sensor from the engine. On diesel models pull out the retaining clip, remove the sensor and recover the sealing ring (see illustrations).

16 With the sensor removed, use a multimeter to check the resistance (see illustration). This should change with temperature.

Refitting

17 Fit a new sealing washer then fit the sensor, tightening it securely.

18 On diesel models, renew the sealing ring and secure the sensor in place with the retaining clip.

19 Reconnect the wiring connector then refill the cooling system as described in the relevant Part of Chapter 1 or top-up as described in Weekly checks.

Engine management system temperature sensor

20 On petrol models, the engine management system coolant temperature sensor (ETC) is located in the in the thermostat housing on the left-hand end of the cylinder head. The

6.15a Remove the U-shaped retainer . . .

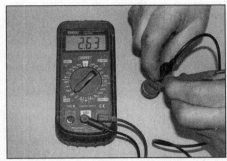

6.16 Check the resistance of the sensor

6.15b . . . and pull the sensor from the housing

6.20 Engine coolant temperature sensor (ECT) – petrol models

upper of the two sensors is the ETC sensor (see illustration).

21 The sensor is a thermistor (see paragraph 11). The fuel injection/engine management electronic control module (ECM) supplies the sensor with a set voltage and then, by measuring the current flowing in the sensor circuit, it determines the engine's temperature. This information is then used, in conjunction with other inputs, to control the injector timing, the idle speed, etc. It is also used to determine the glow plug preheating and post-heating times.

22 If the sensor circuit should fail to provide adequate information, the ECM's back-up facility will override the sensor signal. In this event, the ECM assumes a predetermined setting which will allow the fuel injection/engine management system to run, albeit at reduced efficiency. When this

occurs, the warning light on the instrument panel will come on, and the advice of a Ford dealer or suitably-equipped garage should be sought.

Removal and refitting

23 Refer to the information given in paragraphs 13 to 19.

Radiator fan control unit

24 On some models, a control unit is fitted to the front left-hand side of the engine compartment to operate the cooling fans (see illustrations).

Removal and refitting

25 To remove the unit, release the retaining clips, and disconnect the wiring plugs.

26 Undo the retaining screws and remove the unit.

27 Refitting is a reversal of removal.

6.24a Radiator cooling fans control unit – petrol models . . .

6.24b . . . and some diesel models

7.4 Slacken the coolant pump pulley bolts

7.9 The coolant pump is secured by five bolts

7.12 Fit a new seal to the pump

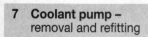

7 Coolant pump –
removal and refitting

Petrol engines

Removal

1 Drain the cooling system as described in Chapter 1A. **Note:** *If an aluminium engine component which comes into contact with the coolant has been renewed, then the coolant must also be renewed. Used coolant will not protect new aluminium from corrosion.*

2 With reference to Chapter 4A, remove the air cleaner assembly.

3 Fully slacken off the right-hand engine mounting nuts, but do not remove them.

4 Slacken the coolant pump pulley bolts **(see illustration).** Do not remove the bolts at this stage.

5 Using a spanner on the tensioner pulley, slacken the auxiliary belt, and slip the belt from the coolant pump pulley.

6 Unbolt the belt tensioner assembly. Use a long lever and a block of wood to move the engine away from the inner wing and then manoeuvre the tensioner from the engine.

7 Fully unbolt and remove the coolant pump pulley.

8 Jack up and support the front of the vehicle (see *Jacking and vehicle support* in the Reference section of this manual). Remove the right-hand roadwheel.

9 Place a suitable container below the coolant pump. Remove the bolts and then remove the coolant pump **(see illustration)**. Note that the lower bolts are difficult to access. The pump may require a sharp tap from a soft-faced mallet to free it from the engine block.

10 Using a long lever, and a suitable block of wood to protect the inner wing, lever the engine away from the inner wing. By levering

the engine away from the inner wing there will be just enough room to remove the coolant pump.

11 Recover the sealing ring.

Refitting

12 Ensure that the pump and cylinder block mating surfaces are clean and dry and position a new seal on the pump **(see illustration)**.

13 Fit the coolant pump to the cylinder block and evenly tighten its retaining bolts to the specified torque setting. Note that due to the offset of the bolt holes, the pump will only fit correctly in one position.

14 The remainder of refitting is a reversal of removal, noting to tighten all nuts/bolts to their specified torque (where available), and refill the cooling system as described in Chapter 1A.

Diesel engines

Removal

15 Drain the cooling system as described in Chapter 1B.

16 Remove the camshaft timing belt as described in Chapter 2B, noting the following points:
  a) The lower part of the timing belt guard need not be removed.
  b) The timing belt should be left in position on the crankshaft sprocket.
  c) Cover the timing belt with a cloth to protect it from coolant.

17 Unscrew the timing belt idler pulley, and push the pulley downwards approximately 30 mm.

18 Unscrew the coolant pump retaining bolts, and remove the pump from the engine block. If the pump is faulty, it must be renewed **(see illustration)**.

Refitting

19 If the coolant pump is being renewed because of a worn bearing the timing belt must be renewed. Refitting is a reversal of removal, bearing in mind the following points.
  a) Fit the coolant pump with a new O-ring.
  b) Lubricate the O-ring with coolant.
  c) Install the pump with the cast lug facing down.
  d) Refill the cooling system as described in Chapter 1B.

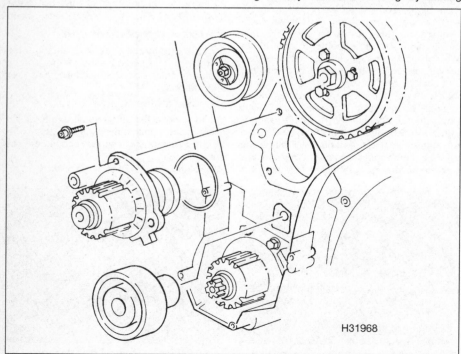

H31968

7.18 Coolant pump removal – diesel engines

Auxiliary coolant pump

20 An additional coolant pump is fitted to all vehicles to supply the rear heater unit.

Removal

21 The pump is mounted on the bulkhead to the rear of the coolant expansion bottle **(see illustration)**.

22 Drain the coolant to below the level of the pump, or fit proprietary hose clamps to the inlet and outlet hoses.

23 Remove the spring clips from the hoses and pull the hoses from the pump.

24 Disconnect the wiring plug and unbolt the pump from the bulkhead.

Refitting

25 Refitting is a reversal of the removal procedure. Top-up the coolant level and check the system for leaks.

8 Heating and ventilation system – general information

1 The heating/ventilation system consists of a fully-adjustable blower motor (housed behind the facia), face level vents in the centre and at each end of the facia, and air ducts to the front footwells.

2 Air distribution ducts also run alongside the centre console to provide air to the rear. A second heater unit for the rear passenger compartment is fitted behind the left-hand load area trim panel. Separate roof-mounted controls are used to operate the rear heater, except on models fitted with climate control. On models with climate control the rear heater is controlled from the main facia-mounted climate control panel.

3 The heater control unit is located in the facia, and the controls operate flap valves to deflect and mix the air flowing through the various parts of the heating/ventilation system. The flap valves are contained in the air distribution housing, which acts as a central distribution unit, passing air to the various ducts and vents.

4 Cold air enters the system through the grille at the lower front edge of the windscreen. If required, the airflow is boosted by the blower,

7.21 The auxiliary coolant pump

and then flows through the various ducts, according to the settings of the controls. Stale air is expelled through ducts at the rear of the vehicle. If warm air is required, the cold air is passed over the heater matrix, which is heated by the engine coolant.

5 The outside air supply to the vehicle can be closed off which is useful to prevent unpleasant odours entering from outside the vehicle. This facility should only be used briefly, as the re-circulated air inside the vehicle will soon become stale.

6 In the event of a fault with the HVAC (heating, ventilation/air conditioning) a fault code will normally be logged. Before dismantling any component parts of the HVAC system it is recommended that the system is interrogated for any stored fault codes by a Ford dealer or suitably-equipped garage.

9 Heater/ventilation components – removal and refitting

General information

1 All models feature air conditioning. The information in this section is only applicable to the components of the heating and ventilation system. The removal and refitting of the specific air conditioning system components is described in Section 11. Also available as options are a booster heater and an additional heater on diesel models. Both heaters ignite fuel supplied from the main tank. Due to the efficiency of the direct

injection diesel engine, not enough heat output is available to provide adequate heating. The booster heater increases the coolant temperature, by burning diesel metered by a separate pump from the main fuel return pipe. If the outside temperature is below 10°C, or the engine coolant temperature is below 75°C, the heater starts automatically. As soon as the coolant temperature reaches 80°C, the heater output is reduced from 3 kW to 1.5 kW. If the temperature reaches 85°C, the heater is switched off. There is no manual control of the booster heater. The additional heater is supplied with fuel from the tank via a separate metering pump, with an additional battery providing the power supply. The switch-on time of the heater can be preset, so that the heater will operate with the engine running, switched off before the engine is started, or switched on or off manually for immediate heat output.

Front control unit

2 Disconnect the battery negative lead. **Note:** *Before disconnecting the battery, refer to 'Disconnecting the battery' at the rear of this manual.*

3 Carefully prise the trim from around the heater control knob **(see illustration)**.

4 Undo the four screws, and pull forward the control panel. Disconnect the wiring plugs as they become visible, noting their locations as they are removed **(see illustration)**.

5 On vehicles fitted with manual AC, it is possible to remove the blower motor fan speed switch from the rear of the panel.

6 Refitting is a reversal of removal, but ensure that the wiring plugs are securely reconnected in their original locations.

Front blower motor

7 Remove the passenger side glovebox as described in Chapter 11.

8 Disconnect the wiring plug from the blower motor **(see illustration)**.

9 Remove the soundproofing, release the retaining tab, turn the motor anti-clockwise, and withdraw it from the housing **(see illustrations)**.

10 Refitting is a reversal of removal.

9.3 Carefully prise the trim from around the heater control knobs

9.4 Undo the screws and remove the panel (arrowed)

9.8 Disconnect the wiring plug

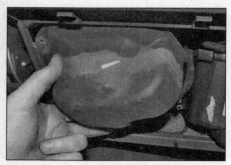

9.9a Remove the insulation . . .

9.9b . . . release the locking tab (arrowed) . . .

9.9c . . . rotate the motor . . .

9.9d . . . and remove it

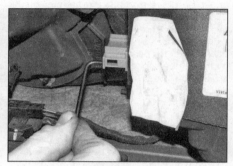

9.12a Remove the bolt . . .

9.12b . . . and remove the resistor

Front blower motor resistor

11 Remove the passenger side glovebox as described in Chapter 11.

12 Disconnect the wiring plug, undo the retaining bolt, and remove the resistor **(see illustrations)**.

13 Refitting is the reverse of removal.

Front heater unit

14 The removal of the heater unit requires the complete removal of both the upper and lower facia panels. Whilst not an especially difficult task, it is a time-consuming one.

15 Have a AC specialist degas and drain the AC system before starting work.

16 Disconnect the battery negative lead. **Note:** *Before disconnecting the battery, refer to 'Disconnecting the battery' at the rear of this manual.*

17 Ensure that engine has cooled completely. and then remove the windscreen cowl panel

and the bulkhead panel, as described in Chapter 11.

18 With reference to Chapter 12, remove the wiper linkage and motor.

19 With the wiper linkage removed, disconnect the wiring plug from the alarm horn. Unbolt the horn from its mounting bracket and then remove the bracket. Slacken, but do not remove the bolt now exposed – this is the mounting for the right-hand side of the air distribution panel **(see illustration)**.

20 With reference to the appropriate routine maintenance Chapter, remove the pollen filter and then unbolt and remove the pollen filter housing. Slacken, but do not remove the left-hand air distribution duct **(see illustrations)**.

21 At the rear of the engine compartment, locate the heater matrix hoses and trace them back to the point where they connect to the bulkhead stub pipes. Place a draining

container underneath the hoses, to catch the coolant that will escape when they are disconnected.

22 Apply proprietary hose clamps to both heater hoses, then release the clips and disconnect the hoses from the bulkhead stubs. Allow the coolant from the heater circuit to collect in the draining container. Alternatively, drain the coolant system as described in the relevant Part of Chapter 1.

23 If you have access to a source of compressed air, apply it carefully at *low pressure* to the left-hand bulkhead stub and blow the remainder of the coolant from the heater matrix.

⚠️ *Warning: Always wear eye protection when working with compressed air.*

24 If you do not have access to compressed air, bear in mind that a large volume of coolant will remain in the heater circuit and that this

9.19 Remove the horn from the bulkhead

9.20a Remove the pollen filter housing . . .

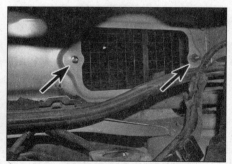

9.20b . . . to access the mounting bolts (arrowed)

9.29 Remove the wiring loom

9.30 Remove the mounting bolts from the crash bar

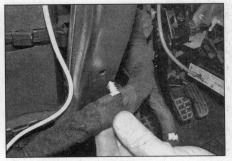

9.34a Release the loom . . .

9.34b . . . cutting the cable-ties as required (arrowed)

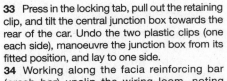

9.36a Remove the upper support strut . . .

9.36b . . . and the pedal box retaining bolt (arrowed)

may escape as the heater unit is removed from the inside of the car.

25 Remove the heater controls, as described in this section.

26 Remove the upper facia panel as described in Chapter 11.

27 Remove the lower facia panel as described in Chapter 11.

28 Working under the bonnet, fully remove the previously-loosened air distribution duct mounting bolts.

29 Note the position of the wiring loom and then remove it from the air distribution panel (see illustration)

30 Work along the steel crash bar and remove the mounting bolts (see illustration).

31 Check that all fixings and wiring connectors have been removed or released and then remove the panel from the vehicle.

32 With reference to Chapter 10 remove the steering wheel and column.

33 Press in the locking tab, pull out the retaining clip, and tilt the central junction box towards the rear of the car. Undo the two plastic clips (one each side), manoeuvre the junction box from its fitted position, and lay to one side.

34 Working along the facia reinforcing bar (crash bar) unclip the wiring loom, noting the location of each section of the loom as it is removed. Several cable-ties will require cutting and at least one loom clip will require unscrewing (see illustrations).

35 Unbolt and remove the left and right-hand earth mounting bolts.

36 Unbolt and remove the reinforcing bar mounting bolts from the bulkhead and pedal box (see illustrations).

37 Unbolt the heater unit from the reinforcing bar, check that all the sections of the wring loom have been removed from the crash bar and then remove the crash bar from the vehicle (see illustrations).

38 Note the locations of the wiring plugs on the heater unit and then disconnect them from the heater unit (see illustration).

39 Disconnect the refrigerant lines from the AC evaporator. Discard the O ring seals – new ones must be fitted.

40 Working under the bonnet, locate and remove the heater unit mounting bolts. These are hidden behind flaps cut into the soundproofing insulation on the bulkhead. Access to these fixings is very limited and a socket set with an assortment of extension bars and a universal joint is essential. On diesel models remove the vacuum solenoids to access one of the fixings

41 Check that all the wiring connectors have been removed and then withdraw the heater unit from the vehicle (see illustrations).

42 Refitting is the reverse of removal, noting the following points.

a) Ensure the ducts, elbows and gaiter are

9.37a Remove the bolts from the heater unit . . .

9.37b . . . and then remove the crash bar

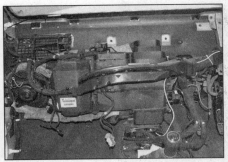

9.38 Unclip and disconnect the remaining sections of the wiring loom

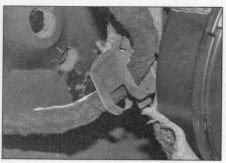

9.41a Release the loom retaining clip as the heater is removed . . .

9.41b . . . and avoid damaging the evaporator drain as the heater unit is withdrawn

9.44a Remove the screws . . .

9.44b . . . and slide the matrix from the heater unit

all securely joined to the housing and the wiring/cables are correctly routed before securing the housing in position.
b) Ensure the coolant hoses are securely reconnected to the matrix.
c) On completion, top-up and bleed the

cooling system as described in the relevant Part of Chapter 1.

Front heater matrix

43 Remove the heater unit as described earlier in this Section, noting that it is only

9.48 Remove the temperature control motor

9.51 Remove the recirculation flap motor (arrowed)

necessary to move the heater unit 40 to 60 mm away from the bulkhead to provide sufficient clearance for the matrix pipes.
44 Undo the screws, and withdraw the heater matrix from the top of the heater unit (see illustrations). Protect your hands as you do this – the matrix fins are sharp and can cause injury.
45 Refitting is a reversal of removal. New heater matrices will be supplied with self-adhesive foam padding strips – these should be affixed to the edges of the core and the upper flange before the matrix is inserted into the heater unit.

Temperature control motor

46 The control motor is located on the top of the heater unit. Remove the lower and upper facia panel as described in Chapter 11.
47 Remove the air distribution panel as described in paragraphs 16 to 29 of this section.
48 Note the position of the index mark on the gears, unplug the wiring connector, unscrew the retaining screw and remove the motor (see illustration).
49 Refitting is a reversal of removal. Align the index marks on the motor and flap gears.

Fresh air/ recirculation flap motor

50 Remove the lower and upper facia panel as described in Chapter 11. Remove the air distribution panel as described in paragraphs 16 to 29 of this section.
51 Unplug the wiring connector, note the position of the index mark on the gears, remove the fixing screws and remove the motor (see illustration).
52 Refitting is a reversal of removal. Align the index marks on the motor and flap gears.

Air distribution flap motor

53 The control motor is located on the right-hand side of the heater unit behind the lower facia panel.
54 Remove the centre console and lower facia panel as described in Chapter 11.
55 Disconnect the wiring plug, remove the three mounting screws and remove the control motor.
56 Refitting is a reversal of removal.

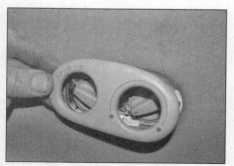

9.57 Remove the trim piece

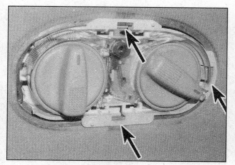

9.58a Release the retaining clips (arrowed) . . .

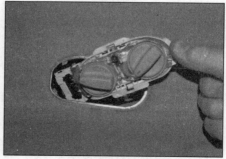

9.58b . . . remove the unit . . .

Rear control unit

57 The rear control unit is fitted into the headlining above the rear doors. Carefully prise the trim from the controls **(see illustration)**.

58 Release the three retaining clips using a small screwdriver and manoeuvre the control panel from the headlining. Disconnect the wiring plugs as the unit is withdrawn **(see illustrations)**. Refitting is a reversal of removal.

Rear blower motor

59 Remove the left-hand rear luggage compartment side trim as described in Chapter 11, Section 33.

60 Disconnect the wiring plug, undo the three screws, and remove the blower motor **(see illustration)**.

61 Refitting is a reversal of removal.

Rear blower motor resistor

62 Remove the left-hand rear luggage compartment trim panel as described in Chapter 11, Section 33.

63 Disconnect the wiring plug, undo the retaining screw, and remove the resistor pack **(see illustrations)**.

64 Refitting is a reversal of removal.

Rear heater unit

65 Remove the left-hand rear luggage compartment side trim panel as described in Chapter 11, Section 33.

66 Place a suitable container underneath the heater hoses, to catch the coolant that will escape when the hoses are disconnected.

67 Apply proprietary hose clamps to both heater hoses, then release the clips and disconnect the hoses from the heater stubs. Allow the coolant from the heater to collect in the draining container **(see illustrations)**. Alternatively, drain the coolant system as described in the relevant Part of Chapter 1.

68 Disconnect the wiring plugs from the blower motor, resistor and temperature control valve.

69 Unscrew the four retaining bolts, and remove the heater unit from the vehicle.

70 Refitting is a reversal of removal. If necessary, top-up the cooling system as described in the relevant Part of Chapter 1.

Rear heater matrix

71 Remove the rear heater unit as described in Paragraphs 65 to 69. On models fitted with rear air conditioning have the AC system evacuated by a Ford dealer or suitably-equipped garage.

72 With the unit on the bench, prise off the metal retaining clips **(see illustration)**.

73 Working around the circumference of the heater unit, release the plastic retaining clips with a small screwdriver. The plastic tabs are extremely fragile, so proceed with caution. If the tabs are damaged during removal it

is possible to obtain additional metal clips. These can be fitted next to the damaged plastic tabs.

74 Separate the two halves of the heater

unit, and lift the matrix from the casing **(see illustrations)**.

75 Refitting is a reversal of removal. New heater matrices may be supplied with

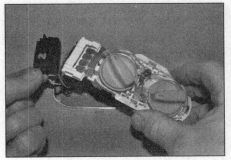
9.58c . . . and disconnect the wiring plug

9.60 Remove the screws (arrowed)

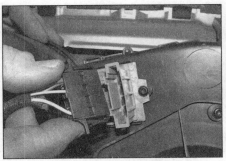
9.63a Disconnect the wiring plug . . .

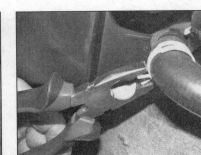
9.63b . . . remove the fixing screw and withdraw the resistor pack

9.67a Clamp the hoses . . .

9.67c . . . and drain the coolant

9.67b . . . release the spring clamps . . .

9.72 Remove the spring clips

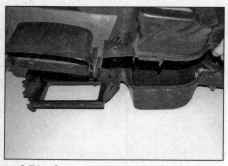

9.74a Separate the two halves of the heater unit . . .

9.74b . . . and remove the matrix

self-adhesive foam padding strips – these should be affixed to the outer circumference of the matrix. Top-up the cooling system as described in the relevant Part of Chapter 1.

Booster heater

76 All diesel-powered vehicles have a fuel-fed booster heater fitted to provide cabin heating **(see illustration)**. This is required because the diesel engine does not initially produce sufficient waste heat to warm the vehicle cabin. The heater operates when the ambient temperature is below 10°C and the coolant temperature is below 75°C. Because the heater is fuel fired a small amount of smoke will be produced when the heater starts up.

77 Chock the front wheels, then jack up the rear of the vehicle and support on axle stands (see *Jacking and vehicle support*).

78 Working underneath the vehicle on the left-hand side in front of the rear wheel, undo the clamp bolt, disconnect the air intake pipe from the heater and pull the pipe from the sill **(see illustration)**.

79 Undo the bolt securing the silencer pipe.

80 Unscrew the two mounting bolts, and lower the unit.

81 Apply proprietary hose clamps to both coolant hoses, then release the clips and disconnect the hoses from the heater stubs. Disconnect the fuel supply pipe.

82 Disconnect the wiring plug, and manoeuvre the heater from under the vehicle **(see illustration)**. No dismantling of the heater is advised.

83 Refitting is a reversal of removal. Top-up

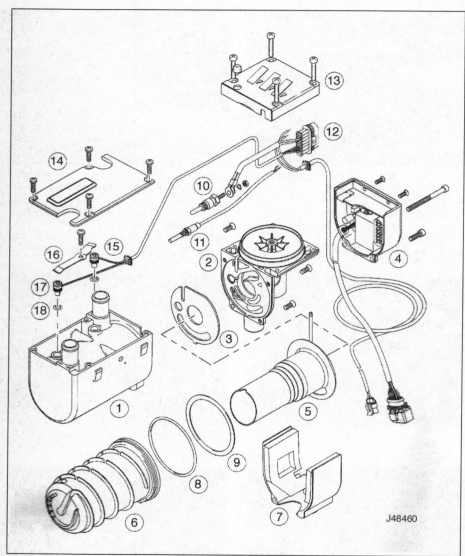

9.76 Diesel booster heater details

1 Water jacket	*7 Blower motor cover*	*13 Cover*
2 Combustion blower	*8 O-ring*	*14 Water jacket cover*
3 Gasket	*9 Gasket*	*15 Temperature sensor*
4 Heater module	*10 Glow plug*	*16 Spring*
5 Combustion chamber	*11 Flame sensor*	*17 Over heat sensor*
6 Heat exchanger	*12 Wiring loom*	*18 O-ring*

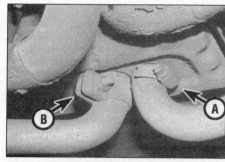

9.78 Booster heater intake pipe clamp (A) and silencer pipe clamp (B)

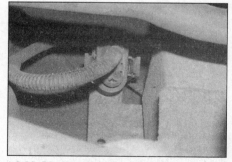

9.82 Disconnect the wiring plug located just behind the booster heater

the coolant level as described in the relevant Part of Chapter 1.

Booster heater fuel metering pump

84 Chock the front wheels, then jack up the rear of the vehicle and support on axle stands (see *Jacking and vehicle support*).
85 The pump is located just in front of the fuel tank, on the right-hand side of the vehicle. Disconnect the wiring plug from the pump, and remove the retaining nut **(see illustration)**.
86 Release the retaining clips, and disconnect the fuel pipes from the pump. Note the fitted positions of the pipes, and be prepared for fuel spillage.
87 Refitting is a reversal of removal.

Additional heater

88 At the time of writing, no information concerning the additional heater was available.

10 Air conditioning system – general information and precautions

General information

1 An air conditioning system is fitted to all models. It combines a conventional air heating system with an air cooling and dehumidifying system. This allows greater control over the temperature and humidity of the air inside the car, giving increased comfort and rapid window demisting. On models equipped with automatic climate control, a rear passenger cabin air conditioning system is also available. The heater/air conditioning control unit is located behind the left-hand rear panel trim, with the conditioned air being routed through ducting by the rear pillar to emerge through vents in the rear passenger headlining.
2 The cooling side of the system works in the same way as a domestic refrigerator. Refrigerant gas, contained in a sealed network of alloy pipes, is drawn into a belt-driven compressor, and is forced through a condenser mounted on the front of the radiator. On entering the condenser, the refrigerant changes state from gas to liquid and releases heat, which is absorbed by the air flowing into the front of the engine compartment through the condenser. The liquid refrigerant passes through an expansion valve to an evaporator, where it changes from liquid under high pressure to gas under low pressure. This change in state is accompanied by a drop in temperature, which cools the evaporator. Air passing through the evaporator is cooled before flowing into the air distribution unit. The refrigerant then returns to the compressor, and the cycle begins again.
3 The cooled air passes to the air distribution unit, where it is blended with hot air blown through the heater matrix to achieve the desired temperature in the passenger compartment. When the air conditioning

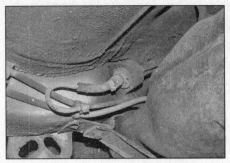

9.85 Disconnect the booster heater fuel metering pump

system is operating in automatic mode, a series of air valves controlled by servo motors automatically regulate the cabin temperature by blending hot and cold air.
4 The heating side of the system works in the same way as on models without air conditioning (see Section 8).
5 The operation of the system can be manually-controlled or automatically-managed by an electronic control unit, which controls the electric cooling fan, the compressor, and the facia-mounted warning light. Any problems with the system should be referred to a Ford dealer or suitably-equipped garage. The system has a built-in, self-diagnostic capability, but specialist equipment is needed to interpret the information it produces.

Precautions

• When working on a vehicle equipped with air conditioning, it is necessary to observe special precautions whenever dealing with any part of the air conditioning system, or its associated components. If for any reason the refrigerant lines must be disconnected, you must entrust this task to a Ford dealer or an air conditioning specialist. Similarly, the system can only be evacuated and recharged by a dealer or air conditioning specialist.

⚠ **Warning: The air conditioning system contains a pressurised liquid refrigerant. If the system is discharged in an uncontrolled manner without the aid of specialist equipment, the refrigerant will boil as soon as it is exposed to the atmosphere, causing severe frostbite if it comes into contact unprotected skin.**

11.5 Undo the bolt and disconnect the refrigerant pipes (arrowed)

In addition, certain refrigerants, in the presence of a naked flame (including a lit cigarette), will oxidise to form a highly poisonous gas. It is therefore extremely dangerous to disconnect any part of the air conditioning system without specialised knowledge and equipment.

• Uncontrolled discharging of the refrigerant can also be damaging to the environment, as certain refrigerants contain CFCs.
• Do not operate the air conditioning system if it is known to be short of refrigerant, as this will damage the compressor.

11 Air conditioning system components – removal and refitting

⚠ **Warning: Do not attempt to discharge the refrigerant circuit yourself (refer to the precautions given in Section 10). It is a criminal offence to knowingly discharge refrigerant to the atmosphere. Have the air conditioning system discharged by a garage or air conditioning specialist. Many specialists now offer a mobile service. On completion of the work, have the system pressure-tested and the AC system re-gassed with the correct amount of refrigerant.**

Compressor

1 Disconnect the negative cable from the battery terminal. **Note:** *Before disconnecting the battery, refer to 'Disconnecting the battery' at the rear of this manual.*
2 Have the air conditioning system discharged by a qualified engineer.
3 Remove the auxiliary drivebelt as described in the relevant Part of Chapter 2.
4 On petrol engine models remove the rear cover plate from the compressor and then remove the upper and lower support brackets.
5 Unscrew the retaining bolt(s) and disconnect the refrigerant lines from the compressor. Remove the O-ring seals and discard them – new ones must be used on reconnection. Plug the open pipes and ports to prevent the ingress of moisture **(see illustration)**.
6 Disconnect the compressor wiring plug **(see illustration)**.

11.6 Disconnect the compressor wiring plug

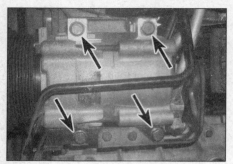

11.7 Undo the bolts (arrowed) and remove the compressor (petrol model shown)

11.11a Remove the spring clips . . .

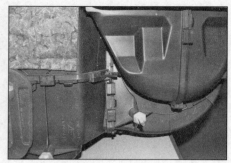

11.11b . . . and release the locking tabs

11.12a Split the housing . . .

11.12b . . . and withdraw the evaporator

7 Unscrew the securing bolts, then remove the compressor from its mounting bracket **(see illustration)**. On diesel and some petrol models the bolts are removed from the front of the compressor.
8 Refitting is a reversal of the removal procedure; ensure that all fixings are tightened to the specified torque, where given. On

completion fit new O-rings (lightly lubricated with the correct compressor oil) to the line connections and then have the system evacuated and recharged.

Front evaporator/heater matrix

9 Observe the warnings at the start of this section and have the AC system discharged

by a suitably-equipped garage or mobile air conditioning specialist.
10 The front evaporator is contained within the main heater unit along with the heater matrix. Remove the complete heater unit as described in paragraphs 14 to 41 in section 9 of this Chapter.
11 With the heater unit on the bench remove the soundproofing insulation, release the spring clips, depress the locking tabs and split the heater unit apart **(see illustrations)**.
12 Withdraw the evaporator from the heater housing **(see illustrations)**.
13 Refitting is the reverse of removal, noting the following points.
  a) *Ensure that the evaporator drain pipe is correctly positioned on the rear of the heater unit.*
  b) *Ensure the wiring/cables are correctly routed before securing the housing in position.*
  c) *Ensure the coolant hoses are securely reconnected to the matrix.*
  d) *Top-up and bleed the cooling system as described in the relevant Part of Chapter 1.*
  e) *On completion fit new O-rings (lightly lubricated with the correct compressor oil) to the line connections and then have the system evacuated and recharged.*

Rear evaporator/heater matrix

14 Have the air conditioning system discharged by a qualified engineer.
15 Ensure that engine has cooled completely before starting work.
16 The rear evaporator is contained within the rear heater unit.
17 Disconnect the negative cable from the battery terminal. **Note:** *Before disconnecting the battery, refer to 'Disconnecting the battery' at the rear of this manual.*
18 Drain the cooling system as described in the relevant Part of Chapter 1.
19 Remove the left-hand luggage compartment trim panel as described in Chapter 11, Section 33.
20 Note their fitted positions (label each connection to avoid confusion on refitting), then disconnect the four wiring plugs from the evaporator/heater housing. Disconnect the water drain pipe from the housing **(see illustration)**.

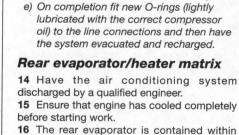

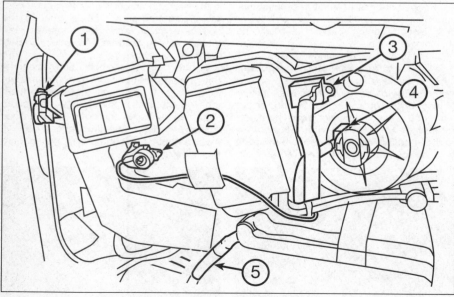

11.20 Rear air conditioning unit

1	*Air distribution servo motor*	
2	*Temperature flap servo motor*	3 *Blower control unit*
		4 *Blower motor*
		5 *Water drain pipe*

21 Where fitted, release the cable-ties, unscrew the retaining bolt, and remove the headlining air duct by pulling it out at the base, and down from the headlining guide.

22 Undo the bolt and detach the refrigerant pipes from the rear expansion valve.

23 Release the retaining clips and disconnect the coolant pipes.

24 Unscrew the four bolts and remove the heater/evaporator housing.

25 Refitting is the reverse of removal, noting the following points.

   a) *Ensure that the evaporator drain pipe is correctly positioned.*

   b) *Ensure the wiring/cables are correctly routed before securing the housing in position.*

   c) *Ensure the coolant hoses are securely reconnected to the matrix.*

   d) *Top-up and bleed the cooling system as described in the relevant Part of Chapter 1.*

   e) *On completion fit new O-rings (lightly lubricated with the correct compressor oil) to the line connections and then have the system evacuated and recharged.*

Receiver/dryer

26 Have the air conditioning system discharged by a qualified engineer.

27 Apply the handbrake, then jack up the front of the vehicle and support it on axle stands (see *Jacking and vehicle support*). The receiver/dryer housing is part of the condenser.

28 With reference to Chapter 11, remove the front bumper cover.

29 Remove the sealing plug. Remove the circlip, insert a M5 bolt into the cap and withdraw the receiver/drier from the housing.

30 Refitting is a reversal of removal. On completion fit new O-rings (lightly lubricated with the correct compressor oil) to the sealing plug and then have the system evacuated and recharged.

High-pressure switch

31 The high-pressure switch is located next to the horns, behind the bumper on the right-hand side.

32 There is no need to have the refrigerant evacuated from the system, as a non-return valve in the receiver/dryer seals the port as the switch is removed. However cautioned should be used, in case the non-return valve is faulty.

33 Disconnect the wiring plug from the switch.

34 Unscrew the switch from the pipe.

35 Install the switch, tightening it to the specified torque.

36 Reconnect the wiring plug, and lower the vehicle to the ground.

Front expansion valve

37 Have the air conditioning system discharged by a qualified engineer. The expansion valve is located on the engine compartment rear bulkhead.

38 Undo the single bolt, and disconnect

11.38 Undo the bolt and disconnect the pipes from the expansion valve

the refrigerant pipe from the valve **(see illustration)**. Discard the O-ring seals, new ones must be fitted.

39 Slacken and remove the two retaining bolts, and remove the expansion valve **(see illustration)**.

40 Refitting is a reversal of removal, noting that the new O-ring seals should be lubricated with refrigerant oil prior to installation.

Rear expansion valve

41 Have the air conditioning system discharged by a qualified engineer.

42 Remove the left-hand seat from the second and third row of seats.

43 Remove the left-hand load space trim panel as described in Chapter 11, Section 33.

44 Undo the single bolt and detach the refrigerant pipes from the expansion valve. Discard the O-ring seals, new ones must be fitted.

45 Undo the retaining bolts, and remove the expansion valve.

46 Refitting is a reversal of removal, noting that the new O-ring seals should be lubricated with refrigerant oil prior to installation.

De-icing switch

47 On petrol engine models, in order to prevent the compressor from icing up, a de-icing switch probe measures the surface temperature of the evaporator cooling fins. If the temperature of the fins drops below 1°C, the switch disengages the electromagnetic clutch of the compressor. As soon as the temperature rises above 2.5°C, the clutch re-engages.

11.54 Remove the bumper bar mounting bolts

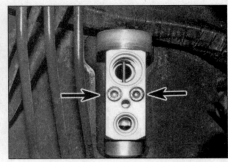

11.39 Remove the bolts (arrowed)

48 Remove the lower and upper facia panels as described in Chapter 11, Section 33.

49 Remove the air distribution panel as described in Section 9 of this Chapter.

50 Pull out the probe from the evaporator. Undo the two Torx screws and remove the switch relay. Remove the switch and harness.

51 Refitting is a reversal of removal.

Condenser

52 Have the air conditioning system discharged by a qualified engineer.

53 Remove the front bumper cover as described in Chapter 11.

54 Unbolt and remove the bumper support bar **(see illustration)**.

55 Remove the bolt from the AC service port support bracket.

56 Unbolt the refrigerant pipes from the condenser. Discard the O-rings.

57 On vehicles built up to 02/2002 the condenser mounting bolts are hidden behind the radiator shroud. Place a block of wood in front of the condenser core and drill four 16 mm holes through the plastic panel to access the mountings.

58 Remove the four bolts and detach the condenser from the radiator **(see illustration)**.

59 Jack up and support the front of the vehicle.

60 Where fitted remove the engine under-shield.

61 Unbolt and remove the radiator mounting bolts.

62 Push the now loose radiator back towards the engine, move the condenser to the left-hand side and then pull it forward to remove it.

11.58 Remove the condenser mounting bolts

11.71 The sunlight sensor

63 Refitting is a reversal of removal, but lubricate the new O-rings with compressor oil before refitting. Have the system recharged by a Ford dealer or AC specialist.

Control panel

Manual air conditioning

64 Refer to heater control panel removal procedure in Section 9 of this Chapter.

Automatic air conditioning

65 Disconnect the battery negative terminal. **Note:** *Before disconnecting the battery, refer to 'Disconnecting the battery' at the rear of this manual.*
66 Remove the trim piece from control unit.
67 Remove the four mounting screws, pull the panel forward and disconnect the wiring plugs.
68 No further dismantling of the control panel is possible.
69 Refitting is a reversal of removal.

Flap valve positioning motors

70 The various heater control motors are accessed in the same manner as the heater unit control motors (see Section 9 of this Chapter. Models with climate control have an additional control motor.

Sunlight photo-sensor

71 Carefully prise the sensor from the vent in the centre of the facia **(see illustration)**. Disconnect the wiring and tie the connector back to prevent it from disappearing down inside the facia.
72 Refitting is a reversal of removal.

Thermal cut-off switch

73 The switch (where fitted) is located in the upper radiator hose. To remove the switch, drain the cooling system to just below the level of the switch, as described in the relevant Part of Chapter 1, or be prepared for coolant spillage.
74 Remove the battery compartment upper and lower panels (see Chapter 5A). Disconnect the wiring plug from the switch.
75 Prise the retaining clip out, and remove the switch. Recover the O-ring seal.
76 Refitting is a reversal of removal. The O-ring seal can be re-used, provided it is in good condition.

Radiator fan third speed switch

77 The switch (where fitted) is located in the upper radiator hose. To remove the switch, drain the cooling system to just below the level of the switch, as described in the relevant Part of Chapter 1, or be prepared for coolant spillage.
78 Remove the battery compartment upper and lower panels (see Chapter 5A). Disconnect the wiring plug from the switch.
79 Prise the retaining clip out, and remove the switch. Recover the O-ring seal.
80 Refitting is a reversal of removal. The O-ring seal can be re-used, provided it is in good condition.

Chapter 4 Part A:
Fuel system – petrol

Contents

Degrees of difficulty

| **Easy,** suitable for novice with little experience | **Fairly easy,** suitable for beginner with some experience | **Fairly difficult,** suitable for competent DIY mechanic | **Difficult,** suitable for experienced DIY mechanic | **Very difficult,** suitable for expert DIY or professional |

Specifications

System type
All models. . . . . Ford EEC V sequential multipoint injection

Recommended fuel
Minimum octane rating. . . . . 95 RON unleaded only

Fuel system data
Fuel pump type . . . . Electric, immersed in fuel tank
Regulated fuel pressure at idling speed:
   Vacuum hose fitted. . . . . 3.5 bar (approx)
   Vacuum hose disconnected . . . . 4.0 bar (approx)
Minimum holding pressure (after 10 minutes) . . . . 2.0 bar
Engine idle speed (non-adjustable, ECM controlled) . . . . 875 rpm
Engine maximum speed. . . . . 6175 rpm
Idle CO content . . . . Not adjustable, ECM-controlled
Fuel tank capacity . . . . 70 litres

Torque wrench settings	**Nm**	**lbf ft**
Camshaft position sensor	5	4
Crankshaft position sensor	4	3
Engine coolant temperature sensor	23	17
Fuel injector bolts	6	4
Fuel pump lock ring	70	52
Fuel pressure regulator	6	4
Fuel rail	23	17
Fuel tank strap bolts	25	18
Idle air control valve to inlet manifold	10	7
Inlet manifold:		
Nuts and bolts	22	16
Studs	14	10
Throttle body to inlet manifold	10	7

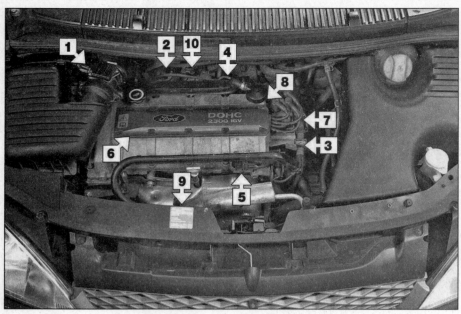

1.1 Petrol engine management components

1 Mass airflow sensor	5 Camshaft position sensor	8 Crankshaft position
2 Throttle position sensor	6 Ignition coils (some	sensor (rear of engine)
3 Coolant temperature	models)/spark plugs cover	9 Oxygen sensor
sensor	7 Ignition coil (some	10 Idle air control
4 Fuel injectors wiring rail	models)	valve

1 General information and precautions

The Ford EEC V sequential multipoint petrol injection system described in this Chapter is a self-contained engine management system, which controls both the fuel injection and the ignition system (see illustration). This Chapter deals with the fuel system components only, however refer to Chapter 5B for details of the ignition system.

The fuel injection system comprises a fuel tank, an electric fuel pump, a fuel filter, fuel supply and return lines, a throttle body, an air mass sensor, a fuel rail, four electronic injectors, a fuel pressure regulator, associated sensors, actuators and wiring. All functions are controlled by an electronic control module

(ECM), often referred to as an ECU (electronic control unit) or in Ford's case a PCM (power control module).

The air mass sensor is located on the air cleaner outlet to the throttle body. Fuel is supplied under pressure to a fuel rail, and then passes to four electronic injectors. The duration of the injection period is determined by the ECM which switches the injectors on and off as required.

The tank-immersed fuel pump delivers a constant supply of fuel through a cartridge filter. The fuel is supplied to a fuel rail, and the fuel pressure regulator maintains a constant fuel pressure to the fuel injectors and returns excess fuel to the tank via the return line. The constant fuel flow system helps to reduce fuel temperature and prevents vaporisation.

The ECM controls starting and warm-up enrichment, together with idle speed regulation and Lambda control. Idle speed

control is achieved by an idle air control valve on the side of the throttle body, and partly by the ignition system. Manual adjustment of the idle speed is not possible.

Intake air is drawn into the engine through the air cleaner, which contains a renewable paper filter element.

The exhaust gas oxygen content is constantly monitored by the ECM via the oxygen sensor, which is mounted in the front section of the exhaust pipe, before the catalytic converter. To comply with legislation a second oxygen sensor is mounted after the catalytic converter. The primary function of this sensor is to monitor the efficiency of the catalytic convertor. The ECM then uses this information to adjust the air/fuel ratio. Manual adjustment of the idle speed exhaust CO content is not possible. A catalytic converter is fitted to the exhaust system on all models. A fuel evaporative control system is fitted, and the ECM controls the operation of the activated charcoal canister – refer to Chapter 4C for further details.

It should be noted that fault diagnosis of all the engine management systems described in this Chapter is only possible with dedicated electronic test equipment. Problems with the system operation should therefore be referred to an Ford dealer or engine management specialist for assessment. Note that all engines are EOBD compliant and the cost of basic fault code readers is now within reach of the home mechanic. Once the fault has been identified, the removal and refitting sequences detailed in the following Sections will then allow the appropriate component(s) to be renewed as required.

⚠ **Warning: Many of the procedures in this Chapter require the removal of fuel lines and connections, which may result in some fuel spillage. Before carrying out any operation on the fuel system, refer to the precautions given in 'Safety first!' at the beginning of this manual, and follow them implicitly. Always switch off the ignition before working on the fuel system. Petrol is a highly-dangerous and volatile liquid, and the precautions necessary when handling it cannot be overstressed.**

Note: Residual pressure will remain in the fuel lines long after the vehicle was last used. Before disconnecting any fuel line, first depressurise the fuel system as described in Section 8.

2 Air cleaner and intake ducts – removal and refitting

Removal

1 Disconnect the wiring plug from the mass airflow sensor (MAF) (see illustration).
2 Release the hose clip securing the air cleaner ducting to the mass airflow sensor housing. Remove the ducting (see illustration).

2.1 Disconnect the MAF sensor

2.2 Remove the outlet pipe

2.3a Remove the screws (arrowed) . . .

2.3b . . . lift off the cover . . .

2.3c . . . and remove the filter

2.4 Recover the PCV filter

2.5 Remove the single screw

2.6 Disconnect the breather hose from the valve cover

3 Remove the cover and take out the air filter **(see illustrations)**.
4 Recover the PCV filter sponge from the air cleaner housing **(see illustration)**. This item is normally supplied with the new air filter.
5 The air cleaner housing is secured by a single screw and three lugs which locate in corresponding grommets in the inner wing. Remove the screw and gently pull the housing until the lugs disengage from the grommets **(see illustration)**.
6 As the air cleaner housing is withdrawn, release the retaining clip and disconnect the crankcase breather hose from the housing or more easily remove the PCV pipe from the valve cover **(see illustration)**.

Refitting

7 Refitting is a reversal of removal.

3	Accelerator cable – removal, refitting and adjustment

Removal

1 Remove the two retaining clips and remove the air intake ducting.
2 Disconnect the accelerator cable from the segment on the throttle body by turning the segment to open the throttle, then releasing the cable and end fitting **(see illustration)**.
3 Disconnect the air inlet temperature sensor wiring plug (where fitted).
4 Undo the three Torx screws and remove the accelerator cable bracket from the

throttle body, complete with the cable **(see illustration)**.
5 Using a pair of pliers, squeeze together the retaining tags and remove the outer cable end fitting from the bracket **(see illustration)**.

3.2 Release the cable end fitting from the quadrant

3.5 Squeeze together the retaining tabs and remove the end fitting from the bracket

6 Working in the passenger compartment, reach up under the facia, pull the cable ferrule from the top of the accelerator pedal, and disconnect the inner cable **(see illustration)**.
7 On automatic transmission models, where

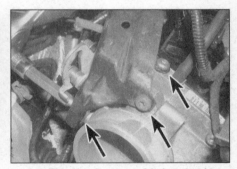

3.4 The accelerator cable bracket is secured by three Torx screws (arrowed)

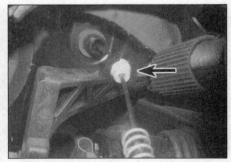

3.6 Pull the ferrule (arrowed) from the pedal and disconnect the cable

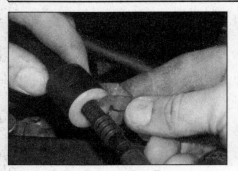

3.10a Remove the clip . . .

3.10b . . . and pull the adjuster and outer cable away from each other

fitted, disconnect the kickdown switch wiring from the outer cable on the engine compartment rear panel in the engine compartment.

8 In the engine compartment, pull the outer cable (complete with plastic end fitting) from the rubber grommet in the bulkhead, and remove it from the vehicle.

Refitting

9 Refitting is a reversal of removal, but adjust the cable as follows. Make sure that the outer cable is located securely in the bulkhead.

Adjustment

10 At the throttle body, pull the clip from the adjuster, and pull the adjuster and outer cable away from each other (see illustrations).

11 Fully depress the throttle pedal, then slowly release it.

12 Refit the clip to the adjuster and outer cable. Depress the throttle pedal fully, and

check that full travel is achieved at the throttle body quadrant.

4 Engine management system components – removal and refitting

Note: *Observe the precautions in Section 1 before working on any component in the fuel system. The ignition must be switched off at all times.*

Mass airflow sensor

1 The mass airflow sensor is located on the air ducting from the air cleaner housing.

2 Disconnect the wiring plug from the sensor (see illustration).

3 Slacken the retaining clip, and disconnect the inlet hose from the sensor.

4 Release the retaining clips and remove the sensor from the air ducting. Check that the

sensor sealing ring is in good condition (see illustration).

5 Refitting is a reversal of removal.

Throttle position sensor

Note: *On automatic transmission models, the ECM 'basic set-up' procedure must be carried out following disconnection of the sensor. This necessitates the use of dedicated diagnostic equipment, and should be entrusted to your local Ford dealer or suitably-equipped specialist.*

6 Remove the mass airflow sensor, as described earlier in this Section. Undo the three screws and remove the bulkhead panel trim. Slide the panel to the right-hand side and manoeuvre it from behind the coolant expansion tank.

7 Disconnect the wiring plug from the inlet air temperature sensor.

8 Slacken the retaining clip and remove the intake ducting from the throttle body (see illustration).

9 Undo the retaining bolts and position the accelerator cable bracket to one side.

10 Unplug the throttle position sensor wiring, and disconnect the inner accelerator cable from the throttle valve.

11 Disconnect the vacuum hose from the throttle body, undo the retaining Torx screws, and remove the throttle body (see illustrations).

12 With the throttle body removed, undo the two Torx screws, and remove the throttle position sensor (see illustration).

13 Refitting is a reversal of removal, ensuring that the sensor is correctly located on the throttle valve shaft. Before refitting the throttle

4.2 Disconnect the mass airflow sensor wiring plug

4.4 Check that the sensor sealing ring is in good condition (arrowed)

4.8 Slacken the retaining clip and disconnect the hose from the throttle body

4.11a Disconnect the vacuum hose

4.11b The throttle body is secured by four Torx screws (two arrowed – two hidden)

4.12 Undo the screws and detach the throttle position sensor

body, check the sealing gasket is in good condition (see illustration). On automatic transmission models, it will now be necessary to carry out the 'basic set-up' procedure using suitable diagnostic equipment.

Inlet air temperature sensor

14 The inlet air temperature sensor is located on the intake ducting between the mass airflow sensor and the throttle body.
15 Disconnect the wiring plug from the inlet air temperature sensor (see illustration).
16 Carefully prise the sensor from the ducting. If required, the sensor can be tested by checking the output voltage and resistance, and comparing the values obtained with those given below.

Air temp °C	Resistance k ohms	Voltage V
−10	183	4.20
0	95	3.87
10	66	3.55
20	38	3.10
30	27	2.70
40	16	2.10

17 Refitting is a reversal of removal, tightening the sensor securely.

Vehicle speed sensor

18 The vehicle speed sensor is fitted into the back of the gearbox. Refer to Chapter 7A or 7B as applicable for the removal and refitting procedure. Any fault with the sensor must be checked by a Ford dealer or suitably-equipped specialist, and if necessary renewed.

Coolant temperature sensor

19 The engine coolant temperature sensor is located on the rear of the thermostat/coolant outlet housing on the left-hand end of the cylinder head (see illustration). The upper sensor is the engine coolant temperature sensor, and the lower sensor is the coolant temperature gauge sender.
20 Disconnect the wiring plug from the sensor.
21 Either drain the cooling system (as described in Chapter 1A) to below the level of the sensor, or be prepared for coolant spillage.
22 Unscrew the sensor from the housing. If required, the sensor can be tested by checking the output voltage and resistance. The values obtained should be identical to those given for the inlet air temperature sensor in Paragraph 16.
23 Refitting is a reversal of removal, tightening the sensor to the specified torque. Refer to Chapter 1A and top-up the cooling system.

Crankshaft position sensor

24 The engine speed sensor is mounted on the rear of the cylinder block, adjacent to the mating surface of the block and transmission bellhousing, just behind the oil filter. Apply the handbrake, then jack up the front of the vehicle and support it on axle stands (see Jacking and vehicle support). Where applicable, remove the splash guard from under the engine compartment.

4.13 The rubber gasket can be re-used if it is in good condition

4.19 Engine coolant temperature sensor

25 Disconnect the wiring plug from the sensor (see illustration).
26 Unscrew the retaining bolt and withdraw the sensor from the cylinder block. If required, the sensor can be tested as follows. Ensure the ignition is turned off, and disconnect the sensor wiring plug. Connect a multimeter between the two sensor terminals, and set the meter to measure resistance. A sensor in good condition should register a resistance of 200 to 450 ohms. If the resistance is outside the range specified, it is likely the sensor is defective.
27 Refitting is a reversal of removal. Tighten the securing bolt to the specified torque.

Throttle body

28 The throttle body removal procedure is incorporated into the throttle position sensor removal procedure described in paragraphs 6 to 12 of this Section.

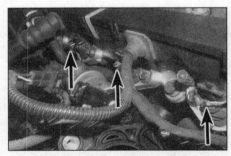
4.33 Release the retaining clips and place the wiring multiplug rail to one side (arrowed)

4.15 Disconnect the inlet air temperature sensor wiring plug

4.25 The crankshaft position sensor is adjacent to the oil filter

Fuel injectors and fuel rail

29 Disconnect the battery negative lead.
Note: Before disconnecting the battery, refer to 'Disconnecting the battery' at the rear of this manual.
30 Remove the air cleaner housing as described in Section 2.
31 Disconnect the inlet air temperature sensor wiring plug.
32 Slacken the retaining clip and remove the air intake ducting from the throttle body.
33 Carefully release the wiring multiplug rail from the top of the injectors, and place it to one side (see illustration).
34 Depressurise the fuel system as described in Section 8.
35 Squeeze together the locking tabs and disconnect the fuel supply and return pipes (see illustration).
36 Undo the Torx screw and remove the fuel pipes retaining clip (see illustration).

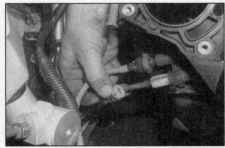
4.35 Squeeze together the locking tabs and disconnect the fuel supply and return pipes

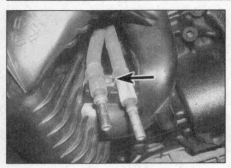

4.36 Undo the hose retaining clip Torx screw (arrowed)

4.38 The fuel rail is secured by two bolts

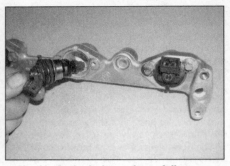

4.40a Undo the bolts and carefully remove the injectors

4.40b Where available, renew the O-ring seals

4.43 Undo the bolts and remove the pressure regulator

4.46 Camshaft position sensor

37 Disconnect the vacuum pipe from the fuel pressure regulator.

38 Undo the retaining bolts and remove the fuel rail complete with pressure regulator and injectors (see illustration).

39 If required, the pressure regulator can be removed by unscrewing the two retaining bolts. Check the availability of a new O-ring seal before discarding the old one.

40 Undo the retaining bolts and carefully prise the injectors from the fuel rail. Check the availability of new O-ring seals before discarding the old ones (see illustrations).

41 Refit the injectors, regulator (if applicable) and fuel rail by following the removal procedure in reverse, noting the following points:

a) The No 4 injector electrical socket must point to the rear of the engine, whilst the remainder face the front.

b) Where available, renew the injector O-ring seals, and smear them with a little clean engine oil before fitting them.

c) Check that the fuel supply and return pipes is reconnected correctly.

d) Check that all vacuum and electrical connections are remade correctly and securely.

e) Reconnect the battery as described in Chapter 5A.

f) On completion, start the engine and check for fuel leaks.

Fuel pressure regulator

42 Remove the fuel rail assembly as described earlier in this Section.

43 Undo the two retaining bolts, and remove the regulator from the fuel rail (see illustration). Check the availability of a new O-ring seal before discarding the old one.

44 Refit the fuel pressure regulator by following the removal procedure in reverse, tightening the retaining bolts to the specified torque.

Camshaft position sensor

45 Disconnect the battery negative lead. Note: Before disconnecting the battery, refer to 'Disconnecting the battery' at the rear of this manual.

46 Disconnect the wiring plug from the sensor (see illustration).

47 Unscrew the mounting bolt and withdraw the sensor from the camshaft cover. Recover the seal. If required, the sensor can be tested as follows. Ensure the ignition is turned off, and disconnect the sensor wiring plug. Connect a multimeter between the two sensor terminals, and set the meter to measure resistance. A sensor in good condition should register a resistance of 200 to 900 ohms. If the resistance is outside the range specified, it is likely the sensor is defective.

48 Refitting is a reversal of removal, tightening the mounting bolt to the specified torque.

Oxygen sensor(s)

49 Disconnect the battery negative lead. Note: Before disconnecting the battery, refer to 'Disconnecting the battery' at the rear of this manual.

50 Apply the handbrake, then jack up the front of the vehicle and support it on axle stands (see Jacking and vehicle support). Undo the two retaining nuts and four bolts (two each side) and remove the engine undershield.

51 Disconnect the wiring plug from the sensor (see illustration).

52 Unscrew and remove the sensor, taking care to avoid damaging the sensor probe as it is removed (see illustration).

4.51 Disconnect the oxygen sensor wiring plug

4.52 Unscrew the sensor from the exhaust pipe

53 Apply a little anti-seize grease to the sensor threads, but avoid contaminating the probe tip. **Note:** *New Oxygen sensors may be supplied with fitting paste on the threads.*
54 Refit the sensor and tighten it securely.
55 Reconnect the wiring plug, refit the engine undershield, and lower the vehicle to the ground.

Electronic control module (ECM)

Caution: Always wait at least 30 seconds after switching off the ignition before disconnecting the wiring from the ECM. When the wiring is disconnected, all the learned values may be erased, however any contents of the fault memory are retained. After reconnecting the wiring, the vehicle must be driven for several miles so that the ECM can learn its basic settings. If the engine still runs erratically, the basic settings may be reinstated by an Ford dealer or specialist using special diagnostic equipment. Note also that if the ECM is renewed, the identification of the new ECM must be transferred to the immobiliser control unit by a Ford dealer or specialist. If a new ECM is fitted, or on automatic transmission models even if the original ECM is refitted, the 'basic set-up' procedure must be carried out using diagnostic equipment, which should be entrusted to a Ford dealer or suitably-equipped specialist.

56 The electronic control module is located behind the facia in the passenger compartment.
57 Disconnect the battery negative (earth) lead. **Note:** *Before disconnecting the battery, refer to 'Disconnecting the battery' at the rear of this manual.*
58 Remove the instrument panel, upper facia and the air distribution panel, as described in Chapter 12.
59 Unbolt and remove the electrical connector **(see illustration)**.
60 Unbolt the ECM mounting bracket and slide the ECM from the housing.
61 Refitting is a reversal of removal, but if the ECM has been renewed it will require programming using suitable diagnostic equipment.

4.59 Undo the bolt and disconnect the ECM wiring plug (shown with facia removed)

Idle air control valve

62 Disconnect the battery negative lead. **Note:** *Before disconnecting the battery, refer to 'Disconnecting the battery' at the rear of this manual.*
63 Release the retaining clips, carefully pull the wiring multiplug rail from the top of the injectors, and position it to one side.
64 Disconnect the wiring plug from the idle air control valve.
65 Unscrew the two retaining bolts and remove the valve **(see illustration)**.
66 Refitting is a reversal of removal. Tighten the valve retaining bolts to the specified torque.

5	Fuel filter –
	renewal

Note: *Observe the precautions in Section 1 before working on fuel system components. Depressurise the system as described in section 8 of this Chapter.*
1 The fuel filter is situated underneath the centre of the vehicle, in front of the fuel tank. Firmly apply the handbrake, then jack up the front of the vehicle and support it securely on axle stands.
2 If available, fit hose clamps to the filter intake and outlet flexible hoses. Even with hose clamps fitted, the old filter will contain some fuel, so have some rags ready to soak up any spillage.

4.65 The idle air control valve is secured to the top of the inlet manifold by two bolts

3 Release the hose clips and detach the hoses from the filter **(see illustration)**. If the fuel hoses show any sign of perishing or cracking, particularly at the hose ends or where the hose enters the metal end fitting, renew the hoses.
4 Before removing the filter, note any direction-of-flow markings on the filter body, and check against the new filter – the arrow should point in the direction of fuel flow (towards the front of the car) **(see illustration)**.
5 Unscrew the two fuel filter housing retaining nuts.
6 Lower the filter and housing from the vehicle body, noting the housing retaining clips need to be pulled down over the mounting studs with the housing. Remove the filter from the housing.
7 Fit the new filter into position in the housing, with the flow marking arrows correctly orientated **(see illustration)**. Push the housing over the retaining studs, and tighten the retaining nuts.
8 Reconnect the fuel hoses using new clips if necessary. Ensure that no dirt is allowed to enter the hoses or filter connections. Where applicable, remove the hose clamps.
9 Start the engine noting that there may be a delay as the system repressurises and the new filter fills with fuel. Let the engine run for several minutes while you check the filter hose connections for leaks, then switch it off.

> ⚠ *Warning: Dispose safely of the old filter; it will be highly flammable, and may explode if thrown on a fire.*

5.3 Release the fuel hose retaining clips

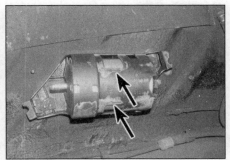

5.4 The arrows on the filter housing points to the front of the vehicle (arrowed)

5.7 Install the new filter with the arrow to the front of the vehicle

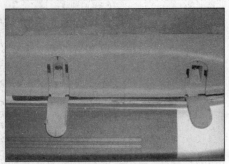

6.5 Pull down the flaps, undo the screws and remove the door sill trim panels

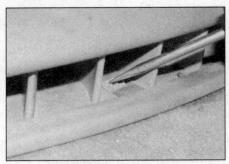

6.6a Depress the retaining clips and lift the cover away . . .

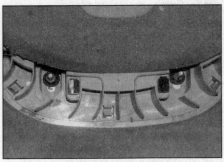

6.6b . . . then undo the two nuts and remove the centre vent

6 Fuel pump and gauge sender unit – removal and refitting

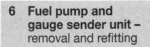

Note: *Observe the precautions in Section 1 before working on fuel system components. Depressurise the system as described in section 8 of this Chapter.*

Removal

1 The fuel pump and gauge sender unit are combined in one assembly, mounted in the fuel tank. Access is via a hatch provided in the load space floor. Removal of the unit exposes the contents of the tank to the atmosphere, so extreme care must be exercised to prevent fire. The area inside and around the car must be well-ventilated to prevent a build-up of fuel fumes. If possible, remove the unit when

6.8 Lift the trims and peel back the carpet

6.11 Disconnect the pump/sender unit wiring plug

the fuel tank is nearly empty, or alternatively siphon the fuel from the tank into a suitable container.

2 Depressurise the fuel system as described in Section 8.

3 Ensure that the vehicle is parked on a level surface, then disconnect the battery negative lead. **Note:** *Before disconnecting the battery, refer to 'Disconnecting the battery' at the rear of this manual.*

4 Pull the weatherstrips from the door apertures adjacent to the sill trim panels.

5 Lever open the plastic flaps, undo the two screws each side, and remove both door sill trim panels **(see illustration)**.

6 Depress the three retaining clips, and lift the floor-mounted centre rear air vent cover. Undo the two nuts and remove the vent **(see illustrations)**.

7 Undo the screws securing the seat mounting trims to the floor for the second row of seats.

6.10 Undo the three screws and remove the access hatch

6.12 Note the arrows on the cover indicating supply and return (arrowed)

8 Carefully prise up the trims at the front edge of the rear carpet, and fold the front half of the carpet to the rear **(see illustration)**.

9 Undo the retaining bolts and remove the seat mounting rail over the access hatch.

10 Slacken and remove the access hatch screws and lift the hatch away from the floorpan **(see illustration)**.

11 Unplug the wiring connector from the pump/sender unit **(see illustration)**.

12 Release the clips and disconnect the fuel supply and return hoses **(see illustration)**. Identify each hose for position – the blue hose is the return circuit.

13 Unscrew the plastic ring securing the pump/sender unit cover to the tank. Ford technicians use a special tool to unscrew the ring, however two screwdrivers engaged with the slots in the ring and crossed over each other may be used with success. Alternatively use a pair of large water pump pliers **(see illustration)**.

14 Lift the sender/pump unit from the tank taking care not to bend or damage the float or arm **(see illustration)**. On some models, the sender unit cover is separate from the pump unit. On these, lift the unit cover and push down and twist the pump unit anti-clockwise, then lift out the assembly. Discard the aperture seal, a new one must be fitted.

15 Inspect the float on the sender unit swinging arm for punctures and fuel ingress, and renew it if it appears damaged. Inspect the sender unit wiper and track; clean off any dirt and debris that may have accumulated and look for breaks in the track. Note the fine

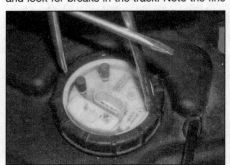

6.13 Unscrew the plastic ring

mesh filter on the base of the pump unit **(see illustration)**. At the time of writing, it would appear that the pump/sender unit is only available as a complete unit.

Refitting

16 Smear the new rubber seal with clean fuel, then locate it on the flange.
17 Where applicable, insert the fuel pump/ sender unit into the tank, then press down and twist it clockwise, or insert the pump/ sender unit into the tank aperture. Ensure that the unit is fitted into its original position **(see illustration)**.
18 Ensure that the arrow on the cover aligns with the mark on the fuel tank **(see illustration)**.
19 Refit and tighten the plastic ring. To ensure the alignment arrows are opposite each other when the ring is fully tight, turn the cover slightly anti-clockwise while the ring is being tightened.
20 Reconnect the fuel supply and return hoses and tighten the clips.
21 Reconnect the wiring connector to the pump/sender unit.
22 Refit the access hatch and tighten the screws.
23 Refit the trim to the load space floor.
24 Reconnect the battery negative (earth) lead.

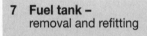
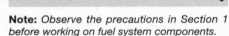

7 Fuel tank – removal and refitting

Note: *Observe the precautions in Section 1 before working on fuel system components.*

Removal

1 Before the tank can be removed, it must be drained of as much fuel as possible. As no drain plug is provided, it is preferable to remove the tank when it is nearly empty. Alternatively, siphon or hand-pump the fuel from the tank into a suitable safe container.
2 Disconnect the battery negative lead. **Note:** *Before disconnecting the battery, refer to 'Disconnecting the battery' at the rear of this manual.*
3 Fold back the front section of the carpet from the load space floor as described in Paragraphs 4 to 9 of the previous Section.
4 Slacken and remove the access hatch screws and lift the hatch away from the floorpan **(see illustration 6.10)**.
5 Unplug the wiring connector from the pump/ sender unit, and disconnect the fuel supply and return hoses. Identify each hose for position. The blue hose is the return circuit.
6 Chock the front wheels, then jack up the rear of the vehicle and support on axle stands (see *Jacking and vehicle support*).
7 Support the fuel tank with a trolley jack and a suitable piece of wood, to prevent the jack head damaging the tank.
8 Undo the four securing bolts, and

6.14 Lift the pump/sender unit from the tank

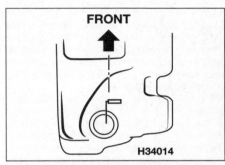
6.17 Install the sender unit with the float arm pointing to the front of the vehicle

remove the fuel tank retaining straps **(see illustrations)**.
9 Using the jack, lower the tank slightly, and release the fuel supply and return pipes from the retaining clips on the tank.

7.8a Fuel tank straps bolts at the front . . .

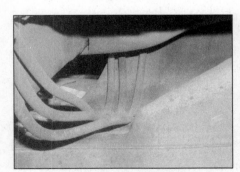
7.10a Release the fuel and breather hoses from the clips on the tank . . .

6.15 At the base of the pump is a fine mesh filter

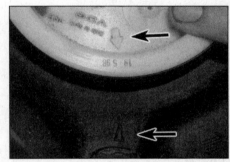
6.18 Ensure the arrow on the cover aligns with the arrow on the tank (arrowed)

10 Release the retaining clips and disconnect the breather pipes from the fuel tank **(see illustrations)**.
11 Slide the fuel filler pipe out as the tank is lowered out of position. Take care not to

7.8b . . . and rear of the tank

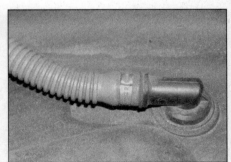
7.10b . . . and the breather hose from the connection on the tank

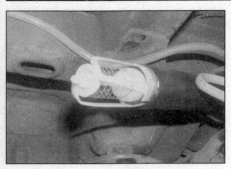

7.11 Take care not to damage the non-return valve on the filler neck as the tank is removed

damage the non-return valve fitted on the end of the fuel filler pipe **(see illustration)**.

12 With the help of an assistant, lower the fuel tank to the ground and remove from under the vehicle.

13 If the tank is contaminated with sediment or water, remove the fuel pump/sender unit (see Section 6) and swill the tank out with clean fuel. The tank is injection-moulded from a synthetic material and if damaged, it should be renewed. However, in certain cases it may be possible to have small leaks or minor damage repaired by a suitable specialist. If required, the filler neck seal can be prised from its location and renewed.

Refitting

14 Refitting is the reverse of the removal procedure noting the following points:
 a) When lifting the tank back into position

8.4 Unscrew the cap from the valve on the fuel rail (arrowed)

9.5 To disconnect the brake servo hose, depress the collar and pull the hose out

take care to ensure none of the hoses get trapped between the tank and vehicle underbody.
 b) Ensure that all pipes and hoses are correctly routed and secured.
 c) Tighten the tank retaining strap bolts.
 d) On completion, refill the tank with fuel and thoroughly check for signs of leakage prior to taking the vehicle out on the road.
 e) Reconnect the battery as described in Chapter 5A.

8 Fuel injection system – depressurisation

⚠️ **Warning: The following procedure will merely relieve the pressure in the fuel system – remember that fuel will still be present in the system components and take precautions accordingly before disconnecting any of them.**

Note: *Observe the precautions in Section 1 before working on fuel system components.*

1 The fuel system referred to in this Section comprises the tank-mounted fuel pump and sender, the fuel filter, the fuel rail and injectors, the fuel pressure regulator, and the metal pipes and flexible hoses of the fuel lines between these components. All these contain fuel which will be under pressure while the engine is running and/or while the ignition is switched on. The pressure will remain for some time after the ignition has been switched off and must be relieved before any of these components are disturbed for servicing work.

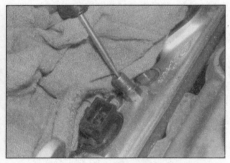

8.5 Depress the valve pin to relieve the fuel pressure

9.6a Pull the crankcase breather pipe from the valve at the front of the engine block . . .

2 Disconnect the battery negative lead. **Note:** *Before disconnecting the battery, refer to 'Disconnecting the battery' at the rear of this manual.*

3 Open the fuel filler flap and briefly remove the filler cap to relieve any pressure in the fuel tank. Refit the cap.

4 Place some cloth rags around the Schrader valve on the right-hand end of the fuel rail **(see illustration)**.

5 Unscrew the valve cap, and depress the valve pin using a small screwdriver (or similar). Try to absorb the fuel spray with the rags **(see illustration)**.

6 On completion, refit the valve cap.

9 Inlet manifold – removal and refitting

Note: *Observe the precautions in Section 1 before working on fuel system components.*

Removal

1 Disconnect the battery negative lead. **Note:** *Before disconnecting the battery, refer to 'Disconnecting the battery' at the rear of this manual.* Drain the cooling system as described in Chapter 1A.

2 With reference to Chapter 11, Section 12, remove the bulkhead panel and then remove the air filter assembly, including the MAF sensor and ducting – see Section 2 of this Chapter.

3 Remove the fuel injectors and throttle body as described in Section 4 of this Chapter.

4 Disconnect the vacuum hose(s) from the manifold. Label the hoses for identification, and note their fitted positions.

5 Disconnect the brake servo vacuum hose from the inlet manifold **(see illustration)**.

6 Undo the bolt securing the crankcase breather pipe to the left-hand end of the engine block. Carefully pull the pipe from the connection at the front of the engine block, and from the connection on the manifold **(see illustrations)**.

7 Disconnect the idle air control valve wiring plug with reference to Section 4.

8 Using a block of wood to spread the load, support the engine on the sump with a suitable jack and remove the right-hand

9.6b . . . and from the inlet manifold

engine mounting as described in Chapter 2A. Remove the earth cable and lower the engine slightly using the jack.

9 Unscrew the nuts and bolts securing the manifold to the cylinder head, and manoeuvre it from the engine compartment. Recover the manifold-to-cylinder rubber seals. Discard the seals, new ones must be fitted **(see illustrations)**.

Refitting

10 Refitting is the reverse of the removal procedure noting the following points:
a) Clean the contact faces of the inlet manifold and cylinder head, and fit new seals.
b) Renew the manifold nuts.
c) Tighten nuts and bolts to the specified torque where given.
d) Check and if necessary adjust the accelerator cable as described in Section 3.
e) Refill/top-up the cooling system with reference to Chapter 1A.
f) Reconnect the battery as described in Chapter 5A.

10 Fuel injection system – testing and adjustment

1 If a fault appears in the fuel injection system first ensure that all the system wiring connectors are securely connected and free of corrosion. Then ensure that the fault is not due to poor maintenance; ie, check that the air cleaner filter element is clean, the spark plugs are in good condition and correctly gapped, the cylinder compression pressures are correct, the ignition timing is correct and the engine breather hoses are clear and undamaged, referring to Chapters 1A, 2A and 5B for further information. Bear in mind that if the battery has been disconnected, the stored values within the engine management ECM will be lost. These values will be relearnt after the vehicle has been driven for 10 to 25 miles. During this period, erratic engine performance may be experienced.

2 If the engine management ECM detects a fault, or if a fault develops within the ECM itself, set values may be substituted by the module which then enters a 'limited

9.9a The inlet manifold is secured by five fasteners (arrowed)

operation strategy' or 'limp home' mode. In this condition some management operations are limited, and engine performance may be reduced. Vehicle speed may be limited to 38 mph on level ground. Once the fault(s) is rectified, and the battery reconnected, the ECM should relearn the necessary operating values over a distance of approximately 10 to 25 miles.

3 If these checks fail to reveal the cause of the problem the vehicle should be taken to a Ford dealer or suitably-equipped specialist for testing. A diagnostic connector, located below the fusebox **(see illustration)**, is incorporated in the engine management system wiring harness, into which dedicated electronic test equipment can be plugged. The test equipment is capable of 'interrogating' the engine management system ECM electronically and accessing its internal fault log. In this manner, faulty components can be highlighted. Testing all the system components individually in an attempt to locate the fault by elimination is a time-consuming operation that is unlikely to be fruitful (particularly if the fault occurs dynamically) and carries high risk of damage to the ECM's internal components. Note however that just because the ECM has logged a unique fault code for a specific component, it does not necessarily follow that the component is faulty. For example the ECM may log a fault code for the idle speed control but the real fault may be a broken wire in the wiring loom. In this case renewing the idle control valve would not rectify the problem.

4 In recent years affordable diagnostic tools have become available and they are a useful

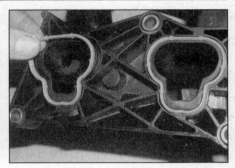
9.9b Fit new seals to the manifold

addition to the home mechanics tool kit **(see illustration)**. Be aware however that these tools will not interrogate the ECM to the same level as professional equipment, as most are based around accessing the mandatory EOBD (European Onboard Diagnostics) emissions fault codes only.

11 Fuel inertia shut-off switch – removal, refitting and resetting

Removal

1 In the event of an accident, this switch is designed to shut-off the fuel supply. Consequently, the switch can also be triggered by sudden vibrations as well, eg, a parking collision. The switch is located in the storage compartment beneath the front passenger seat. Slide the seat as far forward as possible, and remove the storage compartment panel.
2 Ensure the ignition is off, and disconnect the wiring plug from the switch.
3 Undo the two retaining screws and remove the switch **(see illustration)**.

Refitting

4 Refitting is a reversal of removal.

Resetting

5 To reset the switch, ensure the ignition is off, and depress the button on the switch. Turn the ignition switch to position II, pause for a few seconds, then turn the ignition switch to position I.

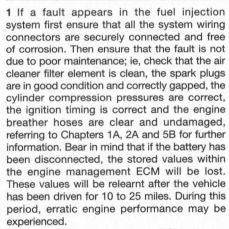

10.3 The diagnostic plug is located below the fusebox (arrowed)

10.4 Using a fault code reader

11.3 Undo the screws and remove the fuel inertia shut-off switch

Notes

Chapter 4 Part B:
Fuel system – diesel

Contents

Degrees of difficulty

Easy, suitable for novice with little experience	**Fairly easy,** suitable for beginner with some experience	**Fairly difficult,** suitable for competent DIY mechanic	**Difficult,** suitable for experienced DIY mechanic	**Very difficult,** suitable for expert DIY or professional

Specifications

General
Engine code by type:*
  66 kW (90 PS) . . . . ANU
  85 kW (115 PS) . . . . AUY
  96 kW (130 PS) . . . . ASZ
  110 kW (150 PS) ASZ1
Firing order 1-3-4-2
Maximum engine speed (intermittent) . . . . 5100 rpm
Engine idle speed. . . . . 900 rpm
Engine fast idle speed . . . . N/A (ECM controlled)
* Note: *See 'Vehicle identification' for the location of the code marking on the engine.*

Fuel injectors
Injection pressure. . . . . 180 to 2050 bar

Tandem pump
Fuel pressure at 1500 rpm . . . . 3.5 bar

Torque wrench settings

	Nm	lbf ft
EGR cooler (to exhaust) bolts	25	18
EGR pipe flange bolts	25	18
EGR valve mounting bolts	25	18
Exhaust clamp nuts	40	30
Exhaust manifold nuts/bolts*	25	18
Exhaust manifold-to-downpipe nuts*	25	18
Exhaust mounting bracket nuts and bolts	25	18
Injector adjusting screw locknut	30	22
Injector clamp bolt:*		
Stage 1	12	9
Stage 2	Angle-tighten a further 270°	
Injector rocker shaft bolt:*		
Stage 1	20	15
Stage 2	Angle-tighten a further 90°	
Inlet manifold flap housing to manifold	10	7
Inlet manifold to cylinder head	25	18
Injector rocker shaft bolts:*		
Stage 1	20	15
Stage 2	Angle-tighten a further 90°	
Intercooler mounting bolts	10	7
Tandem pump bolts:		
Upper	20	15
Lower	10	7
Turbocharger oil return pipe flange bolts	15	11
Turbocharger oil return union bolt	40	30
Turbocharger oil supply pipe nut	25	18
Turbocharger support bracket to engine	40	30
Turbocharger to catalytic converter	25	18
Turbocharger-to-downpipe nuts†	25	18
Turbocharger to exhaust manifold*	25	18
Turbocharger-to-manifold bolts*†	30	22
Turbocharger-to-mounting bracket bolt	25	18

*Use new fasteners
† Use thread-locking compound

1 General information and precautions

General information

All diesel engines fitted to the Ford Galaxy are Volkswagen-sourced PD (Pumpe Duse) engines. Fuel is delivered by a camshaft driven 'tandem pump' at low pressure to the injectors (known as unit injectors). A 'roller rocker' assembly, mounted above the camshaft bearing caps, uses an extra set of camshaft lobes to compress the top of each injector once per firing cycle. This arrangement creates far higher injection pressures. The precise timing of the pre-injection and main injection is controlled by the engine management electronic control module (ECM) and a solenoid on each injector. The resultant effect of this system is improved engine torque and power output, greater combustion efficiency, and lower exhaust emissions.

All engines are fitted with a turbocharger and an exhaust gas recirculation (EGR) emissions control system (Chapter 4C). The EGR is water-cooled on all but the lower power 90 PS (ANU) engines. An 'anti-shudder' control flap fitted to the inlet manifold is closed by the ECM for 3 seconds as the engine is switched off, to minimise the air intake as the engine shuts down. This minimises the vibration felt as the pistons come up against the volume of highly compressed air present in the combustion chambers. A vacuum reservoir mounted on the front of the engine provides the vacuum supply to a vacuum capsule which operates the flap (see illustrations). This valve is not fitted to the low power ANU engine.

As an aid to cold starting and for post-start emissions control, glow plugs are fitted (Chapter 5C). Glow plug operation is controlled by the ECM, as are all engine management functions.

It should be noted that fault diagnosis of the diesel engine management system is only possible with dedicated electronic test equipment. Problems with the system's operation should therefore be referred to a Ford dealer or suitably-equipped specialist for assessment. Once the fault has been identified, the removal/refitting sequences detailed in the following Sections will then allow the appropriate component(s) to be renewed as required.

Precautions

Many of the operations described in this Chapter involve the disconnection of fuel lines, which may cause an amount of fuel spillage. Before commencing work, refer to the warnings below and the information in *Safety first!* at the beginning of this manual.

1.2a Vacuum reservoir for inlet manifold flap valve

1.2b Vacuum capsule on the inlet manifold

2.1 Release the wiring loom

2.2 Remove the screws (arrowed)

2.3 Remove the air filter

2.4 Disconnect the MAF sensor

2.5a Remove the bolt (arrowed) . . .

2.5b . . . and remove the housing

Warning: When working on any part of the fuel system, avoid direct contact skin contact with diesel fuel – wear protective clothing and gloves when handling fuel system components. Ensure that the work area is well ventilated to prevent the build-up of diesel fuel vapour.

- *Fuel injectors operate at extremely high pressures and the jet of fuel produced at the nozzle is capable of piercing skin, with potentially fatal results. When working with pressurised injectors, take care to avoid exposing any part of the body to the fuel spray. It is recommended that a diesel fuel systems specialist should carry out any pressure testing of the fuel system components.*
- *Under no circumstances should diesel fuel be allowed to come into contact with coolant hoses – wipe off accidental spillage immediately. Hoses that have been contaminated with fuel for an extended period should be renewed.*
- *Diesel fuel systems are particularly sensitive to contamination from dirt, air and water. Pay particular attention to cleanliness when working on any part of the fuel system, to prevent the ingress of dirt. Thoroughly clean the area around fuel unions before disconnecting them. Only use lint-free cloths and clean fuel for component cleansing.*
- *Store dismantled components in sealed containers to prevent contamination and the formation of condensation.*

2 Air cleaner assembly – removal and refitting

Removal

1 Unclip the wiring loom from the air filter **(see illustration)**.
2 Remove the cover retaining screws **(see illustration)**.
3 With care the air filter can now be lifted up and out from the main housing **(see illustration)**.
4 To remove the cover completely, disconnect the wiring plug from the MAF sensor **(see illustration)**, compress the spring clip and remove duct from the outlet.
5 The lower half of the air cleaner is secured by a single bolt. Remove the bolt and lift out the air filter housing **(see illustrations)**.

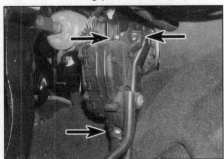

4.1 Undo the bolts (arrowed) and remove the pedal and sensor

Refitting

6 Refit the air cleaner by following the removal procedure in reverse.

3 Accelerator cable – general information

Diesel models do not have an accelerator cable, and instead have an electronically-controlled arrangement known as a 'fly-by-wire' throttle. The throttle position sensor at the accelerator pedal is linked to the engine management ECM, which adjusts the quantity of fuel injected, thus controlling the engine speed. Various sensors are used to enable the ECM to set the quantity of fuel to inject, and the pump timing (commencement of injection).

4 Diesel engine management system – component removal and refitting

Throttle position sensor

1 The position sensor is integral with the accelerator pedal. Remove the driver's side lower facia panel as described in Chapter 11. Disconnect the sensor wiring plug and unscrew the nuts securing the pedal to its mounting bracket **(see illustration)**.

4.4 The coolant temperature sensor (arrowed)

4.8 The fuel temperature sensor

4.9 Remove the sensor

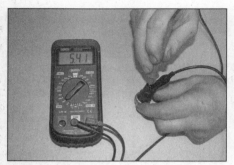

4.10 Checking the sensor resistance with a multimeter

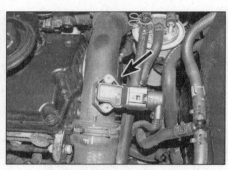

4.12 The MAP sensor (arrowed)

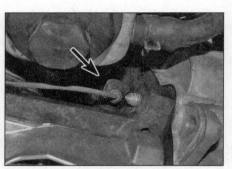

4.14 The crankshaft position sensor (arrowed)

Coolant temperature sensor

Removal

2 Refer to Chapter 1B and drain approximately one quarter of the coolant from the engine. Alternatively, be prepared for coolant spillage as the sensor is removed.
3 Remove the engine cover.
4 The sensor is at the rear of the coolant outlet, at the left-hand end of the cylinder head **(see illustration)**. Unplug the wiring from it at the connector.
5 Remove the clip, then extract the sensor from its housing and recover the O-ring seal.

Refitting

6 Refit the coolant temperature sensor by reversing the removal procedure, using a new O-ring seal. Refer to Chapter 1B or *Weekly checks* and top-up the cooling system.
7 The operation of the coolant sensor can be checked as described in Chapter 3.

Fuel temperature sensor

8 The fuel temperature sensor is located in the fuel line at the front left-hand end of the cylinder head **(see illustration)**.
9 Place a absorbent cloth beneath the sensor, pull out the clip and remove the sensor **(see illustration)**. Disconnect the wiring plug.
10 If required the sensor resistance can be checked with a multimeter **(see illustration)**. The resistance will change as the temperature changes. One suitable test is to refrigerate the sensor for an hour and check that the resistance has increased. Whilst this does not conclusively prove that the sensor is functioning correctly it is a good indication that the sensor is good.

Inlet air temperature sensor

Removal

11 All models have an air temperature sensor built into the manifold absolute pressure (MAP)

sensor. This sensor is often referred to as the 'charge air sensor' or the 'boost pressure sensor' This sensor is an integral part of the MAP sensor and cannot be renewed separately.
12 The sensor is mounted on the left-hand end of the cylinder head **(see illustration)**. Disconnect the wiring plug, remove the screws and remove the sensor.

Refitting

13 Refit the inlet air temperature sensor by reversing the removal procedure, using a new O-ring seal.

Crankshaft position sensor

Removal

14 The crankshaft position sensor is mounted on the front cylinder block, adjacent to the mating surface of the block and transmission bellhousing **(see illustration)**.
15 Remove the engine top cover.
16 Trace the wiring back from the sensor, and disconnect it at the plug behind the oil filter housing.
17 Remove the retaining screw and withdraw the sensor from the cylinder block.

Refitting

18 Refit the sensor by reversing the removal procedure.

Camshaft position sensor

Removal

19 Release the clips and remove the timing belt upper cover.
20 Remove the blanking plug and unbolt the sensor **(see illustrations)**.

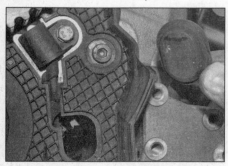

4.20a Remove the blanking plug . . .

4.20b . . . and remove the sensor mounting bolt (arrowed)

4.23 Disconnect the wiring plug

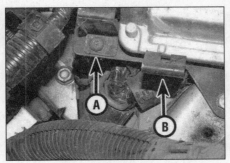

4.38a The bracket retaining screw (A) and one of the ECM retaining tabs (B)

4.38b Remove the bracket

21 Disconnect the wiring plug and feed the sensor through the hole in the timing belt cover.

Refitting

22 Refit the sensor by reversing the removal procedure.

Mass airflow sensor (MAF)

Removal

23 Disconnect the wiring plug from the air mass meter **(see illustration)**.

24 Remove the retaining screws and extract the meter from the air cleaner housing. Recover the O-ring seal.

25 Note that new sensors may be supplied complete with the sensor housing. If this is the case, release the spring clip and unscrew the housing from the air filter outlet.

Caution: Handle the air mass meter carefully – its internal components are easily damaged.

Refitting

26 Refitting is a reversal of removal. Renew the O-ring seal if it appears damaged.

Barometric pressure (altitude) sensor

27 The altitude sensor is an integral part of the ECM, and hence cannot be renewed separately.

Inlet manifold flap housing

28 Where fitted, the control flap is part of the EGR valve. Individual parts are not available and if a mechanical fault develops the EGR must be renewed, as described in Chapter 4C.

29 The default position of the flap is the open position. The flap can be checked by applying a vacuum source to the valve. If the valve operates with vacuum applied check the condition and security of the vacuum hoses to the control solenoid. Connect a vacuum gauge to the control solenoid output, start the engine and then turn it off. The vacuum gauge should momentarily register a vacuum.

Clutch and brake pedal switches

Removal

30 The clutch and brake pedal switches are clipped to mounting brackets directly above their respective pedals.

31 The brake pedal switch operates as a safety device, in the event of a problem with the accelerator position sensor. If the brake pedal switch is depressed while the accelerator pedal is held at a constant position, the engine speed will drop to idle. Thus, a faulty or incorrectly-adjusted brake pedal switch may result in a running problem.

32 The clutch pedal is engaged the switch signal causes the ECM to momentarily reduce the fuel quantity injected into the engine to permit smoother gearchanging.

33 To remove either switch, refer to Chapter 11 and remove the trim panels from under the steering column area of the facia, to gain access to the pedal cluster.

34 The removal and refitting of the brake switch is covered in Chapter 9, Section 17.

35 The removal and refitting of the clutch position switch is covered in Chapter 6, Section 7.

Refitting

36 Refitting is a reversal of removal. Where a brake pedal position switch is fitted in addition to a brake pedal switch, the switches must be synchronised using suitable diagnostic equipment.

Electronic control module (ECM)

Caution: Always wait at least 30 seconds after switching off the ignition before disconnecting the wiring from the ECM. When the wiring is disconnected, all the learned values are erased, however any contents of the fault memory are retained.

4.39 Remove the wiring connectors

If the ECM is renewed, the new ECM must be programmed to the vehicle using suitable diagnostic equipment

Removal

37 The ECM is mounted on the left-hand strut tower behind the battery. Remove the battery cover, battery and the side panels as described in Chapter 5A.

38 Remove the screw from the wiring plug security bracket and remove the bracket **(see illustrations)**.

39 Slide open the locking mechanism on the wiring connectors and remove the connectors **(see illustration)**.

40 The ECM is held in place by locking tabs **(see illustration 4.38a)**.

41 With care release the locking tabs. These tabs are fragile so release them with caution. Remove the ECM **(see illustration)**.

Refitting

42 Refitting is a reversal of removal. Bear in mind the comments made in the Caution.

5 Injectors – general information, removal and refitting

Warning: Exercise extreme caution when working on the fuel injectors. Never expose the hands or any part of the body to injector spray, as the high working pressure can cause the fuel to penetrate the skin, with possibly fatal results. You are strongly advised to

4.41 Remove the ECM

5.4 Undo the adjustment screw until the rocker arm lies against the plunger pin of the injector

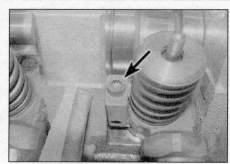

5.6 Remove the clamping block securing bolt (arrowed)

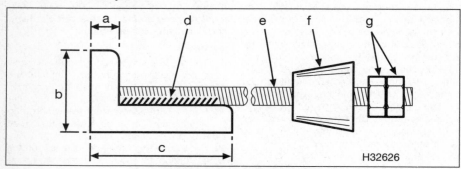

5.8 Unit injector removal tool

a = 5 mm	d Weld/braze the rod to	f Cylindrical weight
b = 15 mm	the angle-iron	g Locknut
c = 25 mm	e Threaded rod	

have any work which involves testing the injectors under pressure carried out by a dealer or fuel injection specialist. Refer to the precautions given in Section 1 of this Chapter before proceeding.

General information

1 Injectors deteriorate with prolonged use, and it is reasonable to expect them to need reconditioning or renewal after 60 000 miles or so. Accurate testing, overhaul and calibration of the injectors must be left to a specialist.

Removal

Note: *Take care not to allow dirt into the injectors or fuel pipes during this procedure.*

Do not drop the injectors or allow the needles at their tips to become damaged. The injectors are precision-made to fine limits, and must not be handled roughly.

2 With reference to Chapter 2B, remove the upper timing belt cover and camshaft cover.
3 Using a spanner or socket, turn the crankshaft pulley until the rocker arm for the injector which is to be removed is at its highest, ie, the injector plunger spring is under the least amount of tension.
4 Slacken the locknut of the adjustment screw on the end of the rocker arm above the injector, and undo the adjustment screw until the rocker arm lies against the plunger pin of the injector **(see illustration)**.

5 Starting at the outside and working in, gradually and evenly slacken and remove the rocker shaft retaining bolts. Lift off the rocker shaft. Check the contact face of each adjustment screw, and renew any that show signs of wear.
6 Undo the clamping block securing bolt and remove the block from the side of the injector **(see illustration)**.
7 Using a small screwdriver, carefully prise the wiring connector from the injector.
8 Ford technicians use a slide hammer (tool No 310-086) to pull the injector from the cylinder head. This is a slide hammer which engages in the side of the injector. If this tool is not available, it is possible to fabricate an equivalent using a short section of angle-iron, a length of threaded rod, a cylindrical weight, and two locknuts. Weld/braze the rod to the angle-iron, slide the weight over the rod, and lock the two nuts together at the end of the rod to provide the stop for the weight **(see illustration)**.
9 Seat the slide hammer/tool in the slot on the side on the injector, and pull the injector out using a few gently taps. Recover circlip, the heat shield and O-rings and discard. New ones must be used for refitting **(see illustration)**.
10 If required, the injector wiring loom/rail can be removed from the cylinder head by undoing the two retaining nuts/bolts at the back of the head. To prevent the wiring connectors fouling the cylinder head casting as the assembly is withdrawn, insert the connectors into the storage slots in the plastic wiring rail. Carefully push the assembly to the rear, and out of the casting **(see illustrations)**.

Refitting

11 Prior to refitting the injectors, the three O-rings, heat insulation washer and clip must be renewed. Due to the high injection pressures, it is essential that the O-rings are fitted without being twisted. Ford recommend the use of three special assembly sleeves to install the O-rings squarely. It may be prudent to entrust O-ring renewal to a Ford dealer or suitably-equipped injection specialist, rather than risk subsequent leaks **(see illustration)**.

5.9 Seat the slide hammer/tool in the slot on the side on the injector, and pull the injector out

5.10a Undo the two nuts at the back of the head and slide the injector loom/rail out

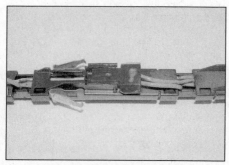

5.10b The injector connectors will slide into the loom/rail to prevent them from being damaged as the assembly is withdrawn/inserted into the cylinder head

5.11 Care must be used to ensure that the injector O-rings are fitted without being twisted

12 After renewing the O-rings, fit the heat shield and secure it in place with the circlip **(see illustration)**.

13 Smear clean engine oil onto the O-rings, and push the injector evenly down into the cylinder head onto its stop.

14 Fit the clamping block alongside the injector, but only hand-tighten the new retaining bolt at this stage.

15 It is essential that the injectors are fitted at right-angles to the clamping block. In order to achieve this, measure the distance from the rear face of the cylinder head to the rounded section of the injector **(see illustrations)**. The dimensions (a) are as follows:

    Cylinder 1 = 332.2 ± 0.08 mm
    Cylinder 2 = 244.2 ± 0.08 mm
    Cylinder 3 = 152.8 ± 0.08 mm
    Cylinder 4 = 64.8 ± 0.08 mm

16 Once the injector(s) are aligned correctly, tighten the clamping bolt to the specified Stage one torque setting, and the Stage two angle tightening setting. **Note:** *If an injector has been renewed, it is essential that the adjustment screw, locknut of the corresponding rocker, and ball-pin are renewed at the same time. The ball-pins simply pull out of the injector spring cap. There is an O-ring in each spring cap to stop the ball-pins from falling out.*

17 Smear some grease onto the contact face of each rocker arm adjustment screw, and refit the rocker shaft assembly to the camshaft bearing caps, tightening the retaining bolts as follows. Starting from the inside out, hand-tighten the bolts. Again, from the inside

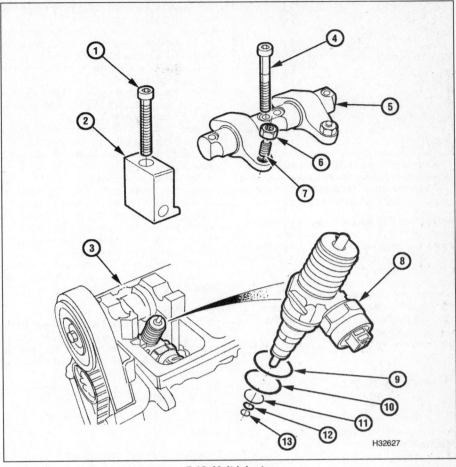

5.12 Unit injector

1 Bolt	4 Bolt	7 Adjuster	11 O-ring
2 Clamping block	5 Rocker arm	8 Unit injector	12 Heat shield
3 Cylinder head	6 Nut	9 O-ring	13 Circlip
		10 O-ring	

out, tighten the bolts to the Stage one torque setting. Finally, from the inside out, tighten the bolts to the Stage two angle tightening setting.

18 The following procedure is only necessary if an injector has been removed and refitted/renewed. Attach a DTI (Dial Test Indicator) gauge to the cylinder head upper surface, and position the DTI probe against the top of the adjustment screw **(see illustration)**. Turn the crankshaft until the rocker arm roller is on the highest point of its corresponding camshaft lobe, and the adjustment screw is at its lowest. Once this position has been established,

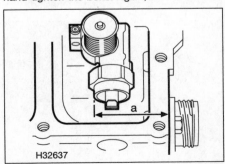

5.15a Measure the distance (a) from the rear of the cylinder head to the rounded section of the injector (see text)

5.15b Use a set square against the edge of the injector ...

5.15c ... and measure the distance to the rear of the cylinder head

5.18 Attach a DTI (Dial Test Indicator) gauge to the cylinder head upper surface, and position the DTI probe against the top of the adjustment screw

remove the DTI gauge, screw the adjustment screw in until firm resistance is felt, and the injector spring cannot be compressed further. Turn the adjustment screw **anti-clockwise** 225°, and tighten the locknut to the specified torque. Repeat this procedure for any other injectors that have been refitted.
19 Reconnect the wiring plug to the injector.
20 Refit the camshaft cover and upper timing belt cover, as described in Chapter 2B.
21 Start the engine and check that it runs correctly.

6 Inlet manifold – removal and refitting

Removal

1 Remove the engine and battery cover. Disconnect the battery and remove the soundproof material from the cylinder head.
2 Remove the bulkhead panel as described in Chapter 11, Section 12.
3 Release the spring clips and remove the inlet pipe ducting from the turbocharger.
4 Remove the turbocharger inlet pipe mounting bolt and crankcase ventilation pipe from the manifold.
5 At the left-hand end of the cylinder head, release the spring clips, unplug the boost pressure sensor (where fitted) and remove the pipe.
6 Disconnect the vacuum hose from the

6.8 Remove the bolts (arrowed)

EGR valve and anti-shudder valve (**see illustrations 12.16a or 12.16b**).
7 On all except the ANU engine, remove the timing belt cover and then remove the valve cover – see Chapter 2B for full details.
8 Unbolt and remove the turbocharger inlet pipe (**see illustration**).
9 On the ANU engines remove the turbocharger oil supply pipe and support bracket (**see illustration 11.1a**).
10 Jack up and support the front of the vehicle and remove the engine undershield.
11 Unbolt the exhaust system flexible pipe section.
12 On vehicles fitted with an EGR cooler, remove the lower radiator hose and drain off sufficient coolant so that the level is below the EGR cooler. Some coolant will remain in the EGR cooler, so anticipate some spillage.
13 Unbolt the EGR valve connector pipe and disconnect the EGR coolant pipe.
14 Remove the inlet manifold mounting bolts and remove the inlet manifold (**see illustration**). Discard the gasket.

Refitting

15 Refitting is a reversal of removal, using new manifold, EGR pipe and manifold flap assembly gaskets. Note that the coated side of the inlet manifold gasket faces the manifold.

7 Fuel filter – renewal

Note: *Observe the precautions in Section 1 before working on any component in the fuel system.*
    Refer to Chapter 1B.

8 Fuel gauge sender unit – removal and refitting

Note: *Observe the precautions in Section 1 before working on any component in the fuel system.*

 Warning: Avoid direct skin contact with fuel – wear protective clothing and gloves when handling

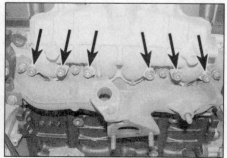

6.14 Remove the bolts (arrowed) – ANU engine shown

fuel system components. Ensure that the work area is well-ventilated to prevent the build-up of fuel vapour.
1 The fuel gauge sender unit is mounted on the top of the fuel tank. Access is via a hatch provided in the load space floor. The unit protrudes into the fuel tank, and its removal involves exposing the contents of the tank to the atmosphere.
2 Refer to the procedures in Chapter 4A, Section 6, for removal and refitting. On petrol models, the gauge sender unit is combined with the fuel pump, so ignore references to the fuel pump.

9 Fuel tank – removal and refitting

Note: *Observe the precautions in Section 1 before working on any component in the fuel system.*
1 Refer to the procedures in Chapter 4A, Section 7. There is no breather pipe to disconnect at the front of the tank – instead, the fuel supply pipe (coloured black) should be disconnected, with the return pipe (coloured blue).

10 Tandem fuel pump – removal and refitting

Removal

1 Remove the engine top cover.
2 Disconnect the charge air pipe, and place it to one side. Disconnect the central connector for the unit injectors (**see illustration**).
3 Release the retaining clip (where fitted) and disconnect the brake servo pipe from the tandem pump (**see illustration**).
4 Disconnect the fuel supply hose (marked white) from the tandem pump (**see illustration 10.3**). Be prepared for fuel spillage.
5 Unscrew the four retaining bolts and move the tandem pump away from the cylinder head (**see illustration 10.3**). As the pump is lifted up, disconnect the fuel return hose (marked blue). Be prepared for fuel spillage. There are no serviceable parts within the tandem pump. If the pump is faulty, it must be renewed.

10.2 Disconnect the injector connectors

Refitting

6 Reconnect the fuel return hose to the pump and refit the pump to the cylinder head, using new rubber seals, and ensuring that the pump pinion engages correctly with the drive slot in the camshaft **(see illustration)**.

7 Refit the pump retaining bolts, and tighten them to the specified torque.

8 Re-attach the fuel supply hose and brake servo hose to the pump.

9 Reconnect the central connector for the unit injectors.

10 Refit the charge air pipe.

11 Disconnect the fuel filter return hose (marked blue), and connect the hose to a hand vacuum pump. Operate the vacuum pump until fuel comes out of the return hose. This primes the tandem pump. Take care not to suck any fuel into the vacuum pump. Reconnect the return hose to the fuel filter.

12 Refit the engine top cover.

13 Have the engine management ECM's fault memory interrogated and erased by a Ford dealer or suitably-equipped specialist.

11 Turbocharger –
general information and precautions

General information

An exhaust manifold mounted turbocharger is fitted to all engines **(see illustrations)**.

The turbocharger increases engine efficiency by raising the pressure in the inlet manifold above atmospheric pressure. Instead of the air simply being sucked into the cylinders, it is forced in. Additional fuel is supplied by the injectors in proportion to the increased amount of air.

Energy for the operation of the turbocharger comes from the exhaust gas. The gas flows through a specially-shaped housing (the turbine housing) and in so doing, spins the turbine wheel. The turbine wheel is attached to a shaft, at the end of which is another vaned wheel, known as the compressor wheel. The compressor wheel spins in its own housing, and compresses the inducted air on the way to the inlet manifold.

Between the turbocharger and the inlet manifold, the compressed air passes through an intercooler. The purpose of the intercooler is to remove some of the heat gained in being compressed from the inducted air. Because cooler air is denser, removal of this heat further increases engine efficiency.

The turbo shaft is pressure-lubricated by an oil feed pipe from the engine oil filter mounting. The shaft 'floats' on a cushion of oil. Oil is returned to the sump via a return pipe that connects to the sump.

The turbocharger is a VGT (variable geometry turbocharger) sometimes referred to as a 'variable vane' or 'variable nozzle turbocharger' (VNT). The angle of the movable vanes is controlled by a vacuum-operated

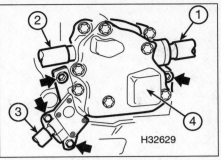

10.3 Fuel tandem pump securing bolts (arrowed)

1 Brake servo hose	3 Fuel return hose
2 Fuel supply hose	4 Tandem pump

10.6 Ensure that the tandem pump pinion engages correctly with the drive slot in the camshaft

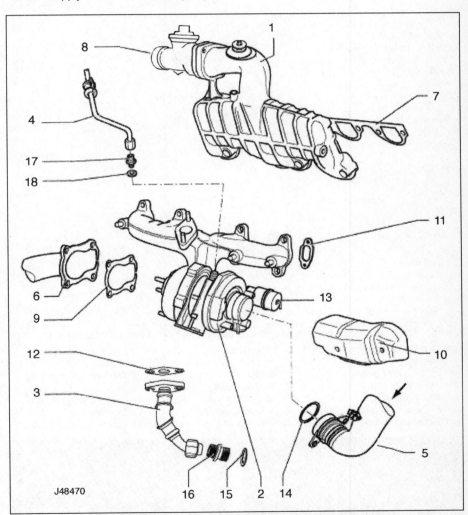

11.1a Turbocharger and associated components (ANU engine)

1 Inlet manifold	7 Inlet manifold gasket	12 Oil return pipe gasket
2 Turbocharger and exhaust manifold	8 EGR and anti-shudder control	13 Vacuum control unit
3 Oil return pipe	9 Exhaust gasket	14 O-ring
4 Oil supply pipe	10 Heat shield	15 Seal
5 Inlet pipe (from air filter)	11 Exhaust manifold gasket	16 Connector
6 Exhaust pipe		17 Connector
		18 Seal

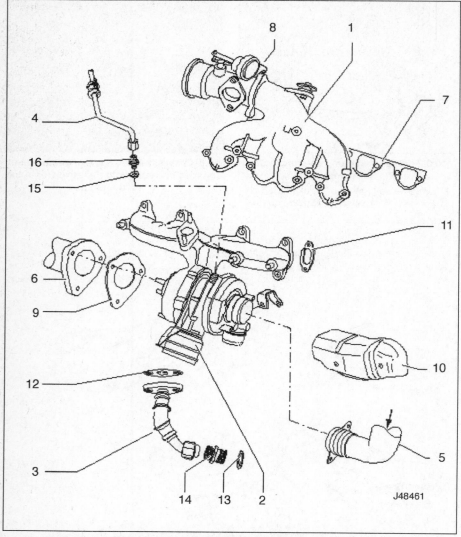

11.1b Turbocharger and associated components (AUY and ASZ engines)

1 Inlet manifold and EGR
   control valve
2 Turbocharger and
   exhaust manifold
3 Oil return pipe
4 Oil supply pipe
5 Inlet pipe (from air filter)

6 Exhaust pipe
7 Inlet manifold
   gasket
8 EGR and anti-shudder
   control
9 Exhaust gasket
10 Heat shield

11 Exhaust manifold
   gasket
12 Oil return pipe gasket
13 Seal
14 Connector
15 Connector
16 Seal

12.3a Remove the exhaust pipe . . .

12.3b . . . and recover the gasket

actuator. At low engine speeds the vanes are used to restrict the exhaust gas supply passage before the gases hit the turbine wheel – this has the effect of increasing the gas flow through the restriction, and the wheel reaches optimum speed faster (reducing turbo 'lag'). At higher engine speeds, the vanes open up the supply passage, which lowers the exhaust back-pressure and reduces fuel consumption.

Precautions

The turbocharger operates at extremely high speeds and temperatures. Certain precautions must be observed to avoid premature failure of the turbo, or injury to the operator.
• Do not operate the turbo with any parts exposed. Foreign objects falling onto the rotating vanes could cause excessive damage and (if ejected) personal injury.
• Cover the turbocharger air inlet ducts to prevent debris entering, and clean using lint-free cloths only.
• Do not race the engine immediately after start-up, especially if it is cold. Give the oil a few seconds to circulate.
• Always allow the engine to return to idle speed before switching it off – do not blip the throttle and switch off, as this will leave the turbo spinning without lubrication.
• Allow the engine to idle for several minutes before switching off after a high-speed run.
• Observe the recommended intervals for oil and filter changing, and use a reputable oil of the specified quality. Neglect of oil changing, or use of inferior oil, can cause carbon formation on the turbo shaft and subsequent failure. Thoroughly clean the area around all oil pipe unions before disconnecting them, to prevent the ingress of dirt. Store dismantled components in a sealed container to prevent contamination.

12 Turbocharger –
removal and refitting

Note: *On all engines the turbocharger is part of the exhaust manifold assembly.*

Removal

1 Apply the handbrake, then jack up the front of the vehicle and support it on axle stands (see *Jacking and vehicle support*). Remove the engine compartment undershield.
2 Remove the bulkhead panel as described in Chapter 11, Section 12.
3 Remove the exhaust pipe from the exhaust manifold and then remove the front section of the exhaust system **(see illustrations)**.
4 On vehicles fitted with an EGR cooler, remove the radiator bottom hose and drain the coolant to below the level of the EGR cooler.
5 Remove the right-hand roadwheel and then remove the outlet pipe from the turbocharger.
6 Remove the engine top cover and the soundproofing from the cylinder head.
7 Disconnect the battery and then support the

engine with a suitable trolley jack. Spread the load on the jack by placing a block of wood between the jack and the sump.

8 Remove the air filter housing as described in Section 2 of this Chapter.

9 With the engine supported, remove the right-hand engine mount (See Chapter 2B).

10 The turbocharger will be removed with the exhaust manifold as a complete assembly. To provide sufficient room to extract the turbocharger the engine must be pulled forward on the trolley jack.

11 With care, pull the engine forwards, checking that no hoses or any of the AC pipes are damaged or strained.

12 Remove the coolant pipe from the EGR cooler and then remove the EGR-to-exhaust manifold pipe (see illustration).

13 Unscrew the union bolt and disconnect the oil supply pipe from the top of the turbocharger; recover the sealing washers, noting their order of fitting. Anticipate some oil spillage as the pipe is removed. Plug or cover the pipe and aperture to prevent entry of dust

12.12 Remove the EGR pipe (arrowed)

12.14 Remove the oil return pipe bolts (arrowed)

and dirt. Remove the small bolt securing the pipe mounting bracket, and remove the pipe.

14 Unscrew the two bolts securing the oil return pipe to the base of the turbocharger (see illustration). Anticipate some oil spillage as the pipe is disconnected, and recover the gasket (obtain a new one for refitting).

15 Disconnect the boost pressure sensor and then remove the inlet pipe from the manifold.

16 Disconnect the vacuum hoses (see illustrations).

17 Unscrew the two nuts and washers securing the heat shield above the turbocharger, and remove the shield.

18 Support the manifold and turbocharger – it is a heavy assembly. Unscrew and remove the eight exhaust manifold retaining nuts, noting that the heat shield mounting bracket

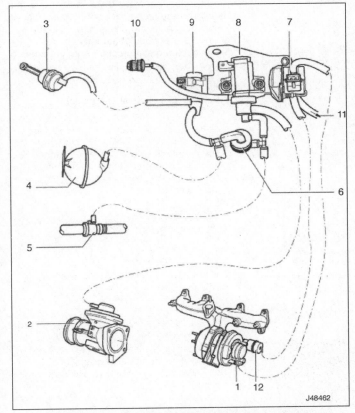

12.16a Turbocharger and associated vacuum hoses (ANU engine)

1 Turbocharger
2 EGR valve
3 Anti-shudder control valve
4 Vacuum reservoir
5 Vacuum supply (from tandem pump)
6 Non-return valve
7 Boost pressure control solenoid
8 EGR control solenoid
9 Anti-shudder control solenoid
10 Vent to atmosphere
11 Connection to air filter
12 Boost pressure control unit

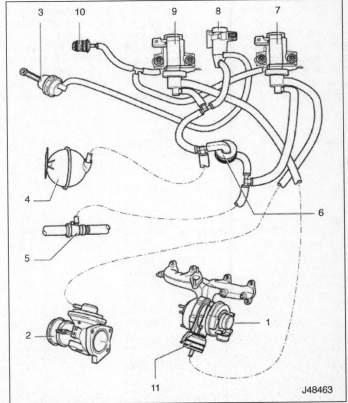

12.16b Turbocharger and associated vacuum hoses (AUY and ASZ engines)

1 Turbocharger
2 EGR valve
3 Anti-shudder control valve
4 Vacuum reservoir
5 Vacuum supply (from tandem pump)
6 Non-eturn valve
7 Boost pressure control solenoid
8 EGR control solenoid
9 Anti-shudder control solenoid
10 Vent to atmosphere
11 Boost pressure control unit

13.2a Remove the inlet hose . . .

13.2b . . . and the outlet hose

is secured by one of the nuts. Use plenty of penetrating oil if the studs are rusty. If a nut appears to be sticking, do not try to force it; tighten the nut back half a turn, apply some more penetrating oil to the stud threads, wait several seconds for it to soak in, then gradually unscrew the nut by one turn. Repeat this process until the nut is free. Note that if these nuts prove difficult to remove, consider removing the inlet manifold as described in Section 6 of this Chapter.

19 In some cases, the manifold studs will come out with the nuts – this poses no great problem, and the studs can be refitted if they are in good condition. For preference, however, a complete set of manifold studs and nuts should be obtained, as the old ones are likely to be in less-than-perfect condition.

20 Carefully separate the manifold from the cylinder head, and slide the manifold off the mounting studs. Manoeuvre the manifold and turbocharger out from below. Recover the manifold gaskets from the cylinder head studs, and discard them.

Refitting

21 Refit the turbocharger by following the removal procedure in reverse, noting the following points:

  a) Renew all gaskets, sealing washers and O-rings.
  b) Before reconnecting the oil supply pipe, fill the turbocharger with fresh oil using an oil can.
  c) Tighten all nuts and bolts to the specified torque, where given.

  d) Ensure that the air hose clips are securely tightened, to prevent air leaks.
  e) Refill the cooling system if required.
  f) When the engine is started after refitting, allow it to idle for approximately one minute to give the oil time to circulate around the turbo shaft bearings. Check for signs of oil or coolant leakage from the relevant unions.

13 Intercooler – removal and refitting

Removal

1 Apply the handbrake, then jack up the front of the vehicle and support it on axle stands (see *Jacking and vehicle support*). Remove the engine compartment undershield.

2 The intercooler is located below the radiator. Remove the inlet and outlet hoses **(see illustrations)**.

3 Working as described in Chapter 3, remove the radiator mounting bolts, and move the radiator to the rear sufficiently to gain access to the intercooler mounting bolts.

4 Undo the intercooler mounting bolts.

5 Manoeuvre the intercooler from underneath the vehicle.

Refitting

6 Refitting is a reversal of removal.

Chapter 4 Part C:
Emission control and exhaust systems

Contents

Degrees of difficulty

Easy, suitable for novice with little experience	Fairly easy, suitable for beginner with some experience	Fairly difficult, suitable for competent DIY mechanic	Difficult, suitable for experienced DIY mechanic	Very difficult, suitable for expert DIY or professional

Specifications

Torque wrench settings	Nm	lbf ft
Catalytic converter to exhaust	55	41
EGR pipe	25	18
EGR valve to inlet manifold	25	18
Exhaust manifold to flexible downpipe	35	26
Exhaust manifold to downpipe (petrol engine).	23	17
Exhaust manifold to cylinder head:		
Diesel engines	25	18
Petrol engines:		
Studs.	14	10
Nuts	23	17
Oxygen sensors	42	31

1 General information

Emission control systems

All petrol engine models are designed to use unleaded petrol and are controlled by engine management systems that are programmed to give the best compromise between driveability, fuel consumption and exhaust emission production. In addition, a number of systems are fitted that help to minimise other harmful emissions. A crankcase emission control system is fitted, which reduces the release of pollutants from the engine's lubrication system, and a catalytic converter is fitted which reduces exhaust gas pollutants. An evaporative loss emission control system is fitted which reduces the release of gaseous hydrocarbons from the fuel tank.

Diesel engine models have a crankcase emission control system, and in addition are fitted with a catalytic converter, and an Exhaust gas recirculation (EGR) system to reduce exhaust emissions. All diesel engines have glow plugs fitted primarily as an aid to cold starting, but under the correct operating conditions they will be operated (by the engine management system) after starting to reduce exhaust emissions. The glow plugs are covered in Chapter 5C.

Crankcase emission control

To reduce the emission of unburned hydrocarbons from the crankcase into the atmosphere, the engine is sealed and the blow-by gases and oil vapour are drawn from inside the crankcase, through a wire mesh oil separator, into the inlet tract to be burned by the engine during normal combustion. All diesel engines have a pressure regulating valve on the camshaft cover, to control the flow of gases from the crankcase. On petrol models the valve is fitted into the tubing from the cylinder block.

Exhaust emission control

Petrol models

To minimise the amount of pollutants which escape into the atmosphere, all petrol models are fitted with a three-way catalytic converter in the exhaust system. The fuelling system is of the closed-loop type, in which an oxygen sensor in the exhaust system provides the engine management system ECM with constant feedback, enabling the ECM to adjust the air/fuel mixture to optimise combustion. Later models are also fitted with a second oxygen sensor after the catalytic converter, to inform the ECM of the oxygen content of the post-catalyst gases.

The oxygen sensor(s) has a heating element built-in that is controlled by the ECM through the oxygen sensor relay to quickly bring the sensor's tip to its optimum operating temperature. The sensor's tip is sensitive to oxygen and relays a voltage signal to the ECM that varies according on the amount of oxygen in the exhaust gas. If the inlet air/fuel mixture is too rich, the exhaust gases are low in oxygen so the sensor sends a low-voltage signal, the voltage rising as the mixture weakens and the amount of oxygen rises in the exhaust gases. Peak conversion efficiency of all major pollutants occurs if the inlet air/fuel mixture is maintained at the chemically-correct ratio for the complete combustion of petrol of 14.7 parts (by weight) of air to 1 part of fuel (the stoichiometric ratio). The sensor output voltage alters in a large step at this point, the ECM using the signal change as a reference point and correcting the inlet air/fuel mixture accordingly by altering the fuel injector pulse width. Details of the oxygen sensor removal and refitting are given in Chapter 4A, Section 4.

An exhaust gas recirculation (EGR) system is also fitted to some models. This reduces the level of nitrogen oxides produced during combustion by introducing a proportion of the exhaust gas back into the inlet manifold, under certain engine operating conditions, via a plunger valve. The system is controlled electronically by the engine management ECM.

2.3 Evaporative loss emission control purge valve

In order to work efficiently, the catalytic converter needs to heated to a temperature of at least 300°C. So that the exhaust gases can heat the catalyst up faster, petrol models are equipped with a secondary air injection system. During the initial warm-up stage, fresh air is injected behind the exhaust valves, this enriches the exhaust gases with oxygen, which causes an 'afterburning' effect, which shortens the catalyst warm-up phase. The activation of the secondary air injection pump and inlet valve, is controlled by the engine management ECM.

Diesel models

An oxidation catalyst is fitted in the exhaust system of all diesel engined models. This has the effect of removing a large proportion of the gaseous hydrocarbons, carbon monoxide and particulates present in the exhaust gas.

An exhaust gas recirculation (EGR) system is also fitted to all diesel engined models. This reduces the level of nitrogen oxides produced during combustion by introducing a proportion of the exhaust gas back into the inlet manifold, under certain engine operating conditions, via a plunger valve. The system is controlled electronically by the diesel engine management ECM.

Evaporative emission control

Petrol models

To minimise the escape of unburned hydrocarbons into the atmosphere, an evaporative loss emission control system (EVAP) is fitted to all petrol models. The fuel

3.1a The crankcase emission regulating valve (arrowed) is fitted to the front of the cylinder block – petrol engines

2.10 Undo the bolt and remove the charcoal canister

tank filler cap is sealed and a charcoal canister is mounted underneath the right-hand wing to collect the petrol vapours released from the fuel contained in the fuel tank. It stores them until they can be drawn from the canister (under the control of the engine management system ECM) via the purge valve(s) into the inlet tract, where they are then burned by the engine during normal combustion.

To ensure that the engine runs correctly when it is cold and/or idling and to protect the catalytic converter from the effects of an over-rich mixture, the purge control valve(s) are not opened by the ECM until the engine has warmed-up, and the engine is under load; the valve solenoid is then modulated on and off to allow the stored vapour to pass into the inlet tract.

Exhaust systems

On petrol models the exhaust system comprises the exhaust manifold, front pipe (with oxygen sensor), catalytic converter, intermediate pipe and silencer, and tailpipe and silencer.

On diesel models, the exhaust system comprises the exhaust manifold, turbocharger, front pipe, catalytic converter, intermediate pipe and silencer, and tailpipe and silencer. The system is supported by rubber bushes and/or rubber mounting rings.

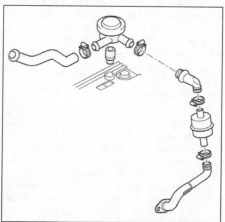

3.1b Crankcase emission regulating valve – diesel engines

Information

1 The evaporative loss emission control system consists of the purge valve, the activated charcoal filter canister and a series of connecting vacuum hoses.
2 The purge valve is located on the bulkhead of the engine compartment, in the vacuum line between the charcoal canister and the inlet manifold. The charcoal canister is mounted inside the right-hand front wheel housing behind the wheel arch liner, in front of the A-pillar.

Component renewal

Purge valve

3 Ensure that the ignition is switched off, then unplug the wiring harness from the purge valve at the connector **(see illustration)**.
4 Undo the valve retaining bolts.
5 Note the fitted locations of the vacuum and vapour hoses, and disconnect them from the valve.
6 Refitting is a reversal of removal.

Charcoal canister

7 Apply the handbrake, then jack up the front of the vehicle and support it on axle stands (see *Jacking and vehicle support*). Remove the right-hand front roadwheel.
8 Partially remove the rear of the right-hand front wheel arch liner to give access to the charcoal canister with reference to Chapter 11.
9 Disconnect the vapour hoses, noting which ports they connect to.
10 Undo the mounting bolt and remove the charcoal canister **(see illustration)**.
11 Refitting is a reversal of removal.

3 Crankcase emission system – general information

1 The crankcase emission control system consists of hoses, and separating valves, connecting the crankcase to the camshaft cover, and the air cleaner or inlet manifold **(see illustrations)**.
2 The systems requires no attention other than to check at regular intervals that the hoses, valve and oil separator are free of blockages and in good condition.

4 Exhaust gas recirculation (EGR) system – component removal

EGR valve

Petrol engine

1 Pull out the battery compartment upper panel.
2 Release the retaining clips/screws and

4.7 Pull the vacuum hose from the EGR valve

4.14a Remove the heat shield

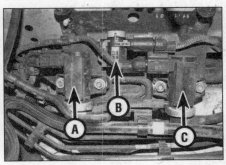

4.14b The EGR control valve is located on the engine compartment bulkhead

A Turbocharger control
B Anti-shudder control
C EGR control

remove the bulkhead cover from the engine compartment. Slide the cover to the right-hand side and manoeuvre it from behind the coolant expansion tank.

3 Unscrew the EGR supply pipe union, and disconnect the pipe from the valve.

4 Slacken and remove the two bolts securing the EGR valve. Disconnect the vacuum hose as the valve is withdrawn. Ford recommend that the exhaust manifold-to-EGR valve pipe is renewed whenever the connecting unions are disturbed – see later in this Section.

5 Refitting is a reversal of removal.

Diesel engines

6 Prise out the cover caps, undo the retaining nuts and remove the plastic cover from the top of the engine.

7 Disconnect the vacuum hose from the top of the valve (see illustration).

8 Undo the bolts securing the EGR pipe to the valve, and recover the gasket.

9 Slacken and remove the retaining bolts, and detach the valve from the manifold. Recover the gasket.

10 Refitting is a reversal of removal. Renew the gaskets and tighten the bolts to the specified torque where given.

EGR control valve

Petrol engine

11 Disconnect the valve wiring plug, located on the engine compartment bulkhead.

12 Undo the two retaining bolts, and disconnect the vacuum pipe as the valve is removed.

13 Refitting is a reversal of removal.

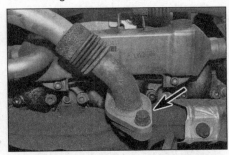

4.30 Undo the bolts securing the EGR pipe to the exhaust manifold (arrowed, with one bolt hidden)

Diesel engines

14 The EGR valve is located on the engine compartment bulkhead. Remove the bulkhead panel, as described in Chapter 11, Section 12. Remove the heat shield. The valve is the right-hand of the two vacuum control solenoids (see illustrations).

15 Note their fitted positions, and disconnect the valve vacuum hoses. Disconnect the wiring plug, undo the two nuts and remove the valve.

16 Refitting is a reversal of removal.

EGR pipe

Petrol engine

17 Drain the cooling system as described in Chapter 1A.

18 At the left-hand end of the cylinder head, disconnect the pressure transducer pipes from the EGR pipe.

19 Release the retaining clips and disconnect the coolant pipes from the outlet housing on the left-hand end of the cylinder head.

20 Disconnect the wiring plug from the engine coolant temperature sensor on the underside of the coolant outlet housing.

21 Disconnect the vacuum hose, and undo the two EGR valve retaining bolts.

22 Undo the two bolts securing the coolant pipe to the left-hand end of the cylinder head.

23 Slacken and remove the two EGR pipe retaining bolts.

24 Release the retaining clip and disconnect the secondary air injection pipe from the EGR pipe.

25 Undo the unions and separate the EGR pipe from the exhaust manifold.

26 Manoeuvre the EGR pipe from the engine complete with the EGR valve. If required, unscrew the union and separate the pipe from the valve. Ford recommend that the EGR pipe should not be re-used.

27 Refitting is a reversal of removal, using a new EGR pipe and gaskets. Tighten the nuts/bolts to the specified torque where given. Refill the cooling system as described in Chapter 1A.

Diesel engines

28 Remove the engine cover and then remove the bulkhead panel (see Chapter 11, Section 12).

29 On the AUY and ASZ engines an EGR cooler is fitted. On these engines it is easier to remove the cooler and connecting pipes as a complete assembly – see below.

30 Slacken and remove the bolts/nuts securing the EGR pipe to the inlet and exhaust manifolds, and manoeuvre the pipe from the engine (see illustration). Recover the gaskets.

31 Refitting is a reversal of removal, using new gaskets, and tightening the nuts/bolts to the specified torque where given.

EGR transducer

Note: No EGR pressure transducer is fitted to diesel engines.

32 Ensure that the ignition is switched off. Unscrew the two transducer retaining nuts (see illustration).

33 Disconnect the wiring plug and system hoses as the transducer is withdrawn.

34 Refitting is a reversal of removal.

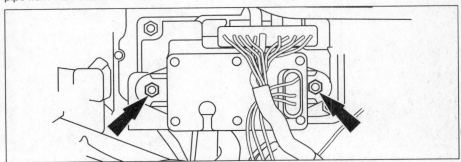

4.32 The pressure transducer is held in place by two nuts (arrowed)

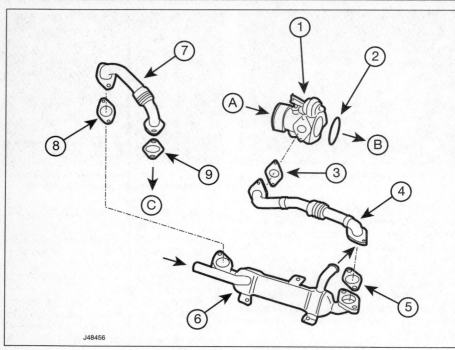

4.37 The EGR cooler and associated parts

1 EGR valve	5 Gasket	9 Gasket
2 O-ring	6 EGR cooler	A From intercooler
3 Gasket	7 Connecting pipe	B To inlet manifold
4 Connecting pipe	8 Gasket	C To exhaust manifold

EGR cooler

Note: *Only fitted to the AUY and ASZ diesel engines*

35 Jack up the front of the vehicle and support it on axle stands (see *Jacking and vehicle support*).

36 Remove engine undershield and the radiator bottom hose. Drain the coolant to below the level of the EGR cooler.

37 Remove the engine cover and disconnect the coolant hoses from the EGR cooler **(see illustration)**.

38 Unbolt the outlet pipe from the EGR control valve – recover the gasket.

39 Unbolt the inlet pipe from the exhaust manifold – recover the gasket.

40 Unbolt the cooler from the inlet manifold

41 Refitting is a reversal of removal, using new gaskets. Refill the cooling system and check for leaks.

5 Exhaust manifold – removal and refitting

Petrol engine models

Removal

1 Remove the EGR pipe (where fitted) as described in the previous Section.

2 Remove the auxiliary drivebelt with reference to Chapter 2A.

3 Where fitted, undo the retaining bolts and remove the exhaust manifold heat shield.

4 Undo the retaining nuts and disconnect the front exhaust pipe from the exhaust manifold.

5 Undo the bolt/nuts securing the bracket to the engine mounting support plate and cylinder head **(see illustration)**.

6 Slacken and remove the alternator top mounting bolt. Pivot the alternator forwards. Undo the nut and bolt, and remove the small bracket above the alternator

7 Unscrew the nut securing the oil dipstick guide tube bracket, and carefully pull the guide tube from the engine block **(see illustration)**.

8 Undo the retaining nuts and remove the exhaust manifold from the engine **(see illustration)**. Recover the gaskets.

Refitting

9 Clean thoroughly the mating surfaces of the manifold and cylinder head.

10 Refitting is a reversal of removal, but fit new gaskets, renew self-locking nuts, and tighten the nuts to the specified torque.

Diesel engine models

11 On all diesel models the exhaust manifold and turbocharger are a complete unit. To remove the exhaust manifold, remove the turbocharger as described in Chapter 4B.

6 Exhaust system – component renewal

⚠️ *Warning: Allow ample time for the exhaust system to cool before starting work. In particular, note that the catalytic converter runs at very high temperatures. If there is any chance that the system may still be hot, wear suitable gloves.*

Removal

1 Each exhaust section can be removed individually, but because the system is located above the rear axle, the system cannot be removed complete.

2 To remove part of the system, first jack up the front or rear of the car and support it on axle stands (see *Jacking and vehicle support*). Alternatively position the car over an inspection pit or on car ramps.

Front pipe

Note: *Handle the flexible, braided section of*

5.5 Remove the bracket from the engine mounting plate to the cylinder head

5.7 Remove the oil dipstick and bracket

5.8 Undo the exhaust manifold nuts (engine removed for clarity)

the front pipe carefully, and do not bend it excessively.

3 On petrol models, trace the oxygen sensor wiring back to the multiplug, and disconnect it.

4 Unscrew the nuts and disconnect the front pipe from the exhaust manifold. Recover the gasket **(see illustrations)**.

5 Support the catalytic converter/short pipe exhaust section on a trolley jack, then unscrew the flange bolts/clamp bolt and separate the front pipe. Recover the gasket.

Catalytic converter

6 Working under the car, support the front pipe and intermediate section on axle stands or trolley jacks.

7 Disconnect the wiring plug from the oxygen sensor (petrol vehicles) unscrew the flange bolts and separate the catalytic converter from the front pipe. Recover the gasket **(see illustration)**.

8 Note the fitted position of the clamp, then unscrew the clamp bolts and separate the catalytic converter from the intermediate section.

Intermediate pipe and silencer

9 Working under the car, support the front pipe on an axle stand or trolley jack.

10 Unscrew the clamp bolts and separate the intermediate pipe from the tailpipe.

11 Note the fitted position of the clamp attaching the intermediate pipe to the catalytic converter or short pipe (the bolts should be on the left-hand side of the clamp, and the lower ends of the bolts should not be below the bottom of the pipe), then unscrew the clamp bolts and separate the catalytic converter.

12 Disconnect the rubber mountings and withdraw the intermediate pipe and silencer from under the car.

Tailpipe and silencer

13 Unscrew the clamp bolts and separate the tailpipe from the intermediate pipe. Note that the fitted position of the clamp should be with the bolts facing the rear of the car, and the bolt ends should not be below the bottom of the pipe.

14 Disconnect the rubber mountings and withdraw the tailpipe and silencer from under the car **(see illustration)**.

Refitting

15 Each section is refitted by a reversal of the removal sequence, noting the following points.

a) Ensure that all traces of corrosion have been removed from the flanges or pipe ends and renew all necessary gaskets.

b) Inspect the rubber mountings for signs

6.4a Undo the nuts to disconnect the front pipe . . .

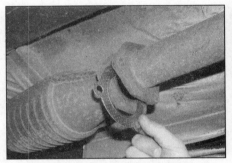
6.7 Recover the gasket between the catalytic converter and the intermediate pipe

6.4b . . . and recover the gasket – petrol model

6.14 Tail pipe/silencer mountings

of damage or deterioration and renew as necessary.

c) Prior to tightening the exhaust system mounting, ensure that all rubber mountings are correctly located and that there is adequate clearance between the exhaust system and vehicle underbody.

d) Do not use any form of jointing compound on the exhaust system on the engine side (upstream) of the catalytic converter, as any residue could cause irreparable damage to its internal components.

7 Catalytic converter – general information and precautions

1 The catalytic converter is a reliable and simple device which needs no maintenance in itself, but there are some facts which an owner should be aware of if the converter is to function properly for its full service life.

All models

a) DO NOT use fuel or engine oil additives – these may contain substances harmful to the catalytic converter.

b) Remember that the catalytic converter operates at very high temperatures.

DO NOT, therefore, park the car in dry undergrowth, over long grass or piles of dead leaves after a long run.

c) Remember that the catalytic converter is FRAGILE – do not strike it with tools during servicing work.

Petrol models

a) DO NOT use leaded petrol – the lead will coat the internal precious metals, reducing their converting efficiency and will eventually destroy the converter.

b) Always keep the ignition and fuel systems well-maintained in accordance with the manufacturer's schedule.

c) If the engine develops a misfire, do not drive the car at all (or at least as little as possible) until the fault is cured.

d) DO NOT push- or tow-start the car further than 50 yards – this will soak the catalytic converter in unburned fuel, causing it to overheat when the engine does start.

e) DO NOT switch off the ignition at high engine speeds.

f) The catalytic converter, used on a well-maintained and well-driven car, should last between 50 000 and 100 000 miles – if the converter is no longer effective it must be renewed.

Chapter 5 Part A:
Starting and charging systems

Contents

Degrees of difficulty

Easy, suitable for novice with little experience	Fairly easy, suitable for beginner with some experience	Fairly difficult, suitable for competent DIY mechanic 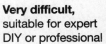	Difficult, suitable for experienced DIY mechanic	Very difficult, suitable for expert DIY or professional

Specifications

General
System type . . . . 12 volt, negative earth

Starter motor
Type . . . . Bosch, pre-engaged

Battery
Ratings:
  Main battery . . . . 44 to 92 Ah (depending on model and market)
  Auxiliary battery . . . . 61 Ah

Alternator
Type . . . . Bosch
Rating. . . . . 70, 90 or 120 amp
Minimum brush length . . . . 5.0 mm

Torque wrench settings

Torque wrench settings	Nm	lbf ft
Alternator mounting bolts.	25	18
Auxiliary drivebelt tensioner bolts	25	18
Battery mounting clamp.	35	26
Starter motor:		
Petrol engines.	35	26
Diesel engines:		
Five-speed transmission.	65	48
Six-speed transmission	80	59

1 General information and precautions

The engine electrical system consists mainly of the charging and starting systems. Because of their engine-related functions, these are covered separately from the body electrical devices such as the lights, instruments, etc, which are covered in Chapter 12. On petrol engine models refer to Part B of this Chapter for information on the ignition system, and on diesel models refer to Part C for the preheating system.

The electrical system is of the 12 volt negative earth type.

The battery is of the maintenance-free (sealed for life) type and is charged by the alternator, which is belt-driven from the crankshaft pulley. On some models, an auxiliary battery is fitted in a floor-level storage compartment, to provide electrical power for the additional heater/air conditioning unit.

The starter motor is of the pre-engaged type, with an integral solenoid. On starting, the solenoid moves the drive pinion into engagement with the flywheel/driveplate ring gear before the starter motor is energised. Once the engine has started, a one-way clutch prevents the motor armature being driven by the engine until the pinion disengages from the flywheel. Two primary earth straps are fitted; one from the battery negative terminal to the body, and one from the engine to the body. Additional earth straps are present throughout the vehicle.

Further details of the various systems are given in the relevant Sections of this Chapter. While some repair procedures are given, the usual course of action is to renew the component concerned.

Precautions

It is necessary to take extra care when working on the electrical system to avoid damage to semi-conductor devices (diodes and transistors), and to avoid the risk of personal injury. In addition to the precautions given in *Safety first!*, observe the following when working on the system:

• *Always remove rings, watches, etc, before working on the electrical system.* Even with the battery disconnected, capacitive discharge could occur if a component's live terminal is earthed through a metal object. This could cause a shock or nasty burn.
• *Do not reverse the battery connections.* Components such as the alternator, electronic control modules, or any other components having semi-conductor circuitry could be irreparably damaged.
• *Never disconnect the battery terminals, the alternator, any electrical wiring or any test instruments when the engine is running.*
• *Do not allow the engine to turn the alternator when the alternator is not connected.*
• *Never test for alternator output by 'flashing' the output lead to earth.*
• *Always ensure that the battery negative lead is disconnected when working on the electrical system.*
• If the engine is being started using jump leads and a slave battery, connect the batteries *positive-to-positive* and *negative-to-negative* (see *Jump starting* at the beginning of the manual). This also applies when connecting a battery charger.
• *Before using electric-arc welding equipment on the car, disconnect the battery, alternator and components such as electronic control units* to protect them from the risk of damage.
Caution:
• *The audio unit fitted as standard equipment has a built-in security code to deter thieves. If the power source to the unit is cut, the anti-theft system will activate. Even if the power source is immediately reconnected, the audio unit will not function until the correct security code has been entered. Therefore, if you do not know the correct security code for the unit, do not disconnect the battery negative terminal or remove the unit from the vehicle.*
• *Disconnecting the main battery will also cause the engine management electronic control module (ECM) to lose its stored values. After reconnection, a journey of approximately 10 to 25 miles may be necessary for the ECM to relearn those values. During this period, the engine performance may be erratic.*

3.1 Remove the cover to access the battery

• *To avoid losing the ECM data, radio code and clock settings, a device known as a 'code saver' may be used in some circumstances. This usually plugs into the cigarette lighter socket, and provides the electrical system with a small 12 volt supply. For details of their recommended usage, refer to your Ford dealer or automotive accessory specialist.*

2 Battery – testing and charging

Caution 1: Battery acid is caustic and corrosive. Wash spillages off skin, clothing or surfaces immediately with plenty of water. If acid gets into the eyes, seek medical advice.
Caution 2: The gas given off by the battery during charging is explosive. Do not smoke or allow naked lights near the battery. Connect the charger to the battery before switching on at the mains, and switch off at the mains before disconnecting the charger when charging is complete.

Testing

1 If the battery cell caps can be removed, a hydrometer may be used to check the state of charge. The specific gravity of the electrolyte in a fully-charged battery should be around 1.270. A reading of 1.130 or below indicates a discharged battery. A difference of 0.040 or more between cells suggests a defective cell.
2 Most modern batteries are sealed for life and maintenance-free. Topping-up and testing of the electrolyte in each cell is not possible. The condition of the battery can therefore only be tested using a battery condition indicator or a digital voltmeter.
3 Certain maintenance-free batteries have a built-in charge condition indicator. The indicator is located in the top of the battery casing, and indicates the condition of the battery from its colour. If the indicator shows green, then the battery is in a good state of charge. If the indicator turns darker, eventually to black, then the battery requires charging, as described later in this Section. If the indicator shows clear or yellow, the electrolyte level in the battery is too low to allow further use, and the battery should be renewed. Do not attempt to charge, load or jump start a battery when the indicator shows clear or yellow.
4 If testing the battery using a digital voltmeter, connect the voltmeter across the battery and note the voltage. The test is only accurate if the battery has not been subjected to charge for the previous six hours. If this is not the case, switch on the headlights for 30 seconds, then switch them off and wait 5 minutes before testing the battery. All other electrical circuits must be switched off, so check that the doors and tailgate are fully shut when making the test.
5 A fully-charged battery should give a reading of at least 12.6 volts. If the reading is

less than 12.2 volts the battery is discharged, whilst a reading of 12.2 to 12.4 volts indicates a partially-discharged condition.
6 If the battery is to be charged, remove it from the vehicle unless the battery charger is specifically stated to be safe for use with the battery connected, otherwise there is a risk of damaging the vehicle's electronics.

Charging

Note: *The following is intended as a guide only. Always refer to the manufacturer's recommendations (often printed on a label attached to the battery) before charging a battery.*
7 Charge the battery at a rate equivalent to no more than 10% of the battery capacity (eg, for a 45 Ah battery charge at 4.5 A maximum) for no more than 12 hours. Stop at once if gasing (a fizzing noise coming from the cells) becomes apparent.
8 Alternatively, a trickle charger charging at the rate of 1.5 A can safely be used overnight.
9 Rapid boost charges can restore the power of the battery in 1 to 2 hours, but they must be strictly controlled to avoid damage through overheating. Suitable equipment is generally found in garage workshops.
10 While charging the battery, note that the temperature of the electrolyte should never exceed 38°C.
11 The maintenance-free battery type takes considerably longer to fully recharge than the standard type, the time taken being dependent on the extent of discharge, but it can take anything up to three days.
12 A constant voltage type charger is required, to be set, when connected, to 13.9 to 14.9 volts with a charger current below 25 amps. Using this method, the battery should be useable within three hours, giving a voltage reading of 12.5 volts, but this is for a partially-discharged battery and, as mentioned, full charging can take far longer.
13 If the battery is to be charged from a fully-discharged state (condition reading less than 12.2 volts), have it recharged by your local automotive electrician, as the charge rate is higher and constant supervision during charging is necessary.

3 Battery – disconnection, removal and refitting

Note: *If the vehicle has a security-coded radio, check that you have a copy of the code number before disconnecting the battery cable; refer to the caution in Section 1.*
Note: *Disconnecting the main battery will also cause the engine management electronic control module (ECM) to lose its stored values. Again, refer to the caution in Section 1.*

Disconnection and removal

Main battery

1 The battery is located at the left-hand side of the engine compartment **(see illustration)**.

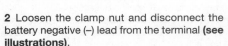

3.2a Undo the negative terminal clamp nut . . .

3.2b . . . and disconnect the terminal

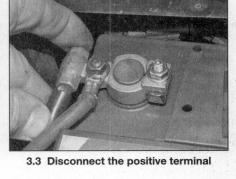

3.3 Disconnect the positive terminal

2 Loosen the clamp nut and disconnect the battery negative (–) lead from the terminal **(see illustrations)**.

3 Lift the plastic flap where fitted, then loosen the clamp nut and disconnect the battery positive (+) lead from the terminal **(see illustration)**.

4 At the base of the battery, unscrew the retaining bolt and remove the clamp **(see illustration)**.

5 Where fitted, disconnect the vent pipe from the battery. Note on some models the vent incorporates a flashback arrester.

6 Lift out the battery and withdraw it from the engine compartment **(see illustration)**.

Additional battery

7 Vehicles equipped with an auxiliary heater are fitted with an additional battery under the passenger seat. At the time of writing, no information concerning removal and refitting of the additional battery was available.

Refitting

8 Clean the battery mounting and apply a little grease to the threads of the clamp bolt.

9 Place the battery in position and refit the clamp. Tighten the bolt to the specified torque.

10 Where fitted, refit the vent pipe.

11 Reconnect the battery positive (+) lead to the terminal and tighten the clamp nut.

12 Reconnect the battery negative (–) lead to the terminal and tighten the clamp nut.

13 Re-activate the radio by inserting the security code where applicable. Refer to Section 1 and the notes at the start of this Section.

4 Battery compartment panels – removal and refitting

Upper panel

1 The upper panel simply pulls from its location **(see illustration)**.

2 Refitting is a reversal of removal, ensuring that the panel edges locate in the grooves of the adjoining panels.

Lower panel

3 Remove battery compartment upper panel, as described in Paragraph 1.

3.4 Undo the bolt and remove the clamp

3.6 Lift the battery from the engine compartment

4 The lower section is bolted into place. Remove the bolts from the loom support bracket and move it to one side. Unclip the wiring loom and hose(s) and then unbolt the panel. Remove the panel **(see illustrations)**.

4.1 The upper panel simply pulls out

4.4a Access the mounting bolts by removing the bracket . . .

4.4b . . . remove the bolts (arrowed) . . .

4.4c . . . and lift the panel out

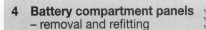

4.8a Remove the bolts (arrowed) . . .

4.8b . . . and lift out the support tray

6 Alternator –
removal and refitting

5 Refitting is a reversal of removal, ensuring that the panel edges locate in the grooves of the adjoining panels.

Battery support tray

Removal

6 Remove the cover and side panels as described above.
7 Unclip the loom supports from the panel
8 Remove the bolts and lift out the support tray **(see illustrations)**.

5 Alternator/charging system –
testing in vehicle

Note: *Refer to Section 1 of this Chapter before starting work.*
1 If the charge warning light fails to illuminate when the ignition is switched on, first check the alternator wiring connections for security. If satisfactory, check that the warning light bulb has not blown, and that the bulbholder is secure in its location in the instrument panel. If the light still fails to illuminate, check the continuity of the warning light feed wire from the alternator to the bulbholder. Check the condition of the auxiliary drivebelt. Check the condition of the regulator within the alternator as described in Section 7 of this Chapter. If all is satisfactory, the alternator is at fault and should be renewed or taken to an auto-electrician for testing and repair.
2 Similarly, if the charge warning light comes on with the ignition, but is then slow to go out when the engine is started, this may indicate

an impending alternator problem. Check all the items listed in the preceding Paragraph, and refer to an auto-electrical specialist if no obvious faults are found.
3 If the charge warning light illuminates when the engine is running, stop the engine and check that the drivebelt is correctly tensioned (see Chapter 1A or 1B) and that the alternator connections are secure. If all is so far satisfactory, check the alternator brushes and slip-rings as described in Section 7. If the fault persists, the alternator should be renewed, or taken to an auto-electrician for testing and repair.
4 If the alternator output is suspect even though the warning light functions correctly, the regulated voltage may be checked as follows.
5 Connect a voltmeter across the battery terminals, and start the engine.
6 Increase the engine speed until the voltmeter reading remains steady; the reading should be approximately 12 to 13 volts, and no more than 14 volts.
7 Switch on as many electrical accessories as possible (eg, the headlights, heated rear window and heater blower), and check that the alternator maintains the regulated voltage at around 13 to 14 volts.
8 If the regulated voltage is not as stated, this may be due to worn brushes, weak brush springs, a faulty voltage regulator, a faulty diode, a severed phase winding or worn or damaged slip-rings. The brushes and slip-rings may be checked (see Section 7), but if the fault persists, the alternator should be renewed or taken to an auto-electrician.

Removal

Petrol engines

1 Disconnect the battery negative lead and position it away from the terminal – refer to the precautions in Section 1.
2 Remove the air cleaner assembly as described in Chapter 4A.
3 Remove the right-hand side headlamp as described in Chapter 12, Section 7.
4 Undo the headlamp shield upper and lower fixing bolts. Release the wiring harness cable-tie.
5 In order to remove the clips securing the trim panel adjacent to the alternator, press in the centre of the clips and prise them from the panel **(see illustration)**. The lower three clips are inserted from the headlamp side of the panel. Remove the trim panel. Note, on later models there is enough room below the headlight housing to remove the alternator upper bolt.
6 Unscrew the remaining headlamp shield fixing bolt, release the two clips and manoeuvre the shield from the engine compartment.
7 Apply the handbrake, then jack up the front of the vehicle and support it on axle stands (see *Jacking and vehicle support*). Undo the four bolts and two nuts, and remove the engine undershield.
8 With a spanner, rotate the auxiliary drivebelt tensioner clockwise, and remove the belt from the alternator pulley.
9 Unscrew the two alternator mounting bolts, and lift the alternator slightly to gain access to the electrical connections **(see illustration)**.
10 Undo the electrical connections and manoeuvre the alternator from the engine compartment **(see illustration)**.

Diesel engines

11 Disconnect the battery negative lead and position it away from the terminal – refer to the precautions in Section 1.
12 Undo the nuts and disconnect the main cable and charging warning light (D+) wire from the rear of the alternator **(see illustrations)**.

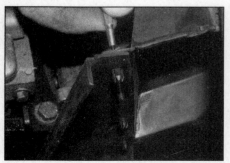

6.5 To remove the clips, push the centres out

6.9 Unscrew the two alternator mounting bolts (arrowed)

6.10 Disconnect the alternator wiring

6.12a Remove the warning light wiring plug

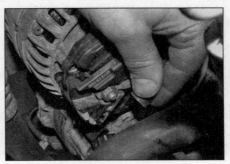

6.12b Remove the cover . . .

6.12c . . . and then unbolt and remove the main cable

13 Using an adjustable spanner on the tensioner arm, rotate the tensioner clockwise and detach the drivebelt from the alternator pulley (see Chapter 2B).

14 Unbolt and remove the automatic belt tensioner (see illustration).

15 Support the alternator, then unscrew and remove the mounting bolts (see illustration). Manoeuvre the alternator from the engine compartment.

Refitting

16 Refitting is a reversal of removal. If an exchange unit is fitted, it may be necessary to adjust the position of the movable pivot (see illustrations). Refer to Chapter 2A or 2B as applicable for details of refitting the main drivebelt. Tighten the alternator mounting bolts to the specified torque.

7 Alternator – brush holder/regulator module renewal

Apart from the drivebelt pulley, no individual parts are available for the alternator. It is considered best practice to use an exchange reconditioned unit.

8 Starting system – testing

Note: Refer to Section 1 of this Chapter before starting work.

1 If the starter motor fails to operate when the ignition key is turned to the appropriate position, the following possible causes may be to blame:

a) The battery is faulty.
b) The electrical connections between the switch, solenoid, battery and starter motor are somewhere failing to pass the necessary current from the battery through the starter to earth.
c) The solenoid is faulty.
d) The starter motor is mechanically or electrically defective.

2 To check the battery, switch on the headlights. If they dim after a few seconds, this indicates that the battery is discharged –

recharge (see Section 2) or renew the battery. If the headlights glow brightly, operate the ignition switch and observe the lights. If they dim, then this indicates that current is reaching the starter motor, therefore the fault must lie in the starter motor. If the lights continue to glow brightly (and no clicking sound can be heard from the starter motor solenoid), this indicates that there is a fault in the circuit or solenoid – see following Paragraphs. If the starter motor turns slowly when operated, but the battery is in good condition, then this indicates that either the starter motor is faulty, or there is considerable resistance somewhere in the circuit.

3 If a fault in the circuit is suspected, disconnect the battery leads (including the earth connection to the body), the starter/solenoid wiring and the engine/transmission earth strap. Thoroughly clean the connections, and reconnect the leads and wiring, then use a

voltmeter or test light to check that full battery voltage is available at the battery positive lead connection to the solenoid, and that the earth is sound. Smear petroleum jelly around the battery terminals to prevent corrosion – corroded connections are amongst the most frequent causes of electrical system faults.

4 If the battery and all connections are in good condition, check the circuit by disconnecting the wire from the solenoid blade terminal. Connect a voltmeter or test light between the wire end and a good earth (such as the battery negative terminal), and check that the wire is live when the ignition switch is turned to the start position. If it is, then the circuit is sound – if not the circuit wiring can be checked as described in Chapter 12.

5 The solenoid contacts can be checked by connecting a voltmeter or test light between the battery positive feed connection on the starter side of the solenoid, and earth. When

6.14 Remove the tensioner

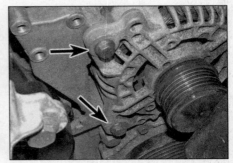

6.15 Remove the mounting bolts (arrowed)

6.16a A socket, bolt and nut can be used . . .

6.16b . . . adjust the sliding pivot

9.3a Remove the main cable cover . . .

9.3b . . . and then unbolt the main cable (arrowed)

9.3c Remove the wiring plug from the solenoid

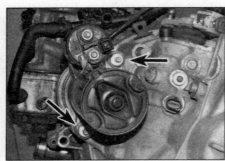

9.4 Undo the two bolts (arrowed) and remove the starter motor (engine removed for clarity)

9 Starter motor – removal and refitting

Removal

1 Disconnect the battery negative (earth) lead (see Section 3).
2 Apply the handbrake, then jack up the front of the vehicle and support it on axle stands (see *Jacking and vehicle support*). Undo the two retaining nuts and four bolts (two each side), then remove the engine undershield.
3 Working underneath the vehicle, disconnect the starter motor wiring connections **(see illustration)**.
4 Undo the two starter motor retaining bolts and manoeuvre the starter motor from under the vehicle **(see illustration)**.

Refitting

5 Refit the starter motor by following the removal procedure in reverse. Tighten the mounting bolts to the specified torque.

10 Starter motor – testing and overhaul

If the starter motor is thought to be defective, it should be removed from the vehicle and taken to an auto-electrician for assessment. In the majority of cases, new starter motor brushes can be fitted at a reasonable cost. However, check the cost of repairs first as it may prove more economical to purchase a new or exchange motor.

the ignition switch is turned to the start position, there should be a reading or lighted bulb, as applicable. If there is no reading or lighted bulb, the solenoid is faulty and should be renewed.
6 If the circuit and solenoid are proved sound, the fault must lie in the starter motor. It may be possible to have the starter motor overhauled by a specialist, but check on the availability and cost of spares before proceeding, as it may prove more economical to obtain a new or exchange motor.

Chapter 5 Part B:
Ignition system – petrol engines

Contents

Degrees of difficulty

Easy, suitable for novice with little experience	**Fairly easy,** suitable for beginner with some experience	**Fairly difficult,** suitable for competent DIY mechanic	**Difficult,** suitable for experienced DIY mechanic	**Very difficult,** suitable for expert DIY or professional

Specifications

Ignition timing . . . .   Not adjustable, ECM-controlled

Spark plugs . . . .   See Chapter 1A Specifications

---

1 General information

The Ford system described in this Chapter is a self-contained engine management system. The EEC V electronic control module (ECM) has overall control of the both the fuel injection and ignition systems. This Chapter deals with the ignition system components only – refer to Chapter 4A for details of the fuel system components.

The ignition system comprises the spark plugs, HT (high tension) leads, electronic ignition coils (or coil pack), and an electronic ignition module together with its associated sensors, actuators and wiring.

The basic operation is as follows: the module supplies a voltage to the input stage of the ignition coil which causes the primary windings in the coil to be energised. The supply voltage is periodically interrupted by the ECM and this results in the collapse of primary magnetic field, which then induces a much larger voltage in the secondary coil, called the HT voltage. This voltage is directed, via the HT leads, to the spark plugs whose pistons rise and fall together, ie, cylinders 1 and 4, 2 and 3. This is known as a wasted-spark DIS (distributorless ignition system). The spark plug electrodes form a gap small enough for the HT voltage to arc across, and the resulting spark ignites the fuel/air mixture in the cylinder. The timing of this sequence of events is critical and is regulated solely by the module.

The ignition timing angle is determined by the engine management ECM, and sent to the ignition module, which compares this signal with that from the crankshaft position sensor, and then determines the optimum exact ignition timing. If the ignition module fails to receive a signal from the engine management ECM, the module determines the ignition timing using the last data received. If no signals are received by the ignition module for five consecutive cycles (10 crankshaft rotations), the module implements a 'limited operation' strategy, and engine performance may be reduced. No manual adjustment of the ignition timing is possible.

All ignition functions are under the control of the engine management EEC V ECM. The DIS coils are fitted directly above Nos 2 and 4 spark plugs, with conventional HT connecting these coils to cylinders No 3 and 1 respectively. Some models have a coil pack – effectively two DIS coils in one unit – fitted to the left-hand end of the cylinder head. These models have four individual HT leads running to the spark plugs.

It should be noted that comprehensive fault diagnosis of all the engine management systems described in this Chapter is only possible with dedicated electronic test equipment. Problems with the systems operation that cannot be pinpointed by following the basic guidelines in Section 2 should therefore be referred to a Ford dealer or suitably-equipped specialist for assessment. Once the fault has been identified, the removal/refitting sequences detailed in the following Sections will then allow the appropriate component(s) to be renewed as required.

2 Ignition system – testing

⚠️ **Warning: Extreme care must be taken when working on the system with the ignition switched on; it is** *possible to get a substantial electric shock from a vehicle's ignition system. Persons with cardiac pacemaker devices should keep well clear of the ignition circuits, components and test equipment. Always switch off the ignition before disconnecting or connecting any component and when using a multimeter to check resistances.*

General

1 Most ignition system faults are likely to be due to loose or dirty connections or to 'tracking' (unintentional earthing) of HT voltage due to dirt, dampness or damaged insulation, rather than by the failure of any of the system's components. Always check all wiring thoroughly before condemning an electrical component and work methodically to eliminate all other possibilities before deciding that a particular component is faulty.
2 The practice of checking for a spark by holding the live end of an HT lead a short distance away from the engine is definitely not recommended.

Engine will not start

3 If the engine either will not turn over at all, or only turns very slowly, check the battery and starter motor. Connect a voltmeter across the battery terminals (meter positive probe to battery positive terminal), then disable the ignition by disconnecting the wiring from the coil(s). Note the voltage reading obtained while turning over the engine on the starter for a maximum of ten seconds. If the reading obtained is less than approximately 10.0 volts, first check the battery, starter motor and charging systems (see Chapter 5A).
4 Check the HT leads and ignition coil(s) with reference to Section 3 of this Chapter.
5 If there is still no spark, then the problem

3.1 Unscrew the ten bolts and remove the cover

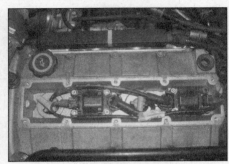

3.2 Release the wiring harness from the clips and disconnect the wiring plugs

3.3 Squeeze the locking tabs and disconnect the HT leads

3.4 Undo the Torx screws and remove the coils

must lie within the engine management system. The vehicle should be referred to a Ford dealer or specialist for assessment.

Engine misfires

6 An irregular misfire suggests either a loose connection or intermittent fault on the primary circuit.

7 With the ignition switched off, check carefully through the system ensuring that all connections are clean and securely fastened. Check the LT circuit as described above.

8 Check that the HT coil(s), and the HT leads are clean and dry. Check the leads themselves and

the spark plugs (by substitution, if necessary).

9 Regular misfiring is almost certainly due to a fault in the HT leads, or spark plugs.

10 If HT voltage is not present on one particular lead, the fault will be in that lead. If HT is present on all leads, the fault will be in the spark plugs.

Other problems

11 Problems with the system's operation that cannot be pinpointed by following the guidelines in the preceding Paragraphs should be referred to a Ford dealer or specialist for assessment.

3 HT coil –
removal and refitting

Removal

1 The coils are either fitted directly above the spark plugs (under a cover) or a single coil pack is fitted to the left-hand end of the cylinder head. Ensure that the ignition is switched off, then unscrew the 10 bolts securing the coils/HT lead cover on the camshaft cover **(see illustration)**.

2 Release the wiring harness from the retaining clips on the coil(s), and disconnect the wiring plug(s) **(see illustration)**.

3 Release the HT leads from the retaining clips on the coil(s), squeeze together the locking tabs and disconnect the HT lead connectors **(see illustration)**.

4 Slacken and remove the retaining screws, and remove the ignition coils **(see illustration)**. Note that the HT connection on the underside of the coil locates directly onto the spark plug beneath it. On models with a coil pack fitted, unbolt and remove the coil pack from the left-hand end of the cylinder head.

Refitting

5 Refitting is a reversal of removal.

4 Ignition timing –
checking and adjusting

The ignition timing is under the control of the engine management system ECM and is not manually-adjustable. The vehicle must be taken to a Ford dealer or suitably-equipped specialist if the timing requires checking.

Chapter 5 Part C:
Preheating system – diesel engines

Contents

Section number   Section number

Degrees of difficulty

Easy, suitable for novice with little experience	Fairly easy, suitable for beginner with some experience	Fairly difficult, suitable for competent DIY mechanic 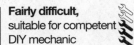	Difficult, suitable for experienced DIY mechanic	Very difficult, suitable for expert DIY or professional

Specifications

Glow plugs

Electrical resistance (typical – no value quoted by Ford)	1.5 ohms
Current consumption (typical – no value quoted by Ford)	8 amps (per plug)

Torque wrench setting	Nm	lbf ft
Glow plug to cylinder head	15	11

1 General information

To assist cold starting, diesel engined models are fitted with a preheating system, which comprises four glow plugs, a glow plug control unit (incorporated in the ECM), a facia-mounted warning light and the associated electrical wiring.

The glow plugs are miniature electric heating elements, encapsulated in a metal case with a probe at one end and electrical connection at the other. Each inlet tract has a glow plug threaded into it, which is positioned directly in line with the incoming spray of fuel. When the glow plug is energised, the fuel passing over it is heated, allowing its optimum combustion temperature to be achieved more readily in the combustion chamber.

The duration of the preheating period is governed by the ECM, which monitors the temperature of the engine via the coolant temperature sensor and alters the preheating time to suit the conditions.

A facia-mounted warning light informs the driver that preheating is taking place. The light extinguishes when sufficient preheating has taken place to allow the engine to be started, but power will still be supplied to the glow plugs for a further period until the engine is started. If no attempt is made to start the engine, the power supply to the glow plugs is switched off to prevent battery drain and glow plug burn-out. If the warning light flashes, or comes on during normal driving, this indicates a fault with the diesel engine management system, which should be investigated by a Ford dealer or suitably-equipped specialist as soon as possible.

After the engine has been started, the glow plugs continue to operate for a further period of time. This helps to improve fuel combustion whilst the engine is warming-up, resulting in quieter, smoother running and reduced exhaust emissions.

2 Glow plugs – testing, removal and refitting

⚠️ *Warning: Under no circumstances should the glow plugs be tested outside the engine. A correctly-functioning glow plug will become red-hot in a very short time. This fact should also be borne in mind when removing the glow plugs if they have recently been in use.*

Testing

1 If the system malfunctions, testing is ultimately by substitution of known good units, but some preliminary checks may be made as described in the following paragraphs.
2 Before testing the system, use a multimeter to check that the battery voltage is at least 11.5 volts. Switch off the ignition.
3 Remove the engine top cover.
4 Disconnect the wiring plug from the coolant temperature sensor at the left-hand end of the engine (left as seen from the driver's seat) – refer to Chapter 3 if necessary. Disconnecting the sensor in this way simulates a cold engine, which is a requirement for the glow plug system to activate.
5 The wiring supply to the glow plugs is a semi-rigid structure. To avoid damage to the wiring loom and connectors, gently ease the wiring loom and connectors from all the glow plugs **(see illustration)**. Connect a suitable multimeter between the wiring connector and a good earth.
6 Have an assistant switch on the ignition for approximately 20 seconds.
7 Battery voltage should be displayed – note that the voltage will drop to zero when the preheating period ends.
8 If no supply voltage can be detected at the glow plug, then either the glow plug relay (where applicable) or the supply wiring must be faulty. Also check that the glow plug fuse or fusible link (usually located on top of the battery) has not blown – if it has, this may indicate a serious wiring fault.
9 To locate a faulty glow plug, first disconnect the battery negative cable and position it away from the terminal. **Note:** *Before disconnecting the battery, refer to 'Disconnecting the battery' at the rear of this manual.*

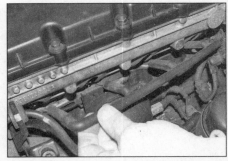

2.5 Ease the electrical supply rail from the glow plugs

2.10 Testing the glow plugs with a multimeter

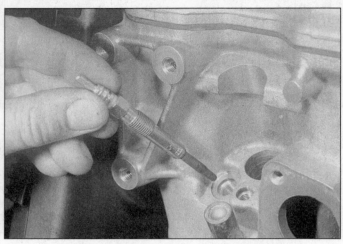

2.15 Remove the glow plug from the cylinder head

10 Disconnect the wiring plug from the glow plug terminal. Measure the electrical resistance between the glow plug terminal and the engine earth **(see illustration)**. At the time of writing, this information is not available – as a guide, a resistance of more than five ohms indicates that the plug is defective.

11 If a suitable ammeter is available, connect it between the glow plug and its wiring connector, and measure the steady-state current consumption (ignore the initial current surge, which will be about 50% higher). As a guide, high current consumption (or no current draw at all) indicates a faulty glow plug.

12 As a final check, remove the glow plugs and inspect them visually, as described in the next sub-Section. If a glow plug is proved to be faulty it is common practice to renew all the glow plugs at the same time. Any known good glow plugs can be kept as emergency spares.

Removal

Note: *Refer to the Warning at the start of this Section before proceeding.*

13 Disconnect the battery negative (earth) lead (see *Disconnecting the battery*).

14 Disconnect the wiring connectors/rail from the glow plugs **(see illustration 2.5)**.

15 Unscrew and remove the glow plug(s) **(see illustration)**. A badly burned or charred stem may be an indication of a faulty fuel injector.

Refitting

17 Refitting is a reversal of removal, but tighten the glow plug to the specified torque.

Chapter 6
Clutch

Contents

Degrees of difficulty

Easy, suitable for novice with little experience	Fairly easy, suitable for beginner with some experience	Fairly difficult, suitable for competent DIY mechanic	Difficult, suitable for experienced DIY mechanic	Very difficult, suitable for expert DIY or professional

Specifications

General

Type	Single dry plate, diaphragm spring with spring-loaded hub
Operation	Hydraulic with slave and master cylinders
Friction disc diameter.	240 mm
Clutch pedal travel	133 ± 5 mm
Friction disc nominal thickness	6.8 mm
Friction disc discard thickness*	6.0mm

* Install a new clutch when the minimum thickness has been reached

Torque wrench settings

	Nm	lbf ft
Clutch slave cylinder mounting bolt:		
5-speed gearbox	11	8
6-speed gearbox	12	9
Pressure plate-to-flywheel bolt*	29	21

* New bolts must be used

1 General information

The clutch is of single dry disc type, incorporating a diaphragm spring pressure plate, and is hydraulically-operated.

The clutch cover (pressure plate) is bolted to the rear face of the flywheel, and the friction disc is located between the pressure plate and the flywheel friction surface. The disc hub is splined to the transmission input shaft and is free to slide along the splines. Friction lining material is riveted to each side of the disc, and the disc hub incorporates cushioning springs to absorb transmission shocks and ensure a smooth take-up of drive.

Some engines have a dual mass flywheel fitted. This is manufactured in two parts. Instead of the conventional single unit, the friction surface has a limited buffered movement in relation to the main flywheel mass bolted to the rear of the crankshaft. This has the effect of absorbing the initial clutch engagement shock and makes for a smoother gearchange. Checking of the dual mass flywheel is covered in Chapter 2B.

When the clutch pedal is depressed, the centrally-mounted slave cylinder forces the release bearing onto the diaphragm spring fingers. As the centre of the spring is pushed in, the outer part of the spring moves out and releases the pressure plate from the friction disc. Drive then ceases to be transmitted to the transmission.

When the clutch pedal is released, the diaphragm spring forces the pressure plate into contact with the linings on the friction disc, and at the same time pushes the disc slightly forward along the input shaft splines into engagement with the flywheel. The friction disc is now firmly sandwiched between the pressure plate and flywheel. This causes drive to be taken up.

As the linings wear on the friction disc, the pressure plate rest position moves closer to the flywheel resulting in the 'rest' position of the diaphragm spring fingers being raised. The hydraulic system requires no adjustment since the quantity of hydraulic fluid in the circuit automatically compensates for wear every time the clutch pedal is operated.

2 Hydraulic system – bleeding

Warning: Hydraulic fluid is poisonous; thoroughly wash off spills from bare skin without delay. Seek immediate medical advice if any fluid is swallowed or gets into the eyes. Certain types of hydraulic fluid are inflammable and may ignite when brought into contact with hot components. Hydraulic fluid is also an effective paint stripper. If spillage occurs onto painted bodywork or fittings, it should be washed off immediately, using copious quantities of cold water. It is also hygroscopic (ie, it can absorb moisture from the air) which lowers the boiling point of the fluid, rendering it dangerous to use in the hydraulic system. Old fluid will have suffered contamination, and should never be re-used.

1 The correct operation of any hydraulic system is only possible after removing all air from the components and circuit; this is achieved by bleeding the system.

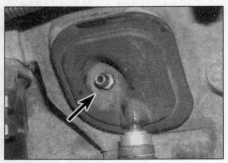

2.10 The clutch bleed nipple is on the top of the transmission bellhousing – five-speed transmission shown (arrowed)

2 During the bleeding procedure, add only clean, unused hydraulic fluid of the recommended type; never re-use fluid that has already been bled from the system. Ensure that sufficient fluid is available before starting work.

3 If there is any possibility of incorrect fluid being already in the system, the hydraulic circuit must be flushed completely with uncontaminated, correct fluid.

4 If hydraulic fluid has been lost from the system, or air has entered because of a leak, ensure that the fault is cured before continuing further.

5 On right-hand drive models, with reference to the relevant Part of Chapter 4, remove the mass airflow sensor and air intake ducting to gain access to the fluid reservoir.

6 Check that all pipes and hoses are secure, unions tight and the bleed screw is closed. The bleed screw is located on the top of the transmission, adjacent to the clutch hydraulic pipe where it enters the transmission casing. Clean any dirt from around the bleed screw.

7 Unscrew the master cylinder fluid reservoir cap (the clutch has the same fluid reservoir as the braking system), and top the master cylinder reservoir up to the upper (MAX) level line. Refit the cap loosely, and remember to maintain the fluid level at least above the lower (MIN) level line throughout the procedure, or there is a risk of further air entering the system.

8 There are a number of one-man, do-it-yourself bleeding kits currently available from motor accessory shops. It is recommended

3.6a Unhook the spring . . .

that one of these kits is used whenever possible, as they greatly simplify the bleeding operation, and reduce the risk of expelled air and fluid being drawn back into the system. If such a kit is not available, the basic (two-man) method must be used, which is described in detail below.

9 If a kit is to be used, prepare the vehicle as described previously, and follow the kit manufacturer's instructions, as the procedure may vary slightly according to the type being used; generally, they are as outlined below in the relevant sub-Section.

Bleeding

Basic (two-man) method

10 Collect a clean glass jar, a suitable length of plastic or rubber tubing which is a tight fit over the bleed screw located on the top of the transmission bellhousing **(see illustration)**, and a ring spanner to fit the screw. The help of an assistant will also be required.

11 Remove the dust cap from the bleed screw. Fit the spanner and tube to the screw, place the other end of the tube in the jar, and pour in sufficient fluid to cover the end of the tube.

12 Ensure that the fluid level is maintained at least above the lower level line in the reservoir throughout the procedure.

13 Have the assistant fully depress the clutch pedal several times to build-up pressure, then maintain it on the final downstroke.

14 While pedal pressure is maintained, unscrew the bleed screw (approximately one turn) and allow the compressed fluid and air to flow into the jar. The assistant should maintain pedal pressure and should not release it until instructed to do so. When the flow stops, tighten the bleed screw again, have the assistant release the pedal slowly, and recheck the reservoir fluid level.

15 Repeat the steps given in paragraphs 13 and 14 until the fluid emerging from the bleed screw is free from air bubbles. If the master cylinder has been drained and refilled allow approximately five seconds between cycles for the master cylinder passages to refill.

16 When no more air bubbles appear, tighten the bleed screw securely, remove the tube and spanner, and refit the dust cap. Do not overtighten the bleed screw.

Using a one-way valve kit

17 As their name implies, these kits consist of a length of tubing with a one-way valve fitted, to prevent expelled air and fluid being drawn back into the system; some kits include a translucent container, which can be positioned so that the air bubbles can be more easily seen flowing from the end of the tube.

18 The kit is connected to the bleed screw, which is then opened. The user returns to the driver's seat, depresses the clutch pedal with a smooth, steady stroke, and slowly releases it; this is repeated until the expelled fluid is clear of air bubbles.

19 Note that these kits simplify work so

much that it is easy to forget the fluid reservoir level; ensure that this is maintained at least above the lower level line at all times.

Using a pressure-bleeding kit

20 These kits are usually operated by the reservoir of pressurised air contained in the spare tyre. However, note that it will probably be necessary to reduce the pressure to a lower level than normal; refer to the instructions supplied with the kit.

21 By connecting a pressurised, fluid-filled container to the hydraulic fluid reservoir, bleeding can be carried out simply by opening the bleed screw and allowing the fluid to flow out until no more air bubbles can be seen in the expelled fluid.

22 This method has the advantage that the large reservoir of fluid provides an additional safeguard against air being drawn into the system during bleeding.

All methods

23 When bleeding is complete, and correct pedal feel is restored, tighten the bleed screw securely and wash off any spilt fluid. Refit the dust cap to the bleed screw, and refit the air cleaner housing and airflow sensor, where necessary.

24 Check the hydraulic fluid level in the master cylinder reservoir, and top-up if necessary (see *Weekly checks*).

25 Discard any hydraulic fluid that has been bled from the system; it will not be fit for re-use.

26 Check the operation of the clutch pedal. If the clutch is still not operating correctly, air must still be present in the system, and further bleeding is required. Failure to bleed satisfactorily after a reasonable repetition of the bleeding procedure may be due to worn master cylinder/release cylinder seals.

---

3 Clutch pedal – removal and refitting

Removal

1 Disconnect the battery negative lead. **Note:** *Before disconnecting the battery, refer to 'Disconnecting the battery' at the rear of this manual.*

2 Remove the lower facia panels from the facia – see Chapter 11, Section 29.

3 Depress the locking tab, and release the upper clip, then release the clips either side and remove the central junction box from its mountings. Using a cable-tie or similar, tie it up to allow access to the pedal pivot.

4 Some models have a cover over the pedal – remove this and then disconnect the wiring plug from the clutch pedal position switch.

5 Turn the clutch pedal position switch anti-clockwise and remove it.

6 Unhook the pedal return spring, and remove the pivot shaft retaining clip **(see illustrations)**. Slide the pivot shaft to the right.

Note that some models have the return spring fitted to the pivot shaft.

7 Unclip the master cylinder pushrod from the pedal, and slide the pedal from the shaft **(see illustration)**. The two sides of the pushrod retaining clip must be pushed in before the clip will release.

Refitting

8 Refitting is a reversal of removal, noting that the pushrod retaining clip must be fitted to the pushrod prior to refitting the pedal. Reconnect the battery negative lead.

3.6b ... and remove the pivot shaft clip

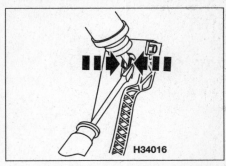

3.7 Unclip the master cylinder pushrod and slide the pedal from the shaft

4 Master cylinder – removal, overhaul and refitting

Note: *Refer to the warning at the beginning of Section 2 regarding the hazards of working with hydraulic fluid.*

Removal

1 The clutch master cylinder is located inside the car on the clutch and brake pedal mounting bracket. Hydraulic fluid for the unit is supplied from the brake master cylinder reservoir.

2 Working at the engine compartment bulkhead, clamp the supply hose from the brake master cylinder (or be prepared for fluid spillage), release the clip and disconnect the hose from the clutch master cylinder. Prise out the clip and pull the pressure pipe from the cylinder **(see illustration)**.

3 Remove the clutch pedal as described the previous Section.

4 Undo the two mounting bolts and manoeuvre the cylinder from under the facia **(see illustration)**.

Overhaul

5 At the time of writing no overhaul kits or information was available. Consult your Ford dealer or local motor factors.

Refitting

6 Refitting is a reversal of removal. Apply a little grease to the clevis pin eye before refitting it. Bleed the clutch hydraulic system as described in Section 2.

5 Slave cylinder/release bearing – removal, overhaul and refitting

Note: *Refer to the warning at the beginning of Section 2 regarding the hazards of working with hydraulic fluid.*
Note: *The slave cylinder should not be re-used. Always fit a new one whenever the gearbox is removed.*

Removal

1 The slave cylinder is located within the bellhousing of the transmission. Remove the transmission as described in Chapter 7A.
2 On the 5-speed gearbox, cover the input shaft splines with adhesive tape to avoid damaging the input shaft oil seal.

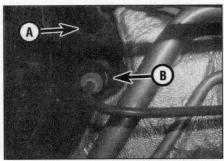

4.2 Clutch cylinder supply hose clip (A) and pressure hose clip (B)

5.3b ... and manoeuvre it from the bellhousing, complete with pipes and bleed nipple

3 Undo the three bolts and manoeuvre the slave cylinder, complete with release bearing and fluid pipes, from the transmission input shaft and bellhousing aperture **(see illustrations)**. No further dismantling is possible, the release bearing is integral with the slave cylinder.

Refitting

4 Refitting is a reversal of removal but renew the cylinder-to-transmission casing O-ring seal – where fitted **(see illustration)**. Consider also renewing the gearbox input shaft oils seal as described in Chapter 7A. Tighten the mounting bolts to the specified torque, refit the transmission (Chapter 7A), and finally bleed the system as described in Section 2.

4.4 Clutch cylinder mounting bolts (arrowed)

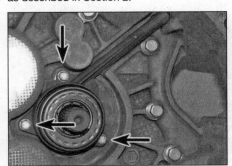

5.3a Undo the slave cylinder mounting bolts (arrowed) ...

5.4 Renew the slave cylinder O-ring

6.4 Remove the pressure plate and friction disc from the flywheel

6 Clutch disc and pressure plate – removal, inspection and refitting

⚠️ **Warning: Dust created by clutch wear and deposited on the clutch components may contain asbestos, which is a health hazard. DO NOT blow it out with compressed air or inhale any of it. DO NOT use petrol or petroleum-based solvents to clean off the dust. Brake system cleaner or methylated spirit should be used to flush the dust into a suitable receptacle. After the clutch components are wiped clean with clean rags, dispose of the contaminated rags and cleaner in a sealed container.**

Removal

1 Access to the clutch is obtained by

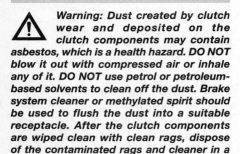

6.11a Note the orientation of the friction disc . . .

6.12 Lock the tool in position

6.6 Examine the fingers of the diaphragm spring for wear or scoring

removing the transmission as described in Chapter 7A.

2 If the clutch components are to be refitted, mark the clutch pressure plate and flywheel in relation to each other.

3 Hold the flywheel stationary, then unscrew the clutch pressure plate bolts progressively in diagonal sequence. With the bolts unscrewed two or three turns, check that the pressure plate is not binding on the dowel pins. If necessary, use a screwdriver to release the pressure plate.

4 Remove all the bolts, then lift the clutch pressure plate and friction disc from the flywheel **(see illustration)**.

Inspection

Note: *Due to the amount of work necessary to remove and refit clutch components, it is usually considered good practice to renew the clutch friction disc, pressure plate assembly*

6.11b . . . and fit the alignment tool

6.13 Fit the clutch assembly

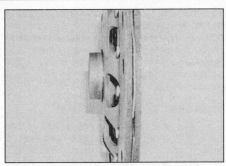

6.8 Examine the friction disc linings for wear and cracking

and release bearing as a matched set, even if only one of these is actually worn enough to require renewal. It is also worth considering the renewal of the clutch components on a preventive basis if the engine and/or transmission have been removed for some other reason.

5 Clean the pressure plate, disc and flywheel. Do not inhale the dust, as it may contain asbestos which is dangerous to health.

6 Examine the fingers of the diaphragm spring pth of wear exceeds half the thickness of the ffor wear or scoring **(see illustration)**. If the deingers, a new pressure plate assembly must be fitted.

7 Examine the pressure plate for scoring, cracking and discoloration. Light scoring is acceptable, but if excessive, a new pressure plate assembly must be fitted.

8 Examine the friction disc linings for wear and cracking, and for contamination with oil or grease **(see illustration)**. The linings are worn excessively if they are worn down to, or near, the rivets. Check the disc hub and splines for wear, by temporarily fitting it on the transmission input shaft. Renew the friction disc as necessary.

9 Examine the flywheel friction surface for scoring, cracking and discoloration (caused by overheating). If excessive, it may be possible to have the flywheel machined by an engineering works, otherwise it should be renewed.

10 Ensure that all parts are clean, and free of oil or grease, before reassembling. Lightly oil the splines of the friction disc hub. **Do not** use copper-based grease. Note that new pressure plates and clutch covers may be coated with protective grease. It is only permissible to clean the grease away from the friction disc lining contact area. Removal of the grease from other areas will shorten the service life of the clutch.

Refitting

11 Commence reassembly by locating the friction disc on the pressure plate, with the raised, torsion spring side of the hub facing outwards. One side of the disc may be marked 'Flywheel side'. Fit the centralising tool **(see illustrations)**.

12 Align the friction disc with the pressure plate and then lock the alignment tool into place **(see illustration)**.

13 Offer the clutch assembly up to the flywheel **(see illustration)** and insert the bolts finger-tight to hold the pressure plate in position.

14 Tighten the pressure plate bolts progressively and in diagonal sequence, until the specified torque setting is achieved, then remove the centralising tool.

15 Refit the transmission with reference to Chapter 7A.

7 Clutch pedal switch – removal, refitting and adjustment

Removal

1 Inside the car, remove the facia panel from below the steering column (refer to Chapter 11, Section 29, if necessary).

2 Depress the retaining clip and disconnect the switch wiring plug.

3 Rotate the switch 90 degrees anti-clockwise and remove the switch **(see illustration)**.

Refitting

4 Refitting is a reversal of removal.

7.3 Turn the switch 90° anti-clockwise and remove it

Chapter 7 Part A:
Manual transmission

Contents

Degrees of difficulty

Easy, suitable for novice with little experience | **Fairly easy,** suitable for beginner with some experience | **Fairly difficult,** suitable for competent DIY mechanic | **Difficult,** suitable for experienced DIY mechanic | **Very difficult,** suitable for expert DIY or professional

Specifications

General

Type	Manual, five or six forward speeds and reverse. Synchromesh on all forward speeds

Identification code:
  5-speed VXT-75
  6-speed MT350

Lubrication

Fluid type . . . . Refer to *Lubricants and fluids*
Oil capacity (approximate):
  5-speed . . . . 2.25 litres
  6-speed . . . . 2.50 litres

Torque wrench settings

	Nm	lbf ft
Battery tray bolts	20	15
Driveshaft intermediate bearing support bracket	27	20
Driveshaft intermediate bearing support bracket (extended type):		
To transmission	40	30
To engine block	45	33
Engine-to-transmission unit bolts:		
5-speed	44	32
6-speed	40	30
6-speed (upper right bolt)	80	59
Engine bracket (to transmission):		
5-speed	98	72
6-speed		
Stage 1	60	44
Stage 2	Angle tighten a further 90°	
Engine left-hand mounting (5-speed transmission):*		
To body:		
Large bolt:		
Stage 1	50	37
Stage 2	Angle tighten a further 90°	
Small bolt	25	18
To transmission:		
Stage 1	90	66
Stage 2	Angle tighten a further 90°	
Engine left-hand mounting (6-speed transmission):*		
To body:		
Large bolt:		
Stage 1	90	66
Stage 2	Angle tighten a further 90°	
Small bolt	25	18
To transmission:		
Stage 1	90	66
Stage 2	Angle tighten a further 90°	
Engine right-hand mounting:		
Stud	10	7
Bolt	61	45
Nut	54	40
Engine roll restrictor to crossmember:		
Stage 1	60	44
Stage 2	Angle tighten a further 90°	
Engine roll restrictor to transmission	100	74
Exhaust-to-manifold nuts	44	32
Starter motor support bracket	20	15
Gearlever housing to body	10	7
Oil drain plug	35	26
Oil filler plug	35	26
Roadwheel bolts	170	125
Starter motor bolts:		
Petrol engines	35	26
Diesel engines:		
Five-speed transmission	65	48
Six-speed transmission	80	59

* Use new nuts/bolts

1 General information

1 The transmission is contained in a cast-aluminium alloy casing bolted to the engine's left-hand end, and consists of the gearbox and final drive differential – often called a transaxle.

2 Drive is transmitted from the crankshaft via the clutch to the input shaft, which has a splined extension to accept the clutch friction disc, and rotates in tapered roller bearings. From the input shaft, drive is transmitted to the output shaft, which also rotates in tapered roller bearings. From the output shaft, the drive is transmitted to the differential crownwheel, which rotates with the differential case and planetary gears, thus driving the sun gears and driveshafts. The rotation of the planetary gears on their shaft allows the inner roadwheel to rotate at a slower speed than the outer roadwheel when the car is cornering.

3 The input and output shafts are arranged side-by-side, parallel to the crankshaft and driveshafts, so that their gear pinion teeth are in constant mesh. In the neutral position, the output shaft gear pinions rotate freely, so that drive cannot be transmitted to the crownwheel.

4 Gear selection is via a floor-mounted lever and selector cables. The selector cables cause the appropriate selector fork to move its respective synchro-sleeve along the shaft, to lock the gear pinion to the synchro-hub.

Since the synchro-hubs are splined to the output shaft, this locks the pinion to the shaft, so that drive can be transmitted. To ensure that gearchanging can be made quickly and quietly, a synchromesh system is fitted to all gears, consisting of baulk rings and spring-loaded fingers, as well as the gear pinions and synchro-hubs. The synchromesh cones are formed on the mating faces of the baulk rings and gear pinions.

5 Five-speed models feature Ford's VXT-75 **(see illustration)** transmission and six-speed models use the MT350 transmission.

2 Transmission oil – draining and refilling

1 This operation is much more efficient if the car is first taken on a journey of sufficient length to warm the engine/transmission up to normal operating temperature.
Caution: If the procedure is to be carried out on a hot transmission unit, take care not to burn yourself on the hot exhaust or the transmission/engine unit.
2 Park the car on level ground, switch off the ignition and apply the handbrake firmly. Jack up the front of the car and support it securely on axle stands. Undo the retaining bolts/nuts and remove the undershield from beneath the engine/transmission unit.
3 Wipe clean the area around the drain plug (located on the end of the transmission on the five-speed gearbox) and position a suitable container underneath.
4 Unscrew the drain plug and allow the transmission oil to drain into the container **(see illustration)**.
5 Allow the oil to drain completely into the container. If the oil is hot, take precautions against scalding.
6 Once the oil has finished draining, ensure the drain plug is clean and refit it to the transmission with a new washer. Tighten the drain plug to the specified torque. Lower the vehicle to the ground.
7 The transmission is refilled via the level plug on the front of the transmission casing.

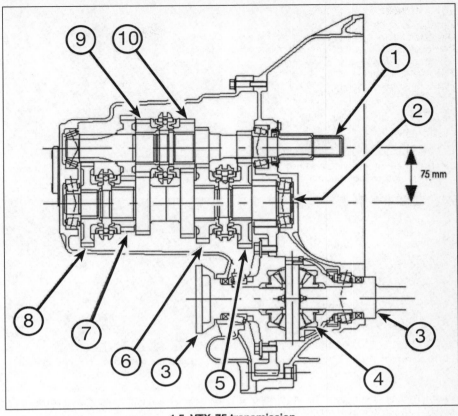

1.5 VTX-75 transmission

1 Transmission input shaft	3 Front driveshafts	5 1st gear	8 Reverse gear
2 Output shaft	4 Differential	6 2nd gear	9 4th gear
		7 5th gear	10 3rd gear

Wipe clean the area around the level plug, and unscrew it from the casing. Refill the transmission with the specified type and amount of oil given in the Specifications, until the fluid begins to trickle out of the level hole **(see illustration)**. Refit the plug and tighten it to the specified torque.
8 Take the vehicle on a short journey so that the new oil is distributed fully around the transmission components.
9 On your return, park the vehicle on level ground and check the transmission oil level as described in Section 9. Refit the engine/transmission undershield.

3 Gearchange mechanism – adjustment

Note: *If working on the 5-speed gearbox, Ford special tool No 308-235 (previously known as 16-083) will be required to hold the position of the gear lever in neutral **(see illustration)**. If the tool is not available, adjustment is still possible by proceeding on a trial-and-error basis, preferably with the help of an assistant to hold the gear lever in the neutral position.*

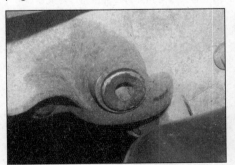

2.4 The drain plug is located on the end of the transmission

2.7 Fill the transmission until the fluid begins to trickle out

3.0 Ford special tool 308-235

3.4 Pull the collars back, and turn them to the left to lock them in place

3.6 Pull the cable gently to take up any free play

3.10 Depress the locking pin (arrowed)

3.11 Lock the gearlever in position with a drill bit (arrowed)

1 Adjustment of the gearchange mechanism is not a routine operation and should only be needed if the mechanism has been removed. If the gearchange action is stiff or imprecise, check that it is correctly adjusted as follows.

2 Prise free the gaiter and remove the trim panel. Pull the gaiter over the gear lever – there is no need to remove it completely.

5-speed gearbox

3 Remove the centre console as described in Chapter 11 and disconnect the wiring plug.

4 Ensure that the transmission is in neutral and then detach the cables from the support bracket. Pull the shift and selector cable locking mechanisms back, and lock them in place by turning the collars anti-clockwise **(see illustration)**.

5 Position the gear lever in the neutral position. Ford specify the use of special tool No 308-235 to ensure the lever is in the correct position. If the tool is available, fit it around the lever, and push it down as far as it will go. If the tool is not available, the lever is in the correct position when it lies between the 3rd and 4th gear gates.

6 Gently pull the selector cable (blue) into the end fitting to take up any free play, and turn the cable locking mechanism to the right to release it **(see illustration)**. Repeat this procedure for the shift cable (black).

7 If fitted, remove the gear lever positioning tool, and check the operation of the lever several times. If the action of the lever is not satisfactory, repeat the adjustment procedure until it is.

8 Plug in the wiring connector and refit the centre console – as described in Chapter 11.

6-speed gearbox

9 With the transmission in neutral, unlock the selector cables at the gearbox. Pull the cables backwards and rotate them anti-clockwise to release the locking mechanism.

10 Push the selector shaft into the gearbox until the locking pin can be pressed into the gearbox housing **(see illustration)**.

11 At the gear lever, fit a 5 mm drill bit into the hole provided and lock the gear lever in position **(see illustration)**.

12 Take up the slack in the selector cables and turn the collar clockwise to lock the cable in position.

13 Release the locking pin at the gearbox and remove the 5 mm drill bit from the gear shift lever.

14 Check the operation of the gear lever. Note that when correctly adjusted and the gear lever is moved across to the first and second gear selection position the selector shaft (at the gearbox) must move down. At this point the selector shaft locking pin can be easily slid into the gearbox. Repeat the adjustment procedure if necessary.

15 Refit the gaiter and gear lever knob.

| 4 | Gearchange mechanism – removal and refitting | |

Removal

1 The gearchange mechanism consists of the gearchange lever, the selector cables and the linkage assembly on the transmission **(see illustration)**. The lever and selector cables can be removed separately.

Gearchange lever and housing

2 Firmly apply the handbrake then jack up

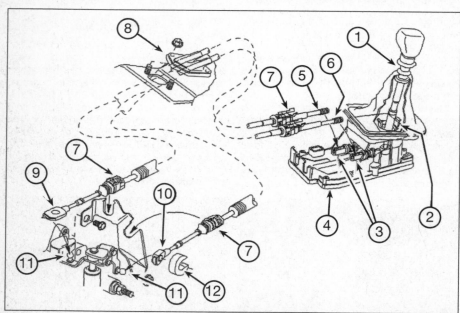

4.1 Gearchange mechanism and cables (5-speed)

1 Gear lever
2 Ford gear lever positioning tool
3 Adjusting sleeves
4 Gear lever housing
5 Selector cable
6 Shift cable
7 Cable end fitting
8 Cable guide
9 Shift cable (blue)
10 Selector cable (black)
11 Balljoints
12 Vibration damper

4.4 Remove the gearchange housing plate from under the vehicle

4.7a Remove the circlips (6-speed) . . .

the front of the vehicle and support it on axle stands. Undo the retaining bolts and remove the undercover from beneath the engine/transmission unit.

3 Undo the retaining nuts from the exhaust system heat shield and slide it backwards. On petrol models unclip the wiring for the rear oxygen sensor and then unbolt and remove the wiring support bracket.

4 Unscrew the four retaining nuts and remove the gearchange housing strengthening plate from under the vehicle **(see illustration)**.

5 Lower the vehicle to the ground and remove the centre console as described in Chapter 11.

6 Ensure that the gear lever and transmission is in neutral. Pull back the cable locking mechanisms, and lock them in place by turning the collars to the left **(see illustration 3.4)**.

7 Squeeze in the tangs of the outer cables end fittings, and press them out from the retaining bracket. On the six-speed transmission remove the locking clips from the support bracket **(see illustrations)**.

8 Lift the lever housing from the floor,

disengaging the cables as the housing is withdrawn. On the six-speed transmission remove the circlips to free the cables.

5-speed gearbox gear lever

9 If not already done so, unscrew the gear knob and recover the compression spring.

10 Invert the housing and note the fitted location of the shank spring. Remove the retaining clip and the spring **(see illustration)**.

11 Carefully lever the cable end fittings from the balljoints. Undo the three screws and remove the upper section of the housing.

12 Using a punch, drive out the cranked lever pivot pin. The lever can now be removed from the housing along with the various components **(see illustration overleaf)**. Examine all components for signs of wear or damage, paying particular attention to the selector rod and lever locating pivot bushes, and renew as necessary.

6-speed gearbox gear lever

13 With the assembly removed from the

vehicle, unbolt and remove the C-shaped retaining clip from the base of the lever.

14 Remove the circlip from selector lever shaft assembly, remove the spring assembly and then remove the shaft from the housing.

15 Depress the spring at the base of the gear lever and remove the locking collar. Note the order of the components and remove them from the gear lever **(see illustration overleaf)**.

16 If required remove the bushes from the cross shaft housing.

Selector and shift cables

17 Remove both front seats as described in Chapter 11.

18 Remove the front heat shield from the exhaust system.

19 Remove the gear selector assembly as previously described.

20 Unbolt and remove the handbrake assembly as described in Chapter 9.

21 Remove the trim piece from the rear heat distribution duct. Remove the three nuts from the ducting.

4.7b . . . or squeeze together the tangs and remove the cable end fittings (5-speed)

4.10 Remove the clip (arrowed) and spring

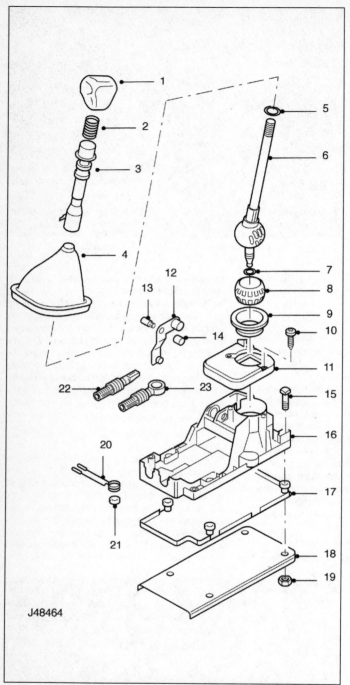

J48464

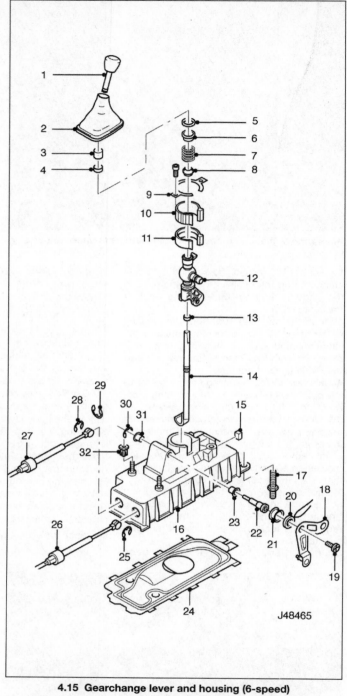

J48465

4.12 Gearchange lever and housing (5-speed)

1 Gear knob	8 Ball	16 Main housing
2 Compression spring	9 Ball cup	17 Gasket
	10 Scew	18 Reinforcing plate
3 Reverse gear sleeve	11 Upper housing	19 Nut
	12 Selector crank arm	20 Spring
4 Gaiter	13 Pivot pin	21 Circlip
5 O-ring	14 Bush	22 Selector cable mounting
6 Gear lever	15 Rectangular-headed bolt	23 Shift cable mounting
7 O-ring		

4.15 Gearchange lever and housing (6-speed)

1 Gear knob	12 Guide	23 Bush
2 Gaiter	13 Damper	24 Reinforcing plate
3 Bush	14 Gear lever	
4 Washer	15 Sound damper	25 Circlip
5 Washer	16 Main housing	26 Selector cable
6 Bush	17 Stud	27 Shift cable
7 Spring	18 Pivot	28 Circlip
8 Bush	19 Screw	29 Circlip
9 Collar	20 Spring	30 Circlip
10 Insert	21 Bush	31 Bush
11 Bearing	22 Pivot	32 Nut

4.25a Release the cables . . .

4.25b . . . and then rotate and release the end fittings on the six-speed transmission . . .

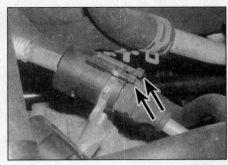

4.25c . . . or squeeze together the tabs of the clip on the five-speed transmission (arrowed)

22 Detach the flooring from both sides of the transmission tunnel.

23 Working under the facia, remove the support bracket.

24 At this point two short cuts must be made in the carpet to allow access to the remaining heater duct fixing screws. Remove the screws and remove the heat distribution duct.

25 At the gearbox unclip the selector cable from the selector shaft and support bracket **(see illustrations)**.

26 Undo the two bolts and remove the gearchange cables' aperture cover **(see illustration)**.

27 Manoeuvre the cables from the vehicle, noting the routing.

28 Examine the cables closely for signs of wear or damage, renewing worn components as necessary.

Refitting

Gearchange lever and housing

29 If necessary, reassemble the lever in the housing, reversing the dismantling procedure. Note that Ford recommend the renewal of all circlips and bushes from the gear lever assembly.

30 Lubricate all pivot points and bearing surfaces with silicone grease then manoeuvre the assembly into position. Working underneath the vehicle, refit the housing strengthener plate, and tighten the retaining nuts securely.

31 Position the exhaust front heat shield, and tighten the nuts securely.

32 Working inside the vehicle, clip the outer cables end fittings into the retaining bracket.

33 Insert the selector and shift cables into the locking mechanisms, and adjust them as described in the pervious Section.

34 Once the gearchange action is satisfactory, refit the centre console and lower the vehicle to the ground.

Selector and shift cables

35 Working from the passenger compartment, guide the cables through the aperture, and into the engine compartment. Note that the cables can only be fitted as a pair.

36 Install the cables in place at the transmission. Note that the shift cable crosses over the selector cable. The outer cables end fittings must clip into place on the retaining bracket, and the inner cable ends push onto the transmission balljoints. The balljoints are different sizes, so it should not be possible to install the cables incorrectly.

37 The remainder of refitting is a reversal of removal. If necessary adjust the cables as described in the previous Section.

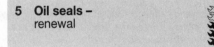

5 Oil seals –
renewal

Driveshaft oil seals

1 Chock the rear wheels, apply the handbrake, then jack up the front of the car and support it on axle stands. Remove the appropriate front roadwheel.

2 Remove the driveshaft as described in Chapter 8. Be prepared for oil spillage.

5-speed gearbox

3 Carefully prise the oil seal out of position using a large flat-bladed screwdriver **(see illustration)**. Note that to improve access to the right-hand side oil seal, we found it helpful to remove the front section of the exhaust pipe (see the relevant Part of Chapter 4).

4 Remove all traces of dirt from the area around the oil seal aperture, then apply a smear of grease to the outer lip of the new oil seal. Ensure the seal is correctly positioned, with its sealing lip and spring facing inwards, and tap it squarely into position, using a suitable tubular drift (such as a socket) which bears only on the hard outer edge of the seal **(see illustration)**. Ensure the seal is fitted flush with the seal housing.

6-speed gearbox

5 On the left-hand side of the gearbox the output flange must be removed. Fit two of the driveshaft fixing bolts into opposite holes in the flange and use a pry bar (or similar) to restrain the flange whilst the centre bolt is removed.

6 On the right-hand side unbolt and remove the bearing carrier and recover the compression spring.

7 Carefully prise the oil seal out of position using a large flat-bladed screwdriver.

8 Remove all traces of dirt from the area around the oil seal aperture, then apply a smear of grease to the outer lip of the new oil seal. Ensure the seal is correctly positioned, with its

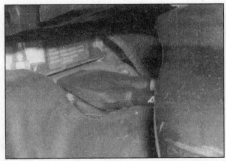

4.26 Undo the two bolts and remove the cable aperture cover

5.3 Carefully prise the driveshaft oil seal from position

5.4 Use a socket to drive in the new seal

5.13 Prise the input shaft seal from the rear of the slave cylinder

5.14 Use a socket to drive in the new seal

5.15 The six-speed transmission oil seal

sealing lip and spring facing inwards, and tap it squarely into position, using a suitable tubular drift (such as a socket) which bears only on the hard outer edge of the seal . Ensure the seal is fitted flush with the seal housing.

9 Refit the drive flange and where appropriate the bearing carrier.

All gearboxes

10 Refit the driveshaft as described in Chapter 8.

11 Refill the transmission with the specified type and amount of oil, as described in Section 2.

Input shaft oil seal

12 The input shaft oil seal is fitted into the rear of the clutch slave cylinder on the five-speed transmission or the gearbox casing on six-speed transmission. All models also feature an O-ring, fitted to the combined slave cylinder and clutch release bearing. Remove the cylinder as described in Chapter 6.

13 Where fitted, carefully prise the seal from the cylinder using a flat-bladed screwdriver **(see illustration)**.

14 Remove all traces of dirt from the seal contact area, and using a tubular drift, press the new seal into place, with the sealing lip and spring facing the rear of the cylinder **(see illustration)**.

15 On the six-speed transmission use a self-tapping screw to remove the oil seal from the transmission casing. Lubricate the new seal and, working evenly around the circumference of the seal, drive it into position with a small block of wood **(see illustration)**.

16 Refit the cylinder as described in Chapter 6.

6 Reversing light switch – testing, removal and refitting

Testing

1 The reversing light circuit is controlled by a switch mounted on the gearchange housing located on the top of the transmission casing (five-speed transmissions) or gearbox casing below the selector shaft **(see illustrations)**.

2 To test the switch, disconnect the wiring connector. Use a multimeter (set to the resistance function) or a battery-and-bulb test circuit to check that there is continuity between the switch terminals only when reverse gear is selected. If this is not the case, and there are no obvious breaks or other damage to the wires, the switch is faulty, and must be renewed.

Removal

3 On diesel engine models, detach the left-hand air charge pipe from the intercooler, and release it from the bracket on the transmission (if necessary refer to Chapter 4B). Unclip the fuel pipes from the pipe and pull it downwards.

4 On vehicles with secondary air injection, release the retaining clip and detach the air hose from the secondary injection pump.

5 Disconnect the wiring connector, then release the retaining clips and remove the

switch from the gearchange housing **(see illustration)**. On the six-speed transmission unscrew the switch.

Refitting

6 Refit the switch to the gearchange housing or screw in the switch to the casing. Reconnect the wiring connector, and the secondary air injection hose, or intercooler pipe as applicable.

7 Transmission – removal and refitting

Note: *The removal of the transmission whilst not difficult is a long and involved procedure. In the interests of safety the use of an engine support bar and the aid of an assistant is highly recommended.*

Removal

1 Mark the position of the bonnet hinges and with the aid of an assistant remove the bonnet – as described in Chapter 11. On diesel engines, remove the engine top plastic cover.

2 Remove the battery as described in Chapter 5A. Remove the battery compartment upper panel, and the bulkhead panel trim panel. On diesel models fitted with the six-speed gearbox detach the fuel filter from the battery tray side panel.

3 Unbolt and move the fusebox to one side. Disconnect the wiring multi-plug and then disconnect the coolant level sensor wiring plug **(see illustration)**.

6.1a The reversing light switch is on the top of the transmission casing (arrowed) . . .

6.1b . . . or on the side of the gearbox

6.5 Release the retaining clips and remove the switch

7.3 Disconnect and remove the wiring plugs

7.4 Remove the battery support tray

7.6 Disconnect the wiring plugs from the ECU

4 Unclip the wiring harness and coolant pipe from the battery tray and then unbolt and remove the battery support tray **(see illustration)**.

5 Remove the air cleaner housing and intake trunking (see the relevant Part of Chapter 4).

6 Remove the retaining bracket and disconnect the wiring plugs from the ECU **(see illustration)**. Move the cables to one side. To avoid any damage to the ECU, unbolt it and remove it from the vehicle. Protect the ECU multiplugs by sealing them inside a polythene bag.

7 With reference to Section 4 of this Chapter remove the gear selector cables and tie them to one side.

8 Remove the circlip and detach the clutch fluid supply pipe. Seal the end of the pipe and slave cylinder. **Note:** *Whilst the hose/pipe is disconnected, do not depress the clutch pedal.*

9 Disconnect the wiring plug from the reversing light switch **(see illustration)**.

10 Remove the metal coolant pipe from the top of the gearbox. Secure it to the top of the engine with cable-ties or stout cord.

11 Chock the rear wheels, then firmly apply the handbrake. Slacken both front roadwheel bolts and the driveshaft hub bolts. Jack up the front of the vehicle, and securely support it on axle stands. There must be sufficient clearance below the car for the transmission to be lowered and removed. Remove both front roadwheels.

12 Remove the engine undershield and then drain the transmission oil as described in Section 2. Alternatively be prepared for oil loss as the driveshafts are removed.

13 Remove both driveshafts as described in Chapter 8.

14 Unbolt and remove the lower rear engine support **(see illustration)**.

15 The engine and transmission must now be supported, as the left-hand mounting must be disconnected. Ford technicians use a support bar which locates in the tops of the inner wings – proprietary engine support bars are available from tool outlets.

16 Due to the steep incline, we fabricated simple brackets to secure the support bar **(see illustration)**. We also used cable-ties to securely anchor the bar to the bonnet hinges.

17 If a support bar is not available, an engine

hoist should be used. With an engine hoist the engine/transmission can be manoeuvred more easily and safely. One solution is to suspend the engine with the hoist, and support the transmission with a trolley jack from below. As both the engine and transmission mountings are removed during this procedure, balancing the engine on a jack is not recommended.

18 Unplug the starter motor solenoid wiring plug and then unbolt the main starter motor supply cable. On the six-speed transmission remove the starter motor completely.

19 Unbolt and remove the starter motor cable support bracket. Disconnect the wiring plug from the vehicle speed sensor at the rear of the gearbox.

20 With reference to Chapter 2A or 2B remove the engine left-hand engine mounting **(see illustration)**. Slacken, but do not remove the left-hand engine mounting bolts. Remove the main earth cable, noting its position.

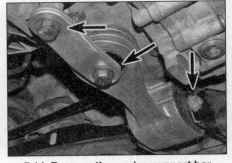

7.9 Disconnect the reversing light switch

7.14 Remove the engine support bar mountings (arrowed)

7.16 A simple bracket secures the support bar in position (arrowed)

7.20 Remove the left-hand engine mounting

21 Unbolt and secure the AC compressor to the radiator shroud. **Do not** disconnect the refrigerant lines.

22 Disconnect the exhaust pipe at the manifold.

23 Ensure all the transmission electrical wiring is disconnected. On diesel models (where fitted) undo the bolts and remove the lower flywheel cover plate.

24 Undo the upper engine-to-transmission nuts and earth lead (where fitted). Unscrew the studs noting their fitted locations.

25 Carefully lower the transmission, so that it clears the crossmember and lower inner wing. At this point we opted to use the engine crane to support the transmission.

26 Slacken and remove the remaining engine-to-transmission bolts and carefully pull the transmission from the engine and free it from its locating dowels. The six-speed transmission must be rotated

10.2a Vehicle speed sensor on the five-speed transmission (arrowed) . . .

10.2b . . . and on the six-speed transmission (arrowed)

10.3a Unscrew the sensor from the drive pinion (5-speed) . . .

10.3b . . . or on the 6-speed transmission unbolt it (arrowed)

anti-clockwise at this point. Once the transmission is free, lower the jack (or engine crane) and manoeuvre the unit out from under the car. Remove the locating dowels from the transmission or engine if they are loose, and keep them in a safe place. **Note:** *If the transmission is to be renewed, check if a starter motor pinion bush is fitted into the casing of the old transmission. If one was, then a new bush must be fitted into the casing of the new transmission, using a suitable drift.*

Refitting

27 The transmission is refitted by a reversal of the removal procedure, bearing in mind the following points.

a) *Ensure the locating dowels are correctly positioned prior to installation.*

b) *Tighten all nuts and bolts to the specified torque (where given).*

c) *Renew the driveshaft oil seals (see Section 5) before refitting the driveshafts.*

d) *Refit the driveshafts as described in Chapter 8.*

e) *Refill the transmission with the correct quantity and specification oil as described in Section 2.*

f) *On completion, adjust the gearchange mechanism as described in Section 3.*

8 Transmission overhaul – general information

1 Overhauling a manual transmission unit is a difficult and involved job for the DIY home mechanic. In addition to dismantling and reassembling many small parts, clearances must be precisely measured and, if necessary, changed by selecting shims and spacers. Internal transmission components are also often difficult to obtain, and in many instances, extremely expensive. Because of this, if the transmission develops a fault or becomes noisy, the best course of action is to have the unit overhauled by a specialist repairer, or to obtain an exchange reconditioned unit.

2 Nevertheless, it is not impossible for the more experienced mechanic to overhaul the transmission, provided the special tools are available, and the job is done in a deliberate step-by-step manner, so that nothing is overlooked.

3 The tools necessary for an overhaul include internal and external circlip pliers, bearing pullers, a slide hammer, a set of pin punches, a dial test indicator, and possibly a hydraulic press. In addition, a large, sturdy workbench and a vice will be required.

4 During dismantling of the transmission, make careful notes of how each component is fitted, to make reassembly easier and more accurate.

5 Before dismantling the transmission, it will help if you have some idea what area is malfunctioning. Certain problems can be closely related to specific areas in the transmission, which can make component examination and renewal easier. Refer to the *Fault finding* Section of this manual for more information.

9 Transmission oil level check

Refer to the relevant Part of Chapter 1.

10 Vehicle speed sensor – removal and refitting

Removal

1 Chock the rear wheels, apply the handbrake, then jack up the front of the vehicle and support it on axle stands (see *Jacking and vehicle support*). Undo the two retaining nuts and four bolts (two each side), and remove the undershield from under the engine compartment.

2 The sensor is fitted on the rear of the transmission casing, above the driveshafts. Lift up the heat shield (where fitted), and disconnect the sensor wiring plug **(see illustrations)**.

3 Unscrew and remove the sensor **(see illustrations)**.

4 On the five-speed transmission (if required) withdraw the roll-pin and pull the sensor drive from the casing, complete with the drive pinion. Discard the O-ring seal, a new one must be fitted.

Refitting

5 If the sensor drive was previously removed on the five-speed transmission, fit a new O-ring to the drive body, and insert it, complete with pinion, into the transmission casing.

6 Ensure that the drive is fully seated, then insert the roll-pin.

7 Screw the sensor onto the drive, tightening it securely. On the six-speed transmission refit the sensor and tighten the nut.

8 Reconnect the sensor wiring plug, and slide the heat shield (where fitted) over the sensor.

9 Refit the engine/transmission undershield, and lower the vehicle to the ground.

Chapter 7 Part B:
Automatic transmission

Contents

Degrees of difficulty

Easy, suitable for novice with little experience	Fairly easy, suitable for beginner with some experience	Fairly difficult, suitable for competent DIY mechanic	Difficult, suitable for experienced DIY mechanic	Very difficult, suitable for expert DIY or professional

Specifications

General

Description . . . . Electro-hydraulically controlled planetary gearbox providing four forward speeds and one reverse speed. Drive transmitted through hydrokinetic torque converter. Lock-up clutch on all four forward speeds, controlled by electronic control module (ECM). Shift points controlled by the ECM using 'Fuzzy logic'

Transmission type number:
  Petrol models AG4
  Diesel models AG5
Automatic transmission fluid . . . . Refer to *Lubricants and fluids*
Automatic transmission fluid capacity:
  AG4:
    Dry (new transmission) . . . . 5.95 litres
    Final drive . . . . 0.8 litres
  AG5:
    Dry (new transmission) . . . . 7.0 litres

Torque wrench settings

	Nm	lbf ft
Engine mountings:*		
Left-hand mounting-to-body bolts:		
Large bolts:		
Stage 1	50	37
Stage 2	Angle-tighten a further 90°	
Small bolt	25	18
Left-hand mounting-to-transmission bolts:		
Stage 1	90	66
Stage 2	Angle-tighten a further 90°	
Final drive fluid drain/filler plug	20	15
Front crossmember to body:		
Stage 1	150	111
Stage 2	Angle-tighten a further 90°	
Heater coolant pipe to transmission	23	17
Oil cooler to transmission	35	26
Right-hand driveshaft oil seal carrier	8	6
Selector cable bracket to transmission	10	7
Starter motor to transmission	11	8
Steering rack to crossmember	48	35
Sump	10	7
Torque converter-to-driveplate nuts:*		
AG4	57	42
AG5	50	37
Transmission bellhousing-to-engine bolts:		
M12 bolts	80	59
M10 bolt	45	33
Transmission fluid drain/level plug	15	11
Transmission range sensor	14	10
Wheel bolts	170	125

* New bolts/nuts must be used

1 General information

An optional automatic transmission unit is available. On petrol models this is a four-speed (plus reverse) transmission unit designated AG4. On diesel models a five-speed transmission (plus reverse) is fitted (AG5). Both transmissions are very similar in operation.

The automatic gearchanges are electronically-controlled, rather than hydraulically as with previous conventional types. The advantage of electronic management is to provide a faster gearchange response. The ECM employs 'Fuzzy logic' to determine the gear up-shift and down-shift points. Instead of having predetermined points for up-shift and down-shift, the ECM takes into account several influencing factors before deciding to shift up or down. These factors include engine speed, driving 'resistance' (engine load), brake pedal position, throttle position, and the rate at which the throttle pedal position is changed. This results in an almost infinite number of shift points, which the ECM can tailor to match the driving style, be that sporty or economic. A kickdown facility is also provided, to enable a faster acceleration response when required.

The transmission consists of three main assemblies, these being the torque converter, which is directly coupled to the engine; the final drive unit, which incorporates the differential unit; and the planetary gearbox, with its multi-disc clutches and brake bands. The transmission is lubricated with automatic transmission fluid (ATF), and is regarded by the manufacturers as being 'filled for life', with no requirement for the fluid to be changed at regular intervals.

The torque converter incorporates an automatic lock-up feature, which eliminates any possibility of converter slip in all forward gears; this aids performance and economy.

Another feature of this transmission is the selector lever lock, with which the selector lever can be set in the P or N position when the engine is running, below about 3 mph. Under these conditions, selection from P or N can only be made by depressing the brake pedal. Correct functioning of the brake light switch is therefore vital for this system to work correctly – see Chapter 9.

The transmission kickdown switch, which acts to select a lower gear (where possible) on full-throttle acceleration, is incorporated into the accelerator cable on petrol models. The switch itself is mounted on the bulkhead in the engine compartment. No adjustment of the switch is possible, beyond ensuring that the basic accelerator cable adjustment is correct – see Chapter 4A. On diesel models the kickdown function is initiated by the ECM monitoring the rate of change of the accelerator pedal position, via the pedal position sensor.

A starter inhibitor/reversing light relay is fitted, to prevent starter motor operation unless the transmission is in P or N, and to switch on the reversing lights when signalled to do so by the transmission range sensor. The relay is located in the left-hand corner of the engine compartment, marked 150.

A transmission range sensor is fitted, and sends signals to the ECM to inform it of the selector shaft position, so that the ECM can initiate such functions as reversing lights, starter inhibition, and cruise control applications. On RHD models, a separate starter inhibitor switch is also fitted on the selector lever. Transmission output speed and turbine shaft speed sensors are also fitted, to inform the ECM of the speed of the output gear, and sun wheel in the planetary gear train. The ECM uses this information to monitor the gear ratio, decide gearchanges, and regulate torque converter slip.

A fault diagnosis system is integrated into the control module, but analysis can only be undertaken with specialised equipment. There is also an emergency running mode, in which only 1st, 3rd and reverse gears can be selected. In any event, it is important that any transmission fault be identified and rectified at the earliest possible opportunity. Delay in doing so will only cause further problems. A

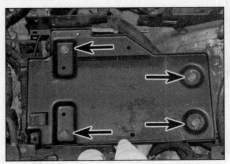

2.4 Remove the battery support tray bolts (arrowed)

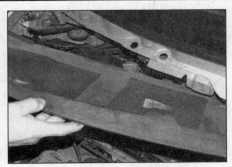

2.5 Remove the bulkhead panel

Ford dealer or suitably-equipped specialist can 'interrogate' the ECM fault memory for stored fault codes, enabling him to pinpoint the fault quickly. Once the fault has been corrected and any fault codes have been cleared, normal transmission operation should be restored.

Because of the need for special test equipment, the complexity of some of the parts, and the need for scrupulous cleanliness when servicing automatic transmissions, the amount which the owner can do is limited. Repairs to the final drive differential are also not recommended. Most major repairs and overhaul operations should be left to a Ford dealer or specialist, who will be equipped with the necessary equipment for fault diagnosis and repair. The information in this Chapter is therefore limited to a description of the removal and refitting of the transmission as a complete unit, the transmission range sensor, and the starter inhibitor switch. The removal, refitting and adjustment of the selector cable is also described.

In the event of a transmission problem occurring, consult a Ford dealer or transmission specialist before removing the transmission from the vehicle, since the majority of fault diagnosis is carried out with the transmission *in situ*.

2 Automatic transmission – removal and refitting

Removal

1 Select a solid, level surface to park the vehicle upon. Give yourself enough space to move around it easily. Apply the handbrake and chock the rear wheels.

2 Mark the position of the bonnet hinges and then (with the aid of an assistant) unbolt and remove the bonnet.

3 Remove both driveshafts (see Chapter 8).

4 Remove the battery, battery compartment panels and the battery support tray **(see illustration)** as described in Chapter 5A

5 Remove the bulkhead panel as described in Chapter 11 **(see illustration)**.

6 Drain the cooling system (see the relevant Part of Chapter 1).

7 Remove the air cleaner housing and intake ducting (see the relevant Part of Chapter 4).

8 Disconnect the hoses from the coolant pipe at the left-hand end of the cylinder head. Undo the two retaining nuts, and move the coolant pipe to one side.

9 Disconnect all the transmission wiring plugs, and release the harnesses from their retaining clips **(see illustrations)**. Note the routing of the harnesses.

10 Remove the front section of the exhaust pipe (see Chapter 4C).

11 Unbolt and remove the oil cooler. Discard the O-ring, a new one must be fitted when the cooler is installed.

12 On all models, ensure the selector lever is in the P position, and unclip the selector inner cable from the lever on the transmission. Unclip the cable outer from the retaining bracket, and position the cable to one side **(see illustration 4.7)**.

13 Remove the front crossmember (see Chapter 10).

14 The engine and transmission must now be supported, as the left-hand mounting must be disconnected. Ford technicians use a support bar which locates in the tops of the inner wings – proprietary engine support bars are available from tool outlets.

15 If a support bar is not available, an engine hoist should be used. With an engine hoist the engine/transmission can be manoeuvred more easily and safely. We found the best solution was to suspend the engine with the hoist, and support the transmission with a trolley jack from below.

16 Completely remove the left-hand transmission mounting (see the relevant Part of Chapter 2).

17 Undo the nuts and bolts securing the engine mounting plate to the mounting and engine. Remove the plate **(see illustration)**.

18 Using a combination of the hoist/and or trolley jack, lower the engine and transmission

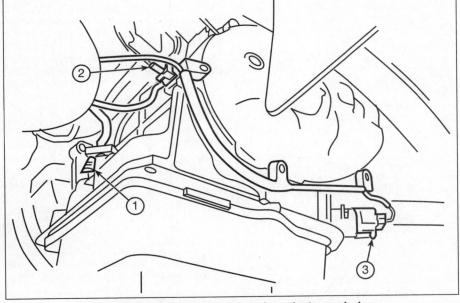

2.9a Disconnect the wiring plugs from the transmission

1 *Valve control solenoid*　　　2 *Large sun gear sensor*　　　3 *Transmission range sensor*

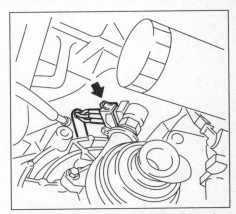

2.9b Disconnect the wiring plug from the vehicle speed sensor (arrowed)

2.17 Remove the engine mounting

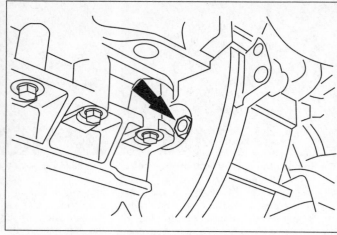

2.19 Unscrew each torque converter nut as it becomes available (arrowed)

unit slightly. Take care not to strain any wiring or hoses.

19 Prise out the rubber plug from front side of the transmission-to-engine adapter plate, and undo the three torque converter-to-driveplate nuts. Use a spanner or socket on the crankshaft pulley nut to rotate the driveplate, and unscrew each nut as it becomes accessible **(see illustration)**.

20 Slacken and remove the bolts securing the transmission to the engine. Note the fitted locations of each bolt to aid refitting.

21 With the help of an assistant, withdraw the transmission from the locating dowels, making sure that the torque converter remains fully engaged with the transmission input shaft. If necessary, use a lever to release the torque converter from the driveplate.

22 When the locating dowels are clear of their

mounting holes, lower the transmission to the ground and remove it from under the vehicle. Strap a retaining bar across the front of the bellhousing to keep the torque converter in place.

> ⚠️ **Warning: Take care to prevent the torque converter from falling out as the transmission is removed.**

Refitting

23 Refitting is a reversal of the removal procedure, but note the following special points:

a) *The transmission-to-engine bolts must be correctly positioned* **(see illustration)**.

b) *Check the fitted depth of the torque converter* **(see illustration)**.

c) *When reconnecting the transmission to the engine, ensure that the location dowels are in position, and the adaptor*

plate is correctly positioned. Check that the transmission is correctly aligned with the locating dowels, before pushing it fully into engagement with the engine.

d) *Tighten all retaining bolts to their specified torque wrench settings (where given).*

e) *Reconnect and adjust the selector cable, as described in Section 4.*

f) *If a new transmission unit has been fitted, it may be necessary to have the transmission ECM 'matched' to the*

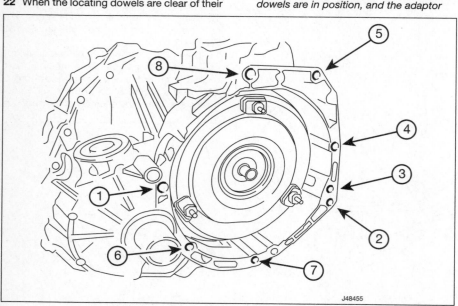

2.23a Install the bolts in the correct locations

1 M12 X 70 mm	3 M12 X 60 mm	5 M12 X 50 mm	7 M10 X 55 mm
2 M10 X 55 mm	4 M12 X 65 mm	6 M10 X 55 mm	8 M12 X 40 mm

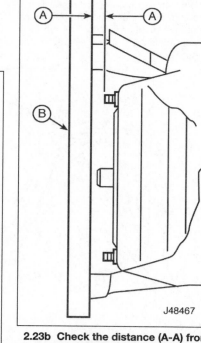

2.23b Check the distance (A-A) from the converter face to the bellhousing mating surface

AG4 = 16.1 ± 0.4 mm
AG5 = 21 mm
B Straight-edge

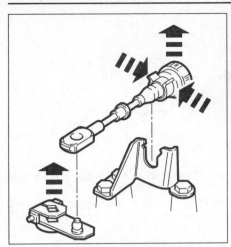

4.7 Disconnect the inner and outer selector cable from the transmission

engine management ECM electronically, to ensure correct operation – seek the advice of your Ford dealer or automatic transmission specialist..

3 Automatic transmission overhaul – general information

In the event of a fault occurring, it will be necessary to establish whether the fault is electrical, mechanical or hydraulic in nature, before repair work can be contemplated. Diagnosis requires detailed knowledge of the transmission's operation and construction, as well as access to specialised test equipment, and so is deemed to be beyond the scope of this manual. It is therefore essential that problems with the automatic transmission are referred to a Ford dealer or automatic transmission specialist for assessment.

Note that a faulty transmission should not be removed before the vehicle has been assessed by a dealer or specialist, as fault diagnosis is carried out with the transmission in situ.

4 Selector cable – removal, refitting and adjustment

Removal

1 Remove the battery as described in Chapter 5A.
2 Move the selector lever to the P position.
3 Firmly apply the handbrake then jack up the front of the vehicle and support it on axle stands. Undo the retaining bolts and remove the undershield from beneath the engine/transmission unit.
4 Undo the retaining nuts, and remove the exhaust system front heat shield.
5 On diesel engine models, detach the left-hand charge air pipe from the intercooler, and release it from the bracket on the

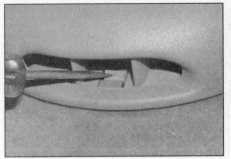

4.12a Depress the clips and lift off the bezel . . .

transmission. Unclip the fuel pipes from the pipe and pull it downwards.
6 If necessary remove the battery side panels. On the AG5 transmission, remove the selector cable support bracket.
7 Carefully prise the selector inner cable end from the lever on the transmission. Squeeze together the outer cable end fitting retaining tabs, and pull it up from the retaining bracket on the transmission **(see illustration)**. On the five-speed gearbox unbolt the support bracket from the transmission.
8 Remove both front seats as described in Chapter 11.
9 Lift the flaps and undo the retaining screws, then remove the sill scuff panel from the passenger side.
10 Remove the left-hand, right-hand and centre heater covers.
11 Remove the centre console as described in Chapter 11.

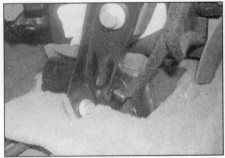

4.15 Undo the bolts and remove the strut

4.16b . . . and one at the rear, then slide the channel to the rear

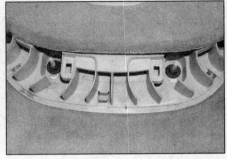

4.12b . . . then undo the nuts and remove the nozzle

12 Depress the retaining clips and lift of the bezel, then undo the two nuts, and remove the footwell heating nozzle **(see illustrations)**.
13 Disengage the two lugs, and pull off the handbrake lever. Pull off the handbrake lever cover.
14 Unclip the handbrake lever floor covering and remove it.
15 Undo the bolts, and remove the strut from the front of the shift assembly baseplate **(see illustration)**.
16 Slacken and remove the three retaining nuts, and slide the rear footwell heating channel backwards **(see illustrations)**.
17 Undo the two bolts and remove the gearchange cable aperture cover. Unbolt and remove the key release cable from the base of the selector lever.
18 Slacken and remove the bolt securing the selector cable to the selector lever **(see illustration)**. Squeeze together the outer cable

4.16a Undo the two nuts at the front . . .

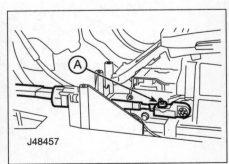

4.18 Selector cable retaining bolt (A)

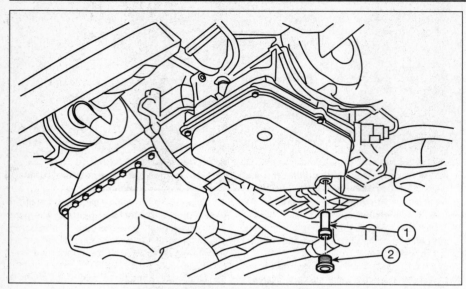

5.2 Drain plug (1) and overflow pipe (2)

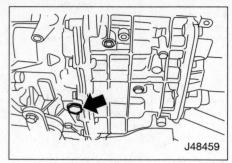

5.3 The five-speed transmission drain plug (arrowed)

29 Refit the engine/transmission undershield, and lower the vehicle to the ground.
30 Ensure that the selector lever is still is position P, then tighten the selector lever clamp bolt.
31 Refit the centre console as described in Chapter 11.
32 Verify the operation of the selector lever by shifting through all gear positions and checking that every gear can be selected smoothly and without delay.

5 Automatic transmission fluid – renewal

Note: *For an accurate fluid level check, Ford technicians use an electronic tester which is plugged into the vehicles diagnostic socket, and establishes that the temperature of the fluid is between 35° and 45°C via a sensor within the transmission casing. However it is possible to measure the fluid temperature using a multimeter with a temperature probe placed down the filler tube.*
Caution: The transmission fluid will be hot when drained. Wear gloves and suitable eye protection.
1 Firmly apply the handbrake then jack up the front of the vehicle and support it on axle stands. Undo the retaining bolts and remove the undershield from beneath the engine/transmission unit.
2 On the four-speed transmission, position a container beneath the combined drain/level plug. Unscrew the centre level plug using an Allen key, then using the same Allen key unscrew the overflow pipe **(see illustration)**. Allow the fluid to drain completely.
3 On the five-speed transmission a separate drain plug is provided **(see illustration)**. Remove the plug and drain the fluid.
4 Refit the overflow pipe (or drain plug), and tighten it securely. **Note:** *The overflow pipe is made of plastic. Do not overtighten it.* Refit the level plug and tighten it to the specified torque.
5 Pull out the retaining clip and pull off the filler pipe blanking plug from the front of the transmission casing **(see illustration)**. On some models, the filler plug is secured by a cap. Prise the cap off with a screwdriver.

end fitting retaining tabs and remove the cable from the bracket.
19 Manoeuvre the cable from the vehicle, noting the routing.
20 Examine the cable closely for signs of wear or damage, renew as necessary.

Refitting

21 Working from the passenger compartment, guide the cable through the aperture, and into the engine compartment.
22 Install the cable in place at the transmission. The outer cable end fittings must clip into place on the retaining brackets and the inner cable end pushes onto the transmission balljoints.
23 If necessary adjust the cable as described

below. The remainder of refitting is a reversal of removal.

Adjustment

24 Ensure the selector lever is in position P.
25 Remove the centre console as described in Chapter 11.
26 Slacken the selector cable clamp bolt sufficiently to release the cable **(see illustration 4.18)**.
27 Firmly apply the handbrake then jack up the front of the vehicle and support it on axle stands. Undo the retaining bolts and remove the undershield from beneath the engine/transmission unit.
28 Check that the transmission selector shaft is in position P. If not, move it to this position.

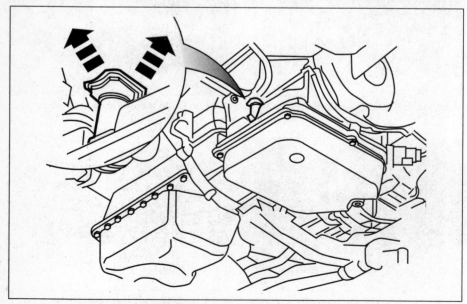

5.5 Pull out the retaining clip and remove the filler pipe plug

6 Measure the amount of fluid removed and then using a suitable funnel, pour in same amount of the correct specification automatic transmission fluid. Note that this amount will not be the total capacity of the transmission, as listed in the specifications, as it is impossible to remove all the fluid from the transmission via the drain plug. Refit the drain plug and lower the vehicle to the ground.

7 Start the engine and move the selector lever through all gear positions. Switch off the engine.

8 At this point Ford technicians connect the IDS diagnostic tester to the vehicles diagnostic socket, and establish that the temperature of the transmission fluid is between 35° and 45°C. A multimeter temperature probe is a suitable alternative solution for the home mechanic. **Note:** *If the level is checked when the temperature is too low, overfilling will occur. If the level is checked when the temperature is too high, underfilling will occur.*

9 With the vehicle still on level ground, start the engine and unscrew the level plug from under the transmission **(see illustration and illustration 5.2)**. If the level is too high, fluid will escape down the overflow pipe. Refit and tighten the level plug when the fluid ceases to drip. If the level is too low, no fluid will escape. Add fluid until it begins to drip from the overflow pipe, then tighten the level plug. Always renew the sealing washer.

10 With the fluid level correct, refit the filler plug and secure it in place with the retaining clip or cap.

11 Refit the undershield.

6 Transmission range sensor – removal and refitting

Note: *On the five-speed (AG5) transmission a special tool is required to align the range sensor, therefore this task is best left to a Ford dealer or suitably-equipped specialist.*

Removal

1 Firmly apply the handbrake then jack up the front of the vehicle and support it on axle stands. Undo the retaining bolts and remove the undershield from beneath the engine/transmission unit.

2 Disconnect the battery negative lead. **Note:** *Before disconnecting the battery, refer to 'Disconnecting the battery' at the rear of this manual.*

3 Drain the automatic transmission fluid as described in the previous Section.

4 The sensor is located on the rear of the transmission casing in front of the left-hand driveshaft. Disconnect the sensor wiring plug, undo the two retaining bolts, and remove the sensor **(see illustration)**.

Refitting

5 Fit a new O-ring to the sensor, and position it in the transmission casing. Tighten the

retaining bolts to the specified torque, and reconnect the wiring plug.

6 Refill the transmission with the correct specification of fluid as described in the previous Section.

7 The remainder of refitting is a reversal of removal.

7 Selector lever lock and key interlock – removal and refitting

Note: *All models feature an electrical selector lever lock and a mechanical key interlock system (see illustration overleaf). The lever lock prevents starting unless the brake pedal is depressed and the lever is in position P (Park) or N (Neutral). The key interlock prevents the removal of the ignition key unless the transmission shift lever is in the P position.*

Selector lever lock

Removal

1 Remove the centre console as described in Chapter 11.

2 Disconnect the electrical wiring plug and unbolt the switch from the housing.

Refitting

3 Refitting is a reversal of removal.

Key interlock cable

Removal

4 Remove the upper and lower steering column shrouds as described in Chapter 11.

5 With the selector lever in the Park position, turn the ignition key to the I (on) position and remove the retaining clip. Remove the cable.

6 Remove the centre console as described in Chapter 11.

7 Remove the selector cable from the gear shift assembly and then unbolt and remove

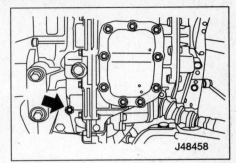

J48458

5.9 The five-speed transmission level plug (arrowed)

the interlock cable. Do not strain the cable.

8 Note the routing of the cable and remove it from the vehicle.

Refitting

9 Refitting is a reversal of removal, but check and adjust (if necessary) the selector cable as described in Section 4 of this Chapter.

8 Driveshaft oil seals – renewal

1 Remove the relevant driveshaft as described in Chapter 8.

Left-hand driveshaft

2 To remove the output flange from the final drive casing, attach a slide hammer to the flange and pull it from the casing. It may take several sharp blows to free the flange. Take care not to pull the vehicle from the axle stands. Alternatively, locate a suitable distance piece (such as a chisel) between the flange and the final drive cover or transmission casing (as applicable), then screw a bolt through the flange onto the distance piece. As

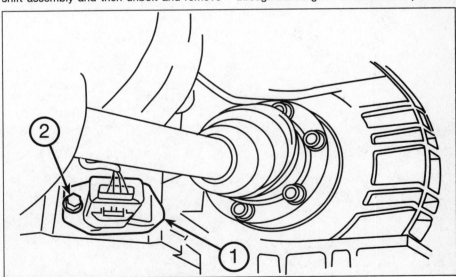

6.4 Disconnect the wiring plug (1), undo the bolts (2) and remove the transmission range sensor

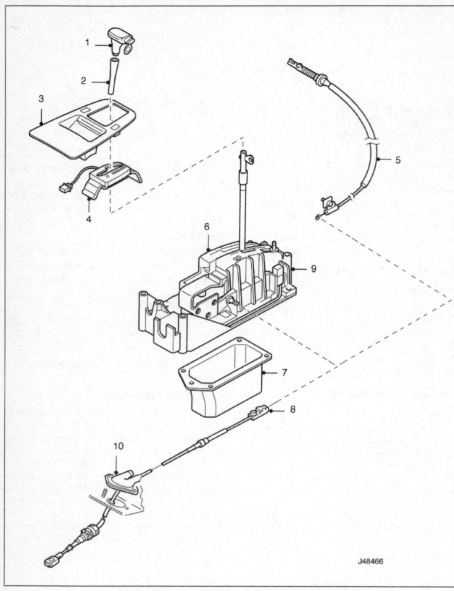

J48466

7.0 Selector lever and key interlock assembly

1 Lever	4 Position	6 Main housing	9 Lever lock
2 Sleeve	indicator	7 Lower cover	connector
3 Trim panel	5 Interlock cable	8 Selector cable	10 Support plate

8.2 Screw a bolt through the driveshaft flange and onto a distance piece placed against the transmission casing

8.3 Lever the oil seal from the casing

the bolt is tightened, the flange will be forced outwards and the circlip released from its groove **(see illustration)**. If the flange is tight, turn it 180º and repeat the removal procedure. Be prepared for oil spillage.

3 With the flange out, note the fitted depth of the oil seal in the housing, then prise it out using a large flat-bladed screwdriver **(see illustration)**.

4 Clean all traces of dirt from the area around the oil seal aperture, then apply a smear of grease to the lips of the new oil seal.

5 Ensure the seal is correctly positioned, with its sealing lip facing inwards, and tap it squarely into position, using a suitable tubular drift (such as a socket) which bears only on the hard outer edge of the seal. If the surface of the flange is good, make sure the seal is fitted at the same depth in its housing as originally fitted.

6 Refit the driveshaft as described in Chapter 8.

Right-hand driveshaft

AG4 transmission

7 Clamp a bearing separator to the final drive output shaft, and lever the intermediate shaft from the casing **(see illustration)**. Be prepared for oil spillage.

8 Disconnect the vehicle speed sensor wiring plug, undo the three retaining bolts, and remove the oil seal carrier **(see illustration)**.

9 Using a punch, drive the oil seal from the carrier.

10 Ensure the oil seal carrier is clean and dry, and fit the seal into the carrier using a tubular drift that bears only on the hard outer edge of the seal. Fit the seal with the sealing lip facing inwards.

11 Fit a new O-ring seal to the final drive casing.

12 Refit the oil seal carrier to the casing, and tighten the retaining bolts securely. Reconnect the vehicle speed sensor wiring plug.

13 With a new O-ring and circlip fitted, insert the intermediate shaft into the casing, and give it a tap with a wooden mallet or similar, to ensure that the shaft circlip engages positively in the differential **(see illustration)**.

14 Refit the driveshaft as described in Chapter 8.

AG5 transmission

15 Place a suitable container below the transmission and remove the centre retaining bolt from the driveshaft flange.

16 Pull out the driveshaft flange and recover the washer and compression spring. Note the orientation of the washer and spring **(see illustration)**.

17 With the flange out, note the fitted depth of the oil seal in the housing, then prise it out using a large flat-bladed screwdriver.

18 Clean all traces of dirt from the area around the oil seal aperture, then apply Vaseline to the space between the inner and outer seal. Do not overfill the space.

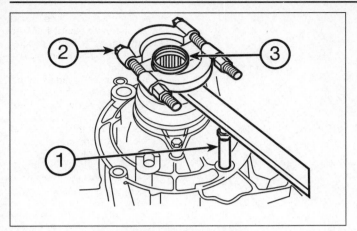

8.7 Output shaft removal

1 M10 x 100 mm bolt   3 Output shaft
2 Separator in O-ring groove

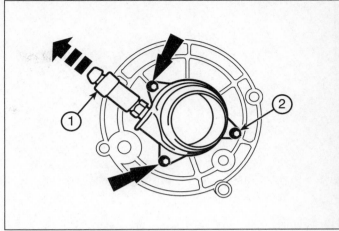

8.8 Disconnect the vehicle speed sensor (1), undo the retaining bolts (2) and remove the seal carrier

19 Ensure the seal is correctly positioned and then tap it squarely into position, using a suitable tubular drift (such as a socket) which bears only on the hard outer edge of the seal. Make sure the seal is fitted at the same depth in its housing as originally fitted.
20 Refit the driveshaft as described in Chapter 8.

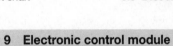

9 Electronic control module (ECM) – removal and refitting

Removal

1 Remove the battery (see Chapter 5A).

2 Working in the left-hand front corner of the engine compartment, disconnect the ECM wiring plug.
3 Undo the securing screw, slide the module to the front and remove it.

Refitting

4 Refitting is a reversal of removal.

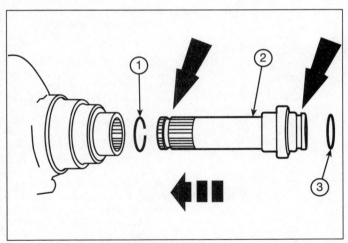

8.13 Output shaft (2), circlips (1) and O-ring (3)

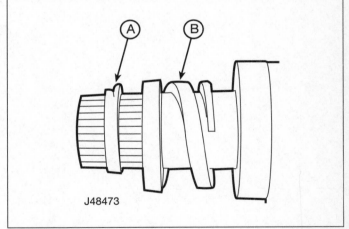

J48473

8.16 Note the position and orientation of the cone (A) and the compression spring (B)

Chapter 8
Driveshafts

Contents

Degrees of difficulty

Easy, suitable for novice with little experience	**Fairly easy,** suitable for beginner with some experience	**Fairly difficult,** suitable for competent DIY mechanic	**Difficult,** suitable for experienced DIY mechanic	**Very difficult,** suitable for expert DIY or professional

Specifications

Lubrication

Type of grease:	
Outer joint	XS4C-M1C203-AA
Inner joint	WSD-M1C230-AA
Quantity of grease per joint:	
Outer joint	180 g
Inner joint:	
Manual gearbox:	
Five-speed	120 g (60 g each side of the joint)
Six-speed	130 g (70 g each side of the joint)
Automatic transmission	120 g (60 g each side of the joint)

Torque wrench settings

	Nm	lbf ft
Anti-roll bar link to suspension strut	100	74
Driveshaft-to-hub bolt:*		
Stage 1	150	111
Stage 2	Angle-tighten a further 90°	
Driveshaft-to-transmission flange bolts	80	59
Lower arm balljoint to hub carrier	55	41
Right-hand driveshaft intermediate bearing bracket to cylinder block	47	35
Right-hand driveshaft intermediate bearing to bracket	27	20
Wheel bolts	170	125

* Do not re-use

2.4 Use a open-ended spanner to stop the balljoint from rotating

2.6 Undo the two Allen bolts – one each side of the balljoint

2.7 Remove the driveshaft bolt and washer

1 General information

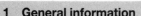

Drive is transmitted from the differential to the front wheels by means of two steel driveshafts of either solid or hollow construction (depending on model). Both driveshafts are splined at their outer ends, to accept the wheel hubs, and are secured to the hub by a large bolt. The inner end of each driveshaft is bolted to the transmission drive flanges on automatic transmission and six-speed manual transmission models. The driveshaft is a push-fit, secured by a circlip on five-speed manual models. The right-hand intermediate driveshaft is supported by a bearing and bracket bolted to the rear of the cylinder block.

Constant velocity (CV) joints are fitted to each end of the driveshafts, to ensure the smooth and efficient transmission of drive at all the angles possible as the roadwheels move up-and-down with the suspension, and as they turn from side-to-side under steering. On all models with five-speed manual transmission, both inner and outer constant velocity joints are of the ball-and-cage type. On models with a six-speed manual or automatic transmission, the outer joint is of the ball-and-cage type, and the inner joint is of the tripod type.

Rubber or plastic gaiters are secured over both CV joints with steel clips. The gaiters contain the grease which lubricates the joints,

and also protect the joints from the entry of dirt and debris.

2 Driveshafts – removal and refitting

Left-hand driveshaft removal

1 Remove the wheel trim/hub cap (as applicable) then apply the handbrake, and partially slacken the relevant hub bolt with the vehicle resting on its wheels – note that the nut is very tight, and a suitable extension bar will probably be required to aid slackening. Also slacken the roadwheel securing bolts.
2 Apply the handbrake, then jack up the front of the vehicle and support it on axle stands (see *Jacking and vehicle support*). Remove the appropriate front roadwheel.
3 Remove the two retaining nuts and four screws (two each side), then remove the undershield from beneath the engine/transmission unit to gain access to the driveshafts.
4 Undo the retaining nut and detach the anti-roll bar link-rod from the suspension strut. Use an open-ended spanner to stop the link-rod balljoint from rotating **(see illustration)**.
5 Release the brake hose and ABS harness from the retaining brackets on the suspension strut.
6 Slacken and remove the two retaining Allen bolts, and separate the lower arm balljoint from the hub carrier **(see illustration)**.
7 Fully unscrew the driveshaft-to-hub bolt

and washer, and pull the hub carrier from the driveshaft end **(see illustration)**.
Caution: Do not allow the driveshaft to hang down under its own weight, or the joint may be damaged.

Automatic and six-speed manual transmissions

8 On the five-speed automatic transmission, disconnect the transmission range sensor wiring plug from the rear of the casing.
9 Using a multi-splined tool **(see illustration)** slacken and remove the bolts securing the inner driveshaft joint to the transmission flange and, where applicable, recover the retaining plates from underneath the bolts. Manoeuvre the driveshaft from under the vehicle.

Five-speed manual transmission

10 Using a lever, carefully prise the inner joint from the final drive casing. Ensure the lever does not damage the seal surfaces of the inner joint. Manoeuvre the driveshaft from under the vehicle. Be prepared for oil spillage.

Right-hand driveshaft removal

Note: *The driveshaft can be removed as a complete assembly with the support bearing and inner driveshaft or as two separate components.*

11 Proceed as described in Paragraphs 1 to 7.

Five-speed manual transmission

12 Using a lever, carefully prise the inner joint from the fixed section of the inner driveshaft.
13 If required unbolt the bearing support bracket and remove the inner driveshaft from the differential casing.

Automatic and six-speed manual transmissions

14 Undo the bolts securing the driveshaft to the intermediate bearing/inner driveshaft and remove the driveshaft **(see illustration)**.
15 If required unbolt the bearing support bracket and remove the inner driveshaft from the differential casing

Left-hand driveshaft refitting

Automatic and six-speed manual transmissions

16 Position the driveshaft inner joint against the transmission output flange, and insert the

2.9 Remove the bolts

2.14 An alternative is to remove the bearing support bolts (arrowed) and remove the driveshaft as an assembly

six retaining bolts. Take care not to damage the transmission range sensor. Tighten the bolts to the specified torque. Reconnect the transmission range sensor wiring plug.

Five-speed manual transmission

17 Fit a new circlip to the inner end of the shaft **(see illustration)**. Insert the driveshaft into the final drive casing, until it can be felt to positively engage. Take care not to damage the oil seal in the casing.

All transmissions

18 Manoeuvre the driveshaft into position, and engage the outer joint with the hub. Fit the new hub bolt and washer, then use it to draw the joint fully into position (a new bolt is normally included in a gaiter kit – check with your supplier).
19 Align the suspension lower arm balljoint, and the hub assembly, then fit lower arm balljoint securing bolts, and tighten them to the specified torque setting.
20 Connect the anti-roll bar link to the suspension strut and tighten the retaining nut to the specified torque.
21 Refit the brake hose and ABS harness into the retaining bracket on the suspension strut.
22 Check the transmission oil level (manual models) or final drive oil level (automatic models) as described in the relevant Part of Chapter 1.
23 Refit the engine/transmission undershield, and front roadwheel(s), then lower the vehicle to the ground.
24 Tighten the driveshaft-to-hub bolt in the two Stages given in the Specifications.
25 Once the driveshaft bolt is correctly tightened, tighten the wheel bolts to the specified torque and refit the wheel trim/hub cap.

Right-hand driveshaft refitting

Automatic and six-speed manual transmissions

26 Fit a new circlip to the inner end of the shaft. Insert the driveshaft into the final drive casing, ensuring the circlip positively engages. Take care not to damage the casing oil seal. Position the intermediate bearing bracket against the cylinder block. Insert the retaining bolts and tighten them to the specified torque.

Five-speed manual transmission

27 Fit a new circlip to the inner end of the shaft. Insert the driveshaft into the final drive casing, ensuring the circlip positively engages. Take care not to damage the casing oil seal. If the driveshaft was removed as a complete assembly (or if the inner driveshaft has been removed) position the intermediate bearing against the support bracket. Insert the retaining bolts and tighten them to the specified torque **(see illustration)**.

All transmissions

28 Proceed as described in Paragraphs 18 to 25.

2.17 Fit a new circlip to the inner end of the driveshaft

2.27 Refit the intermediate bearing flange to the bracket

3 Driveshaft rubber gaiters – renewal

1 Remove the driveshaft from the car, as described in Section 2. Continue as described under the relevant sub-heading. Driveshafts with a tripod type inner joint can be identified by the shape of the inner CV joint; the driveshaft retaining bolt holes are in tabs extending from the joint, giving it a six-pointed star-shaped exterior, in contrast to the smooth, circular shape of the ball-and-cage joint **(see illustrations)**.

Outer CV joint gaiter

2 Secure the driveshaft in a vice equipped with soft jaws, and release the two outer joint gaiter retaining clips. If necessary, the retaining clips can be cut to release them.
3 Slide the rubber gaiter down the shaft to expose the constant velocity joint, and scoop out excess grease.
4 Using a soft-faced mallet, tap the joint off the end of the driveshaft **(see illustration)**.

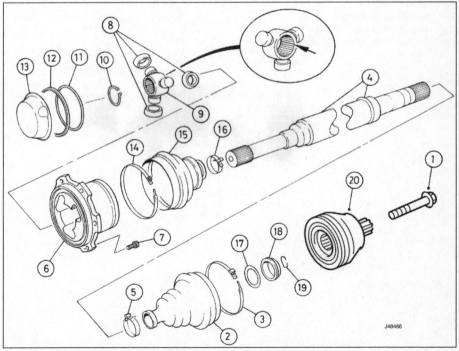

3.1a Driveshaft components – models with press-fit metal cover on inner end of inner CV joint

1 Hub bolt
2 Outer joint gaiter
3 Gaiter securing clip
4 Driveshaft
5 Gaiter securing clip
6 Inner joint
7 Driveshaft-to-transmission flange bolts
8 Tripod roller
9 Tripod
10 Circlip
11 Seal (original)
12 Seal (repair)
13 Metal cover
14 Gaiter securing clip
15 Inner joint gaiter
16 Gaiter securing clip
17 Dished washer
18 Thrust washer
19 Circlip
20 Outer joint

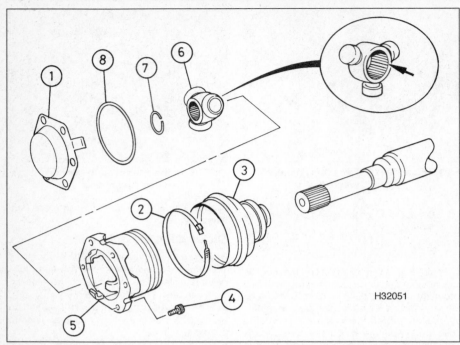

3.1b Inner driveshaft joint components – models with cover on inner end of inner CV joint secured by tabs

1 Metal cover
2 Gaiter securing clip
3 Inner joint gaiter
4 Driveshaft-to-transmission flange bolts
5 Inner joint
6 Tripod/roller assembly (chamfer arrowed faces towards driveshaft)
7 Circlip
8 Seal

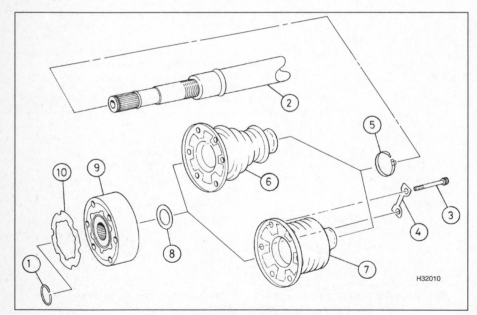

**3.1c Inner driveshaft components –
5-speed manual transmission models**

1 Circlip
2 Driveshaft
3 Driveshaft-to-transmission flange bolts
4 Bolt retaining plate
5 Gaiter securing clip
6 Inner joint gaiter
7 Inner joint gaiter (alternative type)
8 Dished washer
9 Inner joint
10 Gasket

5 Remove the circlip from the driveshaft groove, and slide off the thrust washer and dished washer, noting which way around it is fitted.

6 Slide the rubber gaiter off the driveshaft and discard it.

7 Thoroughly clean the constant velocity joint(s) using paraffin, or a suitable solvent, and dry thoroughly. Carry out a visual inspection as follows.

8 Move the inner splined driving member from side-to-side to expose each ball in turn at the top of its track. Examine the balls for cracks, flat spots or signs of surface pitting.

9 Inspect the ball tracks on the inner and outer members. If the tracks have widened, the balls will no longer be a tight fit. At the same time, check the ball cage windows for wear or cracking between the windows.

10 If on inspection any of the constant velocity joint components are found to be worn or damaged, it will be necessary to renew the complete joint assembly. If the joint is in satisfactory condition, obtain a new gaiter and retaining clips, a constant velocity joint circlip and the correct type of grease. Grease is often supplied with the joint repair kit – if not, use a good-quality molybdenum disulphide grease.

11 Tape over the splines on the end of the driveshaft, to protect the new gaiter as it is slid into place **(see illustration)**.

12 Slide the new gaiter onto the end of the driveshaft, then remove the protective tape from the driveshaft splines.

13 Slide on the dished washer, making sure

3.4 The old driveshaft bolt can be used to force the outer CV joint from the shaft

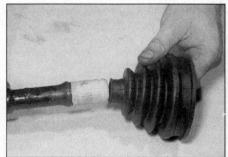

3.11 Tape over the driveshaft splines, then slide the new gaiter along the shaft

3.13a Slide on the dished washer, with its convex side innermost . . .

3.13b . . . then slide on the thrustwasher

3.14a Fit the new circlip to the driveshaft groove . . .

3.14b . . . then locate the joint on the driveshaft splines . . .

3.14c . . . and tap the joint onto the driveshaft

3.16 Seat the gaiter on the outer joint and driveshaft, then lift its inner lip to equalise the air pressure

its convex side is innermost, followed by the thrustwasher (see illustrations).

14 Fit a new circlip to the driveshaft, then tap the joint onto the driveshaft until the circlip engages in its groove (see illustrations). Make sure that the joint is securely retained by the circlip.

15 Pack the joint with the specified type of grease. Work the grease well into the bearing tracks whilst twisting the joint, and fill the rubber gaiter with any excess.

16 Ease the gaiter over the joint, and ensure that the gaiter lips are correctly located on both the driveshaft and constant velocity joint. Lift the outer sealing lip of the gaiter to equalise air pressure within the gaiter (see illustration).

17 Fit the large metal retaining clip to the gaiter. Pull the clip as tight as possible, and locate the hooks on the clip in their slots. Remove any slack in the gaiter retaining clip by carefully compressing the raised section of the clip. In the absence of the special tool, a pair of side-cutters may be used, taking care not to cut the clip (see illustrations). Secure the small retaining clip using the same procedure.

18 Check the constant velocity joint moves freely in all directions, then refit the driveshaft to the vehicle, as described in Section 2.

Tripod inner CV joint gaiter

Press-fit metal cover

19 This type of joint can be recognised from the press-fit metal cover fitted to the end of the CV joint outer member (see illustration 3.1a).

The cover is round. On models where the inner CV joint gaiter has been renewed previously, a metal cover will not be fitted, in which case this type of joint can be recognised during dismantling by the fact that the tripod rollers are a loose fit on the tripod, and will slide off easily (if the rollers are secured to the tripod, proceed as described in paragraphs 45 to 61).

20 Release the two outer joint gaiter retaining clips. If necessary, the retaining clips can be cut to release them. Slide the rubber gaiter down the shaft, away from the joint outer member.

21 Carefully secure the joint outer member in a vice equipped with soft jaws.

22 Drive a screwdriver through the side of the metal cap over the end of the joint outer member, and use the screwdriver to lever the cap off the outer member. If the cap cannot be levered off, drive a second screwdriver through the opposite side of the cap, and use

the two screwdrivers to lever off the cap.

23 Scoop out excess grease from the joint, then remove the O-ring from the groove in the end of the joint outer member.

24 Using a suitable marker pen or a scriber, make alignment marks between the end of the driveshaft, the tripod roller assembly, and the outer member.

25 Support the driveshaft and the joint, and withdraw the outer member from the vice. As the assembly is removed from the vice, make sure that the rollers do not fall off the tripod.

26 Slowly slide the joint outer member down the driveshaft, away from the joint, making sure that the rollers stay on the tripod.

27 Mark the rollers and the arms of the tripod, so that the rollers can be refitted in their original positions, then lift off the rollers and place them to one side on a dry, clean surface.

28 Remove the circlip from the end of the driveshaft.

3.17a Compress the raised section of the gaiter securing clip . . .

3.17b . . . taking great care not to cut through the clip

3.32 Check the tripod rollers and outer member for signs of wear

3.34a Tape over the driveshaft splines to protect the new gaiter . . .

3.34b . . . then lever the gaiter carefully over the ridge on the driveshaft

3.39 Work the grease into the joint outer member

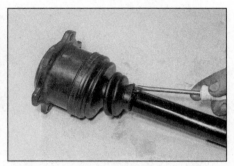

3.41 Lift the gaiter outer end to equalise the air pressure

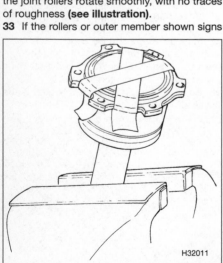

H32011

3.44 Tape over the end of the driveshaft joint

29 Press or drive the driveshaft from the tripod, taking great care not to damage the surfaces of the roller locating arms.

30 Slide the outer member and the rubber gaiter from the end of the driveshaft.

31 Thoroughly clean the joint components using paraffin, or a suitable solvent, and dry thoroughly. Carry out a visual inspection as follows.

32 Inspect the tripod rollers and the joint outer member for signs of wear, pitting or scuffing on their mating surfaces. Check that the joint rollers rotate smoothly, with no traces of roughness (see illustration).

33 If the rollers or outer member shown signs

of wear or damage, it will be necessary to renew the complete driveshaft, since the joint is not available separately. If the joint is in satisfactory condition, obtain a repair kit, consisting of a new gaiter, retaining clips, circlip, and the correct type and quantity of grease.

34 Tape over the splines on the end of the driveshaft, to protect the new gaiter as it is slid into place, then slide the new gaiter and securing clips, and the joint outer member over the end of the driveshaft (see illustrations). Remove the protective tape from the driveshaft splines.

35 Press or drive the tripod onto the end of the driveshaft until it contacts the stop, ensuring that the marks made on the end of the driveshaft and the tripod before dismantling are aligned. Note that the chamfered edge of the internal splines on the tripod should face towards the driveshaft.

36 Fit the new circlip to retain the tripod on the end of the driveshaft.

37 Refit the rollers to the tripod, ensuring that they are refitted in their original locations, as noted before removal.

38 Work half of the grease supplied with the repair kit into the inner end of the joint outer member, then slide the outer member over the tripod, ensuring that the marks made during dismantling are aligned, and clamp the outer member in the vice.

39 Work the rest of the grease supplied with the repair kit into the rear of the joint outer member (see illustration).

40 Slide the rubber gaiter up the driveshaft onto the joint outer member, and secure with the large clip, as described in paragraph 17.

41 Lift the gaiter outer end to equalise the air pressure in the gaiter, then secure the outer gaiter securing clip in position using the method used previously (see illustration).

42 Check that the grease in the joint outer member is evenly distributed around the tripod rollers.

43 Wipe any excess grease from the inner face of the joint outer member, then fit the rectangular profile O-ring provided in the repair kit into the groove in the inner face of the joint outer member. The rectangular profile of the seal acts as a grease seal, and takes the place of the metal cover prised off during dismantling.

44 Check the driveshaft joint moves freely in all directions, then refit the driveshaft to the vehicle, as described in Section 2. To prevent the tripod joint from being pushed back down the driveshaft during refitting, temporarily stick adhesive tape over the open end of the joint outer member (see illustration). Remove the tape just before reconnecting the inner end of the driveshaft to the transmission.

Metal cover secured by tabs

45 This type of joint can be recognised from the metal cover fitted to the end of the CV joint outer member (see illustration 3.1b). The cover fits over the end of the outer member flange, and the driveshaft-to-transmission flange bolts pass through the cover. The cover is secured to the outer member flange by three tabs. If the cover is a press-fit, or if no cover is fitted, proceed as described in paragraphs 19 to 44.

46 Proceed as described in paragraphs 20 and 21.

47 Using a screwdriver, prise up the tabs of the metal cap over the end of the joint outer member. Lever the cover from the joint outer member.

48 Proceed as described in paragraphs 23 and 24.

49 Support the driveshaft and the joint, and withdraw the outer member from the vice. Slide the joint outer member down the driveshaft, away from the joint.

50 Remove the circlip from the end of the driveshaft.

51 Press or drive the driveshaft from the

tripod, taking great care not to damage the rollers.

52 Proceed as described in paragraphs 30 to 36, taking care not to damage the rollers as the tripod is refitted.

53 Work half of the grease supplied with the repair kit into the inner end of the joint outer member, then slide the outer member over the tripod, ensuring that the marks made during dismantling are aligned, and clamp the outer member in the vice.

54 Work the rest of the grease supplied with the repair kit into the rear of the joint outer member.

55 Slide the rubber gaiter up the driveshaft onto the joint outer member, ensuring that the end of the gaiter seats in the groove in the joint outer member, and secure with the large clip as described in paragraph 17.

56 Lift the gaiter outer end to equalise the air pressure in the gaiter, then secure the outer gaiter securing clip in position using the method used previously.

57 Check that the grease in the joint outer member is evenly distributed around the tripod rollers.

58 Wipe any excess grease from the inner face of the joint outer member, then fit the O-ring provided in the repair kit into the groove in the inner face of the joint outer member.

59 Fit the new cover supplied in the repair kit to the inner end of the joint outer member, ensuring that the bolt holes in the outer member and cover are aligned.

60 Secure the cover by bending the securing tabs around the edge of the outer member flange.

61 Check the driveshaft joint moves freely in all directions, then refit the driveshaft to the vehicle, as described in Section 2.

Ball-and-cage type inner CV joint

62 Secure the driveshaft in a vice equipped with soft jaws, then release the gaiter outer securing clip, securing the gaiter to the driveshaft. If necessary, the clip can be cut to release it.

63 Using a hammer and a small drift, carefully drive the inner end of the gaiter from the joint outer member.

64 Slide the gaiter down the driveshaft to expose the constant velocity joint, and scoop out excess grease.

65 Remove the circlip from the end of the driveshaft.

66 Press or drive the driveshaft from the joint, taking great care not to damage the joint. Recover the dished washer fitted between the constant velocity joint and the gaiter.

67 Slide the gaiter from the end of the driveshaft.

68 Proceed as described previously in paragraphs 7 to 12.

69 Slide the dished washer onto the driveshaft, making sure its convex side is innermost.

70 Fit the joint to the end of the driveshaft, noting that the chamfered edge of the internal splines on the joint should face towards the driveshaft. Drive or press the joint into position until it contacts the shoulder on the driveshaft.

71 Fit a new circlip to retain the joint on the end of the driveshaft.

72 It the left-hand driveshaft is being worked on, mark the final installation position of the gaiter outboard end on the driveshaft using tape, or paint – do not scratch the surface of the driveshaft **(see illustration)**.

73 Pack the joint with the recommended quantity of grease (see Specifications), then pack the gaiter with the recommended quantity of grease.

74 Slide the gaiter up the driveshaft, and push or drive the inner end of the gaiter onto the joint outer member.

75 If the left-hand driveshaft is being worked on, slide the outboard end of the gaiter into position using the mark made previously (see paragraph 72), then secure the outer gaiter securing clip in position as described in paragraph 17.

76 If the right-hand driveshaft is being worked on, slide the outboard end of the gaiter into position on the driveshaft, then secure the outer gaiter securing clip in position as described in paragraph 17 **(see illustration)**.

77 Check the driveshaft joint moves freely in all directions, then refit the driveshaft to the vehicle, as described in Section 2.

4 Driveshaft overhaul – general information

If any of the checks described in Chapter 1A or 1B reveal wear in any driveshaft joint, first remove the roadwheel trim or centre cap (as applicable) and check that the hub bolt is tight. If the bolt is loose, obtain a new bolt, and tighten it to the specified torque. If the bolt is tight, refit the centre cap/trim, and repeat the check on the other hub bolt.

Road test the vehicle, and listen for a metallic clicking from the front of the vehicle as the vehicle is driven slowly in a circle on full-lock. If a clicking noise is heard, this indicates wear in the outer constant velocity joint; this means that the joint must be renewed.

If vibration consistent with roadspeed is felt through the car when accelerating, there is a possibility of wear in the inner constant velocity joints.

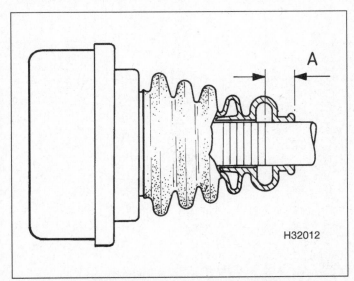

3.72 Installation position of inner joint gaiter on left-hand driveshaft

A = 17.0 mm

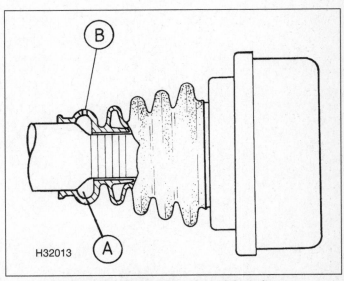

3.76 Installation position of inner joint gaiter on right-hand driveshaft

A Vent chamber in gaiter   B Vent hole

To check the joints for wear, remove the driveshafts, then dismantle them as described in Section 3. If any wear or free play is found, the affected joint must be renewed. Refer to a Ford dealer for information on the availability of driveshaft components.

5 Intermediate driveshaft support bearing – renewal

1 Renewal of the intermediate driveshaft support bearing requires access to a hydraulic press and heat treatment equipment to temporarily shrink the diameter of the driveshaft. If the bearing requires renewal, we recommend that the driveshaft is removed as described in Section 2, and taken to a Ford dealer or specialist.

Chapter 9
Braking system

Contents

Degrees of difficulty

Easy, suitable for novice with little experience	**Fairly easy,** suitable for beginner with some experience	**Fairly difficult,** suitable for competent DIY mechanic	**Difficult,** suitable for experienced DIY mechanic	**Very difficult,** suitable for expert DIY or professional

Specifications

Front brakes

Type	Ventilated disc, with single-piston sliding caliper
Disc diameter	288 mm
Disc thickness:	
New	25 mm
Minimum.	21 mm
Maximum disc run-out	0.10 mm
Brake pad wear limit (including backplate)	7 mm

Rear brakes

Type	Solid disc, with single-piston sliding caliper
Disc diameter	268 mm
Disc thickness:	
New	10 mm
Minimum thickness.	8 mm
Maximum disc run-out	0.05 mm
Brake pad wear limit (including backplate)	7 mm

Torque wrench settings

	Nm	lbf ft
ABS hydraulic unit nuts/bolts:		
Modulator to support bracket	9	7
Support bracket	21	15
Brake disc retaining screw	9	7
Brake pipe union nut	14	10
Front brake caliper:		
Guide pins	28	21
Mounting bracket:		
15 inch wheels	190	140
16 inch wheels	270	199
Handbrake lever mounting bolts	24	18
Master cylinder retaining nuts	25	18
Pedal bracket:		
Bolts	21	15
Nuts	27	20
Rear brake caliper:		
Guide pin bolts	25	18
Mounting bracket bolts	90	66
Servo retaining nuts*	27	20
Splash shield retaining bolts	8	6
Vacuum pump clamp retaining bolt	23	17
Wheel bolts	170	125
Wheel speed sensor retaining bolt	10	7

Use new fasteners

1 General information

1 The braking system is of the servo-assisted, dual-circuit hydraulic type. The arrangement of the hydraulic system is such that each circuit operates one front and one rear brake from a tandem master cylinder. Under normal circumstances, both circuits operate in unison. However, in the event of hydraulic failure in one circuit, full braking force will still be available at two diagonally-opposite roadwheels.

2 All models have disc brakes fitted at the front and rear wheels as standard. ABS is also fitted as standard on all models (refer to Section 18 for further information on ABS operation). Traction control is available as an option (refer to Section 18). Some models also feature an electronic stability feature program (ESP) that uses the ABS system to counteract any tendency to swerve by slowing down the appropriate wheel.

3 The front and rear disc brakes are actuated by single-piston sliding type calipers, which ensure that equal pressure is applied to each disc pad. The handbrake mechanism is built into the rear calipers.

4 On all models, the handbrake provides an independent mechanical (rather than hydraulic) means of rear brake application.

5 Because the diesel engines have no throttle valve, there is insufficient vacuum in the inlet manifold to operate the braking system servo effectively at all times. To overcome this problem, a vacuum pump is fitted to models with diesel engines, to provide sufficient vacuum to operate the servo unit. The pump is mounted to the side of the cylinder block and is driven by the auxiliary shaft.

Note: *When servicing any part of the system,* work carefully and methodically; also observe scrupulous cleanliness when overhauling any part of the hydraulic system. Always renew components (in axle sets, where applicable) if in doubt about their condition, and use only genuine Ford parts, or at least those of known good quality. Note the warnings given in 'Safety first!' and at relevant points in this Chapter concerning the dangers of asbestos dust and hydraulic fluid.

2 Hydraulic system – bleeding

⚠ Warning: *Hydraulic fluid is poisonous; wash off immediately and thoroughly in the case of skin contact, and seek immediate medical advice if any fluid is swallowed or gets into the eyes. Certain types of hydraulic fluid are inflammable, and may ignite when allowed into contact with hot components; when servicing any hydraulic system, it is safest to assume that the fluid is inflammable, and to take precautions against the risk of fire as though it is petrol that is being handled. Hydraulic fluid is also an effective paint stripper, and will attack plastics; if any is spilt, it should be washed off immediately, using copious quantities of fresh water. Finally, it is hygroscopic (it absorbs moisture from the air) – old fluid may be contaminated and unfit for further use. When topping-up or renewing the fluid, always use the recommended type, and ensure that it comes from a freshly-opened sealed container.*

Note: *Ford state that if the ABS hydraulic unit needs to be bled, special test equipment (IDS) must be used. Bearing this in mind it is recommended that the removal and refitting* of the unit is entrusted to a Ford dealer or suitably-equipped specialist. If you do decide to remove and refit the unit yourself, bleed the system as described below, then have the operation of the unit checked at the earliest opportunity by a Ford dealer or specialist.

General

1 The correct operation of any hydraulic system is only possible after removing all air from the components and circuit; this is achieved by bleeding the system.

2 During the bleeding procedure, add only clean, unused hydraulic fluid of the recommended type; *never* re-use fluid that has already been bled from the system. Ensure that a sufficient quantity of new fluid is available before starting work.

3 If there is any possibility of incorrect fluid being already in the system, the brake components and circuit must be flushed completely with uncontaminated, correct fluid, and new seals should be fitted to the various components.

4 If hydraulic fluid has been lost from the system, or air has entered because of a leak, ensure that the fault is cured before proceeding further.

5 Park the vehicle on level ground, securely chock the wheels then release the handbrake.

6 Check that all pipes and hoses are secure, unions tight and bleed screws closed. Clean any dirt from around the bleed screws.

7 Remove the air intake ducting to gain access to the master cylinder reservoir with reference to the relevant Part of Chapter 4. Unscrew the master cylinder reservoir cap, and top the master cylinder reservoir up to the MAX level line; refit the cap loosely, and remember to maintain the fluid level at least above the MIN level line throughout the procedure, or there is a risk of further air entering the system.

8 There are a number of one-man, do-it-yourself brake bleeding kits currently available from motor accessory shops. It is recommended that one of these kits is used whenever possible, as they greatly simplify the bleeding operation, and also reduce the risk of expelled air and fluid being drawn back into the system. If such a kit is not available, the basic (two-man) method must be used, which is described in detail below.

9 If a kit is to be used, prepare the vehicle as described previously, and follow the kit manufacturer's instructions, as the procedure may vary slightly according to the type being used; generally, they are as outlined below in the relevant sub-Section.

10 Whichever method is used, the same sequence must be followed (see paragraphs 11 to 13) to ensure the removal of all air from the system.

Bleeding sequence

11 If the system has been only partially disconnected, and suitable precautions were taken to minimise fluid loss, it should be necessary only to bleed that part of the system (ie, the primary or secondary circuit).

12 If the complete system is to be bled, then it should be done working in the following sequence:

a) Left-hand front brake.
b) Right-hand front brake.
c) Right-hand rear brake.
d) Left-hand rear brake.

Bleeding

Basic (two-man) method

13 Collect a clean glass jar, a suitable length of plastic or rubber tubing which is a tight fit over the bleed screw, and a ring spanner to fit the screw. The help of an assistant will also be required.

14 Remove the dust cap from the first screw in the sequence. Fit the spanner and tube to the screw, place the other end of the tube in the jar, and pour in sufficient fluid to cover the end of the tube.

15 Ensure that the master cylinder reservoir fluid level is maintained at least above the MIN level line throughout the procedure.

16 Have the assistant fully depress the brake pedal several times to build-up pressure, then maintain it on the final downstroke.

17 While pedal pressure is maintained, unscrew the bleed screw (approximately one turn) and allow the compressed fluid and air to flow into the jar.

18 The assistant should maintain pedal pressure, following it down to the floor if necessary, and should not release it until instructed to do so. When the flow stops, tighten the bleed screw again, have the assistant release the pedal slowly, and recheck the reservoir fluid level.

19 Repeat the steps given in paragraphs 16 to 18 inclusive until the fluid emerging from the bleed screw is free from air bubbles. If the

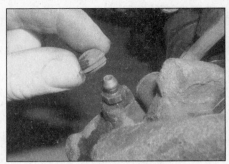

2.23a Remove the dust cap . . .

2.23b . . . and open the bleed nipple with a spanner

master cylinder has been drained and refilled, and air is being bled from the first screw in the sequence, allow approximately five seconds between cycles for the master cylinder passages to refill.

20 When no more air bubbles appear, tighten the bleed screw securely, remove the tube and spanner, and refit the dust cap. Do not overtighten the bleed screw.

21 Repeat the procedure on the remaining screws in the sequence, until all air is removed from the system and the brake pedal feels firm again. On completion, lower the vehicle to the ground (where necessary).

Using a one-way valve kit

22 As their name implies, these kits consist of a length of tubing with a one-way valve fitted, to prevent expelled air and fluid being drawn back into the system; some kits include a translucent container, which can be positioned so that the air bubbles can be more easily seen flowing from the end of the tube.

23 The kit is connected to the bleed screw, which is then opened **(see illustrations)**. The user returns to the driver's seat, depresses the brake pedal with a smooth, steady stroke, and slowly releases it; this is repeated until the expelled fluid is clear of air bubbles.

24 Note that these kits simplify work so much that it is easy to forget to watch the master cylinder reservoir fluid level; ensure that this is maintained at least above the MIN level line at all times, otherwise air will be reintroduced into the system.

Using a pressure-bleeding kit

25 These kits are usually operated by the reservoir of pressurised air contained in the spare tyre. However, note that it will probably be necessary to reduce the pressure to a lower level than normal; refer to the instructions supplied with the kit.

26 By connecting a pressurised, fluid-filled container to the master cylinder reservoir, bleeding can be carried out simply by opening each screw in turn (in the specified sequence), and allowing the fluid to flow out until no more air bubbles can be seen in the expelled fluid.

27 This method has the advantage that the large reservoir of fluid provides an additional safeguard against air being drawn into the system during bleeding.

28 Pressure-bleeding is particularly effective when bleeding difficult systems, or when bleeding the complete system at the time of routine fluid renewal.

All methods

29 When bleeding is complete, and firm pedal feel is restored, wash off any spilt fluid, tighten the bleed screws securely, and refit their dust caps.

30 Check the hydraulic fluid level in the master cylinder reservoir, and top-up if necessary (see *Weekly checks*).

31 Discard any hydraulic fluid that has been bled from the system; it will not be fit for re-use.

32 Check the feel of the brake pedal. If it feels at all spongy, air must still be present in the system, and further bleeding is required. Failure to bleed satisfactorily after a reasonable repetition of the bleeding procedure may be due to worn master cylinder seals. **Note:** *If difficulty is experienced in bleeding the braking circuit, this maybe due to air being trapped in the ABS hydraulic unit. If this is the case then the vehicle should be taken to a Ford dealer so that the system can be bled using special electronic test equipment.*

3 Hydraulic pipes and hoses – renewal

Caution: Disconnect the battery before disconnecting any braking system hydraulic union and do not reconnect the battery until after the hydraulic system has been reconnected and the fluid reservoir is topped-up. Failure to do this could lead to air entering the hydraulic unit requiring the unit to be bled using special Ford test equipment (see Section 2).

Note: *Before starting work, refer to the note at the beginning of Section 2 concerning the dangers of hydraulic fluid.*

1 If any pipe or hose is to be renewed, minimise fluid loss by first removing the master cylinder reservoir cap, then tightening it down onto a piece of polythene to obtain an airtight seal. Alternatively, flexible hoses can be sealed, if required, using a proprietary brake hose clamp; metal brake pipe unions can be

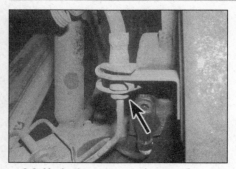

3.2 Undo the union nut (arrowed) and remove the spring clip

plugged (if care is taken not to allow dirt into the system) or capped immediately they are disconnected. Place a wad of rag under any union that is to be disconnected, to catch any spilt fluid.

2 If a flexible hose is to be disconnected, unscrew the brake pipe union nut and remove the spring clip which secures the hose to its mounting bracket **(see illustration)**.

3 To unscrew the union nuts, it is preferable to obtain a brake pipe spanner of the correct size; these are available from most large motor accessory shops. Failing this, a close-fitting open-ended spanner will be required, though if the nuts are tight or corroded, their flats may be rounded-off if the spanner slips. In such a case, a self-locking wrench is often the only way to unscrew a stubborn union, but it follows that the pipe and the damaged nuts must be renewed on reassembly. Always clean a union and surrounding area before disconnecting

it. If disconnecting a component with more than one union, make a careful note of the connections before disturbing any of them.

4 If a brake pipe is to be renewed, it can be obtained, cut to length and with the union nuts and end flares in place, from Ford dealers. All that is then necessary is to bend it to shape, following the line of the original, before fitting it to the car. Alternatively, most motor accessory shops can make up brake pipes from kits, but this requires very careful measurement of the original, to ensure that the new one is of the correct length. The safest answer is usually to take the original to the shop as a pattern.

5 On refitting, do not overtighten the union nuts. It is not necessary to exercise brute force to obtain a sound joint.

6 Ensure that the pipes and hoses are correctly routed, with no kinks, and that they are secured in the clips or brackets provided. After fitting, remove the polythene from the reservoir, and bleed the hydraulic system as described in Section 2. Wash off any spilt fluid, and check carefully for fluid leaks.

4 Front brake pads – renewal

⚠️ **Warning: Renew both sets of front brake pads at the same time – never renew the pads on only one wheel, as uneven braking may result. Note that the dust created by wear of the pads may contain asbestos, which is a health hazard. Never blow it out with**

compressed air, and don't inhale any of it. An approved filtering mask should be worn when working on the brakes. DO NOT use petrol or petroleum-based solvents to clean brake parts; use brake cleaner or methylated spirit only.

1 Apply the handbrake, slacken the roadwheel bolts, then jack up the front of the vehicle and support it on axle stands. Remove the front roadwheels.

2 Insert a small screwdriver under the top of the caliper retaining clip and lever it from the locating hole. Use a pair of pliers to pull the clip out. Repeat the procedure for the lower end of the clip **(see illustrations)**.

3 Remove the dust caps from the guide bushes to gain access to the caliper guide pins **(see illustration)**.

4 Use a 7 mm hexagon key to slacken and remove the caliper guide pins, then lift the caliper away from the mounting bracket **(see illustrations)**. Tie the caliper to the suspension strut using a suitable piece of wire; do not allow it to hang unsupported from the flexible brake hose.

5 If the pad has brake pad wear warning sensor fitted, disconnect the wiring plug, release the cable from the guide and feed it through the caliper as the pad is removed. Pull the inner pad from the caliper piston and remove the outer pad from the mounting bracket **(see illustrations)**.

6 First measure the thickness of each brake pad, including the metal backing plate **(see illustration)**. If either pad is worn at any point to the specified minimum thickness or

4.2a Note how the spring clip locates (arrowed) . . .

4.2b . . . and then use pliers to remove it

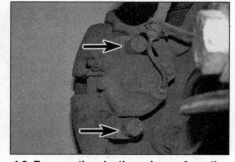

4.3 Remove the plastic end caps from the guide bushes (arrowed)

4.4a Use a 7 mm Allen key to remove the guide pins . . .

4.4b . . . then remove the caliper

4.5a Remove the inner pad . . .

4.5b . . . and the outer

4.6 The thickness of each pad must exceed 7 mm, including the backing plate

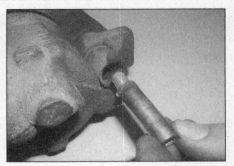

4.8 Check the caliper guide pins move freely

less, **all four** pads must be renewed. Also, the pads should be renewed if any are fouled with oil or grease; there is no satisfactory way of degreasing friction material, once contaminated. If any of the brake pads are worn unevenly, or are fouled with oil or grease, trace and rectify the cause before reassembly.

7 If the brake pads are still serviceable, carefully clean them using a clean, fine wire brush and a proprietary brake cleaning fluid, paying particular attention to the sides and back of the metal backing, paying particular attention to the sides and back of the metal backing. Clean out the grooves in the friction material, and pick out any large embedded particles of dirt or debris. Carefully clean the pad locations in the caliper mounting bracket.

8 Prior to fitting the pads, check that the guide pins are free to slide easily in the caliper body bushes, and are a reasonably tight fit **(see illustration)**. Using brake cleaner, brush the dust and dirt from the caliper and piston, but **do not** inhale it, as it is injurious to health. Inspect the dust seal around the piston for damage, and the piston for evidence of fluid leaks, corrosion or damage. If any of these components requires attention, refer to Section 8.

9 If new brake pads are to be fitted, the caliper piston must be pushed back into the cylinder to make room for them. Either use a piston retraction tool, a G-clamp or use suitable pieces of wood as levers. Clamp off the flexible brake hose leading to the caliper then connect a brake bleeding kit to the caliper bleed nipple. Open the bleed nipple as the piston is retracted; the surplus brake fluid

will then be collected in the bleed kit vessel **(see illustration)**. When the piston is fully retracted, close the bleed nipple and remove the brake pipe clamp. **Note:** *The ABS unit contains hydraulic components that are very sensitive to impurities in the brake fluid. Even the smallest particles can cause the system to fail through blockage. The pad retraction method described here prevents any debris in the brake fluid expelled from the caliper from being passed back to the ABS hydraulic unit.*

10 Clip the inner pad into the caliper piston and fit the outer pad to the mounting bracket, ensuring its friction material is against the brake disc **(see illustrations)**.

11 Manoeuvre the caliper into position then refit the caliper guide pins and tighten them to the specified torque setting **(see illustration 4.4a)**.

12 Refit the end caps to the caliper guide bushes.

13 Fit the retaining spring ends into the

locating holes in the caliper body, then use a pair of pliers to force the sides of the springs over the caliper mounting bracket lugs **(see illustration)**.

14 Depress the brake pedal repeatedly, until the pads are pressed into firm contact with the brake disc, and normal (non-assisted) pedal pressure is restored.

15 Repeat the above procedure on the remaining front brake caliper.

16 Refit the roadwheels, then lower the vehicle to the ground and tighten the roadwheel bolts to the specified torque setting.

17 Check (and if necessary top-up) the hydraulic brake fluid level as described in *Weekly checks*.

⚠ *Warning: New pads will not give full braking efficiency until they have bedded-in. Be prepared for this, and avoid hard braking as much as possible for the first hundred miles or so after pad renewal.*

4.9 Ideally, use a piston retraction tool to push the caliper piston back

4.10a Fit the inner pad . . .

4.10b . . . to the caliper piston . . .

4.10c . . . and the outer pad to the mounting bracket

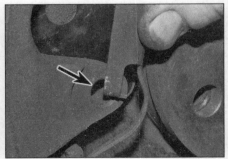

4.13 Ensure the ends of the springs are correctly located (arrowed)

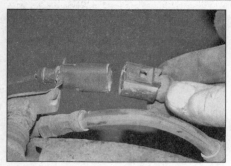
5.3a Disconnect the wiring plug . . .

5.3b . . . remove the cable guide . . .

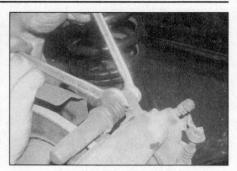
5.3c . . . and then slacken and remove the caliper guide pin bolts

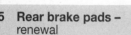

5 Rear brake pads – renewal

⚠ Warning: Renew both sets of rear brake pads at the same time – never renew the pads on only one wheel, as uneven braking may result. Note that the dust created by wear of the pads may contain asbestos, which is a health hazard. Never blow it out with compressed air, and don't inhale any of it. An approved filtering mask should be worn when working on the brakes. DO NOT use petrol or petroleum-based solvents to clean brake parts; use brake cleaner or methylated spirit only.

1 Chock the front wheels, slacken the rear roadwheel bolts, then jack up the rear of the vehicle and support it on axle stands. Remove the rear wheels.

2 Release the handbrake lever then (if necessary) back off the handbrake cable adjuster to obtain maximum free play in the cables and ensure both caliper handbrake levers are against their stops (see Section 14).
3 Where fitted disconnect the wiring connector and remove the cable guide. Slacken and remove the caliper guide pin bolts **(see illustrations)**.
4 Lift the caliper away from the brake pads, and tie it to the suspension strut using a suitable piece of wire. Do not allow the caliper to hang unsupported on the flexible brake hose.
5 Withdraw the two brake pads from the caliper mounting bracket **(see illustration)**.
6 First measure the thickness of each brake pad (including the backing plate) **(see illustration 4.6)**. If either pad is worn at any point to the specified minimum thickness or less, **all four** pads must be renewed. Also,

the pads should be renewed if any are fouled with oil or grease; there is no satisfactory way of degreasing friction material, once contaminated. If any of the brake pads are worn unevenly, or fouled with oil or grease, trace and rectify the cause before reassembly.
7 If the brake pads are still serviceable, carefully clean them using a clean, fine wire brush and a proprietary brake cleaning fluid, paying particular attention to the sides and back of the metal backing. Clean out the grooves in the friction material (where applicable), and pick out any large embedded particles of dirt or debris. Carefully clean the pad locations in the caliper body/mounting bracket.
8 Prior to fitting the pads, check that the guide pins are free to slide easily in the caliper bracket, and check that the rubber guide pin gaiters are undamaged. Soak the caliper and piston with brake cleaner and use a brush to clean them. Inspect the dust seal around the piston for damage, and the piston for evidence of fluid leaks, corrosion or damage. If attention to any of these components is necessary, refer to Section 9.
9 If new brake pads are to be fitted, it will be necessary to retract the piston fully into the caliper bore, by rotating it in a clockwise direction and pressing the piston in at the same time, using a retraction tool, or a pair of pliers. Clamp off the flexible brake hose leading to the caliper then connect a brake bleeding kit to the caliper bleed nipple. Open the bleed nipple as the piston is retracted; the surplus brake fluid will then be collected in the bleed kit vessel **(see illustrations)**. When the

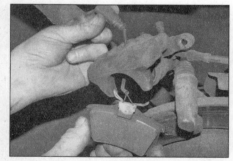
5.5 Feed the brake pad wear warning light cable through the caliper

5.9a Rotate the piston retraction tool clockwise . . .

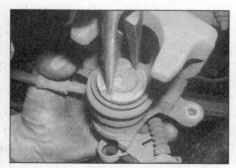
5.9b . . . or use a pair of pliers and push the piston back at the same time

5.9c Clamp the flexible rubber pipe . . .

5.9d . . . and open the bleed nipple (arrowed) as the piston is retracted

5.10a Fit the outer pad . . .

5.10b . . . then the inner pad

5.11 Refit the caliper over the pads

piston is fully retracted, close the bleed nipple and remove the brake pipe clamp. **Note:** *The ABS unit contains hydraulic components that are very sensitive to impurities in the brake fluid. Even the smallest particles can cause the system to fail through blockage. The pad retraction method described here prevents any debris in the brake fluid expelled from the caliper from being passed back to the ABS hydraulic unit.*

10 Fit the pads in the mounting bracket, ensuring that each pad's friction material is facing the brake disc **(see illustrations)**.

11 Slide the caliper back into position over the pads ensuring the pad anti-rattle springs are correctly positioned against the inner surface of the caliper body and are not jammed in the inspection aperture **(see illustration)**.

12 Press the caliper into position, then install the guide pin bolts, tightening them to the specified torque setting **(see illustration 5.3c)**.

13 Repeat the above procedure on the remaining rear brake caliper.

14 Depress the brake pedal repeatedly to force the pads into firm contact with the discs. Once normal pedal feel has returned, check that the discs rotate freely. If necessary, adjust the handbrake as described in Section 14.

15 Refit the roadwheels then lower the vehicle to the ground and tighten the roadwheel bolts to the specified torque setting.

16 Check (and if necessary top-up) the hydraulic fluid level as described in *Weekly checks*.

⚠ **Warning: New pads will not give full braking efficiency until they have bedded-in. Be prepared for this, and avoid hard braking as much as possible for the first hundred miles or so after pad renewal.**

| 6 | Front brake disc – inspection, removal and refitting |

Note: *Before starting work, refer to the note at the beginning of Section 4 concerning the dangers of asbestos dust.*

Note: *If either disc requires renewal, BOTH should be renewed at the same time, to ensure even and consistent braking. New brake pads should also be fitted.*

Inspection

1 Apply the handbrake, slacken the front roadwheel bolts, then jack up the front of the car and support it on axle stands. Remove the appropriate front roadwheel.

2 Slowly rotate the brake disc so that the full area of both sides can be checked; remove the brake pads if better access is required to the inboard surface. Light scoring is normal in the area swept by the brake pads, but if heavy scoring or cracks are found, the disc must be renewed.

3 It is normal to find a lip of rust and brake dust around the disc's perimeter; this can be scraped off if required. If, however, a lip has formed due to excessive wear of the brake pad swept area, then the disc's thickness must be measured using a micrometer. Take measurements at several places around the disc, at the inside and outside of the pad swept area; if the disc has worn at any point to the specified minimum thickness or less, the disc must be renewed.

4 If the disc is thought to be warped, it can be checked for run-out. First secure the disc firmly to the hub by refitting at least two roadwheel bolts – fit plain washers to the roadwheel bolts to ensure that the disc is properly seated on the hub.

5 Either use a dial gauge mounted on any convenient fixed point, while the disc is slowly rotated, or use feeler blades to measure (at several points all around the disc) the clearance between the disc and a fixed point, such as the caliper mounting bracket **(see illustration)**. If the measurements obtained are at the specified maximum or beyond,

the disc is excessively warped, and must be renewed; however, it is worth checking first that the wheel bearing is in good condition (Chapter 10).

6 Check the disc for cracks, especially around the wheel bolt holes, and any other wear or damage, and renew if necessary.

Removal

7 Slacken and remove the two bolts securing the brake caliper mounting bracket to the hub carrier. Slide the whole caliper assembly off the hub and away from the disc, and tie the assembly to the front coil spring, using a piece of wire or string, to avoid placing any strain on the hydraulic brake hose. Unbolt and remove the caliper mounting bracket (see Section 8).

8 Unscrew the countersunk disc retaining screw **(see illustration)**. If the bolt is tight, use an impact driver. Remove the disc, lightly tap its rear face with a hide or plastic mallet to free it from the hub.

Refitting

9 Refitting is the reverse of the removal procedure, noting the following points:
   a) *Ensure that the mating surfaces of the disc and hub are clean and flat.*
   b) *Tighten the disc retaining screw to the specified torque.*
   c) *If a new disc has been fitted, use a suitable solvent to wipe any preservative coating from the disc, before refitting the caliper. Note that new brake pads should always be fitted when the disc is renewed.*
   d) *Prior to installation, clean the caliper*

6.5 Using a DTI gauge to measure disc run-out

6.8 Undo the countersunk screw

7.3 In order to remove the rear disc, the caliper mounting bracket must be removed – two bolts (arrowed)

7.4 The disc is secured by a countersunk screw

bracket mounting bolts. Slide the caliper into position, making sure the pads pass either side of the disc, and tighten the caliper bracket bolts to the specified torque setting.
e) Refit the roadwheel then lower the vehicle to the ground and tighten the wheel bolts to the specified torque. Apply the footbrake several times to force the pads back into contact with the disc before driving the vehicle.

⚠️ *Warning: New pads will not give full braking efficiency until they have bedded-in. Be prepared for this, and avoid hard braking as much as possible for the first hundred miles or so after pad renewal.*

7 Rear brake disc – inspection, removal and refitting

Note: *Before starting work, refer to the note at the beginning of Section 5 concerning the dangers of asbestos dust.*
Note: *If either disc requires renewal, BOTH should be renewed at the same time, to ensure even and consistent braking. New brake pads should be fitted also.*

Inspection

1 Firmly chock the front wheels, engage 1st gear (or P), slacken the rear roadwheel bolts, then jack up the rear of the car and support it on axle stands (see *Jacking and*

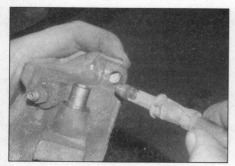

8.6a Rotate the caliper off the brake hose

vehicle support). Remove the appropriate rear roadwheel.
2 Inspect the disc as described in Section 6.

Removal

3 Unscrew the two bolts securing the brake caliper in position, then slide the whole caliper assembly off the disc. Using a piece of wire or string, tie the caliper to the rear suspension coil spring, to avoid placing any strain on the hydraulic brake hose. The caliper mounting bracket must be unbolted and removed (**see illustration**).
4 Undo the countersunk disc retaining screw. If the screw is tight, slacken it using an impact driver (**see illustration**). Remove the disc, lightly tapping its rear face with a hide or plastic mallet to free it from the hub.

Refitting

5 Refitting is the reverse of the removal procedure, noting the following points:
a) Ensure that the mating surfaces of the disc and hub are clean and flat.
b) Tighten the disc retaining screw to the specified torque.
c) If a new disc has been fitted, use a suitable solvent to wipe any preservative coating from the disc, before refitting the caliper. Note that new brake pads should always be fitted when the disc is renewed.
d) Prior to installation, clean the caliper bracket mounting bolts. Slide the caliper into position, making sure the pads pass

8.6b Undo the bolts and remove the caliper mounting bracket

either side of the disc, and tighten the caliper bracket bolts to the specified torque setting.
e) Refit the roadwheel then lower the vehicle to the ground and tighten the wheel bolts to the specified torque. Apply the footbrake several times to force the pads back into contact with the disc before driving the vehicle.

⚠️ *Warning: New pads will not give full braking efficiency until they have bedded-in. Be prepared for this, and avoid hard braking as much as possible for the first hundred miles or so after pad renewal.*

8 Front brake caliper – removal, overhaul and refitting

Note: *Before starting work, refer to the note at the beginning of Section 2 concerning the dangers of hydraulic fluid, and to the warning at the beginning of Section 4 concerning the dangers of asbestos dust.*

Removal

1 Apply the handbrake, slacken the front roadwheel bolts, then jack up the front of the vehicle and support it on axle stands. Remove the front roadwheels.
2 Minimise fluid loss by using a brake hose clamp, a G-clamp or a similar tool to clamp the flexible hose.
3 Where applicable, disconnect the wiring connector from the brake pad wear sensor connector. Unclip the connector from the caliper bracket.
4 Clean the area around the caliper brake pipe union then slacken the union nut.
5 Carefully lever the pad retaining spring out position and remove it from the brake caliper using a flat-bladed screwdriver (**see illustrations 4.2a and 4.2b**). Remove the dust caps from the guide bushes then slacken and remove the caliper guide pins (see Section 4).
6 Lift the caliper out of position. Remove the inner brake pad from the piston and the outer brake pad from the caliper mounting bracket. Disconnect the flexible brake hose by rotating the caliper off the end of the hose. Unbolt and remove the caliper mounting bracket (**see illustrations**).

Overhaul

7 With the caliper on the bench, wipe away all traces of dust and dirt, but *avoid inhaling the dust, as it is injurious to health.*
8 Withdraw the partially-ejected piston from the caliper body, and remove the dust seal.
9 Using a soft flat-bladed instrument, such as a plastic spatula, extract the piston hydraulic seal, taking great care not to damage the caliper bore (**see illustration**).
10 Thoroughly clean all components, using only methylated spirit, isopropyl alcohol or

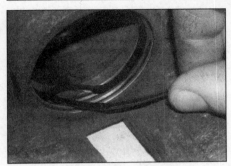

8.9 Use a plastic tool to carefully prise out the piston hydraulic seal

clean brake fluid as a cleaning medium. Never use mineral-based solvents such as petrol or paraffin, as they will attack the hydraulic system's rubber components. Dry the components immediately, using compressed air or a clean, lint-free cloth. Use compressed air to blow clear the fluid passages.

11 Check all components, and renew any that are worn or damaged. Check particularly the cylinder bore and piston; these should be renewed (note that this means the renewal of the complete body assembly) if they are scratched, worn or corroded in any way. Similarly check the condition of the guide pins and the bushes in the caliper body; both pins should be undamaged and (when cleaned) a reasonably tight sliding fit in the bushes. If there is any doubt about the condition of any component, renew it **(see illustration)**.

12 If the assembly is fit for further use, obtain the appropriate repair kit; the components are available from Ford dealers in various combinations. All rubber seals should be renewed as a matter of course; these should never be re-used.

13 On reassembly, ensure that all components are clean and dry.

14 Soak the piston and the new piston (fluid) seal in clean hydraulic fluid. Smear clean fluid on the cylinder bore surface.

15 Fit the new piston (fluid) seal, using only your fingers (no tools) to manipulate it into the cylinder bore groove **(see illustration)**.

16 Fit the new dust seal to the piston groove. Carefully ease the piston squarely into the cylinder bore using a twisting motion. Press the piston fully into position and seat the outer

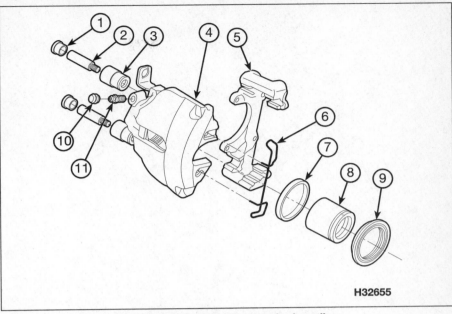

H32655

8.11 Exploded view of the front brake caliper

1 Dust cap	5 Caliper mounting	8 Piston
2 Guide pins	bracket	9 Dust seal
3 Guide bushes	6 Pad retaining spring	10 Dust cap
4 Caliper	7 Piston seal	11 Bleed screw

lip of the dust seal in the caliper body groove **(see illustrations)**.

17 Prior to refitting, fill the caliper with fresh hydraulic fluid by slackening the bleed screw and pumping the fluid through the caliper until bubble-free fluid is expelled from the union hole.

Refitting

18 Bolt the caliper mounting bracket to the hub carrier; and tighten to the specified torque.
19 Reconnect the brake pipe by rotating the caliper onto the pipe.
20 Refit the brake pads to the piston and caliper mounting bracket, with reference to Section 4.
21 Manoeuvre the caliper into position.
22 Fit the caliper guide pins, tightening them to the specified torque setting, and refit the dust caps to the guide bushes.
23 Tighten the brake pipe union nut securely.
24 Fit the pad retaining spring, ensuring its

ends are correctly located in the caliper body holes.
25 Remove the brake hose clamp and bleed the hydraulic system as described in Section 2. Note that, providing the precautions described were taken to minimise brake fluid loss, it should only be necessary to bleed the relevant front brake.
26 Refit the roadwheel, then lower the vehicle to the ground and tighten the roadwheel bolts to the specified torque.

9 Rear brake caliper – removal, overhaul and refitting

Note: *Before starting work, refer to the note at the beginning of Section 2 concerning the dangers of hydraulic fluid, and to the warning at the beginning of Section 5 concerning the dangers of asbestos dust.*

8.15 Fit the new seal into the caliper body

8.16a Insert the piston with the seal fitted into the caliper body . . .

8.16b . . . and seat the outer edge of the seal in the caliper body groove

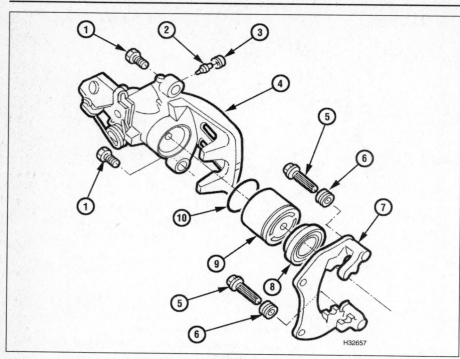

9.13 Exploded view of a rear brake caliper

1 Guide pin bolt	4 Caliper	7 Caliper	8 Dust seal
2 Bleed screw	5 Guide pin	mounting	9 Piston
3 Dust cap	6 Guide pin gaiter	bracket	10 Piston seal

Removal

1 Chock the front wheels, slacken the rear wheel bolts, then jack up the rear of the vehicle and support it on axle stands. Remove the relevant rear wheel.

2 Release the handbrake lever then back off the handbrake cable adjuster to obtain maximum free play in the cables with reference to Section 14.

3 Release the retaining clip and free the handbrake cable from the caliper lever, then free the outer cable from the caliper body.

4 Minimise fluid loss by using a brake hose clamp, a G-clamp or a similar tool to clamp the flexible hose **(see illustration 5.9c)**.

5 Clean the area around the caliper brake hose then slacken the union.

6 Slacken and remove the caliper guide pin bolts.

9.22 Reconnect the handbrake cable to the caliper lever

7 Lift the brake caliper away from the its mounting bracket and unscrew it from the end of the brake hose. Plug/cover the hose end and caliper union to minimise fluid loss and prevent the entry of dirt into the hydraulic system. Wash off any spilt fluid immediately with cold water. Remove the inner and outer brake pads from the caliper mounting bracket. Unbolt and remove the caliper mounting bracket.

Overhaul

Note: *It is not possible to overhaul the brake caliper handbrake mechanism. If the mechanism is faulty, or fluid is leaking from the handbrake lever seal the caliper assembly must be renewed.*

8 With the caliper on the bench, wipe away all traces of dust and dirt, but *avoid inhaling the dust, as it is injurious to health.*

9 Remove the piston from the caliper bore by rotating it in an anti-clockwise direction. This can be achieved using a suitable pair of circlip pliers engaged in the caliper piston slots. Once the piston turns freely but does not come out any further, the piston is held in only by its seal and can be withdrawn by hand.

10 Remove the dust seal from the piston then, using a blunt flat-bladed instrument, carefully extract the piston hydraulic seal from the caliper bore. Take great care not to mark the caliper surface.

11 Withdraw the guide pins from the caliper mounting bracket, and remove the guide pin gaiters.

12 Inspect all the caliper components (as described for the front brake caliper in Section 8), and renew as necessary, noting that the handbrake mechanism must **not** be dismantled.

13 On reassembly, ensure all components are clean and dry **(see illustration)**.

14 Soak the piston and the new piston (fluid) seal in clean hydraulic fluid. Smear clean fluid on the cylinder bore surface. Fit the new piston (fluid) seal, using only your fingers (no tools) to manipulate it into the cylinder bore groove.

15 Fit the new dust seal to the piston groove. Carefully ease the piston squarely into the cylinder bore using a twisting motion. Turn and push the piston in a clockwise direction, using the method employed on dismantling, until it is fully retracted into the caliper bore then seat the outer lip of the dust seal in the caliper groove.

16 Apply the grease supplied in the repair kit, or a copper-based brake grease or anti-seize compound, to the guide pins. Ensure that the gaiters are correctly located in the grooves on the caliper bracket.

17 Prior to refitting, fill the caliper with fresh hydraulic fluid by slackening the bleed screw and pumping the fluid through the caliper until bubble-free fluid is expelled from the union hole.

Refitting

18 Bolt the caliper mounting bracket to the rear hub carrier; and tighten to the specified torque. Refit the brake pads to the caliper mounting bracket with reference to Section 5.

19 Screw the caliper fully onto the brake hose, then manoeuvre the caliper into position over the pads then fit the new guide pin bolts, tightening them to the specified torque setting. Ensure that the pin gaiters are correctly fitted.

20 Tighten the brake hose union, and remove the brake hose clamp.

21 Bleed the hydraulic system as described in Section 2. Note that, providing the precautions described were taken to minimise brake fluid loss, it should only be necessary to bleed the relevant rear brake.

22 Reconnect the handbrake cable to the caliper **(see illustration)**, securing it in position with the retaining clip, and adjust the cable as described in Section 14.

23 Refit the roadwheel, then lower the vehicle to the ground and tighten the roadwheel bolts to the specified torque.

10 Master cylinder – removal, overhaul and refitting

Note: *Before starting work, refer to the warning at the beginning of Section 2 concerning the dangers of hydraulic fluid.*

Removal

1 Slacken both front roadwheel bolts, raise the front of the vehicle and rest it securely on axle stands. Remove both front roadwheels.

10.3 Remove the battery compartment upper panel

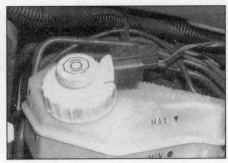

10.7 Disconnect the level sensor wiring plug

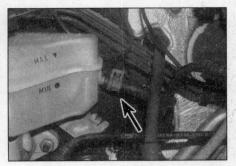

10.8 Release the clip and disconnect the clutch master cylinder feed hose (arrowed)

2 Remove the air cleaner housing, mass airflow sensor, and intake ducting to access the master cylinder, located on the right-hand side of the engine compartment bulkhead (see the relevant Part of Chapter 4).

3 Pull out the battery compartment upper panel **(see illustration)**.

4 With reference to Chapter 11, remove the windscreen cowl panel and the bulkhead panel.

5 On petrol models, remove the throttle body as described in Chapter 4A, Section 4.

6 Connect a length of hose to the right-hand front brake caliper bleed screw, then direct the other end of the hose into a suitable receptacle, as described in Section 2. Open the bleed screw and then depress the brake pedal repeatedly until the level of fluid in the right-hand side of the master cylinder reservoir is below that of the clutch master cylinder supply hose. Close the bleed screw. Repeat the procedure for the left-hand front caliper, to reduce the fluid level in the left-hand side of the reservoir.

7 Pad the area underneath the master cylinder with absorbent rags, to catch any fluid spills. Disconnect the wiring plug from the brake fluid level sensor **(see illustration)**.

8 On manual transmission models, disconnect the clutch master cylinder feed hose from the side of the brake master cylinder and plug the outlet to minimise fluid loss **(see illustration)**.

9 If required, release the retaining tabs, and pull the reservoir up and off the master cylinder **(see illustration)**.

10 Wipe clean the area around the brake pipe

unions on the side of the master cylinder, and place absorbent rags beneath the pipe unions to catch any surplus fluid. Make a note of the correct fitted positions of the unions, then unscrew the union nuts and carefully withdraw the pipes **(see illustration)**. Plug or tape over the pipe ends and master cylinder orifices, to minimise the loss of brake fluid, and to prevent the entry of dirt into the system. Wash off any spilt fluid immediately with cold water.

11 Undo the two nuts and remove the master cylinder **(see illustration)**. Recover the sealing ring.

Overhaul

12 If the master cylinder is faulty, it must be renewed. Repair kits are not available from Ford dealers, so the cylinder must be treated as a sealed unit.

13 The only items which can be renewed are the mounting seals for the fluid reservoir; if these show signs of deterioration, pull out and remove the old seals. Lubricate the new seals with clean brake fluid, and ease them into the master cylinder ports.

Refitting

14 Remove all traces of dirt from the master cylinder and servo unit mating surfaces, and where necessary, fit a new sealing ring to the rear of the master cylinder body.

15 Fit the master cylinder to the servo unit, ensuring that the servo unit pushrod enters the master cylinder bore centrally. Have an assistant depress the brake pedal slightly, so that pushrod is moved towards the master cylinder.

16 Refit the master cylinder mounting nuts and tighten them to the specified torque.

17 Wipe clean the brake pipe unions, then refit them to the master cylinder ports and tighten them to the specified torque.

18 Refit the reservoir into the seals on the top of the master cylinder.

19 On manual transmission models, reconnect the clutch master cylinder hose to the fluid reservoir and securely tighten the retaining clip.

20 Reconnect the fluid level sender unit wiring connector.

21 Refill the master cylinder reservoir with new fluid, and bleed the brake and (if necessary) the clutch hydraulic systems, as described in Section 2 and Chapter 6 respectively.

22 The remainder of refitting is a reversal of removal.

11 Brake pedal – removal and refitting

Removal

1 Disconnect the battery negative lead. **Note:** *Before disconnecting the battery, refer to 'Disconnecting the battery' at the rear of this manual.*

2 Remove the driver's side lower facia panel as described in Chapter 11, Section 29.

3 Lower the central junction box, release the retaining clips each side and at the top, and pull the junction box up and out. Tie the junction box to one side **(see illustrations)**.

10.9 Release the reservoir retaining tabs

10.10 Undo the brake pipe unions

10.11 Undo the two nuts (arrowed) and remove the master cylinder

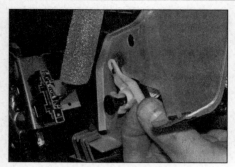

11.3a Release the side clips . . .

11.3b . . . and the central clip (arrowed)

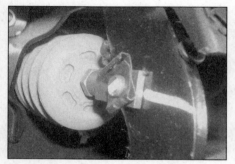

11.5a Release the retaining clip from the servo pushrod

4 Release the brake light switch from its mounting bracket and position it to one side (see Section 17).

5 Remove the servo pushrod pin retaining clip, and slide out the pivot pin. Some later models have a ball and socket type fitting. A special tool is available, but one can also be constructed from an exhaust clamp **(see illustration)**.

6 Detach the pedal pivot shaft retaining clip, slide the shaft towards the clutch pedal, and remove the brake pedal **(see illustration)**.

7 Examine all components for signs of wear or damage, renewing them as necessary.

Refitting

8 Apply a smear of multipurpose grease to the pedal pivot bore.

9 The remainder of the refitting procedure is a reversal of the removal procedure, noting the following points:

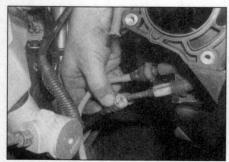

12.5 Disconnect the fuel supply and return couplings

11.6 Remove the pedal shaft retaining clip (arrowed)

a) *Tighten all fixings to the correct torque, where specified.*
b) *Refit and adjust the brake light switch as described in Section 17.*

---

12 Vacuum servo unit – testing, removal and refitting

Testing

1 To test the operation of the servo unit, depress the footbrake several times to exhaust the vacuum, then start the engine whilst keeping the pedal firmly depressed. As the engine starts, there should be a noticeable give in the brake pedal as the vacuum builds-up. Allow the engine to run for at least two minutes, then switch it off. If the brake pedal is now depressed it should feel normal, but further applications should result in the

12.10 Undo the four servo retaining nuts (arrowed)

pedal feeling firmer, with the pedal stroke decreasing with each application.

2 If the servo does not operate as described, first inspect the servo unit check valve as described in Section 13. On diesel engine models, also check the vacuum pump as described in Section 20.

3 If the servo unit still fails to operate satisfactorily, the fault may lie within the unit itself. Repairs to the unit are not possible – if faulty, the servo unit must be renewed.

Removal

4 Remove the master cylinder as described in Section 10.

5 On petrol models, depress the locking tabs, and disconnect the fuel pipes at their quick-release couplings behind the cylinder head **(see illustration)**. Disconnect the evaporative emission pipe below the master cylinder location.

6 Carefully ease the vacuum hose connection out from the servo unit, taking care not to damage the grommet.

7 Working underneath the facia, disconnect the accelerator cable from the pedal, or the wiring plug from the accelerator pedal position sensor – as applicable (see the relevant Part of Chapter 4).

8 Pull out the retaining clip, and pull the pressure pipe from the end of the clutch master cylinder in the engine compartment. Plug the end of the cylinder to prevent fluid loss and dirt ingress.

9 Working underneath the facia, locate the servo unit pushrod and release the retaining clip, and remove the pushrod pin **(see illustration 11.5a or 11.5c)**.

10 Slacken and remove the four nuts securing the servo unit to the bulkhead **(see illustration)**.

11 Manoeuvre the servo unit out of position. Recover the gasket which is fitted between the servo and bulkhead. Examine the gasket for signs of wear or damage and renew if necessary.

Refitting

12 Manoeuvre the pedal bracket back into position, and tighten the retaining bolts/nuts to the specified torque.

13 Ensure the servo unit and bulkhead mating surfaces are clean, fit the gasket to the rear of the servo unit and manoeuvre the unit into position. Fit the new servo unit retaining nuts, and tighten them to the specified torque.

14 The remainder of refitting is a reversal of removal, noting the following points:

a) *Tighten all nuts and bolts to their specified torque where given.*
b) *Bleed the braking system as described in Section 2.*
c) *On manual transmission models, if necessary, bleed the clutch hydraulic system as described in Chapter 6.*
d) *Establish that the braking system is working satisfactorily before driving on the road.*

13 Vacuum servo unit check valve – removal, testing and refitting

Note: *The valve is an integral part of the servo unit vacuum hose and is not available separately.*

Removal

1 Carefully ease the vacuum hose connection out from the servo unit, taking care not to damage the grommet **(see illustration)**.
2 Work back along the hose, freeing it from all the relevant retaining clips whilst noting its correct routing.
3 Slacken the retaining clip then disconnect the vacuum hose from the manifold and/or vacuum pump (as applicable) and remove it from the vehicle. On petrol models depress the collar and pull the hose from the manifold **(see illustration)**.

Testing

4 Examine the vacuum hose for signs of damage, and renew if necessary. The valve may be tested by blowing through it in both directions. Air should flow through the valve in one direction only – when blown through from the servo unit end of the valve. Renew the valve if this is not the case.
5 Examine the servo unit rubber sealing grommet and hose(s) linking the main hose to the manifold/pump (as applicable) for signs of damage or deterioration, and renew as necessary.

Refitting

6 Ensure the sealing grommet is in position in the servo unit then carefully ease the vacuum hose end fitting into position, taking great care not to displace or damage the grommet.
7 Ensure the hose is correctly routed then connect it to the pump/manifold and securely tighten the retaining clip(s).
8 On completion, start the engine and check the check valve-to-servo unit connection for signs of air leaks.

14 Handbrake – adjustment

1 Depress the brake pedal firmly, to settle the rear brake self adjustment mechanism.
2 Chock the front wheels, then jack up the rear of the vehicle and support it on axle stands. Fully release the handbrake lever.
3 Working underneath the vehicle, locate the adjuster locknut at the point where the two handbrake cables join the equaliser plate, and slacken the locknut until the cable levers on the rear calipers return to their stops **(see illustration)**.
4 From inside the vehicle, pull the handbrake on, then release it.
5 Tighten adjuster locknut until the cable

13.1 Carefully prise the hose connection from the servo unit

levers on the calipers begin to move from the stops.
6 Adjust the locknut so that both brakes securely lock the wheels, when the lever has travelled between three and six clicks of the ratchet mechanism. Check that when the lever is released, the rear wheels spin freely.
7 Lower the vehicle to the ground.

15 Handbrake lever – removal and refitting

Removal

1 Chock the front wheels, then jack up the rear of the vehicle and support it on axle stands. Fully release the handbrake lever.
2 Working underneath the vehicle, locate the adjuster locknut at the point where the two handbrake cables join the equaliser plate, and slacken the locknut until the cable levers on the rear calipers return to their stops **(see illustration 14.3)**.
3 Remove the rear centre console as described in Chapter 11. On models without a rear centre console, remove the handbrake lever trim.
4 Lift the carpet over the handbrake and undo the two lever retaining bolts **(see illustrations)**.
5 Release the retaining clip, and disengage the handbrake cable from the base of the lever, then disconnect the wiring switch and remove it from the vehicle.

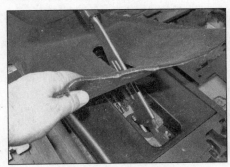
15.4a Lift the carpet . . .

13.3 Depress the retaining collar and pull the vacuum hose from the manifold

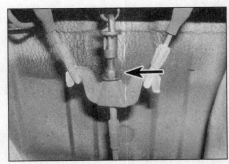
14.3 Handbrake cable adjuster locknut (arrowed)

Refitting

6 Refitting is a reversal of removal, but adjust the handbrake, as described in Section 14, before the rear section of the centre console is refitted.

16 Handbrake cables – removal and refitting

Removal

1 The handbrake cable consists of three sections, a right- and a left-hand section, which are linked to the front cable by an equaliser plate. Each section can be removed individually as follows. Chock the front wheels, then jack up the rear of the vehicle and support it on axle stands. Fully release the handbrake lever.

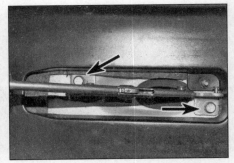
15.4b . . . and undo the handbrake lever bolts (arrowed)

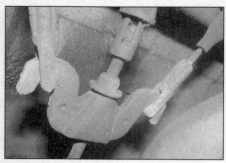

16.5 Unhook the inner cables from the equaliser plate

2 Working underneath the vehicle, locate the adjuster locknut at the point where the two handbrake cables join the equaliser plate, and slacken the locknut until the cable levers on the rear calipers return to their stops.

Front cable

3 Remove the handbrake lever assembly as described in the previous Section.
4 Pull the cable from the rubber gaiter, and disengage it from the equaliser plate rod.

Rear cables

5 Unhook the cable inner from the equaliser plate, and release the outer cable from the retaining bracket **(see illustration)**. If required, repeat this operation on the remaining rear cable.
6 Working at the first rear brake caliper, remove the retaining clip and disconnect the handbrake cable from the caliper lever and retaining bracket **(see illustrations)**. If required, repeat this operation at the remaining caliper.

17.3 Twist the brake light switch clockwise to remove it (early models)

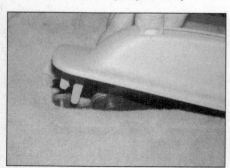

17.8 The handbrake lever trim is clipped to the lever assembly

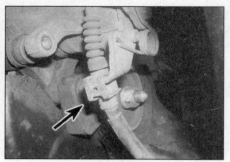

16.6a Pull out the cable retaining clip (arrowed) . . .

7 Work back along the length of each handbrake cable, noting its correct routing, and free it from all the relevant retaining clips and fixings.

Refitting

8 Refitting is a reversal of the removal procedure, ensuring that the cable is correctly routed and retained by all the necessary clips and ties. On completion, adjust the operation of the handbrake as described in Section 14.

17 Braking system switches – removal and refitting

Brake light switch

Removal

1 The brake light switch is located on the pedal bracket behind the facia. On models

17.4 Pull the brake light switch plunger out to its full extent

17.9a Squeeze together the lugs of the retaining clip . . .

16.6b . . . then pull the inner cable end from the caliper lever

with cruise control there are two switches on the brake pedal, the brake light switch is the lower of the two.
2 Remove the driver's side lower facia panel as described in Chapter 11.
3 Twist the switch **clockwise** through 90° and release it from the mounting bracket. Disconnect the wiring plug as the switch is withdrawn **(see illustration)**. On later diesel models the switch requires rotating **clockwise** through 45°.

Refitting

4 Before refitting, pull the switch plunger out to its full extent **(see illustration)**.
5 Depress the brake pedal, insert the switch into the hole in the mounting bracket and rotate it to lock it in place. Slowly release the brake pedal.
6 Reconnect the switch wiring plug. Where a brake pedal position switch is also fitted the switches should be synchronised using suitable diagnostic equipment.
7 Refit the lower facia panel as described in Chapter 11.

Handbrake warning switch

Removal

8 Remove the rear centre console as described in Chapter 11. On models without a centre console, remove the handbrake lever trim **(see illustration)**.
9 Squeeze together the lugs of the retaining clip and remove the switch from the lever **(see illustrations)**.
10 Disconnect the wiring plug as the switch is withdrawn.

17.9b . . . and remove the switch

Refitting

11 Refitting is a reversal of removal. Adjustment of the switch is not possible.

Cruise control pedal switch

Removal

12 The brake pedal switch is located on the pedal bracket behind the facia. The upper of the two switches is the cruise control pedal switch.

13 Remove the driver's side lower facia panel as described in Chapter 11.

14 Disconnect the switch vacuum hose and wiring plug, then unscrew the switch from the bracket (see illustration).

Refitting

15 Refitting is a reversal of removal. With the pedal in the 'at rest' position, screw the switch in until the pedal begins to move, then unscrew the switch a quarter of a turn.

Brake pedal position switch

Removal

16 Remove the driver's side lower facia panel as described in Chapter 11.

17 Twist the switch **anti-clockwise** through 90° and release it from the mounting bracket. Disconnect the wiring plug as the switch is withdrawn.

Refitting

18 Before refitting, pull the switch plunger out to its full extent. Reconnect the wiring plug, depress the brake pedal fully and install the switch by rotating it 90° **clockwise**. The switch should be synchronised with the brake light switch using suitable diagnostic equipment.

18 Anti-lock braking system (ABS) – general information

Note: *On models equipped with traction control, the ABS unit is a dual function unit, controlling both the anti-lock braking system (ABS), and the traction control (TC) system.*

1 ABS is fitted as standard to all models in the range. The system comprises a hydraulic unit, an electronic control module (ECM) and four roadwheel sensors. The hydraulic unit contains the eight hydraulic solenoid valves and the electrically-driven pressure pump. The purpose of the system is to prevent the roadwheels locking during heavy braking. This is achieved by automatic release of the brake on the relevant wheel, followed by re-application of the brake.

2 The solenoid valves are controlled by the ECM, which itself receives signals from the four wheel sensors, which monitor the speed of rotation of each wheel. By comparing these signals, the ECM can determine the speed at which the vehicle is travelling. It can then use this speed to determine when a wheel is decelerating at an abnormal rate, compared to the speed of the vehicle, and therefore

predicts when a wheel is about to lock. During normal operation, the system functions in the same way as a non-ABS braking system. The ABS system only functions at speeds in excess of 3 mph.

3 If the ECM senses that a wheel is about to lock, it activates the relevant solenoid valve in the hydraulic unit, effectively dropping the hydraulic pressure to that caliper, which allows the wheel rotational speed to increase.

4 Once the speed of rotation of the wheel returns to an acceptable rate, the ABS pressure pump is activated, rapidly increasing the pressure to the caliper in accordance with the brake pressure applies by the brake pedal. The ABS unit solenoid valves are de-activated during the pressure build-up phase. This cycle can be carried out many times a second.

5 The action of the solenoid valves and pressure pump creates pulses in the hydraulic circuit. When the ABS system is functioning, these pulses can be felt through the brake pedal.

6 On models with traction control, the ABS system components are used to prevent wheel spin in low traction conditions, such as wet or icy roads. If under acceleration the ECM senses that a wheel is spinning, it uses the hydraulic unit to gradually apply the brake on that wheel until traction is regained. Once the wheel regains traction, the brake is released. With traction control, an extra pair of solenoids are incorporated in to the hydraulic control unit, to supply hydraulic pressure to each of the front brake calipers. The traction control system is active at roadspeeds of up to 30 mph.

7 The operation of the ABS system is entirely dependent on electrical signals. To prevent the system responding to any inaccurate signals, a built-in safety circuit monitors all signals received by the ECM. If an inaccurate signal or low battery voltage is detected, the ABS system is automatically shut down, and the warning light on the instrument panel is illuminated, to inform the driver that the ABS system is not operational. Normal braking should still be available, however.

8 If a fault does develop in the ABS system, the vehicle must be taken to a Ford dealer or suitably-equipped specialist for fault diagnosis and repair.

19 Anti-lock braking system (ABS) components – removal and refitting

Hydraulic unit

Note: *Ford state that if the ABS hydraulic unit needs to be bled, special test equipment (IDS) must be used. Bearing this in mind it is recommended that the removal and refitting of the unit is entrusted to a Ford dealer or suitably-equipped specialist. If you do decide to remove and refit the unit yourself, bleed the system as described in Section 2, then have*

17.14 Brake pedal cruise control switch (brake light switch removed)

the operation of the unit checked at the earliest opportunity by a Ford dealer or specialist.

Removal

1 Remove the battery as described in Chapter 5A.

2 Undo the two bolts securing the coolant expansion tank to the mounting bracket, and disconnect the low coolant level warning switch wiring plug. Place the expansion tank to one side.

3 Pull out the battery compartment upper panel. Release the retaining screws, and remove the engine compartment bulkhead cover. Slide the cover to the right-hand side and manoeuvre it from behind the coolant expansion tank. On vehicles from '98 model year, remove the battery compartment lower panel (see Chapter 5A).

4 Release the locking element and disconnect the ABS hydraulic unit wiring plug (see illustration).

5 On diesel engined models, undo the two retaining bolts, and move the relay box to one side.

6 Slacken both front roadwheel bolts. Raise the front of the vehicle and rest it securely on axle stands, then remove both front roadwheels.

7 Connect a length of hose to the right-hand front brake caliper bleed screw, then direct the other end of the hose into a suitable receptacle, as described in Section 2. Open the bleed nipple and then depress and release the brake pedal until the right-hand side of the brake master cylinder fluid reservoir is empty. Close the bleed screw. Repeat this procedure on the left-hand caliper/reservoir chamber.

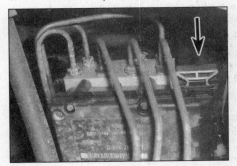

19.4 Pull out the locking element (arrowed) and disconnect the wiring plug

19.8 Undo the pipe union nuts and the unit mounting nuts

19.17 Wheel speed sensor

20.7 On refitting, ensure the slot in the vacuum pump drive gear (arrowed) aligns with the dog on the driveshaft

8 Wipe clean the area around all the pipes unions and mark the locations of the hydraulic fluid pipes to ensure correct refitting. Unscrew the union nuts and disconnect the pipes from the hydraulic unit (see illustration). Be prepared for fluid spillage, and plug the open ends of the pipes and the hydraulic unit unions, to prevent dirt ingress and further fluid loss.
9 Where necessary, release the air conditioning pipes from their retaining clips to gain access to the ABS hydraulic unit mounting bolts.
10 Slacken and remove the hydraulic unit mounting bracket nuts and bolts, then remove the assembly from the engine compartment.

Refitting

Note: *New hydraulic units are supplied pre-filled and fully bled; it is vitally important that the union plugs are not removed until the brake pipes are reconnected, as loss of fluid will introduce air into the unit.*

11 Manoeuvre the hydraulic unit into position, and refit mounting bracket. Tighten the mounting nuts to the specified torque setting.
12 Remove the plugs and reconnect the hydraulic pipes to the correct unions on the hydraulic unit and tighten the union nuts to the specified torque.
13 Reconnect the wiring connector to the hydraulic unit and engage the locking element.
14 The remainder of refitting is a reversal of removal. Bleed the brakes as described in Section 2 – refer to the note at the start of this sub-Section. If necessary, bleed the clutch hydraulic system as described in Chapter 6.

Wheel speed sensor

Removal

15 Apply the handbrake, then jack up the front or rear of the vehicle as applicable, and support securely on axle stands. To improve access, remove the roadwheel.
16 Trace the wiring back from the sensor, releasing it from all the relevant clips and ties whilst noting its correct routing, and disconnect the wiring connector.
17 Slacken and remove the retaining bolt, then carefully pull the sensor out from the hub carrier assembly and remove it from the vehicle (see illustration).

Refitting

18 Ensure that the mating faces of the sensor and hub carrier are clean and dry then lubricate the wheel sensor surfaces with a small quantity of copper-based grease.

19 Insert the wheel speed sensor and tighten the retaining bolt to the specified torque.
20 Ensure the sensor is securely retained then work along the sensor wiring, making sure it is correctly routed, securing it in position with all the relevant clips and ties. Reconnect the wiring connector.
21 Refit the wheel (where removed) then lower the vehicle and (where necessary) tighten the wheel bolts to the specified torque.

20 Vacuum pump (diesel engine models) – removal and refitting

Removal

1 Prise out the covers then unscrew the retaining nuts and remove the plastic cover from the top of the engine. The vacuum pump is situated on the left-hand side of the front face of the cylinder block.
2 Release the retaining clip, and disconnect the vacuum hose from the top of pump.
3 Slacken the retaining clips and remove the charge air pipe from the intercooler to the inlet manifold.
4 Undo the retaining bolt and remove the pump retaining clamp from the cylinder block.
5 Withdraw the vacuum pump from the cylinder block, and recover the sealing ring. Discard the sealing ring, a new one should be used on refitting. According to Ford, no parts are available. If the pump is defective, it must be renewed.

Refitting

6 Fit the new sealing to the vacuum pump and apply a smear of oil to it to aid installation.
7 Manoeuvre the vacuum pump into position, making sure that the slot in the drive gear aligns with the dog on the driveshaft (see illustration).
8 Refit the retaining clamp and tighten its retaining bolt to the specified torque.
9 Reconnect the vacuum hose to the pump, and secure it in position with the retaining clip.
10 Reconnect the air charge pipe, and tighten the retaining clips.
11 Refit the top cover to the engine and securely tighten its retaining nuts/bolts.

Chapter 10
Suspension and steering

Contents

Degrees of difficulty

Easy, suitable for novice with little experience	Fairly easy, suitable for beginner with some experience	Fairly difficult, suitable for competent DIY mechanic	Difficult, suitable for experienced DIY mechanic	Very difficult, suitable for expert DIY or professional

Specifications

Front suspension
Type . . . . Independent MacPherson strut, coil springs, lower suspension arms mounted to the front crossmember, anti-roll bar

Rear suspension
Type . . . . Semi-trailing arm, coil springs, shock absorbers, and anti-roll bar, mounted to the rear crossmember

Steering
Type . . . . Rack-and-pinion, power-assisted

Front wheel alignment and steering angles
Note: All measurements should be taken with the vehicle unladen
Camber angle (negative). . . . . $-0°\ 20'\ \pm\ 0°\ 45'$
Castor angle. . . . . $3°\ 20'\ \pm\ 0°\ 40'$
Front wheel alignment – total toe-out . . . . $0°\ 10'\ \pm\ 0°\ 30'$

Rear wheel alignment
Note: All measurements should be taken with the vehicle unladen
Camber angle (negative). . . . . $-0°\ 20'\ \pm\ 0°\ 30'$
Rear wheel alignment – total toe-in . . . . $0°\ 00'\ \pm\ 0°\ 30'$

Roadwheels
Type . . . . Pressed-steel or aluminium alloy

Tyres
Size. . . . . 195/65 R 16, 205/55 R 16, 215/55 R 16 or 215/45 R17 (depending on model)
Pressures . . . . See end of *Weekly checks*

Torque wrench settings

	Nm	lbf ft
Front suspension		
Anti-roll bar clamp bolts	55	41
Anti-roll bar drop-link balljoint nuts*	100	74
Brake caliper mounting bracket:		
15" wheels	190	140
16" wheels	270	199
Driveshaft bolt:*		
Stage 1	150	111
Stage 2	Angle-tighten a further 90°	
Engine roll restrictor to crossmember:		
Stage 1	60	44
Stage 2	Angle tighten a further 90°	
Engine roll restrictor to transmission	100	74
Front crossmember bolts:*		
Stage 1	150	111
Stage 2	Angle-tighten a further 90°	
Lower arm balljoint retaining bolts	55	41
Lower arm front pivot bolt:†		
Stage 1	90	66
Stage 2	Angle-tighten a further 90°	
Lower arm-to-balljoint locknut:*		
Stage 1	30	22
Stage 2	Angle-tighten a further 90°	
Strut damper rod locknut	60	44
Strut-to-hub carrier bolt	110	81
Strut top mount retaining nut*†	60	44
Wheel bolts	170	125
Rear suspension		
Anti-roll bar bolts	30	22
Brake pipe unions	14	10
Brake caliper mounting bracket	90	66
Rear axle support bracket-to-body bolts	110	81
Rear hub retaining nut/bolt*	200	148
Rear subframe roll restrictor bolt*	260	192
Rear subframe-to-body bolts*	170	125
Shock absorber-to-trailing arm nuts/bolts*†	130	96
Shock absorber upper retaining bolts*	110	81
Trailing arm retaining bolts*†	170	125
Wheel bolts	170	125
Steering		
PAS pipe unions:		
Aluminium pipe	12	9
Pump high-pressure union bolt	41	30
Steel pipe	32	24
PAS pump mounting bolts	23	18
PAS pump pulley bolts	23	18
Steering column lower retaining bolt	11	8
Steering column-to-steering rack pinion pinch-bolt*	24	18
Steering rack mounting bolts:		
Stage 1	30	22
Stage 2	Angle-tighten a further 90°	
Steering rack shield nut	10	7
Steering wheel bolt*	60	44
Track rod end adjuster locknut	55	41
Track rod end balljoint nut:*		
Stage 1	30	22
Stage 2	Angle-tighten a further 90°	
Track rod locking collar	80	59

* Use new nut/bolt
† Tighten when vehicle is resting on its wheels

Note: *Many of the suspension and steering components are secured in position with self-locking 'Nyloc' nuts, recognisable by having a plastic thread insert (often coloured blue). Whenever a self-locking nut is disturbed, it must be discarded and a new nut fitted.*

1 General information

The independent front suspension is of the MacPherson strut type, incorporating coil springs and integral telescopic shock absorbers. The struts are located by transverse lower suspension arms, which use rubber inner mounting bushes. The front wheel bearing housings/hub carriers, which carry the wheel bearings, brake calipers and the hub/disc assemblies, are attached to the MacPherson struts by clamp bolts, and connected to the lower arms through balljoints bolted to the under side of the assembly. A front anti-roll bar is fitted to all models. The anti-roll bar is rubber mounted on the crossmember, and connected to both lower suspension arms by balljointed drop-links.

The rear suspension is of the semi-trailing arm type. These arms pivot from a tubular subframe bolted to the floor pan. A coil spring is fitted between the trailing arms and the floor pan, with separate telescopic shock absorbers fitted to the ends of the arms. The rear hub carriers/wheel bearing housings are incorporated into the trailing arm, with an anti-roll bar clamped to the subframe and trailing arms to prevent excessive body roll.

The steering system comprises an impact-absorbing telescopic steering column, power-assisted steering rack and engine-driven fluid pump, with a fluid reservoir, and connecting pipes and hoses. The adjustable steering column has upper mountings which are designed to detach or deform in the event of a collision, allowing the column to collapse and reduce the risk of injuring the driver. The upper section of the column is splined to accept the steering wheel; the intermediate shaft is joined to the lower shaft by a universal joint, and a further universal joint at the base of the column joins to the splined adapter which attaches the column to the rack pinion. The steering column incorporates a 'clutch' which allows the steering wheel to rotate independently of the column if a force in excess of 145 ± 35 Nm is applied at the wheel. This is designed to prevent would-be car thieves from damaging the steering column lock by force.

The steering rack, which is mounted on the front crossmember, is of conventional design and is connected by two track rods, with balljoints at their outer ends, to bosses projecting rearwards from the hub carriers/wheel bearing housings. The track rod ends are threaded to facilitate adjustment.

Power-assisted steering is standard on all models. The hydraulic steering system is powered by a vane-type pump, which is belt-driven off the crankshaft pulley. Rotary movement of the steering wheel is transferred via the steering column to the valve unit mounted on the steering rack; depending on direction of rotation, fluid

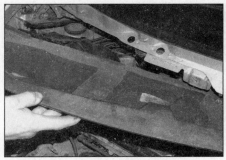

2.2 Remove the bulkhead panel

pressure is applied to one side of the valve or the other, to boost the turning force applied to the pinion, which in turn moves the rack left or right.

2 Front suspension strut –
removal, overhaul and refitting

Removal

1 Apply the handbrake, slacken the roadwheel bolts and the hub retaining bolt, then jack up the front of the vehicle and support it on axle stands. Remove the front roadwheels.

2 With reference to Chapters 11 and 5A remove the battery compartment upper panel. Remove the windscreen cowl panel, release the three retaining bolts, and remove the engine compartment bulkhead cover **(see illustration)**. Slide the cover to the right-hand side and manoeuvre it from behind the coolant expansion tank. On the left-hand side strut, to improve access, remove the battery (see Chapter 5A) and the plastic panel in front of the coolant expansion tank.

3 With an Allen key to prevent the damper rod from rotating, slacken but do not remove the suspension unit top mount nut **(see illustration)**. Note that rain water tends to collect in the top mounts, so thoroughly clean the mounting with a wire brush and liberally apply a proprietary penetrating oil if this is the case.

2.4 Disengage the wheel speed sensor and brake hose from the bracket on the strut

2.3 Insert an Allen key into the damper rod (arrowed)

4 Disengage the flexible brake hose from the retaining bracket on the strut **(see illustration)**.

5 Undo the retaining bolt and remove the wheel speed sensor from the hub carrier, freeing the wiring from any retaining clips – see Chapter 9 for details. Rather than risk damaging the sensor if it has corroded in place, disconnect the wiring harness at the connector on the inner wing.

6 Slacken and remove the two bolts securing the brake caliper mounting bracket to the hub carrier, and suspend the caliper under the wheel arch using a length of wire, or a cable-tie – see Chapter 9 for details. Ensure that no strain is placed on the flexible hose. Do **not** disconnect the brake hose.

7 Unscrew the track rod end balljoint nut, and using a balljoint splitter, detach the balljoint from the hub carrier (see Section 23).

8 Remove and discard the hub retaining bolt. A new one must be fitted.

9 Using an Allen key to prevent the balljoint from rotating, slacken but do not remove, the lower arm balljoint locknut.

10 Using a balljoint splitter, separate the balljoint from the lower arm. Remove the locknut, push the lower arm down, pull the hub carrier outwards and over the end of the driveshaft **(see illustration)**.

Caution: Support the driveshaft by suspending it with wire or string – do not allow it to hang under its own weight, or the joint may be damaged.

11 Slacken and remove the anti-roll bar link

2.10 Use a balljoint splitter to separate the balljoint from the lower arm

2.11 Use an open-ended spanner to prevent the balljoint from rotating whilst slackening the locknut

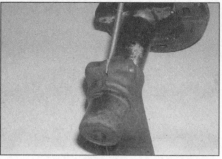

2.13 Use a screwdriver to gently open the hub carrier clamp

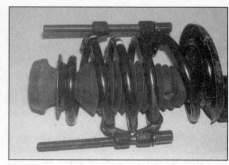

2.14 Compressors must be used to relieve the pressure on the spring seats

upper locknut, and detach the balljoint from the strut **(see illustration)**.

12 Support the strut, and remove the top mount nut. Manoeuvre the strut, complete with the hub carrier, from under the wheel arch.

13 With the assembly on the bench, unscrew the hub carrier clamp bolt and remove the strut. If the strut is reluctant to move, use a screwdriver to gently open the hub carrier clamp **(see illustration)**.

Overhaul

⚠️ *Warning: Before attempting to dismantle the suspension strut, a suitable tool to hold the coil spring in compression must be obtained. Adjustable coil spring compressors are readily available, and are recommended*

for this operation. Any attempt to dismantle the strut without such a tool is likely to result in damage or personal injury.

14 Fit the spring compressors to the coils of the spring **(see illustration)**. Tighten the compressors evenly until the load is taken off the spring seats.

15 Hold the strut piston with an Allen key, then use a spanner to unscrew the damper rod locknut **(see illustration)**.

16 Take off the thrust bearing, followed by the upper spring seat, spring, gaiter and bump stop **(see illustrations)**.

17 With the shock absorber assembly now dismantled, examine all the components for wear and damage. Check the rubber components for deterioration. Examine the shock absorber for damage and signs of fluid

leakage, and check the piston rod for pitting along its entire length. While holding it in an upright position, test the operation of the shock absorber by moving the rod through a full stroke, and then through short strokes of 50 to 100 mm. In both cases, the resistance felt should be smooth and continuous. If the resistance is jerky, or uneven, or if there is any visible sign of wear or damage to the shock absorber, renewal is necessary.

18 If any doubt exists about the condition of the coil spring, gradually release the spring compressor, and check the spring for distortion and signs of cracking. Renew the spring if it is damaged or distorted, or if there is any doubt as to its condition. Note that springs should only be replaced with those that have the same colour-coding – mixing them up will result in a difference in ride heights; springs, like shock absorbers, should be renewed in axle pairs.

19 Inspect all other components for signs of damage or deterioration, and renew any that are suspect.

20 If a new shock absorber is being fitted, hold it vertically and pump the piston a few times to prime it.

21 Reassembly is a reversal of dismantling, noting the following points:

a) Compress the spring before fitting it.

b) Use a new damper rod locknut, and using a torque wrench and adapter, tighten it to the specified torque while holding the strut piston against rotation with an Allen key.

c) Ensure that when the spring is

2.15 Use an Allen key to prevent the damper rod from rotating whilst slackening the locknut

2.16a Remove the locknut and thrust bearing . . .

2.16b . . . followed by the upper spring seat and spring . . .

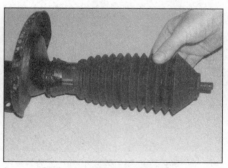

2.16c . . . then the gaiter . . .

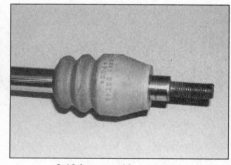

2.16d . . . and bump stop

decompressed, the spring ends fit correctly against the lower spring seat (see illustration).

Refitting

22 Refitting is a reversal of the removal procedure, noting the following points:
  a) *Note the cutaway in the strut leg to accommodate the clamp bolt (see illustration).*
  b) *Renew the strut top mounting nut, but only tighten it once the weight of the vehicle is back on its wheels.*
  c) *Tighten all fixings to the specified torque where given.*
  d) *Refit the ABS wheel sensor and brake caliper as described in Chapter 9.*
  e) *Refit the driveshaft using a new hub bolt.*

3 Front lower arm – removal, overhaul and refitting

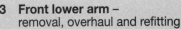

Removal

1 Loosen the wheel bolts, apply the handbrake, then jack up the relevant front wheel and support on axle stands (see *Jacking and vehicle support*). Remove the relevant front wheel.
2 Undo the two retaining nuts and four bolts (two each side), then remove the engine/transmission undershield.
3 Slacken, but do not remove, the lower arm balljoint locknut. Use a balljoint splitter to separate the balljoint. With the balljoint separated, remove the locknut and push the lower arm down and disengage it from the balljoint (see Section 4).
4 Unscrew the lower arm front and rear bolts, and manoeuvre the arm from the vehicle (see illustration).

Overhaul

5 If the arm has suffered damage (from, for example, careless jacking-up or a collision), the arm is best renewed complete. It is advisable to consider renewing both arms in an axle set, rather than just one.
6 To renew the front bush, mount the arm in a vice, and draw the bush from the arm using a length of threaded rod, with several large

2.21 When refitting, the spring end must fit correctly against the lower spring seat (arrowed)

washers and large sockets (see illustration). Use a similar procedure to renew the rear bush.

Refitting

7 Refitting is a reversal of the removal procedure, noting the following points:
  a) *Tighten all fixings to the specified torque where given.*
  b) *Do not fully tighten the lower arm mounting/pivot bolts until the vehicle is resting on its wheels.*

4 Front lower arm balljoint – renewal

1 Loosen the wheel bolts, apply the handbrake, then jack up the relevant front wheel and support on axle stands (see *Jacking and vehicle support*). Remove the front wheel.
2 Slacken, but do not remove, the lower arm balljoint locknut. Use an Allen key in the end of the balljoint to prevent it rotating as the locknut is undone.
3 Use a balljoint splitter to separate the balljoint (see illustration 2.10). With the balljoint separated, remove the locknut and push the lower arm down and disengage it from the balljoint.
4 Slacken and remove the two Allen bolts securing the balljoint to the underside of the hub carrier (see illustration).
5 Refitting is a reversal of removal. Tighten all fixings to the specified torque where given.

2.22 Align the hub carrier clamp bolt with the cutaway in the strut leg (arrowed)

5 Front wheel bearing – renewal

1 Loosen the wheel bolts, and the driveshaft-to-hub bolt, apply the handbrake, then jack up the relevant front wheel and support on axle stands (see *Jacking and vehicle support*). Remove the front wheel.
2 Remove the engine/transmission undershield.
3 Release the flexible brake hose from the retaining bracket on the suspension strut. Do **not** disconnect the brake hose.
4 Undo the retaining bolt and remove the ABS wheel speed sensor (see Chapter 9, Section 19).
5 Undo the two bolts securing the brake caliper mounting bracket to the hub carrier. Slide the caliper from the disc, and using wire or cable-ties, suspend it under the wheel arch.
6 Slacken the track rod balljoint locknut, and using a balljoint splitter, separate the track rod balljoint from the hub carrier. Undo the locknut and lift the track rod balljoint from the hub carrier (see Section 23).
7 Remove and discard the driveshaft-to-hub bolt, a new one must be fitted.
8 Undo the retaining screw, and remove the brake disc. Remove the two retaining bolts, and remove the disc shield from the hub carrier. If necessary, refer to Chapter 9.
9 Slacken and remove the two bolts securing the balljoint to the underside of the hub carrier (see illustration 4.4).

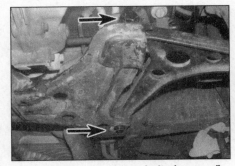

3.4 Undo the lower arm bolts (arrowed)

3.6 Draw the bush from the arm using a length of threaded rod, washers, nuts and large sockets

4.4 Undo the Allen bolts (one each side) and separate the balljoint from the hub carrier

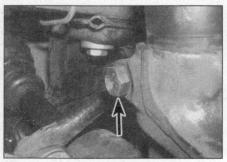

5.10 Undo the hub carrier clamp pinch-bolt (arrowed)

5.13 Drive the flange from the hub

5.14 Remove the bearing inner race from the hub flange

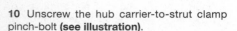

5.15 Remove the bearing retaining circlip

5.18 Try to keep the bearing square to the hub whilst driving it in

5.19 Secure the bearing using a new circlips

10 Unscrew the hub carrier-to-strut clamp pinch-bolt **(see illustration)**.

11 Pull the hub carrier out and over the end of the driveshaft.

12 Using a screwdriver in the gap, spread the hub carrier clamp, and detach the strut **(see illustration 2.13)**.

13 Mount the hub carrier securely in a vice, and using a suitable drift (such as a large socket) drive out the hub flange from the inboard side **(see illustration)**.

14 Mount the drive flange in a vice, then with careful use of a chisel, progressively tap off the bearing race **(see illustration)**. If a bearing puller is available, this is preferable, to avoid risking any damage to the drive flange surfaces.

15 Remove the bearing retaining circlip from the outboard side of the hub **(see illustration)**.

16 Mount the hub carrier in a vice, and drive out the bearing from the inboard side, using a suitable drift.

17 Clean up the hub and drive flange, removing all old grease, and any metal debris from removing the old bearing.

18 Support the inboard side of the hub below the bearing location, and progressively press in the new bearing using a suitable socket or tube which bears only on the bearing outer race. Make sure that the bearing is kept square in the hub until it is fully seated **(see illustration)**.

19 Secure the bearing using a new circlip (usually supplied with the new bearing), then refit the brake disc shield and secure with the bolts **(see illustration)**.

20 Again supporting the inboard side of the hub below the bearing location, align the drive flange squarely into the hub, and tap/press it fully into position **(see illustrations)**.

21 Refitting the hub is a reversal of removal, noting the following points:

a) *Tighten all fasteners to the specified torque where given.*

b) *Use a new hub-to-driveshaft bolt. Tighten the bolt when the weight of the vehicle is on its wheels again.*

c) *Refit the brake disc and ABS wheel sensor as described in Chapter 9.*

6 Front anti-roll bar bushes – renewal

1 Loosen the wheel bolts, apply the handbrake, then jack up the front of the car and support it securely on axle stands (see *Jacking and vehicle support*). Remove the front wheels.

2 Release the two retaining nuts and four bolts (two each side), then remove the engine/transmission undershield.

3 Loosen and remove the nut and bolt for each clamp, and remove the clamp plates from the top of the crossmember **(see illustrations)**.

5.20a Align the drive flange with the bearing . . .

5.20b . . . and drive it in squarely

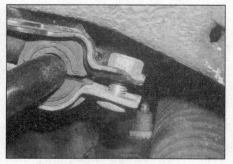

6.3a Undo the clamp bolts . . .

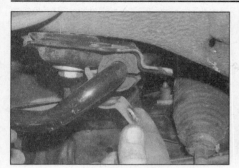

6.3b ... and remove the clamp plates

6.4 As the bushes are split, they can be renewed with the anti-roll bar in place

7.2 Anti-roll bar drop-link lower end (arrowed)

4 The rubber bushes are of split design, so they can be twisted around and removed with the bar *in situ* **(see illustration)**. Once the old bushes are removed, clean up their locations on the bar, and also clean the inner surfaces of the clamp plates.

5 Locate the new bushes in place, then refit the clamp plates and tighten the nuts and bolts to the specified torque.

6 Refit the engine/transmission undershield and the front wheels, then lower the car to the ground.

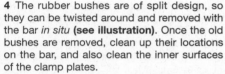

7 Front anti-roll bar drop-links – removal and refitting

Removal

1 Loosen the wheel bolts, apply the handbrake, then jack up the front of the car and support it securely on axle stands (see *Jacking and vehicle support*). Remove the front wheels.

2 Unscrew the nut securing the lower end of each drop-link to the anti-roll bar. It may be necessary to use a second spanner on the inboard side of the roll bar, to prevent the drop-link balljoint shank from turning as the nut is unscrewed **(see illustration)**.

3 Now unscrew the nut at the top end of each link. Remove the drop-link from the vehicle.

Refitting

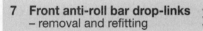

4 If a new link is not being fitted, clean up the balljoint tapers and their mating faces in their fitted locations on the strut and anti-roll bar. Do not apply any lubricant to the tapers, or tightening the balljoint nuts will be made more difficult.

5 Offer the links into position, making sure they are the right way up. Holding the balljoint shanks against rotation as necessary, tighten the upper and lower balljoint nuts to the specified torque.

6 Refit the front wheels, then lower the car to the ground and tighten the wheel bolts to the specified torque.

8 Front anti-roll bar – removal and refitting

Removal

1 Remove the front crossmember as described in Section 9.

2 Loosen and remove the nut and bolt for each anti-roll bar clamp, and remove the clamp plates from the top of the crossmember **(see illustrations 6.3a and 6.3b)**.

3 Lift the anti-roll bar from the crossmember, and remove the bushes as described in Section 6.

Refitting

4 Refitting is a reversal of removal, noting the following points:
   a) *Tighten all fasteners to the specified torque where given.*
   b) *If a new anti-roll bar has been fitted, it is* advisable to fit new bushes, as described in Section 6.

9 Front crossmember – removal and refitting

Note: *New crossmember mounting bolts will be required.*

Removal

1 Loosen the wheel bolts, apply the handbrake, then jack up the front of the car and support it securely on axle stands (see *Jacking and vehicle support*). Do not support under the front crossmember, for obvious reasons. Remove the front wheels.

2 Undo the two retaining nuts and four bolts (two each side), then remove the engine/transmission undershield.

3 Remove the front section of the exhaust pipe as described in Chapter 4C.

4 Unscrew the nuts securing the anti-roll bars drop-links to the ends of the anti-roll bar (see Section 7).

5 Undo the two Allen bolts each side securing the lower arm balljoints to the underside of the hub carriers. Separate the balljoints from the carriers **(see illustration 4.4)**.

6 Undo the four bolts securing the steering rack to the crossmember **(see illustration)**.

7 Slacken and remove the bolt securing the engine roll restrictor to the transmission **(see illustration)**.

8 Before proceeding further, securely support

9.6 Undo the four bolts securing the steering rack to the crossmember (arrowed)

9.7 Remove the bolt securing the roll restrictor to the transmission (arrowed)

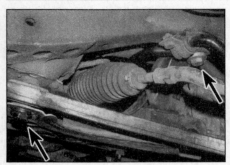

9.9 Two large bolts each side secure the front crossmember (arrowed)

10.3a Undo the nut and bolt securing the shock absorber to the trailing arm . . .

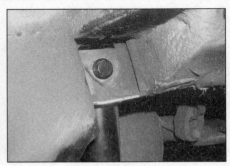

10.3b . . . and the bolt securing it to the vehicle body

the weight of the crossmember. It may also be useful to have an assistant on hand, to help with lowering the crossmember.

9 Remove the four large bolts (two each side) securing the crossmember to the underside of the vehicle. Carefully lower the crossmember, and remove it from under the vehicle **(see illustration)**.

10 If required, undo the clamp bolts and remove the anti-roll bar (see Section 8). The lower arms can be removed by unscrewing the remaining front pivot bolts (see Section 3).

Refitting

11 Where necessary, refit the lower arms and anti-roll bar as described in Sections 3 and 8 respectively. Do not fully tighten the lower arm pivot bolts at this stage.

12 With the help of an assistant, offer up the crossmember, and secure it by the four new crossmember-to-body bolts.

13 Tighten the crossmember-to-body bolts to the specified torque.

14 The remainder of refitting is a reversal of removal. Tighten all fixings to the specified torque where given.

15 Refit the wheels, and lower the car to the ground. Tighten the wheel bolts to the specified torque.

16 With the weight of the car on its wheels, tighten the lower arm pivot bolts to the specified torques.

10 Rear shock absorber – removal, examination and refitting

Removal

1 Loosen the relevant rear wheel bolts, then chock the front wheels and jack up the rear of the car and support on axle stands (see *Jacking and vehicle support*). Remove the relevant rear wheel. Undo the two lower wheel arch liner bolts, and pull the liner out a little.

2 Support the trailing arm with a trolley jack or similar, and slightly compress the suspension spring.

3 Undo the nut and bolt securing the shock absorber to the trailing arm, and the bolt securing the shock absorber to the vehicle body **(see illustrations)**.

4 Manoeuvre the shock absorber from under the vehicle.

Examination

5 Examine the shock absorber for damage and signs of fluid leakage. While holding it in an upright position, test the operation of the shock absorber by moving the rod through a full stroke, and then through short strokes of 50 to 100 mm. In both cases, the resistance felt should be smooth and continuous. If the resistance is jerky, or uneven, or if there is any visible sign of wear or damage to the shock absorber, renewal is necessary.

6 If a new shock absorber is being fitted, hold it vertically and pump the piston a few times to prime it.

Refitting

7 Position the shock absorber against its mounting holes, then insert the upper mounting bolt, and lower nut and bolt. Finger-tighten the lower bolt/nut only at this stage.

8 Slowly lower the trailing arm, and remove the support.

9 Refit the roadwheel, lower the vehicle to the ground. Tighten the shock absorber lower mounting bolt/nut and the roadwheel bolts to their specified torque.

11 Rear suspension spring – removal and refitting

Removal

1 Loosen the relevant rear wheel bolts, chock the front wheels, then jack up the rear of the vehicle and support it on axle stands (see *Jacking and vehicle support*). Remove the relevant rear roadwheel. If you're using a normal, DIY-type trolley jack, the outer trailing arm pivot bolt needs to be at least 43 cm from the ground to provide enough clearance.

2 Unbolt the rear anti-roll bar from the trailing arm as described in Section 12.

3 Support the trailing arm with a trolley jack or similar, and slightly compress the suspension spring.

4 Undo the lower retaining nut/bolt, and remove the shock absorber **(see illustration 10.3a)**.

5 Lower the trailing arm until all tension

is removed from the spring, and it can be manoeuvred out from its locating seats **(see illustration)**.

6 Check the spring for distortion and signs of cracking. Renew the spring if it is damaged or distorted, or if there is any doubt as to its condition. Note that springs should only be replaced with those that have the same colour-coding – mixing them up will result in a difference in ride heights; springs, like shock absorbers, should be renewed in axle pairs.

Refitting

7 Refitting is a reversal of removal. Tighten all fixings to their specified torque where given. Only fully-tighten the lower shock absorber nuts/bolts fully once the weight of the vehicle is on its roadwheels.

12 Rear anti-roll bar and bushes – removal and refitting

Removal

1 Chock the front wheels, then jack up the rear of the vehicle and support it on axle stands (see *Jacking and vehicle support*).

2 Slacken and remove the bolts securing the anti-roll bar clamps to the trailing arms and the rear subframe **(see illustration)**.

3 If required, the anti-roll bar bushes can now be removed **(see illustrations)**. If the anti-roll bar is being renewed, the bushes should also be renewed as a matter of course.

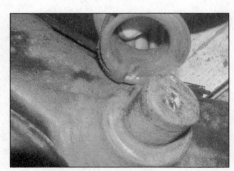

11.5 Rubber inserts are fitted between the spring and its seats

Refitting

4 Once the old bushes are removed, clean up their locations on the bar, and also clean the inner surfaces of the clamp plates.

5 Locate the new bushes in place on the bar. Manoeuvre the anti-roll bar into place, then refit the clamp plates and tighten the bolts to the specified torque.

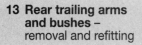

13 Rear trailing arms and bushes –
removal and refitting

Removal

1 Loosen the relevant rear wheel bolts, chock the front wheels, then jack up the rear of the vehicle and support it on axle stands (see *Jacking and vehicle support*). There must be at least 43 cm between the trailing arm outer pivot bolt and the ground to provide enough clearance to lower the arm and remove the spring. Remove the relevant rear roadwheel. **Note:** *If the trailing arm is to be renewed but the wheel bearing retained, slacken the rear hub nut and bolt prior to jacking the vehicle up.*

2 Remove the rear brake caliper as described in Chapter 9. Clamp the flexible hose and disconnect the brake pipe at the retaining bracket **(see illustration)**. Free the brake pipe/hose and handbrake cable from any retaining clips on the trailing arm.

3 Unbolt the rear wheel speed sensor, and free the wiring harness from any retaining clips on the arm.

4 Slacken and remove the brake disc retaining screw, and remove the disc (see Chapter 9).

5 Unscrew the three retaining bolts and remove the brake disc splash shield **(see illustration)**.

6 Undo the clamp bolts and remove the rear anti-roll bar as described in Section 12.

7 Position a trolley jack to support the end of the trailing arm, undo and remove the lower shock absorber nut and bolt.

8 Lower the trailing arm until all tension is removed from the spring, and it can be manoeuvred out from its locating seats.

9 Slacken and remove the inner and outer trailing arm retaining bolts, then manoeuvre

12.2 Rear anti-roll bar clamp bolts (arrowed)

12.3b . . . and remove the inner bushes . . .

the arm from under the vehicle **(see illustration)**.

10 If required, the bushes can be removed by making up your own puller, using a nut and bolt, with several large washers and large sockets

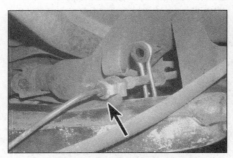

13.2 Clamp the flexible hose, and disconnect the brake pipe at the retaining bracket (arrowed)

12.3a Remove the clamp plates . . .

12.3c . . . and outer bushes

(see illustration). Note: *If the original bushes have an eccentric centre hole, they must be replaced with the same type, fitted in exactly the same position, otherwise the rear wheel geometry will be altered* **(see illustration)**.

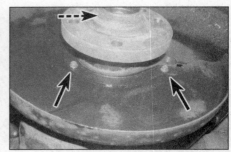

13.5 The brake disc splash shield is retained by three bolts (arrowed – one hidden)

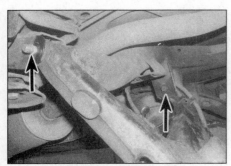

13.9 Slacken and remove the inner and outer trailing arm bolts (arrowed)

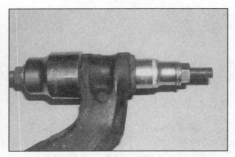

13.10a Use a nut and bolt, several washers and large sockets to remove the trailing arm bushes

13.10b If bushes with eccentric holes were originally fitted, the same type must be fitted, in exactly the same position

14.5a Remove the hub bolt . . .

14.5b . . . and nut . . .

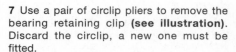

14.5c . . . followed by the sensor ring

11 If the trailing arm is to be renewed, fit the rear hub bearing as described in Section 14.

Refitting

12 With the new bearing and hub in place where applicable, draw the new bushes into place using a combination of sockets, washers, and a nut and bolt.

13 The remainder of refitting is a reversal of removal, tightening all fixings to their specified torque where given. **Note:** *Final tightening of the trailing arm pivot bolts and lower shock absorber nut/bolt should be carried out with the weight of the vehicle on its wheels.*

14 Rear wheel bearing – renewal

1 Loosen the wheel bolts, chock the front wheels, then jack up the relevant rear wheel and support on axle stands (see *Jacking and vehicle support*). Remove the rear wheel.

2 Undo the retaining bolt and remove the rear wheel speed sensor.

3 Undo the caliper bracket retaining bolts, slide the caliper (and mounting bracket) from the disc, and using a length of wire or a cable-tie, suspend the caliper under the wheel arch. Do **not** place the flexible hose under any strain.

4 Undo the retaining screw, and remove the rear brake disc.

5 Slacken and remove the hub securing bolt, nut and washer. Remove the ABS sensor ring **(see illustrations)**. Discard the nut and bolt, new ones must be fitted.

6 Using a slide hammer, pull the hub from the bearings. A DIY slide hammer can be made from a length of threaded rod, four nuts, a suitably-sized socket, a large washer, and a suitable weight **(see illustrations)**.

7 Use a pair of circlip pliers to remove the bearing retaining clip **(see illustration)**. Discard the circlip, a new one must be fitted.

8 With the slide hammer used to remove the hub, and a suitably-sized socket, pull the inner and outer bearing assemblies from the bearing housing **(see illustration)**. If the bearing refuses to be removed by this method, remove the trailing arm as described in Section 13, and either press the bearings out or have the bearing renewed by a Ford dealer or suitably-equipped garage.

9 With the bearing removed, ensure the bearing housing internal surface is clean. Also check the hub surface for cleanliness.

10 Using the threaded rod and suitably-sized washers, socket and nuts, draw the bearing into the housing until the complete circlip groove is visible. Fit the new bearing circlip **(see illustrations)**.

14.6a Use a home-made slide hammer . . .

14.6b . . . with a large socket pulling the hub from the bearings

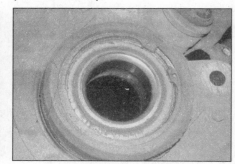

14.7 Remove the bearing circlip

14.8 Use the slide hammer to extract the wheel bearing

14.10a Draw the new bearing into the housing . . .

14.10b . . . and fit a new circlip

11 Again, using the threaded rod, nuts, washers and sockets, draw the hub into the bearings, until the inner race of the outer bearing is up against the hub inner shoulder **(see illustration)**.

12 Insert the new hub retaining bolt and washer, install the ABS sensor ring, and tighten the new nut to the specified torque.

Caution: The hub retaining nut is very tight. Take great care not to pull the vehicle from the axle stands.

13 The remainder of refitting is a reversal of removal. Tighten all fixings to their specified torque where given.

15 Rear subframe – removal and refitting

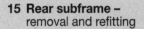

Removal

1 Remove both rear trailing arms as described in Section 13.

2 Slacken and remove the bolt securing the subframe to the roll restrictor **(see illustration)**.

3 Support the weight of the subframe on a jack (or preferably, a pair of jacks). The help of an assistant will also prove useful in lowering the subframe.

4 Undo the three bolts each side securing the support brackets and subframe to the vehicle body **(see illustration)**.

5 With the help of an assistant, lower the subframe and remove from under the car.

Refitting

6 Position the subframe against its mounting points, and support it with a trolley jack or similar. Refit the support brackets and new securing bolts. Only finger-tighten the bolts at this stage.

7 Using a ruler, measure the distance between the edge of the subframe and the inner sill **(see illustration)**. The measurement should be equal on both sides. If the gap is not equal, carefully lever the subframe in the direction of the largest gap, until the position is correct. Tighten the subframe and support brackets retaining bolts to the specified torque.

8 The remainder of refitting is a reversal of removal, noting the following points:
  a) Ford do not state that new subframe-to-body bolts must be used, but they are done up to an extremely high torque, and it would seem sensible to fit new ones. New ones should certainly be fitted if there is any doubt about the old ones.
  b) Tighten all fasteners to the specified torque. The trailing arm and shock absorber mounting bolts should not be fully-tightened until the weight of the vehicle is on its wheels.

14.11 Use the threaded rod, nuts and washers to draw the hub into the bearings

15.4 Remove the three bolts and the support brackets

16 Steering wheel – removal and refitting

Removal

1 Release the steering lock by inserting the ignition key.

2 Remove the airbag unit as described in Chapter 12, then return the steering wheel to the straight-ahead position, and engage the steering lock.

3 Hold the steering wheel to prevent it turning (don't rely on the steering lock for this, as it may not be strong enough, and damage could result), and undo the steering wheel retaining bolt **(see illustration)**. Discard the bolt, a new one must be fitted.

4 Note the alignment marks on the wheel and column **(see illustration)** and then pull

16.3 Remove the bolt

15.2 Undo the roll restrictor bolt

15.7 The gap between the subframe and the edge of the sill must be the same on both sides

the steering wheel from the splined end of the steering column. This should not require great effort, but if it sticks, put the wheel bolt back on by a few threads (to prevent it flying off), and tap the wheel off from behind the boss.

Refitting

5 Locate the steering wheel on the column splines, aligning the index marks. Fit a new bolt and tighten it to the specified torque.

17 Ignition switch, lock barrel and steering column lock – removal and refitting

Ignition switch

Removal

1 Remove the steering column upper and lower shrouds. Two screws retain the upper

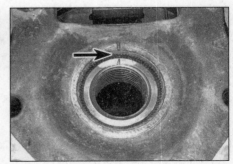

16.4 Note the alignment marks (arrowed)

17.1a Remove the upper screws (arrowed) . . .

17.1b . . . and the lower screws (arrowed)

17.2 Release the retaining clip and disconnect the wiring plug

17.3 Slide the switch from the housing

17.7 Gently pull the transceiver coil from the casing

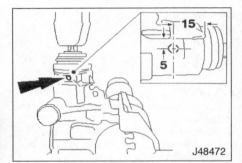

17.8 Drill a 4 mm hole in the casing as shown

shroud, and the lower shroud is retained by three screws **(see illustrations)**. There is no need to remove the steering wheel, simply rotate the wheel to access the upper screws.

2 Disconnect the switch wiring plug **(see illustration)**.

3 Remove the sealant from the screw heads and then slacken off the screws. Slide the switch from the lock casing **(see illustration)**.

Refitting

4 Refitting is the reverse of removal.

Lock barrel

Removal

5 Disconnect the battery negative lead. **Note:** *Before disconnecting the battery, refer to 'Disconnecting the battery' at the rear of this manual.* Remove the ignition key.

6 Remove the steering column upper and

lower shrouds. The upper shroud is retained by two screws, and the lower shroud is retained by three screws **(see illustrations 17.1a and 17.1b)**.

7 Gently pull the anti-theft transceiver coil from the switch **(see illustration)**.

8 Very carefully drill a 4 mm hole in the side of the lock barrel casing as shown **(see illustration)**.

9 Insert the ignition key and turn it to position II. Use a small screwdriver to depress the locking detent and pull the key, with the lock barrel, from the barrel casing.

Refitting

10 Insert the ignition key into the lock barrel, align the key with the locking detent, and insert it into the barrel casing.

11 Push the anti-theft transceiver coil over the end of the switch.

12 The remainder of refitting is a reversal of removal.

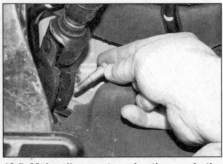

18.5 Make alignment marks, then undo the pinch-bolt

18.6 Unhook the support springs from the column

18 Steering column – removal and refitting

Removal

1 Remove the steering wheel as described in Section 16.

2 Remove the steering column multifunction switches, and airbag rotary contact unit as described in Chapter 12. Note their fitted positions, then cut the cable-tie(s) securing the wiring harnesses to the steering column.

3 Disconnect the multiplugs from the ignition switch and slide the anti-theft transceiver coil over the end of the ignition switch **(see illustrations 17.2 and 17.7)**. Cut the cable-tie and release the loom from the column.

4 Remove the driver's side lower facia trim panel as described in Chapter 11, Section 29, and then unbolt the earth connector

5 At the base of the steering column, make an alignment mark between the flexible coupling clamp and the steering rack pinion shaft. Slacken and remove the coupling-to-pinion shaft clamp bolt **(see illustration)**. Discard the bolt, a new one must be fitted.

6 Unhook the springs from the column **(see illustration)** and then slacken the lower pivot mounting.

7 Remove the column adjuster lever, noting the position of the sliding plate and washers **(see illustrations)**.

8 Disengage the column from the lower pivot and pull the column assembly upwards to remove it **(see illustration)**.

18.7a Remove the bolt . . .

18.7b . . . and slide out the locking assembly

18.8 Remove the column

Refitting

9 Refitting is a reversal of removal, noting the following points:

a) *When the column is first offered in, only tighten the mounting nuts and bolts hand-tight until the column has been engaged correctly with the rack pinion, and the new pinch-bolt tightened to the specified torque.*

b) *If the original column is being refitted, align the previously-made marks on the clamp and pinion.*

c) *Tighten all fasteners to the specified torque where given.*

d) *On completion, check the operation of the steering column lock and indicator self-cancelling before taking the car out on the road.*

19 Steering rack – removal and refitting

Removal

1 Loosen the wheel bolts, apply the handbrake, then jack up the front of the car and support it securely on axle stands (see *Jacking and vehicle support*). Do not support under the front crossmember. Remove the front wheels.

2 Remove the front crossmember as described in Section 9.

3 Working in the passenger cabin, slacken and remove the bolt securing the base of the steering column to the steering rack pinion **(see illustration 18.5)**.

4 Undo the power steering pipe unions from the steering rack, and release the pipes from the clamp on the rack **(see illustrations)**. Discard the O-ring seals, new ones must be fitted.

5 Disconnect the wiring plug from the power steering pressure switch on the rack **(see illustration 19.4b)**.

6 Carefully lower the steering rack to the ground.

7 Where fitted, undo the retaining nut, release the two retaining clips, and remove the shield from the steering rack.

19.4a Disconnect the pipe unions at the front . . .

19.4b . . . and rear of the rack pinion housing

Refitting

8 Refitting is a reversal of removal, noting the following points:

a) *Ensure that the steering rack pinion gaiter is correctly located on the rack before refitting.*

b) *Likewise, engage the rack pinion with the steering column as the crossmember is refitted.*

c) *Renew the fluid pipe union O-ring seals.*

d) *Tighten all fasteners and unions to the specified torque where given.*

e) *On completion, top-up and bleed the power steering system as described in Section 22. Have the front wheel alignment checked and if necessary adjusted as soon as possible.*

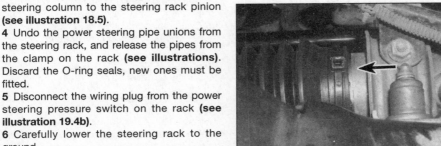

20.3a Ensure the inner (arrowed) . . .

20 Steering rack gaiter – renewal

1 Remove the track rod end balljoint as described in Section 23.

2 Remove the two gaiter securing clips, and slide the gaiter off the rack.

3 Refit in the reverse order of removal. Smear the inner bore of the gaiter with lubricant (often supplied with the gaiter kit) prior to fitting. Renew the balljoint locknut. Use new clips to secure the gaiter, and ensure that the outer end of the gaiter locates correctly in the groove machined into the track rod, without twisting **(see illustrations)**.

4 On completion, have the front wheel alignment checked and if necessary adjusted (see Section 25).

20.3b . . . and outer ends of the gaiter are correctly located

21.3 Rotate the tensioner clockwise to relieve the tension

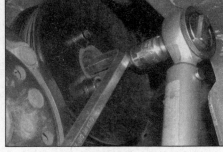

21.4 Prevent the pump pulley from rotating by inserting an Allen key in the centre

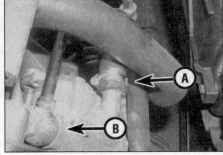

21.8 Power steering pump low-pressure hose (A) and high-pressure pipe (B)

21 Power steering pump – removal and refitting

Petrol models

Removal

1 Disconnect the battery negative lead. **Note:** *Before disconnecting the battery, refer to 'Disconnecting the battery' at the rear of this manual.*

2 Apply the handbrake, then jack up the front of the vehicle and support it on axle stands (see *Jacking and vehicle support*). Release the two retaining nuts and four bolts (two each side), and remove the engine/transmission undershield.

3 With a spanner or socket in the centre of the pulley, rotate the pump drivebelt tensioner clockwise, and remove the belt from the pump pulley **(see illustration)**.

4 Slacken and remove the pump pulley retaining bolts. Prevent the pump from rotating with an Allen key in the centre of the shaft **(see illustration)**.

5 On models with air conditioning, disconnect the compressor wiring plug.

6 Position a container under the fluid inlet hose connection on the pump – be prepared for the contents of the fluid reservoir to drain into it.

7 Undo the bolt securing the high-pressure pipe bracket to the right-hand end of the engine block.

8 Unscrew the high-pressure pipe union

bolt on the pump, and recover the two sealing washers **(see illustration)**. Clean the connection on the pump, then plug it or tape over it to prevent dirt getting in.

9 Slacken the retaining clamp and disconnect the low-pressure hose from the pump **(see illustration 21.8)**. Allow the fluid to drain into the container. Again, clean the connection on the pump, then plug it or tape over it to prevent dirt getting in.

10 Loosen and remove the three mounting bolts, and manoeuvre the pump from the engine bay **(see illustration)**.

Refitting

11 Refitting is a reversal of removal, noting the following points:

a) *Tighten all fasteners and unions to the specified torque where given.*

b) *Renew the high-pressure pipe union sealing washers.*

c) *Refit the drivebelt as described in Chapter 2A.*

d) *On completion, fill the fluid reservoir and bleed the system as described in Section 22.*

Diesel models

Removal

12 Disconnect the battery negative lead. **Note:** *Before disconnecting the battery, refer to 'Disconnecting the battery' at the rear of this manual.*

13 Apply the handbrake, then jack up the front of the vehicle and support it on axle stands (see *Jacking and vehicle support*).

Release the two retaining nuts and four bolts (two each side), and remove the engine/transmission undershield.

14 With a spanner or socket in the centre of the pulley, rotate the pump drivebelt tensioner clockwise, and remove the belt from the pump pulley.

15 Slacken and remove the pump pulley retaining bolts. Prevent the pump from rotating with an Allen key in the centre of the shaft.

16 Position a container under the fluid inlet hose connection on the pump – be prepared for the contents of the fluid reservoir to drain into it.

17 Unscrew the high-pressure pipe union bolt on the pump, and recover the two sealing washers. Clean the connection on the pump, then plug it or tape over it to prevent dirt getting in.

18 Slacken the retaining clip and disconnect the low-pressure hose from the pump. Allow the fluid to drain into the container. Again, clean the connection on the pump, then plug it or tape over it to prevent dirt getting in.

19 Loosen and remove the three mounting bolts on the right-hand end of the pump, and the two on the left-hand end, and manoeuvre the pump from the engine bay **(see illustration)**.

Refitting

20 Refitting is a reversal of removal, noting the following points:

a) *Tighten all fasteners and unions to the specified torque where given.*

b) *Renew the high-pressure pipe union sealing washers*

c) *Refit the drivebelt as described in Chapter 2B.*

d) *On completion, fill the fluid reservoir and bleed the system as described in Section 22.*

22 Power steering system – bleeding

1 With the engine stopped, top-up the fluid reservoir up to the maximum mark with the specified type of fluid.

2 Jack up and support the front of the vehicle, so the that wheels are just off the ground.

21.10 Undo the three bolts and remove the pump

21.19 Power steering pump – diesel models

3 Slowly turn the steering wheel from lock to lock. Constantly check the fluid level, adding fluid if necessary. Stop when the level no longer drops in the reservoir.

4 Have an assistant start the engine, while you keep watch on the fluid level. If the system has been drained during servicing work, be prepared to add more fluid as soon as the engine starts – the fluid level is likely to drop quickly.

5 Once the fluid level has stabilised, turn the engine off.

6 Check that the power steering fluid level is still up to the maximum mark, topping-up if necessary.

7 Start the engine and allow it idle for about 10 seconds, without turning the steering. Stop the engine, then check and top-up the fluid level if necessary.

8 Restart the engine, and turn the steering onto full left-hand lock, holding it there for a few seconds, and then onto full right-hand lock; check all steering hose/pipe unions for signs of leakage. **Note:** *Do not hold the steering at full lock for more than 10 seconds at a time, otherwise the hydraulic system may be damaged.*

9 Stop the engine, and top-up the fluid level if necessary.

10 Start the engine once more, and this time run it for about 2 minutes, turning the steering fully to the right and left.

11 Once all air is removed from the system, stop the engine, and check the fluid level as described in *Weekly checks*. Take the car for a journey of a few miles, then recheck the fluid level with the system fully up to operating temperature – repeat the bleeding process completely if there is any suggestion that air is still present (eg, excessive noise).

12 If the steering is still noisy due to air in the system, attach a vacuum pump to the reservoir and draw a vacuum of approximately 38 cmHg. Turn the steering wheel from lock to lock whilst maintaining the vacuum at the pump. Repeat the procedure if necessary **(see illustration)**.

23 Track rod end balljoint –
removal and refitting

Removal

1 Loosen the wheel bolts, apply the handbrake, then jack up the relevant front wheel and support on axle stands (see *Jacking and vehicle support*). Remove the front wheel.

2 Measure the exposed amount of adjustment thread showing on the inboard side of the track rod end locknut. This will act as a guide to the adjustment position when refitting the track rod end to the track rod.

3 Slacken the track rod end locknut **(see illustration)**.

4 Slacken and remove the track rod end

22.12 Air can be removed from the system with a vacuum pump

balljoint-to-hub carrier locknut, and using a balljoint splitter, separate the balljoint from the hub carrier. Lift the track rod balljoint from the hub carrier. Unscrew the track rod balljoint from the track rod **(see illustration)**. Note that the track rod ends are marked R and L, to indicate right- and left-hand.

5 Carefully clean the balljoint/strut tapers and the track rod threads. Renew the balljoint if its movement is sloppy or too stiff, if it is excessively worn, or if it is damaged in any way; carefully check the stud taper and threads. If the balljoint gaiter is damaged, the complete balljoint assembly must be renewed; it is not possible to obtain the gaiter separately.

Refitting

6 Screw the track rod balljoint and locknut onto the track rod, until the amount of exposed adjustment thread matches that noted on removal. Finger-tighten the locknut.

7 Fit the balljoint into the taper on the hub carrier, then fit a new nut and tighten it to the specified torque.

8 If the tracking is not going to be adjusted immediately the car is lowered, tighten the locknut to the specified torque now.

9 Refit the wheel, then lower the car to the ground and tighten the wheel bolt to the specified torque.

10 On completion, have the tracking (front wheel alignment) checked as soon as possible. A good indication of the need for this will be whether the steering wheel is centralised, but even this isn't foolproof.

23.4 Use a balljoint splitter to separate the track rod end balljoint from the hub carrier

23.3 Slacken the track rod end balljoint

24 Track rods –
removal and refitting

Removal

1 Remove the relevant steering rack gaiter as described in Section 20.

2 Using a large open-ended spanner, unscrew the locking collar securing the track rod to the rack **(see illustration)**.

Refitting

3 Refitting is a reversal of removal, noting the following points:
  a) Use a new track rod balljoint nut.
  b) Hold the track rods parallel to the rack when tightening the track rod locking collar.
  c) Tighten all fasteners to the specified torque (where possible).
  d) On completion, have the front wheel alignment checked at the earliest opportunity.

25 Wheel alignment
and steering angles –
general information

1 Accurate wheel alignment is essential for precise steering and handling, and for even tyre wear. Before carrying out any checking or adjusting operations, make sure that the tyres are correctly inflated, that all steering

24.2 Unscrew the track rod locking collar

and suspension joints and linkages are in sound condition, and that the wheels are not buckled or distorted, particularly around the rims. It will also be necessary to have the vehicle positioned on flat, level ground, with enough space to push the car backwards and forwards through about half its length.

2 Wheel alignment consists of four factors:

Camber

Camber is the angle at which the roadwheels are set from the vertical, when viewed from the front or rear of the vehicle. 'Positive' camber is the angle (in degrees) that the wheels are tilted outwards at the top from the vertical.

Castor

Castor is the angle between the steering axis and a vertical line when viewed from each side of the vehicle. 'Positive' castor is indicated when the steering axis is inclined towards the rear of the vehicle at its upper end.

Steering axis or kingpin inclination

Steering axis or kingpin inclination is the angle, when viewed from the front or rear of the vehicle, between the vertical and an imaginary line drawn between the upper and lower front suspension strut mountings.

Toe setting

Toe setting is the difference, viewed from above, between lines drawn through the roadwheel centres and the car's centre-line. Toe-in is when the roadwheels point inwards, towards each other at the front, while toe-out is when the splay outwards from each other at the front

3 Camber, castor, steering axis inclination and 'thrust angle' are set during manufacture, and are not adjustable. Unless the vehicle has suffered accident damage, or there is gross wear in the suspension mountings or joints, it can be assumed that these settings are correct. If for any reason it is believed that they are not correct, the task of checking them should be left to a Ford dealer or tyre specialist, who will have the necessary special equipment needed to measure the small angles involved.

4 Many tyre specialists check toe settings free, or for a nominal charge.

5 It is, however, within the scope of the home mechanic to check and adjust the front wheel toe setting. To do this, a tracking gauge must first be obtained. Two types of gauge are available, and can be obtained from motor accessory shops. The first type measures the distance between the front and rear inside edges of the roadwheels, as previously described, with the vehicle stationary. The second type, known as a 'scuff plate', measures the actual position of the contact surface of the tyre, in relation to the road surface, with the vehicle in motion. This is achieved by pushing or driving the front tyre over a plate, which then moves slightly according to the scuff of the tyre, and shows this movement on a scale. Both types have their advantages and disadvantages, but either can give satisfactory results if used correctly and carefully.

6 Make sure that the steering is in the straight-ahead position when making measurements, and the vehicle is at normal kerb weight (ie, no-one inside, and no significant load or luggage carried).

Front wheel toe adjustment

7 If adjustment is necessary, apply the handbrake, then jack up the front of the vehicle and support it securely on axle stands. Slacken the track rod end locknuts, then rotate the adjuster threaded section using the nut provided to alter the length of the track rod (as necessary); shortening the track rod will reduce toe-in/increase toe-out. Ensure that the rack gaiter is not twisted during the procedure.

8 When the setting is correct, tighten both the locknuts to the specified torque setting. Check that the rack gaiter is straight.

9 Recheck the toe setting and, if necessary, repeat the adjustment procedure.

Chapter 11
Bodywork and fittings

Contents

Degrees of difficulty

Easy, suitable for novice with little experience

Fairly easy, suitable for beginner with some experience

Fairly difficult, suitable for competent DIY mechanic

Difficult, suitable for experienced DIY mechanic

Very difficult, suitable for expert DIY or professional

Specifications

Torque wrench settings	Nm	lbf ft
Bonnet hinge bolts	25	18
Door latch bolts	12	9
Exterior mirror retaining screws	7	5
Bumper mounting bolts	21	15
Seat bolts	40	30
Seat belts:		
Anchor bolts	40	30
Front pretensioner stalk locknut	20	15
Inertia reel bolt	40	30
Tailgate:		
Mounting nuts	33	24
Latch bolts	12	9
Striker	10	7
Wiper arm mounting nut	20	15

1 General description

One body shape is available, with various seating permutations. The body is of all-steel construction, and incorporates calculated impact crumple zones at the front, and side impact protection beams, with a central safety cell passenger compartment.

During manufacture, the underbody is treated with underseal. The bumpers are plastic mouldings, as are the wheel arch liners.

2 Maintenance – bodywork and underframe

The general condition of a vehicle's bodywork is the one thing that significantly affects its value. Maintenance is easy, but needs to be regular. Neglect, particularly after minor damage, can lead quickly to further deterioration and costly repair bills. It is important also to keep watch on those parts of the vehicle not immediately visible, for instance the underside, inside all the wheel arches, and the lower part of the engine compartment.

The basic maintenance routine for the bodywork is washing – preferably with a lot of water, from a hose. This will remove all the loose solids which may have stuck to the vehicle. It is important to flush these off in such a way as to prevent grit from scratching the finish. The wheel arches and underframe need washing in the same way, to remove any accumulated mud which will retain moisture and tend to encourage rust. Paradoxically enough, the best time to clean the underframe and wheel arches is in wet weather, when the mud is thoroughly wet and soft. In very wet weather, the underframe is usually cleaned of large accumulations automatically, and this is a good time for inspection.

Periodically, except on vehicles with a wax-based underbody protective coating, it is a good idea to have the whole of the underframe of the vehicle steam-cleaned, engine compartment included, so that a thorough inspection can be carried out to see what minor repairs and renovations are necessary. Steam cleaning is available at many garages, and is necessary for the removal of the accumulation of oily grime, which sometimes is allowed to become thick in certain areas. If steam-cleaning facilities are not available, there are some excellent grease solvents available which can be brush-applied; the dirt can then be simply hosed off. Note that these methods should not be used on vehicles with wax-based underbody protective coating, or the coating will be removed. Such vehicles should be inspected annually, preferably just before Winter, when

the underbody should be washed down, and any damage to the wax coating repaired. Ideally, a completely fresh coat should be applied. It would also be worth considering the use of wax-based protection for injection into door panels, sills, box sections, etc, as an additional safeguard against rust damage, where such protection is not provided by the vehicle manufacturer.

After washing paintwork, wipe off with a chamois leather to give an unspotted clear finish. A coat of clear protective wax polish will give added protection against chemical pollutants in the air. If the paintwork sheen has dulled or oxidised, use a cleaner/polisher combination to restore the brilliance of the shine. This requires a little effort, but such dulling is usually caused because regular washing has been neglected. Care needs to be taken with metallic paintwork, as special non-abrasive cleaner/polisher is required to avoid damage to the finish. Always check that the door and ventilator opening drain holes and pipes are completely clear, so that water can be drained out. Brightwork should be treated in the same way as paintwork. Windscreens and windows can be kept clear of the smeary film which often appears, by proprietary glass cleaner. Never use any form of wax or other body or chromium polish on glass.

3 Maintenance – upholstery and carpets

Mats and carpets should be brushed or vacuum-cleaned regularly, to keep them free of grit. If they are badly stained, remove them from the vehicle for scrubbing or sponging, and make quite sure they are dry before refitting. Seats and interior trim panels can be kept clean by wiping with a damp cloth. If they do become stained (which can be more apparent on light-coloured upholstery), use a little liquid detergent and a soft nail brush to scour the grime out of the grain of the material. Do not forget to keep the headlining clean in the same way as the upholstery. When using liquid cleaners inside the vehicle, do not over-wet the surfaces being cleaned. Excessive damp could get into the seams and padded interior, causing stains, offensive odours or even rot. If the inside of the vehicle gets wet accidentally, it is worthwhile taking some trouble to dry it out properly, particularly where carpets are involved. Do not leave oil or electric heaters inside the vehicle for this purpose.

4 Minor body damage – repair

Repairs of minor scratches

If the scratch is very superficial, and does

not penetrate to the metal of the bodywork, repair is very simple. Lightly rub the area of the scratch with a paintwork renovator or a very fine cutting paste to remove loose paint from the scratch, and to clear the surrounding bodywork of wax polish. Rinse the area with clean water.

Apply touch-up paint to the scratch using a fine paint brush; continue to apply fine layers of paint until the surface of the paint in the scratch is level with the surrounding paintwork. Allow the new paint at least two weeks to harden, then blend it into the surrounding paintwork by rubbing the scratch area with a paintwork renovator or a very fine cutting paste. Finally, apply wax polish.

Where the scratch has penetrated right through to the metal of the bodywork, causing the metal to rust, a different repair technique is required. Remove any loose rust from the bottom of the scratch with a penknife, then apply rust-inhibiting paint to prevent the formation of rust in the future. Using a rubber or nylon applicator, fill the scratch with bodystopper paste. If required, this paste can be mixed with cellulose thinners to provide a very thin paste which is ideal for filling narrow scratches. Before the stopper-paste in the scratch hardens, wrap a piece of smooth cotton rag around the top of a finger. Dip the finger in cellulose thinners, and quickly sweep it across the surface of the stopper-paste in the scratch; this will ensure that the surface of the stopper-paste is slightly hollowed. The scratch can now be painted over as described earlier in this Section.

Repairs of dents

When deep denting of the vehicle's bodywork has taken place, the first task is to pull the dent out, until the affected bodywork almost attains its original shape. There is little point in trying to restore the original shape completely, as the metal in the damaged area will have stretched on impact, and cannot be reshaped fully to its original contour. It is better to bring the level of the dent up to a point which is about 3 mm below the level of the surrounding bodywork. In cases where the dent is very shallow anyway, it is not worth trying to pull it out at all. If the underside of the dent is accessible, it can be hammered out gently from behind, using a mallet with a wooden or plastic head. Whilst doing this, hold a suitable block of wood firmly against the outside of the panel, to absorb the impact from the hammer blows and thus prevent a large area of the bodywork from being 'belled-out'.

Should the dent be in a section of the bodywork which has a double skin, or some other factor making it inaccessible from behind, a different technique is called for. Drill several small holes through the metal inside the area – particularly in the deeper section. Then screw long self-tapping screws into the holes, just sufficiently for them to gain a good purchase in the metal. Now the dent can be pulled out by pulling on the protruding heads of the screws with a pair of pliers.

The next stage of the repair is the removal of the paint from the damaged area, and from an inch or so of the surrounding 'sound' bodywork. This is accomplished most easily by using a wire brush or abrasive pad on a power drill, although it can be done just as effectively by hand, using sheets of abrasive paper. To complete the preparation for filling, score the surface of the bare metal with a screwdriver or the tang of a file, or alternatively, drill small holes in the affected area. This will provide a good 'key' for the filler paste.

To complete the repair, see the Section on filling and respraying.

Repairs of rust holes or gashes

Remove all paint from the affected area, and from an inch or so of the surrounding 'sound' bodywork, using an abrasive pad or a wire brush on a power drill. If these are not available, a few sheets of abrasive paper will do the job most effectively. With the paint removed, you will be able to judge the severity of the corrosion, and therefore decide whether to renew the whole panel (if this is possible) or to repair the affected area. New body panels are not as expensive as most people think, and it is often quicker and more satisfactory to fit a new panel than to attempt to repair large areas of corrosion.

Remove all fittings from the affected area, except those which will act as a guide to the original shape of the damaged bodywork (eg headlight shells etc). Then, using tin snips or a hacksaw blade, remove all loose metal and any other metal badly affected by corrosion. Hammer the edges of the hole inwards, to create a slight depression for the filler paste.

Wire-brush the affected area to remove the powdery rust from the surface of the remaining metal. Paint the affected area with rust-inhibiting paint; if the back of the rusted area is accessible, treat this also.

Before filling can take place, it will be necessary to block the hole in some way. This can be achieved with aluminium or plastic mesh, or aluminium tape.

Aluminium or plastic mesh, or glass-fibre matting, is probably the best material to use for a large hole. Cut a piece to the approximate size and shape of the hole to be filled, then position it in the hole so that its edges are below the level of the surrounding bodywork. It can be retained in position by several blobs of filler paste around its periphery.

Aluminium tape should be used for small or very narrow holes. Pull a piece off the roll, trim it to the approximate size and shape required, then pull off the backing paper (if used) and stick the tape over the hole; it can be overlapped if the thickness of one piece is insufficient. Burnish down the edges of the tape with the handle of a screwdriver or similar, to ensure that the tape is securely attached to the metal underneath.

Filling and respraying

Before using this Section, see the Sections on dent, deep scratch, rust holes and gash repairs.

Many types of bodyfiller are available, but generally speaking, those proprietary kits which contain a tin of filler paste and a tube of resin hardener are best for this type of repair which can be used directly from the tube. A wide, flexible plastic or nylon applicator will be found invaluable for imparting a smooth and well-contoured finish to the surface of the filler.

Mix up a little filler on a clean piece of card or board – measure the hardener carefully (follow the maker's instructions on the pack), otherwise the filler will set too rapidly or too slowly. Using the applicator, apply the filler paste to the prepared area; draw the applicator across the surface of the filler to achieve the correct contour and to level the surface. When a contour that approximates to the correct one is achieved, stop working the paste – if you carry on too long, the paste will become sticky and begin to 'pick-up' on the applicator. Continue to add thin layers of filler paste at 20-minute intervals, until the level of the filler is just proud of the surrounding bodywork.

Once the filler has hardened, the excess can be removed using a metal plane or file. From then on, progressively-finer grades of abrasive paper should be used, starting with a 40-grade production paper, and finishing with a 400-grade wet-and-dry paper. Always wrap the abrasive paper around a flat rubber, cork, or wooden block – otherwise the surface of the filler will not be completely flat. During the smoothing of the filler surface, the wet-and-dry paper should be periodically rinsed in water. This will ensure that a very smooth finish is imparted to the filler at the final stage.

At this stage, the 'dent' should be surrounded by a ring of bare metal, which in turn should be encircled by the finely 'feathered' edge of the good paintwork. Rinse the repair area with clean water, until all the dust produced by the rubbing-down operation has gone.

Spray the whole area with a light coat of primer – this will show up any imperfections in the surface of the filler. Repair these imperfections with fresh filler paste or bodystopper, and again smooth the surface with abrasive paper. If bodystopper is used, it can be mixed with cellulose thinners, to form a thin paste which is ideal for filling small holes. Repeat this spray-and-repair procedure until you are satisfied that the surface of the filler, and the feathered edge of the paintwork, are perfect. Clean the repair area with clean water, and allow to dry fully.

The repair area is now ready for final spraying. Paint spraying must be carried out in a warm, dry, windless and dust-free atmosphere. This condition can be created artificially if you have access to a large indoor

working area, but if you are forced to work in the open, you will have to pick your day very carefully. If you are working indoors, dousing the floor in the work area with water will help to settle the dust which would otherwise be in the atmosphere. If the repair area is confined to one body panel, mask off the surrounding panels; this will help to minimise the effects of a slight mismatch in paint colours. Bodywork fittings (e.g. chrome strips, door handles etc) will also need to be masked off. Use genuine masking tape, and several thickness of newspaper, for the masking operations.

Before starting to spray, agitate the aerosol can thoroughly, then spray a test area (an old tin, or similar) until the technique is mastered. Cover the repair area with a thick coat of primer; the thickness should be built up using several thin layers of paint, rather than one thick one. Using 400 grade wet-and-dry paper, rub down the surface of the primer until it is smooth. While doing this, the work area should be thoroughly doused with water, and the wet-and-dry paper periodically rinsed in water. Allow to dry before spraying on more paint.

Spray on the top coat, again building up the thickness by using several thin layers of paint. Start spraying at one edge of the repair area, and then, using a side-to-side motion, work until the whole repair area and about 2 inches of the surrounding original paintwork is covered. Remove all masking material 10 to 15 minutes after spraying on the final coat of paint.

Allow the new paint at least two weeks to harden, then, using a paintwork renovator or a very fine cutting paste, blend the edges of the paint into the existing paintwork. Finally, apply wax polish.

Plastic components

With the use of more and more plastic body components by the vehicle manufacturers (e.g. bumpers, spoilers, and in some cases major body panels), rectification of more serious damage to such items has become a matter of either entrusting repair work to a specialist in this field, or renewing complete components. Repair of such damage by the DIY owner is not feasible, owing to the cost of the equipment and materials required for effecting such repairs. The basic technique involves making a groove along the line of the crack in the plastic, using a rotary burr in a power drill. The damaged part is then welded back together, using a hot air gun to heat up and fuse a plastic filler rod into the groove. Any excess plastic is then removed, and the area rubbed down to a smooth finish. It is important that a filler rod of the correct plastic is used, as body components can be made of a variety of different types (e.g. polycarbonate, ABS, polypropylene).

Damage of a less serious nature (abrasions, minor cracks etc) can be repaired by the DIY owner using a two-part epoxy filler repair material which can be used directly from the tube. Once mixed in equal proportions, this is used in similar fashion to the bodywork filler used on metal panels. The filler is usually cured in twenty to thirty minutes, ready for sanding and painting.

If the owner is renewing a complete component himself, or if he has repaired it with epoxy filler, he will be left with the problem of finding a suitable paint for finishing which is compatible with the type of plastic used. At one time, the use of a universal paint was not possible, owing to the complex range of plastics met with in body component applications. Standard paints, generally speaking, will not bond to plastic or rubber satisfactorily, but professional matched paints, to match any plastic or rubber finish, can be obtained from some dealers. However, it is now possible to obtain a plastic body parts finishing kit which consists of a pre-primer treatment, a primer and coloured top coat. Full instructions are normally supplied with a kit, but basically the method of use is to first apply the pre-primer to the component concerned, and allow it to dry for up to 30 minutes. Then the primer is applied, and left to dry for about an hour before finally applying the special-coloured top coat. The result is a correctly coloured component, where the paint will flex with the plastic or rubber, a property that standard paint does not normally possess.

5 Major body damage – repair

Where serious damage has occurred, or large areas need renewal due to neglect, it means that complete new panels will need welding-in, and this is best left to professionals. If the damage is due to impact, it will also be necessary to check completely the alignment of the bodyshell, and this can only be carried out accurately by a Ford dealer using special jigs. If the body is left misaligned, it is primarily dangerous, as the car will not handle properly, and secondly, uneven stresses will be imposed on the steering, suspension and possibly transmission, causing abnormal wear, or complete failure, particularly to such items as the tyres.

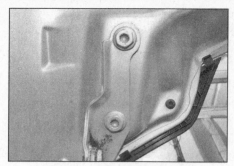

7.2 Mark the position of the hinges

6 Door rattles – tracing and rectification

1 Check first that the door is not loose at the hinges, and that the latch is holding the door firmly in position. Check also that the door lines up with the aperture in the body. If the door is out of alignment, adjust it as described in Section 23.
2 If the latch is holding the door in the correct position, but the latch still rattles, the lock mechanism is worn and should be renewed.
3 Other rattles from the door could be caused by wear in the window operating mechanism, interior lock mechanism, loose glass channels or loose wiring.

7 Bonnet – removal, refitting and adjustment

Removal
1 Fully open the bonnet, then place some cardboard or rags beneath the corners by the hinges to protect the bodywork.
2 Carefully mark the position of the bonnet hinges and then loosen, but **do not** remove the mounting bolts **(see illustration)**.
3 Unclip and remove the bonnet support strut.
4 With the help of an assistant fully remove the hinge bolts and remove the bonnet from the vehicle.

5 Store the bonnet up right and cover it with an old blanket to protect it.

Refitting and adjustment
6 Refitting is a reversal of removal. Ensure that the hinges are adjusted to their original positions. Close the bonnet very carefully initially; misalignment may cause the edges of the bonnet to damage the bodywork. If necessary, adjust the hinges to their original positions and check that the bonnet is level with the surrounding bodywork. If necessary, adjust the height of the bonnet front edge by screwing the rubber buffers in or out.
7 Check that the bonnet lock operates in a satisfactory manner. In particular, check that the safety catch holds the bonnet after the bonnet release cable has been pulled.

8 Bonnet lock and release cable – removal and refitting

Removal
1 Open the bonnet and locate the bonnet lock mechanism, mounted in the crossmember at the front of the engine compartment. Use a marker pen or similar to make alignment marks between the lock and the mounting panel **(see illustration)**.
2 Release the bonnet cable from the retaining clips in the engine compartment.
3 Remove the four grille upper mounting bolts. This provides enough room to manoeuvre the release handle from the grille.
4 Slacken and remove the two retaining bolts and lift the bonnet lock and backing plate from the crossmember **(see illustration)**.
5 Separate the backing plate from the lock and detach the release cable outer and inner, as the lock is withdrawn.
6 If required, the bonnet release cable can now be removed as follows.
7 Working in the driver's side footwell, undo the two screws and remove the release handle from the trim panel **(see illustration)**.
8 Disengage the outer cable, then the inner cable from the handle **(see illustrations)**.
9 Tie a length of cord to the inner end of the release cable in the driver's footwell, and carefully pull the complete cable through the

8.1 Mark the position of the mounting bolts

8.4 Remove the lock and backing plate

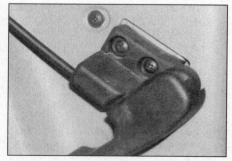

8.7 Undo the two screws and remove the release handle

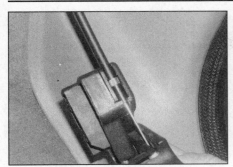

8.8a Disconnect the outer . . .

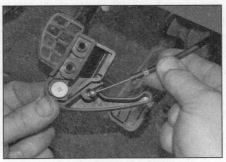

8.8b . . . and inner cable

bulkhead and into the engine compartment, leaving the length of cord in place of the release cable. Undo the cord from the cable, and leave the cord ends exposed in the engine compartment and footwell.

Refitting

10 Refit in the reverse order of removal. Tie the inner end of the cable to the exposed cord in the engine compartment, carefully pull the cable through to the release handle, then untie the cord.

11 When positioning the cable in the engine compartment, ensure that it is rerouted correctly to avoid kinks, sharp bends and chafing. Check for satisfactory operation of the cable and the lock before closing the bonnet. Ensure that the bonnet locks properly when closed, and also that the safety catch operates correctly when the bonnet release cable is actuated.

9 Bumpers – removal and refitting

Front bumper

Removal

1 Jack up and support the front of the vehicle (see *Jacking and vehicle support* in the reference Chapter).

2 Working at each front wheel arch in turn, undo the three Torx screws each side to release the trailing edges of the bumper from the wheel arch liner **(see illustration)**.

3 Unscrew and remove the three retaining bolts at the centre, rear edge of the bumper from below.

4 Remove the four upper grille locating screws. With care it is now possible to remove

the bumper, however removal is considerable easier if the front headlights are removed first – see Chapter 12.

5 Carefully withdraw the bumper assembly by sliding it squarely away from the front of the vehicle and out from the guides on the front wings. Disconnect the front foglamps wiring plugs as the bumper is withdrawn. Where fitted disconnect the wiring plug from the front parking sensors and the headlight washer hose.

6 If required, the bumper support bar can be removed by unscrewing the four bolts securing it to the chassis. The support panel may also be removed from the wing **(see illustrations)**.

Refitting

7 Refitting is a reversal of removal. Tighten the bumper support bar retaining bolts to the specified torque.

Rear bumper

Removal

8 Pull the rubber tailgate weatherstrip from the tailgate aperture **(see illustration)**.

9 Jack up and support the rear of the vehicle (see *Jacking and vehicle support*). Remove the spare wheel, as described in *Roadside repairs* and then remove both rear wheels.

10 Working at each rear wheel arch in turn, undo the three screws each side to release the leading edges of the bumper from the wheel arches **(see illustrations)**. Note that on vehicles fitted with mudflaps these will need to be removed first to access the bumper screws.

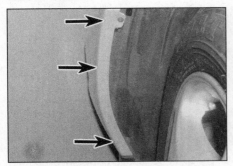

9.2 Three screws each side secure the bumper to the wheel arch liner (arrowed)

9.6a Remove the support bar mounting bolts – left hand side shown (arrowed)

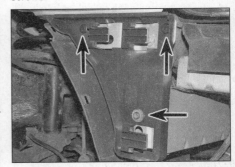

9.6b The side panel is secured with two 'scrivets' and a single bolt (arrowed)

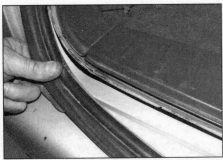

9.8 Pull the weatherstrip from the bumper flange

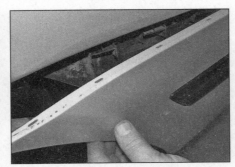

9.10a Release the edge of the bumper from the mounting bracket on the rear wing

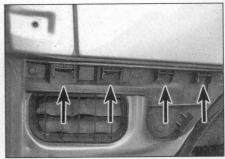

9.10b With the bumper removed, note the position of the locking tabs (arrowed)

9.11 Loosen the bolt

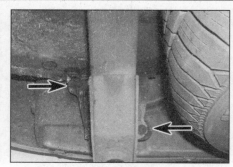

9.13 Remove the lower bolts (arrowed)

9.14 Remove the rear bumper

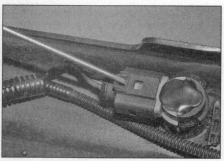

9.15a A thin-bladed screwdriver can be used to release the wiring connector

9.15b Gently release the locking tabs from the parking sensors . . .

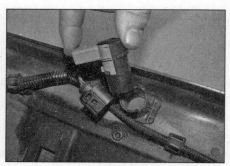

9.15c . . . and then remove them

11 Carefully prise free and remove the trim piece from below both rear lamps and then loosen, but do not remove the bumper cover upper mounting bracket bolts **(see illustration)**.

12 Where fitted unplug the wiring connector for the rear parking sensors – accessible from below the bumper.

13 Working up behind the rear bumper, slacken and remove the two bolts on each side securing the bumper to the vehicle **(see illustration)**.

14 The bumper should now be held in place by the previously-loosened upper bolts. Remove the bolts and with the aid of an assistant pull the bumper from the bodywork **(see illustration)**.

15 If required the bumper cover can be unbolted and removed from the bumper. Complete the removal by unclipping the rear parking sensors – where fitted **(see illustrations)**.

Refitting

16 Refit in the reverse order of removal. Loosely fit all retaining bolts and screws before fully tightening them. Tighten the retaining bolts to the specified torque.

10 Radiator grille – removal and refitting	

Removal

1 Whilst the grille is a separate item, we found it impossible to separate the grille from the bumper whilst the bumper was still fitted to the vehicle. To remove the grille, remove the front bumper as described in the previous Section.

2 With the bumper on the floor and protected from damage with an old blanket gently prise free the retaining tabs from the bumper and remove the grille.

Refitting

3 Refitting is a reversal of removal.

11 Wheel arch liners – removal and refitting	

Removal

1 Chock the wheels, apply the handbrake, then loosen the relevant wheel bolts. Jack up and support the front (or rear) of the car on axle stands (see *Jacking and vehicle support*). Remove the relevant roadwheel.

2 The liner is secured by Torx screws. Remove the screws and manoeuvre the liner from under the front wing **(see illustrations)**.

Refitting

3 Refitting is a reversal of removal.

12 Windscreen cowl panel – removal and refitting	

Removal

1 Open the bonnet and remove the windscreen wiper arms as described in Chapter 12, Section 11.

2 On early models (up to 11/2003) remove the cowl side panels **(see illustration)** and then

11.2a Remove the fixing screws . . .

11.2b . . . and manoeuvre the liner out from the wing (front shown)

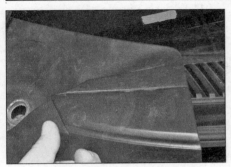

12.2 Remove the side panels

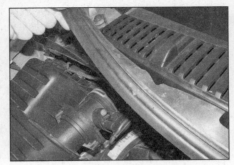

12.3 Remove the weatherstrip

12.4a Disconnect the screen washer hose . . .

unbolt and partially remove the cowl centre panel. If the panel will not release, access the lower mounting bolts and remove it complete with the support panel

3 On all models remove the weatherstrip **(see illustration)** before partially removing the cowl.

4 Disconnect the washer hose and where fitted disconnect the electrical wiring plug from the heated washer jets **(see illustrations)**.

5 Turn the cowl panel over and unclip the washer hose and wiring loom from the panel **(see illustration)**.

6 The lower panel can now be removed. It is secured in place by bolts adjacent to the bonnet hinges and a single central bolt **(see illustrations)**.

Refitting

7 Refitting is a reversal of removal.

13 Tailgate – removal and refitting

Removal

1 Open the tailgate, then unclip the upper trim. Note that later models also have two screws hidden under covers that must be removed.

2 Working on the lower edge of the tailgate, prise out the plastic caps, undo the two retaining screws and carefully remove the pull-down handle.

3 Pull the trim away from the lock end of the tailgate, then release the four clips securing the trim to the panel below the window.

4 With the trim removed, disconnect the wiring plugs to the rear lamps and wiper motor. Release the wiring harness from the retaining clips. Make a note of the fitted position of the harness.

5 Remove the cable-tie from the wiring loom and release the tailgate latch and handle multiplugs from the foam insulation. Disconnect the wiring plugs.

6 Disconnect the rubber washer hose from the jet **(see illustration)**.

7 Unclip the wiring loom from the various securing clips. Prise out the rubber grommets adjacent to the hinges, and pull the harness

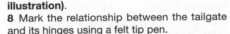
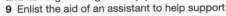

12.4b . . . and then unplug the wiring connector (where fitted)

and washer tube from the tailgate **(see illustration)**.

8 Mark the relationship between the tailgate and its hinges using a felt tip pen.

9 Enlist the aid of an assistant to help support

12.6a Remove the bolts (left-hand side bolt shown) . . .

13.6 Unplug the washer hose

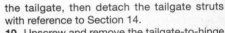

12.5 Remove the support clips from the bulkhead

the tailgate, then detach the tailgate struts with reference to Section 14.

10 Unscrew and remove the tailgate-to-hinge securing bolts, and lift the tailgate clear of the vehicle.

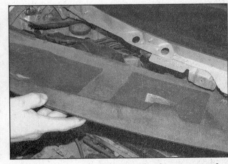

12.6b . . . and slide out the lower panel

13.7 Unclip the cover and pull the loom and washer tube from the tailgate

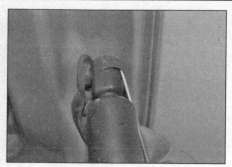

14.2 Prise the clip free

Refitting

11 Refit in the reverse order of removal. Check that the tailgate is correctly aligned before fully-tightening the tailgate hinge bolts.
12 The fit and closing tension of the tailgate can be adjusted by altering the positions of the rubber buffers at the upper and lower edges of the tailgate.

14 Tailgate support strut(s) – removal and refitting

Removal

1 Open the tailgate and support it with a prop (or with the aid of an assistant).
2 Disconnect the strut(s) at the upper and lower balljoints by lifting the spring clips, and prising the joint free **(see illustration)**.

15.3a Remove the Torx screws and . . .

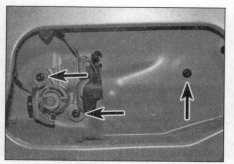

15.8 Remove the bolts (arrowed)

3 If a strut is defective in operation, it must be renewed. Do not attempt to dismantle and repair the strut. Note that the struts are filled with pressurised gas, and so should not be punctured or disposed of by incineration.
4 If required the undo the retaining bolts and separate the upper strut mounting plate from the tailgate.

Refitting

5 Refit in the reverse order of removal. The thinner, piston rod end of the strut(s) must be attached to the bodywork. Ensure that the strut is securely engaged with the balljoints.

15 Tailgate latch, handle and cylinder – removal and refitting

1 Remove the tailgate trim panel with reference to Section 32. Disconnect the battery negative terminal. **Note:** *Before disconnecting the battery, refer to 'Disconnecting the battery' at the rear of this manual.*

Latch

Removal

2 Cut the cable-tie that secures the wiring loom in place.
3 Remove the three screws from the lower edge of the tailgate and manoeuvre the latch from the tailgate , disconnect the wiring plugs as the latch is removed **(see illustrations)**.
4 If required the locking motor can be removed from the latch assembly, however Ford do not supply this as a separate item.

15.3b . . . manoeuvre the latch from the tailgate

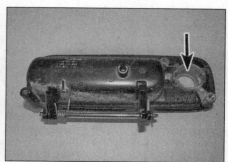

15.12 The location of the O-ring (arrowed)

Refitting

5 Refit in the reverse order of removal using a new cable-tie to secure the wiring loom.

Lock

Removal

6 To remove the lock, the latch assembly must be removed first – as described above.
7 Cut the cable-tie that secures the wiring loom in place.
8 Working inside the tailgate unbolt the lock assembly. Manoeuvre the lock from position, and disconnect the wiring plugs as the lock assembly is withdrawn. Note that it is just as easy to remove the lock and handle as a single unit **(see illustration)**.

Refitting

9 Refit in the reverse order of removal using a new cable-tie to secure the wiring loom.

Handle

Removal

10 Remove the tailgate latch assembly, as described in Paragraphs 2 and 3.
11 Working inside the tailgate, unplug the lock cylinder assembly wiring plugs, undo the two Torx screws and remove the cylinder assembly.
12 Unscrew the remaining Torx screw and remove the handle assembly. An O-ring seal is fitted to the lock cylinder housing in the handle **(see illustration)**. Remove the O-ring and fit it to the key barrel when reassembling the lock and handle.

Refitting

13 Refitting is a reversal of removal.

Cylinder assembly

Removal

14 Remove the lock cylinder assembly as described in Paragraphs 6 to 8 of this Section.
15 At the time of writing no separate parts were available for the cylinder assembly, however if the action of the key in the lock barrel is suspect, it may be worth stripping and cleaning the key barrel and cylinder.
16 To remove the lock cylinder, insert the key, and prise off the circlip at the inner end of the cylinder **(see illustration)**.

15.16 Remove the circlip

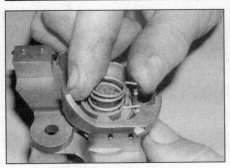

15.17a Remove the spring . . .

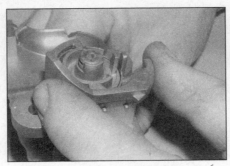

15.17b . . . and the operating lever . . .

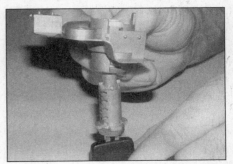

15.17c . . . then remove the cylinder

17 Lift off the spring and the operating lever. The cylinder can now be withdrawn from the underside of the assembly. **Do not** invert the assembly as the cylinder sleeve and spacer will fall out (**see illustrations**).

Refitting

18 The remainder of refitting is a reversal of removal.

16 Door trim panel – removal and refitting

Front door trim

Removal

1 Remove the door pull handle retainer clip and then lever up and remove the door pull trim panel. Disconnect the wiring plug as the trim panel is removed (**see illustrations**).

2 With the pull handle removed, locate and remove the three fixing screws (**see illustration**).

3 Using a plastic trim or upholstery tool release the door trim from the door – expect some of the trim clips to be damaged during removal.

4 As the panel is removed disconnect the wiring plugs from the door mirror and alarm LED (**see illustrations**).

5 Unhook the door latch remote cable from the panel and remove the panel from the vehicle (**see illustration**).

6 After removal of the loudspeaker, if required the door membrane can be removed. This membrane can be removed by carefully cutting through the mastic seal with a sharp knife. If the mastic is keep clean during any work the membrane can normally be easily refixed.

16.1a Prise free the inner section of the handle . . .

Refitting

7 Replace any damaged trim clips and then refit in the reverse order of removal.

16.1b . . . and then the complete handle

16.1c Disconnect the wiring plug as the handle is removed

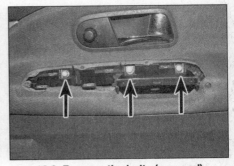

16.2 Remove the bolts (arrowed)

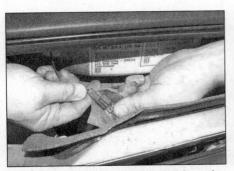

16.4a Disconnect the wiring plug from the alarm LED . . .

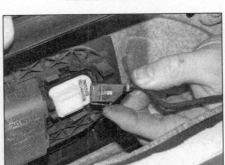

16.4b . . . and the door mirror switch

16.5 Unhook the release cable

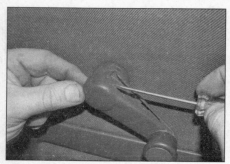

16.8a Lever the cover free . . .

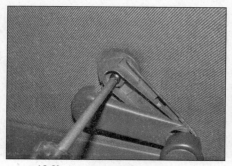

16.8b . . . remove the screw . . .

16.8c . . . pull off the handle and recover the washer

16.10 Remove the bolts

16.11 A broad-bladed plastic trim tool can be used to release the trim panel

Rear door trim

Removal

8 On vehicles fitted with manual windows, remove the cover from the handle then unbolt and remove the handle (see illustration).

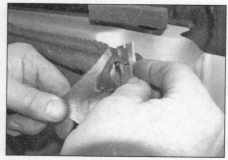

17.2 Use a sharp blade to cut through the sealant

17.4b . . . and remove the shield

9 Using a small flat-bladed screwdriver or plastic trim tool, lift up and remove the pull handle (see illustrations 16.1a and 16.1b). On vehicles fitted with electric windows disconnect the wiring plug as the handle is removed.

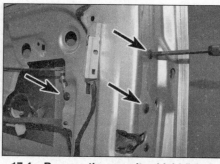

17.4a Remove the security shield fixing screws (arrowed) . . .

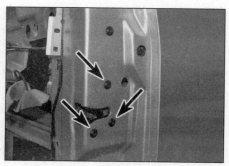

17.5 Remove the screws (arrowed)

10 Behind the pull handle are two fixing bolts – remove them (see illustration).
11 Using a plastic trim or upholstery tool release the door trim from the door – expect some of the trim clips to be damaged during removal (see illustration). On the illustrated vehicle some of the retaining clips were difficult to remove. We used an electric torch to locate them and levered them free with a large screwdriver.
12 As the panel is removed unhook the remote cable from the door release handle (see illustration 16.5) and disconnect the wiring plug from the small speaker. Note that some models have a warning lamp fitted to the door trim panel. Disconnect the wiring plug as the panel is removed.

Refitting

13 Renew any damaged trim clips and then refit in the reverse order of removal.

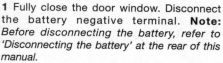

17 Door latch –
removal and refitting

Front door

Removal

1 Fully close the door window. Disconnect the battery negative terminal. **Note:** *Before disconnecting the battery, refer to 'Disconnecting the battery' at the rear of this manual.*
2 Remove the door trim panel and speaker (see Section 16).
3 Using a sharp knife or blade, cut through the sealant between the plastic membrane and the door frame (see illustration). Carefully peel the membrane away from the door. **Note:** *Do not attempt to peel away the membrane without first cutting through the sealant.*
4 A security shield is fitted over the key cylinder and latch assembly. Remove the shield (see illustrations).
5 Slacken and remove the three Torx screws securing the door latch to the door frame (see illustration).
6 Manoeuvre the latch from the door frame. If necessary remove the exterior door handle as described in the next Section. Disconnect

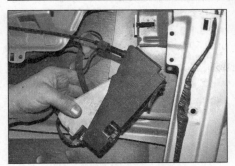

17.6a Remove the latch . . .

17.6b . . . and disconnect the wiring plug

17.7a Open the cover . . .

17.7b . . . and remove the cable

17.8 Rotate the barrel adjuster on the latch assembly to eliminate any play in the cable

17.12 Remove the Torx screws from the latch

the wiring connector as the latch assembly is removed (see illustrations).

7 If required the plastic cover from the latch assembly can be opened and the release cable removed (see illustrations)

Refitting

8 Refitting is a reversal of the removal procedure, ensuring that the exterior handle engages correctly with the latch actuating lever. The interior release handle cable should be checked and adjusted as the trim panel is refitted (see illustration)

Rear door

Removal

9 Fully close the door window. Disconnect the battery negative terminal. **Note:** *Before disconnecting the battery, refer to 'Disconnecting the battery' at the rear of this manual.*

10 Remove the door trim panel and speaker (see Section 16).

11 Using a sharp knife or blade, cut through the sealant between the plastic membrane and the door frame. Carefully peel the membrane away from the door (see illustration 17.2). **Note:** *Do not attempt to peel away the membrane without first cutting through the sealant.*

12 Slacken and remove the three Torx screws securing the door latch to the door frame (see illustration).

13 Slacken the exterior handle retaining screw and then manoeuvre the latch assembly from the door frame. If necessary remove the exterior door handle as described in the next

Section. Disconnect the wiring connector as the latch assembly is removed (see illustration).

Refitting

14 Refitting is a reversal of the removal procedure

18 Door handles and lock cylinder – removal and refitting

Exterior door handle

Removal

1 Fully close the door window. Disconnect the battery negative terminal. **Note:** *Before disconnecting the battery, refer to 'Disconnecting the battery' at the rear of this manual.*

17.13 Remove the latch

2 Remove the door trim panel and speaker (see Section 16).

3 Using a sharp knife, cut through the sealant between the plastic membrane and the door frame. Carefully peel the membrane away from the door. **Note:** *Do not attempt to peel away the membrane without first cutting through the sealant.*

4 Where fitted prise out the rubber grommet in the end of the door frame, and undo the exterior handle retaining screw (see illustration).

5 Slacken and remove the three Torx screws securing the door latch to the door frame (see illustration 17.5). If working on the front door handle remove the security plate from the latch assembly as described in Section 17 above.

6 To disengage the lock from the handle, carefully pull the latch inward and down as the exterior handle is pulled outwards.

7 Slide the exterior handle towards the

18.4 The access point to release the door handle (arrowed)

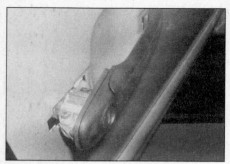

18.7 Pull the rear of the handle assembly out first

18.8a Check that the handle return spring is correctly located before refitting (arrowed)

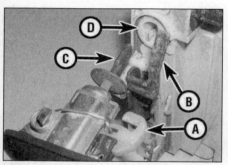

18.8b Shown removed, the exterior handle lug (A) engages with the lever (B) and the cylinder rod (C) locates into the slot (D)

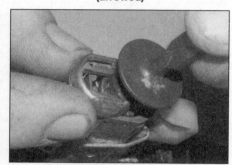

18.10a Slide out the circlip . . .

Refitting

8 Refitting is a reversal of removal, but ensure that the handle return spring is correctly located, before fitting the handle. The front door handle lock must locate correctly in the latch **(see illustrations)**.

Lock cylinder

Removal

9 Remove the exterior door handle as described in Paragraphs 1 to 7.
10 Slide out the cylinder retaining clip and remove the lock components. **Note:** *The components retained by the clip are spring pressurised. Slide out the clip, and release the components slowly* **(see illustrations)**.
11 Insert the key into the barrel, turn the barrel through 90° anti-clockwise, and pull the key, complete with the barrel, from the housing **(see illustration)**.

Refitting

12 Refitting is a reversal of removal.

Interior door handle

Removal

13 Fully close the appropriate door window. Disconnect the battery negative terminal. **Note:** *Before disconnecting the battery, refer to 'Disconnecting the battery' at the rear of this manual.*
14 Remove the door trim panel (see Section 16).
15 Place the door panel on a clean surface and release the locking tabs from the handle.

front of the vehicle, and pull the rear end of the handle out from the door. Now slide the

handle towards the rear of the vehicle, and out from the door **(see illustration)**.

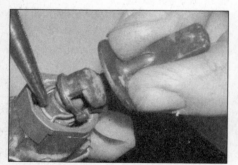

18.10b . . . remove the operating rod . . .

18.10c . . . and the spring

18.10d . . . then lift out the lever . . .

18.10e . . . followed by the collar

18.11 Turn the key 90° anti-clockwise and remove the barrel

18.15a Release the locking tabs (arrowed) . . .

18.15b . . . and then remove the door mirror switch, if working on the driver's door

The mirror control switch or loudspeaker can be removed from the handle if required (see illustrations).

Refitting

16 Refitting is a reversal of removal.

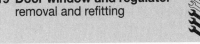

19 Door window and regulator – removal and refitting

Door window glass

Removal

1 Remove the door trim, loudspeaker and membrane as described in Section 16.
2 Temporarily reconnect the window switch and move the window until the clamps' securing Torx screws are accessible. Mark the position of the clamps on the glass using tape or a permanent marker to record the relationship between the clamp jaws and the glass. This will aid alignment during refitting. On models with manual rear windows, temporarily refit the winder handle and position the window so that the Torx screws are accessible (see illustrations).
3 Slacken and remove the screws, then release the window glass from the clamps. Lower the glass to the bottom of the door.
4 Carefully remove the weather seal from the outside of the door and then partially remove the rubber guide channel from the rear of the door frame (see illustrations). Protect the paintwork with masking tape if necessary.
5 Rotate the glass in the door frame and carefully remove the glass towards the outside of the door frame.

Refitting

6 Refitting is a reversal of removal. On refitting the glass, align the previously-made marks between the clamps and the glass, but do not fully tighten the clamp screws until the glass is in the fully-raised position.

Window regulator

Removal

7 Remove the door trim, loudspeaker and membrane as described in Section 16.
8 Where applicable, temporarily reconnect the window switch (or winder handle) and move the window until the clamps' securing

19.2 Position the door glass so that the clamp plates are accessible

Torx screws are accessible. Mark the position of the clamps on the glass using tape or a permanent marker to record the relationship between the clamp jaws and the glass. This will aid alignment during refitting.
9 Slacken and remove the screws, then release the window glass from the clamps. Lift the glass to the top of the door, and tape or wedge it in place (see illustration).
10 Where applicable, push the wiring plug upwards to disconnect it from the electric window motor. Release any wiring harness cable-ties secured to the regulator (see illustrations).
11 Slacken and withdraw the five retaining screws, and release the two retaining clips, then manoeuvre the regulator from the door (see illustrations).
12 If required, the electric window motor

19.4a Remove the external weather seal . . .

19.4b . . . and partially remove the rubber glass guide channel from the door frame

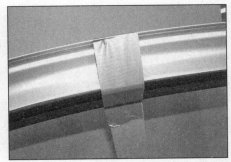

19.9 Secure the glass with strong adhesive tape

19.10a Cut the cable-tie(s)

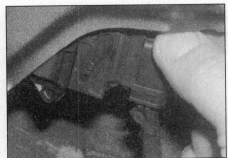

19.10b Slide the connector upwards to disconnect it

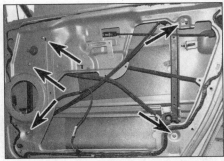

19.11a Remove the mounting screws (arrowed) . . .

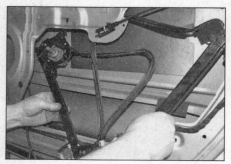

19.11b ... and withdraw the regulator from the door frame

20.6a Remove two Torx bolts (arrowed) ...

20.6b ... and screw them into the holes (arrowed) to secure the regulator to the baseplate

(where fitted), can now be removed as described in the next Section.

Refitting

13 Refitting is a reversal of removal.

20 Electrically-operated windows – general information and motor renewal

Window switches

1 Refer to Chapter 12, Section 6.

Window winder motors

Removal

2 Slacken the clamps and tape or wedge the glass in the closed position, as described in the previous Section.

20.7 Undo the remaining bolts and separate the motor from the regulator

21.2 Remove the operating arm screw

3 Disconnect the wiring plug from the motor and cut the cable-ties to free the wiring loom.
4 Unplug the wiring connector from the central locking control and detach the wring from the cable clips. Move the loom to the side.
5 Remove the window regulator as described in Section 19.
6 Remove two regulator-to-motor Torx bolts and screw them into the regulator casing (see illustrations). This secures the baseplate to the regulator.
7 Undo the remaining Torx bolts and separate the motor from the regulator (see illustration).

Refitting

8 Refitting is a reversal of removal, but note that the motor is not available from Ford as separate part.

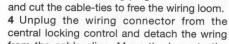

20.11 Unclip the rod (A), undo the screws (B) and remove the complete motor assembly

21.3 Remove the single screw from the glass

9 Once the window operation is known to be correct, refit the inner trim panel as described in Section 16.

Rear side window motors

Removal

10 Remove the D-pillar trim as described in Section 33.
11 Unclip the window opening rod from the motor (see illustration).
12 Disconnect the motor wiring plug, undo the two retaining screws and remove the motor complete with the bracket.

Refitting

13 Refitting is a reversal of the removal procedure.

21 Rear opening side window – removal and refitting

Removal

1 Remove the trim from the D-pillar with reference to Section 33.
2 On models with an electrically-powered opening side window, undo the screw securing the motor operating arm to the window (see illustration).
3 On models with manually-opened rear windows, undo the screw securing the catch to the D-pillar (see illustration).
4 Disconnect the aerial connection (see illustrations). Carefully prise away the trim

21.4a Remove the trim piece ...

from the front inner edge of the glass, undo the two retaining screws and remove the glass.

5 Partially remove the weatherstrip from the C-pillar and then remove the trim panel from the C-pillar. Note that this panel is bonded to the pillar with double-sided adhesive tape. It may be necessary to cut through the adhesive tape with a sharp knife.

6 Have and assistant hold the glass securely and then remove the mounting bolts from the C-pillar.

7 If required the operating latch or motor can be unbolted and removed from the D-pillar.

Refitting

8 Refitting is a reversal of removal, but all traces of the adhesive tape must be removed from the trim panel. New double-sided tape will be required. Tighten all fasteners securely.

22 Front quarter light glass –
removal and refitting

Removal

1 Remove the relevant A-pillar trim with reference to Section 33.

2 Undo the three retaining nuts, and remove the window and seal from the vehicle body **(see illustration)**.

Refitting

3 Refitting is a reversal of removal.

23 Doors –
removal and refitting

Removal

1 Disconnect the battery negative lead. **Note:** *Before disconnecting the battery, refer to 'Disconnecting the battery' at the rear of this manual.*

2 Where fitted, depress the retaining clip and remove the door check strap plastic shield.

3 Rotate the door harness wiring plug collar 90° anti-clockwise, and separate it from the pillar socket **(see illustration)**.

4 Undo the single nut and bolt, and disconnect the door check strap **(see illustration)**.

5 Unscrew the door hinge locking bolts, and lift the door from its hinges **(see illustration)**.

Refitting

6 Refitting is a reversal of the removal procedure.

7 On completion, shut the door and check it for closure and alignment. Check the depth at which the striker enters the lock. If adjustment is required, slacken the securing bolts and reposition the striker plate **(see illustration)**.

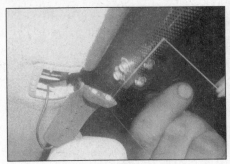

21.4b . . . and unplug the aerial connection

24 Windscreen and
tailgate glass –
general information

The windscreen and tailgate glass are directly bonded to the metalwork. Their removal and refitting requires the use of special tools not readily available to the home mechanic. This work should therefore be left to a Ford dealer, or a specialist glass renewal company.

25 Sunroof –
general

1 Removal and refitting of the complete sunroof is best entrusted to a Ford garage, as specialised tools are required, and the complete headlining must be removed.

23.3 Rotate the connector anti-clockwise to unplug it

23.5 Slacken the locking bolt and lift off the door

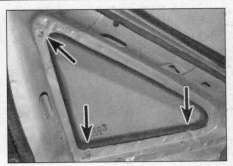

22.2 Remove the three nuts and remove the glass

2 The sunroof panel motor can be removed and refitted as described in Chapter 12. If the motor malfunctions when the roof panel is in the open position, it can be wound shut manually (see Chapter 12).

3 If the sunroof appears to be leaking it is possible to check and adjust the position of the glass within the sunroof aperture. Fully close the roof panel and insert a 1 mm thick and at least 150 mm long spacer between the panel and the rear edge of the roof. Loosen the mounting screws and adjust the panel so that it is flush with the roof and sits squarely in the aperture. Tighten the fixing bolts.

4 If the sunroof water drain hoses become blocked, they may be cleared by probing them with a length of suitable cable (an old speedometer drive cable is ideal) or with an airline. Insert the cleaning tool into the top of the hoses, accessible when the sunroof is fully open. The front drain tubes terminates just in

23.4 Remove the nut and bolt and disconnect the check strap

23.7 If necessary slacken the bolts and reposition the striker plate

26.2 Disconnect the wiring plug

26.3 Remove the screw covers

26.4 Support the mirror and then remove the Torx screws

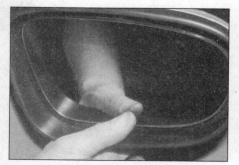

26.6a Press the lower edge in . . .

26.6b . . . lever the top edge out . . .

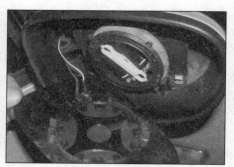

26.6c . . . and disconnect the heated glass wiring plugs

front of the A-pillars, behind the wheel arch liners. The rear drain tubes terminate behind the leading edges of the rear bumper.

26 Door mirror – renewal

Mirror assembly

1 Remove the door trim as described in Section 16, and carefully peel back the door membrane in the corner adjacent to the mirror.
2 Detach the electrical connector and disconnect the wiring plug (see illustration).
3 Prise out the two plastic covers from the door frame (see illustration).
4 Unscrew the two Torx retaining screws, and withdraw the mirror (see illustration).

5 Fit the new mirror housing using a reversal of the removal procedure.

Mirror

⚠️ **Warning: Wear gloves and eye protection when carrying out this operation, particularly if the mirror glass is broken.**

6 To remove the mirror, first press the lower edge of the mirror in, then using a wide flat-bladed tool, lever the top of the mirror out. Where applicable, disconnect the mirror wiring plugs (see illustrations).
7 To refit, press firmly at the centre of the mirror glass to engage the retaining clips. On completion, check the operation of the mirror adjustment mechanism using the adjustment knob/buttons.

27 Centre console – removal and refitting

Removal

1 On manual transmission models carefully pull the gaiter up the gear lever (see illustration). It is not necessary to remove the gaiter completely. On automatic transmission models move the selector lever to the neutral position.
2 Gently ease the trim panel from the console, using a plastic trim removal tool if necessary (see illustrations).
3 Disconnect the wiring connector from the trim panel as it is removed (see illustration) and then lift the panel over the gear lever.

27.1 Release the gaiter

27.2a Release the trim panel . . .

27.2b . . . and remove it

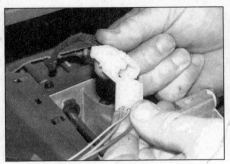

27.3 Unplug the wiring connector

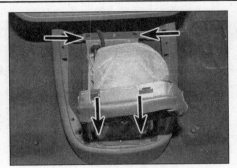

27.4 Remove the screws (arrowed)

4 Remove the four fixings from below the trim panel **(see illustration)** and lift the centre console, up and over the gear lever. On automatic transmission models move the gear selector to the park position to remove the console.

Refitting

5 Refitting is a reversal of the removal procedure.

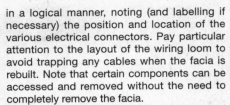

28 Overhead console – removal and refitting

Removal

1 Disconnect the battery negative lead. **Note:** *Before disconnecting the battery, refer to 'Disconnecting the battery' at the rear of this manual.*

2 Open the storage compartment and remove the two fixing screws.
3 Lower the front edge of the console and unhook the rear. Disconnect the wiring plugs as the console is removed.

Refitting

4 Refitting is a reversal of the removal procedure.

29 Facia and associated panels – removal and refitting

Removal

1 The facia is composed of an upper and lower section. The lower section must be removed before the upper section can be removed. Complete removal of the facia whilst not difficult is a time-consuming task. Proceed

in a logical manner, noting (and labelling if necessary) the position and location of the various electrical connectors. Pay particular attention to the layout of the wiring loom to avoid trapping any cables when the facia is rebuilt. Note that certain components can be accessed and removed without the need to completely remove the facia.
2 Disconnect the battery negative lead. **Note:** *Before disconnecting the battery, refer to 'Disconnecting the battery' at the rear of this manual.*
3 Remove the centre console as described in Section 27 this Chapter.

Lower facia panel

4 Open the fusebox cover on the driver's side of the facia, pulling the panel downwards, then outwards, and remove it from the vehicle. Note that the cover may prove difficult to remove and can be left in position, but access to the lower fixing screws of the main panel will be restricted with it in place.
5 On the driver's side remove the facia end panel and the trim panel from below the air distribution vent. Both panels are simply clipped into position **(see illustrations)**.
6 Remove the now exposed two upper and two lower screws from the driver's side lower panel **(see illustrations)**. Unplug the wiring connectors to the switches and unclip the data link connector (DLC) as the panel is removed.
7 On the passenger's side remove the long decorative trim piece. This is a fragile item, so proceed carefully using a plastic trim removal tool. Remove the facia end panel **(see illustrations)**

29.5a Remove the end panel . . .

29.5b . . . and the decorative trim piece

29.6a Remove the screws . . .

29.6b . . . and release the panel

29.7a Use a trim tool to free the panel . . .

29.7b . . . and then remove it carefully

29.10a Use a thin screwdriver to release the cup holders

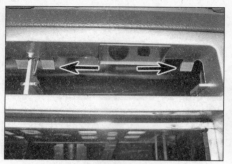

29.10b With the holders removed the locking tabs are visible (arrowed)

29.10c Push out the switches . . .

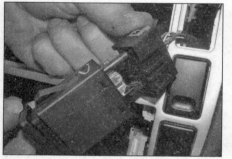

29.10d . . . and disconnect them

29.12a Remove the lamp . . .

29.12b . . . and the switch

8 Open the glovebox and remove the trim panel. Compress the check straps on the glovebox and remove the glovebox. Remove the upper trim panel from the glovebox aperture.

9 Remove the audio unit as described in Chapter 12 and remove the heating and ventilation controls (or climate controls, depending on the model) as described in Chapter 3.

10 Open the cup holders and then using a thin screwdriver remove the cup holders. Reach through the audio unit housing, push out the switches and disconnect the wiring plugs **(see illustrations)**.

11 Remove the screws from the heating control trim panel. Note that two small clips must be removed from the lower edge of the panel. Disconnect the remaining wiring connectors as the panel is removed.

12 Working at the passenger side remove the glovebox light switch and lamp **(see illustrations)**. Where fitted disconnect and remove the footwell illumination lamp.

13 Unbolt and remove the bolts from the passenger side lower panel and then remove the bolt from the lower central support bracket **(see illustrations)**.

14 Remove the screws and clips from the top edge of the lower panel. Note the position of the different length screws as they are removed. As the panel is removed disconnect the glovebox lamp wiring loom and the driver's side footwell lamp wiring loom **(see illustration)**.

15 With the aid of an assistant remove the panel from the vehicle **(see illustration)**.

Upper facia panel

16 Remove the A-pillar panels as described in Section 33 of this Chapter.

17 Open the centre storage compartment, remove the fixing screws and then remove the compartment **(see illustration)**.

18 Open the passenger side upper storage compartment, remove the fixing screws

29.13a Remove the lower fixing bolts . . .

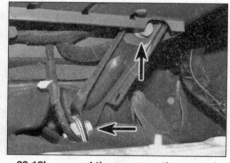

29.13b . . . and then remove the central support bracket bolts (arrowed)

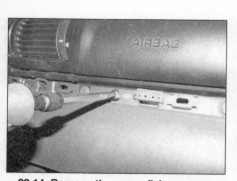

29.14 Remove the upper fixing screws

29.15 Remove the panel from the vehicle

29.17 Remove the central storage compartment

29.18 Remove the passenger side storage compartment

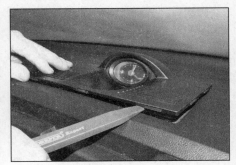

29.21 Remove the clock

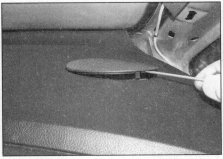

29.22a Remove the speaker cover . . .

29.22b . . . the speaker . . .

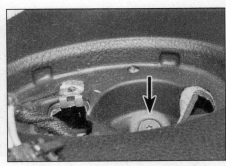

29.22c . . . and the screw (arrowed)

and then remove the compartment **(see illustration)**.

19 Some models have a storage compartment above the instrument panel. Open the compartment and pull the compartment rearward to remove it. Remove the three upper facia mounting bolts hidden by the storage compartment.

20 Remove the upper and lower steering column shrouds and then remove the instrument panel as described in Chapter 12, Section 10. With the panel removed unscrew the upper facia mounting bolt.

21 Use a plastic trim tool and remove the clock trim panel **(see illustration)**. Disconnect the wiring plug as the panel is removed.

22 Remove the speaker grilles from both sides and then unbolt and unplug the loudspeakers. Remove the facia mounting screw now revealed **(see illustrations)**.

23 Where fitted unclip the sunlight sensor from the centre of the facia. Disconnect the wiring connector.

24 Remove the centre and side air distribution vents. Disconnect the wiring connectors as the vents are removed.

25 Locate and unplug the electrical connector for the passenger side airbag **(see illustration)**.

26 Work along the upper surface of the panel and remove the fixing screws **(see illustration)**. Remove the fixing screws from the front of the panel. Disconnect the wiring plugs from the ends of the facia, if not already done so.

27 Check carefully that all fixings have been removed and then lift up the front of the upper facia panel. With the aid of an assistant pull the panel rearward and remove it from the vehicle **(see illustration)**.

28 If you are removing the facia to access the heater unit refer to Chapter 3 for further information.

Refitting

29 Refitting is a reversal of the removal procedure.

---

30 Glovebox and lock – removal and refitting

Removal

1 Pull the small trim piece free from the left-hand side of the glovebox **(see illustration)**.

2 Open the glovebox, and pull it to the rear to remove it. Complete the removal by removing the upper trim panel **(see illustrations)**.

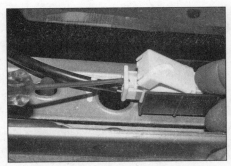

29.25 Disconnect the wiring plug from the passenger airbag

29.26 Remove the screws from the support struts

29.27 Remove the upper facia panel from the vehicle

30.1 Remove the trim panel

30.2a Remove the glovebox . . .

30.2b . . . and the upper trim panel

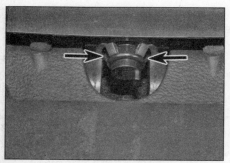

30.3 Release the tabs (arrowed) to remove
the lock cylinder

3 To remove the lock assembly, prise free the
locking tabs. This is a difficult procedure as
two of the tabs are hidden (see illustration).

Refitting

4 Refit in the reverse order of removal.

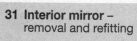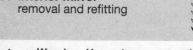

31 Interior mirror –
removal and refitting

⚠ *Warning: Use extreme care whilst
attempting this procedure. The
windscreen is easily cracked.*

Standard mirror

1 Twist the mirror support arm 90° anti-
clockwise, and remove it from the mounting
plate.
2 To refit, position the support arm at 90° to
the vertical, then carefully turn it clockwise

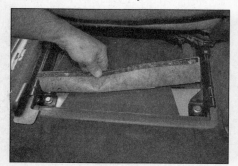

32.3 Lift the carpet to access the rear
mounting bolts

31.2 Position the a... ... of ... to the ...
then twis... ... clockwise ...
to the point where the ... ...
engage (see illustration).
3 If the mirror mounting plate becomes
detached, clean away the old glue, then apply
a suitable glass-to-metal glue in accordance
with the glue manufacturer's instructions, and
refit the mounting plate into position. Ensure
that the plate is correctly orientated, so that
when the mirror is fully fitted to it, the mirror
support arm is vertical.

Auto dimming mirror

4 Remove the weatherstrip from right hand
side A-pillar and then remove the A-pillar trim
panel as described in Section 33.
5 Remove both sunvisors as described in
Section 36 of this Chapter.
6 Remove the interior lamp as described in
Chapter 12 Section 8.
7 Remove the two mounting bolts and
partially lower the headlining.

32.6 Remove the rear mounting bolts

8 Unclip the trim panel from the mirror and
disconnect the wiring connector from the rear
of the mirror.
9 Rotate the mirror anti-clockwise to remove
it.

... ...sconnecting
... ...g plug on
...models ... ...ide airbags,
*it is essential you are electrostatically
discharged by briefly touching a door lock,
or the vehicle body.*

Removal

1 Move the seat forwards to the extent of
its travel, and on models with seat height
adjustment raise it to its maximum height.
2 Check beneath both front seats for
any wiring connectors, if any are present
disconnect the battery negative cable and
wait at least 10 minutes before proceeding.
Note: *Before disconnecting the battery, refer
to 'Disconnecting the battery' at the rear of
this manual.*
3 Behind the front seat, remove the cover
plate (where fitted) or lift up the carpet (see
illustration).
4 Where applicable, disconnect the seat
heater wiring plug, and the side airbag
connector.
5 Detach the side airbag wiring harness
(where fitted) from the retaining bracket.
6 Unscrew and remove the rear seat rail
mounting bolts (see illustration).
7 Lower the seat and move it fully to the rear.
8 At the front of the seat, remove the inboard
and outboard bolt cover trim pieces (see
illustration).
9 Undo the two front seat rail mounting bolts
(see illustration).
10 Lift up the front of the seat and check
that all the wiring connectors have be
disconnected. Feed the wiring cables and
connectors through the access hole as
necessary and then remove the seat.

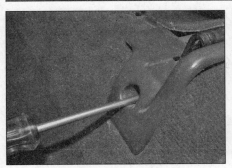

32.8a Unscrew the cover . . .

32.8b . . . and remove it

32.9 Remove the front mounting bolts

Refitting

11 Refit the seat in the reverse order of removal. **Note:** *If after refitting the seat(s), the airbag warning light on the dash signals a fault, take the vehicle to a Ford dealer or suitably-equipped specialist to have the self diagnosis system interrogated and the fault code erased.*

Rear seat

Removal

12 Due to the vehicle's design, the rear seats can be moved to give numerous seating configurations. To remove a seat, fold the seatback forwards, pull the lever at the side of the seat and lift the rear of the seat.

13 With the seat fully folded, squeeze together the release levers between the front mountings, and lift the seat from the floor.

Refitting

14 Squeeze together the release levers, and insert the front mountings into the desired location. Release the levers, and unfold the seat.

33 Interior trim –
general information,
removal and refitting

Trim panels

1 The interior trim panels are secured using either screws or various types of trim fasteners, usually studs or clips.

2 Check that there are no other panels overlapping the one to be removed; usually there is a sequence that has to be followed, and this will only become obvious on close inspection.

3 Remove all obvious fasteners, such as screws. If the panel will not come free, it is held by hidden clips or fasteners. These are usually situated around the edge of the panel and can be prised up to release them; note, however that they can break quite easily so new ones should be available. The best way of releasing such clips without the correct type of tool, is to use a large flat-bladed screwdriver. Note in many cases that the adjacent sealing strip must be prised back to release a panel.

4 When removing a panel, **never** use excessive force or the panel may be damaged; always check carefully that all fasteners or other relevant components have been removed or released before attempting to withdraw a panel.

5 The pillars at the front of the passenger cabin, level with the windscreen are known as the A-pillars. The subsequent pillars are known as the B-, C- and D-pillars. The D-pillars are level with the tailgate.

A-pillar trim

6 Pull the weatherstrip from the door aperture in the area of the A-pillar **(see illustration)**. Lever up and remove the lower A-pillar trim panel.

7 On early vehicles, unclip and remove the facia trim panel adjacent to the pillar.

8 On later vehicles remove the three trim panel fixing screws. Note that on vehicles fitted with side curtain airbags there is a fixing bolt behind the upper cover. Remove the plastic cover and undo the pillar trim screw.

9 Unclip and remove the A-pillar trim **(see illustration)**.

10 Refitting is the reverse of the removal procedure; secure the fasteners by pressing them firmly into place and ensure that all disturbed components are correctly secured to prevent rattles.

B-pillar trim

11 Remove the front seat belt upper and lower mounting point covers, and remove the mounting bolts **(see illustrations)**.

12 Undo the pillar trim retaining screw, and pull the door weatherstrips from either side of the trim **(see illustration)**.

13 The trim panel is in two sections. Unclip

33.6 Partially remove the weatherstrip

33.9 Remove the trim piece

33.11a Remove the upper cover . . .

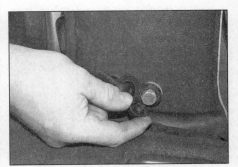

33.11b . . . the lower cover . . .

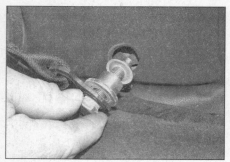

33.11c . . . and the bolts

33.12 Remove the single screw

33.13a Disconnect the wiring plug from the upper panel . . .

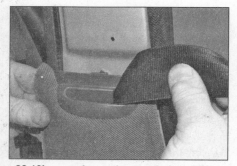

33.13b . . . release the seat belt webbing and remove the lower panel

33.16a Open the cover . . .

33.16b . . . and remove the bolt

and remove the upper trim, disconnecting the alarm sensor as the panel is removed. Feed the seat belt from the lower trim section and remove it (see illustrations).

14 Refitting is the reverse of the removal procedure; secure the fasteners by pressing them firmly into place and ensure that all disturbed components are correctly secured to prevent rattles.

C-pillar trim

15 On vehicles built up to September 2001, remove the second row seat belt upper mounting point cover, and remove the mounting bolt.

16 On later vehicles the cover is hinged and should be opened, but not removed. Remove the mounting bolt (see illustrations).

17 Pull the door weatherstrip from the door aperture adjacent to the C-pillar trim.

18 Undo the C-pillar retaining screw (see illustration) and unclip the trim from the pillar.

19 Refitting is the reverse of the removal procedure; secure the fasteners by pressing them firmly into place and ensure that all disturbed components are correctly secured to prevent rattles.

D-pillar trim

20 Remove the rear seat belt upper mounting point cover (early vehicles) or open the hinged cover (later vehicles) and remove the mounting bolt.

21 If necessary pull the weatherstrip from the tailgate aperture adjacent to the D-pillar trim.

22 Remove the fixing screw covers and remove the screws. Remove the trim.

23 Refitting is the reverse of the removal procedure; secure the fasteners by pressing

them firmly into place and ensure that all disturbed components are correctly secured to prevent rattles.

Luggage area side trim

24 Remove the rear seats. Next remove the C- and D-pillar trims on the appropriate side.

25 Prise up and remove the luggage area scuff panel.

26 Detach the weatherstrip and tuck it behind the tailgate struts to keep it out of the way.

27 On the appropriate side remove the cover from the tailgate guide plate and then remove the fixing bolts (see illustrations).

28 Unbolt and remove the rear lower seat belt mounting (see illustrations).

29 Remove the single plastic bolt from the lower edge of the panel and then slide the seat belt webbing from the guide plates (see illustration)

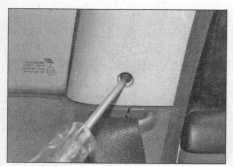

33.18 Remove the fixing screw

33.27a Remove the screw . . .

33.27b . . . and then remove the cover

33.28a Remove the cover . . .

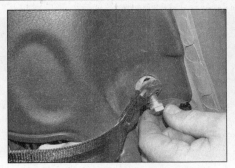

33.28b . . . and then remove the bolt

33.29 Remove the single plastic screw

33.31a Use a short screwdriver to remove the screws . . .

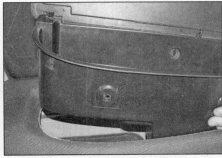

33.31b . . . and then remove the storage compartment

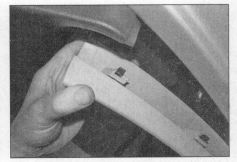

33.34 Remove the upper trim panel

30 If working on the left-hand panel remove the rear lamp cover and unplug the 12V power socket. Where fitted remove and disconnect the load space lamps.

31 On the right-hand trim panel unbolt and remove the CD multi-disk player (where fitted). Where no CD player is fitted, remove the storage compartment (see illustrations).

32 Pull the bottom edge of the panel inwards to release it and then push the panel upwards to unhook it. As the panel is removed, disconnect the wiring plug from the loudspeaker and feed the seat belt webbing through the slot in the panel. Some vehicles will also have a temperature sensor fitted to the left-hand panel. Disconnect the wiring plug as the panel is removed.

33 Refitting is the reverse of the removal procedure; secure the fasteners by pressing them firmly into place and ensure that all

disturbed components are correctly secured to prevent rattles.

Tailgate trim

34 Using a broad-bladed screwdriver, or a plastic trim tool, carefully lever the upper panel free from the tailgate (see illustration).

35 Unbolt and remove the interior pull handle (see illustration) and then remove the two covers from the tailgate-mounted lamps.

36 Remove the fixing screws (see illustration) and then detach the lower panel. Slide it forward to fully remove the panel.

37 If required the trim clips can be removed from the tailgate.

38 Refitting is the reverse of the removal procedure; secure the fasteners by pressing them firmly into place and ensure that all disturbed components are correctly secured to prevent rattles.

Kick panel and door step trim

39 Partially remove the weatherstrip from the door frame and then remove the B-pillar trim as described above.

40 If you are working on the right-hand kick panel, unbolt and remove the bonnet release handle.

41 Remove the screw from the kick panel (see illustration) and where fitted open the covers and remove the screws from the door step section. Remove the panel from the vehicle.

42 Refitting is the reverse of the removal procedure; secure the fasteners by pressing them firmly into place and ensure that all disturbed components are correctly secured to prevent rattles.

Headlining

43 The headlining is clipped to the roof and

33.35 Remove the pull handle

33.36 Remove the screws

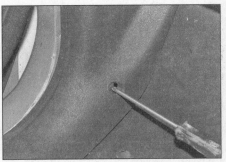

33.41 Remove the single screw from the footwell

35.4a Remove the single bolt from the pretensioner . . .

35.4b . . . and then unbolt and remove the inertia reel

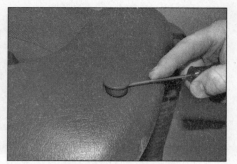

35.6a Remove the blanking plug . . .

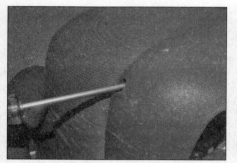

35.6b . . . and remove the screw(s) . . .

35.6c . . . to access the stalk mounting bolt (arrowed)

can be withdrawn only once all fittings such as the grab handles, sunvisors, sunroof (if fitted), windscreen, rear quarter windows and related trim panels have been removed, and the door, tailgate and sunroof aperture sealing strips (as applicable) have been prised clear.

44 Note that headlining removal and refitting requires considerable skill and experience if it is to be carried out without damage and is therefore best entrusted to an expert.

34 Seat belt pretensioning mechanism – general information

All models are fitted with front seat belt pretensioners. The system is designed to instantaneously take up any slack in the seat belt in the case of a direct or oblique frontal impact, therefore reducing the possibility of injury to the occupants. Each front seat is fitted with its own tensioner, which is situated behind the lower B-pillar trim panel/sill scuff plate.

The seat belt tensioner is triggered by a frontal impact above a predetermined force. Lesser impacts and impacts to the rear of the vehicle will not trigger the system.

When the system is triggered, the explosive gas in the tensioner mechanism retracts and locks the seat belt through a cable which acts on the inertia reel. This prevents the seat belt moving and keeps the occupant firmly in position in the seat. Once the tensioner has been triggered, the seat belt will be permanently locked and the assembly

must be renewed, together with the impact sensors.

Note the following warnings before contemplating any work on the front seat belts.

⚠️ **Warning:**
- **Do not expose the tensioner mechanism to temperatures in excess of 100ºC.**

- **If the tensioner mechanism is dropped, it must be renewed, even it has suffered no apparent damage.**

- **Do not allow any solvents to come into contact with the tensioner mechanism.**

- **Do not attempt to open the tensioner mechanism as it contains explosive gas.**

- **Tensioners must be discharged before they are disposed of, but this task should be entrusted to a Ford dealer.**

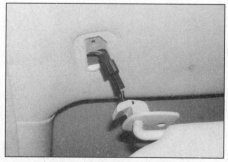

36.1 Disconnect the wiring plug as the sunvisor is withdrawn

35 Seat belts – general

Note: *Refer to the warnings in Section 34 before working on the seat belts.*

1 Periodically check the belts for fraying or other damage. If evident, renew the belt.

2 If the belts become dirty, wipe them with a damp cloth, using a little liquid detergent only.

3 Check the tightness of the anchor bolts, and if they are ever disconnected, make quite sure that the original sequence of fitting of washers, bushes, and anchor plate is retained.

4 Access to the front belt height adjuster and inertia reel units can be made by removing the trim from the B-pillar and door step on the side concerned **(see illustrations)**. Handle the assembly with caution and take great care not to knock the tensioner against anything. Once removed from the vehicle store the inertia reel and pretensioner in a secure location.

5 The rear seat belt anchorages/inertia reel units can be checked by removing the C-pillar trims (second row of seats), or the luggage compartment side trims – see Section 33.

6 The seat belt stalks are fitted to the sides of the seat bases. Undo the screws, remove the trim and unscrew the stalk mounting bolt. On the front seats remove the height adjustment lever first **(see illustrations)**.

7 The torque wrench settings for the seat belt anchor bolts and other attachments are given in the Specifications at the start of this Chapter.

8 Never modify the seat belts, or alter the attachments to the body, in any way.

36 Sunvisors – removal and refitting

Removal

1 Swing the sunvisor out of its retaining clip. Undo the screw and remove the sunvisor. On models with and illuminated vanity mirror, disconnect the wiring plug as the sunvisor is withdrawn **(see illustration)**.

2 To remove the sunvisor retaining clip, prise

off the plastic cap and remove the retaining screws **(see illustration)**.

Refitting

3 Refitting is a reversal of removal.

37 Grab handles –
removal and refitting

Removal

1 Hold down the grab handle, and prise up the plastic covers. Undo the retaining screws and remove the handles **(see illustration)**.

Refitting

2 Refitting is a reversal of removal.

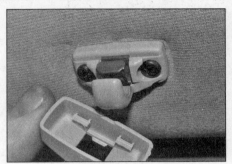

36.2 Remove the cover to access the screws

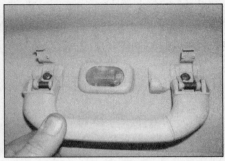

37.1 Prise up the covers and undo the grab handle screws

Notes

Chapter 12
Body electrical system

Contents

Degrees of difficulty

Easy, suitable for novice with little experience 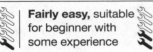	Fairly easy, suitable for beginner with some experience	Fairly difficult, suitable for competent DIY mechanic	Difficult, suitable for experienced DIY mechanic	Very difficult, suitable for expert DIY or professional

Specifications

System type .... 12 volt, negative earth

Bulbs	Power rating (watts)
Brake/tail lights	21/5
Clock	1.2
Foglight:	
Front	55
Rear	21
Footwell, entrance lights	5
Glovebox light	3
Grab handle	5
Headlights (halogen):	
Main beam	55
Dipped beam	55
Headlights (xenon):	
Main beam	55
Dipped beam	35
Indicators:	
Front	21
Rear	21
Side repeaters	5
Interior lights	10
Interior mirror light	3
Luggage compartment	5
Number plate light	5
Reading lights	10
Reversing light	21
Sidelights	5
Side repeaters	5
Tail lights	5
Vanity lights	3

Torque wrench settings

	Nm	lbf ft
Airbag control module	10	7
Airbag securing plate-to-steering wheel screws	4	3
Airbag unit-to facia-screws	4	3
Headlight screws	8	6
Seatbelt anchor bolts	40	30
Seatbelt pretensioner locknut	20	15
Side impact sensor retaining bolts	9	7
Side curtain airbag nuts	8	6
Side curtain airbag screws	4	3
Tailgate wiper arm nut	20	15
Windscreen wiper arm nuts	34	25
Windscreen wiper linkage bolts	20	15
Windscreen wiper motor	6	4
Windscreen wiper motor crank arm nut	26	19

1 General information and precautions

⚠️ *Warning: Before carrying out any work on the electrical system, read through the precautions given in 'Safety first!' at the beginning of this manual, and in Chapter 5A.*

1 The electrical system is of 12 volt negative earth type. Power for the lights and all electrical accessories is supplied by a lead-acid type battery which is charged by the alternator.

2 This Chapter covers repair and service procedures for the various electrical components not associated with the engine. Information on the battery, alternator and starter motor can be found in Chapter 5A.

3 It should be noted that prior to working on any component in the electrical system, the battery negative terminal should first be disconnected to prevent the possibility of electrical short-circuits and/or fires. **Note:** *Before disconnecting the battery, refer to 'Disconnecting the battery' at the rear of this manual.*

2 Electrical fault finding – general information

Note: *Refer to the precautions given in 'Safety first!' and in Chapter 5A before starting work. The following tests relate to testing of the main electrical circuits, and should not be used to test delicate electronic circuits (such as anti-lock braking systems), particularly where an electronic control module is used.*

General

1 Typically, electrical circuit consists of an electrical component, any switches, relays, motors, fuses, fusible links or circuit breakers related to that component, and the wiring and connectors which link the component to both the battery and the chassis. To help to pinpoint a problem in an electrical circuit, wiring diagrams are included at the end of this Chapter.

2 Have a good look at the appropriate wiring diagram, before attempting to diagnose an electrical fault, to obtain a complete understanding of the components included in the particular circuit concerned. The possible sources of a fault can be narrowed down by noting if other components related to the circuit are operating properly. If several components or circuits fail at one time, the problem is likely to be related to a shared fuse or earth connection.

3 An electrical problem will usually stem from simple cause, such as loose or corroded connections, a faulty earth connection, a blown fuse, a melted fusible link, or a faulty relay (refer to Section 3 for details of testing relays). Visually inspect the condition of all fuses, wires and connections in a problem circuit before testing the components. Use the wiring diagrams to determine which terminal connections will need to be checked in order to pinpoint the trouble-spot.

4 The basic tools required for electrical fault-finding include a circuit tester or voltmeter (a 12 volt bulb with a set of test leads can also be used for certain tests); a self-powered test light (sometimes known as a continuity tester); an ohmmeter (to measure resistance); a battery and set of test leads; and a jumper wire, preferably with a circuit breaker or fuse incorporated, which can be used to bypass suspect wires or electrical components. Before attempting to locate a problem with test instruments, use the wiring diagram to determine where to make the connections.

5 Sometimes, an intermittent wiring fault (usually caused to a poor or dirty connection, or damaged wiring insulation) can be pinpointed by performing a wiggle test on the wiring. This involves wiggling the wiring by hand to see if the fault occurs as the wiring is moved. It should be possible to narrow down the source of the fault to a particular section of wiring. This method of testing can be used in conjunction with any of the tests described in the following sub-Sections.

6 Apart from problems due to poor connections, two basic types of fault can occur in an electrical circuit: open-circuit, or short-circuit.

7 Largely, open-circuit faults are caused by a break somewhere in the circuit, which prevents current from flowing. An open-circuit fault will prevent a component from working, but will not cause the relevant circuit fuse to blow.

8 Low resistance or short-circuit faults are caused by a 'short'; a failure point which allows the current flowing in the circuit to 'escape' along an alternative route, somewhere in the circuit. This typically occurs when a positive supply wire touches either an earth wire, or an earthed component such as the bodyshell. Such faults are normally caused by a breakdown in wiring insulation. A short circuit fault will normally cause the relevant circuit fuse to blow.

9 Fuses are designed to protect a circuit from being overloaded. A blown fuse indicates that there may be problem in that particular circuit and it is important to identify and rectify the problem before renewing the fuse. Always renew a blown fuse with one of the correct current rating; fitting a fuse of a different rating may cause an overloaded circuit to overheat and even catch fire.

Finding an open-circuit

10 One of the most straightforward ways of finding an open-circuit fault is by using a circuit test meter or voltmeter. Connect one lead of the meter to either the negative battery terminal or a known good earth. Connect the other lead to a connector in the circuit being tested, preferably nearest to the battery or fuse. Switch on the circuit, bearing in mind that some circuits are live only when the ignition switch is moved to a particular position. If voltage is present (indicated either by the tester bulb lighting or a voltmeter reading, as applicable), this means that the section of the circuit between the relevant connector and the battery is problem-free. Continue to check the remainder of the circuit in the same fashion. When a point is reached at which no voltage is present, the problem must lie between that point and the previous test point with voltage. Most problems can be traced to a broken, corroded or loose connection.

3.3a Pull down the cover panel to access the main fusebox . . .

3.3b . . . or lift the lid on the auxiliary fusebox

3.10 Relays on the central junction box (viewed with the facia removed)

Finding a short-circuit

11 Loading the circuit during testing will produce false results and may damage your test equipment, so all electrical loads must be disconnected from the circuit before it can be checked for short circuits. Loads are the components which draw current from a circuit, such as bulbs, motors, heating elements, etc.

12 Keep both the ignition and the circuit under test switched off, then remove the relevant fuse from the circuit, and connect a circuit test meter or voltmeter to the fuse connections.

13 Switch on the circuit, bearing in mind that some circuits are live only when the ignition switch is moved to a particular position. If voltage is present (indicated either by the tester bulb lighting or a voltmeter reading, as applicable), this means that there is a short-circuit. If no voltage is present, but the fuse still blows with the load(s) connected, this indicates an internal fault in the load(s).

Finding an earth fault

14 The battery negative terminal is connected to 'earth': the metal of the engine/transmission and the car body – and most systems are wired so that they only receive a positive feed, the current returning through the metal of the car body. This means that the component mounting and the body form part of that circuit. Loose or corroded mountings can therefore cause a range of electrical faults, ranging from total failure of a circuit, to a puzzling partial fault. In particular, lights may shine dimly (especially when another circuit sharing the same earth point is in operation), motors (eg, wiper motors or the radiator cooling fan motor) may run slowly, and the operation of one circuit may have an apparently unrelated effect on another. Note that on many vehicles, earth straps are used between certain components, such as the engine/transmission and the body, usually where there is no metal-to-metal contact between components due to flexible rubber mountings, etc.

15 To check whether a component is properly earthed, disconnect the battery and connect one lead of an ohmmeter to a known good earth point. Connect the other lead to the wire or earth connection being tested.

The resistance reading should be zero; if not, check the connection as follows.

16 If an earth connection is thought to be faulty, dismantle the connection and clean back to bare metal both the bodyshell and the wire terminal or the component earth connection mating surface. Be careful to remove all traces of dirt and corrosion, then use a knife to trim away any paint, so that a clean metal-to-metal joint is made. On reassembly, tighten the joint fasteners securely; if a wire terminal is being refitted, use serrated washers between the terminal and the bodyshell to ensure a clean and secure connection. When the connection is remade, prevent the onset of corrosion in the future by applying a coat of petroleum jelly or silicone-based grease or by spraying on (at regular intervals) a proprietary ignition sealer or a water dispersant lubricant.

3 Fuses and relays – general information

Central junction box

1 All models feature a facia mounted central junction box which incorporates not only the relays and fuses, but also an ECM (electronic control module) known as a GEM (generic electronic module). This module is the 'switching centre' of the vehicle. Depending on the vehicle trim level, it controls the windscreen wiper interval, front and rear window heating interval, windscreen washer system, central locking, electric windows, radio remote control, anti-theft warning system with ultrasonic monitoring, and the bulb failure monitoring system. The central junction box is located under the driver's side of the facia.

Main fuses

2 The fuses are located in the central junction box under the driver's side of the facia, and in an auxiliary fusebox in the left-hand corner of the engine compartment.

3 Access to the fuses is gained by pulling open the cover panel (central fusebox), or lifting the lid (auxiliary fusebox) **(see illustrations)**.

4 Each fuse is numbered; the fuses' ratings and circuits they protect are listed on the rear face of the cover panel.

5 On some models (depending on specification), some additional fuses are located in separate holders next to the relays.

6 To remove a fuse, first switch off the circuit concerned (or the ignition), then pull the fuse out of its terminals. The wire within the fuse should be visible; if the fuse is blown the wire will have a break in it, which will be visible through the plastic casing.

7 Always renew a fuse with one of an identical rating; never use a fuse with a different rating from the original or substitute anything else. Never renew a fuse more than once without tracing the source of the trouble. The fuse rating is stamped on top of the fuse; note that the fuses are also colour-coded for easy recognition.

8 If a new fuse blows immediately, find the cause before renewing it again; a short to earth as a result of faulty insulation is most likely. Where a fuse protects more than one circuit, try to isolate the defect by switching on each circuit in turn (if possible) until the fuse blows again.

9 Always carry a supply of spare fuses of each relevant rating on the vehicle, a spare of each rating should be clipped into the base of the fusebox.

Relays

10 The relays are mounted in the central junction box under the driver's side facia, and also in the auxiliary fusebox in the engine compartment **(see illustration)**. The seat heating relays are located under the relevant seat.

11 The relays are of sealed construction, and cannot be repaired if faulty. The relays are of the plug-in type, and may be removed by pulling directly from their terminals. In some cases, it will be necessary to prise the two plastic clips outwards before removing the relay.

12 If a circuit or system controlled by a relay develops a fault and the relay is suspect, operate the system; if the relay is functioning, it should be possible to hear it click as it is energised. If this is the case, the fault lies with the components or wiring of the system. If the relay is not being energised, then either the relay is not receiving a main supply or a switching voltage, or the relay itself is faulty. Testing is by the substitution of a known

4.2 Rotate the steering wheel to access the two screws (arrowed)

4.3a Remove the lower screws

4.3b Release the trim piece from below the instrument panel . . .

4.3c . . . and remove the shrouds

4.4a Cut the cable-tie . . .

4.4b . . . and remove the wiring connector plug

good unit, but be careful; while some relays are identical in appearance and in operation, others look similar but perform different functions.

13 To renew a relay, first ensure that the ignition switch is off. The relay can then simply be pulled out from the socket and the new relay pressed in.

4 Ignition switch – removal and refitting

1 Disconnect the battery negative lead (see *Disconnecting the battery* in the Reference Chapter).
2 Rotate the steering wheel to access the two shroud screws **(see illustration)**
3 Remove the three lower column shroud screws and then remove the upper and lower column shrouds. **(see illustrations)**.
4 Cut the cable-tie and remove the ignition switch wiring connector from the rear of the steering column lock **(see illustrations)**.
5 Slacken the two screws and release the switch **(see illustration)**.
6 Refitting is a reversal of the removal process, but renew the cable-tie after the switch has been refitted.

4.5 Remove the paint and slacken the screws (arrowed)

5.3a Remove the upper screws (arrowed) . . .

5 Steering column combination switch – removal and refitting

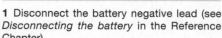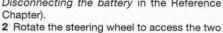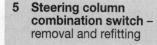

Removal

1 Disconnect the battery negative lead (see *Disconnecting the battery* in the Reference Chapter).
2 With reference to this Chapter (Section 22) and Chapter 10, remove the airbag and steering wheel.
3 With the steering column in its lowest and rearmost position, undo the retaining screws

5.3b . . . the lower screws (arrowed) . . .

5.3c . . . and remove the shrouds

5.4 Slacken the retaining screw (arrowed)

5.6a Depress the locking tab (arrowed) . . .

5.6b . . . and separate the switch

and remove the steering column shrouds **(see illustrations)**.

4 Undo the combination switch retaining screw **(see illustration)**.

5 Note their fitted locations and disconnect the switch wiring multiplugs. Note that the design of the plugs is such that it is impossible to reconnect them to the wrong switches.

6 Remove the switch and separate the two halves **(see illustrations)**. No further dismantling of the switch is recommended.

Refitting

7 Refitting is a reversal of removal.

6	Switches – removal and refitting

Facia-mounted light switch

1 Disconnect the battery negative lead (see *Disconnecting the battery* in the Reference Chapter).

2 Select the position O on the switch. Push the switch in, turn the switch clockwise and pull the switch from the panel **(see illustrations)**.

3 Disconnect the wiring plugs as the switch panel is withdrawn.

4 Refit in the reverse order of removal.

Headlight range switch and dash illumination switch

5 Remove the end panel from the facia and the decorative trim piece from the switch panel as described in Section 29 of Chapter 11.

6.2a Pull the switch free

6 Disconnect the wiring plug **(see illustration)**.

7 Use a small screwdriver to depress the locking tabs and then push the switch from the panel **(see illustrations)**.

8 Refit in the reverse order of removal.

6.6 Disconnect the wiring plug

6.2b Viewed from the rear, this locking tab is retracted when the switch is depressed and rotated (arrowed)

Door mirror adjuster switch

9 Gently prise the front edge of the switch panel from the door release handle trim. Disconnect the switch wiring plug as the switch panel is withdrawn **(see illustrations)**.

6.7a Depress the tabs . . .

6.7b . . . and release the switch

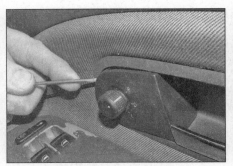

6.9a Prise the switch free . . .

6.9b . . . and disconnect the wiring plug

6.11 Carefully prise the interior light/
switch panel from the overhead console

6.15a Remove the seal . . .

13 release the four retaining tabs, and pull the switch from the panel.
14 Refit in the reverse order of removal.

Courtesy light switch

15 The courtesy lights are controlled by switches fitted to the lower corners of the door apertures. The luggage compartment light is controlled by a switch incorporated into the tailgate lock (see Chapter 11, Section 15). To remove a door switch, disconnect the battery negative terminal, and carefully lever the switch from the door aperture. Disconnect the wiring plug as the switch is withdrawn **(see illustrations)**. **Note:** *Before disconnecting the battery, refer to 'Disconnecting the battery' at the rear of this manual.*
16 Refitting is a reversal of removal.

Handbrake warning switch

17 Remove the two sections of the handbrake cover, unclip the rear heater vent and then lift the carpet over the handbrake **(see illustrations)**.
18 Squeeze together the retaining clip lugs, and remove the switch from the bracket. Disconnect the wiring plugs as the switch is withdrawn **(see illustrations)**.
19 Refit in the reverse order of removal.

Electric window switch

Door-mounted

20 The switch panel is part of the door pull handle assembly.
21 Remove the pull handle as described in Chapter 11, Section 16.

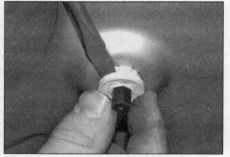

6.15b . . . lever the courtesy light switch
from the door aperture . . .

6.15c . . . and disconnect the wiring plug

10 Refit in the reverse order of removal.

Sunroof control switch

11 With a pad of soft material between the screwdriver and the surround to prevent any damage, gently prise the interior light/sliding roof operating switch panel from the overhead console **(see illustration)**.
12 Note their fitted positions, and disconnect the wiring plugs as the panel is withdrawn.

6.17a Lift off the upper cover . . .

6.17b . . . the lower cover . . .

6.17c . . . the heater vents . . .

6.17d . . . and lift the carpet over the
handbrake

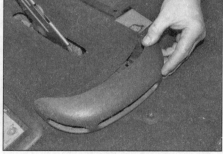

6.18a Squeeze together the clip lugs . . .

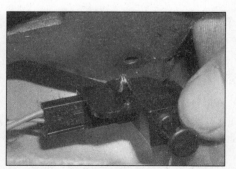

6.18b . . . and remove the handbrake
warning switch

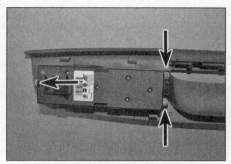

6.22 Remove the screws (arrowed)

6.25a Push the appropriate switch free from the rear through the audio unit aperture . . .

6.25b . . . or remove a blanking plug and push the switch free

22 Remove the fixing screws and release the switch assembly **(see illustration)**.
23 Refitting is a reversal of removal.

Facia-mounted

24 Remove the audio unit as described in Section 17.
25 With the audio unit removed, reach through the aperture and push the appropriate switch free from the rear. An alternative approach is to remove one of the blanking switch covers to release the switch **(see illustrations)**. Note that attempting to prise the switch free from the front will damage the switch.
26 Disconnect the wiring plug as the switch is removed **(see illustration)**.
27 Refitting is a reversal of removal.

Brake light switch

28 Refer to Chapter 9.

Steering column switch

29 Refer to Section 5.

Luggage area light switch and tailgate ajar switch

30 Remove the tailgate trim panel as described in Chapter 11, Section 33.
31 Disconnect the switch wiring plug.
32 Release the retaining clip and remove the switch **(see illustration)**.
33 Refitting is a reversal of removal.

Heated windows switch, seat heating switch and auxiliary heater switch

34 The removal and refitting procedure for these switches is identical to that given for the facia-mounted switches, in Paragraphs 24 to 27 in this Section.

Hazard warning switch

35 The removal and refitting procedure for these switches is identical to that given for the facia-mounted switches, in Paragraphs 24 to 27 in this Section.

Parking sensor switch

36 The removal and refitting procedure for these switches is identical to that given for the facia-mounted switches, in Paragraphs 24 to 27 in this Section.

ESP switch

37 The removal and refitting procedure for these switches is identical to that given for the facia-mounted switches, in Paragraphs 24 to 27 in this Section.

Reversing light switch

38 Refer to Chapter 7A.

Heater blower motor switch

39 Use a small screwdriver to gently prise out the heater control panel trim. Use a pad of soft material between the screwdriver and the panel to prevent any accidental damage **(see illustration)**.
40 Remove the screws and disconnect the wiring plugs as the control unit is pulled forward **(see illustration)**.
41 At the time of writing the switch was not

available separately from the heater control panel.

Rear quarter light switch

42 Where motorised rear quarter light windows are fitted the switches are mounted on the floor console.
43 Prise up and lift up the gear lever gaiter.
44 Push the switch out from the rear, disconnecting the wiring as the switch is removed.

7 Exterior light units and bulbs – removal and refitting

1 Whenever a bulb is renewed, note the following points:
  a) Ensure the ignition is turned off.

6.26 Disconnect the wiring plug

6.32 Release the retaining clip and remove the tailgate ajar switch (arrowed)

6.39 Remove the trim piece

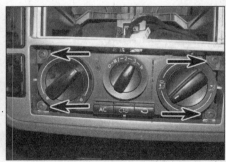

6.40 Remove the screws (arrowed)

7.3a Slide up the plastic panel . . .

b) *Remember that if the light has just been in use, the bulb may be extremely hot.*
c) *Always check the bulb contacts and holder, ensuring that there is clean metal-to-metal contact between the bulb and its live(s) and earth. Clean off any corrosion or dirt before fitting a new bulb.*
d) *Wherever bayonet-type bulbs are fitted, ensure that the live contact(s) bear firmly against the bulb contact.*
e) *Always ensure that the new bulb is of the correct rating and that it is completely clean before fitting it; this applies particularly to headlight/foglight bulbs (see below).*

Halogen headlight

Dipped beam

2 The access to all the headlight mounted bulbs is poor and given that removing the complete headlight unit is relatively

7.3b . . . and then unclip and remove the cover

straightforward it may prove easier to remove the headlight to change the bulbs.
3 Lift up the retaining clip and remove the cover from the rear of the headlight **(see illustrations)**. Unplug the wiring connector from the rear of the relevant bulb.
4 Release the metal retaining clip and withdraw the bulb **(see illustrations)**.
5 Refitting is a reversal of removal. Insert the new bulb so that the lug on the bulb aligns with the slot in the reflector **(see illustration)**. Do not touch the glass of the new bulb with bare fingers. If the glass is accidentally touched, clean it with methylated spirit.

Main beam

6 Remove the cover from the headlight as described above and then remove the wiring plug **(see illustration)**.
7 Release the spring clip and then remove the bulb **(see illustrations)**.
8 Refitting is a reversal of removal. Insert the

new bulb so that the flat edge of the bulb is correctly located. Do not touch the glass of the new bulb with bare fingers. If the glass is accidentally touched, clean it with methylated spirit.

Xenon headlight

⚠️ *Warning: Gloves and safety glasses must be worn at all times when working with xenon lighting systems. Failure to follow these precautions may result in personal injury.*

9 On vehicles fitted with xenon (often referred to as HID – high intensity discharge – headlights) the headlight must be removed from the vehicle, as described in Section 9 of this Chapter. **Note:** *If the left-hand unit is removed, the headlight system will require recalibrating with the Ford IDS diagnostic tool.*
10 Before removing the rear cover the wiring plug must be disconnected.
11 Remove the rear cover and then unplug the wiring connector to the dipped beam. Rotate the bulb anti-clockwise to remove it
12 To remove the main beam bulb, disconnect the wiring plug and release the U-shaped bulb retainer. Remove the bulb.
13 Refitting is a reversal of removal, but do not handle the bulb with bare fingers. Observe the safety warning given above at all times.

Sidelight

14 Turn the roadwheel to gain access to the sidelight. Remove cover from the wheel arch by sliding it upwards **(see illustration)**.

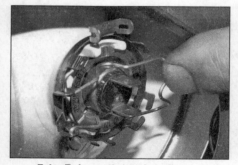

7.4a Release the spring clip . . .

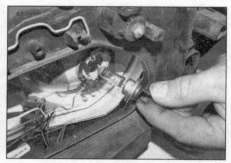

7.4b . . . and remove the bulb

7.5 Make sure the tab on the bulb aligns with the slot in the reflector (arrowed)

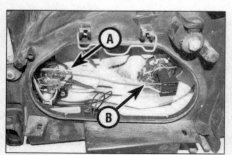

7.6 The rear of the headlight showing the main beam bulb (A) and the dipped beam bulb (B)

7.7a Release the spring clip . . .

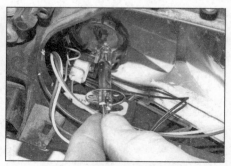

7.7b . . . and remove the bulb

15 Rotate the bulbholder anti-clockwise and remove it complete with the bulb. Remove the bulb from the bulb holder **(see illustration)**.

16 Refitting is a reversal of removal.

Front foglights

17 The front foglights are fitted into the front bumper. The right-hand front bulb is easily accessible, but the left-hand unit will require lifting of the front of the vehicle and partial removal of the wing liner.

18 To remove the complete foglight, remove the trim piece from the foglight. Remove the mounting screws **(see illustrations)**.

19 At the rear of the bumper, pull the foglight free. On the left-hand foglight release the trim clips and partially free the wing liner to access the lamp assembly. Disconnect the wiring plug.

20 To renew the bulb, rotate the lamp cover anti-clockwise and remove it **(see illustration)**.

21 Disconnect the wiring plug, release the retaining clip and remove the bulb from the unit **(see illustrations)**.

22 Refitting is a reversal of removal.

Front direction indicator

23 Turn the road wheel to gain access to the indicator. Remove the cover from the wheel arch by sliding it upwards.

24 Rotate the bulbholder anti-clockwise and withdraw it from the light unit **(see illustration)**.

25 Pull the capless type bulb from the bulbholder.

26 Refitting is a reversal of removal.

Direction indicator side repeater

27 Great care must be exercised when attempting to remove the side repeater lamps, as it is only possible to remove them in one direction (depending on the position in which they previously fitted), and impossible to recognise which side of the repeater the spring clip or the mounting sits. Push the lens towards the front or rear of the vehicle to compress the spring clip, then tilt it out at the rear or front to release the lens from the bodywork **(see illustration)**.

28 Rotate the bulbholder anti-clockwise, extract the bulbholder from the lens, then pull the bulb from the bulbholder **(see illustrations)**.

29 Refitting is a reversal of removal.

Rear lights

Body-mounted

30 Open the tailgate, and open the access flap on the left-hand side trim, on

7.14 Slide up the cover

7.15 Remove the capless type sidelight bulb from the bulbholder

7.18a Remove the trim piece . . .

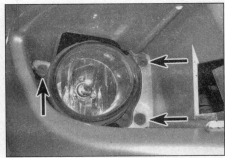
7.18b . . . and remove the mounting screws (arrowed)

7.20 Remove the cover

7.21a Remove the wiring plug . . .

7.21b . . . release the clip and remove the bulb

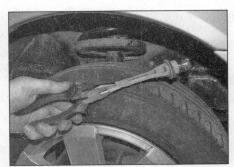
7.24 Use a pair of pliers to easily remove the indicator bulb

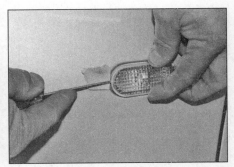
7.27 Protect the bodywork with card or tape whilst levering out the side repeater

7.28a Remove the bulbholder . . .

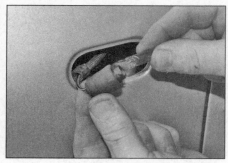
7.28b . . . and then pull the bulb from the holder

7.30a Remove the cover and . . .

7.30b . . . unclip the bulbholder assembly

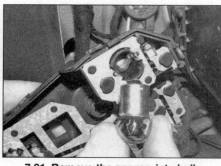
7.31 Remove the appropriate bulb

7.32 Remove the trim piece

the right-hand side open the jack storage compartment. Release the locking tab and remove the bulbholder (see illustrations).
31 Press and twist the relevant bulb anti-clockwise, and withdraw it from the bulbholder (see illustration).

32 To remove the light unit first remove the trim piece from below the lamp, using a plastic trim removal tool if necessary (see illustrations).
33 Release the plastic clip at the side by pushing the central peg inwards and then prising the main section free. Remove the

bumper mounting bracket fixing bolt (see illustrations).
34 Remove the rear access panel or storage compartment cover, as appropriate, and unplug the wiring connector.
35 Use a deep reach socket and extension bar to access the rear fixing nuts (see illustration). Remove the nuts and then manoeuvre the lamp free from the vehicle. Note that the lamp assembly must be manoeuvred around the bumper bracket by slightly distorting the bracket.
36 Refit in the reverse order of removal, ensuring that the seal is correctly positioned. Remove the small plastic peg from the plastic clip before refitting the clip (see illustration). On completion check for the satisfactory operation of all rear lights.

Tailgate-mounted

37 Open the tailgate, and remove the access flap.

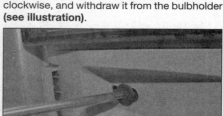
7.33a Push the central peg inwards to release the clip . . .

7.33b . . . and remove the bumper mounting bolt

7.35 Remove the mounting nuts (arrowed)

7.36 Refit the plastic locking peg

7.38 Remove the bulbholder

7.39 Remove the appropriate bulb

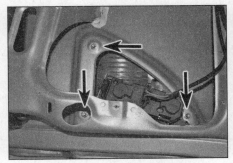

7.41 Remove the nuts (arrowed)

7.43 Remove the screws

7.44 Remove the bulb

7.48a With the trim piece removed,
unscrew . . .

7.48b . . . and then unplug the lamp

38 Depress the spring retainer and remove the bulbholder assembly **(see illustration)**.
39 Depress and twist the bulb, then withdraw it from the bulbholder **(see illustration)**.
40 To remove the light unit first remove the tailgate trim panel as described in Chapter 11, Section 33.
41 Slacken and remove the retaining nuts, and remove the light assembly from the tailgate **(see illustration)**. Disconnect the wiring plug as the lamp is removed.
42 Refit in the reverse order of removal, ensuring that the seal is correctly positioned. On completion check for the satisfactory operation of all rear lights.

Number plate lights

43 The number plate lights are located in the tailgate, just above the number plate. Undo the two retaining screws and remove the lamp **(see illustration)**.
44 The bulb is a festoon type bulb and can be removed by gently opening the locating arms of the bulbholder **(see illustration)**.
45 Refit in the reverse order of removal, and check the light for satisfactory operation.

High-level brake light

46 Open the tailgate and carefully remove the glass trim panel.
47 The high level brake light uses LEDs and not a conventional bulb. If a fault develops the complete assembly must be renewed.
48 Disconnect the wiring plug, remove the two fixing screws and withdraw the lamp **(see illustrations)**.
49 Before condemning the lamp use a

multimeter to check that there is battery voltage at the lamp when the brake pedal is pressed. The ignition must be on to conduct this test.
50 Refitting is a reversal of removal.

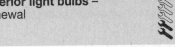

8 Interior light bulbs – renewal

1 Whenever a bulb is renewed, note the following points:
a) *Remember that if the light has just been in use, the bulb may be extremely hot.*
b) *Always check the bulb contacts and holder, ensuring that there is clean metal-to-metal contact between the bulb and its live(s) and earth. Clean off any corrosion or dirt before fitting a new bulb.*
c) *Wherever bayonet-type bulbs are fitted, ensure that the live contact(s) bear firmly against the bulb contact.*

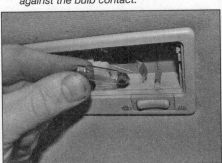

8.3 Remove the bulb

d) *Always ensure that the new bulb is of the correct rating and that it is completely clean before fitting it.*

Interior/reading lights

Front/centre interior lights

2 Unclip the lens from the light unit. Use a pad of soft material under the screwdriver to prevent damage to the surround.
3 Remove the bulb from its holder. The light is fitted with a festoon bulb which can be prised from its spring contacts **(see illustration)**.
4 Refit in the reverse order of removal.

Reading lights

5 Using a screwdriver, carefully prise the light unit from its location. Where a reading light is incorporated into the same unit as an interior light, the complete unit must be prised from position **(see illustrations)**.
6 With the unit removed, twist the bulbholder

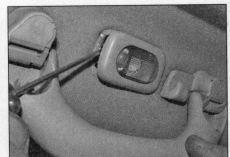

8.5a Remove the complete lamp from the lights above the grab handles . . .

8.5b ... or remove the complete combined light from the headlining

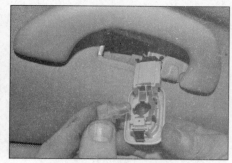

8.6a Remove the bulbholder ...

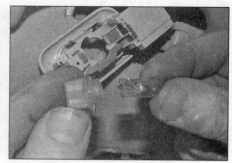

8.6b ... and pull the bulb free

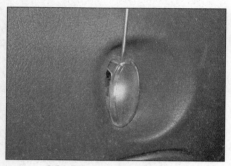

8.8a Prise the lamp free ...

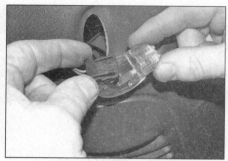

8.8b ... disconnect the wiring plug ...

8.8c ... and remove the bulb

anti-clockwise, and pull the capless bulb from the holder **(see illustrations)**.

7 Refitting is a reversal of removal.

Luggage area light, glovebox light, engine compartment light, and passenger footwell light

8 Prise free the light unit and extract the festoon bulb from its holder. When removing the glovebox light unit, prise the top of the lens out first **(see illustrations)**.

9 Refit in the reverse order of removal, and check for satisfactory operation.

Sunvisor/vanity mirror light

10 Prise free the mirror frame from the sunvisor. The festoon bulbs can be extracted from their holders **(see illustrations)**.

11 Refit in the reverse order of removal.

Instrument panel illumination

12 Remove the instrument panel as described in Section 10 of this Chapter.

13 There are no renewable bulbs in the instrument panel. LED type bulbs are used to illuminate the panel. If they are faulty the complete instrument panel will require renewal.

14 Refit in the reverse order of removal. If the panel has been renewed it will require programming, using suitable diagnostic equipment.

Cigar lighter illumination

15 In order to access the cigar lighter illumination bulbholder, it is necessary to remove the centre console trim panel as described in Chapter 11.

16 Leaving the cigar lighter in the panel, lift the plastic wiring cover from the rear, push out the metal body and then remove the green illuminated surround **(see illustrations)**.

17 Unclip the bulbholder, separate the two halves and remove the bulb **(see illustration)**.

18 Refit in the reverse order of removal.

Switch illumination

19 All switch illumination bulbs are built into the switch itself, and cannot be renewed separately. Refer to Section 6 and remove/renew the switch.

Heater control illumination

20 The heater controls are illuminated with LED type lights. If a fault develops the entire control unit must be renewed.

8.10a Prise the mirror frame from the sunvisor ...

8.10b ... and remove the bulb(s)

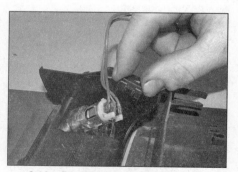

8.16a Remove the wiring cover ...

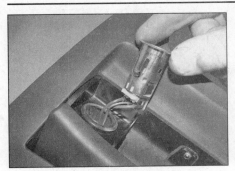

8.16b . . . push out the metal body . . .

8.16c . . . and then the surround

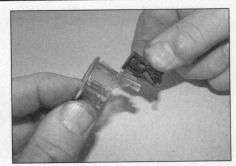

8.17a Remove the bulbholder . . .

Clock illumination

21 Carefully prise the clock from the centre of the facia. Use a pair of pliers to unscrew the bulbholder from the rear of the unit. The illumination bulb is integral with the bulbholder **(see illustrations)**.

22 Refitting is a reversal of removal.

| 9 | Headlights –
removal, refitting
and beam adjustment |

Headlight unit

 Warning: If working on a vehicle equipped with xenon headlights, gloves and safety glasses must be worn at all times.

Removal

1 The headlight assembly combines the

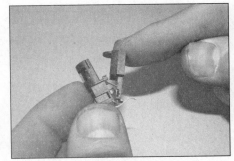

8.17b . . . separate the two halves . . .

8.17c . . . and use a small section of screen washer hose to remove the bulb

sidelights and direction indicators all into one single unit.

2 Open the bonnet and, to ease access to the lower mountings, remove the grille mounting screws **(see illustration)**. This allows the grille to be moved forward slightly.

3 Remove the covers from the upper mounting bolts and then remove the bolts **(see illustrations)**.

4 Remove the lower mounting bolts and pull the unit forward to remove it **(see illustrations)**.

8.21a Prise the clock free from the facia . . .

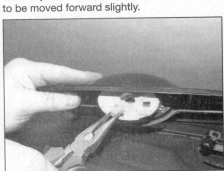

8.21b . . . and remove the bulbholder from the rear of the clock

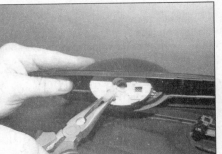

9.2 Remove the screws from the grille

9.3a Remove the covers and . . .

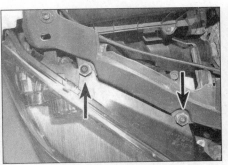

9.3b . . . then remove the bolts (arrowed)

9.4a Remove the lower mounting bolts . . .

9.4b . . . and then pull the headlight forward

9.9 Remove the screws

9.11a Remove the motor . . .

9.11b . . . and disconnect the wiring plug

9.14 The headlight aim adjusters (arrowed)

5 As the unit is removed disconnect the wiring plug from the rear of the unit.

Refitting

6 Refitting is a reversal of the removal procedure. On completion check for satisfactory operation, and have the headlight beam adjustment checked as soon as possible (see below).

Headlight levelling motor

Removal

7 Remove the headlight as described in the previous Section.
8 Remove the rear cover as described in Section 7 of this Chapter.
9 Undo the two control motor retaining screws (see illustration).
10 Use a thin-bladed screwdriver to release the motor from the mounting bracket.

11 Rotate the motor and remove it from the lamp. Disconnecting the wiring plug as the motor is removed (see illustrations).

Refitting

12 Install the range control motor wiring into the headlight unit wiring plug. The remainder of refitting is a reversal of removal. On completion, check for satisfactory operation, and have the headlight beam adjustment checked as soon as possible.

Beam adjustment

Halogen headlights

13 Accurate adjustment of the headlight beam is only possible using optical beam setting equipment, and this work should therefore be carried out by a Ford dealer or suitably-equipped workshop. All MOT test centres must have this equipment.

14 For reference, the headlights can be adjusted using the adjuster screws, accessible via the top of each light unit (see illustration).

Xenon headlights

15 To comply with the legal requirements all xenon headlights are self-adjusting and all have a headlight washer system fitted.
16 The left-hand headlight is the master unit and if this, or any of the level sensing units (fitted to the front and rear axle assemblies) are removed the system will require recalibrating using suitable diagnostic equipment. At the time of writing only Ford's own IDS diagnostic tool was capable of performing this task.

---

10 Instrument panel – removal and refitting

Removal

1 Disconnect the battery negative lead (refer to Section 1 and Chapter 5A) and lower the steering column. **Note:** *Before disconnecting the battery, refer to 'Disconnecting the battery' at the rear of this manual.*
2 With reference to Section 4 of this Chapter, detach and remove both the column shrouds and then remove the right-hand lower facia panel (see Chapter 11, Section 29).
3 Slacken and remove the two lower retaining screws and release the clip fixing from the top of the instrument panel (see illustration).
4 Tilt the panel towards the steering wheel, and manoeuvre it through the facia aperture. Disconnect the wiring plug(s) as the unit is withdrawn (see illustration).
5 No further dismantling of the instrument panel is possible. If any of the instrument panel components are faulty then the complete panel must be renewed.

Refitting

6 Refitting is a reversal of removal, but note that if a new panel is being fitted it will require programming to the vehicle with suitable diagnostic equipment.

10.3 Use a trim tool to free the instrument panel from the facia

10.4 Unplug the instrument panel as the unit is withdrawn

11.3a Mark the position of the blades with adhesive tape . . .

11.3b . . . then undo the nut and ease the arm from the spindle

11.3c Specialist tools are available to aid removal of the wiper arm if necessary

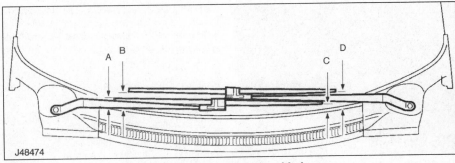

11.4 Position of the wiper blades

A = 16 to 26 mm   B = 64 to 74 mm   C = 19 to 29 mm   D = 56 to 66 mm

11.8 Remove the mounting bolts and recover the special washer (centre one shown)

11 Windscreen wiper components – removal and refitting

Wiper blades

1 Refer to *Weekly checks.*

Wiper arms

2 If the wipers are not in their parked position, switch on the ignition, and allow the motor to automatically park.

3 Before removing an arm, mark its parked position on the glass with a strip of adhesive tape. Prise off the cover and unscrew the spindle nut approximately two turns. Ease the arm from the spindle by rocking it slowly from side-to-side, then completely unscrew the nut and remove the arm (see illustrations).

4 Refitting is a reversal of removal, but before tightening the spindle nuts, position the wiper blades as marked before removal. If the original position of the arms has been lost, position the arm/blades as shown (see illustration).

Wiper linkage

Removal

5 Remove the wiper arms as described previously in this Section.

6 Remove the windscreen cowl and bulkhead panel as described in Section 12 of Chapter 11.

7 The wiper linkage is removed with the wiper motor as a single item.

8 Unbolt and remove the three mounting bolts (see illustration).

9 Remove the linkage from the vehicle, disconnect the wiring plug and unclip the wiring conduit as the linkage is removed (see illustrations).

Refitting

10 Refitting is a reversal of removal.

Wiper motor

Removal

11 Remove the linkage as described above and lever off the link arm.

12 Precisely mark the position of the crank arm and then remove it.

13 Remove the three wiper motor mounting bolts and then remove the motor.

Refitting

14 Refitting is the reverse of removal ensuring the that the crank arm is correctly positioned and the mounting bolts are tightened to the specified torque.

11.9a Disconnect the wiring plug . . .

11.9b . . . unclip the wiring conduit . . .

11.9c . . . and remove the linkage

12.2a Prise the pump free . . .

12.2b . . . disconnect the wiring . . .

12c . . . pull free the washer hoses . . .

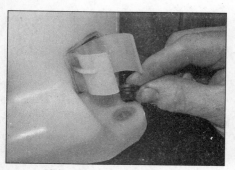

12d . . . and recover the seal

12.8 The washer jet is a push-fit in the wiper motor spindle

12 Washer system – general information

1 All models are fitted with a windscreen and tailgate window washer system. Some models are fitted with headlight washers.
2 The fluid reservoir for the windscreen washer (and where applicable, for the headlight washers) is located in the engine compartment behind the left-hand headlight. The fluid pump is attached to the side of the reservoir body (see illustrations). Some models may also have a level sensor fitted. Access to the reservoir and pump is achieved by removing the front bumper assembly – see Chapter 11. To remove the reservoir the front left-hand headlight must also be removed. **Note:** *On xenon headlight models, this will*

necessitate recalibration of the system with the Ford IDS diagnostic tool.
3 The tailgate washer is fed by the same reservoir and pump, operating in the reverse direction. Models that have the headlight washer system fitted have a separate washer pump fitted to the reservoir.
4 The reservoir fluid level must be regularly topped-up with windscreen washer fluid containing an antifreeze agent, but not cooling system antifreeze – see Weekly checks.
5 The supply hoses are a simple push-fit onto their various connections and if required, can be detached by simply pulling them free from the appropriate connector.
6 The windscreen washer jets can not be adjusted. It is possible to clean them out with a fine pin.
7 To remove a washer jet, remove the windscreen cowl, pull off the hose, disconnect

the wiring plug, and depress the locking tabs to remove the jet.
8 To remove the tailgate washer jet, open the wiper arm cover and pull the jet free from the wiper motor (see illustration).
9 Access to the headlight washer components is achieved by removing the front bumper cover (see Chapter 11).

13 Tailgate wiper motor – removal and refitting

Removal

1 Ensure that the wiper arm is in the parked position and then disconnect the battery negative lead. **Note:** *Before disconnecting the battery, refer to 'Disconnecting the battery' at the rear of this manual.*
2 Mark the position of the wiper arm. Lift up the plastic cover and remove the nut from the spindle.
3 Work the wiper arm free from the spindle (see illustration).
4 Remove the tailgate trim panel as described in Chapter 11, Section 33.
5 Detach the wiring connector and the washer supply hose from the wiper motor (see illustration).
6 Undo the bolts and remove the motor from the tailgate glass. If required the grommet can be removed from the glass.

Refitting

7 Refit in the reverse order of removal. Refit the wiper arm and blade so that the arm is parked correctly.

14 Horns – removal and refitting

Removal

1 Remove the front bumper as described in Chapter 11.
2 With the bumper removed, undo the horn unit retaining nut(s) and disconnect the wiring connector(s) (see illustration).

13.3 Remove the wiper arm

13.5 Remove the wiring plug and washer hose (arrowed)

Refitting

3 Refit in the reverse order of removal. Check for satisfactory operation on completion.

---

15 Sunroof motor – removal and refitting

Closing sunroof manually

1 If the motor malfunctions when the roof panel is in the open position, it can be wound shut manually. To do this, carefully prise the interior light assembly from the roof console, then undo the two console trim panel retaining screws, and push the trim panel to the rear. Release the manual cranking tool which is clipped to motor. Turn the cap on the lever hole in the direction of the arrow, insert the cranking tool into the hole at the end of the motor shaft. The tool can then be turned to close the sunroof as required.

Motor

Removal

2 Ensure that the sunroof is fully closed – refer to paragraph 1 if the motor has failed. Disconnect the battery negative lead (refer to Section 1 and Chapter 5A). **Note:** *Before disconnecting the battery, refer to 'Disconnecting the battery' at the rear of this manual.*

3 Carefully prise the interior light assembly from the roof console, and disconnect the wiring plugs. Take care not to damage the light surround.

4 Undo the two console retaining screws in the interior light aperture, and slide the console to the rear and withdraw it from the roof panel **(see illustration)**.

5 Disconnect the motor wiring plug, undo the two retaining screws, and remove the motor **(see illustration)**.

Refitting

6 Refit in the reverse order of removal, noting the following points:

a) *As with removal, it is important that the roof panel be in the closed position to ensure correct engagement. If the motor was activated whilst it was removed, or if a new motor is being fitted, it must be set for correct engagement before fitting. To do this, connect up the switch wiring to it and turn the switch to the closed position. This will activate the motor so that it is set at the closed position, ready for fitting.*

b) *Check for satisfactory operation of the sunroof on completion.*

---

16 Central locking system – general information

1 All models are equipped with a central door locking system, which automatically locks all doors and the rear tailgate in unison with the manual locking of either front door. The system is operated electronically with motors/switches incorporated into the door lock assemblies. The system is controlled by the generic electronic module (GEM) incorporated into the central junction box under the driver's side of the facia.

2 The control unit is equipped with a self-diagnosis capability. Should the system develop a fault, have the control unit interrogated by a Ford dealer or suitably-equipped specialist. Once the fault has been established, refer to the relevant Section of Chapter 11 to renew the door or tailgate lock.

---

17 Audio unit – removal and refitting

Note: *This Section applies only to standard-fit audio equipment.*

Removal

1 The radio/cassette/CD player is fitted with special mounting clips, requiring the use of dedicated removal tools. These tools are widely available.

2 Insert the removal rods in the holes provided on the upper and lower edges of the unit.

3 Slide the removal tools fully into the slots until they locate **(see illustration)**.

4 Withdraw the audio unit from the mounting case, then disconnect the wiring and aerial connectors. Note that some audio units also have a fuse fitted on the rear face.

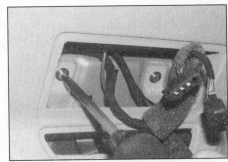

15.4 Undo the overhead console retaining screws

17.3 Slide the removal tools into the slots, gently push them to the outside, and pull the unit from the centre panel

14.2 The horns are accessible after the front bumper had been removed

Refitting

5 Refitting is a reversal of removal, but push the radio fully into its case until the spring clips are engaged. If the radio is of the security code type, it will be necessary to enter the code.

---

18 CD autochanger – removal and refitting

Note: *This Section applies only to standard-fit audio equipment.*

Removal

1 Raise the right-hand rear storage compartment lid, and remove the foam packing piece.

2 Undo the two retaining screws, and lift the autochanger from the storage compartment **(see illustration)**.

15.5 The sunroof motor is secured by two screws (arrowed)

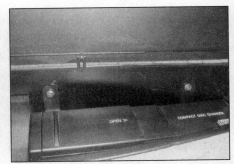

18.2 The CD autochanger is secured by two screws

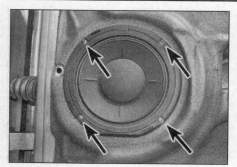

20.3 The door mounted mid-range speakers are retained by four screws (arrowed)

3 Depress the locking tab and disconnect the wiring plug.
4 If necessary, undo the Torx screws and remove the mounting brackets from each side of the unit.

Refitting

5 Refitting is a reversal of removal.

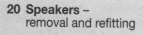

19 Radio aerial –
removal and refitting

1 The aerial is built into the right-hand rear side window. To remove the window, refer to Chapter 11, Section 21.

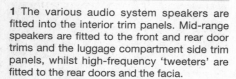

20 Speakers –
removal and refitting

1 The various audio system speakers are fitted into the interior trim panels. Mid-range speakers are fitted to the front and rear door trims and the luggage compartment side trim panels, whilst high-frequency 'tweeters' are fitted to the rear doors and the facia.

Door-mounted speaker

2 To remove a door-mounted mid-range speaker, remove the appropriate door trim as described in Chapter 11.
3 Undo the four retaining screws, and disconnect the wiring plug(s) as the speaker is withdrawn (see illustration).
4 Refit in the reverse order of removal.

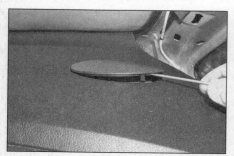

20.11 If necessary use a pad of soft material to prevent damage to the facia whilst prising out the speaker

20.6 Luggage compartment side trim speaker

Luggage area speaker

5 Remove the relevant luggage compartment side trim panel as described in Chapter 11, Section 33.
6 Disconnect the speaker wiring plug, undo the retaining nuts, and remove the speaker (see illustration).
7 Refitting is a reversal of removal.

Door-mounted tweeter

8 Remove the appropriate door trim as described in Chapter 11.
9 Disconnect the wiring plug to the speaker, release the four locking tabs with a small screwdriver, and remove the speaker (see illustration).
10 Refit in the reverse order of removal.

Facia-mounted tweeter

11 Using a small screwdriver, carefully prise the speaker cover from the facia (see illustration).
12 Remove the single mounting screw (see illustration) and disconnect the wiring plug as the speaker is withdrawn.
13 Refitting is a reversal of removal.

21 Airbag system –
general information and precautions

⚠️ **Warning:**
• *Before carrying out any operations on the airbag system, disconnect the battery negative terminal (see Chapter 5A), and wait at least 15*

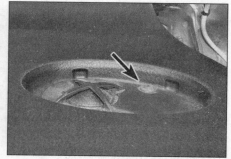

20.12 Remove the single screw (arrowed)

minutes before starting any operation. Ensure that the battery negative lead cannot accidentally be reconnected. Note: Before disconnecting the battery, refer to 'Disconnecting the battery' at the rear of this manual.
• *Before working on the airbag(s) or seat belt pretensioners, ensure you are electrostatically discharged by touching a suitable metal part, eg, a metal bench, or mains water pipe.*
• *Do not use a 'code saver' device when working on the supplementary restraint system.*
• *When operations are complete, make sure no one is inside the vehicle when the battery is reconnected.*
• *Note that the airbag(s) must not be subjected to temperatures in excess of 90°C. When the airbag is removed, ensure that it is stored the correct way up (padded surface uppermost) to prevent possible inflation.*
• *Do not allow any solvents or cleaning agents to contact the airbag assemblies. They must be cleaned using only a damp cloth.*
• *The airbags and control unit are both sensitive to impact. If either is dropped or damaged they should be renewed.*
• *Disconnect the airbag control unit wiring plug prior to using arc-welding equipment on the vehicle.*

A driver's airbag and a passenger airbag are fitted as standard to the Galaxy range. Side and curtain airbags are available as options. The driver's airbag is fitted to the centre of the steering wheel. The passenger's airbag is fitted to the upper surface of the facia. The airbag system comprises of the airbag unit(s) (complete with gas generators), an impact sensor (or sensors for vehicles fitted with multiple airbags) the control unit and a warning light in the instrument panel. All models feature front seat belt pretensioners. The deployment of the airbags is controlled by a centrally-located control module.

The airbag system is triggered in the event of a direct or offset frontal impact above a predetermined force. The airbag is inflated within milliseconds, and forms a safety cushion between the driver and the steering wheel or (where applicable) the passenger and

20.9 Disconnect the wiring plug, release the clips and remove the speaker

22.3 Note the position of the airbag retaining clip (arrowed)

22.5 Release the wiring plug

22.8 Remove the mounting nuts

the facia. This prevents contact between the upper body and the steering wheel, column and facia, and therefore greatly reduces the risk of injury. The airbag then deflates almost immediately through vents in the side of the airbag.

Every time the ignition is switched on, the airbag control unit performs a self-test. The self-test takes approximately 5 seconds, and during this time the airbag warning light on the facia is illuminated. After the self-test has been completed, the warning light should go out. If the warning light fails to come on, remains illuminated after the initial 5-second period, or comes on at any time when the vehicle is being driven, there is a fault in the airbag system. The vehicle should then be taken to a Ford dealer or a local garage, providing that they have suitable diagnostic equipment to interrogate the system.

22 Airbag system components – removal and refitting

Note: *Refer to the warnings in Section 21 before carrying out the following operations.*
1 Disconnect the battery negative terminal (see Section 1 and Chapter 5A), and wait at least 15 minutes before starting any procedure involving any airbag, control unit or sensor. **Note:** *Before disconnecting the battery, refer to 'Disconnecting the battery' at the rear of this manual.*

Driver's airbag

2 Set the steering wheel to straight-ahead, then turn it 90° to the left or right. Release the steering column adjustment lever, and pull the wheel out and down as far as possible.
3 The airbag is held in position by two hidden spring clips that are accessed from the rear of the steering wheel **(see illustration)**.
4 Rotate the steering wheel to improve access to the retaining clips and then release the clips using a flat-bladed screwdriver.
5 Return the steering wheel to the straight-ahead position, then carefully lift the airbag assembly away from the steering wheel and disconnect the wiring connector(s) from the rear of the unit **(see illustration)**. Note that the airbag must not be knocked or dropped, and

should be stored the correct way up with its padded surface uppermost.
6 On refitting, reconnect the wiring connector(s) and seat the airbag unit in the steering wheel, making sure the wire does not become trapped. Ensure the passenger compartment is unoccupied, then reconnect the battery negative lead.

Passenger airbag

7 The passenger side airbag is located below the upper facia panel. With reference to Chapter 11, remove the upper facia.
8 Slacken and remove the four retaining nuts and remove the passenger airbag from the support panel **(see illustration)**. Note that the airbag must not be knocked or dropped, and should be stored with its curved surface uppermost. Note that if the original airbag has been deployed, carefully check the facia for any signs of cracking, distortion, or whitening (indicating that the area has been stressed). If any of these defects are present, the facia must be renewed, as described in Chapter 11.
9 Refitting is a reversal of removal. Ensure that the wiring connector is securely reconnected.
10 Ensure that no-one is inside the vehicle, then reconnect the battery negative lead.

Airbag wiring contact unit (clock spring)

11 Position the steering wheel in the straight-ahead position and remove the key from the steering lock. Remove the driver's airbag as described in this Section and then remove the steering wheel as described in Chapter 10.
12 Release and remove the column shrouds.

Locate the three lower screws and two upper that hold the shrouds in position. Remove the screws and then remove the shrouds **(see illustrations 5.3a and 5.3b)**.
13 Release the locking tabs and pull the clock spring free from the multifunction switch **(see illustrations)**. Disconnect the wiring plugs from the horn and airbag. On models fitted with stability assist disconnect the wiring connector from the steering wheel position sensor.
14 Carefully withdraw the contact unit from the steering wheel. Do not attempt rotate the clock spring once removed from the vehicle. On vehicle fitted with stability assist (and no locking plunger) tape the two sections of the clock spring together.
15 Refit the contact unit to the steering wheel, and carry out the following centralisation procedure:
a) *Depress the locking plunger.*
b) *Rotate the outer rotor anti-clockwise until it becomes tight.*
c) *Rotate the outer rotor clockwise approximately 4.5 turns.*
d) *Rotate the outer rotor anti-clockwise until the plunger locks the rotor in position – this will be after approximately 2.75 revolutions. On vehicles with stability assist the raised arrow marking will align with a mark on the steering wheel position sensor.*

16 The remainder of refitting is a reversal of removal. On vehicles fitted with stability assist the system should be reconfigured using suitable diagnostic equipment.

22.13a Release the locking tabs (arrowed) . . .

22.13b . . . and remove the clock spring

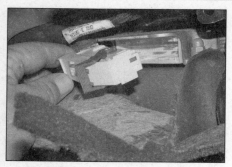

22.18 Remove the wiring connector

Airbag control unit

17 The control unit is located forward of the centre console. It is possible to remove with the centre console in position, but access is greatly improved if the console is removed as described in Chapter 11.

18 Release the locking tab and release the two-stage locking connector from the unit. Stage one disengages the connector terminals, and stage two releases the connector from the control unit **(see illustration)**.

19 Undo the three retaining nuts and remove the control unit.

20 Refitting is a reversal of removal.

Side airbags

21 The side airbags are incorporated into the side of the front seats. Remove the appropriate front seat as described in Chapter 11.

22 Carefully lever the seat back adjuster free with a suitable broad-bladed screwdriver or plastic trim tool.

23 On models with rotating front seats remove the cover from the lever and then unscrew and remove the lever.

24 If equipped, remove the armrest. Prise the cover plug free and remove the retaining screw.

25 Remove the plug from the lumbar adjuster and then remove the control knob and plastic surround.

26 Next remove the seat outer trim panel. This is secured by a single screw, a clip and a locking tab.

27 Working at the rear of the seat remove the trim cover and retaining pins and then remove the folding tray.

25.1 The temperature sensor (arrowed)

28 On a clean surface invert the seat and detach the wiring harness for the airbag from the side of the seat. The cable-ties must be cut to release the wiring loom.

29 Pull down and release the back rest outer cover retaining strap. Partially roll up the cover to access the front and back cover tensioning clips. Release the clips and spreader. Roll up the seat back cover to expose the upper tensioning bar.

30 Detach the upper tensioning bar, fully roll up the seat cover and use a 5 mm hex key to release the airbag lower mounting.

31 Unbolt the upper airbag mounting and pull forward the upper portion of the airbag. Lift out the airbag and disconnect the wiring plug. Remove and discard the airbag retaining clip and sleeve.

32 Refitting is a reversal of the removal procedure, but a new retaining sleeve and nuts must be fitted. These are normally part of the service kit supplied with the new airbag.

Crash sensors for side airbags

33 The sensors are located under each front seat. Remove the appropriate front seat as described in Chapter 11.

34 Remove the trim panel, note the wiring harness routing, and disconnect the sensor wiring plug.

35 Unscrew the two retaining bolts. Remove the sensor.

36 Refitting is a reversal of removal. Ensure the passenger compartment is unoccupied prior to reconnecting the battery negative lead.

Curtain airbag

37 Some models feature a side curtain airbag. The renewal of the side curtain airbag requires the removal of the vehicle headlining. This work should be trusted to a local Ford dealer or fully equipped specialist garage.

Crash sensors for curtain airbags

38 Remove the rear seats and the C-pillar trim panel as described in Chapter 11.

39 Prise free the lower section of the D-pillar trim panel and where fitted remove the luggage compartment cover.

40 Unbolt and remove the lower rear seat belt anchorage and then remove the load space cover locating bracket.

26.4a Slacken the screws . . .

41 On the appropriate side remove the load space trim panel as described in Chapter 11, Section 33.

42 Unplug the wiring connector and then unbolt the crash sensor.

43 Refitting is a reversal of removal. Ensure the passenger compartment is unoccupied prior to reconnecting the battery negative lead.

23 Anti-theft alarm system – general information

An engine immobiliser is fitted as standard, and a volumetric sensing perimeter alarm is available as an option.

Should the system(s) become faulty, the vehicle should be taken to a Ford dealer or suitably-equipped specialist for examination. They will have access to a special diagnostic tester which will assist in tracing any fault present in the system.

24 Clock – removal and refitting

Removal

1 Using a screwdriver, carefully prise the clock from the centre of the fascia **(see illustration 8.21a)**.

2 Disconnect the wiring plug as the clock is removed. If required the bulb can be renewed as described in Section 8 of this Chapter.

Refitting

3 Refitting is a reversal of removal.

25 Ambient air temperature sensor – removal and refitting

Removal

1 The sensor is located behind the front bumper at the left-hand side of the vehicle **(see illustration)**.

2 Jack up and support the front of the vehicle, reach up and unclip the sensor.

3 Disconnect the sensor wiring plug as the sensor is removed.

Refitting

4 Refitting is a reversal of removal.

26 Fuel filler flap lock motor – removal and refitting

Removal

1 Working in the luggage compartment, remove the vehicle jack storage cover.

2 Prise out and remove the seat belt guide from the luggage compartment side panel.

3 Undo the retaining screws and remove the rear storage box. On models fitted with a multi-disk CD player, remove the unit as described in Section 18 of this Chapter.
4 Disconnect the lock motor wiring plug, slacken the two retaining bolts, unhook the operating lever and remove the motor (**see illustrations**).

Refitting

5 Refitting is a reversal of removal.

27 Cruise control system – general information, and component renewal

General information

Both petrol and diesel versions of the Galaxy can be specified with cruise control. On petrol models, the system comprises an electronic control module (ECM), a vacuum pump, a brake pedal switch/vacuum valve, a clutch pedal switch/vacuum valve (manual transmission models only), an accelerator pedal vacuum servo, and the driver's control switches.

The electrically-driven vacuum pump provides an independent vacuum supply to the speed control unit which operates directly on the accelerator pedal. The clutch and brake pedal switches also incorporate a vacuum supply configured so that as soon as the brake or clutch pedal are used the vacuum to the accelerator control is vented and the throttle is immediately closed.

On diesel models, the cruise control system is purely electronic, comprising of brake and clutch pedal switches, and driver control switches. The system control is incorporated into the electronic diesel control ECM, which regulates the amount of fuel injected into the engine to maintain the desired speed.

Component renewal

Driver's speed control switch

1 The driver's speed control switch is an integral part of the steering column combination switch – refer to Section 5.

Brake pedal switch/vacuum valve (petrol models)

2 Open the central fusebox cover on the driver's side of the lower facia. Hinge the cover down and pull it from the hinges.
3 Remove the right-hand lower facia trim panel (see Chapter 11, Section 29).
4 Disconnect the wiring plug and the vacuum hose from the switch/valve (**see illustration**).
5 Unscrew the switch from the mounting bracket.
6 To refit the switch, hold the pedal in the rest position, and screw the switch into the bracket until the plunger reaches its stop position (**see illustration**). Reconnect the wiring plug and the vacuum pipe. The remainder of refitting is a reversal of removal.

26.4b . . . and remove the fuel filler flap motor (shown with the trim panel removed)

Clutch pedal switch/vacuum valve (petrol models)

7 The procedure for the clutch switch is identical to that given for the brake pedal switch earlier in this Section.

Brake pedal switch (diesel models)

8 Open the central electrical box cover on the driver's side of the lower facia. Hinge the cover down and pull it from the hinges.
9 Undo the retaining screws and remove the lower facia trim panel.
10 Disconnect the switch wiring plug, and turn the switch anti-clockwise to remove it.
11 Refitting is a reversal of removal.

Clutch pedal switch (diesel models)

12 The procedure for the clutch switch is identical to that given for the brake pedal switch earlier in this Section.

27.4 Disconnect the vacuum hose and wiring plug from the switch

27.14 Disconnect the wiring plug as the ECM is removed

Speed electronic control module (ECM)

13 Remove the fusebox and relay plate as described in Section 3 of this Chapter.
14 Unscrew the retaining nut, and disconnect the wiring plug as the ECM is removed (**see illustration**).
15 Refitting is a reversal of removal.

Vacuum pump

16 The vacuum pump is located behind the front bumper. Remove the front bumper as described in Chapter 11.
17 Disconnect the wiring plug and the vacuum hose.
18 Unbolt and remove the pump.
19 Refitting is a reversal of removal.

Accelerator pedal vacuum servo

20 Open the fusebox cover on the driver's side of the lower facia. Hinge the cover down and pull it from the hinges.
21 Undo the six retaining screws and remove the lower facia trim panel (see Chapter 11, Section 29).
22 Disconnect the vacuum pipe from the servo (**see illustration**).
23 Using a screwdriver, carefully prise the servo actuating rod from the accelerator pedal.
24 Undo the retaining nut and remove the servo.
25 To refit the servo, position the unit in the mounting bracket and tighten the retaining nut securely.
26 Push the actuating rod back onto the accelerator pedal, and reconnect the vacuum pipe.

27.6 Screw in the switch until the plunger is fully retracted

27.22 Disconnect the vacuum pipe from the servo unit

27 To reset the servo, turn the adjusting sleeve anti-clockwise, and pull it fully forward.
28 Check, and if necessary, adjust the accelerator cable (see Chapter 4A).

29 Push the servo adjusting sleeve backwards until all play at the pedal is eliminated. Turn the adjusting sleeve clockwise to lock it in position. Check the accelerator pedal for freedom of movement.
30 The remainder of refitting is a reversal of removal.

Ford Galaxy wiring diagrams

Diagram 1

At the time of writing, certain wiring diagram technical information was unavailable. As a result these diagrams are intended as a representative set covering most major electrical systems typically encountered on this model range.

 WARNING: This vehicle is fitted with a supplemental restraint system (SRS) consisting of a combination of driver (and passenger) airbag(s), side impact protection airbags and seatbelt pre-tensioners. The use of electrical test equipment on any SRS wiring systems may cause the seatbelt pre-tensioners to abruptly retract and airbags to explosively deploy, resulting in potentially severe personal injury. Extreme care should be taken to correctly identify any circuits to be tested to avoid choosing any of the SRS wiring in error.
For further information see airbag system precautions in body electrical systems chapter.
Note: The SRS wiring harness can normally be identified by yellow and/or orange harness or harness connectors.

Key to symbols

Solenoid actuator

Earth point and location

Wire colour (blue with white tracer) — Bu/Wh

Dashed outline denotes part of a larger item, containing in this case an electronic or solid state device (pins 23 and 24 of connector 2).

Bulb

Switch

Fuse/Fusible link F26

Resistor

Variable resistor

Variable resistor

Wire splice, soldered joint, or unspecified connector

Connecting wires

Diode

Light-emitting diode

Item number 12

Motor/pump

Heating element

Passenger fusebox ⑤

F1	10A	Engine management
F2	10A	Electric windows, electric mirrors, rear vent windows
F3	5A	Automatic speed control, glovebox light, clock, sunroof, navigation, automatic temperature control, heated seats
F4	10A	Engine management
F5	15A	Automatic transmission, reversing light
F6	10A	Horn
F7	25A	Cigar lighter
F8	15A	Luggage compartment accessory connector 1
F9	5A	Auxiliary heating (without heated seats)
	15A	Heated seats
F10	15A	Luggage compartment accessory connector 2
F11	20A	Headlight washer (without trailer)
	25A	Trailer
F12	25A	Auxiliary heater
F13	3A	Engine management (petrol)
	10A	Engine management (Diesel)
F14	25A	Engine management (Diesel)
	20A	Engine management (petrol)
	30A	Engine management (petrol)
F15	10A	Stop lights
F16	15A	Air conditioning
F17	10A	Automatic transmission
F18	5A	Engine cooling fan
F19	5A	Central locking, park assist, audio, diagnostics, automatic temperature control, instrument cluster
F20	5A	Front/rear wiper
F21	25A	Air conditioning
F22	30A	Air conditioning
F23	10A	Heated mirrors
F24	30A	Front wiper
F25	30A	Starter/immobiliser
F26	15A	Front foglights
F27	25A	Power supply, interior lighting
F28	3A	Number plate light, headlight levelling, lighting dimmer
F29	20A	Engine management (Diesel)
F30	20A	Audio system
F31	3A	Audio system
F32	5A	Engine management
F33	30A	Front heater blower
F34	5A	Engine management (petrol)
	10A	Engine management (Diesel)
F51	20A	Heated rear window, heared mirrors
F52	20A	Direction indicators
F53	10A	Cut-off
F54	10A	Alarm
F55	5A	Power supply
F56	5A	RH side light
F57	5A	LH side light
F58	10A	Daytme running light
F59	5A	LH dip beam
F60	5A	RH dip beam
F61	10A	LH main beam
F62	10A	RH main beam

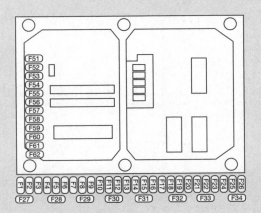

H47396

Colour codes

Wh	White	**Og**	Orange
Bu	Blue	**Rd**	Red
Gy	Grey	**Pk**	Pink
Ye	Yellow	**Gn**	Green
Bn	Brown	**Vt**	Violet
Bk	Black	**Sr**	Silver
Na	Natural	**Lg**	Light green

Key to items

1 Battery
2 Engine fusebox
3 Starter motor
4 Alternator
5 Ignition switch
6 Passenger fusebox
a = compressor clutch control unit
R149 = load reduction relay
R182 = horn relay
R191 = starter relay
R245 = cooling fan run-on relay

8   Horn (high tone)
9   Horn (low tone)
10 Steering wheel clock spring
11 Horn switch
12 Luggage comp. accessory socket 1
13 Luggage comp. accessory socket 2
14 Cigar lighter
15 Cooling fan control unit
16 Cooling fan 1
17 Cooling fan 2
18 Engine management control unit

19 Heater blower switch
20 Three way pressure switch
21 Outside air thermo-switch
22 Thermo-switch

Diagram 2

H47397

Starting and charging

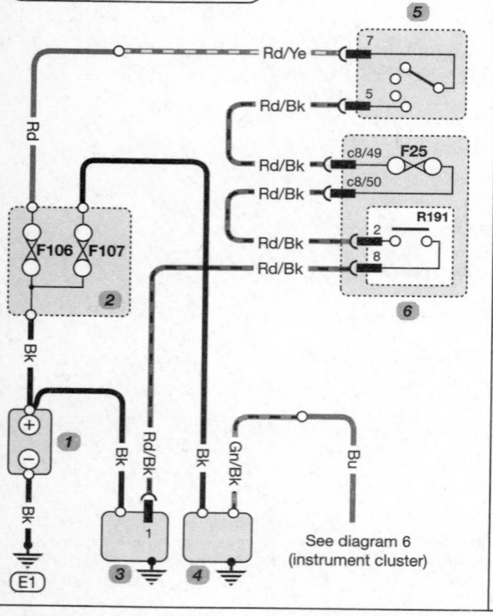

Horn

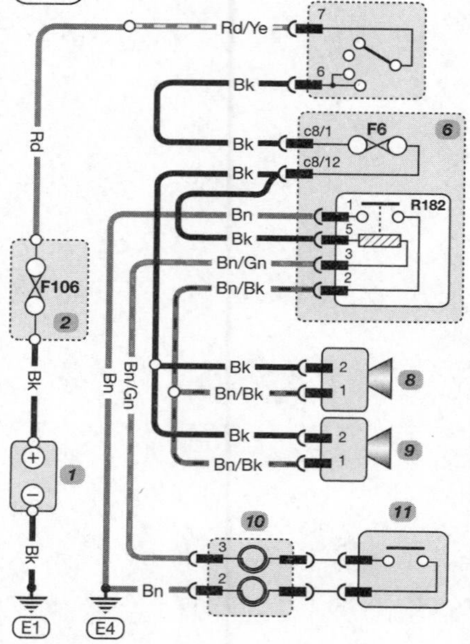

Cigarette lighter & accessory sockets

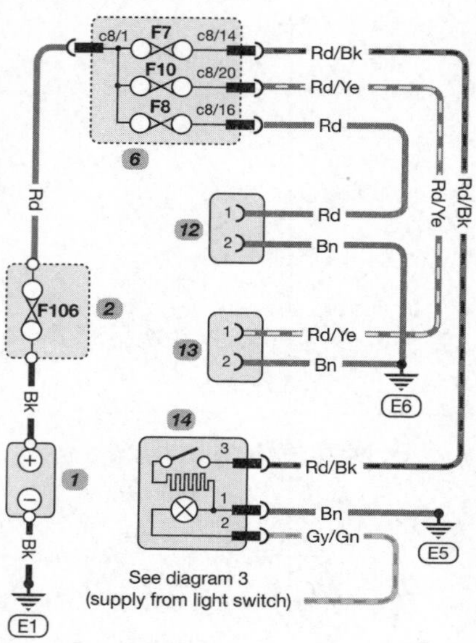

See diagram 6 (instrument cluster)

See diagram 3 (supply from light switch)

Engine cooling fan

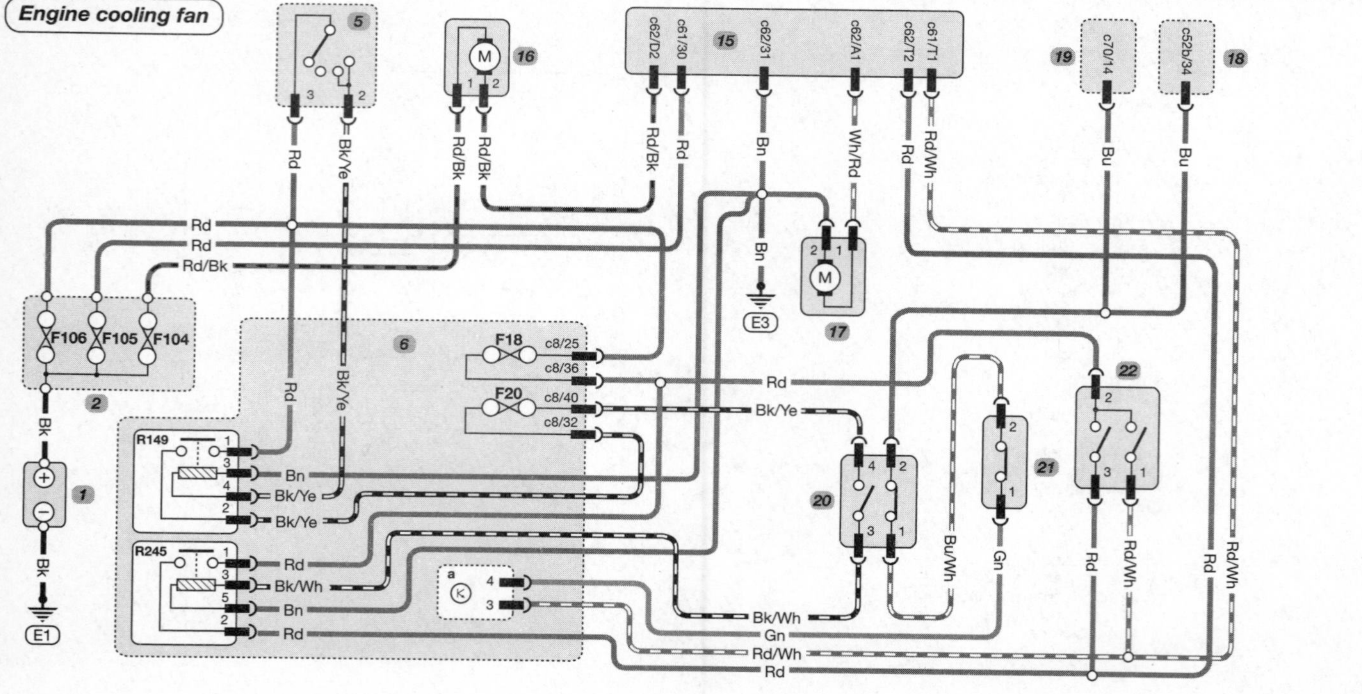

Colour codes

Wh	White	Og	Orange
Bu	Blue	Rd	Red
Gy	Grey	Pk	Pink
Ye	Yellow	Gn	Green
Bn	Brown	Vt	Violet
Bk	Black	Sr	Silver
Na	Natural	Lg	Light green

Key to items

1 Battery
2 Engine fusebox
5 Ignition switch
6 Passenger fusebox
   b = control unit
7 Instrument cluster
25 Stop light switch
26 Reversing light switch
27 LH tailgate light unit
   a = reversing light
   b = foglight

28 RH tailgate light unit
   a = reversing light
   b = foglight
29 LH rear light assembly
   a = stop light
   b = tail light
   c = direction indicator
30 RH rear light assembly
   a = stop light
   b = tail light
   c = direction indicator

31 High level brake light
32 Light switch
   a = side/headlight switch
   b = foglight switch
33 Steering column switch
   a = parking light
   b = direction indicator
34 LH headlight unit
   a = side light
   b = direction indicator

35 RH headlight unit
   a = side light
   b = direction indicator
36 Number plate light
37 Hazard warning light
38 LH indicator side repeater
39 RH indicator side repeater
40 LH front foglight
41 RH front foglight

Diagram 3

H47398

Stop & reversing lights

Engine management/
Automatic transmission/
ABS (not shown)

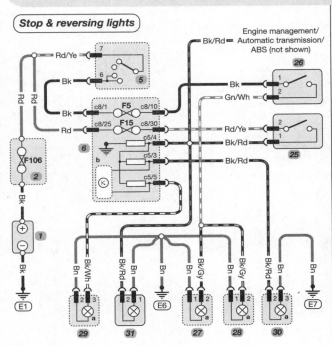

Side, tail & number plate lights

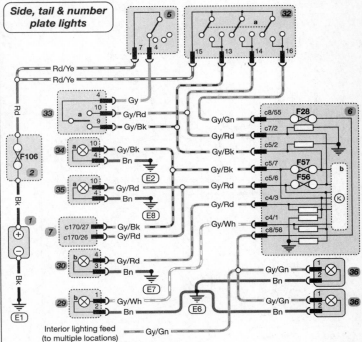

Interior lighting feed
(to multiple locations)

Fog lights

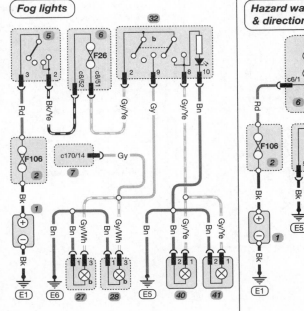

**Hazard warning lights
& direction indicators**

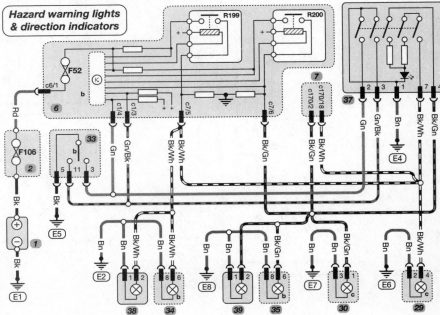

Colour codes

Wh	White	**Og**	Orange
Bu	Blue	**Rd**	Red
Gy	Grey	**Pk**	Pink
Ye	Yellow	**Gn**	Green
Bn	Brown	**Vt**	Violet
Bk	Black	**Sr**	Silver
Na	Natural	**Lg**	Light green

Key to items

1 Battery
2 Engine fusebox
5 Ignition switch
6 Passenger fusebox
   b = control unit
   R96 = interior light delay relay
   R126 = accessory delay relay
32 Light switch
   a = side/headlight switch

34 LH headlight unit
   c = dip/main beam
   d = headlight levelling adjuster
35 RH headlight unit
   (c and d as above)
45 Headlight levelling switch
46 Footwell light
47 Glove box light
48 Glove box light switch

49 Door entry light
50 Luggage compartment light
51 Interior light front
52 Interior light rear
53 Map reading light
54 Vanity mirror light
55 Map reading light (3rd row seat)

Diagram 4

H47399

Headlights

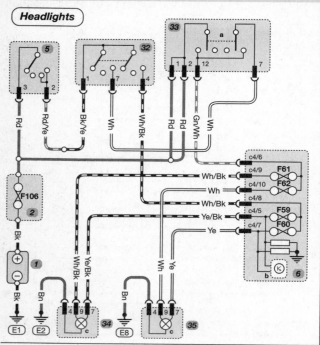

Headlight levelling

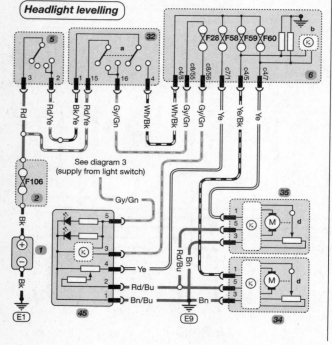

See diagram 3
(supply from light switch)

Interior lighting

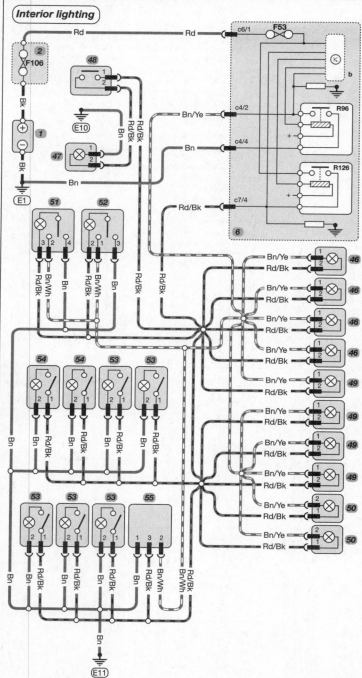

Diagram 5

Colour codes

Wh	White	**Og**	Orange
Bu	Blue	**Rd**	Red
Gy	Grey	**Pk**	Pink
Ye	Yellow	**Gn**	Green
Bn	Brown	**Vt**	Violet
Bk	Black	**Sr**	Silver
Na	Natural	**Lg**	Light green

Key to items

1 Battery
2 Engine fusebox
5 Ignition switch
6 Passenger fusebox
  b   = control unit
  R1 = heated rear window relay
  R149 = load reduction relay
  R164 = heated mirror relay
  R251 = heated mirror relay
33 Steering column switch
  c   = front wiper

  d   = front washer & rear wash/wipe
  e   = variable wiper
58 Front wiper motor
59 Rear wiper motor
60 Front/rear washer pump
61 Heated rear window
62 LH mirror assembly
  a   = heating element
63 RH mirror assembly
  a   = heating element
64 Heated rear window switch

65 Heated windscreen switch
66 LH heated windscreen element
67 RH heated windscreen element
68 LH heated washer jet
69 RH heated washer jet

H47400

Wash/wipe

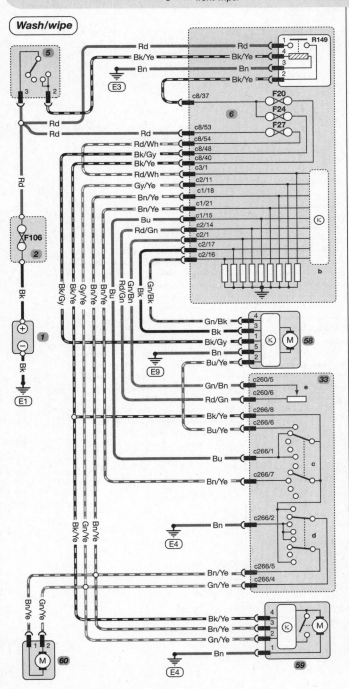

Heated front/rear screen & heated washer jets

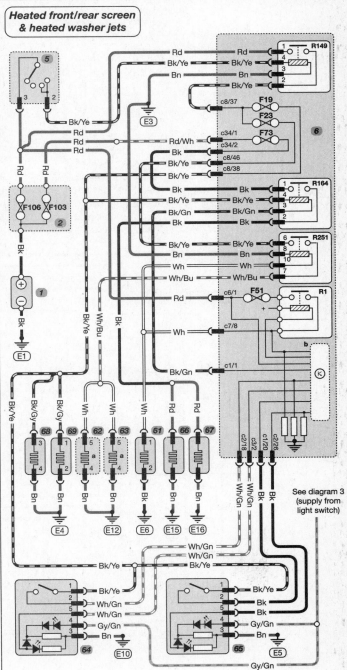

See diagram 3
(supply from
light switch)

Colour codes

Wh	White	**Og**	Orange
Bu	Blue	**Rd**	Red
Gy	Grey	**Pk**	Pink
Ye	Yellow	**Gn**	Green
Bn	Brown	**Vt**	Violet
Bk	Black	**Sr**	Silver
Na	Natural	**Lg**	Light green

Key to items

1 Battery
2 Engine fusebox
5 Ignition switch
6 Passenger fusebox
  b   = control unit
18 Engine management control unit
33 Steering column switch
72 Vehicle speed sensor
73 Low brake fluid switch
74 Handbrake switch
75 Low oil pressure switch
76 Low washer fluid level sensor
77 Outside air temperature sensor
78 Fuel pump/fuel level sensor
79 Coolant level sensor

80 Tailgate switch
81 LH front door switch
82 LH rear door switch
83 RH front door switch
84 RH rear door switch
85 LH front pad wear sensor
86 LH rear pad wear sensor
87 RH front pad wear sensor
88 RH rear pad wear sensor
89 Instrument cluster
  a   = illumination
  b   = ABS warning light
  c   = TCS warning light
  d   = speedometer
  e   = alternator warning light

f = low coolant level warning light
g = coolant temperature sensor
h = fuel gauge
i = low fuel warning light
j = glow plug warning light
k = low oil pressure warning light
l = low washer fluid
m = ice warning light
n = low brake fluid/handbrake warning light
o = bulb failure warning light
p = door ajar warning light
q = trip computer
r = pad wear warning light
90 Diagnostic connector

Diagram 6

H47401

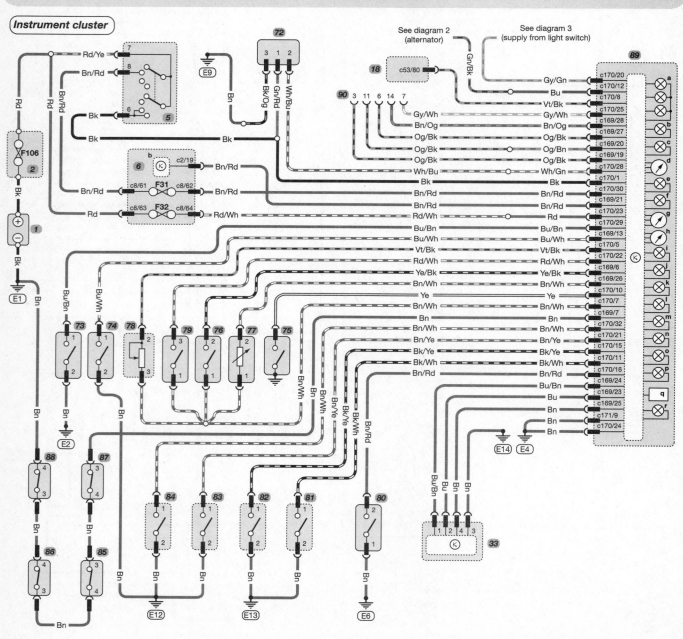

Instrument cluster

Colour codes

Wh	White	**Og**	Orange
Bu	Blue	**Rd**	Red
Gy	Grey	**Pk**	Pink
Ye	Yellow	**Gn**	Green
Bn	Brown	**Vt**	Violet
Bk	Black	**Sr**	Silver
Na	Natural	**Lg**	Light green

Key to items

1 Battery
2 Engine fusebox
5 Ignition switch
6 Passenger fusebox
  b = control unit
  R149 = load reduction relay
18 Engine management control unit
19 Heater blower switch
62 LH mirror assembly
  b = up/down motor
  c = left/right motor

63 RH mirror assembly
  b = up/down motor
  c = left/right motor
95 Heater blower resistors
96 Heater blower motor
97 Sunroof motor assembly
98 Sunroof switch
99 Audio unit
100 LH front door speaker
101 LH front tweeter
102 LH rear speaker

103 RH front door speaker
104 RH front tweeter
105 RH rear speaker
106 Electric mirror control switch

Diagram 7

H47402

Heater blower
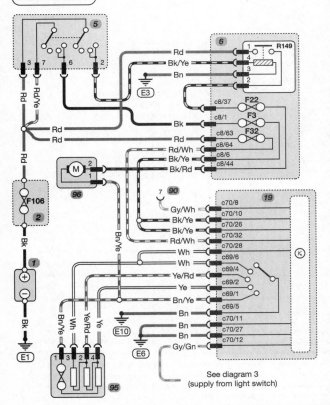

Sunroof
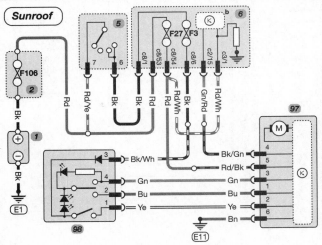

Audio system
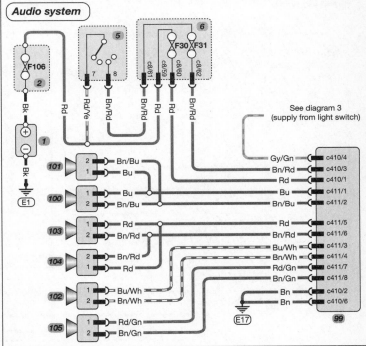

Electric mirrors
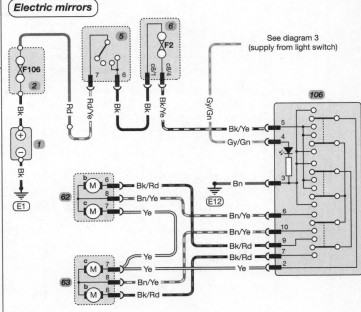

Colour codes

Wh	White	**Og**	Orange
Bu	Blue	**Rd**	Red
Gy	Grey	**Pk**	Pink
Ye	Yellow	**Gn**	Green
Bn	Brown	**Vt**	Violet
Bk	Black	**Sr**	Silver
Na	Natural	**Lg**	Light green

Key to items

1 Battery
2 Engine fusebox
5 Ignition switch
6 Passenger fusebox
80 Tailgate switch
81 LH front door switch
82 LH rear door switch
83 RH front door switch
84 RH rear door switch

110 Driver's window switch
   a = door lock switch
111 Driver's door lock motor
112 Passenger's door lock motor
113 LH rear door lock motor
114 RH rear door lock motor
115 Fuel filler flap lock motor
116 Tailgate lock motor
117 Driver's door lock switch

118 Passenger's door lock switch
119 Tailgate lock switch
120 Alarm 'on' indicator
121 Tailgate outside switch

Diagram 8

H47403

Central locking

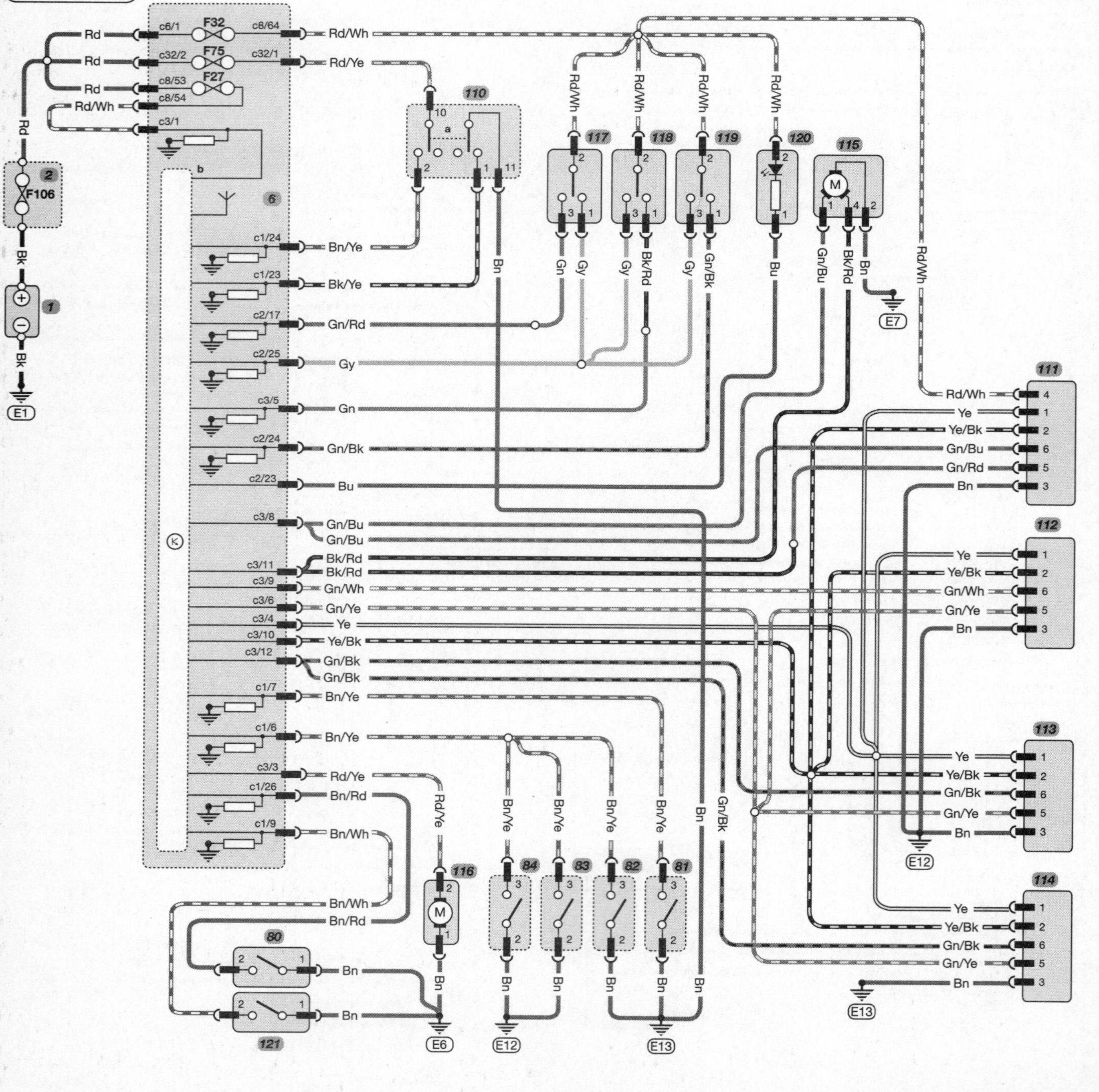

Colour codes

Wh	White	**Og**	Orange
Bu	Blue	**Rd**	Red
Gy	Grey	**Pk**	Pink
Ye	Yellow	**Gn**	Green
Bn	Brown	**Vt**	Violet
Bk	Black	**Sr**	Silver
Na	Natural	**Lg**	Light green

Key to items

1   Battery
2   Engine fusebox
5   Ignition switch
6   Passenger fusebox
  b = control unit
110 Driver's window switch
  b = driver's window switch
  c = passenger's window
  d = RH rear window switch

e = LH rear window switch
f = rear window isolator switch
117 Driver's door lock switch
125 Driver's door control unit
126 Passenger's door control unit
127 LH rear door control unit
128 RH rear door control unit
129 Passenger's window switch
130 LH rear window switch

131 RH rear window switch

Diagram 9

H47404

Electric windows

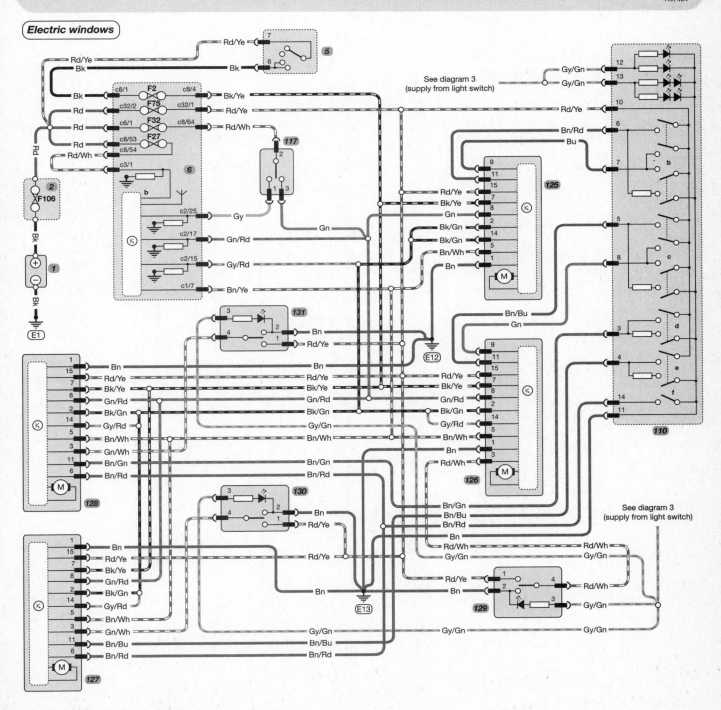

Dimensions and weights

Note: *All figures are approximate, and may vary according to model. Refer to manufacturer's data for exact figures.*

Dimensions
Overall length	4641 mm
Overall width (excluding mirrors)	1810 mm
Overall height (unladen)	1707 to 1820 mm
Turning circle	11.7 m

Weights
Kerb weight:
Petrol engine models	1669 to 1977 kg (manual) or 1699 to 2007 kg (automatic)
Diesel engine models	1724 to 2003 kg (manual) or 1757 to 2014 kg (automatic)

Permissible gross weight:
Petrol engine.	2470 kg
Diesel engine model	2510 kg
Maximum roof rack load	75 kg

Fuel economy

Although depreciation is still the biggest part of the cost of motoring for most car owners, the cost of fuel is more immediately noticeable. These pages give some tips on how to get the best fuel economy.

Working it out

Manufacturer's figures

Car manufacturers are required by law to provide fuel consumption information on all new vehicles sold. These 'official' figures are obtained by simulating various driving conditions on a rolling road or a test track. Real life conditions are different, so the fuel consumption actually achieved may not bear much resemblance to the quoted figures.

How to calculate it

Many cars now have trip computers which will

display fuel consumption, both instantaneous and average. Refer to the owner's handbook for details of how to use these.

To calculate consumption yourself (and maybe to check that the trip computer is accurate), proceed as follows.

1. Fill up with fuel and note the mileage, or zero the trip recorder.
2. Drive as usual until you need to fill up again.
3. Note the amount of fuel required to refill the tank, and the mileage covered since the previous fill-up.
4. Divide the mileage by the amount of fuel used to obtain the consumption figure.

For example:

Mileage at first fill-up (a) = 27,903
Mileage at second fill-up (b) = 28,346
Mileage covered (b - a) = 443
Fuel required at second fill-up = 48.6 litres

The half-completed changeover to metric units in the UK means that we buy our fuel

in litres, measure distances in miles and talk about fuel consumption in miles per gallon. There are two ways round this: the first is to convert the litres to gallons before doing the calculation (by dividing by 4.546, or see Table 1). So in the example:

48.6 litres ÷ 4.546 = 10.69 gallons
443 miles ÷ 10.69 gallons = 41.4 mpg

The second way is to calculate the consumption in miles per litre, then multiply that figure by 4.546 (or see Table 2).

So in the example, fuel consumption is:

443 miles ÷ 48.6 litres = 9.1 mpl
9.1 mpl x 4.546 = 41.4 mpg

The rest of Europe expresses fuel consumption in litres of fuel required to travel 100 km (l/100 km). For interest, the conversions are given in Table 3. In practice it doesn't matter what units you use, provided you know what your normal consumption is and can spot if it's getting better or worse.

Table 1: conversion of litres to Imperial gallons

litres	1	2	3	4	5	10	20	30	40	50	60	70
gallons	0.22	0.44	0.66	0.88	1.10	2.24	4.49	6.73	8.98	11.22	13.47	15.71

Table 2: conversion of miles per litre to miles per gallon

miles per litre	5	6	7	8	9	10	11	12	13	14
miles per gallon	23	27	32	36	41	46	50	55	59	64

Table 3: conversion of litres per 100 km to miles per gallon

litres per 100 km	4	4.5	5	5.5	6	6.5	7	8	9	10
miles per gallon	71	63	56	51	47	43	40	35	31	28

Maintenance

A well-maintained car uses less fuel and creates less pollution. In particular:

Filters

Change air and fuel filters at the specified intervals.

Oil

Use a good quality oil of the lowest viscosity specified by the vehicle manufacturer (see *Lubricants and fluids*). Check the level often and be careful not to overfill.

Spark plugs

When applicable, renew at the specified intervals.

Tyres

Check tyre pressures regularly. Under-inflated tyres have an increased rolling resistance. It is generally safe to use the higher pressures specified for full load conditions even when not fully laden, but keep an eye on the centre band of tread for signs of wear due to over-inflation.

When buying new tyres, consider the 'fuel saving' models which most manufacturers include in their ranges.

Driving style

Acceleration

Acceleration uses more fuel than driving at a steady speed. The best technique with modern cars is to accelerate reasonably briskly to the desired speed, changing up through the gears as soon as possible without making the engine labour.

Air conditioning

Air conditioning absorbs quite a bit of energy from the engine – typically 3 kW (4 hp) or so. The effect on fuel consumption is at its worst in slow traffic. Switch it off when not required.

Anticipation

Drive smoothly and try to read the traffic flow so as to avoid unnecessary acceleration and braking.

Automatic transmission

When accelerating in an automatic, avoid depressing the throttle so far as to make the transmission hold onto lower gears at higher speeds. Don't use the 'Sport' setting, if applicable.

When stationary with the engine running, select 'N' or 'P'. When moving, keep your left foot away from the brake.

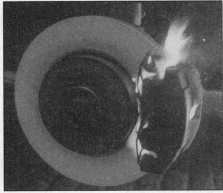

Braking

Braking converts the car's energy of motion into heat – essentially, it is wasted. Obviously some braking is always going to be necessary, but with good anticipation it is surprising how much can be avoided, especially on routes that you know well.

Carshare

Consider sharing lifts to work or to the shops. Even once a week will make a difference.

Electrical loads

Electricity is 'fuel' too; the alternator which charges the battery does so by converting some of the engine's energy of motion into electrical energy. The more electrical accessories are in use, the greater the load on the alternator. Switch off big consumers like the heated rear window when not required.

Freewheeling

Freewheeling (coasting) in neutral with the engine switched off is dangerous. The effort required to operate power-assisted brakes and steering increases when the engine is not running, with a potential lack of control in emergency situations.

In any case, modern fuel injection systems automatically cut off the engine's fuel supply on the overrun (moving and in gear, but with the accelerator pedal released).

Gadgets

Bolt-on devices claiming to save fuel have been around for nearly as long as the motor car itself. Those which worked were rapidly adopted as standard equipment by the vehicle manufacturers. Others worked only in certain situations, or saved fuel only at the expense of unacceptable effects on performance, driveability or the life of engine components.

The most effective fuel saving gadget is the driver's right foot.

Journey planning

Combine (eg) a trip to the supermarket with a visit to the recycling centre and the DIY store, rather than making separate journeys.

When possible choose a travelling time outside rush hours.

Load

The more heavily a car is laden, the greater the energy required to accelerate it to a given speed. Remove heavy items which you don't need to carry.

One load which is often overlooked is the contents of the fuel tank. A tankful of fuel (55 litres / 12 gallons) weighs 45 kg (100 lb) or so. Just half filling it may be worthwhile.

Lost?

At the risk of stating the obvious, if you're going somewhere new, have details of the route to hand. There's not much point in achieving record mpg if you also go miles out of your way.

Parking

If possible, carry out any reversing or turning manoeuvres when you arrive at a parking space so that you can drive straight out when you leave. Manoeuvering when the engine is cold uses a lot more fuel.

Driving around looking for free on-street parking may cost more in fuel than buying a car park ticket.

Premium fuel

Most major oil companies (and some supermarkets) have premium grades of fuel which are several pence a litre dearer than the standard grades. Reports vary, but the consensus seems to be that if these fuels improve economy at all, they do not do so by enough to justify their extra cost.

Roof rack

When loading a roof rack, try to produce a wedge shape with the narrow end at the front. Any cover should be securely fastened – if it flaps it's creating turbulence and absorbing energy.

Remove roof racks and boxes when not in use – they increase air resistance and can create a surprising amount of noise.

Short journeys

The engine is at its least efficient, and wear is highest, during the first few miles after a cold start. Consider walking, cycling or using public transport.

Speed

The engine is at its most efficient when running at a steady speed and load at the rpm where it develops maximum torque. (You can find this figure in the car's handbook.) For most cars this corresponds to between 55 and 65 mph in top gear.

Above the optimum cruising speed, fuel consumption starts to rise quite sharply. A car travelling at 80 mph will typically be using 30% more fuel than at 60 mph.

Supermarket fuel

It may be cheap but is it any good? In the UK all supermarket fuel must meet the relevant British Standard. The major oil companies will say that their branded fuels have better additive packages which may stop carbon and other deposits building up. A reasonable compromise might be to use one tank of branded fuel to three or four from the supermarket.

Switch off when stationary

Switch off the engine if you look like being stationary for more than 30 seconds or so. This is good for the environment as well as for your pocket. Be aware though that frequent restarts are hard on the battery and the starter motor.

Windows

Driving with the windows open increases air turbulence around the vehicle. Closing the windows promotes smooth airflow and

reduced resistance. The faster you go, the more significant this is.

And finally . . .

Driving techniques associated with good fuel economy tend to involve moderate acceleration and low top speeds. Be considerate to the needs of other road users who may need to make brisker progress; even if you do not agree with them this is not an excuse to be obstructive.

Safety must always take precedence over economy, whether it is a question of accelerating hard to complete an overtaking manoeuvre, killing your speed when confronted with a potential hazard or switching the lights on when it starts to get dark.

Conversion factors

Length (distance)

Inches (in)	x 25.4	= Millimetres (mm)	x 0.0394	= Inches (in)
Feet (ft)	x 0.305	= Metres (m)	x 3.281	= Feet (ft)
Miles	x 1.609	= Kilometres (km)	x 0.621	= Miles

Volume (capacity)

Cubic inches (cu in; in³)	x 16.387	= Cubic centimetres (cc; cm³)	x 0.061	= Cubic inches (cu in; in³)
Imperial pints (Imp pt)	x 0.568	= Litres (l)	x 1.76	= Imperial pints (Imp pt)
Imperial quarts (Imp qt)	x 1.137	= Litres (l)	x 0.88	= Imperial quarts (Imp qt)
Imperial quarts (Imp qt)	x 1.201	= US quarts (US qt)	x 0.833	= Imperial quarts (Imp qt)
US quarts (US qt)	x 0.946	= Litres (l)	x 1.057	= US quarts (US qt)
Imperial gallons (Imp gal)	x 4.546	= Litres (l)	x 0.22	= Imperial gallons (Imp gal)
Imperial gallons (Imp gal)	x 1.201	= US gallons (US gal)	x 0.833	= Imperial gallons (Imp gal)
US gallons (US gal)	x 3.785	= Litres (l)	x 0.264	= US gallons (US gal)

Mass (weight)

Ounces (oz)	x 28.35	= Grams (g)	x 0.035	= Ounces (oz)
Pounds (lb)	x 0.454	= Kilograms (kg)	x 2.205	= Pounds (lb)

Force

Ounces-force (ozf; oz)	x 0.278	= Newtons (N)	x 3.6	= Ounces-force (ozf; oz)
Pounds-force (lbf; lb)	x 4.448	= Newtons (N)	x 0.225	= Pounds-force (lbf; lb)
Newtons (N)	x 0.1	= Kilograms-force (kgf; kg)	x 9.81	= Newtons (N)

Pressure

Pounds-force per square inch (psi; lbf/in²; lb/in²)	x 0.070	= Kilograms-force per square centimetre (kgf/cm²; kg/cm²)	x 14.223	= Pounds-force per square inch (psi; lbf/in²; lb/in²)
Pounds-force per square inch (psi; lbf/in²; lb/in²)	x 0.068	= Atmospheres (atm)	x 14.696	= Pounds-force per square inch (psi; lbf/in²; lb/in²)
Pounds-force per square inch (psi; lbf/in²; lb/in²)	x 0.069	= Bars	x 14.5	= Pounds-force per square inch (psi; lbf/in²; lb/in²)
Pounds-force per square inch (psi; lbf/in²; lb/in²)	x 6.895	= Kilopascals (kPa)	x 0.145	= Pounds-force per square inch (psi; lbf/in²; lb/in²)
Kilopascals (kPa)	x 0.01	= Kilograms-force per square centimetre (kgf/cm²; kg/cm²)	x 98.1	= Kilopascals (kPa)
Millibar (mbar)	x 100	= Pascals (Pa)	x 0.01	= Millibar (mbar)
Millibar (mbar)	x 0.0145	= Pounds-force per square inch (psi; lbf/in²; lb/in²)	x 68.947	= Millibar (mbar)
Millibar (mbar)	x 0.75	= Millimetres of mercury (mmHg)	x 1.333	= Millibar (mbar)
Millibar (mbar)	x 0.401	= Inches of water (inH$_2$O)	x 2.491	= Millibar (mbar)
Millimetres of mercury (mmHg)	x 0.535	= Inches of water (inH$_2$O)	x 1.868	= Millimetres of mercury (mmHg)
Inches of water (inH$_2$O)	x 0.036	= Pounds-force per square inch (psi; lbf/in²; lb/in²)	x 27.68	= Inches of water (inH$_2$O)

Torque (moment of force)

Pounds-force inches (lbf in; lb in)	x 1.152	= Kilograms-force centimetre (kgf cm; kg cm)	x 0.868	= Pounds-force inches (lbf in; lb in)
Pounds-force inches (lbf in; lb in)	x 0.113	= Newton metres (Nm)	x 8.85	= Pounds-force inches (lbf in; lb in)
Pounds-force inches (lbf in; lb in)	x 0.083	= Pounds-force feet (lbf ft; lb ft)	x 12	= Pounds-force inches (lbf in; lb in)
Pounds-force feet (lbf ft; lb ft)	x 0.138	= Kilograms-force metres (kgf m; kg m)	x 7.233	= Pounds-force feet (lbf ft; lb ft)
Pounds-force feet (lbf ft; lb ft)	x 1.356	= Newton metres (Nm)	x 0.738	= Pounds-force feet (lbf ft; lb ft)
Newton metres (Nm)	x 0.102	= Kilograms-force metres (kgf m; kg m)	x 9.804	= Newton metres (Nm)

Power

Horsepower (hp)	x 745.7	= Watts (W)	x 0.0013	= Horsepower (hp)

Velocity (speed)

Miles per hour (miles/hr; mph)	x 1.609	= Kilometres per hour (km/hr; kph)	x 0.621	= Miles per hour (miles/hr; mph)

Fuel consumption*

Miles per gallon, Imperial (mpg)	x 0.354	= Kilometres per litre (km/l)	x 2.825	= Miles per gallon, Imperial (mpg)
Miles per gallon, US (mpg)	x 0.425	= Kilometres per litre (km/l)	x 2.352	= Miles per gallon, US (mpg)

Temperature

Degrees Fahrenheit = (°C x 1.8) + 32   Degrees Celsius (Degrees Centigrade; °C) = (°F - 32) x 0.56

It is common practice to convert from miles per gallon (mpg) to litres/100 kilometres (l/100km), where mpg x l/100 km = 282

Spare parts are available from many sources, including maker's appointed garages, accessory shops, and motor factors. To be sure of obtaining the correct parts, it will sometimes be necessary to quote the vehicle identification number. If possible, it can also be useful to take the old parts along for positive identification. Items such as starter motors and alternators may be available under a service exchange scheme – any parts returned should be clean.

Our advice regarding spare parts is as follows.

Officially appointed garages

This is the best source of parts which are peculiar to your car, and which are not otherwise generally available (eg, badges, interior trim, certain body panels, etc). It is also the only place at which you should buy parts if the car is still under warranty.

Accessory shops

These are very good places to buy materials and components needed for the maintenance of your car (oil, air and fuel filters, light bulbs, drivebelts, greases, brake pads, touch-up paint, etc). Components of this nature

sold by a reputable shop are usually of the same standard as those used by the car manufacturer.

Besides components, these shops also sell tools and general accessories, usually have convenient opening hours, charge lower prices, and can often be found close to home. Some accessory shops have parts counters where components needed for almost any repair job can be purchased or ordered.

Motor factors

Good factors will stock all the more important components which wear out comparatively quickly, and can sometimes supply individual components needed for the overhaul of a larger assembly (eg, brake seals and hydraulic parts, bearing shells, pistons, valves). They may also handle work such as cylinder block reboring, crankshaft regrinding, etc.

Engine reconditioners

These specialise in engine overhaul and can also supply components. It is recommended that the establishment is a member of the Federation of Engine Re-Manufacturers, or a similar society.

Tyre and exhaust specialists

These outlets may be independent, or members of a local or national chain. They frequently offer competitive prices when compared with a main dealer or local garage, but it will pay to obtain several quotes before making a decision. When researching prices, also ask what extras may be added – for instance fitting a new valve, balancing the wheel and tyre disposal all both commonly charged on top of the price of a new tyre.

Other sources

Beware of parts or materials obtained from market stalls, car boot sales, on-line auctions or similar outlets. Such items are not invariably sub-standard, but there is little chance of compensation if they do prove unsatisfactory. In the case of safety-critical components such as brake pads, there is the risk not only of financial loss, but also of an accident causing injury or death.

Second-hand components or assemblies obtained from a car breaker can be a good buy in some circumstances, but this sort of purchase is best made by the experienced DIY mechanic.

Vehicle identification numbers

Modifications are a continuing and unpublicised process in vehicle manufacture, quite apart from major model changes. Spare parts manuals and lists are compiled upon a numerical basis, the individual vehicle identification numbers being essential to correct identification of the component concerned.

When ordering spare parts, always give as much information as possible. Quote the car model, year of manufacture, body and engine numbers as appropriate.

The vehicle identification number is in the form of plate visible through the windscreen on the passenger's side and on the bulkhead panelling in the centre-rear of the engine

compartment (**see illustrations**). The vehicle identification plate is situated adjacent to the left-hand strut tower (**see illustration**).

The *engine number* is stamped on the front side of the cylinder block, adjacent to the transmission joint. Diesel engine models also have a sticker on the timing belt cover.

Vehicle Identification Number (VIN) located on the left-hand front edge of the windscreen

The VIN located on the scuttle panel, below the windscreen

The VIN plate located adjacent to the left-hand strut tower

Whenever servicing, repair or overhaul work is carried out on the car or its components, observe the following procedures and instructions. This will assist in carrying out the operation efficiently and to a professional standard of workmanship.

Joint mating faces and gaskets

When separating components at their mating faces, never insert screwdrivers or similar implements into the joint between the faces in order to prise them apart. This can cause severe damage which results in oil leaks, coolant leaks, etc upon reassembly. Separation is usually achieved by tapping along the joint with a soft-faced hammer in order to break the seal. However, note that this method may not be suitable where dowels are used for component location.

Where a gasket is used between the mating faces of two components, a new one must be fitted on reassembly; fit it dry unless otherwise stated in the repair procedure. Make sure that the mating faces are clean and dry, with all traces of old gasket removed. When cleaning a joint face, use a tool which is unlikely to score or damage the face, and remove any burrs or nicks with an oilstone or fine file.

Make sure that tapped holes are cleaned with a pipe cleaner, and keep them free of jointing compound, if this is being used, unless specifically instructed otherwise.

Ensure that all orifices, channels or pipes are clear, and blow through them, preferably using compressed air.

Oil seals

Oil seals can be removed by levering them out with a wide flat-bladed screwdriver or similar implement. Alternatively, a number of self-tapping screws may be screwed into the seal, and these used as a purchase for pliers or some similar device in order to pull the seal free.

Whenever an oil seal is removed from its working location, either individually or as part of an assembly, it should be renewed.

The very fine sealing lip of the seal is easily damaged, and will not seal if the surface it contacts is not completely clean and free from scratches, nicks or grooves. If the original sealing surface of the component cannot be restored, and the manufacturer has not made provision for slight relocation of the seal relative to the sealing surface, the component should be renewed.

Protect the lips of the seal from any surface which may damage them in the course of fitting. Use tape or a conical sleeve where possible. Where indicated, lubricate the seal lips with oil before fitting and, on dual-lipped seals, fill the space between the lips with grease.

Unless otherwise stated, oil seals must be fitted with their sealing lips toward the lubricant to be sealed.

Use a tubular drift or block of wood of the appropriate size to install the seal and, if the seal housing is shouldered, drive the seal down to the shoulder. If the seal housing is unshouldered, the seal should be fitted with its face flush with the housing top face (unless otherwise instructed).

Screw threads and fastenings

Seized nuts, bolts and screws are quite a common occurrence where corrosion has set in, and the use of penetrating oil or releasing fluid will often overcome this problem if the offending item is soaked for a while before attempting to release it. The use of an impact driver may also provide a means of releasing such stubborn fastening devices, when used in conjunction with the appropriate screwdriver bit or socket. If none of these methods works, it may be necessary to resort to the careful application of heat, or the use of a hacksaw or nut splitter device. Before resorting to extreme methods, check that you are not dealing with a left-hand thread!

Studs are usually removed by locking two nuts together on the threaded part, and then using a spanner on the lower nut to unscrew the stud. Studs or bolts which have broken off below the surface of the component in which they are mounted can sometimes be removed using a stud extractor.

Always ensure that a blind tapped hole is completely free from oil, grease, water or other fluid before installing the bolt or stud. Failure to do this could cause the housing to crack due to the hydraulic action of the bolt or stud as it is screwed in.

For some screw fastenings, notably cylinder head bolts or nuts, torque wrench settings are no longer specified for the latter stages of tightening, "angle-tightening" being called up instead. Typically, a fairly low torque wrench setting will be applied to the bolts/nuts in the correct sequence, followed by one or more stages of tightening through specified angles.

When checking or retightening a nut or bolt to a specified torque setting, slacken the nut or bolt by a quarter of a turn, and then retighten to the specified setting. However, this should not be attempted where angular tightening has been used.

Locknuts, locktabs and washers

Any fastening which will rotate against a component or housing during tightening should always have a washer between it and the relevant component or housing.

Spring or split washers should always be renewed when they are used to lock a critical component such as a big-end bearing retaining bolt or nut. Locktabs which are folded over to retain a nut or bolt should always be renewed.

Self-locking nuts can be re-used in non-critical areas, providing resistance can be felt when the locking portion passes over the bolt or stud thread. However, it should be noted that self-locking stiffnuts tend to lose their effectiveness after long periods of use, and should then be renewed as a matter of course.

Split pins must always be replaced with new ones of the correct size for the hole.

When thread-locking compound is found on the threads of a fastener which is to be re-used, it should be cleaned off with a wire brush and solvent, and fresh compound applied on reassembly.

Special tools

Some repair procedures in this manual entail the use of special tools such as a press, two or three-legged pullers, spring compressors, etc. Wherever possible, suitable readily-available alternatives to the manufacturer's special tools are described, and are shown in use. In some instances, where no alternative is possible, it has been necessary to resort to the use of a manufacturer's tool, and this has been done for reasons of safety as well as the efficient completion of the repair operation. Unless you are highly-skilled and have a thorough understanding of the procedures described, never attempt to bypass the use of any special tool when the procedure described specifies its use. Not only is there a very great risk of personal injury, but expensive damage could be caused to the components involved.

Environmental considerations

When disposing of used engine oil, brake fluid, antifreeze, etc, give due consideration to any detrimental environmental effects. Do not, for instance, pour any of the above liquids down drains into the general sewage system, or onto the ground to soak away. Many local council refuse tips provide a facility for waste oil disposal, as do some garages. You can find your nearest disposal point by calling the Environment Agency on 08708 506 506 or by visiting www.oilbankline.org.uk.

Note: It is illegal and anti-social to dump oil down the drain. To find the location of your local oil recycling bank, call 08708 506 506 or visit www.oilbankline.org.uk.

The jack supplied with the vehicle tool kit should only be used for changing the roadwheels – see *Wheel changing* at the front of this manual. When carrying out any other kind of work, raise the vehicle using a hydraulic trolley jack, and always supplement the jack with axle stands positioned under the vehicle jacking points.

When using a trolley jack or axle stands, always position the jack head or axle stand head under, or adjacent to one of the relevant wheel changing jacking points under the sills **(see illustration)**. Use a block of wood between the jack or axle stand and the sill.

Do not attempt to jack the vehicle under the front crossmember, the sump, or any of the suspension components.

The jack supplied with the vehicle locates in the jacking points on the underside of the sills – see *Wheel changing* at the front of this manual. Ensure that the jack head is correctly engaged before attempting to raise the vehicle.

Never work under, around, or near a raised vehicle, unless it is adequately supported in at least two places.

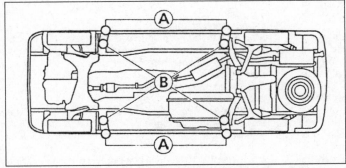

Position the vehicle jack under points (A) and axle stands or a trolley jack under points (B)

Disconnecting the battery

Caution: After reconnecting the battery, the safety function of the electric windows will not be re-instated until the windows have been reprogrammed. This could potentially cause severe pinching injuries.

Several of the systems require battery power to be available at all times (permanent live). This is either to ensure their continued operation (such as the clock), or to maintain electronic memory settings which would otherwise be erased. Whenever the battery is to be disconnected, first note the following points, to ensure there are no unforeseen consequences:

a) Firstly, on any vehicle with central door locking, it is a wise precaution to remove the key from the ignition, and to keep it with you. This avoids the possibility of the key being locked inside the car, should the central locking engage when the battery is reconnected.

b) If a security-coded audio unit is fitted, and the unit and/or the battery is disconnected, the unit will not function until the correct security code has been entered. Therefore, if you do not know the correct security code for the radio/cassette unit, **do not** disconnect either of the battery terminals, or remove the radio/cassette unit from the vehicle. The code appears on a code card supplied with the car when new. Details for entering the code appear in the vehicle handbook. Should the code have been misplaced

or forgotten, on production of proof of ownership, a Ford dealer or in-car entertainment specialist may be able to help.

c) The engine management system ECM is of the 'self-learning' type, meaning that, as it operates, it adapts to changes in operating conditions, and stores the optimum settings found (this is especially true for idle speed settings). When the battery is disconnected, these 'learned' settings are lost, and the ECM reverts to the base factory settings. When the engine is restarted, it may idle and run roughly until the ECM has 'relearned' the best settings. To further this 'learning' process, take the car for a road test of at least 15 minutes' duration, covering as many engine speeds and loads as possible, and concentrating on the 2000 to 4000 rpm range. On completion, let the engine idle for at least 10 minutes, turning the steering wheel occasionally and switching on high-current-draw equipment such as the heater fan or heated rear window. If the engine does not regain its normal performance, have the system checked for faults by a Ford dealer or suitably-equipped garage.

d) On vehicles equipped with an original equipment anti-theft alarm system, before disconnecting the battery, de-activate the alarm system, otherwise the alarm will be triggered.

e) After the battery has been reconnected, the electric windows positions must be reprogrammed as follows: Turn the ignition on (or start the vehicle) and lower the window. Hold the switch in the down position for 5 or more seconds. Raise the window and hold the switch in the closed position for 5 or more seconds. Repeat the procedure for all power windows.

f) When starting a petrol engine for the first time after having disconnected the battery, turn on the ignition for 30 seconds, then switch off the ignition – the engine may now be started.

Devices known as 'memory-savers' or 'code-savers' can be used to avoid some of the above problems. Precise details of use vary according to the device used. Typically, it is plugged into the cigarette lighter socket, and is connected by its own wiring to a spare battery; the vehicle battery is then disconnected from the electrical system, leaving the memory-saver to pass sufficient current to maintain audio unit security codes, and other memory values, and also to run permanently-live circuits such as the clock.

⚠ Warning: Some of these devices allow a considerable amount of currect to pass, which can mean that many of the vehicle's systems are still operational when the main battery is disconnected. If a memory-saver is used, ensure that the circuit concerned is actually 'dead' before carrying out any work on it.

Introduction

A selection of good tools is a fundamental requirement for anyone contemplating the maintenance and repair of a motor vehicle. For the owner who does not possess any, their purchase will prove a considerable expense, offsetting some of the savings made by doing-it-yourself. However, provided that the tools purchased meet the relevant national safety standards and are of good quality, they will last for many years and prove an extremely worthwhile investment.

To help the average owner to decide which tools are needed to carry out the various tasks detailed in this manual, we have compiled three lists of tools under the following headings: *Maintenance and minor repair, Repair and overhaul,* and *Special.* Newcomers to practical mechanics should start off with the *Maintenance and minor repair* tool kit, and confine themselves to the simpler jobs around the vehicle. Then, as confidence and experience grow, more difficult tasks can be undertaken, with extra tools being purchased as, and when, they are needed. In this way, a *Maintenance and minor repair* tool kit can be built up into a *Repair and overhaul* tool kit over a considerable period of time, without any major cash outlays. The experienced do-it-yourselfer will have a tool kit good enough for most repair and overhaul procedures, and will add tools from the *Special* category when it is felt that the expense is justified by the amount of use to which these tools will be put.

Maintenance and minor repair tool kit

The tools given in this list should be considered as a minimum requirement if routine maintenance, servicing and minor repair operations are to be undertaken. We recommend the purchase of combination spanners (ring one end, open-ended the other); although more expensive than open-ended ones, they do give the advantages of both types of spanner.

☐ *Combination spanners:*
Metric - 8 to 19 mm inclusive
☐ *Adjustable spanner - 35 mm jaw (approx.)*
☐ *Spark plug spanner (with rubber insert) - petrol models*
☐ *Spark plug gap adjustment tool - petrol models*
☐ *Set of feeler gauges*
☐ *Brake bleed nipple spanner*
☐ *Screwdrivers:*
Flat blade - 100 mm long x 6 mm dia
Cross blade - 100 mm long x 6 mm dia
Torx - various sizes (not all vehicles)
☐ *Combination pliers*
☐ *Hacksaw (junior)*
☐ *Tyre pump*
☐ *Tyre pressure gauge*
☐ *Oil can*
☐ *Oil filter removal tool (if applicable)*
☐ *Fine emery cloth*
☐ *Wire brush (small)*
☐ *Funnel (medium size)*
☐ *Sump drain plug key (not all vehicles)*

Repair and overhaul tool kit

These tools are virtually essential for anyone undertaking any major repairs to a motor vehicle, and are additional to those given in the *Maintenance and minor repair* list. Included in this list is a comprehensive set of sockets. Although these are expensive, they will be found invaluable as they are so versatile - particularly if various drives are included in the set. We recommend the half-inch square-drive type, as this can be used with most proprietary torque wrenches.

The tools in this list will sometimes need to be supplemented by tools from the *Special* list:

☐ *Sockets to cover range in previous list (including Torx sockets)*
☐ *Reversible ratchet drive (for use with sockets)*
☐ *Extension piece, 250 mm (for use with sockets)*
☐ *Universal joint (for use with sockets)*
☐ *Flexible handle or sliding T "breaker bar" (for use with sockets)*
☐ *Torque wrench (for use with sockets)*
☐ *Self-locking grips*
☐ *Ball pein hammer*
☐ *Soft-faced mallet (plastic or rubber)*
☐ *Screwdrivers:*
Flat blade - long & sturdy, short (chubby), and narrow (electrician's) types
Cross blade - long & sturdy, and short (chubby) types
☐ *Pliers:*
Long-nosed
Side cutters (electrician's)
Circlip (internal and external)
☐ *Cold chisel - 25 mm*
☐ *Scriber*
☐ *Scraper*
☐ *Centre-punch*
☐ *Pin punch*
☐ *Hacksaw*
☐ *Brake hose clamp*
☐ *Brake/clutch bleeding kit*
☐ *Selection of twist drills*
☐ *Steel rule/straight-edge*
☐ *Allen keys (inc. splined/Torx type)*
☐ *Selection of files*
☐ *Wire brush*
☐ *Axle stands*
☐ *Jack (strong trolley or hydraulic type)*
☐ *Light with extension lead*
☐ *Universal electrical multi-meter*

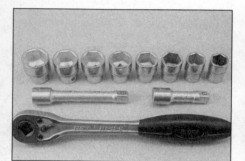
Sockets and reversible ratchet drive

Brake bleeding kit

Torx key, socket and bit

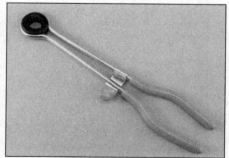
Hose clamp

Angular-tightening gauge

Special tools

The tools in this list are those which are not used regularly, are expensive to buy, or which need to be used in accordance with their manufacturers' instructions. Unless relatively difficult mechanical jobs are undertaken frequently, it will not be economic to buy many of these tools. Where this is the case, you could consider clubbing together with friends (or joining a motorists' club) to make a joint purchase, or borrowing the tools against a deposit from a local garage or tool hire specialist.

The following list contains only those tools and instruments freely available to the public, and not those special tools produced by the vehicle manufacturer specifically for its dealer network. You will find occasional references to these manufacturers' special tools in the text of this manual. Generally, an alternative method of doing the job without the vehicle manufacturers' special tool is given. However, sometimes there is no alternative to using them. Where this is the case and the relevant tool cannot be bought or borrowed, you will have to entrust the work to a dealer.

- [ ] *Angular-tightening gauge*
- [ ] *Valve spring compressor*
- [ ] *Valve grinding tool*
- [ ] *Piston ring compressor*
- [ ] *Piston ring removal/installation tool*
- [ ] *Cylinder bore hone*
- [ ] *Balljoint separator*
- [ ] *Coil spring compressors (where applicable)*
- [ ] *Two/three-legged hub and bearing puller*
- [ ] *Impact screwdriver*
- [ ] *Micrometer and/or vernier calipers*
- [ ] *Dial gauge*
- [ ] *Tachometer*
- [ ] *Fault code reader*
- [ ] *Cylinder compression gauge*
- [ ] *Hand-operated vacuum pump and gauge*
- [ ] *Clutch plate alignment set*
- [ ] *Brake shoe steady spring cup removal tool*
- [ ] *Bush and bearing removal/installation set*
- [ ] *Stud extractors*
- [ ] *Tap and die set*
- [ ] *Lifting tackle*

Buying tools

Reputable motor accessory shops and superstores often offer excellent quality tools at discount prices, so it pays to shop around.

Remember, you don't have to buy the most expensive items on the shelf, but it is always advisable to steer clear of the very cheap tools. Beware of 'bargains' offered on market stalls, on-line or at car boot sales. There are plenty of good tools around at reasonable prices, but always aim to purchase items which meet the relevant national safety standards. If in doubt, ask the proprietor or manager of the shop for advice before making a purchase.

Care and maintenance of tools

Having purchased a reasonable tool kit, it is necessary to keep the tools in a clean and serviceable condition. After use, always wipe off any dirt, grease and metal particles using a clean, dry cloth, before putting the tools away. Never leave them lying around after they have been used. A simple tool rack on the garage or workshop wall for items such as screwdrivers and pliers is a good idea. Store all normal spanners and sockets in a metal box. Any measuring instruments, gauges, meters, etc, must be carefully stored where they cannot be damaged or become rusty.

Take a little care when tools are used. Hammer heads inevitably become marked, and screwdrivers lose the keen edge on their blades from time to time. A little timely attention with emery cloth or a file will soon restore items like this to a good finish.

Working facilities

Not to be forgotten when discussing tools is the workshop itself. If anything more than routine maintenance is to be carried out, a suitable working area becomes essential.

It is appreciated that many an owner-mechanic is forced by circumstances to remove an engine or similar item without the benefit of a garage or workshop. Having done this, any repairs should always be done under the cover of a roof.

Wherever possible, any dismantling should be done on a clean, flat workbench or table at a suitable working height.

Any workbench needs a vice; one with a jaw opening of 100 mm is suitable for most jobs. As mentioned previously, some clean dry storage space is also required for tools, as well as for any lubricants, cleaning fluids, touch-up paints etc, which become necessary.

Another item which may be required, and which has a much more general usage, is an electric drill with a chuck capacity of at least 8 mm. This, together with a good range of twist drills, is virtually essential for fitting accessories.

Last, but not least, always keep a supply of old newspapers and clean, lint-free rags available, and try to keep any working area as clean as possible.

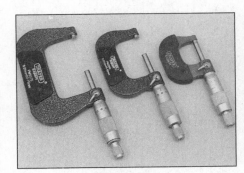

Micrometers

Dial test indicator ("dial gauge")

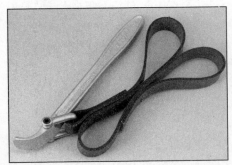

Oil filter removal tool (strap wrench type)

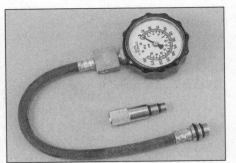

Compression tester

Bearing puller

This is a guide to getting your vehicle through the MOT test. Obviously it will not be possible to examine the vehicle to the same standard as the professional MOT tester. However, working through the following checks will enable you to identify any problem areas before submitting the vehicle for the test.

It has only been possible to summarise the test requirements here, based on the regulations in force at the time of printing. Test standards are becoming increasingly stringent, although there are some exemptions for older vehicles.

An assistant will be needed to help carry out some of these checks.

The checks have been sub-divided into four categories, as follows:

1 Checks carried out **FROM THE DRIVER'S SEAT**

2 Checks carried out **WITH THE VEHICLE ON THE GROUND**

3 Checks carried out **WITH THE VEHICLE RAISED AND THE WHEELS FREE TO TURN**

4 Checks carried out on **YOUR VEHICLE'S EXHAUST EMISSION SYSTEM**

---

1 Checks carried out **FROM THE DRIVER'S SEAT**

Handbrake (parking brake)

☐ Test the operation of the handbrake. Excessive travel (too many clicks) indicates incorrect brake or cable adjustment.
☐ Check that the handbrake cannot be released by tapping the lever sideways. Check the security of the lever mountings.

☐ If the parking brake is foot-operated, check that the pedal is secure and without excessive travel, and that the release mechanism operates correctly.
☐ Where applicable, test the operation of the electronic handbrake. The brake should engage and disengage without excessive delay. If the warning light does not extinguish when the brake is disengaged, this could indicate a fault which will need further investigation.

Footbrake

☐ Depress the brake pedal and check that it does not creep down to the floor, indicating a master cylinder fault. Release the pedal,

wait a few seconds, then depress it again. If the pedal travels nearly to the floor before firm resistance is felt, brake adjustment or repair is necessary. If the pedal feels spongy, there is air in the hydraulic system which must be removed by bleeding.

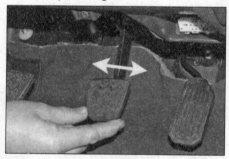

☐ Check that the brake pedal is secure and in good condition. Check also for signs of fluid leaks on the pedal, floor or carpets, which would indicate failed seals in the brake master cylinder.
☐ Check the servo unit (when applicable) by operating the brake pedal several times, then keeping the pedal depressed and starting the engine. As the engine starts, the pedal will move down slightly. If not, the vacuum hose or the servo itself may be faulty.

Steering wheel and column

☐ Examine the steering wheel for fractures or looseness of the hub, spokes or rim.
☐ Move the steering wheel from side to side and then up and down. Check that the steering wheel is not loose on the column, indicating wear or a loose retaining nut. Continue moving the steering wheel as before, but also turn it slightly from left to right.

☐ Check that the steering wheel is not loose on the column, and that there is no abnormal movement of the steering wheel, indicating wear in the column support bearings or couplings.
☐ Check that the ignition lock (where fitted) engages and disengages correctly.
☐ Steering column adjustment mechanisms (where fitted) must be able to lock the column securely in place with no play evident.

Windscreen, mirrors and sunvisor

☐ The windscreen must be free of cracks or other significant damage within the driver's field of view. (Small stone chips are acceptable.) Rear view mirrors must be secure, intact, and capable of being adjusted.

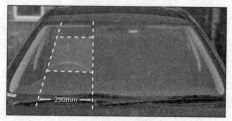

☐ The driver's sunvisor must be capable of being stored in the "up" position.

Seat belts and seats

Note: *The following checks are applicable to all seat belts, front and rear.*

☐ Examine the webbing of all the belts (including rear belts if fitted) for cuts, serious fraying or deterioration. Fasten and unfasten each belt to check the buckles. If applicable, check the retracting mechanism. Check the security of all seat belt mountings accessible from inside the vehicle, ensuring any height adjustable mountings lock securely in place.
☐ Seat belts with pre-tensioners, once activated, have a "flag" or similar showing on the seat belt stalk. This, in itself, is not a reason for test failure.
☐ The front seats themselves must be securely attached and the backrests must lock in the upright position.

Doors

☐ Both front doors must be able to be opened and closed from outside and inside, and must latch securely when closed.

Bonnet and boot/tailgate

☐ The bonnet and boot/tailgate must latch securely when closed.

2 Checks carried out WITH THE VEHICLE ON THE GROUND

Vehicle identification

☐ Number plates must be in good condition, secure and legible, with letters and numbers correctly spaced – spacing at (A) should be 33 mm and at (B) 11 mm. At the front, digits must be black on a white background and at the rear black on a yellow background. Other background designs (such as honeycomb) are not permitted.

☐ The VIN plate and/or homologation plate must be permanently displayed and legible.

Electrical equipment

☐ Switch on the ignition and check the operation of the horn.
☐ Check the windscreen washers and wipers, examining the wiper blades; renew damaged or perished blades. Also check the operation of the stop-lights.

☐ Check the operation of the sidelights and number plate lights. The lenses and reflectors must be secure, clean and undamaged.
☐ Check the operation and alignment of the headlights. The headlight reflectors must not be tarnished and the lenses must be undamaged.
☐ Switch on the ignition and check the operation of the direction indicators (including the instrument panel tell-tale) and the hazard warning lights. Operation of the sidelights and stop-lights must not affect the indicators - if it does, the cause is usually a bad earth at the rear light cluster. Indicators should flash at a rate of between 60 and 120 times per minute – faster or slower than this could indicate a fault with the flasher unit or a bad earth at one of the light units.
☐ Check the operation of the rear foglight(s), including the warning light on the instrument panel or in the switch.
☐ The ABS warning light must illuminate in accordance with the manufacturers' design. For most vehicles, the ABS warning light should illuminate when the ignition is switched on, and (if the system is operating properly) extinguish after a few seconds. Refer to the owner's handbook.

Footbrake

☐ Examine the master cylinder, brake pipes and servo unit for leaks, loose mountings, corrosion or other damage. If ABS is fitted, this unit should also be examined for signs of leaks or corrosion.

☐ The fluid reservoir must be secure and the fluid level must be between the upper (**A**) and lower (**B**) markings.

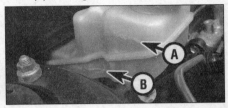

☐ Inspect both front brake flexible hoses for cracks or deterioration of the rubber. Turn the steering from lock to lock, and ensure that the hoses do not contact the wheel, tyre, or any part of the steering or suspension mechanism. With the brake pedal firmly depressed, check the hoses for bulges or leaks under pressure.

Steering and suspension

☐ Have your assistant turn the steering wheel from side to side slightly, up to the point where the steering gear just begins to transmit this movement to the roadwheels. Check for excessive free play between the steering wheel and the steering gear, indicating wear or insecurity of the steering column joints, the column-to-steering gear coupling, or the steering gear itself.
☐ Have your assistant turn the steering wheel more vigorously in each direction, so that the roadwheels just begin to turn. As this is done, examine all the steering joints, linkages, fittings and attachments. Renew any component that shows signs of wear or damage. On vehicles with power steering, check the security and condition of the steering pump, drivebelt and hoses.
☐ Check that the vehicle is standing level, and at approximately the correct ride height.

Shock absorbers

☐ Depress each corner of the vehicle in turn, then release it. The vehicle should rise and then settle in its normal position. If the vehicle continues to rise and fall, the shock absorber is defective. A shock absorber which has seized will also cause the vehicle to fail.

Exhaust system

☐ Start the engine. With your assistant holding a rag over the tailpipe, check the entire system for leaks. Repair or renew leaking sections.

3 Checks carried out **WITH THE VEHICLE RAISED AND THE WHEELS FREE TO TURN**

Jack up the front and rear of the vehicle, and securely support it on axle stands. Position the stands clear of the suspension assemblies. Ensure that the wheels are clear of the ground and that the steering can be turned from lock to lock.

Steering mechanism

☐ Have your assistant turn the steering from lock to lock. Check that the steering turns smoothly, and that no part of the steering mechanism, including a wheel or tyre, fouls any brake hose or pipe or any part of the body structure.
☐ Examine the steering rack rubber gaiters for damage or insecurity of the retaining clips. If power steering is fitted, check for signs of damage or leakage of the fluid hoses, pipes or connections. Also check for excessive stiffness or binding of the steering, a missing split pin or locking device, or severe corrosion of the body structure within 30 cm of any steering component attachment point.

Front and rear suspension and wheel bearings

☐ Starting at the front right-hand side, grasp the roadwheel at the 3 o'clock and 9 o'clock positions and rock gently but firmly. Check for free play or insecurity at the wheel bearings, suspension balljoints, or suspension mount-ings, pivots and attachments.
☐ Now grasp the wheel at the 12 o'clock and 6 o'clock positions and repeat the previous inspection. Spin the wheel, and check for roughness or tightness of the front wheel bearing.

☐ If excess free play is suspected at a component pivot point, this can be confirmed by using a large screwdriver or similar tool and levering between the mounting and the component attachment. This will confirm whether the wear is in the pivot bush, its retaining bolt, or in the mounting itself (the bolt holes can often become elongated).

☐ Carry out all the above checks at the other front wheel, and then at both rear wheels.

Springs and shock absorbers

☐ Examine the suspension struts (when applicable) for serious fluid leakage, corrosion, or damage to the casing. Also check the security of the mounting points.
☐ If coil springs are fitted, check that the spring ends locate in their seats, and that the spring is not corroded, cracked or broken.
☐ If leaf springs are fitted, check that all leaves are intact, that the axle is securely attached to each spring, and that there is no deterioration of the spring eye mountings, bushes, and shackles.

☐ The same general checks apply to vehicles fitted with other suspension types, such as torsion bars, hydraulic displacer units, etc. Ensure that all mountings and attachments are secure, that there are no signs of excessive wear, corrosion or damage, and (on hydraulic types) that there are no fluid leaks or damaged pipes.
☐ Inspect the shock absorbers for signs of serious fluid leakage. Check for wear of the mounting bushes or attachments, or damage to the body of the unit.

Driveshafts (fwd vehicles only)

☐ Rotate each front wheel in turn and inspect the constant velocity joint gaiters for splits or damage. Also check that each driveshaft is straight and undamaged.

Braking system

☐ If possible without dismantling, check brake pad wear and disc condition. Ensure that the friction lining material has not worn excessively, (A) and that the discs are not fractured, pitted, scored or badly worn (B).

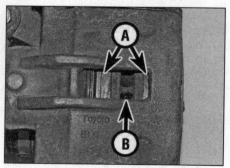

☐ Examine all the rigid brake pipes underneath the vehicle, and the flexible hose(s) at the rear. Look for corrosion, chafing or insecurity of the pipes, and for signs of bulging under pressure, chafing, splits or deterioration of the flexible hoses.
☐ Look for signs of fluid leaks at the brake calipers or on the brake backplates. Repair or renew leaking components.
☐ Slowly spin each wheel, while your assistant depresses and releases the footbrake. Ensure that each brake is operating and does not bind when the pedal is released.

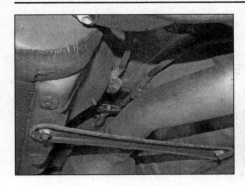

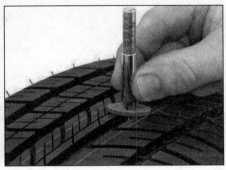

□ Examine the handbrake mechanism, checking for frayed or broken cables, excessive corrosion, or wear or insecurity of the linkage. Check that the mechanism works on each relevant wheel, and releases fully, without binding.

□ It is not possible to test brake efficiency without special equipment, but a road test can be carried out later to check that the vehicle pulls up in a straight line.

Fuel and exhaust systems

□ Inspect the fuel tank (including the filler cap), fuel pipes, hoses and unions. All components must be secure and free from leaks. Locking fuel caps must lock securely and the key must be provided for the MOT test.

□ Examine the exhaust system over its entire length, checking for any damaged, broken or missing mountings, security of the retaining clamps and rust or corrosion.

Wheels and tyres

□ Examine the sidewalls and tread area of each tyre in turn. Check for cuts, tears, lumps, bulges, separation of the tread, and exposure of the ply or cord due to wear or damage. Check that the tyre bead is correctly seated on the wheel rim, that the valve is sound and properly seated, and that the wheel is not distorted or damaged.

□ Check that the tyres are of the correct size for the vehicle, that they are of the same size and type on each axle, and that the pressures are correct.

□ Check the tyre tread depth. The legal minimum at the time of writing is 1.6 mm over the central three-quarters of the tread width. Abnormal tread wear may indicate incorrect front wheel alignment or wear in steering or suspension components.

□ If the spare wheel is fitted externally or in a separate carrier beneath the vehicle, check that mountings are secure and free of excessive corrosion.

Body corrosion

□ Check the condition of the entire vehicle structure for signs of corrosion in load-bearing areas. (These include chassis box sections, side sills, cross-members, pillars, and all suspension, steering, braking system and seat belt mountings and anchorages.) Any corrosion which has seriously reduced the thickness of a load-bearing area (or is within 30 cm of safety-related components such as steering or suspension) is likely to cause the vehicle to fail. In this case professional repairs are likely to be needed.

□ Damage or corrosion which causes sharp or otherwise dangerous edges to be exposed will also cause the vehicle to fail.

Towbars

□ Check the condition of mounting points (both beneath the vehicle and within boot/hatchback areas) for signs of corrosion, ensuring that all fixings are secure and not worn or damaged. There must be no excessive play in detachable tow ball arms or quick-release mechanisms.

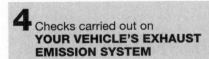

4 Checks carried out on **YOUR VEHICLE'S EXHAUST EMISSION SYSTEM**

Petrol models

□ The engine should be warmed up, and running well (ignition system in good order, air filter element clean, etc).

□ Before testing, run the engine at around 2500 rpm for 20 seconds. Let the engine drop to idle, and watch for smoke from the exhaust. If the idle speed is too high, or if dense blue or black smoke emerges for more than 5 seconds, the vehicle will fail. Typically, blue smoke signifies oil burning (engine wear);

black smoke means unburnt fuel (dirty air cleaner element, or other fuel system fault).

□ An exhaust gas analyser for measuring carbon monoxide (CO) and hydrocarbons (HC) is now needed. If one cannot be hired or borrowed, have a local garage perform the check.

CO emissions (mixture)

□ The MOT tester has access to the CO limits for all vehicles. The CO level is measured at idle speed, and at 'fast idle' (2500 to 3000 rpm). The following limits are given as a general guide:

    At idle speed – Less than 0.5% CO
    At 'fast idle' – Less than 0.3% CO
    Lambda reading – 0.97 to 1.03

□ If the CO level is too high, this may point to poor maintenance, a fuel injection system problem, faulty lambda (oxygen) sensor or catalytic converter. Try an injector cleaning treatment, and check the vehicle's ECU for fault codes.

HC emissions

□ The MOT tester has access to HC limits for all vehicles. The HC level is measured at 'fast idle' (2500 to 3000 rpm). The following limits are given as a general guide:

    At 'fast idle' – Less then 200 ppm

□ Excessive HC emissions are typically caused by oil being burnt (worn engine), or by a blocked crankcase ventilation system ('breather'). If the engine oil is old and thin, an oil change may help. If the engine is running badly, check the vehicle's ECU for fault codes.

Diesel models

□ The only emission test for diesel engines is measuring exhaust smoke density, using a calibrated smoke meter. The test involves accelerating the engine at least 3 times to its maximum unloaded speed.

Note: *On engines with a timing belt, it is VITAL that the belt is in good condition before the test is carried out.*

□ With the engine warmed up, it is first purged by running at around 2500 rpm for 20 seconds. A governor check is then carried out, by slowly accelerating the engine to its maximum speed. After this, the smoke meter is connected, and the engine is accelerated quickly to maximum speed three times. If the smoke density is less than the limits given below, the vehicle will pass:

    Non-turbo vehicles: 2.5m-1
    Turbocharged vehicles: 3.0m-1

□ If excess smoke is produced, try fitting a new air cleaner element, or using an injector cleaning treatment. If the engine is running badly, where applicable, check the vehicle's ECU for fault codes. Also check the vehicle's EGR system, where applicable. At high mileages, the injectors may require professional attention.

Engine

- ☐ Engine fails to rotate when attempting to start
- ☐ Engine rotates, but will not start
- ☐ Engine difficult to start when cold
- ☐ Engine difficult to start when hot
- ☐ Starter motor noisy or excessively-rough in engagement
- ☐ Engine starts, but stops immediately
- ☐ Engine idles erratically
- ☐ Engine misfires at idle speed
- ☐ Engine misfires throughout the driving speed range
- ☐ Engine hesitates on acceleration
- ☐ Engine stalls
- ☐ Engine lacks power
- ☐ Engine backfires
- ☐ Oil pressure warning light illuminated with engine running
- ☐ Engine runs-on after switching off
- ☐ Engine noises

Cooling system

- ☐ Overheating
- ☐ Overcooling
- ☐ External coolant leakage
- ☐ Internal coolant leakage
- ☐ Corrosion

Fuel and exhaust systems

- ☐ Excessive fuel consumption
- ☐ Fuel leakage and/or fuel odour
- ☐ Excessive noise or fumes from exhaust system

Clutch

- ☐ Pedal travels to floor – no pressure or very little resistance
- ☐ Clutch fails to disengage (unable to select gears)
- ☐ Clutch slips (engine speed increases, with no increase in vehicle speed)
- ☐ Judder as clutch is engaged
- ☐ Noise when depressing or releasing clutch pedal

Manual transmission

- ☐ Noisy in neutral with engine running
- ☐ Noisy in one particular gear
- ☐ Difficulty engaging gears
- ☐ Jumps out of gear
- ☐ Vibration
- ☐ Lubricant leaks

Automatic transmission

- ☐ Fluid leakage
- ☐ General gear selection problems
- ☐ Transmission will not downshift (kickdown) with accelerator pedal fully depressed
- ☐ Engine will not start in any gear, or starts in gears other than Park or Neutral
- ☐ Transmission slips, shifts roughly, is noisy, or has no drive in forward or reverse gears

Driveshafts

- ☐ Vibration when accelerating or decelerating
- ☐ Clicking or knocking noise on turns (at slow speed on full-lock)

Braking system

- ☐ Vehicle pulls to one side under braking
- ☐ Noise (grinding or high-pitched squeal) when brakes applied
- ☐ Excessive brake pedal travel
- ☐ Brake pedal feels spongy when depressed
- ☐ Excessive brake pedal effort required to stop vehicle
- ☐ Judder felt through brake pedal or steering wheel when braking
- ☐ Pedal pulsates when braking hard
- ☐ Brakes binding
- ☐ Rear wheels locking under normal braking

Steering and suspension

- ☐ Vehicle pulls to one side
- ☐ Wheel wobble and vibration
- ☐ Excessive pitching and/or rolling around corners, or during braking
- ☐ Wandering or general instability
- ☐ Excessively-stiff steering
- ☐ Excessive play in steering
- ☐ Lack of power assistance
- ☐ Tyre wear excessive

Electrical system

- ☐ Battery will not hold a charge for more than a few days
- ☐ Ignition/no-charge warning light remains illuminated with engine running
- ☐ Ignition/no-charge warning light fails to come on
- ☐ Lights inoperative
- ☐ Instrument readings inaccurate or erratic
- ☐ Horn inoperative, or unsatisfactory in operation
- ☐ Windscreen/tailgate wipers inoperative, or unsatisfactory in operation
- ☐ Windscreen washers inoperative, or unsatisfactory in operation
- ☐ Electric windows inoperative, or unsatisfactory in operation

Introduction

The vehicle owner who does his or her own maintenance according to the recommended service schedules should not have to use this section of the manual very often. Modern component reliability is such that, provided those items subject to wear or deterioration are inspected or renewed at the specified intervals, sudden failure is comparatively rare. Faults do not usually just happen as a result of sudden failure, but develop over a period of time. Major mechanical failures in particular are usually preceded by characteristic symptoms over hundreds or even thousands of miles. Those components which do occasionally fail without warning are often small and easily carried in the vehicle.

With any fault finding, the first step is to decide where to begin investigations. Sometimes this is obvious, but on other occasions, a little detective work will be necessary. The owner who makes half a dozen haphazard adjustments or replacements may be successful in curing a fault (or its symptoms), but will be none the wiser if the fault recurs, and ultimately may have spent more time and money than was necessary. A calm and logical approach will be found to be more satisfactory in the long run. Always take into account any warning signs or abnormalities that may have been noticed in the period preceding the fault – power loss, high or low gauge readings, unusual smells,

etc – and remember that failure of components such as fuses or spark plugs may only be pointers to some underlying fault.

The pages which follow provide an easy-reference guide to the more common problems which may occur during the operation of the vehicle. These problems and their possible causes are grouped under headings denoting various components or systems, such as Engine, Cooling system, etc. The Chapter and/or Section which deals with the problem is also shown in brackets. Whatever the fault, certain basic principles apply. These are as follows:

Verify the fault. This is simply a matter of being sure that you know what the symptoms are before starting work. This is particularly important if you are investigating a fault for someone else, who may not have described it very accurately.

Don't overlook the obvious. For example, if the vehicle won't start, is there fuel in the tank? (Don't take anyone else's word on this particular point, and don't trust the fuel gauge either). If an electrical fault is indicated, look for loose or broken wires before digging out the test gear.

Cure the disease, not the symptom. Substituting a flat battery with a fully-charged one will get you off the hard shoulder, but if the underlying cause is not attended to, the new battery will go the same way. Similarly, changing oil-fouled spark plugs for a new set will get you moving again, but remember that the reason for the fouling (if it wasn't simply an incorrect grade of plug) will have to be established and corrected.

Don't take anything for granted. Particularly, don't forget that a 'new' component may itself be defective (especially if it's been rattling around in the boot for months), and don't leave components out of a fault diagnosis sequence just because they are new or recently-fitted. When you do finally diagnose a difficult fault, you'll probably realise that all the evidence was there from the start.

Consider what work, if any, has recently been carried out. Many faults arise through careless or hurried work. For instance, if any work has been performed under the bonnet, could some of the wiring have been dislodged or incorrectly routed, or a hose trapped? Have all the fasteners been properly tightened? Were new, genuine parts and new gaskets used? There is often a certain amount of detective work to be done in this case, as an apparently-unrelated task can have far-reaching consequences.

Diesel fault diagnosis

The majority of starting problems on small diesel engines are electrical in origin. The mechanic who is familiar with petrol engines but less so with diesel may be inclined to view the diesel's injectors and pump in the same light as the spark plugs and distributor, but this is generally a mistake.

When investigating complaints of difficult starting for someone else, make sure that the correct starting procedure is understood and is being followed. Some drivers are unaware of the significance of the preheating warning light – many modern engines are sufficiently forgiving for this not to matter in mild weather, but with the onset of winter, problems begin. Glow plugs in particular are often neglected – just one faulty plug will make cold-weather starting very difficult.

As a rule of thumb, if the engine is difficult to start but runs well when it has finally got going, the problem is electrical (battery, starter motor or preheating system). If poor performance is combined with difficult starting, the problem is likely to be in the fuel system. The low-pressure (supply) side of the fuel system should be checked before suspecting the injectors and high-pressure pump. The most common fuel supply problem is air getting into the system, and any pipe from the fuel tank forwards must be scrutinised if air leakage is suspected.

Engine

Engine fails to rotate when attempting to start

- [ ] Battery terminal connections loose or corroded (see *Weekly checks*).
- [ ] Battery discharged or faulty (Chapter 5).
- [ ] Broken, loose or disconnected wiring in the starting circuit (Chapter 5).
- [ ] Defective starter solenoid or switch (Chapter 5).
- [ ] Defective starter motor (Chapter 5).
- [ ] Starter pinion or flywheel/driveplate ring gear teeth loose or broken (Chapter 2 and 5).
- [ ] Engine earth strap broken or disconnected (Chapter 5).

Engine rotates, but will not start

- [ ] Fuel tank empty.
- [ ] Battery discharged (engine rotates slowly) (Chapter 5).
- [ ] Battery terminal connections loose or corroded (see *Weekly checks*).
- [ ] Ignition components damp or damaged – petrol models (Chapters 1 and 5).
- [ ] Broken, loose or disconnected wiring in the ignition circuit – petrol models (Chapters 1 and 5).
- [ ] Worn, faulty or incorrectly-gapped spark plugs – petrol models (Chapter 1).
- [ ] Preheating system faulty – diesel models (Chapter 5).
- [ ] Fuel injection system fault – petrol models (Chapter 4).
- [ ] Stop solenoid faulty – diesel models (Chapter 4).
- [ ] Air in fuel system – diesel models (Chapter 4).
- [ ] Major mechanical failure (e.g. timing chain/belt) (Chapter 2).

Engine difficult to start when cold

- [ ] Battery discharged (Chapter 5).
- [ ] Battery terminal connections loose or corroded (see *Weekly checks*).
- [ ] Worn, faulty or incorrectly-gapped spark plugs – petrol models (Chapter 1).
- [ ] Preheating system faulty – diesel models (Chapter 5).
- [ ] Fuel injection system fault – petrol models (Chapter 4).

- [ ] Other ignition system fault – petrol models (Chapters 1 and 5).
- [ ] Low cylinder compressions (Chapter 2).

Engine difficult to start when hot

- [ ] Air filter element dirty or clogged (Chapter 1).
- [ ] Fuel injection system fault – petrol models (Chapter 4).
- [ ] Low cylinder compressions (Chapter 2).

Starter motor noisy or excessively-rough in engagement

- [ ] Starter pinion or flywheel ring gear teeth loose or broken (Chapter 2 and 5).
- [ ] Starter motor mounting bolts loose or missing (Chapter 5).
- [ ] Starter motor internal components worn or damaged (Chapter 5).

Engine starts, but stops immediately

- [ ] Loose or faulty electrical connections in the ignition circuit – petrol models (Chapters 1 and 5).
- [ ] Vacuum leak at the throttle body or inlet manifold – petrol models (Chapter 4).
- [ ] Blocked injector/fuel injection system fault – petrol models (Chapter 4).
- [ ] Air in fuel system – diesel models (Chapter 4).

Engine idles erratically

- [ ] Air filter element clogged (Chapter 1).
- [ ] Vacuum leak at the throttle body, inlet manifold or associated hoses – petrol models (Chapter 4).
- [ ] Worn, faulty or incorrectly-gapped spark plugs – petrol models (Chapter 1).
- [ ] Uneven or low cylinder compressions (Chapter 2).
- [ ] Camshaft lobes worn (Chapter 2).
- [ ] Timing chain/belt incorrectly fitted (Chapter 2).
- [ ] Blocked injector/fuel injection system fault – petrol models (Chapter 4).
- [ ] Air in fuel system – diesel models (Chapter 4).
- [ ] Faulty injector(s) – diesel models (Chapter 4).

Engine (continued)

Engine misfires at idle speed

- [ ] Worn, faulty or incorrectly-gapped spark plugs – petrol models (Chapter 1).
- [ ] Faulty spark plug HT leads – petrol models (Chapter 1).
- [ ] Vacuum leak at the throttle body, inlet manifold or associated hoses – petrol models (Chapter 4).
- [ ] Blocked injector/fuel injection system fault – petrol models (Chapter 4).
- [ ] Faulty injector(s) – diesel models (Chapter 4).
- [ ] Uneven or low cylinder compressions (Chapter 2).
- [ ] Disconnected, leaking, or perished crankcase ventilation hoses (Chapter 4).

Engine misfires throughout the driving speed range

- [ ] Fuel filter choked (Chapter 1).
- [ ] Fuel pump faulty, or delivery pressure low – petrol models (Chapter 4).
- [ ] Fuel tank vent blocked, or fuel pipes restricted (Chapter 4).
- [ ] Vacuum leak at the throttle body, inlet manifold or associated hoses – petrol models (Chapter 4).
- [ ] Worn, faulty or incorrectly-gapped spark plugs – petrol models (Chapter 1).
- [ ] Faulty spark plug HT leads – petrol models (Chapter 1).
- [ ] Faulty injector(s) – diesel models (Chapter 4).
- [ ] Faulty ignition coil(s) – petrol models (Chapter 5).
- [ ] Uneven or low cylinder compressions (Chapter 2).
- [ ] Blocked injector/fuel injection system fault – petrol models (Chapter 4).

Engine hesitates on acceleration

- [ ] Worn, faulty or incorrectly-gapped spark plugs – petrol models (Chapter 1).
- [ ] Vacuum leak at the throttle body, inlet manifold or associated hoses – petrol models (Chapter 4).
- [ ] Blocked injector/fuel injection system fault – petrol models (Chapter 4).
- [ ] Faulty injector(s) – diesel models (Chapter 4).

Engine stalls

- [ ] Vacuum leak at the throttle body, inlet manifold or associated hoses – petrol models (Chapter 4).
- [ ] Fuel filter choked (Chapter 1 and 4).
- [ ] Fuel pump faulty, or delivery pressure low – petrol models (Chapter 4).
- [ ] Fuel tank vent blocked, or fuel pipes restricted (Chapter 4).
- [ ] Blocked injector/fuel injection system fault – petrol models (Chapter 4).
- [ ] Faulty injector(s) – diesel models (Chapter 4).

Engine lacks power

- [ ] Timing chain/belt incorrectly fitted or tensioned (Chapter 2).
- [ ] Fuel filter choked (Chapter 1 and 4).
- [ ] Fuel pump faulty, or delivery pressure low – petrol models (Chapter 4).
- [ ] Uneven or low cylinder compressions (Chapter 2).
- [ ] Worn, faulty or incorrectly-gapped spark plugs – petrol models (Chapter 1).
- [ ] Vacuum leak at the throttle body, inlet manifold or associated hoses – petrol models (Chapter 4).
- [ ] Blocked injector/fuel injection system fault – petrol models (Chapter 4).

- [ ] Faulty injector(s) – diesel models (Chapter 4).
- [ ] Injection pump timing incorrect – diesel models (Chapter 4).
- [ ] Brakes binding (Chapters 1 and 9).
- [ ] Clutch slipping (Chapter 6).
- [ ] Air filter element clogged (Chapter 1).

Engine backfires

- [ ] Timing chain/belt incorrectly fitted or tensioned (Chapter 2).
- [ ] Vacuum leak at the throttle body, inlet manifold or associated hoses – petrol models (Chapter 4).
- [ ] Incorrect HT firing sequence – petrol models (Chapter 5)
- [ ] Blocked injector/fuel injection system fault – petrol models (Chapter 4).

Oil pressure warning light illuminated with engine running

- [ ] Low oil level, or incorrect oil grade (Weekly checks).
- [ ] Faulty oil pressure switch (Chapter 2).
- [ ] Worn engine bearings and/or oil pump (Chapter 2).
- [ ] High engine operating temperature (Chapter 3).
- [ ] Oil pressure relief valve defective (Chapter 2).
- [ ] Oil pick-up strainer clogged (Chapter 2).

Engine runs-on after switching off

- [ ] Excessive carbon build-up in engine (Chapter 2).
- [ ] High engine operating temperature (Chapter 3).
- [ ] Fuel injection system fault – petrol models (Chapter 4).
- [ ] Faulty stop solenoid – diesel models (Chapter 4).

Engine noises

Pre-ignition (pinking) or knocking during acceleration or under load

- [ ] Ignition system fault – petrol models (Chapters 1 and 5).
- [ ] Incorrect grade of spark plug – petrol models (Chapter 1).
- [ ] Vacuum leak at the throttle body, inlet manifold or associated hoses – petrol models (Chapter 4).
- [ ] Excessive carbon build-up in engine (Chapter 2).
- [ ] Blocked injector/fuel injection system fault – petrol models (Chapter 4).

Whistling or wheezing noises

- [ ] Leaking inlet manifold or throttle body gasket – petrol models (Chapter 4).
- [ ] Leaking exhaust manifold gasket or pipe-to-manifold joint (Chapter 4).
- [ ] Leaking vacuum hose (Chapters 4 and 9).
- [ ] Blowing cylinder head gasket (Chapter 2).

Tapping or rattling noises

- [ ] Worn valve gear or camshaft (Chapter 2).
- [ ] Ancillary component fault (coolant pump, alternator, etc) (Chapters 3, 5, etc).

Knocking or thumping noises

- [ ] Worn big-end bearings (regular heavy knocking, perhaps less under load) (Chapter 2).
- [ ] Worn main bearings (rumbling and knocking, perhaps worsening under load) (Chapter 2).
- [ ] Piston slap (most noticeable when cold) (Chapter 2).
- [ ] Ancillary component fault (coolant pump, alternator, etc) (Chapters 3, 5, etc).

Cooling system

Overheating

- [ ] Insufficient coolant in system (*Weekly checks*).
- [ ] Thermostat faulty (Chapter 3).
- [ ] Radiator core blocked, or grille restricted (Chapter 3).
- [ ] Electric cooling fan or thermostatic switch faulty (Chapter 3).
- [ ] Inaccurate temperature gauge sender unit (Chapter 3).
- [ ] Airlock in cooling system.
- [ ] Expansion tank pressure cap faulty (Chapter 3).

Overcooling

- [ ] Thermostat faulty (Chapter 3).
- [ ] Inaccurate temperature gauge sender unit (Chapter 3).

External coolant leakage

- [ ] Deteriorated or damaged hoses or hose clips (Chapter 1).

- [ ] Radiator core or heater matrix leaking (Chapter 3).
- [ ] Pressure cap faulty (Chapter 3).
- [ ] Coolant pump internal seal leaking (Chapter 3).
- [ ] Coolant pump-to-housing seal leaking (Chapter 3).
- [ ] Boiling due to overheating (Chapter 3).
- [ ] Core plug leaking (Chapter 2).

Internal coolant leakage

- [ ] Leaking cylinder head gasket (Chapter 2).
- [ ] Cracked cylinder head or cylinder block (Chapter 2).

Corrosion

- [ ] Infrequent draining and flushing (Chapter 1).
- [ ] Incorrect coolant mixture or inappropriate coolant type (see *Weekly checks*).

Fuel and exhaust systems

Excessive fuel consumption

- [ ] Air filter element dirty or clogged (Chapter 1).
- [ ] Fuel injection system fault – petrol models (Chapter 4).
- [ ] Faulty injector(s) – diesel models (Chapter 4).
- [ ] Ignition system fault – petrol models (Chapters 1 and 5).
- [ ] Brakes binding (Chapter 9).
- [ ] Tyres under-inflated (see *Weekly checks*).

Fuel leakage and/or fuel odour

- [ ] Damaged fuel tank, pipes or connections (Chapter 4).

Excessive noise or fumes from exhaust system

- [ ] Leaking exhaust system or manifold joints (Chapters 1 and 4).
- [ ] Leaking, corroded or damaged silencers or pipe (Chapters 1 and 4).
- [ ] Broken mountings causing body or suspension contact (Chapter 1).

Clutch

Pedal travels to floor – no pressure or very little resistance

- [ ] Faulty master or slave cylinder (Chapter 6).
- [ ] Faulty hydraulic release system (Chapter 6).
- [ ] Broken clutch release bearing or arm (Chapter 6).
- [ ] Broken diaphragm spring in clutch pressure plate (Chapter 6).

Clutch fails to disengage (unable to select gears)

- [ ] Faulty master or slave cylinder (Chapter 6).
- [ ] Faulty hydraulic release system (Chapter 6).
- [ ] Clutch disc sticking on gearbox input shaft splines (Chapter 6).
- [ ] Clutch disc sticking to flywheel or pressure plate (Chapter 6).
- [ ] Faulty pressure plate assembly (Chapter 6).

Clutch slips (engine speed increases, with no increase in vehicle speed)

- [ ] Faulty hydraulic release system (Chapter 6).

- [ ] Clutch disc linings excessively worn (Chapter 6).
- [ ] Clutch disc linings contaminated with oil or grease (Chapter 6).
- [ ] Faulty pressure plate or weak diaphragm spring (Chapter 6).

Judder as clutch is engaged

- [ ] Clutch disc linings contaminated with oil or grease (Chapter 6).
- [ ] Clutch disc linings excessively worn (Chapter 6).
- [ ] Faulty or distorted pressure plate or diaphragm spring (Chapter 6).
- [ ] Worn or loose engine or gearbox mountings (Chapter 2).
- [ ] Clutch disc hub or gearbox input shaft splines worn (Chapter 6).

Noise when depressing or releasing clutch pedal

- [ ] Worn clutch release bearing (Chapter 6).
- [ ] Worn or dry clutch pedal pivot (Chapter 6).
- [ ] Faulty pressure plate assembly (Chapter 6).
- [ ] Pressure plate diaphragm spring broken (Chapter 6).
- [ ] Broken clutch friction plate cushioning springs (Chapter 6).

Manual transmission

Noisy in neutral with engine running

☐ Input shaft bearings worn (noise apparent with clutch pedal released, but not when depressed) (Chapter 7A).*
☐ Clutch release bearing worn (noise apparent with clutch pedal depressed, possibly less when released) (Chapter 6).

Noisy in one particular gear

☐ Worn, damaged or chipped gear teeth (Chapter 7A).*

Difficulty engaging gears

☐ Clutch fault (Chapter 6).
☐ Worn or damaged gear linkage (Chapter 7A).
☐ Worn synchroniser units (Chapter 7A).*

Jumps out of gear

☐ Worn or damaged gear linkage (Chapter 7A).

☐ Worn synchroniser units (Chapter 7A).*
☐ Worn selector forks (Chapter 7A).*

Vibration

☐ Lack of oil (Chapter 1).
☐ Worn bearings (Chapter 7A).*

Lubricant leaks

☐ Leaking oil seal (Chapter 7A).
☐ Leaking housing joint (Chapter 7A).*
☐ Leaking input shaft oil seal (Chapter 7A).

Although the corrective action necessary to remedy the symptoms described is beyond the scope of the home mechanic, the above information should be helpful in isolating the cause of the condition, so that the owner can communicate clearly with a professional mechanic.

Automatic transmission

Note: *Due to the complexity of the automatic transmission, it is difficult for the home mechanic to properly diagnose and service this unit. For problems other than the following, the vehicle should be taken to a dealer service department or automatic transmission specialist. Do not be too hasty in removing the transmission if a fault is suspected, as most of the testing is carried out with the unit still fitted.*

Fluid leakage

☐ Automatic transmission fluid is usually dark in colour. Fluid leaks should not be confused with engine oil, which can easily be blown onto the transmission by airflow.
☐ To determine the source of a leak, first remove all built-up dirt and grime from the transmission housing and surrounding areas using a degreasing agent, or by steam-cleaning. Drive the vehicle at low speed, so airflow will not blow the leak far from its source. Raise and support the vehicle, and determine where the leak is coming from.

General gear selection problems

☐ Chapter 7B deals with checking and adjusting the selector mechanism on automatic transmissions. The following are common problems which may be caused by a poorly-adjusted mechanism:
a) *Engine starting in gears other than Park or Neutral.*
b) *Indicator panel indicating a gear other than the one actually being used.*

c) *Vehicle moves when in Park or Neutral.*
d) *Poor gear shift quality or erratic gear changes.*
☐ Refer to Chapter 7B for the selector mechanism adjustment procedure.

Transmission will not downshift (kickdown) with accelerator pedal fully depressed

☐ Low transmission fluid level (Chapter 1).
☐ Incorrect selector mechanism adjustment (Chapter 7B).

Engine will not start in any gear, or starts in gears other than Park or Neutral

☐ Incorrect selector mechanism adjustment (Chapter 7B).

Transmission slips, shifts roughly, is noisy, or has no drive in forward or reverse gears

☐ There are many probable causes for the above problems, but unless there is a very obvious reason (such as a loose or corroded wiring plug connection on or near the transmission), the car should be taken to a franchise dealer or automatic transmission specialist for the fault to be diagnosed. The transmission control unit incorporates a self-diagnosis facility, and any fault codes can quickly be read and interpreted by a dealer or specialist with the proper diagnostic equipment.

Driveshafts

Vibration when accelerating or decelerating

☐ Worn inner constant velocity joint (Chapter 8).
☐ Bent or distorted driveshaft (Chapter 8).
  Clicking or knocking noise on turns (at slow speed on full-lock)

☐ Worn outer constant velocity joint (Chapter 8).
☐ Lack of constant velocity joint lubricant, possibly due to damaged gaiter (Chapter 8).

Braking system

Note: *Before assuming that a brake problem exists, make sure that the tyres are in good condition and correctly inflated, that the front wheel alignment is correct, and that the vehicle is not loaded with weight in an unequal manner. Apart from checking the condition of all pipe and hose connections, any faults occurring on the anti-lock braking system should be referred to a Ford dealer or specialist for diagnosis.*

Vehicle pulls to one side under braking

☐ Worn, defective, damaged or contaminated front or rear brake pads on one side (Chapters 1 and 9).
☐ Seized or partially-seized front or rear brake caliper (Chapter 9).
☐ A mixture of brake pad lining materials fitted between sides (Chapter 9).
☐ Brake caliper mounting bolts loose (Chapter 9).
☐ Worn or damaged steering or suspension components (Chapters 1 and 10).

Noise (grinding or high-pitched squeal) when brakes applied

☐ Brake pad friction lining material worn down to metal backing (Chapters 1 and 9).
☐ Excessive corrosion of brake disc – may be apparent after the vehicle has been standing for some time (Chapters 1 and 9).
☐ Foreign object (stone chipping, etc) trapped between brake disc and shield (Chapters 1 and 9).

Excessive brake pedal travel

☐ Faulty master cylinder (Chapter 9).
☐ Air in hydraulic system (Chapter 9).
☐ Faulty vacuum servo unit (Chapter 9).
☐ Faulty vacuum pump – diesel models (Chapter 9).

Brake pedal feels spongy when depressed

☐ Air in hydraulic system (Chapter 9).
☐ Deteriorated flexible rubber brake hoses (Chapters 1 and 9).

☐ Master cylinder mountings loose (Chapter 9).
☐ Faulty master cylinder (Chapter 9).

Excessive brake pedal effort required to stop vehicle

☐ Faulty vacuum servo unit (Chapter 9).
☐ Disconnected, damaged or insecure brake servo vacuum hose (Chapters 1 and 9).
☐ Faulty vacuum pump – diesel models (Chapter 9).
☐ Primary or secondary hydraulic circuit failure (Chapter 9).
☐ Seized brake caliper (Chapter 9).
☐ Brake pads incorrectly fitted (Chapter 9).
☐ Incorrect grade of brake pads fitted (Chapter 9).
☐ Brake pads contaminated (Chapter 9).

Judder felt through brake pedal or steering wheel when braking

☐ Excessive run-out or distortion of brake disc(s) (Chapter 9).
☐ Brake pad linings worn (Chapters 1 and 9).
☐ Brake caliper mounting bolts loose (Chapter 9).
☐ Wear in suspension or steering components or mountings (Chapters 1 and 10).

Pedal pulsates when braking hard

☐ Normal feature of ABS – no fault

Brakes binding

☐ Seized brake caliper piston(s) (Chapter 9).
☐ Incorrectly-adjusted handbrake mechanism (Chapter 9).
☐ Faulty master cylinder (Chapter 9).

Rear wheels locking under normal braking

☐ Rear brake pad linings contaminated (Chapters 1 and 9).
☐ Rear brake discs warped (Chapters 1 and 9).

Steering and suspension

Note: *Before diagnosing suspension or steering faults, be sure that the trouble is not due to incorrect tyre pressures, mixtures of tyre types, or binding brakes.*

Vehicle pulls to one side

- ☐ Defective tyre (see *Weekly checks*).
- ☐ Excessive wear in suspension or steering components (Chapters 1 and 10).
- ☐ Incorrect front wheel alignment (Chapter 10).
- ☐ Accident damage to steering or suspension components (Chapters 1 and 10).

Wheel wobble and vibration

- ☐ Front roadwheels out of balance (vibration felt mainly through the steering wheel) (Chapter 10).
- ☐ Rear roadwheels out of balance (vibration felt throughout the vehicle) (Chapter 10).
- ☐ Roadwheels damaged or distorted (Chapter 10).
- ☐ Faulty or damaged tyre (*Weekly checks*).
- ☐ Worn steering or suspension joints, bushes or components (Chapters 1 and 10).
- ☐ Wheel bolts loose (Chapter 1 and 10).

Excessive pitching and/or rolling around corners, or during braking

- ☐ Defective shock absorbers (Chapters 1 and 10).
- ☐ Broken or weak coil spring and/or suspension component (Chapters 1 and 10).
- ☐ Worn or damaged anti-roll bar or mountings (Chapter 10).

Wandering or general instability

- ☐ Incorrect front wheel alignment (Chapter 10).
- ☐ Worn steering or suspension joints, bushes or components (Chapters 1 and 10).
- ☐ Roadwheels out of balance (Chapter 10).
- ☐ Faulty or damaged tyre (*Weekly checks*).
- ☐ Wheel bolts loose (Chapter 10).
- ☐ Defective shock absorbers (Chapters 1 and 10).

Excessively-stiff steering

- ☐ Seized track rod end balljoint or suspension balljoint (Chapters 1 and 10).

- ☐ Broken or incorrectly adjusted auxiliary drivebelt (Chapter 1).
- ☐ Incorrect front wheel alignment (Chapter 10).
- ☐ Steering gear damaged (Chapter 10).

Excessive play in steering

- ☐ Worn steering column universal joint(s) (Chapter 10).
- ☐ Worn steering track rod end balljoints (Chapters 1 and 10).
- ☐ Worn steering gear (Chapter 10).
- ☐ Worn steering or suspension joints, bushes or components (Chapters 1 and 10).

Lack of power assistance

- ☐ Broken or incorrectly-adjusted auxiliary drivebelt (Chapter 1).
- ☐ Incorrect power steering fluid level (*Weekly checks*).
- ☐ Restriction in power steering fluid hoses (Chapter 10).
- ☐ Faulty power steering pump (Chapter 10).
- ☐ Faulty steering gear (Chapter 10).

Tyre wear excessive

Tyres worn on inside or outside edges

- ☐ Incorrect camber or castor angles (Chapter 10).
- ☐ Worn steering or suspension joints, bushes or components (Chapters 1 and 10).
- ☐ Excessively-hard cornering.
- ☐ Accident damage.

Tyre treads exhibit feathered edges

- ☐ Incorrect toe setting (Chapter 10).

Tyres worn in centre of tread

- ☐ Tyres over-inflated (*Weekly checks*).

Tyres worn on inside and outside edges

- ☐ Tyres under-inflated (*Weekly checks*).
- ☐ Worn shock absorbers (Chapter 10).

Tyres worn unevenly

- ☐ Tyres/wheels out of balance (*Weekly checks*).
- ☐ Excessive wheel or tyre run-out (Chapter 10).
- ☐ Worn shock absorbers (Chapters 1 and 10).
- ☐ Faulty tyre (*Weekly checks*).

Electrical system

Note: *For problems associated with the starting system, refer to the faults listed under 'Engine' earlier in this Section.*

Battery will not hold a charge for more than a few days

- ☐ Battery defective internally (Chapter 5).
- ☐ Battery electrolyte level low – where applicable (*Weekly checks*).
- ☐ Battery terminal connections loose or corroded (*Weekly checks*).
- ☐ Auxiliary drivebelt worn – or incorrectly adjusted, where applicable (Chapter 1).
- ☐ Alternator not charging at correct output (Chapter 5).

- ☐ Alternator or voltage regulator faulty (Chapter 5).
- ☐ Short-circuit causing continual battery drain (Chapters 5 and 12).

Ignition/no-charge warning light remains illuminated with engine running

- ☐ Auxiliary drivebelt broken, worn, or incorrectly adjusted (Chapter 1).
- ☐ Internal fault in alternator or voltage regulator (Chapter 5).
- ☐ Broken, disconnected, or loose wiring in charging circuit (Chapter 5).

Electrical system (continued)

Ignition/no-charge warning light fails to come on
- [ ] Broken, disconnected, or loose wiring in warning light circuit (Chapter 12).
- [ ] Alternator faulty (Chapter 5).

Lights inoperative
- [ ] Bulb blown (Chapter 12).
- [ ] Corrosion of bulb or bulbholder contacts (Chapter 12).
- [ ] Blown fuse (Chapter 12).
- [ ] Faulty relay (Chapter 12).
- [ ] Broken, loose, or disconnected wiring (Chapter 12).
- [ ] Faulty switch (Chapter 12).

Instrument readings inaccurate or erratic

Fuel or temperature gauges give no reading
- [ ] Faulty gauge sender unit (Chapters 3 and 4).
- [ ] Wiring open-circuit (Chapter 12).
- [ ] Faulty gauge (Chapter 12).

Fuel or temperature gauges give continuous maximum reading
- [ ] Faulty gauge sender unit (Chapters 3 and 4).
- [ ] Wiring short-circuit (Chapter 12).
- [ ] Faulty gauge (Chapter 12).

Horn inoperative, or unsatisfactory in operation

Horn operates all the time
- [ ] Horn contacts permanently bridged or horn buttons stuck down (Chapter 12).

Horn fails to operate
- [ ] Blown fuse (Chapter 12).
- [ ] Cable or cable connections loose, broken or disconnected (Chapter 12).
- [ ] Faulty horn (Chapter 12).

Horn emits intermittent or unsatisfactory sound
- [ ] Cable connections loose (Chapter 12).
- [ ] Horn mountings loose (Chapter 12).
- [ ] Faulty horn (Chapter 12).

Windscreen/tailgate wipers inoperative, or unsatisfactory in operation

Wipers fail to operate, or operate very slowly
- [ ] Wiper blades stuck to screen, or linkage seized or binding (*Weekly checks* and Chapter 12).
- [ ] Blown fuse (Chapter 12).
- [ ] Cable or cable connections loose, broken or disconnected (Chapter 12).
- [ ] Faulty relay (Chapter 12).
- [ ] Faulty wiper motor (Chapter 12).

Wiper blades sweep over too large or too small an area of the glass
- [ ] Wiper arms incorrectly positioned on spindles (Chapter 12).
- [ ] Excessive wear of wiper linkage (Chapter 12).
- [ ] Wiper motor or linkage mountings loose or insecure (Chapter 12).

Wiper blades fail to clean the glass effectively
- [ ] Wiper blade rubbers worn or perished (*Weekly checks*).
- [ ] Wiper arm tension springs broken, or arm pivots seized (Chapter 12).
- [ ] Insufficient windscreen washer additive to adequately remove road film (*Weekly checks*).

Windscreen washers inoperative, or unsatisfactory in operation

One or more washer jets inoperative
- [ ] Blocked washer jet (Chapter 12).
- [ ] Disconnected, kinked or restricted fluid hose (Chapter 12).
- [ ] Insufficient fluid in washer reservoir (*Weekly checks*).

Washer pump fails to operate
- [ ] Broken or disconnected wiring or connections (Chapter 12).
- [ ] Blown fuse (Chapter 12).
- [ ] Faulty washer switch (Chapter 12).
- [ ] Faulty washer pump (Chapter 12).

Electric windows inoperative, or unsatisfactory in operation

Window glass will only move in one direction
- [ ] Faulty switch (Chapter 12).

Window glass slow to move
- [ ] Regulator seized or damaged, or in need of lubrication (Chapter 11).
- [ ] Door internal components or trim fouling regulator (Chapter 11).
- [ ] Faulty motor (Chapter 11).

Window glass fails to move
- [ ] Blown fuse (Chapter 12).
- [ ] Faulty relay (Chapter 12).
- [ ] Broken or disconnected wiring or connections (Chapter 12).
- [ ] Faulty motor (Chapter 12).

Central locking system inoperative, or unsatisfactory in operation

Complete system failure
- [ ] Blown fuse (Chapter 12).
- [ ] Faulty relay (Chapter 12).
- [ ] Broken or disconnected wiring or connections (Chapter 12).

Latch locks but will not unlock, or unlocks but will not lock
- [ ] Faulty switch (Chapter 12).
- [ ] Broken or disconnected latch operating rods or levers (Chapter 11).
- [ ] Faulty relay (Chapter 12).

One lock fails to operate
- [ ] Broken or disconnected wiring or connections (Chapter 12).
- [ ] Faulty motor (Chapter 11).
- [ ] Broken, binding or disconnected lock operating rods or levers (Chapter 11).
- [ ] Fault in door lock (Chapter 11).

A

ABS (Anti-lock brake system) A system, usually electronically controlled, that senses incipient wheel lockup during braking and relieves hydraulic pressure at wheels that are about to skid.

Air bag An inflatable bag hidden in the steering wheel (driver's side) or the dash or glovebox (passenger side). In a head-on collision, the bags inflate, preventing the driver and front passenger from being thrown forward into the steering wheel or windscreen.

Air cleaner A metal or plastic housing, containing a filter element, which removes dust and dirt from the air being drawn into the engine.

Air filter element The actual filter in an air cleaner system, usually manufactured from pleated paper and requiring renewal at regular intervals.

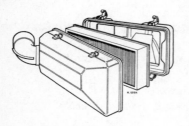

Air filter

Allen key A hexagonal wrench which fits into a recessed hexagonal hole.

Alligator clip A long-nosed spring-loaded metal clip with meshing teeth. Used to make temporary electrical connections.

Alternator A component in the electrical system which converts mechanical energy from a drivebelt into electrical energy to charge the battery and to operate the starting system, ignition system and electrical accessories.

Alternator (exploded view)

Ampere (amp) A unit of measurement for the flow of electric current. One amp is the amount of current produced by one volt acting through a resistance of one ohm.

Anaerobic sealer A substance used to prevent bolts and screws from loosening. Anaerobic means that it does not require oxygen for activation. The Loctite brand is widely used.

Antifreeze A substance (usually ethylene glycol) mixed with water, and added to a vehicle's cooling system, to prevent freezing of the coolant in winter. Antifreeze also contains chemicals to inhibit corrosion and the formation of rust and other deposits that would tend to clog the radiator and coolant passages and reduce cooling efficiency.

Anti-seize compound A coating that reduces the risk of seizing on fasteners that are subjected to high temperatures, such as exhaust manifold bolts and nuts.

Anti-seize compound

Asbestos A natural fibrous mineral with great heat resistance, commonly used in the composition of brake friction materials. Asbestos is a health hazard and the dust created by brake systems should never be inhaled or ingested.

Axle A shaft on which a wheel revolves, or which revolves with a wheel. Also, a solid beam that connects the two wheels at one end of the vehicle. An axle which also transmits power to the wheels is known as a live axle.

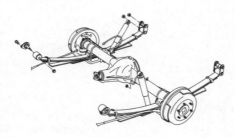

Axle assembly

Axleshaft A single rotating shaft, on either side of the differential, which delivers power from the final drive assembly to the drive wheels. Also called a driveshaft or a halfshaft.

B

Ball bearing An anti-friction bearing consisting of a hardened inner and outer race with hardened steel balls between two races.

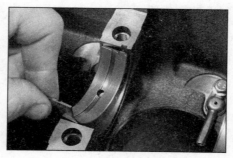

Bearing

Bearing The curved surface on a shaft or in a bore, or the part assembled into either, that permits relative motion between them with minimum wear and friction.

Big-end bearing The bearing in the end of the connecting rod that's attached to the crankshaft.

Bleed nipple A valve on a brake wheel cylinder, caliper or other hydraulic component that is opened to purge the hydraulic system of air. Also called a bleed screw.

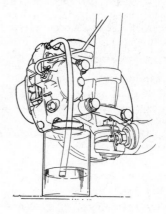

Brake bleeding

Brake bleeding Procedure for removing air from lines of a hydraulic brake system.

Brake disc The component of a disc brake that rotates with the wheels.

Brake drum The component of a drum brake that rotates with the wheels.

Brake linings The friction material which contacts the brake disc or drum to retard the vehicle's speed. The linings are bonded or riveted to the brake pads or shoes.

Brake pads The replaceable friction pads that pinch the brake disc when the brakes are applied. Brake pads consist of a friction material bonded or riveted to a rigid backing plate.

Brake shoe The crescent-shaped carrier to which the brake linings are mounted and which forces the lining against the rotating drum during braking.

Braking systems For more information on braking systems, consult the *Haynes Automotive Brake Manual*.

Breaker bar A long socket wrench handle providing greater leverage.

Bulkhead The insulated partition between the engine and the passenger compartment.

C

Caliper The non-rotating part of a disc-brake assembly that straddles the disc and carries the brake pads. The caliper also contains the hydraulic components that cause the pads to pinch the disc when the brakes are applied. A caliper is also a measuring tool that can be set to measure inside or outside dimensions of an object.

Camshaft A rotating shaft on which a series of cam lobes operate the valve mechanisms. The camshaft may be driven by gears, by sprockets and chain or by sprockets and a belt.

Canister A container in an evaporative emission control system; contains activated charcoal granules to trap vapours from the fuel system.

Canister

Carburettor A device which mixes fuel with air in the proper proportions to provide a desired power output from a spark ignition internal combustion engine.

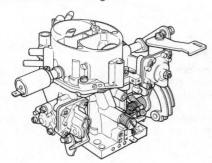

Carburettor

Castellated Resembling the parapets along the top of a castle wall. For example, a castellated balljoint stud nut.

Castellated nut

Castor In wheel alignment, the backward or forward tilt of the steering axis. Castor is positive when the steering axis is inclined rearward at the top.

Catalytic converter A silencer-like device in the exhaust system which converts certain pollutants in the exhaust gases into less harmful substances.

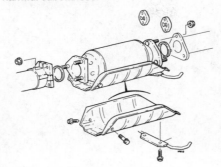

Catalytic converter

Circlip A ring-shaped clip used to prevent endwise movement of cylindrical parts and shafts. An internal circlip is installed in a groove in a housing; an external circlip fits into a groove on the outside of a cylindrical piece such as a shaft.

Clearance The amount of space between two parts. For example, between a piston and a cylinder, between a bearing and a journal, etc.

Coil spring A spiral of elastic steel found in various sizes throughout a vehicle, for example as a springing medium in the suspension and in the valve train.

Compression Reduction in volume, and increase in pressure and temperature, of a gas, caused by squeezing it into a smaller space.

Compression ratio The relationship between cylinder volume when the piston is at top dead centre and cylinder volume when the piston is at bottom dead centre.

Constant velocity (CV) joint A type of universal joint that cancels out vibrations caused by driving power being transmitted through an angle.

Core plug A disc or cup-shaped metal device inserted in a hole in a casting through which core was removed when the casting was formed. Also known as a freeze plug or expansion plug.

Crankcase The lower part of the engine block in which the crankshaft rotates.

Crankshaft The main rotating member, or shaft, running the length of the crankcase, with offset "throws" to which the connecting rods are attached.

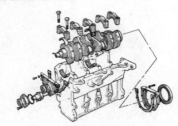

Crankshaft assembly

Crocodile clip See Alligator clip

D

Diagnostic code Code numbers obtained by accessing the diagnostic mode of an engine management computer. This code can be used to determine the area in the system where a malfunction may be located.

Disc brake A brake design incorporating a rotating disc onto which brake pads are squeezed. The resulting friction converts the energy of a moving vehicle into heat.

Double-overhead cam (DOHC) An engine that uses two overhead camshafts, usually one for the intake valves and one for the exhaust valves.

Drivebelt(s) The belt(s) used to drive accessories such as the alternator, water pump, power steering pump, air conditioning compressor, etc. off the crankshaft pulley.

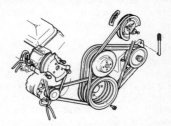

Accessory drivebelts

Driveshaft Any shaft used to transmit motion. Commonly used when referring to the axleshafts on a front wheel drive vehicle.

Driveshaft

Drum brake A type of brake using a drum-shaped metal cylinder attached to the inner surface of the wheel. When the brake pedal is pressed, curved brake shoes with friction linings press against the inside of the drum to slow or stop the vehicle.

Drum brake assembly

E

EGR valve A valve used to introduce exhaust gases into the intake air stream.

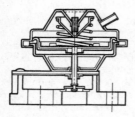

EGR valve

Electronic control unit (ECU) A computer which controls (for instance) ignition and fuel injection systems, or an anti-lock braking system. For more information refer to the *Haynes Automotive Electrical and Electronic Systems Manual.*

Electronic Fuel Injection (EFI) A computer controlled fuel system that distributes fuel through an injector located in each intake port of the engine.

Emergency brake A braking system, independent of the main hydraulic system, that can be used to slow or stop the vehicle if the primary brakes fail, or to hold the vehicle stationary even though the brake pedal isn't depressed. It usually consists of a hand lever that actuates either front or rear brakes mechanically through a series of cables and linkages. Also known as a handbrake or parking brake.

Endfloat The amount of lengthwise movement between two parts. As applied to a crankshaft, the distance that the crankshaft can move forward and back in the cylinder block.

Engine management system (EMS) A computer controlled system which manages the fuel injection and the ignition systems in an integrated fashion.

Exhaust manifold A part with several passages through which exhaust gases leave the engine combustion chambers and enter the exhaust pipe.

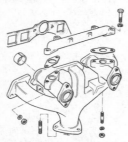

Exhaust manifold

F

Fan clutch A viscous (fluid) drive coupling device which permits variable engine fan speeds in relation to engine speeds.

Feeler blade A thin strip or blade of hardened steel, ground to an exact thickness, used to check or measure clearances between parts.

Feeler blade

Firing order The order in which the engine cylinders fire, or deliver their power strokes, beginning with the number one cylinder.

Flywheel A heavy spinning wheel in which energy is absorbed and stored by means of momentum. On cars, the flywheel is attached to the crankshaft to smooth out firing impulses.

Free play The amount of travel before any action takes place. The "looseness" in a linkage, or an assembly of parts, between the initial application of force and actual movement. For example, the distance the brake pedal moves before the pistons in the master cylinder are actuated.

Fuse An electrical device which protects a circuit against accidental overload. The typical fuse contains a soft piece of metal which is calibrated to melt at a predetermined current flow (expressed as amps) and break the circuit.

Fusible link A circuit protection device consisting of a conductor surrounded by heat-resistant insulation. The conductor is smaller than the wire it protects, so it acts as the weakest link in the circuit. Unlike a blown fuse, a failed fusible link must frequently be cut from the wire for replacement.

G

Gap The distance the spark must travel in jumping from the centre electrode to the side

Adjusting spark plug gap

electrode in a spark plug. Also refers to the spacing between the points in a contact breaker assembly in a conventional points-type ignition, or to the distance between the reluctor or rotor and the pickup coil in an electronic ignition.

Gasket Any thin, soft material - usually cork, cardboard, asbestos or soft metal - installed between two metal surfaces to ensure a good seal. For instance, the cylinder head gasket seals the joint between the block and the cylinder head.

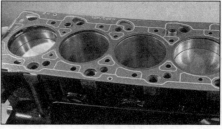

Gasket

Gauge An instrument panel display used to monitor engine conditions. A gauge with a movable pointer on a dial or a fixed scale is an analogue gauge. A gauge with a numerical readout is called a digital gauge.

H

Halfshaft A rotating shaft that transmits power from the final drive unit to a drive wheel, usually when referring to a live rear axle.

Harmonic balancer A device designed to reduce torsion or twisting vibration in the crankshaft. May be incorporated in the crankshaft pulley. Also known as a vibration damper.

Hone An abrasive tool for correcting small irregularities or differences in diameter in an engine cylinder, brake cylinder, etc.

Hydraulic tappet A tappet that utilises hydraulic pressure from the engine's lubrication system to maintain zero clearance (constant contact with both camshaft and valve stem). Automatically adjusts to variation in valve stem length. Hydraulic tappets also reduce valve noise.

I

Ignition timing The moment at which the spark plug fires, usually expressed in the number of crankshaft degrees before the piston reaches the top of its stroke.

Inlet manifold A tube or housing with passages through which flows the air-fuel mixture (carburettor vehicles and vehicles with throttle body injection) or air only (port fuel-injected vehicles) to the port openings in the cylinder head.

J

Jump start Starting the engine of a vehicle with a discharged or weak battery by attaching jump leads from the weak battery to a charged or helper battery.

L

Load Sensing Proportioning Valve (LSPV) A brake hydraulic system control valve that works like a proportioning valve, but also takes into consideration the amount of weight carried by the rear axle.
Locknut A nut used to lock an adjustment nut, or other threaded component, in place. For example, a locknut is employed to keep the adjusting nut on the rocker arm in position.
Lockwasher A form of washer designed to prevent an attaching nut from working loose.

M

MacPherson strut A type of front suspension system devised by Earle MacPherson at Ford of England. In its original form, a simple lateral link with the anti-roll bar creates the lower control arm. A long strut - an integral coil spring and shock absorber - is mounted between the body and the steering knuckle. Many modern so-called MacPherson strut systems use a conventional lower A-arm and don't rely on the anti-roll bar for location.
Multimeter An electrical test instrument with the capability to measure voltage, current and resistance.

N

NOx Oxides of Nitrogen. A common toxic pollutant emitted by petrol and diesel engines at higher temperatures.

O

Ohm The unit of electrical resistance. One volt applied to a resistance of one ohm will produce a current of one amp.
Ohmmeter An instrument for measuring electrical resistance.
O-ring A type of sealing ring made of a special rubber-like material; in use, the O-ring is compressed into a groove to provide the sealing action.

O-ring

Overhead cam (ohc) engine An engine with the camshaft(s) located on top of the cylinder head(s).
Overhead valve (ohv) engine An engine with the valves located in the cylinder head, but with the camshaft located in the engine block.
Oxygen sensor A device installed in the engine exhaust manifold, which senses the oxygen content in the exhaust and converts this information into an electric current. Also called a Lambda sensor.

P

Phillips screw A type of screw head having a cross instead of a slot for a corresponding type of screwdriver.
Plastigage A thin strip of plastic thread, available in different sizes, used for measuring clearances. For example, a strip of Plastigage is laid across a bearing journal. The parts are assembled and dismantled; the width of the crushed strip indicates the clearance between journal and bearing.

Plastigage

Propeller shaft The long hollow tube with universal joints at both ends that carries power from the transmission to the differential on front-engined rear wheel drive vehicles.
Proportioning valve A hydraulic control valve which limits the amount of pressure to the rear brakes during panic stops to prevent wheel lock-up.

R

Rack-and-pinion steering A steering system with a pinion gear on the end of the steering shaft that mates with a rack (think of a geared wheel opened up and laid flat). When the steering wheel is turned, the pinion turns, moving the rack to the left or right. This movement is transmitted through the track rods to the steering arms at the wheels.
Radiator A liquid-to-air heat transfer device designed to reduce the temperature of the coolant in an internal combustion engine cooling system.
Refrigerant Any substance used as a heat transfer agent in an air-conditioning system. R-12 has been the principle refrigerant for many years; recently, however, manufacturers have begun using R-134a, a non-CFC substance that is considered less harmful to the ozone in the upper atmosphere.

Rocker arm A lever arm that rocks on a shaft or pivots on a stud. In an overhead valve engine, the rocker arm converts the upward movement of the pushrod into a downward movement to open a valve.
Rotor In a distributor, the rotating device inside the cap that connects the centre electrode and the outer terminals as it turns, distributing the high voltage from the coil secondary winding to the proper spark plug. Also, that part of an alternator which rotates inside the stator. Also, the rotating assembly of a turbocharger, including the compressor wheel, shaft and turbine wheel.
Runout The amount of wobble (in-and-out movement) of a gear or wheel as it's rotated. The amount a shaft rotates "out-of-true." The out-of-round condition of a rotating part.

S

Sealant A liquid or paste used to prevent leakage at a joint. Sometimes used in conjunction with a gasket.
Sealed beam lamp An older headlight design which integrates the reflector, lens and filaments into a hermetically-sealed one-piece unit. When a filament burns out or the lens cracks, the entire unit is simply replaced.
Serpentine drivebelt A single, long, wide accessory drivebelt that's used on some newer vehicles to drive all the accessories, instead of a series of smaller, shorter belts. Serpentine drivebelts are usually tensioned by an automatic tensioner.

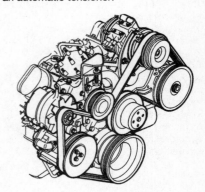
Serpentine drivebelt

Shim Thin spacer, commonly used to adjust the clearance or relative positions between two parts. For example, shims inserted into or under bucket tappets control valve clearances. Clearance is adjusted by changing the thickness of the shim.
Slide hammer A special puller that screws into or hooks onto a component such as a shaft or bearing; a heavy sliding handle on the shaft bottoms against the end of the shaft to knock the component free.
Sprocket A tooth or projection on the periphery of a wheel, shaped to engage with a chain or drivebelt. Commonly used to refer to the sprocket wheel itself.

Starter inhibitor switch On vehicles with an automatic transmission, a switch that prevents starting if the vehicle is not in Neutral or Park.

Strut See MacPherson strut.

T

Tappet A cylindrical component which transmits motion from the cam to the valve stem, either directly or via a pushrod and rocker arm. Also called a cam follower.

Thermostat A heat-controlled valve that regulates the flow of coolant between the cylinder block and the radiator, so maintaining optimum engine operating temperature. A thermostat is also used in some air cleaners in which the temperature is regulated.

Thrust bearing The bearing in the clutch assembly that is moved in to the release levers by clutch pedal action to disengage the clutch. Also referred to as a release bearing.

Timing belt A toothed belt which drives the camshaft. Serious engine damage may result if it breaks in service.

Timing chain A chain which drives the camshaft.

Toe-in The amount the front wheels are closer together at the front than at the rear. On rear wheel drive vehicles, a slight amount of toe-in is usually specified to keep the front wheels running parallel on the road by offsetting other forces that tend to spread the wheels apart.

Toe-out The amount the front wheels are closer together at the rear than at the front. On front wheel drive vehicles, a slight amount of toe-out is usually specified.

Tools For full information on choosing and using tools, refer to the *Haynes Automotive Tools Manual.*

Tracer A stripe of a second colour applied to a wire insulator to distinguish that wire from another one with the same colour insulator.

Tune-up A process of accurate and careful adjustments and parts replacement to obtain the best possible engine performance.

Turbocharger A centrifugal device, driven by exhaust gases, that pressurises the intake air. Normally used to increase the power output from a given engine displacement, but can also be used primarily to reduce exhaust emissions (as on VW's "Umwelt" Diesel engine).

U

Universal joint or U-joint A double-pivoted connection for transmitting power from a driving to a driven shaft through an angle. A U-joint consists of two Y-shaped yokes and a cross-shaped member called the spider.

V

Valve A device through which the flow of liquid, gas, vacuum, or loose material in bulk may be started, stopped, or regulated by a movable part that opens, shuts, or partially obstructs one or more ports or passageways. A valve is also the movable part of such a device.

Valve clearance The clearance between the valve tip (the end of the valve stem) and the rocker arm or tappet. The valve clearance is measured when the valve is closed.

Vernier caliper A precision measuring instrument that measures inside and outside dimensions. Not quite as accurate as a micrometer, but more convenient.

Viscosity The thickness of a liquid or its resistance to flow.

Volt A unit for expressing electrical "pressure" in a circuit. One volt that will produce a current of one ampere through a resistance of one ohm.

W

Welding Various processes used to join metal items by heating the areas to be joined to a molten state and fusing them together. For more information refer to the *Haynes Automotive Welding Manual.*

Wiring diagram A drawing portraying the components and wires in a vehicle's electrical system, using standardised symbols. For more information refer to the *Haynes Automotive Electrical and Electronic Systems Manual.*

Note: *References throughout this index are in the form* "**Chapter number**" • "**Page number**". *So, for example, 2C•15 refers to page 15 of Chapter 2C.*

Note: *References throughout this index are in the form* "**Chapter number**" • "**Page number**". *So, for example, 2C•15 refers to page 15 of Chapter 2C.*

Note: *References throughout this index are in the form* "**Chapter number**" • "**Page number**". *So, for example, 2C•15 refers to page 15 of Chapter 2C.*

Note: *References throughout this index are in the form* "**Chapter number**" • "**Page number**". *So, for example,* 2C•15 *refers to page 15 of Chapter 2C.*

Note: *References throughout this index are in the form* "**Chapter number**" • "**Page number**". *So, for example, 2C•15 refers to page 15 of Chapter 2C.*

Haynes Manuals – The Complete UK Car List

Title	Book No.
ALFA ROMEO Alfasud/Sprint (74 - 88) up to F *	0292
Alfa Romeo Alfetta (73 - 87) up to E *	0531
AUDI 80, 90 & Coupe Petrol (79 - Nov 88) up to F	0605
Audi 80, 90 & Coupe Petrol (Oct 86 - 90) D to H	1491
Audi 100 & 200 Petrol (Oct 82 - 90) up to H	0907
Audi 100 & A6 Petrol & Diesel (May 91 - May 97) H to P	3504
Audi A3 Petrol & Diesel (96 - May 03) P to 03	4253
Audi A4 Petrol & Diesel (95 - 00) M to X	3575
Audi A4 Petrol & Diesel (01 - 04) X to 54	4609
AUSTIN A35 & A40 (56 - 67) up to F *	0118
Austin/MG/Rover Maestro 1.3 & 1.6 Petrol (83 - 95) up to M	0922
Austin/MG Metro (80 - May 90) up to G	0718
Austin/Rover Montego 1.3 & 1.6 Petrol (84 - 94) A to L	1066
Austin/MG/Rover Montego 2.0 Petrol (84 - 95) A to M	1067
Mini (59 - 69) up to H *	0527
Mini (69 - 01) up to X	0646
Austin/Rover 2.0 litre Diesel Engine (86 - 93) C to L	1857
Austin Healey 100/6 & 3000 (56 - 68) up to G *	0049
BEDFORD CF Petrol (69 - 87) up to E	0163
Bedford/Vauxhall Rascal & Suzuki Supercarry (86 - Oct 94) C to M	3015
BMW 316, 320 & 320i (4-cyl) (75 - Feb 83) up to Y *	0276
BMW 320, 320i, 323i & 325i (6-cyl) (Oct 77 - Sept 87) up to E	0815
BMW 3- & 5-Series Petrol (81 - 91) up to J	1948
BMW 3-Series Petrol (Apr 91 - 99) H to V	3210
BMW 3-Series Petrol (Sept 98 - 03) S to 53	4067
BMW 520i & 525e (Oct 81 - June 88) up to E	1560
BMW 525, 528 & 528i (73 - Sept 81) up to X *	0632
BMW 5-Series 6-cyl Petrol (April 96 - Aug 03) N to 03	4151
BMW 1500, 1502, 1600, 1602, 2000 & 2002 (59 - 77) up to S *	0240
CHRYSLER PT Cruiser Petrol (00 - 03) W to 53	4058
CITROËN 2CV, Ami & Dyane (67 - 90) up to H	0196
Citroën AX Petrol & Diesel (87 - 97) D to P	3014
Citroën Berlingo & Peugeot Partner Petrol & Diesel (96 - 05) P to 55	4281
Citroën BX Petrol (83 - 94) A to L	0908
Citroën C15 Van Petrol & Diesel (89 - Oct 98) F to S	3509
Citroën C3 Petrol & Diesel (02 - 05) 51 to 05	4197
Citroen C5 Petrol & Diesel (01-08) Y to 08	4745
Citroën CX Petrol (75 - 88) up to F	0528
Citroën Saxo Petrol & Diesel (96 - 04) N to 54	3506
Citroën Visa Petrol (79 - 88) up to F	0620
Citroën Xantia Petrol & Diesel (93 - 01) K to Y	3082
Citroën XM Petrol & Diesel (89 - 00) G to X	3451
Citroën Xsara Petrol & Diesel (97 - Sept 00) R to W	3751
Citroën Xsara Picasso Petrol & Diesel (00 - 02) W to 52	3944
Citroen Xsara Picasso (03-08)	4784
Citroën ZX Diesel (91 - 98) J to S	1922
Citroën ZX Petrol (91 - 98) H to S	1881
Citroën 1.7 & 1.9 litre Diesel Engine (84 - 96) A to N	1379
FIAT 126 (73 - 87) up to E *	0305
Fiat 500 (57 - 73) up to M *	0090
Fiat Bravo & Brava Petrol (95 - 00) N to W	3572
Fiat Cinquecento (93 - 98) K to R	3501
Fiat Panda (81 - 95) up to M	0793
Fiat Punto Petrol & Diesel (94 - Oct 99) L to V	3251
Fiat Punto Petrol (Oct 99 - July 03) V to 03	4066
Fiat Punto Petrol (03-07) 03 to 07	4746
Fiat Regata Petrol (84 - 88) A to F	1167
Fiat Tipo Petrol (88 - 91) E to J	1625
Fiat Uno Petrol (83 - 95) up to M	0923
Fiat X1/9 (74 - 89) up to G *	0273
FORD Anglia (59 - 68) up to G *	0001

Title	Book No.
Ford Capri II (& III) 1.6 & 2.0 (74 - 87) up to E *	0283
Ford Capri II (& III) 2.8 & 3.0 V6 (74 - 87) up to E	1309
Ford Cortina Mk I & Corsair 1500 ('62 - '66) up to D*	0214
Ford Cortina Mk III 1300 & 1600 (70 - 76) up to P	*0070
Ford Escort Mk I 1100 & 1300 (68 - 74) up to N *	0171
Ford Escort Mk I Mexico, RS 1600 & RS 2000 (70 - 74) up to N *	0139
Ford Escort Mk II Mexico, RS 1800 & RS 2000 (75 - 80) up to W *	0735
Ford Escort (75 - Aug 80) up to V *	0280
Ford Escort Petrol (Sept 80 - Sept 90) up to H	0686
Ford Escort & Orion Petrol (Sept 90 - 00) H to X	1737
Ford Escort & Orion Diesel (Sept 90 - 00) H to X	4081
Ford Fiesta (76 - Aug 83) up to Y	0334
Ford Fiesta Petrol (Aug 83 - Feb 89) A to F	1030
Ford Fiesta Petrol (Feb 89 - Oct 95) F to N	1595
Ford Fiesta Petrol & Diesel (Oct 95 - Mar 02) N to 02	3397
Ford Fiesta Petrol & Diesel (Apr 02 - 07) 02 to 57	4170
Ford Focus Petrol & Diesel (98 - 01) S to Y	3759
Ford Focus Petrol & Diesel (Oct 01 - 05) 51 to 05	4167
Ford Galaxy Petrol & Diesel (95 - Aug 00) M to W	3984
Ford Granada Petrol (Sept 77 - Feb 85) up to B *	0481
Ford Granada & Scorpio Petrol (Mar 85 - 94) B to M	1245
Ford Ka (96 - 02) P to 52	3570
Ford Mondeo Petrol (93 - Sept 00) K to X	1923
Ford Mondeo Petrol & Diesel (Oct 00 - Jul 03) X to 03	3990
Ford Mondeo Petrol & Diesel (July 03 - 07) 03 to 56	4619
Ford Mondeo Diesel (93 - 96) L to N	3465
Ford Orion Petrol (83 - Sept 90) up to H	1009
Ford Sierra 4-cyl Petrol (82 - 93) up to K	0903
Ford Sierra V6 Petrol (82 - 91) up to J	0904
Ford Transit Petrol (Mk 2) (78 - Jan 86) up to C	0719
Ford Transit Petrol (Mk 3) (Feb 86 - 89) C to G	1468
Ford Transit Diesel (Feb 86 - 99) C to T	3019
Ford Transit Diesel (00-06)	4775
Ford 1.6 & 1.8 litre Diesel Engine (84 - 96) A to N	1172
Ford 2.1, 2.3 & 2.5 litre Diesel Engine (77 - 90) up to H	1606
FREIGHT ROVER Sherpa Petrol (74 - 87) up to E	0463
HILLMAN Avenger (70 - 82) up to Y	0037
Hillman Imp (63 - 76) up to R *	0022
HONDA Civic (Feb 84 - Oct 87) A to E	1226
Honda Civic (Nov 91 - 96) J to N	3199
Honda Civic Petrol (Mar 95 - 00) M to X	4050
Honda Civic Petrol & Diesel (01 - 05) X to 55	4611
Honda CR-V Petrol & Diesel (01-06)	4747
Honda Jazz (01 - Feb 08) 51 - 57	4735
HYUNDAI Pony (85 - 94) C to M	3398
JAGUAR E Type (61 - 72) up to L *	0140
Jaguar MkI & II, 240 & 340 (55 - 69) up to H *	0098
Jaguar XJ6, XJ & Sovereign; Daimler Sovereign (68 - Oct 86) up to D	0242
Jaguar XJ6 & Sovereign (Oct 86 - Sept 94) D to M	3261
Jaguar XJ12, XJS & Sovereign; Daimler Double Six (72 - 88) up to F	0478
JEEP Cherokee Petrol (93 - 96) K to N	1943
LADA 1200, 1300, 1500 & 1600 (74 - 91) up to J	0413
Lada Samara (87 - 91) D to J	1610
LAND ROVER 90, 110 & Defender Diesel (83 - 07) up to 56	3017
Land Rover Discovery Petrol & Diesel (89 - 98) G to S	3016
Land Rover Discovery Diesel (Nov 98 - Jul 04) S to 04	4606
Land Rover Freelander Petrol & Diesel (97 - Sept 03) R to 53	3929
Land Rover Freelander Petrol & Diesel (Oct 03 - Oct 06) 53 to 56	4623

Title	Book No.
Land Rover Series IIA & III Diesel (58 - 85) up to C	0529
Land Rover Series II, IIA & III 4-cyl Petrol (58 - 85) up to C	0314
MAZDA 323 (Mar 81 - Oct 89) up to G	1608
Mazda 323 (Oct 89 - 98) G to R	3455
Mazda 626 (May 83 - Sept 87) up to E	0929
Mazda B1600, B1800 & B2000 Pick-up Petrol (72 - 88) up to F	0267
Mazda RX-7 (79 - 85) up to C *	0460
MERCEDES-BENZ 190, 190E & 190D Petrol & Diesel (83 - 93) A to L	3450
Mercedes-Benz 200D, 240D, 240TD, 300D & 300TD 123 Series Diesel (Oct 76 - 85)	1114
Mercedes-Benz 250 & 280 (68 - 72) up to L *	0346
Mercedes-Benz 250 & 280 123 Series Petrol (Oct 76 - 84) up to B *	0677
Mercedes-Benz 124 Series Petrol & Diesel (85 - Aug 93) C to K	3253
Mercedes-Benz A-Class Petrol & Diesel (98-04) S to 54)	4748
Mercedes-Benz C-Class Petrol & Diesel (93 - Aug 00) L to W	3511
Mercedes-Benz C-Class (00-06)	4780
MGA (55 - 62) *	0475
MGB (62 - 80) up to W	0111
MG Midget & Austin-Healey Sprite (58 - 80) up to W *	0265
MINI Petrol (July 01 - 05) Y to 05	4273
MITSUBISHI Shogun & L200 Pick-Ups Petrol (83 - 94) up to M	1944
MORRIS Ital 1.3 (80 - 84) up to B	0705
Morris Minor 1000 (56 - 71) up to K	0024
NISSAN Almera Petrol (95 - Feb 00) N to V	4053
Nissan Almera & Tino Petrol (Feb 00 - 07) V to 56	4612
Nissan Bluebird (May 84 - Mar 86) A to C	1223
Nissan Bluebird Petrol (Mar 86 - 90) C to H	1473
Nissan Cherry (Sept 82 - 86) up to D	1031
Nissan Micra (83 - Jan 93) up to K	0931
Nissan Micra (93 - 02) K to 52	3254
Nissan Micra (03-07) 52 to 57	4734
Nissan Primera Petrol (90 - Aug 99) H to T	1851
Nissan Stanza (82 - 86) up to D	0824
Nissan Sunny Petrol (May 82 - Oct 86) up to D	0895
Nissan Sunny Petrol (Oct 86 - Mar 91) D to H	1378
Nissan Sunny Petrol (Apr 91 - 95) H to N	3219
OPEL Ascona & Manta (B Series) (Sept 75 - 88) up to F *	0316
Opel Ascona Petrol (81 - 88)	3215
Opel Astra Petrol (Oct 91 - Feb 98)	3156
Opel Corsa Petrol (83 - Mar 93)	3160
Opel Corsa Petrol (Mar 93 - 97)	3159
Opel Kadett Petrol (Nov 79 - Oct 84) up to B	0634
Opel Kadett Petrol (Oct 84 - Oct 91)	3196
Opel Omega & Senator Petrol (Nov 86 - 94)	3157
Opel Rekord Petrol (Feb 78 - Oct 86) up to D	0543
Opel Vectra Petrol (Oct 88 - Oct 95)	3158
PEUGEOT 106 Petrol & Diesel (91 - 04) J to 53	1882
Peugeot 205 Petrol (83 - 97) A to P	0932
Peugeot 206 Petrol & Diesel (98 - 01) S to X	3757
Peugeot 206 Petrol & Diesel (02 - 06) 51 to 06	4613
Peugeot 306 Petrol & Diesel (93 - 02) K to 02	3073
Peugeot 307 Petrol & Diesel (01 - 04) Y to 54	4147
Peugeot 309 Petrol (86 - 93) C to K	1266
Peugeot 405 Petrol (88 - 97) E to P	1559
Peugeot 405 Diesel (88 - 97) E to P	3198
Peugeot 406 Petrol & Diesel (96 - Mar 99) N to T	3394
Peugeot 406 Petrol & Diesel (Mar 99 - 02) T to 52	3982

* Classic reprint

Title	Book No.
Peugeot 505 Petrol (79 - 89) up to G	0762
Peugeot 1.7/1.8 & 1.9 litre Diesel Engine (82 - 96) up to N	0950
Peugeot 2.0, 2.1, 2.3 & 2.5 litre Diesel Engines (74 - 90) up to H	1607
PORSCHE 911 (65 - 85) up to C	0264
Porsche 924 & 924 Turbo (76 - 85) up to C	0397
PROTON (89 - 97) F to P	3255
RANGE ROVER V8 Petrol (70 - Oct 92) up to K	0606
RELIANT Robin & Kitten (73 - 83) up to A *	0436
RENAULT 4 (61 - 86) up to D *	0072
Renault 5 Petrol (Feb 85 - 96) B to N	1219
Renault 9 & 11 Petrol (82 - 89) up to F	0822
Renault 18 Petrol (79 - 86) up to D	0598
Renault 19 Petrol (89 - 96) F to N	1646
Renault 19 Diesel (89 - 96) F to N	1946
Renault 21 Petrol (86 - 94) C to M	1397
Renault 25 Petrol & Diesel (84 - 92) B to K	1228
Renault Clio Petrol (91 - May 98) H to R	1853
Renault Clio Diesel (91 - June 96) H to N	3031
Renault Clio Petrol & Diesel (May 98 - May 01) R to Y	3906
Renault Clio Petrol & Diesel (June '01 - '05) Y to 55	4168
Renault Espace Petrol & Diesel (85 - 96) C to N	3197
Renault Laguna Petrol & Diesel (94 - 00) L to W	3252
Renault Laguna Petrol & Diesel (Feb 01 - Feb 05) X to 54	4283
Renault Mégane & Scénic Petrol & Diesel (96 - 99) N to T	3395
Renault Mégane & Scénic Petrol & Diesel (Apr 99 - 02) T to 52	3916
Renault Megane Petrol & Diesel (Oct 02 - 05) 52 to 55	4284
Renault Scenic Petrol & Diesel (Sept 03 - 06) 53 to 06	4297
ROVER 213 & 216 (84 - 89) A to G	1116
Rover 214 & 414 Petrol (89 - 96) G to N	1689
Rover 216 & 416 Petrol (89 - 96) G to N	1830
Rover 211, 214, 216, 218 & 220 Petrol & Diesel (Dec 95 - 99) N to V	3399
Rover 25 & MG ZR Petrol & Diesel (Oct 99 - 04) V to 54	4145
Rover 414, 416 & 420 Petrol & Diesel (May 95 - 98) M to R	3453
Rover 45 / MG ZS Petrol & Diesel (99 - 05) V to 55	4384
Rover 618, 620 & 623 Petrol (93 - 97) K to P	3257
Rover 75 / MG ZT Petrol & Diesel (99 - 06) S to 06	4292
Rover 820, 825 & 827 Petrol (86 - 95) D to N	1380
Rover 3500 (76 - 87) up to E *	0365
Rover Metro, 111 & 114 Petrol (May 90 - 98) G to S	1711
SAAB 95 & 96 (66 - 76) up to R *	0198
Saab 90, 99 & 900 (79 - Oct 93) up to L	0765
Saab 900 (Oct 93 - 98) L to R	3512
Saab 9000 (4-cyl) (85 - 98) C to S	1686
Saab 9-3 Petrol & Diesel (98 - Aug 02) R to 02	4614
Saab 9-3 Petrol & Diesel (02-07) 52 to 57	4749
Saab 9-5 4-cyl Petrol (97 - 04) R to 54	4156
SEAT Ibiza & Cordoba Petrol & Diesel (Oct 93 - Oct 99) L to V	3571
Seat Ibiza & Malaga Petrol (85 - 92) B to K	1609
SKODA Estelle (77 - 89) up to G	0604
Skoda Fabia Petrol & Diesel (00 - 06) W to 06	4376
Skoda Favorit (89 - 96) F to N	1801
Skoda Felicia Petrol & Diesel (95 - 01) M to X	3505
Skoda Octavia Petrol & Diesel (98 - Apr 04) R to 04	4285
SUBARU 1600 & 1800 (Nov 79 - 90) up to H *	0995

Title	Book No.
SUNBEAM Alpine, Rapier & H120 (67 - 74) up to N *	0051
SUZUKI SJ Series, Samurai & Vitara (4-cyl) Petrol (82 - 97) up to P	1942
Suzuki Supercarry & Bedford/Vauxhall Rascal (86 - Oct 94) C to M	3015
TALBOT Alpine, Solara, Minx & Rapier (75 - 86) up to D	0337
Talbot Horizon Petrol (78 - 86) up to D	0473
Talbot Samba (82 - 86) up to D	0823
TOYOTA Avensis Petrol (98 - Jan 03) R to 52	4264
Toyota Carina E Petrol (May 92 - 97) J to P	3256
Toyota Corolla (80 - 85) up to C	0683
Toyota Corolla (Sept 83 - Sept 87) A to E	1024
Toyota Corolla (Sept 87 - Aug 92) E to K	1683
Toyota Corolla Petrol (Aug 92 - 97) K to P	3259
Toyota Corolla Petrol (July 97 - Feb 02) P to 51	4286
Toyota Hi-Ace & Hi-Lux Petrol (69 - Oct 83) up to A	0304
Toyota RAV4 Petrol & Diesel (94-06) L to 55	4750
Toyota Yaris Petrol (99 - 05) T to 05	4265
TRIUMPH GT6 & Vitesse (62 - 74) up to N *	0112
Triumph Herald (59 - 71) up to K *	0010
Triumph Spitfire (62 - 81) up to X	0113
Triumph Stag (70 - 78) up to T *	0441
Triumph TR2, TR3, TR3A, TR4 & TR4A (52 - 67) up to F *	0028
Triumph TR5 & 6 (67 - 75) up to P *	0031
Triumph TR7 (75 - 82) up to Y *	0322
VAUXHALL Astra Petrol (80 - Oct 84) up to B	0635
Vauxhall Astra & Belmont Petrol (Oct 84 - Oct 91) B to J	1136
Vauxhall Astra Petrol (Oct 91 - Feb 98) J to R	1832
Vauxhall/Opel Astra & Zafira Petrol (Feb 98 - Apr 04) R to 04	3758
Vauxhall/Opel Astra & Zafira Diesel (Feb 98 - Apr 04) R to 04	3797
Vauxhall/Opel Astra Petrol (04 - 08)	4732
Vauxhall/Opel Astra Diesel (04 - 08)	4733
Vauxhall/Opel Calibra (90 - 98) G to S	3502
Vauxhall Carlton Petrol (Oct 78 - Oct 86) up to D	0480
Vauxhall Carlton & Senator Petrol (Nov 86 - 94) D to L	1469
Vauxhall Cavalier Petrol (81 - Oct 88) up to F	0812
Vauxhall Cavaiier Petrol (Oct 88 - 95) F to N	1570
Vauxhall Chevette (75 - 84) up to B	0285
Vauxhall/Opel Corsa Diesel (Mar 93 - Oct 00) K to X	4087
Vauxhall Corsa Petrol (Mar 93 - 97) K to R	1985
Vauxhall/Opel Corsa Petrol (Apr 97 - Oct 00) P to X	3921
Vauxhall/Opel Corsa Petrol & Diesel (Oct 00 - Sept 03) X to 53	4079
Vauxhall/Opel Corsa Petrol & Diesel (Oct 03 - Aug 06) 53 to 06	4617
Vauxhall/Opel Frontera Petrol & Diesel (91 - Sept 98) J to S	3454
Vauxhall Nova Petrol (83 - 93) up to K	0909
Vauxhall/Opel Omega Petrol (94 - 99) L to T	3510
Vauxhall/Opel Vectra Petrol & Diesel (95 - Feb 99) N to S	3396
Vauxhall/Opel Vectra Petrol & Diesel (Mar 99 - May 02) T to 02	3930
Vauxhall/Opel Vectra Petrol & Diesel (June 02 - Sept 05) 02 to 55	4618
Vauxhall/Opel 1.5, 1.6 & 1.7 litre Diesel Engine (82 - 96) up to N	1222
VW 411 & 412 (68 - 75) up to P *	0091
VW Beetle 1200 (54 - 77) up to S	0036
VW Beetle 1300 & 1500 (65 - 75) up to P	0039

Title	Book No.
VW 1302 & 1302S (70 - 72) up to L *	0110
VW Beetle 1303, 1303S & GT (72 - 75) up to P	0159
VW Beetle Petrol & Diesel (Apr 99 - 07) T to 57	3798
VW Golf & Jetta Mk 1 Petrol 1.1 & 1.3 (74 - 84) up to A	0716
VW Golf, Jetta & Scirocco Mk 1 Petrol 1.5, 1.6 & 1.8 (74 - 84) up to A	0726
VW Golf & Jetta Mk 1 Diesel (78 - 84) up to A	0451
VW Golf & Jetta Mk 2 Petrol (Mar 84 - Feb 92) A to J	1081
VW Golf & Vento Petrol & Diesel (Feb 92 - Mar 98) J to R	3097
VW Golf & Bora Petrol & Diesel (April 98 - 00) R to X	3727
VW Golf & Bora 4-cyl Petrol & Diesel (01 - 03) X to 53	4169
VW Golf & Jetta Petrol & Diesel (04 - 07) 53 to 07	4610
VW LT Petrol Vans & Light Trucks (76 - 87) up to E	0637
VW Passat & Santana Petrol (Sept 81 - May 88) up to E	0814
VW Passat 4-cyl Petrol & Diesel (May 88 - 96) E to P	3498
VW Passat 4-cyl Petrol & Diesel (Dec 96 - Nov 00) P to X	3917
VW Passat Petrol & Diesel (Dec 00 - May 05) X to 05	4279
VW Polo & Derby (76 - Jan 82) up to X	0335
VW Polo (82 - Oct 90) up to H	0813
VW Polo Petrol (Nov 90 - Aug 94) H to L	3245
VW Polo Hatchback Petrol & Diesel (94 - 99) M to S	3500
VW Polo Hatchback Petrol (00 - Jan 02) V to 51	4150
VW Polo Petrol & Diesel (02 - May 05) 51 to 05	4608
VW Scirocco (82 - 90) up to H *	1224
VW Transporter 1600 (68 - 79) up to V	0082
VW Transporter 1700, 1800 & 2000 (72 - 79) up to V *	0226
VW Transporter (air-cooled) Petrol (79 - 82) up to Y *	0638
VW Transporter (water-cooled) Petrol (82 - 90) up to H	3452
VW Type 3 (63 - 73) up to M *	0084
VOLVO 120 & 130 Series (& P1800) (61 - 73) up to M *	0203
Volvo 142, 144 & 145 (66 - 74) up to N *	0129
Volvo 240 Series Petrol (74 - 93) up to K	0270
Volvo 262, 264 & 260/265 (75 - 85) up to C *	0400
Volvo 340, 343, 345 & 360 (76 - 91) up to J	0715
Volvo 440, 460 & 480 Petrol (87 - 97) D to P	1691
Volvo 740 & 760 Petrol (82 - 91) up to J	1258
Volvo 850 Petrol (92 - 96) J to P	3260
Volvo 940 petrol (90 - 98) H to R	3249
Volvo S40 & V40 Petrol (96 - Mar 04) N to 04	3569
Volvo S40 & V50 Petrol & Diesel (Mar 04 - Jun 07) 04 to 07	4731
Volvo S60 Petrol & Diesel (01-08)	4793
Volvo S70, V70 & C70 Petrol (96 - 99) P to V	3573
Volvo V70 / S80 Petrol & Diesel (98 - 05) S to 55	4263

DIY MANUAL SERIES

Title	Book No.
The Haynes Air Conditioning Manual	4192
The Haynes Car Electrical Systems Manual	4251
The Haynes Manual on Bodywork	4198
The Haynes Manual on Brakes	4178
The Haynes Manual on Carburettors	4177
The Haynes Manual on Diesel Engines	4174
The Haynes Manual on Engine Management	4199
The Haynes Manual on Fault Codes	4175
The Haynes Manual on Practical Electrical Systems	4267
The Haynes Manual on Small Engines	4250
The Haynes Manual on Welding	4176

* Classic reprint

CL24.08/09

Preserving Our Motoring Heritage

> The Model J Duesenberg
> Derham Tourster.
> Only eight of these
> magnificent cars were
> ever built – this is the
> only example to be found
> outside the United States
> of America

Almost every car you've ever loved, loathed or desired is gathered under one roof at the Haynes Motor Museum. Over 300 immaculately presented cars and motorbikes represent every aspect of our motoring heritage, from elegant reminders of bygone days, such as the superb Model J Duesenberg to curiosities like the bug-eyed BMW Isetta. There are also many old friends and flames. Perhaps you remember the 1959 Ford Popular that you did your courting in? The magnificent 'Red Collection' is a spectacle of classic sports cars including AC, Alfa Romeo, Austin Healey, Ferrari, Lamborghini, Maserati, MG, Riley, Porsche and Triumph.

A Perfect Day Out

Each and every vehicle at the Haynes Motor Museum has played its part in the history and culture of Motoring. Today, they make a wonderful spectacle and a great day out for all the family. Bring the kids, bring Mum and Dad, but above all bring your camera to capture those golden memories for ever. You will also find an impressive array of motoring memorabilia, a comfortable 70 seat video cinema and one of the most extensive transport book shops in Britain. The Pit Stop Cafe serves everything from a cup of tea to wholesome, home-made meals or, if you prefer, you can enjoy the large picnic area nestled in the beautiful rural surroundings of Somerset.

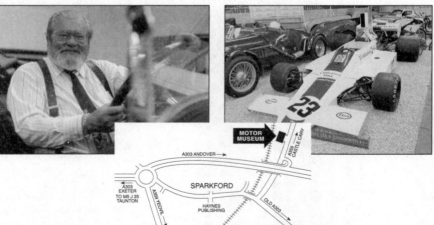

*John Haynes O.B.E.,
Founder and
Chairman of the
museum at the wheel
of a Haynes Light 12.*

*Graham Hill's Lola
Cosworth Formula 1
car next to a 1934
Riley Sports.*

The Museum is situated on the A359 Yeovil to Frome road at Sparkford, just off the A303 in Somerset. It is about 40 miles south of Bristol, and 25 minutes drive from the M5 intersection at Taunton.
Open 9.30am - 5.30pm (10.00am - 4.00pm Winter) 7 days a week, *except Christmas Day, Boxing Day and New Years Day*
Special rates available for schools, coach parties and outings Charitable Trust No. 292048